Technology, Management and the Evangelical Church

ALSO BY JOHN WEAVER
AND FROM MCFARLAND

*The New Apostolic Reformation:
History of a Modern Charismatic Movement* (2016)

*The Failure of Evangelical Mental Health Care:
Treatments That Harm Women, LGBT Persons
and the Mentally Ill* (2015)

*Evangelicals and the Arts in Fiction:
Portrayals of Tension in Non-Evangelical
Works Since 1895* (2013)

Technology, Management and the Evangelical Church

JOHN WEAVER

McFarland & Company, Inc., Publishers
Jefferson, North Carolina

This book has undergone peer review.

ISBN (print) 978-1-4766-7816-0
ISBN (ebook) 978-1-4766-3885-0

LIBRARY OF CONGRESS AND BRITISH LIBRARY
CATALOGUING DATA ARE AVAILABLE

Library of Congress Control Number 2020012130

© 2020 John Weaver. All rights reserved

No part of this book may be reproduced or transmitted in any form or by any means, electronic or mechanical, including photocopying or recording, or by any information storage and retrieval system, without permission in writing from the publisher.

Front cover image © 2020 Shutterstock

Printed in the United States of America

*McFarland & Company, Inc., Publishers
Box 611, Jefferson, North Carolina 28640
www.mcfarlandpub.com*

With much love to
Gina Eckert, Deb Hibbard,
and Mikhail Gofman

Table of Contents

Acknowledgments — viii
Preface — 1
Acronyms — 6
Introduction — 8

1. The Origins of Evangelical Management Culture — 25
2. The Church Growth Movement and the Birth of Modern Metricspirituality — 95
3. Cybernetics, Computers and Christ: How Systems Theory Helped Found the Modern Religious Right — 115
4. Networked Churches and the Rise of Church Toyota — 194
5. The Christian Right's Technological Infrastructure — 239
6. The Evangelical Web — 274

Conclusion: Managing the Future — 296
Glossary — 311
Chapter Notes — 319
Works Cited — 325
Index — 351

Acknowledgments

This book would not have been possible without the help of many gracious people. Foremost of these was Mikhail Gofman, who through countless discussions and book recommendations, allowed me to gain an understanding of the basic outlines of systems theory and cybernetics (any errors remaining in the text are obviously entirely my own). Chester Jezierski also provided technical input on occasion. I also wish to thank John Sterlacci for his helpful suggestions regarding the economic concepts presented in this book. Although Dr. Sterlacci and I come from somewhat different vantage points on the political spectrum, his willingness to engage with me on economic issues was very helpful.

As always, Rachel Tabachnick, Bruce Wilson, and Frederick Clarkson provided helpful insight for this book. I particularly thank Bruce for his helpful suggestions on Christian Right influences in Silicon Valley, some of which made their way into this book. Rachel's read-throughs of numerous drafts also helped me clarify many issues within this text. The book would be a much poorer effort without the input of these three individuals.

Several people in the evangelical community proved helpful interlocutors during the writing of this text. I particularly would like to thank the members of the ODM blog Herescope for our interchanges. I am also exceedingly grateful for the interchanges I have had with evangelical science fiction writers, notably Steve Rzasa, Kerry Nietz, Chris Walley, and Al Bohl. Such interchanges, as well as my own research into evangelical science fiction, helped me reframe the conclusion of the book. Chris Walley's influence goes even deeper than that, as he profoundly, if unknowingly, influenced my understanding of the libertarian aspects of Silicon Valley.

I wish to thank my friends and family for their help. At Broome Community College, I particularly thank Mary Seel, Chris Origer, Joshua Lewis, Alexis Katchuk, Carol Silverberg, Virginia Shirley, Deb Hibbard, and Gina Eckert. Special thanks go to Gina for getting me out of the doldrums on several occasions and helping me to refocus on writing. Alexis also helped me stop writing on one or two occasions where that was equally badly needed. At SUNY Binghamton, I offer my thanks to Collen Burke, Collen Bailey, Donna Berg, and Rose McNierney.

I especially thank my family: Edie and Dan Weaver, all the Jezierskis (Chet, Mooney, Carol, Jane, John), my brother David and sister Rachel, my cousins Keelie, Kieren, and Courtney, my uncle Mike and my aunt Evelyn. Finally, I honor the memory of my late grandparents, Mary and James (Jim) Sheridan, for all their help over the years, which I can never repay.

Preface

I began writing this book in the spring of 2016. At the time, I thought the task would be simple. I realized that the Christian Right at times utilized sophisticated management theory. However, my vision of the Christian Right gave too great a weight to the power of theological beliefs, rather than pragmatic considerations, over its management philosophy. This is, in many ways, quite a statement to make, as my previous writing, which aligns with the research approach of independent researchers like Bruce Wilson and Rachel Tabachnick, already leaned heavily to a pragmatic interpretation of Christian Right activities. What shocked me in writing *Technology, Management and the Evangelical Church* was the depth and sophistication of this pragmatic orientation, which far exceeds even the worst fears of the American left.

A number of foundational influences shaped this work. Three bear special mention. The first is the input and continued mentorship of Rachel Tabachnick. Although much of the material I found in *Technology, Management and the Evangelical Church* came about as the result of my own odd interest in management theory, Tabachnick served as a valuable resource for much of this work. It was at Tabachnick's instigation that I began looking for ways of relating this book to broader concerns regarding neoliberalism. She also played a central role in my continuing education regarding the New Right and Austrian school economics; the importance of this influence was so great that it fundamentally shaped the last three chapters of this book, and additionally led to a major rethink of the first few chapters. Moreover, Tabachnick's belief in the importance of the Leadership Network to the contemporary Christian Right served as one of the core assumptions that motivated my initial research. This work bears out in detail the correctness of Tabachnick's assumption about the Leadership Network.

Also important to me was the writings of authors sympathetic to the mission of Political Research Associates (PRA), most notably Frederick Clarkson. While this influence is less marked than that exerted by Tabachnick, it helped mold much of this book. Through authors like Clarkson and

Kapya Kaoma, I was able to gain a much fuller understanding of the Christian Right than would have otherwise been possible.

Finally, much of my interest in the material in this book has been shaped by the documentaries of Adam Curtis, a three-time UK BAFTA winner ("Adam Curtis: Awards" 2017) whose central concerns have revolved around issues of governance. While I am not a Curtis "groupie," I have found that the connections in seemingly disparate forms of governance that he posits in many of his major documentaries—notably *Century of the Self*, *Pandora's Box*, *The Trap*, and *All Watched Over by Machines of Loving Grace*—are nearly entirely accurate. Furthermore, while popular press accounts of Curtis portray him as a hyperbolic scaremonger,[1] the connections he posits are frequently widely conceded in mainstream academic writing.[2] In any case, what gives Curtis's documentaries their considerable power is their ability to take issues of governance outside the realm of reified academic abstractions and translate them to everyday people in a manner that is understandable, but not condescending. Therefore, whatever my personal disagreements with Curtis might be,[3] this work has been shaped by Curtis's connective approach to different forms of governance, as well as by his desire to communicate these connections in a translatable manner.

There are a number of factors that distinguish *Technology, Management and the Evangelical Church* from other works concerned with evangelical governance and management practices. The first is the historical breadth of this work, which is far more expansive than any other attempt at tracing these links. Not only does this work explore these links over a period that lasts more than a century, but it also explores the techniques of governance that the Christian Right uses in areas that are seldom explored by other academics, most notably in the work's rather idiosyncratic approach to the Christian Right's appropriation of information communications technologies (ICT[s]).

Secondly, this work seeks to problematize simplified readings of the Christian Right by noting the movement's surprising affinities with network theory, systems theory, cybernetics, complexity science, futurism and game theory, all part of or related to the so-called "cyborg sciences" as historian Philip Mirowski puts it (see Mirowski, 2002, 12–17). As this book extensively documents from Chapter 3 on, by the 1970s and accelerating thereafter, practices of church governance were increasingly aligned with almost all of these fields, most notably systems theory. Moreover, this work contends that it is almost futile to understand the governance policies of both evangelical and mainline churches without reference to these fields.

Although there are a number of other differences between this work and other works concerned with church governance, the only other difference I wish to highlight is an ideological one. My research is predicated on two core loyalties: the first is to progressive politics, despite my frustrations with the American left. The second is my commitment to serving my former co-religionists in the evangelical movement. Although I am only nominally religious today (a "broad church" Anglican), I grew up as a fundamentalist Protestant. Though my intellectual training was heavily Calvinist, my sympathies and theological commitments were mainly shaped by Arminian and pietist theologies. Because I grew up surrounded by *deeply* fundamentalist and anti-consumerist churches, I realize that drawing any one-to-one correspondence between the wider evangelical movement's theology and capitalism is potentially problematic. While there are certainly affinities between the two, such links should not be viewed as a natural state of being for American evangelicalism, but a fusion of concepts that should be problematized by academics. At the same time, my commitment to a progressive vision of religion means that I am deeply suspicious of any attempts to normalize neoliberal economics as a state of evangelical normativity that should not be interrogated. It is this concern that fundamentally distances me from the numerous scholars of evangelicalism associated with the Templeton Foundation. These scholars, most notably Donald E. Miller in *Reinventing American Protestantism: Christianity in the New Millennium* (1999) and Brad Christerson and Richard Flory's *The Rise of Network Christianity: How Independent Leaders Are Changing the Religious Landscape* (2017) promote a naïve rendering of the Christian Right's adoption of neoliberal and "new economy" management practices. Thus, while these works are certainly useful to interested scholars—particularly Miller's work, whose insights into new paradigm churches (NPC) are of historical importance not only to academics, but to how network Christianity viewed itself—they must be treated with caution. As my previous work, *The New Apostolic Reformation: History of a Modern Charismatic Movement* (2016) documents, the Templeton Foundation has extensive links to the Christian Right (see Weaver 2016, 13–16, as well as Weaver, 2015). Moreover, Miller oversaw a major research initiative on Pentecostalism and Charismatic Christianity undertaken by the Templeton Foundation ("Donald E. Miller"). Likewise, Richard Flory was an important participant in Templeton-funded research on Pentecostalism and collaborated with Miller on several projects ("Richard Flory: Associate Professor [Research] of Sociology" 2017; "Pentecostal and Charismatic Research Initiative" n.d.). As I have argued elsewhere, the links between Templeton research and the Christian Right are so extensive—for instance, Donald E. Miller was on C. Peter Wagner's dissertation committee (Wagner 1977, i)—that it is impossible to consider this research objective. Nevertheless, for those interested in issues of Christian governance and management practices, the two works of Miller, Christerson and Flory are a good place to start.

As far as works that I would recommend on Christian management and governance practices, two particularly stand out. The first, *Protestants and American Business Methods* (1979) is by far the most detailed historical examination of the adoption of Taylorist business practices by churches. The second work of special significance to *Technology, Management and the Evangelical Church*'s interpretation of Christian Right governance practices is Robert Doornenbal's dissertation "Crossroads: An Exploration of the Emerging-Missional Conversation with a Special Focus on 'Missional Leadership' and Its Challenges for Theological Education" (2012). While Doornenbal's work focuses on the Emergent Missional Conversation (EMC)—which is usually and, to my mind problematically, seen as somehow separate from the Christian Right—it has broad applications to how the Christian Right is interpreted. As this book extensively documents, many of the management practices of the EMC have their origins in the Leadership Network (LN), and nevertheless have garnered the support of this powerful subsection of "liberal" Protestantism; moreover, as *Technology, Management and the Evangelical Church* explores, much of the organizational methodology of the EMC and LN is reflected throughout the Christian Right as well. Finally, I would also point interested readers to Warner Anderson Smith's dissertation "An Analysis of Church Consultation in the North American Church, 1960–2003" (2006).

Astute readers will note that two of the three sources recommended here are dissertations. This is not a coincidence. Any breadth or depth that this work possesses is in many ways chiefly attributable to the fact that I have relied first on dissertation research, secondly on primary resources written by Christian Right or mainline promoters of church growth and related fields (such as church marketing and church health), and only lastly on academic monographs. While this decision was initially motivated by monetary considerations, the fundamental reason I chose to approach my research in this manner soon became academic. Research undertaken by students—here, almost exclusively Ph.D. candidates—has been both *far more thorough and far more objective* about the Christian Right than that undertaken by already-published authors. Such research also often covers fields understudied or simply unstudied by academics. The vision of an ideologically unsophisticated Christian Right leadership that is promoted by certain elements of both the left and the Christian Right itself is rendered suspect by even a cursory reading of the dissertations produced by evangelical intellectual powerhouses, such as Fuller Seminary and its offshoots, the Southern Baptist Theological Seminary (SBTS), Westminster Seminary, and New Orleans Baptist Theological Seminary (NOBTS). Therefore, I not only unapologetically utilize dissertations as a major venue of research, but make a much stronger claim, or plea. The claim is simply this: continued efforts at researching the Christian Right that rely primarily on publicly available print sources, such as books, or alternately archival research, increasingly runs the risk of giving academia a "tunnel vision" concerning the Christian Right, one that leaves academics unable to understand the true complexity and sophistication of the Christian Right. While I would not dream of suggesting that academics simply abandon the archives or publicly available print sources, such research must also increasingly take into account digital archives or databases, as well as Web sources, if scholars are to gain a complete understanding of the Christian Right. My ability to engage with the history of the Leadership Network in far greater detail than Christerson and Flory, for instance, is as attributable to my methodology of research as it is to the ideological differences that shape our contrasting worldviews.

Acronyms

CAS(s)—Complex Adaptive System(s)
CG—Church Growth
CGM—Church Growth Movement
CH—Church Health
CHM—Church Health Movement
COR—Club of Rome
CP—Church Planting
CPI—Committee on Public Information
CPM—Church Planting Movement
DAWN—Disciple a Whole Nation
EFF—Electronic Frontier Foundation
EMC—Emerging Missional Conversation
FLF—Fort Lauderdale Five
GBN—Global Business Network
GST—General Systems Theory
HMB—Home Mission Board
IACG—Institute for American Church Growth
ICT(s)—Information and Communication Technology/Technologies
ID—Intelligent Design
IWM—Interchurch World Movement
JP—Jesus People
JPM—Jesus People Movement
LN—Leadership Network
LST—Living Systems Theory
MARC—Missions Advanced Research Center
MBO—Management by Objectives/Ministry by Objectives
MCM—Missional Change Model
MRFM—Men and Religion Forward Movement
NAE—National Association of Evangelicals
NAR—New Apostolic Reformation
NCC—National Council of Churches

NCD—Natural Church Development
NPC—New Paradigm Church
NPM—New Public Management
NRM—New Religious Movement(s)
NTL—National Training Laboratory
OSI—Open Systems Interconnection
PFF—Progress and Freedom Foundation
PRA—Political Research Associates
PTP—Project Test Pattern
RCT—Rational Choice Theory
RISE—Research in Strategic Evangelization
SBC—Southern Baptist Convention
SGM—Sovereign Grace Ministries
SIL—Summer Institute of Linguistics
SM—Shepherding Movement
TQM—Total Quality Management/Total Quality Ministry
WCA—Willow Creek Association
WELL—Whole Earth "Lectronic" Link
YFC—Youth for Christ
YLN—Young Leadership Network
ZPG—Zero Population Growth

Introduction

Technology, Management and the Evangelical Church traces the history of management and governance practices within the evangelical movement over the last century. Such an expansive vision means that, of necessity, some aspects of this history must be left out. To truly explore every aspect of such governance would involve exploring many more fields than this book has the time to cover. For instance, the evangelical movement's approach to conflict management, environmental management, nuclear policy, and psychology could all be considered legitimate areas of exploration under a broad definition of governance practices. This work therefore primarily focuses on the evangelical church's increasing appropriation of business practices from the secular world as solutions to organizational problems. But as the history of this governance progresses, an increasing focus on the importance of quantifying spiritual life and rendering such data quickly and effectively led many Protestant churches, both mainline and evangelical, to adopt techniques developed by the "cyborg sciences" to more effectively manage and control churches. Such techniques included direct borrowings from cybernetics, systems theory, system dynamics, strategic planning, and scenario planning and could align the Christian Right (not to mention mainline Protestants) with some surprisingly odd bedfellows.

Chapter 1 covers the development of Taylorist principles within evangelical and mainline Protestant churches at the beginning of the 20th century, though these principles actually slightly predate Taylorism in some ways. Particularly important to understand is the desire for efficiency Taylorism promulgated throughout the whole of American society. Although Taylorist ideas were adopted by both mainline Protestants and evangelicals, they appear to have been more systematically accepted in mainline denominations. Mainline denominations, for better or worse, came to be seen as bureaucratically oriented, while evangelical denominations, and particularly non-denominational parachurch organizations, were associated with more decentralized organizational principles. Chapter 1 then traces the adoption of decentralized organizational models in a number of successive evangelical movements, such as the parachurch movement (represented here by groups such as the Navigators and Campus Crusade for Christ), the shepherding movement, the Jesus People Movement (also sometimes known as the Jesus Movement, but hereafter abbreviated as JPM), and the small group/cell church movement. The chapter also explores early connections made between the National Training Laboratory (NTL) and mainline Protestantism, which is necessary for an understanding of Protestant group life. Protestant appropriation of NTL's encounter groups, as well as Kurt Lewin's revolutionary insights into organizational life, is now widespread. This chapter serves to offer some explanations as to why this is the case.

Chapter 2 offers up a history of the church growth movement (CGM), whose promotion of social science methods and the importation of quantifiable data are central to understanding the continued employment of spiritual metrics and "cyborg sciences" by the Christian Right. This chapter, along with Chapter 3, also lays the groundwork for understanding debates in the evangelical movement surrounding equilibrium concepts and the Second Law of Thermodynamics. This work contends that the CGM and most of its allies were motivated by cornucopian assumptions that markets faced few or no "limits to growth"; these assumptions were grounded in a nearly religious belief, foundational in both the Christian Right and neoliberalism, that human innovation negates any limits to growth that entropy might impose on the global economy.

Chapter 3 traces the adoption of cybernetics and systems theory, especially as a means of governance, by both mainline Protestants and the Christian Right. Particularly important in this history is an understanding of the influential role the Club of Rome's *Limits to Growth* (1972) report played in influencing both mainline Protestant and evangelical thought. The chapter traces the influence of "limits to growth" thinking and systems theory on the church health movement, particularly Christian Schwarz's model of Natural Church Development (NCD), a theory of church health grounded in the bio-cybernetic ideology of Frederic Vester that is quite popular among both evangelicals and mainline Protestants. The chapter concludes with an exploration of the influence of systems theory on the emergent-missional conversation, as well as the EMC's extensive appropriation of other elements of "cyborg science."

Chapter 4 explores the rise of networked Christianity. Informed primarily by the research of Sara Diamond and Rachel Tabachnick, but also referencing the New Paradigm Church (NPC) model that Miller promoted, this chapter looks at a number of evangelical movements that have taken on aspects of networked Christianity, such as Willow Creek, the Leadership Network (LN), New Calvinism, and the church planting movement. Through this exploration, a number of characteristics of networked Christianity are teased out, particularly its allegiance to Toyotist forms of organizational management.

Chapter 5 looks at the union of cyber-libertarian and Christian Right ideology, paying particular attention to a few seminal figures—Kevin Kelly and *Wired* Magazine, as well as George Gilder and Discovery Institute. Chapter 5 attempts to draw out major inconsistencies between the evangelical beliefs of Gilder and Kelly and their embrace of the discourses of neoliberalism, the new economy, and bionomics. Chapter 5 then segues into a broader appraisal and evaluation of the Christian Right's development of information and communication technology (ICT), particularly its use of Web 2.0. The cumulative effect of the research in Chapters 4 and 5 suggests that the ideological affinities, and, in many cases, organizational connections between such notable cyber-libertarians as John Perry Barlow, Stewart Brand, Esther Dyson, and the Christian Right is much deeper than is commonly understood.

Chapter 6 explores the creation of modern evangelicalism's information infrastructure. Besides looking at the creation of what could be called an evangelical Web, this chapter explores specific IT practices followed by many evangelical churches. After looking at evangelical applications of Big Data, the chapter concludes with an exploration of evangelicalism's attempts to shape Silicon Valley culture.

Definition of Evangelicalism

One of the favored definitions for evangelicalism is advanced by British historian D.W. Bebbington. Bebbington outlines four distinguishing characteristics of evangelical belief: "conversionism, the belief that lives need to be changed; activism, the expression of the gospel in effort; biblicism, a particular regard for the Bible and what may be called crucicentrism, a stress on the sacrifice of Christ on the cross" (Bebbington 1989, 2–3). Although Bebbington's work in evangelical studies is valuable, this definition questionably privileges rightwing explanations of evangelical belief. The biblicist element, in particular, does not seem relevant to a modern evangelicalism that is starting to form both conservative and liberal forms of postmodernist scriptural critique that question the traditional evangelical literalist hermeneutic. Bebbington's definition also ignores the significant similarities that have existed historically between traditional evangelicalism and mainline Protestantism.

Similarly, as I have argued in *Evangelicals and the Arts in Fiction* (2013), denominational definitions are a problematic tool for classifying evangelicals. Many denominations have both evangelical and mainline wings, ranging from the Mennonites to the Southern Baptists. Also, even groups which are traditionally thought of as mainline denominations have large evangelical wings (see Sweeney 2005, 19). Since denominational identities are not fixed, the historical time period in which one is looking at is also important to understanding whether a denomination is evangelical. For instance, the denominational ancestors of the United Churches of Christ would have arguably been considered evangelical during the early 19th century, but not today. Fixed denominational definitions of evangelical belief therefore simply do not work (Weaver 2013, 11). I therefore utilize, with a few caveats, the system offered up by Fritz Detwiler. Detwiler divides the religious right into six parts (one of which is Catholicism). The five major divisions of evangelical belief that Detwiler argues for are fundamentalists, Holiness, Pentecostal/charismatic, born-again evangelicals (which in this work are referred to as neo-evangelicals) and Reformed Christians (Detwiler 1999, 150–155). Fundamentalism is a theological movement originally characterized by its opposition to theological modernism and evolutionary theory (Marsden 2006, 3–4). Holiness Christianity is notable mainly for the primacy it places on the pietistic life as the mark of true Christian behavior (Detwiler 1999, 152). Neo-evangelicalism is largely distinguishable from fundamentalism, its spiritual progenitor, by a greater willingness to embrace a diversity of hermeneutical viewpoints concerning Scripture, and by a tendency to try to engage with culture, instead of fight against it. Pentecostalism is a major subset of modern Christianity characterized by strong belief in the gifts of the spirit, such as speaking in tongues, prophecy, the casting out of demons, and so on.

Reformed Christianity is a theological system that is much too complex to simply and neatly define. However, in popular evangelical usage today, it typically refers to those evangelicals who draw their theological inspiration from the "teachings of John Calvin" (Detwiler 1999, 154), or, much more rarely, one of the other early Reformed leaders, such as Guillaume Farel. Opponents of Reformed Christianity often simplify its core doctrines to simply a belief in predestination or the famous, and frequently misused, TULIP designation (Total depravity, Unconditional election, Limited atonement, Irresistible grace, and Perseverance of the saints). However, Reformed beliefs go beyond such simplifications. As Molly Worthen notes, the Reformed tradition focused on "the depravity of humankind, the awesome sovereignty of God, and the Christian mandate to transform earthly society according to God's command" (Worthen 2013, loc. 276). Central to most modern Reformed thought (outside of now mainline Reformed denominations), is a strong belief in the value of pastoral care, a firm belief in the value of church discipline, and a preoccupation with correct ecclesiology. Two factions of the modern Reformed movement are particularly prominent in this work, Christian Reconstructionists and New Calvinists. For the sake of simplicity, I follow William C. Martin's parsimonious, if inadequate, definition of Christian Reconstructionism, which contends that "[b]roadly speaking, Reconstructionists believe that Christians have a mandate to rebuild, or reconstruct, all of human society, beginning with the United States and moving outward. They contend that the Bible, particularly Mosaic Law, offers the perfect blueprint for the shape a reconstructed world would take" (Martin 2005, 353). Reconstructionism is most well-known for its infamous desire to make homosexuality, adultery, blasphemy and repeated disobedience on the part of children punishable by death (Martin 2005, 353). While some non–Calvinists may consider themselves Reconstructionists, the vast majority of the movement aligns itself with Reformed philosophy. The movement's influence, however, extends considerably beyond the Reformed movement, despite frequent academic denials to the contrary. Reconstructionism is sometimes seen as synonymous with dominionism, but this assumption is erroneous. Dominionism itself is a "theocratic idea that regardless of theological view or eschatological timetable Christians are called by God to exercise dominion over society by taking control of political and cultural institutions" (Rachel Tabachnick and Frederick Clarkson 2015, personal communication). However, as Tabachnick and Clarkson point out, while Reconstructionism was "crucial to the spread of Dominionism among Neocharismatics and subsidiary movements within Pentecostalism," dominionist ideas within the Pentecostal and Charismatic movements can be traced back even earlier, to the Latter Rain movement (Tabachnick and Clarkson 2015, personal communication). For the purpose of this book, the crucial element to understand is that Reconstructionism played an influential role on evangelical approaches to organizational decentralization (see McVicar 2010, 326–331, 334 and Ingersoll 2015, 169–170, 239). Another ill-defined group of evangelicals, the seeker-sensitive church movement, has no set denominational affiliation, but concentrates mainly on gaining new followers and creating massive megachurches. As a general rule, if seeker-sensitive churches do have a denominational or theological leaning, it is to the Word of Faith movement (Prosperity Gospel), which has its roots in Charismatic teaching, or to the Third Wave Charismatic movement, whose most influential contemporary figure is C. Peter Wagner.

A significant difference between this work's definition of evangelicalism and my first two books is that this work contends that the difference between Charismatic and Pentecostal belief (two theological systems which are both devoted to the "gifts of the spirit") is much larger than most scholars have previously realized. In popular evangelical *lingua franca*, churches are often labeled Charismatic as a means of denoting them from what many see as the more extreme Pentecostal brand of Christianity. In fact, if one looks into the history of the Charismatic movement as it has developed over the last fifty years, the opposite image emerges. While the initial impetus toward Charismatic belief arose in mainline Protestantism during the 1960s and was therefore seen by some as a liberal alternative to the then disreputable mainstream Pentecostal churches, the Charismatic Renewal became increasingly hardline over the course of its existence. When the Renewal eventually hit non-mainline churches—that is mainstream evangelicalism—it would morph into what is commonly called the Third Wave of Pentecostalism. Much of this wave, in turn, evolved into the New Apostolic Reformation (NAR), a movement that bypasses traditional Pentecostal denominational hierarchies in favor of a top-down system of almost dictatorial control on the part of certain "apostolic" leaders. A plethora of terminology is used to describe the Pentecostal and Charismatic movement. The difference between Charismatics and Pentecostals is important to understand, but the problem is that the difference is often irrelevant to the actual spiritual and political practice of the two groups. In addition, there is a huge overlap between classical (traditional denominationally based) Pentecostalism and the Charismatic movement, particularly in many Third Wave Charismatic churches. Nor is the scholarship on Pentecostal and Charismatic terminology very helpful. Much of the scholarship on Third Wave Pentecostals for instance, emphasizes the Third Wave movement's rather restrained character. C. Peter Wagner, for instance, has characterized the movement's "acceptance of tongues" as "low-key" and has said the movement avoids "divisiveness at almost any cost" (Wagner 2002, 1141). Yet anyone with any knowledge of the contemporary Charismatic movement knows that the most radical theology coming out of the movement today either originated in the Third Wave or was adopted by the Third Wave from First Wave (classic Pentecostal) and Second Wave (Charismatic Renewal) Charismatics.

There is no good way to refer to Pentecostal belief as a whole. The use of the term Charismatic/Pentecostal is too unwieldy, and while Margaret Poloma's abbreviation of that to C/P in *Main Street Mystics* (Poloma 2003, passim) is serviceable, I have found that its usage tends to jar the reading of a text. I therefore have typically used the term Charismatic to refer to the movement as a whole, Pentecostal to refer specifically to classical and denominational Pentecostalism, and Charismatic Renewal to refer to the second wave of the Charismatic movement. When needed, I have also used the term Third Wave Charismatic, the rubric under which the majority of NAR adherents would fall.

The present book's approach to the emergent and missional churches—referred to hereafter as the Emerging Missional Conversation (EMC)—has been largely guided by Robert Doornenbal's excellent and exhaustive treatment of that movement, "Crossroads: An Exploration of the Emerging-Missional Conversation with a Special Focus on 'Missional Leadership' and Its Challenges for Theological Education" (2012). As Doornenbal notes, there is no universally accepted definition of the EMC. In general, churches that adhere to the model emphasize flexibility, the importance of community, decentralized power structures, a fondness for technology, and postmodern hermeneutics (Doornenbal 2012, 3, 10, 12–13). I largely also follow Doornenbal's description of the missional part of this conversation. The key insight of missional theology is that the church should move from an attractional mindset, in which the world comes to the church, to an incarnational mindset, where the church goes to the world. I would caution the reader, however, that Doornenbal does underestimate how pervasive the missional movement is within evangelicalism. Doornenbal sees missional Christianity's leadership as primarily mainline (Doornebal 2012, 5), a position which at this point in time must be significantly more qualified than when Doornenbal's dissertation was published in 2012.

Mainline Protestantism plays a much more prominent role in this work than in my previous books, so I will attempt to address it more carefully than I have in the past. As Jason Lantzer notes, defining mainline Protestantism can often seem deceptively obvious. Traditionally, the mainline was seen as a core group of seven denominations: "The Congregational Church (now a part of the United Church of Christ), the Episcopal Church, the Evangelical Lutheran Church, the Presbyterian Church (USA), the United Methodist Church, the American Baptist Convention, and the Disciples of Christ" (Lantzer 2012, 1). Among some evangelicals, mainline Protestantism is often seen as synonymous with liberal Protestantism. This definitional equivalency is problematic on a number of counts. For one thing, mainline Protestants have often wrangled over the meaning of theological liberalism within their own tradition.[1] Moreover, mainline Protestantism has a large and vocal renewal movement which is often sympathetic to evangelicalism. Therefore, for the purpose of this book, mainline Protestants are defined as members of the seven core mainline denominations, who generally but not universally subscribe to politically liberal and theologically modernist beliefs.

Notes on Terminology

One of the most crucial terms that the reader must understand before one can address the use of management and governance practices in churches is the concept of managerialism. There is no universally held definition of managerialism. However, for the purpose of this work, I build off of the research of Jean Isabel Matthews, who wrote about managerialism in the context of her study of the British National Health Services. Matthews contends that managerialism "generates the notion that organizational order ceases to be pre-ordained and is the arena for management intervention and control"

(Matthews 2000, 7). This notion is centered in the belief "that systems are controllable and should be controlled," leading to a "machine like perspective of the organization and a partiality for cybernetic and ideological philosophies of management" (Matthews 2000, 7).

A crucial contention of this book, which may shock readers familiar with cybernetics and systems theory, is that much of Protestant management practice is now rooted in the same cybernetic orientation to the control of personnel. Upon reflection, however, the adoption of these practices by both mainline Protestants and the Christian Right appears to be more inevitable than noteworthy. Mainline Protestants consistently rank among the most well-educated of Americans,[2] so their adoption of systems theory follows naturally from similar appropriations of systems theory in most secular fields as well. Nor is the Christian Right's appropriation of cybernetic and systems perspectives at all surprising. As demonstrated in Chapter 3, leaders in the Christian Right have long understood the implication of systems concepts, including those derived from general systems theory (GST). In any case, the popularization of systems concepts in the wake of the publication of Peter Senge's *The Fifth Discipline* (1990) ensured the ideology's adoption by the Christian Right. As Chapter 3 demonstrates, this adoption occurred far earlier in the evangelical movement than most scholars would presuppose.

Obviously, adopting a cybernetic or systems-based approach to managing congregational life has far reaching theological and ideological implications. The belief that systems "are controllable and should be controlled" leads many churches, both mainline and conservative, to view their congregants in highly mechanistic terms (see Matthews 2000, 7, on this characteristic of systems). Discussions of feedback loops, open systems, living systems, input and output and other terminology associated with systems concepts is fairly rife through much of church management literature.[3] Moreover, the appropriation of systems concepts by church management gurus leads to the dangerous simplification of organizational metaphors. The ideal 21st-century church, as shown in Chapter 3, is reified as a living system, in contrast to the previous "bureaucratic" or "institutional" church of the past. In the process, a holistic approach to understanding congregational life has gained ascendancy. Doornenbal has noted that such institutional metaphors have proven particularly attractive to those involved in the EMC. EMC authors often utilize the term as ideological shorthand for what they are discarding (Doornenbal 2012, 137). Doornenbal has noted with some concern the affinity that modern holistic metaphors have with fascistic forms of holistic thinking developed by the Nazis (Doornenbal 2012, 138). These concerns are hardly unrealistic. As I myself pointed out in *The New Apostolic Reformation*, similar organic metaphors have been utilized by the New Apostolic Reformation, many times with a distinctly *volkisch* connotation (Weaver 2016, 170–184).

Doornenbal and I are not alone in questioning the appropriateness of utilizing holistic metaphors as the language of managerial control in churches. Lyndon Shakespeare, for instance, has contended that organizational theorists' vision of the body "as a mechanical organism" has led to a form of reductionism in which "the body" of an organization is preserved, while the "actual agent," the organizational ghost in the machine, "remains overlooked" (Shakespeare 2016, loc. 2337–2343). Managerialism's tendency to view human beings as little more than metric data problematically casts individuals as merely cogs in an organizational machine; cogs that can be controlled via carefully modulated feedback loops in which ministry teams methodically organize what their church systems output and what those same systems allow to be input into their organization.

Managerialism is a practice that is often intertwined with neoliberalism, though as Thomas Klikaeur notes, they are not synonymous (Klikaeur 2015, 1107). Understanding neoliberalism is also quite important in understanding the ideological project that motivates church management and governance practices. David Harvey, a leading writer on neoliberalism, notes that the most important aspect of neoliberal ideology is its promotion of "strong private property rights, free markets, and free trade" in the ideological interest of creating "individual entrepreneurial freedom" (David Harvey 2005, 2). Within a neoliberal framework, the objectives of the state are clearly delineated. It should ensure that the value of the nation's currency is not called into question. Moreover, the state must promote those political bodies that protect "private property rights," such as the armed forces and the judicial system. Without the existence of these elements of society, the markets cannot function. Neoliberal thinkers argue that where markets have not been established, they should be formed. Neoliberalism presupposes, however, that interventionist policies undertaken by the state to control markets are doomed to failure, and it is therefore preferable to let the markets, as much as possible, regulate themselves (David Harvey 2005, 2). Neoliberal ideology brings with it a particular theory of state "governance" which has specific implications for how the state should ideally view both the corporate world and itself. Neoliberal states emphasize "competitiveness, interest, and decentralization," with the decentralization aspect being particularly important. Instead of embracing centralized authority, the ideal neoliberal state cedes as much power as possible to "smaller localized units," which are run on market principles. From a neoliberal perspective, the goal of the state is not first and foremost the promotion of "the public good" but instead the promotion of "profits." Neoliberals hope to achieve this kind of organizational efficiency by a host of techniques borrowed from the corporate world, such as the use of strategic planning, quantitative benchmarks, and the use of rational choice theory (RCT) to promote an organizational mindset that "internalize[s] and thus normalize[s] market-oriented behavior" (Steger and Roy 2010, 12–13). Neoliberal ideology, particularly within the New Public Management (NPM) framework deemphasizes the value of bureaucratic structures and instead argues for the empowerment of state workers to achieve their goals via the entrepreneurial techniques of the market. In this model, citizens are seen as "customers" whose consumer needs should be satiated via the mechanisms of the market (Steger and Roy 2010, 12–13). NPM models typically emphasize such values as "administrative efficiency, effectiveness, and accountability" (Steger and Roy, 2010, 13).

Neoliberalism led to the public sector taking on many aspects of the private sector, including the managerial ideology of the corporations. Given contemporary theories about organizational isomorphism,[4] it is therefore not surprising that managerialism has not only infected the public sector and the private sector, but the spiritual "sector" as well. As this book consistently demonstrates, churches are not immune to the force of institutional change that shapes other societal organizations. Thus, the shaping of the Christian Right and even many parts of mainline Protestantism around neoliberal principles is the predictable outgrowth of the more global adoption of neoliberal economic ideas. While in an ideal world, churches should be able to resist the pressures that force them to take on corporate organizational techniques, realistically such a situation is not likely to occur. Protestant churches have in many ways acted no worse than other societal institutions in their co-opting of business techniques; indeed, in some cases, both among conservative and liberal Protestants, they have arguably put up a spirited resistance against these homogenizing tendencies.

Two other closely related theories, game theory and RCT, are also of importance in understanding contemporary Protestant approaches to governance. Game theory emphasized a view of "human rationality" in which two entities aimed to develop strategies that optimized "their expected utilities" (Amadae 2003, 76). Amadae contends that for neoliberalism, the model "neoliberal citizen and consumer is the strategic rational actor modeled by orthodox game theory" (Amadae, 2015 xvi–xvii). RCT, as Amadae notes, advances the same argument. This model of rational agents, grounded in Cold War concerns about U.S. nuclear strategy created an image of rational actors as motivated by a morality that was "consequentialist, realist, individualistic, and amoral" (Amadae, 2015 xvi–xvii). As Amadae points out, the "canonical rational actor," through the policy dilemmas that faced the American establishment during the Cold War, was transformed from a figure that was known to be fictional to a "stand-in for ideal rational agents throughout international relations, civil politics, and even evolutionary biology" (Amadae 2015, xvi–xvii). Game theorists saw "strategic rationality" as an "all-encompassing theory of rational decision making" (Amadae 2015, xvi–xvii). Thus, the assumptions of strategic rationality, were applied by RCT theorists (such as the advocates of NPM) to the political sphere (Amadae 2015, xvi–xvii).

What this meant in principle is actually relatively simple to explain. Classical liberal capitalism, while it had its problems, was predicated on a moral, rather than amoral, reading of the market, and therefore promoted a "no harm principle" (Amadae 2015, i). This meant that classical liberal capitalism at least acknowledged the importance of "individual human dignity" and mutual social responsibility. Neoliberalism, however, utilizing noncooperative game theory, saw individual rational agents as engaged in a battle for "scare resources" in which "every individual seeks dominance" (Amadae 2015, i). For advocates of neoliberal applications of noncooperative game theory and RCT, "solidarity and good will" no longer exists and all human relationships are viewed as operating on a "quid pro quo basis" (Amadae 2015, i).

While there are relatively few references to RCT and game theory in church growth or church management literature, the fundamental assumptions of these fields regarding human nature are reflected through much of the church growth movement's (CGM), church health movement's (CHM), EMC movement's, and Leadership Network's approach to church governance. In particular, most of these movements, particularly the church growth movement and the Leadership Network, share the ideological preference of neoliberalism and RCT for modeling human agency based on noncooperative assumptions. Although these noncooperative assumptions are often rooted, either explicitly or implicitly in Calvinist notions of humanity's fundamentally selfish nature, rather than in game theory or RCT, the acceptance of this view of human nature has helped pave the way for the dominance of neoliberal economic models among evangelicals.

Recent models of Protestant management and governance practices, which have been notably more open about mainline Protestant and evangelical adaptations of cybernetics and systems theory, have also borrowed notably from complex systems theory, alternately known as "second order cybernetics" or complexity science. While the exact principles of complexity science are outlined in Chapter 3, for the purpose of this introduction the important thing to realize about complexity science is that it seeks to explain how "systems adapt, evolve, and self-organize not in spite of crisis but through the very means of crisis" (Cooper 2011, 373). This theory has considerable attraction to neoliberalism for two reasons. First, neoliberals, led by Friedrich von Hayek, saw complexity theory as a means of supporting deregulatory efforts. Hayek believed that "the natural complexity of market phenomena was such that no centralized authority could hope to predict, much less control, the precise evolution of individual elements in the system" (Cooper 2011, 373). Thus, complexity science was a perfect tool to advance both deregulatory efforts and government policy predicated on a "hands off" approach to market regulation (Cooper 2011, 376). Neither mainline Protestantism nor the Christian Right were slow to realize the potential implications for governance that complexity science created. The metaphors of complexity science have been used by various evangelical and mainline movements and institutions, most notably the Alban Institute, the Leadership Network, and the EMC, to advance explicitly "deregulatory" visions of church structure, church leadership, and even theology. The adoption of complexity science by the Christian Right, and mainline Protestantism thus provides an important backdrop to the second half of this book.

Neoliberals liked the idea of complexity science for another reason. It fit in well with another Austrian school economist's views on disequilibrium states. This economist was Joseph Schumpeter, who popularized the concept of "creative destruction" (Fisher 2007, 99). Creative destruction is a theoretical process that involves businesses forming "new wants and products" while at the same time, making "older wants, commodities and jobs obsolete." Schumpeter saw creative destruction as fundamental to "economic growth," but it also made capitalist economies subject to frequent states of market disequilibrium. However, for Schumpeter, these periods of market disequilibrium were part of a "benevolent, positive, and progressive ... process of disequilibrium" (Fisher 2007, 99). The role of the government in stopping these market disturbances is to do precisely nothing, since the process of creative destruction is ultimately beneficial to the economy (Fisher 2007, 99). The evangelical movement has readily borrowed from Schumpeter on this score, with the CGM's and LN's deployment of Everett Rogers diffusion of innovation research being a particular open example of the debt evangelical organizational gurus owe to Schumpeter's admittedly idiosyncratic rendering of Austrian School economics.

At points in this book I have described current forms of evangelical governance as having Toyotist characteristics. While there are debates about the historical uniqueness of Toyotism as an organizational paradigm, for the purpose of this work what I seek to highlight are certain aspects of evangelical governance practices that resemble characteristics of Toyotism. As a whole, Toyotism is characterized by "just in time" supply systems which help reduce inventory sizes, better quality control practices that ideally lead to "near zero defects"; better resource allocation; greater worker involvement in the production process; particularly through the incorporation of ideas of teamwork; and "flat" governance structures. As we will see, churches follow Toyotist organizational principles in surprising ways (Castells 2010a, 169). When it comes to debates surrounding Toyotism, the differences between my work and Templeton-financed scholars is narrower than in other areas. The major difference, which in particular tends to separate me from Donald E. Miller, is that Toyotist practices are, for me, primarily seen as valuable from a descriptive standpoint, whereas Miller appears to be more prescriptive in his approach to these practices.

Toyotism had specific effects on spirituality's place in the workplace. This is particularly true of New Age and Eastern spirituality. Much of the evangelical church's appropriation of systems theory occurred via popularizers of New Age or Eastern systems concepts. The characteristics of this new workplace spirituality were as, Anne Dyer-Witherford notes, strikingly similar to the workplace organizational ideology of Toyotism or post–Fordism as it eventually gelled together in the modern workplace (Dyer-Witherford 2017, 30–31, 216–219). Both Nigel Thrift and R. John Williams have noted similar trends. Thrift has pointed out the emphasis on "new paradigms" within the New Age movement, as well as the transmission of new workplace values through centers/purveyors of the human potential movement, such as est (Thrift 2005, 63). New Age techniques are also imported into management via the application of "New Age training" which is popular in management circles because it seeks to recognize such scientific fields as "quantum physics, cybernetics … and chaos theory" (Thrift 2005, 41). Thrift contends that this fusion of New Age ideas with thinking in the hard sciences allows managers to market the importance of "soft skills," particularly "intuition" and "vision" to the workforce (Thrift 2005, 41). R. John Williams has noted a similar trend, more a direct borrowing, of what he terms "oriental systems theory," by management (R. John Williams 2016, 478, 485). This form of systems thinking Williams has characterized, in juxtaposition to the "computationalist, rationalist" cybernetics tradition, as "narratological … avant gardist, quasi-religious, and generally committed to various Oriental philosophies" (R. John Williams 2016, 477, 478). Whatever the terminology employed, when the use of systems theory, complexity theory, and other sophisticated forms of management practice gained widespread currency in the evangelical movement, their early proselytizers often transmitted them via thinkers such as Peter Senge or Margaret Wheatley, who were closely associated with "new paradigm" thinking, "neospirituality" or "Oriental Systems theory." These thinkers typically utilized a deliberately mystified discourse on contemporary physics—aligning them with so-called "popular physics" promoters—combined with various management tools that utilized more or less conscious management appropriations of cognitive reframing practices.[5] The promotion of New Paradigm thinking has led to widespread concerns in the evangelical public about the potential spiritual implications of the shift from Fordist models of spirituality to post–Fordist or Toyotist models of spirituality. Within this text, this theme is pursued most strongly in Chapter 4 and the Conclusion, but remains an important consideration throughout.

Finally, this work is deeply indebted to scholars who engage with "Whole Earth" or "whole systems" discourse. This discourse was primarily created in the 1960s as an attempt to affirm an ecologically centered understanding of the world. Much of this discourse revolved around Stewart Brand, the fascinating publisher of *The Whole Earth Catalog*. In contrast to ecological paradigms that saw nature and technology as fundamentally in conflict, Brand sought to legitimate forms of technology which could productively interact with their natural environment. "Whole systems" technologies, informed by cybernetics, most notably the computer, thus became fundamental to the mission of this discourse (Bryant 2006, 1). Chapters 4 and 5 both engage with this discourse, which had a surprisingly large influence on the evangelical movement.

I have explored these somewhat complicated terminological questions in depth because they are reflective of a trend that is broadly characteristic of both neoliberalism and evangelical governance practices: de-democratization. The contemporary justification for de-democratization has a diverse number of roots, but among their chief pillars of support is a philosophy known as the Californian ideology, and which is also referred to in this book as cyber-libertarianism or the digital discourse. The Californian ideology arose in the Bay Area as a fusion of counterculture ideas and pro-computer empowerment rhetoric and was popularized by key segments of the counterculture, especially supporters of Whole Earth discourse (Barbrook and Cameron 1996, 1, 3; Turner 2002, 25, 34–35). The ideology combined its countercultural ideals with technological utopian beliefs derived from "the convergence of media, computing and telecommunications" (Barbrook and Cameron 1996, 3). Like the rest of neoliberal ideology, the Californian ideology promoted the creation of a radically decentralized society. Californian Ideology Proponents, however, went further than this, by attempting to demonstrate that the creation of the Internet had the ability to create a society almost free of hierarchies, based on "an idealized neoclassical market" (Turner 2002, 18). Ideologues who supported the Californian ideology or cyber-libertarianism often used metaphors derived "from science fiction ('cyberspace'), American history ('electronic frontier') and mystical theology ('noosphere')" to construct their vision of an idyllic future based on leveled sociopolitical hierarchies and human beings who had been "empowered" by the Net (Turner 2002, 6). Others, as we will see, adapted biological concepts, in which the Internet was portrayed as a transitional evolutionary point to "a new stage in human evolution" (Turner 2002, 6). This new economy would act like an "'ecosystem'" (Turner 2002, 6). The Whole Earth movement legitimized and popularized this informational discourse. Ideologically, Whole Earth advocates advanced a "countercultural discourse" which sought to combine elements of ecological utopianism with new forms of technology that were seen as both humane and environmentally friendly (see Bryant 2006, 1).

Cyber-libertarians such as John Perry Barlow promoted the idea that governance in the online world took a radically different form than in the "material world." In the material world, coercion was utilized by governments to force certain behaviors on the citizenry. Governance online, however, was created by two factors. First, the computer codes and protocols on which the Internet was built served as the underlying organizational "structure" of the Net. Secondly, order was created as an emergent property of the "conversational norms of individuals" who participated in online environments. This led to a system in which control was not exerted via "centralized authority" but through "distributed systems" (Turner 2002, 8). As Turner notes, this was "an informational model of an economic market" (Turner 2002, 11). Promoters of the Californian ideology claimed that in this new informational economy, the power of government and the nation state should be reduced, to be replaced by the feedback of information "between autonomous individuals and their software" (Barbrook and Cameron 1996, 7). In an interview with Adam Curtis, noted economic historian Philip Mirowski highlights how this rationalized view of governance helped legitimate neoliberal economic beliefs:

> In this game theory view of the world, everyone is out for their own personal advantage ... [It's a] very narrow view of politics. But of course it has to be, because it's a narrow view of the human being. But what it does is it reduces what it means to be a human being to a few relatively mechanical processes. That individuals are little information processors but the market is the best information processor and voting or a democracy is a weak information processor ... inefficient [Curtis, 2007].

The neoliberal supposition that governments could no longer respond effectively to the needs of their citizenries had profound implications. Foremost of these was the promotion of a new form of democracy, "market democracy," in which the market "would take over the responsibility for running much of society from the politicians" (Curtis, 2007). As Frank notes, in the works of market democratic ideologues like Walter Wriston, the market and democracy become synonymous terms (Thomas Frank 2000, 55) and therefore the traditional tools of democratic governance, such as voting are no longer effective.

As in other areas of society, churches, particularly in the church growth movement, have adopted many aspects of market democracy. This has led "market-driven" churches, such as those that make up the CGM, to embrace "responsiveness" as their underlying rationale (Kenneson and Street 2003, 133–134). By a consistent push for effectiveness based on setting measurable goals, enacting plans, soliciting feedback, and then evaluating that feedback, church marketers and the church growth movement created a "marketized" church, which encouraged congregants to view the church as a product or service, rather than as a community to whom certain mutual obligations were owed (Kenneson and Street 2003, 66, 137). This had two major effects, neither of which were salutary. First, it encouraged congregations to view the church through a consumer lens, based on customer satisfaction. Secondly, and more detrimentally, this marketized view of the church had profound implications for the continued existence of democratic governance within modern Protestantism. As I have documented in my books *The Failure of Evangelical Mental Health Care* and *The New Apostolic Reformation*, democratic forms of church governance have become increasingly precarious in the wake of the New Apostolic Reformation and the rapid rise of extreme practices of church discipline among New Calvinists. Within the church, as in the secular world, democracy relies on the belief that individuals are bound by a social contract that is dependent on mutually reinforcing obligations. Without the shared belief in the social contract, congregation members become merely autonomous agents motivated by purely selfish desires and all too easily manipulatable by the logic of the market. In such a system the church becomes ruled by metrics and measures of effectiveness, understood through the lens of market responsiveness, which becomes the benchmark for organizational success (see Kenneson and Street 2003, 127–133).

Having now dispensed with these terminological questions, we can now begin our exploration of Protestant management and governance practices. This century-long quest has its roots in the dreams of an efficient society born out of the Progressive era. But over the course of a century, that dream, molded by changes in church culture and the popularization of the "cyborg sciences" during World War II and the Cold War, would fundamentally alter how Protestant Christians viewed their churches. The effects of those changes are still felt in modern American Protestantism.

1

The Origins of Evangelical Management Culture

Prior to the institutionalization of formal management practices into the church, clergymen primarily viewed their congregants through the lens of pastoral care. This did not mean that bureaucratic structures did not impose certain control mechanisms on congregations. However, the increasing regimentalization of pastoral care did not fully blossom until the late 20th century. To understand both the effectiveness and limits of the governance systems Protestant churches eventually set up, one should look at the intersection between Protestantism and pastoral care. Four forms of pastoral care—Lutheran, Anglican, Reformed, and Catholic—have dominated the United States (Holifield 1983, 16). In terms of American Protestant history, the first three forms tend to be the most significant.

Whatever the tradition, those engaged in pastoral care primarily wanted to deal with sin's consequences (Holifield 1983, 17). Pastoral counselors sought to allay fears about sin while also correcting those who engaged in sinful behavior (Holifield 1983, 17–18). For instance, early Catholic church confessional practice involved confessors engaging in spiritual assessments of penitents to determine the best cure for their soul's ailments (Kidder 2010, 26). Initial writings in the penitential tradition emphasized the commonalities between sin and disease and thus began a longstanding connection between medical discourse, pastoral care and (eventually) management. This early literature emphasized sin's contagious and harmful nature, while also proclaiming that confessors served as "'spiritual physicians'" (Kidder 2010, 34). The early New Testament church saw itself as a fraternally united community, which placed a burden of "mutual edification" on believers. Christians wished to address problems between believers in-house, so that the Church could present a united front to its non–Christian neighbors (John T. McNeill 1951, 85).

As a result of these developments, the "penitential discipline" triumphed in the Western Church by the beginning of the 13th century. Confession, once a corporate and uncommon expression of belief, transformed into a private and ubiquitous practice (John T. McNeill 1951, 112). The penitential system eventually became enshrined as a sacrament, in which priests absolved parishioners of their sins (Kidder 2010, 34-35). During the 14th and 15th century, distinctions between sacramental and mystical theology grew within the church. The fraught relationship between the functions of spiritual directors and confessors dramatized this conflict. These two forms of ministry came to have "distinct functions" in soul care during this period. Although the role of confessor remained the prerogative of the priestly class, increasingly the laity could perform the function of spiritual director. This included such duties as "'preaching' and teaching, exhortation and spiritual guidance," thus giving the laity a more prominent role in the church, but also ensuring that the lines between priest and spiritual director were increasingly nebulous. In response, the Church sought to tighten its control of the sacramental system; unfortunately, this exposed it to criticisms of clerical corruption. The reforms that Martin Luther tried to initiate were designed, in part, to address these perceived abuses of clerical power (Kidder 2010, 100).

One of the crucial distinctions that shaped Luther's rejection of Catholic theology was his concentration on "faithlessness" as a general human state rather than a specific condition of specific penitents. Consequentially, Luther believed even "good" deeds could cloak sinful desires. During the rise of the Lutheran Pietist tradition in the 17th century—a tradition that had a significant influence on conservative American Christianity—pietist believers put a greater emphasis on the experience of spiritual "'rebirth.'" For the Pietists, a lack of this feeling was sinful and denoted a state of "spiritual deadness" (Holifield 1983, 19-20). Much subsequent Pietist theology, as well as movements borrowing from Pietism, such as Methodism and the Keswick movement, would be shaped by this flight from spiritual deadness.

In many ways, however, the Reformed tradition played the most significant role in the history of American pastoral care. Reformed pastoral care concentrated on sin's idolatrous nature. Reformed Protestants devoted themselves to spiritually taxonomizing the human condition. The Puritans, not surprisingly, became soul specialists, teasing out the various states of the religious affections and "hidden intentions" (Holifield 1983, 22-23). Many Puritan and Pietist individuals of this era suffered from spiritually troubled states, which they attributed to the influence of "religious melancholy" or the demonic world. Typically, the only way to gain peace of mind from such religious melancholy came through gaining "assurance of grace," the certitude that one was among God's chosen people. Julius Rubin notes the paradoxical nature of these two movements' attempts to promote assurance while also at the same time heightening uncertainty through a "lengthy, difficult, and uncertain" process of conversion (Rubin 1994, 55). In addition, often even the elect doubted their own salvation (Rubin 1994, 55). The constant self-doubt that many American Protestants faced became a powerful tool of social control in modern Protestantism.

The system of church government that John Calvin (1509–1564) advocated made distinctions between a number of church offices. Pastors were responsible for exhortation, prayer, the administration of the sacraments and church governance. The church's benevolent activities were administered by the deaconate, while teachers' duty was religious educational instruction. It was the elders, however, who administered church discipline and oversaw the everyday life of local communities (Kidder 2010, 154). Historically, in much of the Reformed movement that adopted Calvin's model of governance, the power of religious elders has given church and denominational governments a representational, and in some ways, republican character based on presbytery-led rule. McNeill notes that the Reformed church tended to practice a more vigorous form of church discipline than that found in the Lutheran tradition (McNeill 1951, 217)—this point holds equally true today, with conservative churches in the Reformed tradition continuing to emphasize church discipline as the prime means of ensuring doctrinal conformity among believers.

When it came to church governance, as opposed to pastoral care, the Pietist tradition's influence on church governance practices was likely greater than that exhibited by the Reformed tradition. Pietists, as followers of Martin Luther (1483–1546), promoted the idea that the Christian priesthood was open to all Christians. From the Pietist standpoint, all Christians had a duty to communicate and instruct one another, as well as convert others. A principle frequently employed to achieve this aim was mutual edification within homes (Kidder 2010, 127). Pietists believed in the continuous regeneration of the soul via the Holy Spirit (Kidder 2010, 127); the experiential nature of their faith would, through the Moravian influence on Methodism, become a major bedrock of American revivalism (Kidder 2010, 127, 134). Lutheran pastor Jakob Spener (1635–1705), the most prominent advocate of the Pietist tradition, sought for a radical equalization of the clergy and laity, including in matters pertaining to church discipline (Kidder 2010, 127–128). Spener's most crucial contribution to the future development of Christian governance theories, however, was the distinction he made between ministering to the unfaithful and the faithful. The unfaithful, Spener contended, needed the Bible read to them, as well as conversion. However, the faithful, Spener argued, were better served by small groups in which believers gathered together and studied the Scriptures. These groups offered the twin advantages of mutual admonition and accountability (Kidder 2010, 130).

Moravianism's most important early advocate was Count Nikolaus Ludwig von Zinzendorf (1700–1760), whose beliefs directly originated from the Pietism of the 18th century (Spener had personally blessed Zizendorf in his youth) (Hadaway, Dubose and Wright 1987, 49–50; Kidder 2010, 131–132). Zinzendorf helped settle a small group of Bohemian Brethren—that is Moravians—on his estate in the early 18th century. Zinzendorf promoted the idea of using "brotherly agreements" to resolve disputes within the community. Community members were split into small groups named bands, or sometimes choirs. Shepherds or elders controlled the bands and made periodic visits to congregants to see to their needs. In effect, despite the informal nature of the bands, the whole community fell under intense spiritual discipline (Comiskey 2014, loc. 1732–1736). These bands proved to be phenomenally successful and soon the small group movement flourished within Moravianism (Kidder 2010, 132). From Moravianism, the small group concept soon spread into the Methodist movement through the influence of John Wesley (1703–1791) (Kidder 2010, 134–135). Methodist small groups were organized into "societies"; usually, such societies, governed by practical considerations, were based on territorial proximity. Members pledged to maintain a pious life under the headship of a class leader. As in Moravianism, these bands promoted mutual accountability and confession (Kidder 2010, 136). By 1742, these small groups had taken on pastoral care duties, with the functions of personal counsel and reproof now explicitly tied to the group (Kidder 2010, 136–137). While the small group movement arguably dates back as far as the early New Testament, the influence of Pietist, Moravian, and Methodist traditions has been particularly pronounced in the modern church's understanding of small groups and small group dynamics.

Protestant churches utilized small groups as increasingly influential control mechanisms in the centuries that followed the Methodist adoption of the small group method. However, for early Protestantism, the preferred means of social control was the religious denomination itself. The initial denominations planted on America's soil did not necessarily embrace the idea of voluntary association that characterizes modern denominationalism (Richey 2013, 2, 4–5, 31). The existence of denominationalism presupposes that religious association embraces the corollary principle of voluntary association; toleration of rival belief systems and the principle of "religious freedom" are foundational to the system of denominationalism (Richey 2013, 2). The religious denomination takes its form from "modernity" and embraces some of the same functions of political factions, the media, and free markets (Richey 2013, 3). Denominations understand themselves as legitimate religious factions, churches, or religious movements while embracing voluntarism. They do not, however, necessarily concede that all other religious factions or denominations deserve toleration (Richey 2013, 3).

Nevertheless, the principles of religious toleration and separation of church and state, which the Founders encoded in American civic culture,

1. The Origins of Evangelical Management Culture

presented a dilemma for Protestant churches of the late 1700s and early 1800s. Due to the disestablishment of state churches, clergymen could no longer enforce compliance to the creedal or financial commitments previously imposed onto congregants by municipal or state governments. Denominational churches, as a matter of survival, relied on voluntaristic principles of association. This meant, in turn, that churches had to promote pious ardency in their parishioners and their communities (Primer 1979, 14).

In the era immediately following the American Revolution, most of the major denominations formed governance structures that in theory, played the same role for the denominations that Congress did for the national government. Practically, however, this pastoral setup did not approximate our contemporary theories regarding organizational culture. People valued churches primarily for their pastoral function; the conception of how denominations and denominational agencies functioned was profoundly localized (Primer 1979, 13). This situation began to change in the 1850s. Pastors and other clerics were now seen as religious professionals; denominational hierarchies controlled career advancement. Advancing in that hierarchy required pastors to show allegiance to the denominational system they belonged to. Preaching ability and skillful pastoral care no longer ensured a cleric's ascension to the top of church life; increasingly, networking and organizational aptitude were also important considerations (Beth Barton Schweiger 1994, 203). But denominations suffered numerous organizational problems at the time, including inefficiency and a lack of centralized administration. As Southern and Northern pastors and denominations began splitting from each other in the leadup to the Civil War, Southern religious leaders, following northern religious leaders' lead, started constructing highly centralized leadership structures, characterized by modernized bureaucratic techniques, within their denominations (Schweiger 1994, 190, 195).

During the lead-up to the Civil War, religious agency structures arose, most of which were not denominational in character (Chaves 1998, 179). Today's modern religious agency structures are groups with formal ties to denominations that engage in various religious outreach, administrative, and support efforts. These efforts can include "foreign and home missions; producing Sunday School and other educational material; publishing tracts, reports and books; administering pension funds; giving or loaning money to congregations for building projects; and organizing denominational efforts in higher education" (Chaves 1998, 179). In addition to their lack of denominational emphasis, early religious agencies conceptualized the idea of membership in terms of individuals rather than congregations. Financing occurred via direct solicitations of members (Chaves 1998, 179).

During the early 1800s, the nationalization of religious agencies began increasing, particularly with the creation of The American Bible Society

(1816), formed largely through the efforts of prominent lawyer and bank director Elias Boudinot (1740–1821) (Primer 1979, 19; Wosh 1988, 21). In the 19th century, the ABS proved to be one of the most forward looking and creative philanthropies in the country, creating new organizational systems to "Christianize the nation" (Wosh 1988, 2–3, 106). Boudinot promoted the streamlining of state Bible societies and the elimination of redundant organizational features. His activism promoted increasing the available financial resources available to Bible societies. Boudinot gained the support of a number of prominent Americans, perhaps most notably Arthur and Lewis Tappan (Primer 1979, 19). The ABS initially hoped to adopt a locally run model to achieve their goal of national Christianization. This idea foundered; the use of autonomous local organizations presented enormous financial hurdles. Instead, the ABS relied on professional paid agents who traveled throughout the country and promoted the organization and its mission (Wosh 1988, 106). The agency system that the ABS utilized, part of a larger philanthropic trend among American religious organizations, plays an important but often unacknowledged role in the history of American Protestant organizational structures. Protestant aid and benevolent societies felt that they could no longer rely solely on the support of local institutions to sustain them, particularly as their own missions increasingly became national in scope. This led to the creation of what Peter J. Wosh calls the "rootless religious professional," untied to local congregational structures. These new religious professionals, no longer bound by local ties, eventually contributed to the birth of the American parachurch movement, thus fundamentally reshaping the organizational ideology that motivates conservative American Protestantism (Wosh 1988, 107).

Significantly, the ABS wanted to take all the disparate bible societies that existed at the town or local level and build a national organizational structure to unite them. To realize this goal the ABS had to avoid interdenominational acrimony. Therefore, local Bible societies were asked to pledge that the Bibles they distributed would be given out "'without note or comment.'" The ABS hoped that by promoting this theologically minimalist vision of orthodoxy, it could avoid entanglement in debates between different confessional traditions (Wosh 1988, 110). Most modern parachurch organizations, even within the conservative Protestant tradition, tend to follow this model, adopting a "mere Christian" model that seeks to avoid doctrinal disputes not directly related to the organization's mission (Scheitle 2008, 45–47).

The interdenominational character of the ABS and similar organizations such as the American Tract Society and the American Sunday School Union, had a profound effect on the relationship between the laity and clerical professionals. Professionals, often businessmen, dominated these organizations and exerted a tight control over the governing boards of philanthropic institutions. Clergymen increasingly took second place to these individuals. Thus,

1. The Origins of Evangelical Management Culture

the organizational pioneers of the ABS and other interdenominational agencies created the modern concept of "lay governance," in which an informal lay establishment, rather than clerics, dominated religious benevolent societies and parachurch organizations (Wosh 1988, 59).

The success of the American Bible Society and similar voluntaristic organizations during this period is not hard to explain. These organizations enjoyed the support of wealthy and influential Americans. In addition, the leaders of these various voluntaristic associations had a sophisticated understanding of contemporary business and management techniques. These men emphasized the need to engage in "systematic'" operations, promoted the centralization of bureaucracies, engaged in advertising campaigns and formed the financial superstructure under which the agency structures could operate (Primer 1979, 20).

Alarmed by the rise of multidenominational agency structures, the various Protestant denominations engaged in the formation of their own missions, publishing, and charitable groups beginning in the early 1800s. These new ventures, however, remained small until the close of the 19th century (Primer 1979, 27). By that point, the agency structures, which had typically promoted a united Protestant front, had been succeeded by new denominational efforts (Primer 1979, 35). Supporters of denominational agencies contended that these organizations could spread the Protestant message far more effectively than individual churches. Churches themselves, they argued, were of little value; it was the cause the church promoted that mattered (Schweiger 1994, 355). However, these denominational efforts were handicapped by the fact that like the agency structures of the past, denominational agencies tended to focus on "limited, single objectives," thus promoting the proliferation of denominational agencies (Primer 1979, 35). But even at this late date the power of religious agencies was relatively minor compared to the "traditional pastoral structures" that controlled the church (Primer 1979, 39).

Although many narratives describing late 19th century American Protestantism depict a movement suffering a crisis of identity, Protestantism was still in fact a virile force in this period. Many of the denominational agencies expressed more concern about structural problems that the church faced rather than debates over the usefulness of the Social Gospel. Because denominations were increasingly being called upon to serve national, rather than simply local, functions, many church leaders felt that the older pastoral orientation of their denominations was now passé. Moreover, denominational agencies' bureaucratic structures faced numerous inefficiencies. Older methods of church financing had proved both inadequate and needlessly irritating to denominational members. Denominations' administrative branches felt increasingly unable to handle the numerous functions demanded of them.

The denominations suffered from "mission creep," as various new demands were placed on them, needlessly straining resources. However, at the time, most church administrators and clergymen did not have a good grasp on how to handle these problems (Primer 1979, 43–55).

As Ben Primer notes, the inability of fin-de-siècle Protestants to understand the problems confronting them is understandable. Denominational leaders did not yet realize the power of new centralized bureaucracies to eliminate waste and redundancy. Moreover, real fears existed that administrative shake-ups would sacrifice those at the center of power in order to appease the administrative new order. Understandably, some denominational leaders expressed resistance to organizational change (Primer 1979, 56).

A new relationship between business methodology and the church appeared after the Civil War. For instance, among Southern Baptists, clerics were increasingly seen not only as purveyors of spiritual succor, but also administrative personnel, tasked with the duty of running increasingly complex organizational structures. In the new vision of the ministerial role, the clergy's role took on a mechanistic character, with "observable results" becoming the benchmark of a ministry's success (William Gene Moore 2003, 181). This, in turn, provoked a great degree of consternation within the Southern Baptist community, as many Baptists worried that in emphasizing statistical success, the church was leaving out other important, but less quantifiable metrics. The general move to quantify spirituality, which can be seen as broadly characteristic of most late 19th century Christianity (Primer 1979, passim), also deeply troubled Southern Baptists (William Gene Moore 2003, 230). Some Southern Baptists worried that assessing their pastorate based on numerical growth would harm the pastorate, forcing clerical assessment to take on a "worldly" form in which "success," rather than Godliness, marked sincere faith (William Gene Moore 2003, 232). Helping start a pattern that reoccurred in the CGM, Southern Baptists established "numerical growth" as the benchmark for organizational efficiency in their churches (William Gene Moore 2003, 226). To achieve this goal, Southern Baptists, began creating numerous new laity-centered organizations, hoping to increase lay commitment to Christian ministry (William Gene Moore 2003, 183, 205).

Beginning roughly around the turn of the 20th century, churches started employing efficiency specialists as troubleshooters in church administration. These specialists ensured that the church's spiritual and administrative functions were streamlined in order to both minimize redundancy and ensure efficient resource allocation (Schlect 2015, 75). From 1870 on, an increasing focus on efficient business practice led American churches to more proactively integrate principles derived from the psychological sciences into spiritual life (Tommy Dale Johnson Jr. 2014, 5). Protestant churches, such as the Southern Baptists, saw that America had entered an era characterized by cultural and

1. The Origins of Evangelical Management Culture

organizational complexity. Big business had abandoned lax efficiency standards, and churches believed they must follow suit. These businesses served as the new benchmark by which the church measured the success of its efforts. These new metrics, moreover, were measured in functional and pragmatic, not spiritual, terms (William Gene Moore 2003, 242).

Management theory had only come into its own at the beginning of the 20th century. One crucial figure who defined its future evolution was Frederick W. Taylor (1856–1915). Taylor gained renown for his use of time studies and for his promotion of what became known as "scientific management" or Taylorism. Taylor argued that there needed to be a shift in how business management related to labor. He argued that both labor and management should focus on achieving a "common productive goal" in order to avoid political conflicts. Scientific managers did this by finding the most efficient way of running the company or factory. As Stephen Waring points out, Taylorism embodied an attempt to articulate a purportedly non-ideological view of the workplace, in which the "naturalness of capitalism" was assumed. The good of company and society was defined primarily through the prism of "productive growth and efficiency," which could be measured apolitically and dispassionately using "scientific calculations" that appealed to economic rationalism (Waring 1991, 11–12; Sheldrake 2002, 16–17).

The philosophy of Taylorism was applied to a whole host of social problems at the turn of the 20th century. Baptist ecumenicist and church leader Shailer Matthews (1863–1941) became an early proponent of utilizing Taylorist ideas in the church. Matthews' background was "thoroughly middle class," and that middle-class heritage is clearly evident in his book, *Scientific Management in the Churches* (1912), which played an important role in the growing acceptance of Taylorist administrative practices among Protestants (Schlect 2015, 81; Dorrien 2003, 182). Newer religious organizations modeled themselves along Taylorist lines, leading both to the promotion of management theory and to a growing emphasis on the professionalization and bureaucratization of spirituality. The Social Gospel movement, in particular, sought to utilize the social sciences in order to advance its agenda of a more just and economically perfected world (Moorhead 2003, 485). But it was not simply slum-reforming Social Gospelers who saw Taylorism's value. During the early 20th century, denominational leaders themselves became convinced that both their organizational culture needed to be enhanced and their operational controls expanded (Primer 1979, 70). Finances, too, needed to be regularized and systemized (Primer 1979, 71). Furthermore, this vast new vision required the implementation of "systems of control" at the local level (Primer 1979, 71). On the foreign field, the proliferation of missions agencies led to support for more effective church bureaucracies (Moorhead 2003, 485). Missions agencies sought alliances with business and corporate interests and spoke the same Taylorist efficiency language that the denominational leaders did (Moorhead 2003, 485).

Churches felt trapped in a life and death struggle with secular organizational cultures. Many blamed contemporary struggles centering on immigration and changes in theology on the failure of Protestantism to adapt to the dynamic nature of innovation that characterized Progressive-era America. While the flood of immigrants could not easily be cut off nor the tide of modernism silenced, Protestantism could work to implement a new organizational culture (Primer 1979, 73). Those who worked in furtherance of the "efficiency church" had the promise of this vision to bolster them up (Primer 1979, 73–74).

Utopian visions of an "efficiency church" found a ready audience. Shailer Matthews's call for "Scientific Management in the Churches" led to the publication of numerous similar works, as well as the introduction of educational courses devoted to promoting efficient church practices. Representative examples of the former included *The Reconstruction of the Church* (1915), written by Paul Moore Strayer (1871–1929), a Rochester Presbyterian, *The Social Engineer*, which was penned by Christian sociologist Edwin Earp (1867–1950); and the numerous writings of church management guru Albert F. McGarrah (1878–1962). These new church efficiency advocates usually advocated church structures dominated by committees, who were then responsible to a lead pastor. Running an efficient church was seen as godly, as it promoted the advance of the Christian "kingdom" (Moorhead 2003, 488; William Gene Moore 2003, 288). Denominational leaders echoed this call, arguing that the church was a business. Many denominational leaders felt that outside consultants and efficiency experts were needed to streamline the functions of their organizations (Primer 1979, 76). Other innovations were also introduced at a denominational level. Southern Baptists, for instance, used numerical goal-setting to spur organizational efficiency (William Gene Moore 2003, 269–270). Various churches experimented with the introduction of "standards of excellence" for the assessment of ministry effectiveness (William Gene Moore 2003, 271–272). Obviously, such assessment strategies were reflective of the Taylorist thinking prevalent during this era. It also reflected a changed conception of human nature. While many critics of managerial Christianity have charged that it views human beings mechanistically, it also tended to see human nature as a natural resource to be exploited. Conservation efforts in the Progressive era often viewed the environment through the lens of "resource management." Eventually, the push for effective resource management began pushing its way into other fields (see Lowe 2013, 85), including churches.

In addition to effective resource management, financial management, as well as public relations, became markedly more sophisticated during the

1. The Origins of Evangelical Management Culture

opening decades of the 20th century. Denominational executives hoped to manipulate the press through advertising and the use of "Information Bureaus"; in function, these agencies appeared little different from the public relations efforts of the controversial Edward Bernays (see Primer 1979, 78). Denominations implemented a new financing technique, "systematic finance," to replace the older models of fundraising that existed in many denominations. "Systematic Finance," adopted by most denominations in the initial decades following the turn of the 20th century, derived its efficiency from its commitment to weekly giving, rather than the more sporadic yearly giving that had once been common (Primer 1979, 94. 101, 120). This program allowed for more accurate charting of church finances, eliminating some of the inefficiencies that had plagued earlier church financing efforts (Primer 1979, 101, 120).

Supporters of the new church financing techniques argued that it would restore confidence in American Protestantism. They maintained that accurate bookkeeping and paying of bills could gain the church the admiration of the secular world (Primer 1979, 118). While "systematic finance" allowed for American Protestantism to reach a level of economic efficiency theretofore undreamt of, it came at a price. As Primer notes, one of the unfortunate by-products of "systematic finance" occurred in the way Protestantism chose to "define its goals" (Primer 1979, 114). Increasingly, Protestant leaders saw the Church as "much a business as a religious institution" (Primer 1979, 114). This limited Protestantism's ability to engage in prophetic critique of the societal issues that plagued America over the course of the 20th century (Primer 1979, 114, 120).

In reshaping church finances, denominational leaders again reshaped church bureaucracies. The need to accurately plot out strategic objectives led to an emphasis on more long-term and strategic planning. Primer notes that many Protestant agencies "engaged in a process of internal bureaucratization, manifested in departmentalization, specialization, and intensified oversight and coordination" (Primer 1979, 127). Even more emphasis was placed on organizational streamlining. Power became increasingly centralized in the denominational bureaucracy and lead management (Primer 1979, 127). By the end of World War I, multiple denominations had hired management consultants; increasing emphasis was placed on "internal coordination" of departmental functions (Primer 1979, 133). Denominations emphasized the need for better inter-agency communication, and denominational leaders increasingly utilized their prerogative to closely monitor internal denominational activities. Properly filled out paperwork became a paramount concern, leading to complaints about "red tape" (Primer 1979, 134).

New questions arose about the meaning of the cult of business efficiency in the churches. For some Protestants, the push towards organizational efficiency built up community; it allowed Americans to engage in the "boosterism" that has so long characterized American Protestantism (Schweiger 1994, 387–388). There were concerns, however, about how Taylorist practices affected pastoral care. What was the dividing line, Americans wondered, that separated the administrative and religious functions of the church? Many Protestant churches bypassed the theological questions that such commitment to business efficiency prompted. Moreover, church administrators had refashioned the experience of "doing church" itself. Increasingly, as Christopher Schlect reflects, church was seen as an impersonal experience. By tying local churches more tightly to denominational structures, church administrators also increased the power of Protestant denominations, raising troubling questions about the centralization of that power within church hierarchies (Schlect 2015, 75–76).

The questions Protestants faced about the separating of the administrative functions of the church from its pastoral functions were pressing ones (Schlect 2015, 77). Already by the early 1900s efforts were afoot to apply the theories of the social sciences to pastoral care. A prominent early example was the Emmanuel Movement, which provided an embryonic form of modern pastoral counseling; the Movement was an important early advocate for psychotherapy in the United States, despite its eventual battle with the clinicians of the period (Holifield 1983, 202–207). These ideas spread widely throughout the Protestant Church. One early advocate was Gaines Dobbins (1886–1978). Appointed to Southern Seminary in 1920, Dobbins applied behavioral science methods to Southern Baptist pastoral care, in an attempt to unite the insights of pastoral care, the behavioral sciences, and church management theory into one complete ideological package (Johnson Jr. 2014. 23, 79).

Dobbins derived his ideas on church management not only from Taylorism and scripture, but also from secular educational theorists like John Dewey (1859–1952) and Baptist Sunday school advocate Arthur Flake (1862–1952) (who had sought to apply the ideas of business efficiency to pastoral education) (Johnson Jr. 2014. 70). As the mania for systematic organization and efficiency were applied to the American economy in the early 1900s, these ideas gradually attracted the attention of other parts of American society, including educational theory. Progressive educational theory quickly followed suit. Because Dobbins was a religious educator, he quickly became aware of the growing influence of Dewey over American education (Johnson Jr. 2014, 70–71, 83). Efficiency and management guru Harrington Emerson (1853–1931) also influenced Dobbins. He eventually constructed a test of efficiency that he claimed was based on New Testament principles. Dobbins promoted the idea that pastors should be the primary church administrators but should delegate key functions to subordinate officers (Johnson Jr. 2014, 75–78). To make this grand pastoral and educational vision work, Dobbins ended up relying heavily on the methodologies of social scientists, "especially tests and measurements," which had been developed by scientific thinkers like G. Stanley Hall (1846–1924) and E.L. Thorndike (1874–1949) (Johnson Jr. 2014, 82).

Dobbins's reformist impulses not only profoundly influenced Southern Baptists, but were also characteristic of a broader move to organizational efficiency in pastoral care. Protestant pastors in the first quarter of the 20th century were advised to divide their churches by department, with each member taking on a specific role within the organizational layout. In a denomination like the Southern Baptists, pastors themselves were now expected to be seminary educated, since seminary introduced future pastors to concepts of organizational efficiency. This approach resulted less from efficiency-mania than a concern that effective pastoral care for the spiritually suffering could not be truly implemented until the organizational reforms that Dobbins and others introduced had taken root. Nevertheless, the continued emphasis on functional measurements of organizational success led many Christians to worry that the church's main mission was being abandoned (William Gene Moore 2003, 244–245, 267–268).

But debates over pastoral care hardly represented the only areas of contention that the new push for an "efficiency church" provoked. Denominational leaders also expressed concern about challenges to their authority resulting from the new organizational philosophy that characterized Taylorist denominational structures. Moreover, because Protestantism was also dependent on efficiency and centralized power structures for its survival, many denominational leaders took challenges to their authority as threats to the survival of the Church itself (Primer 1979, 155). Both the centralized leadership of the denominations and the agencies under them became intolerant of the power struggles of those underneath them (Primer 1979, 156–157). Denominational leadership figures engaged in carefully laid plans which aimed to minimize local dissent, but such strategic planning was limited by real fear of "interest groups" within the denominational structure (Primer 1979, 164). As we will see in Chapters 3 and 4, such systemized planning would take on a shocking degree of sophistication by the early 21st century.

Many Protestants of the Progressive Era expressed concern at the fusion of management theory and Protestant thought. Yet the pressures of urbanization necessitated such a union. By the late 1800s, many churches had begun diversifying their functions. Instead of just providing a space for proselytizing and worship, churches in the late 1800s began to take on a large number of auxiliary functions, ranging from providing church socials, to organizing youth groups and reforming societies. The larger a church became, the more complex the organizational apparatus needed to maintain it. The ideal of pastors devoted solely to pastoral care seemed impractical. Administrators were needed to rearrange the business of church every bit as much as they were the business of business (Holifield 1983, 173–175, Schlect 2015, 77, 89 151). Reading about the reorganization of the Progressive-era church, one can easily sympathize with the motives of many early church efficiency experts. Efficiency was clearly relevant to pastoral life; if a church could not, for instance, maintain a balanced bank account, it could neither support itself nor engage in the kind of missions' work and social activism that were demanded of it.

However, critics expressed important concerns about the drive for ecclesiastical efficiency, charges that reoccurred into the 21st century. One important criticism, first pointed out in a *Nation* editorial on Presbyterian efficiency guru Mark Matthews (1867–1940), was that church efficiency experts blurred the distinction between administrative and pastoral work. The *Nation*, as Christopher R. Schlect notes, contended that while "administration is impersonal … shepherding souls is deeply personal" (Schlect 2015, 89). The tendency to promote efficiency as the standard of the church undermined the clergy's pastoral function, leaving it handicapped in its ability to properly administer soul care (Schlect 2015, 86–90). Moreover, the *Nation* editorialists further charged that Christian administrative specialists, in seeking to quantify, measure, and time spirituality, ended up trivializing spirituality and thus offered up an atomized spirituality (a charge also made against the CGM) (Schlect 2015, 89–90).

The use of the efficiency gospel to crush dissent represented another problematic aspect of the movement and played an important role in the disintegrating relationship between modernists and fundamentalists. The centralization of power that occurred within denominations during the Progressive era also allowed those possessing the most power to direct the mission and theological outlook of the denomination. Voices that dissented against mainstream denominational views were silenced. Because of this, there was a sudden imbalance between those advocating the social gospel and those advocating evangelism, with the former temporarily gaining more power within many of the mainline churches. As John Michael Utzinger states, "in effect, denominational consolidations placed modernists in stronger places to implement their ideas of church vocation and their attendant programs" (Utzinger 2000, 144). This in turn led to rancor among evangelism-oriented Protestants, who saw social gospel advocates taking over positions that they felt rightly belonged to them (Utzinger 2000, 144). Fundamentalists viewed themselves as a "populist protest" movement against those who controlled the Protestant hierarchy. To combat theological modernism, "soul saving" evangelicals prioritized the development of effective parachurch networks. In turn, liberal Protestants, who controlled the social hierarchy of Protestantism, tried to ensure the failure of fundamentalism's attempts to circumvent the social gospel (Utzinger 2000, 17).

1. The Origins of Evangelical Management Culture

Yet in spite of these criticisms, Protestant Christianity prior to World War I was marked by a gradual, if not uniform, push to greater Christian unity in the name of efficiency. These two goals, in the minds of religious progressives, were interlinked (Ernst 1968, 59). The voluntary associations that had characterized 19th century Protestantism had played an important role in interdenominational cooperation during that period. Particularly notable, in addition to the ABS, was the Evangelical Alliance, an organization devoted to creating a unified system of religious dogmas by which Protestants could cooperate. However, gradually the Evangelical Alliance came to be seen as too restrictive in its doctrinal limitations on Christian union. The Evangelical Alliance handicapped itself by the minimal attention it paid to influencing Christians at the denominational level, a handicap that many voluntary associations suffered from (Ernst 1968, 60). Thus, those who called for unity and interdenominational cooperation could count on a sympathetic reception from many Protestants during this period (Ernst 1968, 60).

One of the important moves to greater interdenominational cooperation was the 1893 Foreign Missions Conference of North America, which was a consultation on creating interdenominational unity on the mission field. Soon, other agencies were created to aid in the move towards, an interdenominational, "federative" Protestantism, ranging from missions-oriented agencies towards those dealing with Sunday School. The most influential and successful of these agencies, the Federal Council of the Churches of Christ in America would replace the Evangelical Alliance as the dominant interdenominational body in America (Ernst 1968, 61).

Due in large part to such calls for Christian unity, as well as the tensions such calls produced, World War I marked the defining point in the intersection of secular management practices and Christian belief in the United States. The war and its aftereffects caused American Protestants to emphasize efficiency with even greater zeal (Schlect 2015, 120). Many Protestants now saw themselves as spreading both the gospel of God and of democracy (Sizer 2012, 27). Agreement as to the means of disseminating this new gospel proved difficult. Liberal Protestants declaimed religious "dogmatism" and argued for revisions to Christian doctrine and practice. Theological conservatives contended that World War I had shown the dangers of devotion to bureaucracy and ecumenicism. Meanwhile, efficiency gospel advocates contended that through organizational restructuring, many of the problems the War had highlighted could be solved, most notably "ignorance and inefficiency" (Sizer 2012, 27–28). Increasingly, American Protestants diverged from each other on the proper methods "for coordinating and systemizing the practice of their faith" (Schlect 2015, 120).

The conflict over the gospel of democracy pitted different democratizing factions against each other. Establishment liberal Protestants believed that reform must take place, although the organizational structure of the church could likely remain intact. The famous Protestant minister Harry Emerson Fosdick (1878–1969) represented the dominant voice in this tradition. More radical liberals argued that World War I had highlighted fundamental problems in the structure of the church, comparing the new democratic ideals the church espoused with its historical "antidemocratic tendencies." These critics argued that the church would have to be organizationally "reshaped" in line with "modern sensibilities." The refusal to do this, they argued, could lead to the emergence of an anti-democratic form of religiosity. A third faction, advocating a conservative vision of democratization, emphasized "the prerogatives and insights of the local church." This localist vision of democratization contested the corporatist models of ecclesiastical reform being offered up by some modernists, notably advocates of the gospel of efficiency. Much like modern critics of the CGM, these conservative democratizers saw the gospel of managerial Christianity as dehumanizing. For them, applying business logic to Christianity turned human beings, and thereby religion, into mechanisms only important for their production value, rather than their intrinsic worth (Sizer 2012, 28–31). These critics were particularly fearful of the new emphasis on the efficiency gospel being utilized as an excuse for establishing top-down rule by theological elites. This, they feared, led to the promotion of an ecumenicism not bound by the doctrinal orthodoxies of a sponsoring denomination. The push for "organic union" of denominations, in which the denominational control mechanisms of several denominations were unified, struck conservative democratizers as a dangerous centralization of power (Sizer 2012, 31).

Meanwhile, a final faction, dubbed "administrative democratizers" by Aaron W. Sizer, sought to combine the functions of mass democracy with centralized leadership structures. This faction argued that democracy did not automatically entail "personal self-determination," but rather the social engineering of the average churchman for theological citizenship (Sizer 2012, 32). As Sizer notes, this faction of Christian democratizers held a vision of social reform akin to that of "political Progressives" (Sizer 2012, 32). During the first quarter of the 20th century, many in the middle class became haunted by the image of the newly liberated "masses," unbound by traditional rules concerning class deference and hierarchy. These masses, middle class intellectuals maintained, had to be fit into a new social order for which they had not been prepared. Unlike the middle class, which could be trained in rationality, the "crowd," as French social psychologist Gustave Le Bon (1841–1931) contended, was solely reactionary (Ewan 1996, 61, 65–67). To cope with this problem, some American progressives, most notably the immensely influential Walter Lippmann (1889–1974), argued that social scientists and other policy elites must engage in social engineering to maintain public order (Ewan

1996, 64). Within this social context, an increased focus on "group dynamics" and the interior life of individuals became paramount (Ewan 1996, 64). Sizer's "administrative democractizers" differed little from Lippmann and company in this regard. Their view of ecclesiastical democracy focused on the use of the church itself as a tool of social engineering (Sizer 2012, 31–32).

Many Protestant churchmen had been fascinated with Woodrow Wilson's (1856–1924) use of propaganda techniques to win over the American public during the First World War. One particularly effective government tool that intrigued church leaders was the Committee on Public Information (CPI) (Sizer 2012, 45). The CPI utilized publicity methods, first pioneered by Progressives, to direct public opinion (Ewan 1996, 110–111). Essentially, CPI employed sales techniques from the advertising world to sell the American public on the need for war (Ewan 1996, 113). The CPI was an inspiration to many Protestants who wished to borrow the techniques of the Committee to build "ideological consensus and institutional solidarity" in their own churches (Sizer 2012, 46). After the war, many Protestant leaders advocated the use of such techniques (Cannon 2015, 3).

The desire for such large-scale coordination of Protestantism motivated much discussion of Protestantism's post-war role. After the war, a systemic attempt to remodel Protestantism along Taylorist grounds occurred through the organization of the Interchurch World Movement (IWM), which benefited from the involvement of John D. Rockefeller, Jr. (1874–1960) (Schlect 2015, 128). The organization aimed to merge the pastoral care and missions' functions of all the major Protestant groups (Schlect 2015, 128). The IWM would serve as a harbinger of the interdenominational cooperative ventures that would characterize mainline Protestantism in the 20th century (Ernst 1968, Abstract). Despite the negative reception the IWM received among fundamentalists (Ernst 1968, 357–358), it likely played an important role in encouraging the development of parachurch ventures among evangelicals. The IWM sought to bring to Protestant Christianity the same sort of global vision that characterized the League of Nations (Ernst 1968, 129).

The IWM was influenced by a number of earlier cooperative ventures, many bearing a similarity to the Evangelical Alliance. Organizations as diverse as the World Sunday School Association, the Y.M.C.A., the Red Cross, and several major temperance organizations also shaped the movement's vision. However, four interchurch cooperative movements created the ideological backbone of the movement and served as its most foundational influences: "the Student Volunteer Movement, the Missionary Education Movement, the Laymen's Missionary Movement, and the Men and Religion Forward Movement" (Ernst 1968, 62).

The Student Volunteer Movement was shaped by evangelist D.L. Moody (1837–1899). It dedicated itself to the promotion of foreign missions, encouraging preexistent denominational missions-sending groups to engage in this cause. However, it did not try to promote itself as an alternative to these groups. It aimed simply to serve those denominational missions agencies that already existed. The movement gained an international following, recruiting hundreds of missionaries to serve abroad, revolutionizing how evangelical Protestants viewed missions. It was also responsible for influencing many of the most influential Protestant leaders of the early 20th century, notably John R. Mott (1865–1955) (Ernst 1968, 64). Though less influential, the Missionary Education Movement also helped promote missions' education (Ernst 1968, 64–65).

More important was the Laymen's Missionary Movement. Founded in 1906, the movement centered itself on the vision of John B. Sleman, Jr., who had also participated in the Student Volunteer Movement. Sleman was heartbroken by missions' boards' inability to maintain financial self-sufficiency, and decided to create a movement among the laity to address this issue. The movement quickly gained accolades, as it was efficiently organized and capable of speedily achieving difficult goals. The movement's impressive fundraising ability and its adoption of a "standardized large-scale campaign organization and technique," that included effective use of public relations and propaganda techniques, committee meetings, special speakers, and numerous other strategies borrowed from the business and political world, gained the movement widespread support. The movement became particularly adept at utilizing the "every member canvas" giving technique to regularize church financing at the time, further promoting its important place within the efficiency gospel movement (Ernst 1968, 65–67).

However, the most foundational influence on the IWM was the Men and Religion Forward Movement (Ernst 1968, 67), a movement whose influence would reappear at the close of the 20th century via its influence on the Promise Keepers (Fenimore Jr. 2009, 72). An effort meant to mobilize Christian men for social reform and global evangelism, the Men and Religion Forward Movement (MRFM) sought to apply the lessons of the Laymen's Missionary Movement on a far more massive canvas. More even than the Laymen's Missionary Movement, the Men and Religion Forward Movement sought to create a synergy between progressive religion, business, and philanthropic enterprise. Like the Laymen's Missionary Movement, the MRFM campaigns were thorough and systematic. Meetings in select urban locations were planned weeks in advance and utilized important national religious leaders as experts. "Institutes" were conducted in which these religious elites would meet with important local leaders. The MRFM saw itself not as a permanent body, but as a change catalyst in contemporary religious organizations. The Movement systematically produced its own literature and formed highly organized sub-departments. The Movement intensely committed itself to both

1. The Origins of Evangelical Management Culture 43

evangelism and the social gospel, while incorporating—as was characteristic of many efficiency gospel advocates of the era—the most advanced social science research methods then available (Ernst 1968, 67–73).

Immediately prior to the start of the IWM, a number of denominations began developing an agenda for aggressive expansion of their financing, programming and resource management. Four denominations–The Disciples of Christ, Methodists, Presbyterians, and Northern Baptists—proved particularly influential in this push (known as the denominational forward movements). Fundraising campaigns and advanced surveying techniques figured prominently in these campaigns (Ernst 1968, 102–113).

Likewise, the IWM's plans called for the surveying of nations throughout the world in order to develop efficiency standards for missions' work that could then be applied "through rational administrative measures" (Schlect 2015, 130). Churches had developed an intense fascination with social science survey techniques due to their experiences during World War I, where such techniques were utilized as a social engineering tool, in concert with advertising (Sizer 2012, 48–49). Rockefeller contended that Protestant missions work was inefficiently run and advanced a plan to vertically integrate church work in the same manner that his father had revolutionized the oil industry. The IWM's missions' surveys reflected a rationalized spirituality. The IWM went into target areas, assessed their spiritual needs and resources and then sought to connect spiritual suppliers with spiritual consumers. Techniques derived from Frank and Lilian Gilbreth's motion-saving studies were directly applied to evangelization and outreach efforts. The IWM's vision of missions work and pastoral care sounded at times eerily like Henry Ford's (1863–1947) ideas on mass production. Pastors were seen as "interchangeable" parts that could be effortlessly applied to one parish or another like a spiritual widget. Because of the IWM's desire to avoid partisan bickering, in part a byproduct of its involvement with the Rockefeller family, the movement's vision of pastoral care predicated itself on the idea that creedal and liturgical assumptions need not affect the relationship between pastors and their flocks. And the IWM, much like Shailer Matthews, would be criticized for its allegiance to impersonal efficiency rather than personalized spiritual care (Schlect 2015, 128–134).

Organizationally, the IWM resembled a boardroom, not a denomination or clerical structure. Its functions were not particularly dependent on pastors and elders (Schlect 2015, 134–135). The IWM's structure closely modeled itself after that of big business (Ernst 1968, 210). The IWM was quite forward looking in envisioning its potential future role within global Protestantism. It envisioned itself as a potential "clearing house ... factfinding and data-processing firm ... and ... promotion agency" for Protestant religion, all of these functions being undertaken under "as efficient and economical a basis as possible" (Ernst 1968, 222). The use of advanced social science surveys by the IWM came to be seen as an important function of the IWM; data-processing, far from being ancillary to the movement's mission, was central (Ernst 1968, 224) Moreover, the organization realized that Protestantism needed better command and control structures to coordinate efforts among different organizations and individuals (Ernst 1968, 222). Besides allowing for the spread of the gospel, the adoption of such techniques would have had obviously beneficial implications in reducing interdenominational duplication of efforts. The IWM's use of advanced advertising techniques helped revolutionize religious promotionalism in the United States (Ernst 1968, 224). A direct line can be traced from the Interchurch World Movement to the Institute of Social and Religious Research (ISRR) to the modern church growth movement. Funded by Rockefeller money and incorporating the survey department of the IWM, the ISRR sought to utilize the most exacting scientific techniques to study religious, ethical, and moral questions. John Mott was president of the ISRR throughout the short history of the organization. In a move that would prove fateful for modern evangelicalism, ISRR chose to fund J. Waskom Pickett's (1890–1981) research into mass religious movements in India, using ISRR techniques. The results of the survey would eventually be compiled in a book entitled *Christian Mass Movements in India*. This study in turn served as a foundational text in church growth theory and helped the movement concentrate its attention on research (McPhee 2007, 44–47, 51).

Schlect points out that the IWM came to represent the epitome of "the religious ideals of centralized leadership, coordinated operations, and integrated resources" (Schlect 2015, 134–135). The organizational apparatus the movement set up, however was not ideal and the organization expended a great deal of energy simply to avoid duplicating its own efforts, let alone synching them with those of other Protestant organizations (Ernst 1968, 210). Ironically, the organization collapsed because of its own economic inefficiencies (Schlect 2015, 134–135). After the IWM collapsed, the church efficiency movement continued to utilize the IWM's insights throughout the 1920s. Moreover, the idea of applying a technocratically based plan to spiritually map the world occurred repeatedly throughout the course of the 20th century, most notably in the movements descended from the IWM-influenced church growth movement, such as the Christian Right's AD 2000 campaign, which created the practice of spiritual mapping (Schlect 2015, 134–135).

Concepts of scientific management entered the modern Christian Right through a number of means. As Schlect points out, the organizational paradigm shift caused by Taylorism affected how conservative Protestants saw doctrinal issues. For these leaders, "doctrinal standardization" was seen as a means of promoting orthodoxy, thus precipitating the fundamentalist crisis. Administrators of large denominations ended up rejecting the orthodox position, not so much out of disagreement with it, as out of fear of alienating important backers within their denominations. Yet, not all conservatives went along with this fundamentalist process of doctrinal standardization, fearing it could replace longstanding creedal forms (Schlect 2015, 121). As Brendan Pietsch and Schlect have contended, the desire for standardization of theological beliefs within the contemporary Protestantism of the 1920s reflected a Christian mind which Pietsch has characterized as "taxonomic." Believers were now applying the technocratic standards of engineering to their faith commitments (Schlect 2015, 151; Pietsch 2011, 70).

The Southern Baptist Convention's desire to remodel itself along Taylorist principles during the latter half of the 19th century and the first half of the 20th century particularly contributed to the growth of management and business influences over evangelicalism during this period. SBC leaders sought to apply key components of progressivism, such as "efficiency, uplift, [and] manhood" to perpetuating Southern religious values. The push for the scientific rationalization of the denomination's structure gained widespread support as a means of defeating theological modernism. Through this organizational remodeling, the SBC provided a model for modern fundamentalism's appropriation of management theory and the technological mechanisms it employs in its evangelism (Paul Harvey 1992, 476–477). Starting long before the "official" rise of scientific church management, Southern Baptists began organizing around corporatist ideas, utilizing "the language of modern business" and seeing individual church members as "shareholders," with the "denominational leaders serving as a board of directors." This meant that those who provided pastoral care were now viewed through the lens of "'denominational efficiency'"; this mindset permanently marked the model of pastoral care and denominational organization within the SBC (Paul Harvey 1992, 495–496) and thus likely served as an inspiration for the many evangelicals and fundamentalists who were either members of the SBC, or influenced by Southern Baptist connections.

As Ben Primer notes, the implementation of modern organizational culture into American Protestantism likely saved American Protestant churches from extinction. By contrast, European Protestant churches became shells of their former selves over the same period. Primer posits an important question, however, when he asks whether the American Protestant church structure that remained was only a "secular ghost" of its previous self (Primer 1979, 186). For Primer, writing in 1978, this question was unanswerable. Even today, the debate about the "secularization" hypothesis remains unsettled. The critics of secularization theory may now have the stronger case. In the coming chapters, this work implicitly advances the contention that while conservative Protestants did not secularize spiritually or theologically over the course of the 20th century, their ecclesiology did secularize. This has led evangelical ecclesiology to assume an increasingly pragmatic character. That pragmatism characterizes not simply the church growth movement bur also increasingly affects how conservative American Protestants approach the social sciences, information sciences, and the mission field.

The Mainline's Centralization

Immediately following World War II, mainline Protestant denominations began a major push towards centralization. This push for centralization and interdenominational cooperation was especially notable within the field of church education (McElligott 1995, 51). Efforts were made to shape new church educational agendas, often through highly innovative and experimental techniques (McElligott 1995, 51). The Presbyterian Church in the U.S.A. began this process even before the end of World War II, and most other mainline Protestant denominations initiated it sometime in the 1950s (McElligott 1995, 51–52).

Writing in 1967, Lloyd Warner et al. concluded that denominational growth up to that point had been characterized by three main impulses. The first was a growing tendency to expand administrative personnel. The second tendency was an increased "centralized control of fund-raising and budgeting" (Warner et al. 1967, 431). Finally, denominational staffing was becoming increasingly specialized (Warner et al. 1967, 431). Because of the pragmatic character of American Protestantism, denominational staffs increasingly required specialized labor, much of it professionally trained management figures. This in turn led to conflicts between denominational bureaucracies, which operated on bureaucratic and professional assumptions, and their adherents in the pews. Clergy in this period were often forced to choose between viewing their career as a vocation or as a job. Denominational staffs, by contrast, had a more "cosmopolitan" mindset. As denominational size and complexity increased, conflict also tended to increase as well (Warner et al. 1967, 438).

As the mainline denominations reached the 1960s, however, cracks began to appear in their administrative armor. One particularly clear demonstration of this was the organizational difficulties that beset the National Council of Churches (NCC) in the postwar period. Coordination between the various bureaus and boards that helped run the NCC proved to be impossible. Administrative personnel within the NCC found themselves conflicted between their loyalties to their denomination and their loyalty to the NCC. In such an environment, there was little hope of creating a unified political or policy agenda by which the NCC could develop a comprehensive approach to the religious questions of the day. In reaction to this, the NCC tried to develop a more centralized control system in the mid–1960s. The NCC also

1. The Origins of Evangelical Management Culture 47

hoped to spread this preference for centralized planning to its member denominations (Warner et al. 1967, 442).

Although the NCC's reform plan was well-intentioned, by the early 1960s such "corporate models" of the denomination proved unfeasible. The mistrust between those in the pews and denominational "managers and trustees" was increasingly a central issue within denominational conflicts. Debates within denominational culture over American imperialism made the mission-orientation of many denominations, even mainline ones, seem culturally "chauvinist." Moreover, mainline Protestant growth had crested in 1965 and the size of denominational infrastructures in the post–World War II era was unsustainable. This led to budgetary reductions, which in turn led to increasing dissent in the pews and a spiraling decrease of committed members (Dykstra and James Hudnut Beumler 1992, 318–319). In response to these kinds of organizational problems, a number of groups, such as the Alban Institute, were set up to provide consulting services for mainline churches.

The oversight of denominations was also increasingly circumscribed by congregations' desire for new religious curricula; often, the best material was more preferably purchased from outside agencies rather than denominational publishers. Nationalized programs everywhere gave way to localized efforts focusing on appealing to special-interest groups. The small group movement was one byproduct of this trend (Dykstra and Hudnut Beumler 1992, 320). Denominations came to be seen less as corporations and more as "regulatory agencies" (Dykstra and Hudnut Beumler 1992, 321). But unlike the early corporate model, which had been enthusiastically embraced by many advocates at the turn of the century, the regulatory model found few defenders (Dykstra and Hudnut Beumler 1992, 321). To the Americans of post–Watergate America, governmental bodies held little respect, a trend only accelerated with the rise of New Public Management (NPM) and trickle-down economics (Dykstra and Hudnut-Beumler 1992, 321).

The radically changed nature of church organizational life following the peak of the mainline in the mid–1960s encouraged many denominations to adopt concepts borrowed from secular management to solidify support for their agendas (Reifsnyder 1984, 34). Besides centralization, denominational restructuring was a primary goal in this process in almost all denominations (Reifsnyder 1984, 33–36). Regardless of the denominations' move towards a regulatory, rather than corporate, view of governance, mainline Protestant organizational life was still characterized by large-scale adaptations of corporate-based ideology and management practices.

Richard. G. Hutcheson, Jr., writing in 1979, gave eloquent testimony to the profound nature of this change. Hutcheson, a prominent authority on organizational life in the Presbyterian Church in the United States (Hutcheson Jr. 1979, 7), noted that even by the late 1970s, management seminars had become institutionalized forms of professional training for religious leaders. The religious application of the Peter Drucker-inspired Management by Objectives (MBO) management philosophy was already widespread (Hutcheson Jr. 1979, 15). Congregational goals and even spiritual renewal were reframed through corporate language, heavily tinged with Druckerian jargon (Hutcheson Jr. 1979, 15–16). Perhaps the most important byproduct of this corporatization of mainline Protestantism, brought about by the adoption of systems-based perspectives on congregational culture, was the adoption of an "'instrumentalist'" outlook on the church, in which congregational culture was viewed primarily through the lens of "social 'output'" and input (Hutcheson Jr. 1979, 50). This, in turn raised the specter of the church being viewed simply as a "means to social ends" (Hutcheson Jr. 1979, 50). Hutcheson critiqued progressive Protestant critics for adopting such instrumentalism, but this outlook would actually be most ardently embraced by evangelical adopters of systems perspectives, notably the Leadership Network (see Hutcheson Jr. 1979, 50 on Progressive Protestantism and instrumentalism). Supporters of metricspiritual practices and theology would rely heavily on the pragmatic logic of instrumentalism to justify their actions.

Along with the push towards denominational centralization, there was an increasing awareness of the centrality of group life in American culture. Critics, notably Philip Rieff (1922–2006), charged that by the late 1950s, the cultural center of the United States had shifted from church and government to the hospital. This shift in cultural values led to a renewed emphasis on self-examination. Unlike Puritanical introspection, however, which had focused primarily on guilt, sin, and repentance, the new American Self being constructed at the dawn of the 1960s was a therapeutic self, preoccupied with "self-expression and self-direction" (Holifield 1983, 308). Before the close of the decade, a new therapeutic ethos dominated the country. Previously outlandish therapeutic concepts received widespread support, including Wilhelm's Reich's eccentric ideas about the human body and Frederick Perls Gestalt therapy. By 1967, Perls' employer Esalen, one of the leading influences on the counterculture was raking in profits exceeding $1 million dollars a year. A slew of new therapies had developed in the wake of Esalen's success, among them "psychodrama ... bioenergetics, a bodily therapy invented by a student of Reich; rolfing, a form of deep-muscle manipulation created by a biologist turned therapist; psychosynthesis, a combination of group and individual methods" (Holifield 1983, 308–309). The 1960s therefore saw an explosion of interest in small groups (Holifield 1983, 309; Wuthnow 1994, 43). The groups that emerged in the sixties, often the product of the counterculture, avoided the didacticism of previous small group models in favor of "mutual interaction" which offered a consensus-oriented approach to group development (Wuthnow 1994, 43).

1. The Origins of Evangelical Management Culture 49

These new therapeutic schools vaguely coalesced around the label of "humanistic psychology." Mainstream practitioners of humanistic psychology, such as Abraham Maslow and Carl Rogers, emphasized the importance of self-actualization and personal fulfillment. Proponents of humanistic psychology, interacting with advocates of the small group movement of the period, eventually formed what has been called the "'human potential movement,'" a loose association of individuals, training facilities, and small groups dedicated to self-actualization (Holifield 1983, 307–310). The ideology of the human potential movement, particularly so-called encounter groups, influenced the "self-oriented" rhetoric that came to dominate much CG and mainline small group literature. Indeed, the evangelical church began adopting the organizational tools of the counterculture before the counterculture was even formed.

The encounter group, the model on which much of American small group life was based, originated in the fertile mind of Gestalt psychologist Kurt Lewin (1890–1947). Lewin had created small groups known as "T-groups" as mechanisms for understanding the interaction of individuals within groups and the function of groups themselves. After Lewin's death, National Training Laboratories (Labs) held a number of well-regarded T-group sessions (Milton 2002, 136–137). The basic format of these sessions was quite similar. Usually participants were taken to a remote area where they engaged in a multi-week program of workshops. These workshops involved a process of mutual criticism and feedback. Participants were encouraged to assess themselves, others, and the group itself. Those who promoted the T-group contended that it created more efficient organizations by allowing management to more effectively communicate with subordinates. Simultaneously, the open venting of feelings by subordinates allowed emotional tensions to unwind harmlessly (Alden 2012, 283).

Mainline Protestant churches became early advocates of the T-group approach. In order to develop an effective educational agenda, the Episcopalian church began networking with the National Training Laboratory in Group Dynamics. Starting in 1953, the denomination began holding Church and Group Life Laboratories. These laboratories taught small group dynamics within a church context, as well as teaching Episcopalian leaders the basic psychological theories that underpinned NTL methodology. Although these laboratories were heavily criticized, they became a major part of leadership development among Episcopalians (McElligott 1995, 80, 132).

Critics nonetheless charged that the laboratories allowed the utilization of secular methods within the church context. Many also felt that the Church and Group Life Laboratories ended up creating a spiritual "'elite.'" (McElligott 1995, 131–132). Early adopters of the NTL small group model were keenly aware of this problem. They realized that while NTL's approach to group dynamics offered enormous advantages, its educational philosophy was opposed to the top down hierarchicalism that characterized traditional small group leadership structures (Braun 1960, 215). Therefore, at a crucial early meeting in October 1952 which helped shape Episcopalians' adoption of NTL's group dynamics approach, Episcopalians who had participated in NTL began to adopt a framework for applying NTL's ideas to their denomination. In order to facilitate the training and perhaps provide for a more receptive learning audience, the leaders suggested that the Church recruit from those who had had previous contact with the church's own training program (Braun 1960, 216).

The Group and Life Laboratories that the Episcopalian church underwrote were major innovations in how mainline small group life was conceptualized. Ostensibly, the purpose of these laboratories was to reinvigorate the denomination's commitment to community life (Braun 1960, 216). Its more prosaic goals, however, were far more practical. The initial Group and Life Laboratory[1] was committed to leadership development. Much of the rest of the structure of the Laboratory was modeled heavily on NTL practices, with small training groups—equivalent to NTL T-groups—engaging in small group meetings, as well as attending seminars devoted to theory in which all members of a lab attended, and practicums which allowed individuals to test their skills (Braun 1960, 217). Training group facilitators deliberately took a passive role at first, letting the groups work out their own direction. This, in turn, allowed group members to engage in experimentation concerning various forms of interpersonal behavior (Braun 1960, 217–218). In the theory sessions, participants discussed a wide range of topics ranging from the covert agendas that might motivate individual members to the dangers of authoritarianism on "non-conforming members" (Braun 1960, 219). It should be emphasized that at this point in history there is no reason to necessarily suppose that the agenda of the Group and Life Laboratories, much less NTL, was necessarily malign. NTL's founder, Kurt Lewin, who had died in 1947, had been a major opponent of authoritarianism and many of the methods NTL initially adopted were designed to combat that authoritarianism (Waring 1991, 108–109).

Towards the close of 1958, the National Council of the Episcopal Church decided to stop conducting the Church and Group Life Laboratories, but shortly thereafter the Church's Leadership Training Division started sponsoring local labs that were conducted within a diocese or a group of dioceses (McElligott 1995, 133). Even when locally focused, the use of NTL methods remained controversial for the Episcopalian church. Nevertheless, the denomination went ahead with an ambitious program to enhance its understanding of education and group dynamics. Leaders were encouraged to look at new ways of preparing individuals for church service. Meanwhile, multiple departments within the church utilized NTL's laboratories on "Community Relations." During 1965, they conducted an "Advanced Training Institute in Social Change," which harnessed the thought of well-known community activist Saul Alinsky (McElligott 1995, 134–135).

The changes wrought in the Episcopal church were part of a broader shift in mainline denominations that favored the adoption of NTL's approach to group dynamics. In the years following World War II, many denominations grew concerned about the need for effective adult education. Mainline churches were as keen to achieve such educational standards as their evangelical and fundamentalist counterparts and from 1957 on the National Council of Churches of Christ in America began employing a full-time staff-person to oversee adult education. The increased emphasis on adult education was consistent with contentions being made in educational theory, then just reaching full public awareness, that adult learners could be effectively instructed if proper educational theory was utilized. This presented a problem for local churches, who often lacked effectively trained personnel and teaching staff. Moreover, there was a disconnect between the education being targeted at religious consumers and those consumers' spiritual and felt needs (Lela Susan Wright 1968, 4–5). Steeped in adherence to a 2,000-year-old text, many denominations faced difficulty in adopting their curricular agendas to a modern idiom. Others faced equally strong challenges making their material accessible to the average lay reader. Moreover, there was considerable tension within denominations about the most effective group instructional methods, as well as both the possibilities of "free inquiry" when stacked against the need for denominational authority (Lela Wright 1968, 4–5).

Thanks to its successes in the Episcopalian church, NTL soon became an important center for church leaders looking for information on group dynamics. The National Council of Churches of Christ in America (NCC), the country's foremost interdenominational mainline Protestant body, started an innovative series of NTL-led laboratories that individual denominations were invited to participate in 1953 (Lela Wright 1968, 5–6, 26). By 1957, the Methodist Church had adopted many of the techniques used by the Episcopalian leadership in its own leadership development program (Lela Wright 1968, 5–6). The American Baptist denomination, meanwhile, whose theology leaned towards majority mainline beliefs, had developed its own Laboratory School in 1957 (Lela Wright 1968, 10). Such training sessions, much like those conducted by the Episcopalians, introduced lay leaders of various denominations to the underpinnings of organizational theory, particularly group dynamics. Group members were encouraged to develop effective assessment techniques for dealing with group problems. Once these skills were developed, they could then be deployed back in the group member's home congregation (Lela Wright 1968, 57). As Lela Wright notes in her discussion of

American Baptist laboratory schools, what was revolutionary about the laboratory school approach was that it incorporated the insights of group dynamics thinkers into the church's analysis of groups. Laboratory schools analyzed the process of group formation, what prevented groups from being formed, the social dynamics of groups, and how groups were socially maintained. Group members were encouraged to understand the interconnected nature of group relations; thus, sensitivity training was heavily emphasized, both as a means of group norming and as a tool to encourage self-actualization among individual group members (Lela Wright 1968, 57–58).

The success of the small group movement within mainline Protestant churches paralleled similar developments that occurred within the evangelical movement. To understand how evangelicals approached small groups, three evangelical movements must be examined: the parachurch movement, the shepherding movement and the Jesus People Movement. For without these key movements, the evangelical small group movement would not have the power it now possesses.

Parachurch and the Rebirth of Evangelical Small Groups

Although initially behind mainline Protestants in their use of small groups, evangelicals and other conservative Protestants soon proved quite adept at applying this venerated form of pastoral care in the spheres of evangelism and social control. One of the major inspirations for the growth in small groups was the birth of the parachurch movement. The parachurch movement laid the groundwork for much of the subsequent organizational innovation that took place in evangelicalism during the second half of the 20th century.

Parachurch groups have taken on a wide number of functions in the post–World War II environment. As Robert Wuthnow notes in his discussion of "special purpose organizations"—a term he utilizes that is broader than but encompasses the parachurch movement—these organizations aim to serve highly specialized "constituencies." For instance, some are specifically geared to meet the needs of businessmen, or athletes, or lawyers. Others have been founded over commonly shared recreational activities. Still others aim to enact specific policy objectives, such as the promotion of creationism in the public schools (Wuthnow 1994, 108–110). Wuthnow argues that as denominationalism has become less important, the parachurch movement has taken on added importance. Wuthnow speculates that the growth of the state following World War II led to the creation of special interest groups, including the parachurch, to either combat that growth, or to stimulate it in

1. The Origins of Evangelical Management Culture 53

different directions (Wuthnow 1994, 113–116). Organizationally, parachurch organizations have an easier time cutting through red tape than organizations run by denominational boards. Because of this, the parachurch movement can create effective alliances on policy issues that might not be possible for denominational bodies. Moreover, membership in parachurch organizations does not typically require the same level of creedal commitment that belonging to a denomination does.

The parachurch movement is crucial to understanding the political power of the Christian Right. Sara Diamond, a leading writer on the Christian Right, has argued that it was the establishment of the parachurch that "laid the groundwork for later evangelical political activity" (Diamond 1995, 98). Starting in the early 1940s, the evangelical movement began an extensive networking campaign to establish itself as a political force within American society. Parachurch ministries played a key role in this campaign. Often times, as Diamond relates, an organization, often parachurch or transdenominational in origin, would be started for religious purposes, only to later morph into a politically oriented group. During the Cold War, the implicit aim of many of these organizations was to fight Communism through red-baiting mainline Protestants. This aim, of course, served evangelicalism's long-term objectives, by equating its foremost theological enemy with a political group widely perceived as tyrannical (Diamond 1995, 95). Reformed historian George Marsden has gone even further, arguing that parachurch organizations have become the central wellspring of Christian identity in contemporary evangelicalism (Marsden 1984, xiv). Moreover, the ability of the parachurch to bypass denominational bickering and infighting via its transdenominational networks allows these organizations to also assume a transnational character. This ability has made them crucial to efforts at religious proselytization by evangelicals (Brouwer, Gifford and Rose 1996, 183). In some cases, parachurch organizations take on the characteristics of corporate multinationals, serving a number of different constituencies (Brouwer, Gifford and Rose 1996, 183).

The corporate nature of parachurch organizations makes them ideal partners for business leaders, many of whom prefer parachurch organizational practices and spirituality to that promoted by traditional congregations. Organizations such as *Christianity Today*, Wheaton College, and the Billy Graham Evangelistic Association received important backing from the business community, including such prominent business leaders as J. Howard Pew (D. Michael Lindsay 2007, 194). The more efficient model of leadership that parachurch organizations offered often allowed for more influence on the part of businessmen than could be seen in congregational structures. D. Michael Lindsay also notes, on the basis of numerous interviews with evangelical business leaders, that many members of the evangelical corporate elite prefer the parachurch movement because of its ability to adapt to the changing world of Internet connectivity (D. Michael Lindsay 2007. 194–195). The even more adaptive parachurch models that came about during the 1990s, known as church networks, will likely contribute to greater corporate-parachurch connections due to their Toyotist characteristics, even as this model evolves these connections in patterns radically different from past parachurch organizations.

Although its international arm can be dated back much earlier, the parachurch, as an American phenomenon, evolved mainly out of the voluntary societies that characterized early 19th century Christianity (Scheitle 2008, 16–18, 25). Originally local in scope, groups like Bible societies, for instance, began wanting to have a national (later, sometimes, an international outreach). These organizations also realized they could avoid duplication of efforts and increase their productivity if they cooperated amongst each other. In addition, Bible and tract societies were motivated by the fact that mass printing technology was becoming available, but was prohibitively expensive for local societies. By establishing national groups, these proto-parachurch organizations could pool their assets, increasing their effectiveness (Scheitle 2008, 25). However, tensions between denominations led to the creation of agency structures within denominations, leading to the decline of parachurch activities until about halfway through the 20th century (Scheitle 2008, 27).

Theologically and ideologically, the parachurch movement was shaped by many of the same foundational influences that created the modern small group movement. From Phillip Spener, for instance, they inherited a laity-centered mission emphasis and a focus on biblical study (Hunsicker 1998, 60–61). David B. Hunsicker also makes a persuasive case that German Pietism has played a major role in creating the ideology of the parachurch movement. German Pietism is known for its "experiential" view of Christianity, which emphasizes living a pure life. Even before the export of Spener's and Wesley's teachings to America, experiential Christianity had established a strong foothold in the future United States. What Spener, as well as John Wesley did, was accelerate that trend (Hunsicker 1998, 125). The influence of Pietism also subtly shifted the emphases of American Protestantism, leading it to focus more on conversion and holy living and less on theological and ecclesiological issues (Hunsicker 1998, 126–127). This shift in emphasis had major implications for how these newly pietistic Christians conceptualized church. German Pietism had not worried about denominationalism; the movement was transdenominational in character. Spener was more concerned with how Christians lived their lives than with their denominational affiliations (Hunsicker 1998, 128). Moreover, the emphasis on laity involvement within the movement played a profound role (Hunsicker 1998, 128–129) in many of the CG-influenced forms of parachurch thought.

Largely due to its pietistic roots, the parachurch movement profoundly

1. The Origins of Evangelical Management Culture 55

influenced the United States (Hunsicker 1998, 110). As the 19th century drew to a close, a number of evangelism-centered movements spread to the fore of evangelicalism, many of them inspired by revivalistic impulses. Groups like the YMCA and the Student Volunteer Movement spread this new emphasis to a national audience (Hunsicker 1998, 147). Interdenominational Bible schools also significantly shaped the expansion of the parachurch movement. Many of the leading figures in the parachurch movement had direct ties to Bible institutes or schools (Hunsicker 1998, 149). Hunsicker notes that the pervasiveness of German Pietistic thought within American Protestantism accelerated the acceptance of the parachurch in the United States because pietism ended up having an almost ubiquitous influence on even those theologies most hostile to it, such as the Reformed movement. Moreover, the perpetual revivalism in American Protestantism allowed American evangelicalism to develop an entrepreneurial approach to religion which encouraged ecclesiological innovation (Hunsicker 1998, 121).

An early and important modern parachurch organizations was the Navigators, founded by Dawson Trotman (1906–1956). Trotman's Christian formation was shaped by his reading of famous Christian missionaries, such as David Brainerd and Hudson Taylor (Hunsicker 1998, 178). With the help of his high school science teacher, Irene Mills, Trotman concentrated on improving his public speaking following his 1926 conversion (Hankins Jr. 2011, 53, 59). Trotman's discipling methodology, his key gift to the parachurch movement, was shaped by the influence of Dr. Vernon Morgan, the leader of an L.A-based evangelism ministry which specialized in training evangelists (Hankins Jr. 2011, 61–62). Morgan's methods so inspired Trotman that he applied and refined them in his next three ministry opportunities (Hankins Jr. 2011, 62). Along with a friend, Trotman helped establish an organization named the Minute Men, an organization devoted to pious living and evangelism (Hankins Jr.2011, 64). While this organization was initially unsuccessful, it eventually evolved into The Navigators organization. Initially aimed mainly at servicemen, the Navigators proved to be a smash hit among servicemen (Hankins Jr. 2011, 65–67). Trotman's various ministry endeavors, including the Navigators, consistently emphasized the importance of the "spiritual disciplines" in the life of a believer, notably scripture reading, proselytization, prayer and the mutual support of other believers (Hankins Jr. 2011, 72).

Regarding ecclesiology, Trotman broke significantly from confessional and denominational-centered definitions of Christian fellowship. Trotman cared little for the church as a "corporate body"; rather his focus was on individual souls. While not opposed to local congregations, Trotman also did not think the local congregation was particularly necessary to the promulgation of the Christian message and thus had no problem with members of his organization viewing the Navigators as their church body. Trotman's vision of Christianity was interdenominational; at the end of his career, he became an important advocate of cooperation among evangelicals. Trotman freely shared his personal network of contacts and Navigator workers with other evangelical ministries, arguing that the Great Commission required that evangelicals work in unison. Moreover, despite the size and influence of the Navigators, Trotman resisted calls to transform the Navigators into some sort of denominational structure, and was reluctant even to formally incorporate it. Only after working with Billy Graham, did Trotman fully realize the benefits to missions that local congregations could offer (Felts 1989, 84–89).

Trotman's rejection of traditional evangelical ecclesiology points to the important fissures that would rise between advocates of traditional denominationalism and the parachurch, fissures that eventually led to the parachurch supplanting the denomination as the dominant religious force within conservative Protestantism. Denominations, particularly after the rise of efficiency-oriented practices borrowed from scientific management, sought to utilize "central planning" and to regulate and control their "religious markets." By contrast, parachurch organizations adopted an explicitly consumer-oriented approach that eschewed the "centralized control" of the religious economy that denominations aimed for in favor of a more market-oriented approach. Parachurch leaders such as Demos Shakarian (1913–1993) and Bill Bright (1921–2003) ended up "effectively blending the priorities of evangelism within the new corporate structure" (Darran Dochuk 2011, 185). In many ways, the competition between market-oriented parachurch organizations and the centralized planning offered by denominations mirrored the rivalry between capitalist and communist models of economic regulation that arose during the Cold War period.

The ability of parachurch organizations to work beyond denominational structures has opened them up to considerable criticism. Many evangelicals argue that these organizations violate Scriptural precepts, since the efforts parachurch organizations oversee can be effectively undertaken by local churches, without the need of the parachurch. Critics who hold this position contend that denominationalism is more consistent with historic Christianity than the parachurch movement, since denominations are bound to work within systems—rather than outside them—and are at least theoretically responsible to churches for their conduct. Neither of these restrictions, by contrast bind the parachurch organization (Schleite 2008, 42). Christopher Schleite argues, however, that this position is something of a red herring. Criticisms of the market-oriented nature of parachurch organizations obscures the fact that religious organizations in the United States have never operated outside a market-oriented model. Scheitle sees criticisms of the parachurch as rooted in contestations for power, rather than simply "scriptural interpretation." For Scheitle, congregations and denominational entities are seats of

1. The Origins of Evangelical Management Culture 57

power, and thus do not want to compete with parachurch entities for control of the religious market. It is this desire for regulated markets, more than scriptural concerns, that characterizes objections to the parachurch (Scheitle 2008, 42–43). Scheitle notes that many of the objections to parachurch organization resemble how corporations will valorize:

> the virtues of an unregulated market system until they become the dominant player in the market. Then, all of a sudden they praise the virtues of laws protecting their patents and copyrights and other mechanisms limiting the ability of competitors to challenge it [the corporation] [Scheitle 2008, 43].

Scheitle's comments are perceptive to a point. Certainly, many denominationally oriented conservative Christians have expressed loathing for parachurch organizations and in some cases this loathing can be traced to concerns about loss of prestige and power. Moreover, the rise of the parachurch has often privileged Pentecostal and Charismatic organizations which many evangelicals—as well as other Protestants—see as representative of an inferior class culture. Thus, cultural prejudice against newly emergent powers within conservative Protestantism definitely plays a part in objections to parachurch Christianity. Nor is Scheitle incorrect to note that the broad-tent orientation of the parachurch has garnered it considerable criticism, some of it doubtlessly unjust (see Scheitle 2008, 43–45). However, Scheitle ignores significant objections to his position. Many evangelicals who oppose the parachurch movement do not operate from a position of privilege. Some of its most vocal critics are members of discernment ministries or "spiritual abuse" survivors, who have expressed concern about many of the soul care practices of the parachurch movement. And it is here that Trotman's foundational influence on the American parachurch movement again shows itself, due to his influence on modern evangelical mentoring and discipling practices.

One of the reasons why Trotman is such an important figure in the birth of modern evangelical managerial practices is his approach to discipleship, much of which, as later re-interpreted through philosophies like shepherding, would prove disastrous to the survival of democratic values within the evangelical movement. Indeed, James Douglas Hankins, Jr., argues that the modern concept of discipleship was largely created by Trotman and the Navigators (Hankins Jr. 2011, 128). Early 20th century conservative evangelicalism and its fundamentalist offshoots were dominated by a concern for "soul winning," the converting of non-believers to Christ. Far more than in other centuries, conversion became the primary tool of Christians, leading to the embrace of a missions-oriented emphasis and a move away from other aspects of the Christian life (Hankins Jr. 2011, 33). Charles Spurgeon, for instance, emphasized that only those who evangelized were truly worthy of

God's benevolence (Hankins Jr. 2011, 35), a belief echoed by other evangelical leaders at the turn of the 20th century, notably D.L Moody (Hankins Jr. 2011, 35–36).

Trotman's message "Born to Reproduce" (1955), a sermon which he gave a number of times over the last two years of his life, offered a paradigm-shifting view of Christian mentoring for numerous evangelical organizations, including Campus Crusade, the BGEA, and Trotman's own Navigators. Throughout his career, Trotman emphasized three key aspects of discipleship: the use of so-called "follow up ministry" in addition to proselytization, the promotion of a "theology of spiritual reproduction," and the modernization of the concept of discipleship to include aspects of modern mentoring relationships (Hankins Jr. 2011, 123, 128, 138). For Trotman, the concept of spiritual reproduction denoted that aspects of Christians' spiritual lives closely resembled how humans are organically created. This had important consequences for spiritual formation. Just as children needed adults to raise them as they matured, so too did young Christians need "spiritual adults" to help them grow. Without this attention to spiritual growth, young Christians' spiritual formation became stunted, handicapping the Christian community's ability to perpetuate itself (Hankins Jr. 2011, 140). This belief in spiritual reproduction was the impetus for Trotman adopting the idea of "follow up" ministry (Hankins Jr. 2011, 141).

It was follow-up ministry that was the most revolutionary aspect of Trotman's approach to spiritual mentoring. Early on in his career, Trotman had been inclined to the soul-winning approaches that characterized D.L. Moody (Hankins Jr. 2011, 139). Moody had little patience for what he called "lifeboat" (Hankins Jr. 2011, 35) approaches to evangelism. Thus, discipleship played little role in Moody's theological life. Trotman, by contrast, tried to develop a "holistic" model of discipleship, in which those who converted a non-believer then began to mentor them as well (Hankins Jr. 2011, 139). Trotman felt that this kind of holistic approach avoided created a "bifurcated" relationship between evangelism and discipleship. For Trotman, discipleship was literally inseparable from evangelism (Jeffrey Paul Reynolds 2014, 79). Moreover, Trotman was influenced by a bias, shared by CGM proponents, that ministerial education tended to leave seminary-trained pastors poorly equipped for mentoring relationships; the discipling model he offered up was a corrective to this trend, as it focused more on pragmatic aspects of conversion and membership retention, rather than abstract theorizing (Reynolds 2014, 85–86).

Trotman's approach to discipling may reflect the particular theological ideas that shaped the formative period of his Christian life. The fundamentalism that Trotman encountered as a young believer has been characterized by Hankins Jr. as a "soul-winning-or-bust" approach (Hankins Jr. 2011, 39).

1. The Origins of Evangelical Management Culture

Viewing this approach to conversion in economic terms, the issue of retention becomes a major problem. Soul-winning campaigns could be massively effective, but if no attention was paid to resource (i.e., believer) retention, all the benefits of these campaigns would be lost. Moreover, a truly effective discipleship model could not only minister to the newly converted, but to the "backslidden" or simply to other evangelicals whom parachurch organizations or small groups believed were not toeing the theological "party line." Pragmatically, even simplistic attempts at retention proved useful to the embryonic parachurch movement, particularly as justifications for the movement's existence outside denominational structures. Nor was Trotman unsophisticated in his retention methods. When Billy Graham (1918–) and Trotman consulted on how to approach follow-up ministry, the two men hit upon a method that combined elements of revivalism with modern social science techniques including the using of counseling and statistical metrics (Hankins Jr. 2011, 17–18).

Trotman's application of the follow-up approach in Graham's crusades showed a keen desire to professionalize and systemize Graham's evangelism's efforts. Trotman instituted a standardized counselor training technique. All counselors used the same material, thus helping minimize deviations from organizational norms. Trotman developed some sensible basic rules for the counseling process as well. He contended that the counseling process should be age-segregated whenever possible (Hankins Jr. 2011, 176–177). Another mark of the professionalization of revivalism that Trotman insisted on was counselor confidentiality for new converts. He rejected any coercive form of proselytization. The counseling process, much like that practiced by NTL, was non-directive in nature (Hankins Jr. 2011, 177). Unlike NTL, however, Trotman preferred "one-on-one" mentoring rather than group training to enhance the change of "spiritual reproduction" on discipleship (Felts 1989, 113). Trotman's emphasis on individual mentoring in part likely reflected the pietistic influences on his life. Pietistic movements have always had the tendency to utilize relatively small organizational entities to achieve effectiveness. In addition, Trotman was concerned about the need for leadership training, something that became a constant concern among future movement thinkers (Felts 1989, 115). Moreover, Trotman believed that the nature of human relationships limited the number of individuals one could mentor effectively (Felts 1989, 114). While the use of church growth principles within modern Protestantism has put finite limits on the degree to which personal discipleship is possible, most churches do aspire to some form of personal discipleship as an ideal. Indeed, the adoption of the small group model is intended to further the efficiency of discipleship, not supplant it.

Trotman not only revolutionized discipleship and evangelical retention practices, but also helped improve the data-processing capabilities of Graham's revivals, improving efficiency tremendously. Trotman and his co-workers employed a sophisticated system of decision card collection and organization, which gave them such information as the congregational and denominational affiliation of new converts. A follow-up letter campaign sent multiple letters to converts. Trotman tried to get local congregations involved in the converts lives quickly (Hankins Jr. 2011, 177–178), which likely aided in convert retention. Due to Trotman's influence, Graham also began insisting on better localized training for counselors. Trotman conducted training sessions within areas targeted for a revival to teach counselors Navigator discipling techniques (Hankins Jr. 2011, 177). Trotman also established a carefully outlined post-revival pastor response plan, showing pastors how to effectively engage in "follow-up" ministry with new converts (Hankins Jr. 2011, 180). After their introduction via the Graham campaigns, Trotman's methodology and material quickly became the benchmark for organizational efficiency among evangelists. "Follow up" ministry soon became standard practice in evangelical circles (Felts 1989, 95).

The impact of Trotman on future evangelical leaders was enormous. Trotman was a foundational influence on Campus Crusade's approach to discipleship (James Douglas Hankins, Jr. 2011, 24). Trotman's promotion of "follow up" ministry at Billy Graham crusades became a fundamental aspect of Graham's ministry. Graham not only borrowed Trotman's expertise, but employed Navigator materials in his ministry's follow-up endeavors (James Douglas Hankins Jr. 2011, 26). Trotman also influenced Jack Wyrtzen (1913–1996), founder of the influential Word of Life Bible Institute (James Douglas Hankins 2011, 23–24). Trotman's influence was felt keenly among Charismatics, whose practice of discipleship closely resembled that of the Navigators (S. David Moore 2003, 73).[2]

Trotman's Navigators were not the only evangelical parachurch organization to be birthed by the Great Depression and the War years. Evangelical leaders, like their mainline counterparts, expressed concern about the potential effect the Depression and the War might have on youth (Martin 2005, 25). Christian leader Torrey Johnson (1909–2002) began to target servicemen for evangelism and began helping numerous young preachers jumpstart their ministries, including Billy Graham. By July 1945, Johnson had helped found Youth for Christ (YFC), with Billy Graham serving as a crucial organizational representative and Johnson taking the role of president. Adapting methods that were later refined by the CGM, megachurch, and EMC movements, YFC aimed immediately for a modern, youth-directed approach to evangelization. Leaders adopted what they thought were hip clothes and music that resembled big band as much as the church choir. The movement also sought to engage the service of celebrity preachers, entertainers, sports stars, servicemen, and business leaders (Martin 2005, 26). The movement offered magical acts, ventriloquist shows, and bible quiz games (Martin 2005, 26). While these methods appear quaint by the standards of today's youth-oriented evangelicalism, many were highly innovative in the mid–1940s (Martin 2005, 26). Typically, rallies were held at locations deemed as non-divisive by local church leaders and were normally organized by one or two important leaders who took on the considerable risk of promoting what was then still a somewhat controversial form of revivalism (Senter 1989, 131).

The YFC movement, along with similar youth-oriented parachurch movements, responded to a number of perceived problems in conservative Protestant responses to youth culture. In the 1930s and 1940s, evangelical youth curricular planning began looking at youth evangelism in terms of students' felt needs, rather than centering on the inward pietistic values that had characterized evangelical culture previously (Senter 1989, 128–129). This shift in emphases was responsive to broader psychologizing trends in American society. Traditional denominational youth movements were unprepared for the changes then taking place in American youth culture. These organizations were characterized by a "'top-down'" approach that centered power in the hands of adults. From a marketing standpoint, even the concerns of these group were insufficiently shaped by youth's felt needs. Denominational organizations did not engage in effective advertising and marketing of their youth groups, leading to stagnation on the part of denominational youth organizations (Senter 1989, 128–129).

YFC, by contrast, benefited from its effective utilization of both mass media and mass evangelism. Stadium-sized revival meetings enticed American youth who were not yet used to urbanization. YFC's methods of radio evangelism, pioneered by evangelical youth advocate Jack Wrytzen,[3] proved attractive to many young people. There was also the allure of becoming a Christian celebrity oneself, as YFC recruited teens to rework traditional gospel music into a modern idiom (Bergler 2000, 109–110). The rallies proved so popular that even non–Christians occasionally attended; meanwhile, evangelical youth, often suffering from restrictive rules at homes, saw this new revivalism as "nearly irresistible" (Bergler 2000, 109–110).

YFC was one of a number of evangelical parachurch organizations birthed in the 1940s and 1950s that targeted young people. Many of these organizations worked under the aegis, or via the model of, the National Association of Evangelicals (NAE). The NAE aimed for a "mere Christian" approach to evangelical identity, something akin to what C.S. Lewis offers in *Mere Christianity*. Its goal was to reduce "the gospel message" to its most basic components so that Christians could target as many prospective evangelical Christians as possible. By adopting this broad tent approach, the NAE and its satellite ministries proved to be far more effective than denominationally linked youth ministries. These churches could bypass denominational bureaucracies and adapt new methods and techniques that traditional denominational churches were unable to experiment with (Shires 2007, 44–45). The YFC, under Torrey Johnson's leadership, adopted this non-denominational approach, avoiding the factionalism that then characterized conservative fundamentalism. Since YFC's main goal, much like the Navigators, was "soul winning," it was crucial that the organization avoid doctrinal conflicts (Hunsicker 1998, 380–381). Johnson also made a fateful decision for the future of parachurch organizations in the United States: He conceded to denominational churches the right to doctrinally instruct any youth evangelized by YFC. YFC's position was that it was to work alongside of, rather than supplant, denominational organizations (Hunsicker 1998, 381–382).

Faced with unprecedented success, YFC movement leadership sought to systemize their form of revivalism to meet the needs of a new form of religious consumer. During the early 1950s, the Bible club movement served as a way of channeling newly converted evangelical youth into local congregations (Bergler 2000, 116). Bible clubs had started developing in the 1930s and early 1940s and their long-term influence equaled that of the evangelical youth rally (Senter 1989, 162). High school Bible clubs were explicitly parachurch oriented and much like the Navigators, were often the vision of one formative early influence. As such, they often existed outside the bounds of traditional denominational structures (Senter 1989, 164). Because of the countless number of Bible clubs spawned in the 1930s, it is wrong to trace YFC's adoption of the Bible club model to any one group. However, one of the most formative influences was the Miracle Book Club, started in 1933 through the influence of Evelyn McClusky (Senter 1989, 165). As a woman, McClusky's influence is unusual during this period. Part of that influence on the evangelical youth movement can be attributed to the fact that her ministry was aimed at teens in the public schools and thus did not fall under the purview of most traditional denominational ministries (Senter 1989, 165). The club adopted a lecture format that meshed with McClusky's considerable storytelling ability. McClusky demanded such skills out of the leadership of her movement, ensuring that the movement was seen as entertaining by youth. Perhaps even more crucially, McClusky frowned upon public calls to conversion. Her tactics involved the "soft sell" of Christian spirituality, a position entirely in keeping with her Presbyterian background (Senter 1989, 168–169). Towards the close of the 20th century, Willow Creek Community Church applied similar insights and thus the soft sell emerged as a formative early influence on the megachurch movement; this approach has often been seen as one of the foundational reasons for the perceived shallowness of various early metricspiritual movements, such as church marketing and the CGM. Like the YFC, McClusky avoided doctrinal battles between modernists and fundamentalists in order to build broad-based support (Senter 1989, 170).

1. The Origins of Evangelical Management Culture 63

McClusky also made three significant organizational deviations from the traditional Sunday school. Unlike traditional Sunday schools, the opening fifteen minutes of Bible Club hour were youth-led, rather than directed by adults. Secondly, McClusky focus on narrative and teaching skills evidently had a positive influence on the movement; its teaching methods were seen as more effective than similar Christian organizations. Finally, the group did not meet just on Sunday, but during the week (Senter 1989, 171).

Young Life, the paradigmatic evangelical high school youth organization, grew out of the Good News Club and was influenced by its model, albeit heavily refined through its founder Jim Rayburn (1909–1970) (Senter 1989, 174–177). However, a number of features helped Young Life stand out from other evangelical youth organizations of the period and turn its model into the dominant expression of youth evangelism. First, Young Life was characterized by strong support by the business community and Rayburn insisted on a business-oriented organizational model in order to cut down on inefficiency (Hunsicker 1998, 301–302). Hunsicker also speculates that Rayburn's desire to construct a broad tent organization might have encouraged him to mimic corporate models when establishing Young Life (Hunsicker 1998, 302).

Rayburn believed that Young Life needed to develop a business-oriented fundraising model. Besides the obvious efficiency of mimicking effective non-profit fundraising practices, this donation model mitigated worries on donors' parts about funding an organization unmoored from any denominational body (Hunsicker 1998, 302–303). Rayburn, like Trotman, saw leadership training as a crucial to gaining and keeping new converts and thus did value the importance of discipleship as an important ministry technique (Hunsicker 1998, 305).

Rather than being centered on Bible study, as the Miracle Book Club was, Young Life was evangelism centered (Senter 1989, 180, 183). Young Life emphasized the importance of adult leadership for young people. This, as Senter points out, put the movement "out of step with the democratic ideals of progressive education" and also separated the movement from denominational churches, which did try to develop their own cadres of young leaders. Meetings were expected to be well coordinated and when student participation proved ineffective, adult leaders were encouraged to intervene (Senter 1989, 181–182). To encourage this leader-oriented model, Rayburn insisted on a paid leadership in any city where Young Life was established (Senter 1989, 183). As with the YFC, Young Life emphasized worship and music. Talks were supposed to be conversational and short, although Rayburn did discourage some more contemporary evangelism practices, such as the use of food and drinks to bring people in (Hunsicker 1998, 313–315).

YFC paralleled the streamlined efficiency of Young Life and the Navigators. For the YFC, Bible clubs fulfilled the same role that follow-up ministry and discipleship did for Billy Graham and Dawson Trotman, ensuring not only conversion but retention of converts, creating a "supply network that would feed their rallies" (Bergler 2000, 116). The Bible club movement gave the Christian Right a base of operations within the public schools, which many evangelicals worried were becoming increasingly secularized (Bergler 2000, 116). Essentially YFC rallies in miniature, the Bible club movement instituted the same effective PR and advertising techniques that the YFC had pioneered. Teens were encouraged to engage in energetic singing and prayer and utilize skits to drum up support (Bergler 2000, 119). Although retention was important, the organization was still primarily conversion-focused, like most evangelical ministries in the growth-oriented mid-century evangelical religious economy. To gain members, Bible clubs also showed Christian movies, utilized the popular police procedural "Dragnet" as a model for their own programs, and in one extreme case, formed a hot-rodders group. Since evangelicalism needed to be trendy to compete with other cliques in the public schools, YFC encouraged participants in Bible Clubs to wear "distinctive pins, sweaters and jackets," setting them apart from other individuals in the school and serving as advertisements for potential converts (Bergler 2000, 120).

Yet there were limits to how effectively YFC could utilize these new evangelism methods. So long as contemporary cultural practices in cinema, television, and music did not conflict with the church, YFC had little problem using them. However, the organization was opposed to employing elements of pop culture that stood in opposition to its gospel message. In the highly charged political climate of the 1950s, this meant that rock music and dancing were seen as deeply threatening (Bergler 2000, 141). As a result, the advantages that could be accrued to the church from adopting these youth culture practices did not occur until fundamentalism lost much of its cultural hold over the rest of evangelicalism.

YFC's methods were effective, but they did provoke criticism. The YFC was accused of turning evangelism into a form of "'streamlined revivalism,' complete with duplicitous media campaigns (Harold E. Fey 1945, qtd. in Hunsicker 1998, 393). Mainline Protestants saw YFC's theology as embarrassingly naïve (Martin 2005, 27). Others were deeply worried by William Randolph Hearst's promotion of the organization; as a youth movement born in the immediate wake of the Hitler Youth, the YFC suffered from criticisms, doubtlessly ill-founded, that it could turn into an organization resembling that ill-fated creation of the Nazi past (Martin 2005, 27). More recently, the YFC has been critiqued for its participation in American Cold War politics. According to Eileen Lohr, YFC, in addition to its support of Cold War "containment policies," also created an ideologically colonialist worldview through which privileged first world YFC youth could view their peers in the

1. The Origins of Evangelical Management Culture 65

developing world. This worldview combined elements of more old-fashioned imperialism with a more contemporary desire to present the evangelical church, including its youth wing, as a modern, non-racist alternative to colonialism (Eileen Lohr 2015, 296–297, 303, 305).

One final group deserves special mention for its influence on the parachurch movement: Campus Crusade for Christ. Campus Crusade was founded by Bill Bright. Henrietta Mears, an influential Californian evangelical leader, spearheaded Bright's rise to prominence. Mears encouraged Bright to join a highly selective Bible study group which allowed him to develop a network of contacts with the new emerging generation of evangelical leaders, among them Billy Graham (Dochuk 2011, 178–179). Towards the end of his time at Fuller Seminary, Bright determined that his Christian vocation was to develop an evangelism and discipling ministry aimed primarily at college students (Martin 2005, 28; Travis Fleming 2006, 33–35). But the ministry represented far more than simple evangelism to Bright. Bright came to believe that Campus Crusade could stand as a "bulwark against secularism, moral decay and communism" (Martin 2005, 28). This aspect of Bright's vision led both Campus Crusade and Bright himself to be prominent warriors for the American Right. For instance, during the sixties many CC employees actively supported Barry Goldwater, and his organization famously tried to conquer Berkley for Christ in 1967 (Martin 2005, 91–93).

Initially aiming his movement at UCLA, Bright's Campus Crusade quickly transformed into a nationwide ministry (Dochuk 2011, 179). The success of Bright's parachurch ministry depended on a few key factors. Bright's ministry was tightly controlled, with a strict hierarchical system of leadership, in which Bright himself exercised authoritarian control over the group. Like Trotman, Bright emphasized the importance of pious living rooted in Keswick theology (Martin 2005, 28; John G. Turner 2005, 61–63). Campus Crusade applied militaristic rhetoric to evangelism, developing a sophisticated 4-pronged strategy to converting campuses to Christ: "Penetration, Concentration, Saturation and Continuation" (Martin 2005, 28). Undergirding this was Bright's concept of the Four Spiritual Laws, a simple, easy to understand spiritual message that, as the 1960s rolled on, increasingly was used as a tool for depoliticizing converted former sixties radicals while endorsing certain aspects of sixties culture that were seen as consistent with Christianity (Martin 2005, 28; Shires 2007, 86–87).

Yet, despite these appeals to sixties radicalism, Campus Crusade, like most parachurch organizations, relied on techniques borrowed from big business. The very fact of the ministry's rapid expansion forced it to operate like a "multinational corporation" complete with a sophisticated fundraising apparatus and slickly marketed evangelism tools (Dochuk 2011, 186). Influenced by the positive thinking rhetoric of his era, Bright adopted marketing techniques from leading positivity promoters. He also openly espoused a connection between Christian and business salesmanship, seeing "soulwinning" as a form of product placement in which salvation was pitched to potential consumers (John G. Turner 2005, 106). In order to help potential religious consumers confront psychological obstacles to salvation, Bright adopted psychologized explanations for human problems borrowed from positive psychology. Given the optimism of the fifties boom years, this was another smart sales choice on his part. Christianity was pitched as a solution to life problems (John G. Turner 2005, 108). Campus Crusade specifically targeted influential members of the campus community for conversion: fraternity brothers, sorority sisters, athletes, etc. The organization also made sure to try to win over members of the student government. In addition, Campus Crusade utilized specially designed surveys to determine what individuals would and would not be likely converts. Ideally, the campaign functioned as smoothly as theological clockwork in bringing the non-believers to a point of decision, though in practice the campaign did not always work this way (John G. Turner 2005, 109–110).

Yet, as influential as Campus Crusade for Christ was as a parachurch organization, its greatest influence on the future of the evangelical movement would be its approach to discipleship. Bright's philosophy of discipleship differed little from Trotman's, on whom it was partly modeled (Travis Fleming 2006, 174–176). In particular the emphasis on holistic discipleship characterized Bright's approach every bit as much as Trotman's (Travis Fleming 2006, 175–176). Flavil Yeakley has traced the roots of the discipling movement in the Churches of Christ to the influence of parachurch ministries, which promoted authoritarian teachings; he notes that the Charismatic shepherding movement grew out of similar influences. Since the discipling movement in the Churches of Christ is, by most accounts, just another form of shepherding, it is certain that Bright's ministry was a formative influence on shepherding practices in the Charismatic movement as well (see Don E. Vizant 1988, 128–130).

The Rise of Shepherding and Small Groups in Evangelicalism

The rise of the small group movement in evangelicalism resulted from a number of factors. First, much like its secular equivalent, the evangelical small group movement was shaped by the counterculture, particularly the Jesus movement. Additionally, evangelical small groups were shaped by the continued rise of the parachurch movement within evangelical circles. And finally, the evangelical small group movement was profoundly shaped by the practice of shepherding. Without these three factors, the evangelical movement might never have adopted the small group model to the extent it has today.

Although historically the Jesus People Movement (JPM) is said to have arisen in California, one of its foremost chroniclers, Richard Bustraan, has contended—plausibly enough—that the movement's origins were more organic than this. While California profoundly influenced the JPM, effectively "homogenizing" the movement, it was not its only center of influence (Bustraan 2014, 38). Although the JPM quickly petered out, it played a profound role in shaping evangelical culture. The movement set the standards by which the evangelical movement subsequently interacted with youth culture. It also gave evangelical insiders an outlet by which they could connect to the wider subculture without compromising their evangelical beliefs (Eskridge 2005, 18–19, 21).

The Jesus People (JP) did this by embracing much of the ethos of the counterculture, but with a Christian spin. Experiential Pentecostal and Charismatic beliefs replaced the psychedelic outlook of the hippies, yet the movement was something of an outsider even among the Pentecostal community whose beliefs it had embraced. Moreover, the anti-establishmentarianism that characterized the hippies was also characteristic of the JP as well (Bustraan 2014, 27). Larry Eskridge points out that while the Jesus People's rise can be seen as surprising, it was hardly unlikely given the spiritual climate of the time. The counterculture was often distinctively spiritual, so the religious "experimentation" that characterized the JPM proved hardly unusual. Moreover, many hippies had a profound respect for Christ and a fascination with eschatology, aspects of their beliefs that the evangelical movement later exploited. But perhaps most importantly, the JPM developed because a few innovative pastors from outside the counterculture saw within it the possibility for more effective youth outreach. These pastors targeted promising youth for evangelism, converted them, and then quickly discipled them into leadership positions. Those youth recruited among their peers, creating a feedback system that allowed for continuous replenishment of the JPM's ranks (Eskridge 2005, 66–67).

Organizationally, initially the early JPM was centered around coffeehouses and storefront churches which catered to countercultural clientele during the period. Evangelists who desired to recruit from the counterculture, as well as JP themselves, utilized locations like this as points of contact with the counterculture. For street evangelists, the coffeehouse movement, in particular, allowed them centralized locations from which they conducted evangelism campaigns, while providing a central recruiting station for prospective new members of the JPM. For the counterculture, the coffeehouses provided food, shelter, and, quite frequently, Christian instruction (Shires 2007, 94; Bustraan 2014, 32).

Yet the movement did not stop its organizational efforts at coffee houses. The JPM's roots in both the counterculture and evangelical Christianity eventually led the movement to experiment with communal living arrangements. For the Jesus People, communal living represented the ideals of the book of Acts, where the goods of the early Church were held in common. Financial pressures also motivated the movement to embrace the possibilities of communalism. But for the future shaping of church governance practices, the most important factor was a growing concern among both members of the JPM and outsiders that there was not sufficient discipline in the movement. Older Christians feared that JP might relapse into sinfulness or lapse in their Christian witness. Much as with the Navigators, "follow up" ministry was a real concern. Therefore, the communal experience allowed the JPM an ideal means of providing Christian instruction while also teaching "basic life skills." As a result, "Jesus houses" frequently drew up lengthy lists of "rules, regulations and expectations" for their members (Eskridge 2005, 142–147, Bustraan 2014, 32; Scott Lee Guffin 1999, 241).

One of the most influential of these commune movements came out of Calvary Chapel Costa Mesa. Calvary Chapel was founded by Chuck Smith (1927–2013), a product of the International Church of the Foursquare Gospel, a Pentecostal denomination founded by evangelist Aimee Semple McPherson (1890–1944). Like McPherson, Smith ended up adopting an innovative approach to evangelism. Long before most other evangelical leaders saw a need for it, Smith decided to embrace youth culture, not fight it (Shires 2007, 125–126). Utilizing the organizational brilliance and leadership of evangelist Lonnie Frisbee (1951–1993), Smith's church quickly baptized over 15,000 converts. The church also adopted modern musical methods and opened a commune for drug addicts under Frisbee's direction (Shires 2007, 125–126). These communes rapidly multiplied until the church controlled a whole network of "Jesus houses" (Eskridge 2005, 123–124).

At the Calvary Chapel communes, "servanthood" was heavily emphasized. Because the commune was viewed as a family, communes emphasized accountability structures. The communes discouraged reflecting on the past and instead encouraged their members to engage in Biblical reflection. Like other Christian communes (see Young 2011, 84–86), social isolation proved difficult to find and communal life was highly structured. What mattered most significantly for the future history of evangelicalism, however, was the leadership structure of the communes and Calvary Chapel itself. Elders led households and oversaw deacons. The latter were frequently trained by an elder, after which they started their own communes (Kevin John Smith 2002, 173–175). However, while the upper leadership of Calvary Chapel was characterized by organizational innovativeness, many of the commune leaders were poorly trained and lacked effective experience in organizational management and pastoral care (Kevin John Smith 2002, 198). Meanwhile, Calvary Chapel Costa Mesa was repeatedly blessed with leaders of tremendous oratorical and organizational power. Smith himself was a highly gifted public speaker, while an early colleague, John Wimber (1934–1997), became even more influential than Smith himself (see Shires 2007, 126–128). However, because of the top-down authority structure that the JPM communes promoted and that Wimber's teachings later accentuated, many of the movements that descended out of Calvary Chapel, such as the Vineyard movement and the Revival Alliance, were characterized by authoritarianism.

Initially, JPM communes relied on the sponsorship of local denominational groups. Chuck Smith's Calvary Chapel played a large part in sponsoring such communes. Other communes, however, created their own networked structures. But the commune movement also struggled to maintain peace with local legal restrictions (Young 2011, 31). In general, those communes that thrived were connected to established churches rather than originating organically from within the JPM. While its connection to "indigenous" hippie elements was crucial, organizationally the JPM was ill equipped to provide the kind of pastoral care and discipline needed to sustain a long-standing movement culture (Kevin John Smith 2002, 191–192).

Perhaps partly in response to this perceived weakness, the JPM communes peaked around 1971, and organizationally the JPM soon reverted to again utilizing the coffee house as its main organizational tool. By the early 1970s, however, the JP were no longer so countercultural; increasingly, being one of the Jesus People was the "in thing" to be. Because of this, the coffee houses now began targeting a different, less countercultural clientele. In many communities, coffee houses became community fixtures by which evangelists and youth workers tapped into both the counterculture and their own native youth culture. While financing and organizational stability were often a major concern, functionally most of the coffee houses served the same purposes: They were Christian hangouts, entertainment centers, and outreach points for Jesus People (Eskridge 2005, 227–228). Without the organizational grid that these coffee houses provided the movement, the JPM might not have had the long-term effect that it did.

From the outset, the JPM faced a number of organizational hurdles. Extreme Biblicism characterized many JPM communes, leading to a lack of theological balance that handicapped them in maintaining organizational stability. The movement's leadership structure veered towards a leader-centered authority model, with charismatic figureheads having enormous power over their followers. The movement deliberately cast itself in an apostolic and prophetic light, setting the stage for the co-opting of the JPM by the shepherding movement and later Third Wave Pentecostalism. The JPM also was notably dependent on charismatic orators and grassroots support (Kevin John Smith 2002, 100). The disproportionate authority vested in the JPM's prophets and apostles was accentuated by young converts' countercultural viewpoints, which predisposed them to both radical utopianism and a willingness to form "social networks" that were not bound by parental strictures (Kevin John Smith 2002, 156). Not surprisingly, given its connections to Bill Bright (see John G. Turner Jr. 2005, 256–259) and the parachurch movement, the JPM was heavily influenced by Watchman Nee (1903–1972), whose teachings are often seen by critics as authoritarian (Kevin John Smith 2002, 271). While this made the movement more attractive to prospective converts, it also made its membership vulnerable to abuse, as JPM converts frequently were cut off from parental and cultural influences that contradicted charismatic authority figures. Because of the millennialism of the JPM, it also gravitated to doctrinal extremes (Young 2011, 42–43).

Critics of JPM communes have noted their tendency to degenerate into authoritarian control systems, where the pastorate holds disproportionate power (Young 2011, 114). In recent years, critics of the prominent JPUSA commune have critiqued it for what they see as an overemphasis on "control and secrecy" (Young 2011, 98), a charge that has been frequently made against both the JPM and the shepherding movement as well. Ex-commune members of JPUSA have complained about privacy-violations and an inability to maintain "personal boundaries" as reasons for leaving the movement (Young 2011, 257). These criticisms, too, are broadly characteristic of critiques of both the JPM and shepherding (see Diamond 1989, 112, 116–118, Eskridge 2005, 308–310). Kevin John Smith has perceptively noted that the interpretation of discipleship promoted by both the parachurch movement and the JPM tended to avoid crucial doctrinal and ecclesiological issues. Within both the parachurch movement and the JPM, discipling was seen as the be-all and end-all of Christian instruction and its focus tended to be decidedly non-ecclesiological in character. This, in turn, had the tendency to distort JPM, parachurch and also shepherding instruction into a mindless anti-denominationalism, in which the issue of ecclesiological and doctrinal authority were given insufficient attention (Kevin John Smith 2002, 275–276). This tendency towards anti-denominationalism became institutionalized in the shepherding movement, CGM, and NAR, to the point where today it even has its own religious catchphrase ("Christianity is not a religion, it's a relationship"). As I have argued in *The New Apostolic Reformation*, the anti-denominationalism of such movements, particularly the NAR, makes them more, not less, vulnerable to abuse (Weaver 2016, 26). Without the legislative checks and balances that govern denominational structures, the JPM offered little accountability for poor or abusive decision making. The valuation of charismatic authority figures that it and its successor movements emphasized also tended to promote personality cults that make movement followers vulnerable to exploitation.

Yet the success of the JPM in paving the way for the small group movement, as well as for movements like the CGM and NAR, cannot be overstated. As Kevin John Smith notes, the JPM's success cannot be explained simply by its preference for charismatic authority figures. As important as those figures were, other factors also played into the JPM's success, including sophisticated mass media manipulation, skilled leadership training, and effective discipling techniques (Kevin John Smith 2002, 197). Innovations were introduced and diffused through the evangelical movement by the JPM, which were then adopted by early adopters like Chuck Smith. The counterculture served as an ideal milieu to experiment with new ways of doing church, all while under the pastoral leadership of mainstream evangelical churches (Kevin John Smith 2002, 197). For instance, the movement's emphasis on using modern musical idioms and the mass media to reach youth became a mainstay of evangelical youth ministry and gained widespread acceptance from thinkers in the CGM, notably C. Peter Wagner (1930–2016) (Guffin 1999, 259, 265–267).

Those who introduced these new innovations, such as John Wimber and Chuck Smith, also introduced a mode of leadership that focused on "entrepreneurialism" and that existed in a "non-professional" and "deregulated" ecclesiastical space. Movement leadership encouraged experimentation and risk-taking. While the charismatic figureheads of the movement held considerable authority, this authority tended to exist "off the grid," with institutionalized hierarchical relationships being frowned on in favor of those based on relational connections. Mentoring was the key to influence in the movement (Kevin John Smith 2002, 203–205). The CGM and the NAR, both heavily influenced by John Wimber and his friend C. Peter Wagner, have seen the organizational advantages in this arrangement and have thus continued to promote an emphasis on innovations in theology, worship, and dress, while minimizing creedal differences beyond a basic commitment to doctrinal orthodoxy.[4] The pragmatic nature of CG and church health (CH) proponents, taken to its fullest extent in the writings of Christian Schwarz (1960–), make the movement ideally equipped to survive in a competitive religious marketplace, where commitment to creedal orthodoxy and institutionalism leaves organizations poorly equipped to deal with the rapid pace of cultural change.

Yet the JPM alone cannot account for the massive changes that gave birth to the modern small group and church growth movement. To fully account for these developments, one must also look at the shepherding movement, for it is in the shepherding movement (SM) that many of the most long-ranging theological innovations of the sixties and seventies came to pass. And the consequences of these innovations would have nearly global repercussions in the decades to come.

The Shepherding Movement

The theological innovations that characterized the SM, such as they are, were broadly consistent with earlier developments in Charismatic and Pentecostal Christianity. Like the 1948 Latter Rain Revival, the Shepherding movement was characterized by an ardent belief in the fivefold gospel of "apostle, prophet, evangelist, pastor and teacher" (Weaver 2016, 28; Darrand and Shupe 1983, 67). Much like the JPM, with which it often shared overlapping leadership and doctrinal interests, the SM's preference was for charismatic leadership characterized by anti-denominationalism and an emphasis on relatively flat chains of command.

In part, the SM was formed in response to the excesses of the JPM. Elements of the JPM, notably the infamous Children of God movement, had veered into behavior widely perceived as cultic. The shepherds believed that one way to correct such excesses was to engage in prolonged periods of discipling and shepherding in which new and young Christians could be instructed in correct dogma, as well as the spiritual "disciplines." The movement sought to establish "strict lines of authority" in order to set clear boundary lines for correct Christian behavior (Eskridge 2005, 299).

A number of major influences shaped the shepherding movement. The parachurch movement played a large formative role in creating the movement's underlying ideology (Don Vizant 1988, 128–130).[5] As with the parachurch movement and the JPM the teachings of Watchman Nee strongly influenced the shepherding movement and tended to greatly accentuate its authoritarian character. Nee held an important leadership role in Chinese Christianity during the 1920s and 1930s and established a system of "ecclesiastical answerability and authoritarian congregational control" that were important ideological influences on the SM's leaders, known as the Fort Lauderdale Five (FLF), and particularly on Ern Baxter. Nee's emphasis on "complete submission" to authority would also characterize the FLF's teachings and is particularly evident if one peruses the movement's flagship magazine, *New Wine*, in any depth (Hunt 2009, 300). Another influence was Juan Carlos Ortiz (1934–). Ortiz's *Call to Discipleship* was a how-to manual for shepherding leaders. Notably, one of this shepherding leader's main emphases centered on the importance of "cell groups" to evangelism (Diamond 1989, 115). Shepherding movement supporters argued that a major reason for the decline of the church was that the traditional "authority structures" that had governed the church were no longer operant (Hadaway, Dubose, and Wright 1987, 151). This preference for long-standing authority structures extended beyond the walls of the church, as the SM was a strong supporter of patriarchy and conservative government (Diamond 1989, 127–130, Cuneo 2001, 123). The shepherding movement contended that Jesus's mentoring practices were steeped

1. The Origins of Evangelical Management Culture 73

in Middle Eastern culture and rejected the individualistic bias of traditional Western spiritual mentoring in favor of a far greater delegation of authority to leadership figures (Hadaway, Wright and Dubose 1987, 154–155).

Ecclesiologically, the shepherding movement drew heavily on Restorationist ideas. Restorationism is essentially a form of Christian primitivism. Those Christians who subscribe to Restorationist principles argue that "something went very wrong very early in the history of the Christian Church." Because of this, the basic teachings of the church's early apostles became corrupted, resulting in the rise of Catholicism. Most Restorationists also believe that since the Protestant Reformation, the church has progressively regained its spiritual bearings (S.L. Ware 2002, 1019–1021). Restorationism is in some degree characteristic of all Protestantism, but has always been strongly emphasized in Pentecostalism. Both the British house church movement (often simply called Restorationism within the U.K.) and the American shepherding movement drink strongly from Restorationist ideas. Eschatologically, the SM never truly embraced the gospel of despair that characterized dispensationalism, seeing it as an "escapist" theology (S. David Moore 2003, 81). Postmillennial influences could be detected in their theology, as well as the influence of G. Eldon Ladd's "already but not yet" eschatological beliefs, which played a formative influence on the spirituality of John Wimber (S. David Moore 2003, 81). Because of this complex set of beliefs about past and future Christianity, the SM and its cousins in the British house church movement were strongly inclined to ecclesiological primitivism. This primitivism infected virtually every part of the SM's ecclesiology. Moore notes that there was a basic disjunction in the SM between faith and praxis, contending that "[o]n the one hand, their [SM leaders] restorationism made them inherently anti-institutional, and the leaders seemed repulsed by the idea of becoming a denomination. Yet, on the other hand, as they were forced to organize themselves ... they became functionally and increasingly institutional" (S. David Moore 2003, 83). The movement, like other Charismatic movements, thus suffered over tensions governing what Margaret Poloma has called the "routinization of charisma," or the tendency of Charismatic movements to become gradually rigidified into more traditional organizational and spiritual forms (see Poloma 2003, 15–16; S. David Moore 2003, 83–84). The leadership of the SM sought to "decentralize and dismantle" the ecclesiological institutions that governed the church, instead relying on relational connections. However, the movement still was effectively institutionalized (S. David Moore 2003, 83–84). Yet Moore correctly notes that the movement had some notable success in using relational networking to bypass the hurdles created by denominational bureaucracies (S. David Moore 2003, 84). This emphasis on relational networking, a byproduct of the attention the movement paid to covenant relationships, would give its descendants in the NAR leadership structure a profound advantage when they competed against more top-heavy evangelical organizations.

The leadership structure of the American shepherding movement itself centered on the FLF: Bob Mumford (1930–), Charles Simpson (1937–), Derek Prince (1915–2003), Ern Baxter (1914–1993) and Don Basham (1926–1989) (Diamond 1989, 114). The FLF began a number of conferences devoted to spreading their message and utilized their monthly publication, *New Wine Magazine*, as a vehicle for disseminating that message. New Wine sought to provide a relatively formal doctrinal unity to the otherwise disparate groups that made up the Charismatic Renewal (Hunt 2009, 299).[6]

The leadership structure of the SM resembled that of a pyramid scheme. At the bottom of the hierarchy were average congregants. Typically, above them were house group leaders, followed by shepherds, then area leaders, and elders (Hunt 2009, 299–300; Hardaway, Wright, and Dubose 1987, 200). This structure was necessitated by the particular cultural politics of the era. Those who participated in the Charismatic Renewal were deeply opposed to "notions of clerical caste" (Scotland 2000, 86–87). Like many people in the sixties, Charismatics declined vesting authority in traditional power structures, instead preferring to put their faith in individuals, an emphasis that was accentuated by their commitment to the "equipping of the laity" for spiritual service (Scotland 2000, 86–87). The movement therefore believed in the necessity of recovering the leadership of the apostolate, even if the American shepherds did not use that technical term (British apostles, by contrast, did) (Scotland 2000, 89–90). In the U.K., these apostles, early advocates of the New Apostolic paradigm, would have a primarily mission-oriented viewpoint of their ministry (Scotland 2000, 91–92). The apostolic networks that developed in the U.K., similar in form to both the shepherding networks for the time and modern NAR apostolic networks, relied on the principles of charismatic leadership. Tradition took a distinct back seat to the personal leadership qualities of the guiding apostle (Kay 2007, 20) Hunt characterizes the movement's hierarchy as rigidly "authoritarian" and while this is true Hunt overlooks the fact that the movement's lack of connection to traditional denominational oversight gave its leadership the ability to make wide-ranging decisions more quickly and easily than was possible in traditional denominational churches. This, of course, promoted widespread abuses of power but also gave the movement organizational advantages that were later adopted by the NAR (Diamond 1989, 117–118; Hunt 2009, 299–300; S. David Moore 2003, 188–189; Hardaway, Wright, and Dubose 1987, 200).

Like the JPM, the successes and failures of the SM often relied on its leadership development practices. In the hands of a good shepherd, the system could be tremendously helpful. However, much like the JPM, the movement's emphasis on equipping lay leaders for ministry meant that many unqualified individuals took on important leadership positions, especially since the movement suffered from a lack of shepherds and pastors equipped to disciple congregants. This trait so severely characterized the SM that as it ebbed in 1984, four of the shepherds held a major eight-day Pastoral Training Institute in order to give its pastors a crash course on pastoral care and other theologically related subjects, a process that was repeated with different theological and teaching emphases two more times within the next year. The leadership recruitment practices of the SM handicapped the movement's leadership training as well. Few shepherds had received seminary-level instruction, and the majority of shepherds tended to be young and often the product of the JPM. Moreover, because of the shepherds' frequent allegiance to the JPM, the movement's leadership often lacked any institutional affiliations, no doubt exacerbating the movement's simplistic notions about denominational affiliations (Hadaway, Wright, Dubose 1987, 143–144; S. David Moore 2003, 153; Scotland 2000, 114). Moore notes that the emphasis on rapid leadership development may have hurt the spiritual formation of many SM leaders. These leaders were often placed in locales far removed from the FLF. While Moore contests that the FLF did not endorse the abuses of authority that occurred within the shepherding system, he acknowledges that the very teachings the movement used to counter authoritarian leadership, in practice invited such leaders into the movement, especially young ones. Moreover, the SM represented a prime example of demand outstripping supply. The movement simply wanted more effective leaders than it could ever possibly recruit (S. David Moore 2003, 149, 186). The movement's utopian character also predisposed it to authoritarianism (S. David Moore 2003, 149). Such rigidity was likely seen as necessary for organizational functionality.

Another fault that characterized the SM was a tendency for apostolic leaders and shepherds to create a division between their congregations and other Christian groups. This, according to Kay, led the movement to develop theological and ecclesiological emphases that resulted more from the apostle's personal preference than correct theology or wise policy (Kay 2007, 39). Because of all these factors, the shepherding system, by its very nature, was prone to abuse.

Within the Shepherding Movement, two widely held concepts contributed to such abuses. The first was the idea of covering. Under the doctrine of "covering," many major and some minor life decisions made by disciples had to have the preapproval of the individual discipling them. Shepherds hoped that this accountability system could encourage spiritual maturation and enforce the prominence of the spiritual "disciplines." Much like the communalism of the JPM, the emphasis on the spiritual disciplines in the SM gave the movement a monastic character (Scotland 2000, 114–115). Shepherds and other members of the shepherding system's leadership structure were supposed to provide a spiritual "covering" for those under them. In the process, however, this control often became disturbingly authoritarian, reaching into such everyday decisions as "employment, vacation time, appointments with professionals ... marriage, and even how often a husband and wife could have sex" (Moriarty 1992, 76). The second central organizing idea of the movement is the concept of "covenant relationships." Covenant relationships were compared to marriages by movement leadership. The movement leaders took on the role of establishing mutual accountability for each other's religious life (Diamond 1989, 114–115). This system of mutual accountability was universally seen as necessary because movement members, including leadership, believed that even the leadership must submit to authority and peer critique (Walker 1998, 164–165) These concepts, in turn, led to widespread reports of abuses in many of these areas (Eskridge 2005, 309). Diamond, writing during the heyday of the anticult movement, reported that many individuals leaving the SM experienced "profound psychological trauma" from their experiences (Diamond 1989, 117–118). More than two decades later, I encountered similar reports while researching for my book *The Failure of Evangelical Mental Health Care*.

Yet despite such abuses, the SM represented a form of pastoral care (S. David Moore 2003, 181), but one of a more "intense" nature than that characterized by typical discipling practices. Traditional discipling in the SM's cousin British house church movement, for instance, involved "House group leaders being instructed to keep a firm hand on the people placed in their group," while in neo-evangelicalism it often means little more than informal mentoring (Scotland 2000, 112–113). Those house church leaders who supported discipling over shepherding set down formalized guidelines governing finances, tithing, and interpersonal connections. By contrast, shepherds tended to place a much greater emphasis on reviewing their disciples' personal lives, often going so far as to take notes; the movement also tended to put a greater emphasis on counseling relationships, sometimes borrowing from the Reformed teachings of biblical counseling guru Jay Adams (1929–) (Scotland 2000, 112–113; Weaver 2016, 158). Nigel Scotland notes that as a form of pastoral care, shepherding suffers from a crucial weakness: its tendency to encourage dependency in its followers. He argues that this made the movement vulnerable to the same kind of controlling practices that characterize new religious movements (NRM) (Scotland 2000, 114–115). The movement's discipling emphasis also tended to "blur the distinction between church and home" giving the movement a totalistic character lacking in many other forms of Charismatic spirituality practiced at the time (Walker 1998, 183). Moreover, traditional Protestant pastoral counseling and spiritual mentoring does not have "a bottom line," in which a specific pastoral counselor's authority cannot be crossed. Walker notes that in shepherding and discipling

1. The Origins of Evangelical Management Culture 77

relationships, abuse tends to be noted mainly when shepherds' decisions are considered as a "bottom line" that cannot be questioned. In this respect, the counseling system of both the SM and the British house church movement resembles that of Catholicism, where a priest can refuse absolution for recalcitrant sinners (Walker 1998, 184–185). But without the bureaucratic safeguards Catholicism sets in place to prevent the abuse of such priest-penitent relationships, the SM's application of pastoral counseling was, from the start, fare more inherently prone to abuse than Catholicism.

The parallels and overlap between JPM and SM communes are so notable that it is difficult to talk about them as separate movements. Charismatic communities formed in the wake of the British house church movement were held together by covenant pledges, which included, among other things, mutual admonition and confession and a "lifetime commitment" to the community (Scotland 2000, 25). Patriarchy was strongly emphasized in such communities and communally owned businesses were not uncommon (Scotland 2000, 26). Much like JPM communes, communes descended from British Restorationist and Shepherding Movement influences engaged in aggressive evangelism. Communal living was practiced, usually of a rather austere type. Most forms of mass media, notably TV, were avoided and commune members personal decisions were often referred up to elders (Scotland 2000, 26).

In an ideological move that had longstanding implications for the evangelical movement, the leadership of the Shepherding Movement, notably Charles Simpson and Bob Mumford, became convinced that a return to the house church was necessary for the advancement of the Christian gospel (S. David Moore 2003, 52–53, 56). Simpson emphasized that a proper Christian ecclesiology would focus on the centrality of the house church to the church's mission. It was in the context of these beliefs that both Simpson and Mumford began much of their early experimentation with discipling relationships (S. David Moore 2003, 52–53). Prince, meanwhile, had a similar ministry emphasis. He contended that churches should be organized geographically rather than denominationally, with house churches or church cell groups forming the nexus of a city's organizational structure (S. David Moore 2003, 55). As Moore notes, the practice of discipling and house church fit like a kid glove. The discipling emphasis required an effective mentoring system and the house church idea provided a mutual accountability system that ensured that covenant relationships were honored. In turn, it also promoted the pastoral care for members of small groups and cells that the SM believed essential (S. David Moore 2003, 56).

Because of the organizational structure the SM supported, the movement saw the promotion of small groups as a central organizational principle. In part, this was due to what Moore characterizes as the SM's "relational emphasis" (S. David Moore 2003, 77). SM advocates in both the U.S. and UK strongly emphasized the importance of mutual fellowship (Scotland 2000, 31). In addition, SM supporters wanted to develop ecclesiological systems that reflected biblical principles (S. David Moore 2003, 77). Since the Shepherding Movement's success was predicated on how well covenant relationships worked, developing smoothly functioning Christian communities was a must. This fueled the movement's need for a constant stream of effective leaders. Leadership development played a paramount role in the SM because the movement relied on small groups for organizational effectiveness. Perhaps unfortunately for the movement, its small group leaders and shepherds usually lacked quality training, with most of the training they had received being a direct byproduct of the shepherding system itself (S. David Moore 2003, 77). The Shepherding Movement's often weak understanding of ecclesiology and theology, especially when compared to equivalent small group movements within Reformed and fundamentalist Christianity, is notable. This weakness was exploited by the apostles of the NAR, who used their followers' lack of doctrinal instruction to establish an aegis of influence unimaginable for leaders in other parts of the Christian Right. Moreover, in order to become a leader within the SM, a man typically had to prove his willingness to submit to authority. Thus, to get into the leadership track of the movement, disciples had to first prove their willingness to be led (S. David Moore 2003, 77–78). While this obviously created a strongly loyal core group, it also has exacerbated tensions between shepherding advocates and their critics in the Christian Right.

Despite the problems inherent in shepherding, it had a number of advantages that led to the adoption of much of its philosophy by the NAR. The foremost of these was that the movement played an important part in accelerating the adoption of the network as the dominant organizational paradigm for the modern church. Many of these traits were shared with the JPM. Like the JPM, the relational networking that characterized the SM allowed the movement to avoid needless competition and work towards achieving common objectives. Because the movement relied on relational networking, it never had to formulate "legal documents" (see Kay 2007, 31).[7] Yet there was one other key element that contributed to the effectiveness of apostolic networks, as well as network churches outside the NAR: The rise of an independent evangelical small group movement.

The Rise of the Small Group Movement

The rise of the cell church, which helped give birth to the small group movement, occurred in the early 1960s. The movement originated with South

Korean pastor David Yonggi Cho (1936–), who was looking for better ways to delegate responsibility for church functions after a major illness. Cho organized the church into home groups, based on geographical divisions. The church, located in Seoul, divided the city into 13 districts, with a senior pastor at the top of each district, reporting to Cho. Below these districts were 309 sub-districts, and below those, 4,374 sections. Below the sections were divisions of five cell groups, with each cell group holding at a maximum 10 families. When a cell group exceeded its potential, it subdivided and created a new cell. Each cell group contained a cell leader, who provided oversight over an assistant leader. That assistant leader was typically being groomed to take control of another cell. The cell groups relied primarily on biblical instruction, rather than Western based felt-needs orientations, to attract membership (Kay 2007, 192–193). Latin American evangelicals also soon picked up the cell church model and implemented it (Kay 2007, 193).

There are a number of reasons why the cell church model became one of the primary tools for the spread of the small group movement. One was simply the success of Cho's Yoido Full Gospel Church, still the largest church in the world (Matthew Bell 2017). Much as Asian corporations and the systems concepts associated with them proved popular with a certain class of secular management guru, so too did Yoido's cell strategy prove influential in the wider evangelical world. The church's success brought an influential visitor, CGM pioneer Donald McGavran (1897–1990), to visit the church. McGavran, impressed by the success of Cho's ministry, persuaded him to mentor other pastors on how to implement the model. This led to the formation of Church Growth International in 1976, which has spread Cho's methods to thousands of pastors globally through its seminars and conferences. Cho's message also has gained influence because of *Successful Home Cell Groups* (1982), a work in which he outlined the cell church method in clear, accessible prose. C. Peter Wagner also became an important advocate of cell churches, ensuring the idea's acceptance in the NAR (Comiskey 2014, loc. 3089–3096, Cho 1981, passim).

The typical cell structure continues to follow Cho's organizational model. Each cell contains 5 to 15 members. These individuals, in turn, are overseen by a zone "elder" who looks over 5 cells. Above the zone elder is a zone pastor, who is responsible for 5 zone elders. When necessary, a district pastor is placed above a zone pastor (Arthur Tucker 2003, 163). The most significant variant to this system is the G12 system advocated by Columbian apostle César Castellanos, which is organized around groups of twelve. The goal is to make each person within the group of twelve the leader of their own cell. Individuals were therefore to be both mentored in a cell, and be a mentor of a cell. Cells were considered perfected "when each of the 12 people in your first cell were themselves leaders of 12 cells" (Kay 2007, 199). This model promoted rapid growth, but it has also been criticized because of its leadership structure and perceived authoritarian nature (Kay 2007, 198–199).

Nevertheless, despite such criticisms of cell church theology, the cell church model lost little time in finding its way to American shores. Here, its main promoter was Ralph Neighbour (1929–), who initially utilized the model in Houston, Texas. In 1969, Neighbour started People Who Care, a church based on the cell model. In the early 1970s, he followed this up with the establishment of TOUCH Outreach Ministries, a group geared to promulgate the idea of cell churches. Soon, Neighbour started running national conferences on the cell model (Hastings 2000, 174; McKinley 1999, 11, 13). Neighbour eventually saw the cell church model as a small group format universally applicable to all cultures. Neighbour initially did not have as much luck with the model as Cho, but he was responsible for promulgating the cell model in the United States and his influence in the developing world, notably on Lawrence Khong's Faith Community Baptist Church, was significant (Kay 2007, 194; McKinley 1999, 44).

For Neighbour, one of the main roadblocks to the spread of the Christian message was what he called the "Program Base Design" (P.B.D.) church. P.B.D. churches were based on "large group structures" which Neighbour contended were bureaucratically top-heavy and inefficient (Neighbour 1990, 38–47). Neighbour believed that traditional churches promoted needless over-specialization, which led to wasteful resource allocation (Neighbour 1990, 47). By contrast, Neighbour argued that churches should network around cell groups based on people's naturally formed social networks, utilizing the thinking of Christian systems theorist E. Mansell Patisson to support that position (Neighbour 1990, 114–116). Not only was this organizationally more efficient, but it had important implications for evangelism. The program-based model, from Neighbour's standpoint, relied too much on an individual-based approach to evangelism. By contrast, the cell model was more a team-based approach (McKinley 1999, 103). This affected how churches tried to recruit new Christians. Traditional, program-based churches were committed to a "centripedal" model in which the church was a community center to which people came to. By contrast, the cell church went out into the community to find new potential Christians. Its model was a "go structure" and thus was based on a much more proactive recruitment strategy (McKinley 1999, 117; Arthur Tucker 2003, 159). This mission-based, team-based approach to missions was thus similar to how secular Toyotist organizations operated.

The cell church strategy typically is utilized to achieve several important goals. Those who utilize the model hope that the cell model proves conducive to mutual community building and communal care. The cell model is also heavily oriented to a mentoring model of leadership, from the top to the bottom. The model also beneficially orients towards a strong commitment to

1. The Origins of Evangelical Management Culture

evangelism, and thus is ideally suited for churches focused on recruiting new membership (Hastings 2000, 175). The cell-based church, as envisioned by Neighbour, is primarily committed to a focus on cells. The model also provides for regional gatherings, known as congregations and larger assemblies called celebrations (McKinley 1999, 2). However, while the model provides for congregation-sized and celebration-sized gatherings, the main focus of the model is centered on cells (Hastings 2000, 176). Unlike the Meta strategy (discussed below), however, Neighbour's vision of cell church did not incorporate a systems perspective, though such systems perspectives are strongly evident in other leaders' vision of cell ministry, most prominently David Yonggi Cho (Hastings 2000, 176).

In Neighbour's model of cell church, the cell is responsible for anything of importance in church life. Thus, the cell church does not typically relate to other ministries or small groups, except in celebration-sized events (Hastings 2000, 177). Like the Serendipity model (discussed below), the cell church strategy does not engage in demographic or psychographic segmentation (Hastings 2000, 179–180). Cell churches often hand out a weekly instructional guide for cell leaders, often based on the pastor's sermons or targeted at some perceived need of the membership. Such curricular planning allows cell churches to anticipate for ineffective cell leaders, or cell leaders unequipped to come up with quality material on their own. As Hastings puts it, this practice ensures "quality control" because theoretically every group has a good lesson if the basic material is sound. Moreover, the strategy also allows for the standardization of theological instruction, thus harmonizing any potential disagreements within the church (Hastings 2000, 182). From a Toyotist perspective, this is a major advantage to any church, as it minimizes the risk of wasted production runs created by lost membership or, worse, breakoff cells and church splits. Neighbour's theory of cell multiplication is likely designed to avoid wasted production runs, as he requires that cells multiply once they reach at least fifteen members, with the leader taking one half of the group and the mentee the other and forming new groups. This practice allows for the movement to try to anticipate for and correct leadership burnout. Moreover, in order to prevent wasteful resource commitment, groups showing insufficient growth are shut down, with their members being split off into other cell groups (Hastings 2000, 193).

Cell churches offer a number of advantages. Because of the way cell churches are organizationally put together, their growth potential is greater than churches based on the traditional Fordist model. From a resource management and distribution perspective, cell churches also offer a "much more cost effective" model than that embraced by program-oriented churches (Hastings 2000, 195). Cell church advocate Ralph Neighbour has also plausibly argued that in terms of resource utilization, cell churches are far "more efficient than traditional churches," where "only ten to fifteen percent of the membership are engaged in the tasks required to make the church function" (Neighbour 1990, 20). Given that the evangelical church faced increasing competition from other societal institutions switching to "lean" manufacturing principles, that kind of bureaucratic outlay clearly was not sustainable (Neighbour 1990, 20). Because cell ministry is "integrated ... both organizationally and financially," it is able to reduce operational bureaucracy, and function with a "far simpler organizational and leadership structure" than that of traditional churches (Arthur Tucker 2003, 170).

The process of leadership development and discipling in cell churches is another area where the model outshines traditional church structures. The model's leadership development system, according to Hastings, is well developed (Hastings 2000, 195). Within the cell model, discipling is constantly reinforced by the pastor, and the pastor constantly reinforces discipling (Arthur Tucker 2003, 198). From a Toyotist perspective, this reflects what is called the principle of "continuous improvement," in which the production process continuously "revolutionizes" the quality of the product, which is here Christian disciples (Sidorick 2009, loc. 667). Moreover, as Tucker notes, "the input data" that the cell proselytizer uses "can be adapted to be in accord with the developmental level of those in the group" (Arthur Tucker 2003, 198). Thus, more intellectualized messages can be aimed at skeptical crowds, while simpler messages can be aimed at teenagers or the earnestly faithful.

Jui Hui Judy Han, a prominent secular commentator on the evangelical movement, has observed that the cell church model is based on an organic "operational logic" (Han 2009, 63–64). The church's "reproductive capacity" is cast in terms of its ability to cellularly replicate, and this term is commonly referred to as cell multiplication in the evangelical literature (Han 2009, 63–64).[8] In the cells that Han encountered as an outsider studying the movement, cellular development was supported by aggressive attempts to evangelize quickly and within "finite but unspecified time frame[s]" (Han 2009, 63–65). This organic justification for church outreach and evangelism efforts should be noted, because it will reoccur again with the church health and organic church movements.

Han notes that in addition to the organic metaphor, there is another analogous term to the "cell church," which is the revolutionary cell. Han contends that *the rhetoric* of the cell church often invokes the *foquismo* form of Marxist revolutionary thinking promoted by Che Guevara, also known as focalism. Focalism supports the idea that "small, localized focal power can successfully form the vanguard for insurrection and revolutionary change" (Han 2009, 65). Focalism sought to avoid establishing centralized leadership structures because the destruction of such structures could fatally undermine a revolution. Instead, focalism required revolutionaries to rely on small guerrilla bands. Han, however, contends that the evangelical cell church's operational *praxis* is actually closer to Leninist party cell operations, which relied on "highly selective recruitment of members, intensive indoctrination, and uncompromising ideological conformity, for the objective of overthrowing the existing political system and implementing revolutionary change in society" (Han 2009, 66). I would argue, however, that the correct position to take would be that the cell church *aims* to be more of a fusion of focalism and Leninist approaches. In actual *practice*, however, Han is probably right in arguing that the movement is closer to Leninist organizational principles than those advocated by Focalism.

Whatever its similarities to Marxist organizational paradigms, however, cell churches operate on capitalist logic. Indeed, from a marketing perspective, cell churches have a number of advantages. Given their small size, cell churches have the ability to inject themselves more deeply into local societal superstructures. They require little financial outlay, are easy to begin and quick to unwind if they prove unpopular. Because they are so small, cells can "target specific cultural, interest, social and ethnic groups that will not feel at home in the congregation until a significant number are involved as worshipers." Moreover, cells can be tailored to attendees' scheduling needs, an increasingly important factor (Arthur Tucker 2003, 194). Cell churches are also quite sensitive to consumer needs. They can provide nearly instantaneous "feedback from cell groups as to missional effectiveness, and specific problems and areas of concern among cell members that allows the leadership to adapt quickly to changing situations" (Arthur Tucker 2003, 195). This allows a church's leadership to tailor its outreach efforts to community concerns (Arthur Tucker 2003, 195). Given all these advantages, therefore, it is unsurprising that the cell church model has become so ubiquitous.

There are many other strategies of doing small groups besides cell church, so I will concentrate on just two. The Serendipity model is one of the earliest and was created by Lyman Coleman (1933–), a pioneering figure in the small group movement. Influenced especially by the Navigators, Coleman's ministry started pioneering his Serendipity model in the 1960s. Spreading his message on small groups in the ensuing decades, his model was eventually accepted by thousands of churches (Hastings 2000, 139). Coleman began college in the 1950s, as the secular small group theory was just being perfected. Coleman's subsequent work benefited from the fact that he familiarized himself with this literature during its formulative period (Fowler 1983, 15, 23). In the late fifties, Coleman began promoting "Growth Groups" (Fowler 1983, 32). While incorporating biblical instruction, Coleman also innovatively applied theories from group dynamics research (Fowler 1983, 33). During the early sixties, he consulted with churches about how to implement small groups into their ministry. His ideas were broadly consistent with the philosophy promoted by the encounter movement, except that Coleman preferred positively reinforcing people rather than using the shame-based "confrontational" approach that characterized encounter groups (Fowler 1983, 34). The coffee house movement popularized Coleman's ideas, which received widespread acclaim among those who used it (Fowler 1983, 35–36).

Serendipity's model was program-based, rather than seeking to implement cells through the entire church (the cell church model) and was initially not inclined to the systems view. Coleman, did, however, move the model closer to a systems theory outlook in later years (Hastings 2000, 140). Because Coleman's model of small groups was program-based, he compartmentalized small groups, with small groups being a department of the church, like other departments. However, Coleman noted that other aspects of the church should take on elements of small group life, including utilizing small group dynamics theory (Hastings 2000, 140). Coleman also avoided segmenting populations into target groups, a common aspect of demographic and psychographic advertising (Hastings 2000, 141). The leadership teams of Serendipity groups were made up of a leader, another individual being trained to lead, and a person who hosted the small group/cell. Although Coleman recognized the value of democratically led groups, he preferred using curriculum-centered groups in which "the curriculum is the real leader" (Hastings 2000, 143). To ensure proper leadership development, the Serendipity model encourages leaders to recruit and train their own co-leaders and historically offered a plentiful supply of curriculum to get meetings running (Hastings 2000, 143–144). However, since the curriculum was the real leader of Serendipity material, churches were encouraged to use recruiting practices that centered on religious faithfulness and willingness to be instructed, rather than leadership skills, the assumption being that the heavy lifting in the Serendipity model is done by the curriculum itself, rather than small group leaders. To ensure that the group engaged in proper leadership delegation, Coleman argued for what he called a "Starburst model," in which five groups and their leaders would be presided over by one coach. Larger churches, in turn, would have coordinators to watch over coaches and pastoral staff to watch over coordinators (Hastings 2000, 144, 147).

The Serendipity model offered several advantages to those who adopted it. Because of its program-based nature, it provided a good fit for mainline churches, with their department-based organizational structure. Moreover, because of the movement's curricular focus, it was easily implementable without having to overinvest in expensive leadership development. Hastings contends that this allowed for potentially rapid cell multiplication, because the model did not have to rely on equipping an extensively trained leadership group (Hastings 2000, 166–167).

Yet the Serendipity model suffered from a number of significant weak-

1. The Origins of Evangelical Management Culture 85

nesses that would eventually lead the small group movement to shift away from the Serendipity approach. The movement's curricular focus meant that it tended to be weak on leadership development and recruitment, which leaders in the small group movement correctly understood as a necessary component for organizational success. Also immediately apparent when looking at the material is the weakness of its approach to leadership supervision. Moreover, as far as evangelicals were concerned, the Serendipity model focused more on retention than growth practices. This did not endear the strategy to the evangelical small group movement and made its policy towards membership recruitment suspect in their eyes (Hastings 2000, 167, 173). Hastings also argues that the Covenant strategy, of which Serendipity is a prominent example, is likely to lead to poor leadership retention. Since Serendipity is designed to be used in program-based, primarily mainline churches, many of its leaders will be expected to also extensively participate in other worship activities. And though the Covenant strategy allows for leadership vacations, in most other respects it does not pay attention to "spans of care" issues. This problem is accentuated by the lack of focus Serendipity gives to leadership mentoring. Without this focus, groups may grow larger than the capacity of one person to handle, again leading to burnout issues (Hastings 2000, 168).

The Serendipity model also tended to have a weaker understanding of changes in evangelical ecclesiology brought about by the rise of the Toyotist church. It tended to view the church through the lens of traditional institutional structures, with a notable focus on congregation-sized structures, as befits a ministry which often catered to mainline Protestant institutions. Because of this, the model failed to fully utilize the possibilities that both Celebration-sized events and small groups offered up. Churches modeled more on the Fordist principles characteristic of the pre–New Paradigm Church (NPC) movement suffered from an over-investment of resources and financing in buildings. In a program-based church, buildings had to offer up room for numerous groups, including "Sunday school classes, men's groups, women's groups and choirs" (Hastings 2000, 169). This required numerous different room sizes, complicating facility-building and eroding church resources. By contrast, both cell churches and mega churches only utilized building space for worship, without the need of room for "mid-size groups" (Hastings 2000, 168). This problem was also accentuated by the fact that Fordist churches' institutional-based nature makes them over-commit resources to staffing, as well as buildings. Simply put, from an economic standpoint, both the Meta-Church and Cell-Church models represented more economically competitive and sustainable small group models (Hastings 2000, 170).

Churches that overcommitted to the institutionalism characteristic of the Fordist model did not sufficiently provide for growth. Churches structured on traditional models tended to maximize their growth-potential at about 10,000 members, typically because of the restrictions caused by their approach to pastoral care and facility management. Because paid staff were improperly equipped to delegate responsibilities in these models, they were unable to provide quality pastoral care, leading to a high rate of staff burnout. Again, the Meta Model and Cell Church model typically proved themselves superior in this respect because they allowed for the distribution of work responsibilities among a much wider group of people. Like many "lean" groups that have arisen in recent years, both of these models had figured out how to do more with less. Programmatic churches also tended to encourage departmental competition, leading to a problematic lack of institutional unity. By contrast, some advocates of the cell model advocated the systems perspective and the Meta church model adopted systems theory out right, allowing for a more robust resistance to this kind of infighting (Hastings 2000, 170–171, 176).

Carl George, the inventor of the Meta model, began his ministry career as a Baptist pastor. After reading C. Peter Wagner's *Your Church Can Grow* (1976), he studied under Wagner and John Wimber in the summer of 1977. In 1978, he became the head of the Charles E. Fuller Institute of Evangelism and Church Growth, which he ran until 1998 (Hastings 2000, 201–202; Wagner 1988, 235). Beginning in 1986, George began designing and field-testing a method of running the church which eventually evolved into his Meta-Church theory. The publication of *Prepare Your Church for the Future* (1991) served as the introduction of the Meta-Church model to most pastors. Within three years, four hundred churches were making use of George's model (Hastings 2000, 202).

The Meta Church principle was developed in part to deal with some of the handicaps of older congregational organizational structures. George's key insights largely derived from the success of the cell church. He realized that while the cell church had been fully successful, there were many churches that could not adopt the model due to limitations they had inherited from their current organizational structure. Thus, to be truly effective, the Meta-Church paradigm had to adapt a systems perspective, as only this viewpoint could take into account both where churches were and where they wanted to be (McMahan 1998, 163).

This understanding informed one of George's key organizational insights involving the relationship between organizational effectiveness and church size. George contended that any time churches grow, their overall quality lessens, which requires that they in turn "implement a new organizational system geared to their current size" (George 1992, 42–43). Obviously, however, this presents huge problems, since the persistent implementation of new organizational systems is both costly and likely to slow growth. Moreover, it prevents the church from having a consistent organizational philosophy. The

Meta Church's "social architecture," therefore, was designed to address issues of scale that other church organizational philosophies were unequipped to deal with (George 1992, 52, 57).

George realized that churches suffered from an inability to reconcile their desire for growth with their organizational ability to structure for growth without "disruption of quality" (George 1992, 43). For new paradigm churches, which were based on "lean" models of organizational effectiveness, this presents a serious problem. What George is contending is that without reforms, churches face the problem of "limits to growth," a dilemma faced within all known systems.[9] "Plateaued" churches (churches where growth had stalled) also faced these same limitations, which is part of the reason that George adopted a systems perspective in his approach to church turnaround management (McMahan 1998, 164). Martin Alan McMahan notes that "when attempting to install new paradigms for growth into existing, plateaued churches it is critical to know how any intervention will be received and how it may alleviate or exacerbate existing conditions or problems" (McMahan 1998, 164). This requires an ability to do systems analysis (George and Bird 1993, 68; McMahan 1998, 163).

A major part of George's application of systems analysis within church settings involved trying to convince churches to adopt an "open systems" versus "closed systems" perspective. George argues that congregation-sized structures typically are so concerned with their nucleus that they lack the ability to "relate to the changing needs represented by ... newcomers" (George 1992, 80). An open systems perspective towards church growth, however, holds that for any system, the system itself is "as big as you draw the box" (George 1992, 80). Traditional congregational structures, often based on Fordist/Taylorist assumptions, were organizationally handicapped by how they mapped out their organizational systems (McMahan 1998, 178; see George 1992, 79–81 for why McMahan argues that George is adopting an open systems approach). A congregational model built on an open systems perspective, when properly designed and implemented, allows for smooth growth transitions, whereas the closed system approach used by traditional congregations was less adaptive to change.

The Meta Church model, like the cell church model, tried to move away from a programmatic emphasis to a cell emphasis. George believed that small groups in churches could typically be reconceptualized as cells very easily. Furthermore, when church leadership thought through the organizational structure of a church's larger groups, they realized that most of these larger structures were in fact composed of small groups (George 1992, 88–89). To make the Meta Church model work, George organizationally divided the model into two separate groupings: task and nurture groups (George 1992, 89).

George saw nurture groups as the prime center of the Meta Church model (George 1992, 96). He believed that small groups should be laity-led. Much of the reason for this is detailed below, but in terms of pastoral care, a crucial reason for adopting a laity-led model was the fear that pastoral change might "derail" and "destabilize" any effective small group organizational structure the pastor had set up (George 1992, 98). George's preference for adopting a cell-celebration model rather than fully embracing medium size congregations was motivated primarily by the question of pastoral care. He argued that traditional congregations operated with the "underlying assumption ... that a pastor or skilled lay leader can provide adequate care" for groups ranging from 50 to 100 people (George 1992, 67). However, this assumption was erroneous in his estimation because it ended up promoting "limited intimacy and ... accountability" (George 1992, 67). The organizational model that congregational size churches furthered also was characterized by cliquishness and an overly bureaucratic structure, making new membership recruitment difficult.[10] This was unideal from a both humanitarian and practical standpoint. First, it prevented the church from adequately helping people who were dealing with crisis situations. From a practical standpoint, George feared that the organizational deficiencies of the "congregation paradigm" led to insufficient member retention (George 1992, 68–69). Thus, providing of better and more humanitarian pastoral care represented not only an ethical imperative but a pragmatic necessity if evangelical churches hoped to remain competitive with other societal institutions. What the meta church model theoretically did was allow the larger churches to scale up in size, while scaling down the number of pastoral care recipients per care giver that churches required. George, like cell church advocates, feared that allowing cell groups to go beyond an optimal size reduced the quality of pastoral care received (George 1992, 104). The nature of program-based churches, however, lends them to form group structures that are suboptimal in qualitative performance, handicapping *both* growth capacity and quality pastoral care. Thus, when George and other advocates of cell multiplication promote the multiplication of cells, their concern is not solely rooted in a greed for growth, but also in the simple reality that without cell multiplication churches will likely either face a plateaued church or overburdened leadership teams that cannot provide quality spiritual care. Moreover, as we will see in Chapter 4, from the standpoint of network theory, this point is eminently sensible for any system that communicates information. For instance, if one overburdens a network server on the Internet, it becomes strained because it has too many clients. The same exact principle, likely adopted consciously by CG advocates, applies to pastoral care.

A reader who first encounters George's description of problematic church members—"extra grace required (EGR) people"—may be disturbed at

1. The Origins of Evangelical Management Culture 89

the usage of such terminology. However, again, George's analysis here reflects not simply questionable pragmatic commitments to CG principles, but also concerns over providing qualitatively superior pastoral care. George notes that certain disturbed or troubled church members may quickly drain off the quality of pastoral care provided to other members of small groups, who themselves may need pastoral care of a lesser degree. To ensure the fullest quality coverage, George recommends creating a referral system to quickly provide assistance to those members who are beyond a cell leader's or cell coach's ability to handle. In the most extreme of situations, such members can even be referred to medical personnel (George 1992, 105). By creating this referral system, George anticipates the needs of problem members while making sure that other pastoral care issues are not left unaddressed. In the hands of a caring and competent pastor, therefore, George's model is likely to increase the effectiveness of pastoral care, rather than decrease it.

For George's system to work, of course, high quality leadership is required. Hastings contends that the "heart of Meta Church strategy is leadership development," a fact that was often overlooked by pastors who viewed it as just "one more small group system" (Hastings 2000, 203). According to Walter G. Hastings, the Meta church model attempts to "prioritize cell-celebration and effectively blends evangelism and pastoral care with leadership development" (Hastings 2000, 201). As such, the model does obviously emphasize small groups, because George saw small groups as "ideal" vehicles for "evangelism and assimilation, as well as discipling, nurture and pastoral care" (Hastings 2000, 203). But the model prioritizes leadership development (Hastings 2000, 203). Indeed, George sees small groups as leadership development laboratories, where leaders can be formed and tested (George and Bird 1994, 311). As with so many other aspects of "lean" churches, such leadership development required what evangelicals term the "equipping of the laity." For George, this involved delegating as much responsibility for church development to the laity as possible. Churches were to be restructured and organized along a new laity-centered model (George 1992, 155). This delegation of authority allowed pastors to shift their emphasis away from concerns on what Toyotists would term the church's factory floor to higher level organizational decisions that were becoming increasingly necessary with urbanization and the growth of large-scale churches and apostolic networks. As with other Toyotist managerial models that became prominent during this era, the emphasis on putting more of the leadership burden on the laity was implemented in order to ensure a lack of leadership burnout (George 1992, 60).

George's understanding of how leadership development relates to pastoral care is based on a sophisticated understanding of communications theory. He demonstrates the need for relatively small groupings with a simple example. In any communication of information between two people, the "interplay involves two exchanges: what you are signaling to Person B, and what person B is signaling back to you" (George 1992, 125). But what if one adds a third person? The addition of a third person creates the possibility of 9 possible interchanges. The addition of a fourth person creates 28 possible signals. A fifth person creates 75 different potential signals. By the time one raises the group level to 10 people, there are 5,110 possible signals (George 1992, 125–126). George notes a number of reasons why this is a problem. First, it makes the organization unresponsive to community needs (George 1992, 125). An axiom that governs business operations is that businesses that are unresponsive to customer demand die off. The same principle applies to churches unable to meet the demands or felt needs of their congregants, whatever those needs may be. The fewer number of signals a system requires, the less likely it is to face sustained or terminal damage from hiccups or malfunctions in the system. In an organization where a pastor is forced to listen to "a hundred voices at once" (George 1992, 125), miscommunication or burnout is inevitable, as the server—the pastor—suffers from trying to handle too many connections at once. George's small group model is based on the same idea and offers a similar solution. Just as companies will add extra servers to provide better connection, George's model tries to anticipate flaws in the system by creating an apprentice system and a coaching system for cell group leaders, insuring that the system is backed up to the maximum degree possible (George 1992, 128).

The Meta Church model does not subscribe to the program-based model of institutional church, but can more easily work with it than Neighbor's "pure cell" model. This is because the Meta-Church model allows for organizational flexibility by looking at the preferable degree to "cellularize" a church (George 1994, 276; Hastings 2000, 206). While Meta Church wants to move towards the "bull's eye" of cell church, it is willing to achieve less than ideal results, recognizing that different churches will have different degrees of cell optimization in this regard (George 1994, 276–277).

Because of its commitment to a "Cell-Celebration" format (George 1992, 59–61), rather than a traditional congregational one, the Meta Church model adopts a flat organizational structure. Whether talking about the flow of authority from senior pastor to small group participant or people to pastor communication, the model aims for quality control via quick responsiveness to problematic organizational issues (see George 1992, 182–183). This reflects another longstanding practice of lean manufacturing which is the immediate resolution of problems. The closer one gets production to zero defects on the assembly line, the more likely one will produce qualitatively better products, making a company more economically competitive. Quantitative benefits can also be gained from the implementation of this principle as well, since it allows for companies to invest more money in both manufacturing and quality control (Sidorick 2009, loc. 646–663). A major reason churches adopted small group models was to create better economies of scale. This has increased the corporate character of these churches in recent years. Given the growth of urbanization, the demand for larger churches was probably inevitable, especially until the house church movement's "go small" approach gained some traction recently. But scaling up church size forced churches to change their leadership styles as well, with the leaders of larger churches increasingly taking on the role of "middle manager" or "managing director" with staff members and team members under them. Despite the criticisms made against the megachurch movement, it is difficult to see how the movement could have achieved this economy of scale without the adoption of a corporate model (Jennifer G. Turner 2000, 28). For that matter, house churches have not been totally immune to the effect of corporatization either. It is not surprising, therefore, that evangelical small group advocate Robert E. Slocum notes the pull between Fordist and Toyotist advocates of small groups. Many Fordist-oriented leaders still argued for "centralization, synchronization, [and] standardization" in church formats, even as newer expressions of Christian belief argued for reorienting the church around more Toyotist principles of decentralization, flexibility and relatively leaderless organizations, in which control of the system is "distributed widely among gifted lay people" (Jennifer G. Turner 2000, 43–44; Slocum 1990, 70–77). Obviously, Serendipity and similar models, with their program-based approach, have more to gain from a Fordist orientation while cell models and the Meta church approach were more responsive to a Toyotist approach.

In order to achieve flexibility with all size scales, the Meta Church model not only decentralizes its communications process, but virtually all aspects of church life. Evangelism and assimilation of membership are to be achieved by delegating authority to cell groups. Even the creation of new leadership is ideally created more via the cell system than its upper echelons (see George 1992, 190). This is because a Fordist system in which recruitment of cell leaders is centralized simply cannot keep up with company demand for new leadership material. Again, George's system protects itself against the charge of poor leadership recruitment practices made against some other communally oriented evangelical movements, notably the JPM and SM (George 1992, 190).

Although George contends that leadership development is the true heart of his model, a large part of what makes this approach viable is his adoption of a systems perspective. The evangelical movement's embrace of systems theory was noted in the introduction and will be explored in greater detail in Chapter 3, but it is also important to understand how the use of the model helped refine George's small group approach. McMahan warns that "all systems tend toward homeostasis." Thus, to create sustained growth, "systems interventions" must occur in as many areas of the church as feasible. A systemic intervention that focuses only on one person or a few people is unlikely to produce sustained change (McMahan 1998, 182). Because George embraces systems theory and utilizes an open systems model, the Meta Church's emphasis on "systemic replication" allows for infinite cell replication, though McMahan concedes that this will not happen, as it would not in any other system social scientists know of. The important thing, though, is that structurally, the box the Meta Church draws is of universe-size, not congregation size, and therefore is implementable on a far larger scale than program-based churches, or churches that use piecemeal, program-based formats, such as the advocates of the Covenant strategy (McMahan 1998, 182).

Both Hastings and McMahan were clearly impressed with the Meta Church model and given its clear superiority over covenant-based strategies, there's no reason to dispute them on this score (McMahan 1998, 235–236). If one concedes the desirability of maintaining high quality Protestant churches with the potential to quantitatively grow, the model has numerous advantages. Organizationally, the Meta-Church model is also more flexible than the Cell Church format and more adaptive to the demands of American culture. Walter G. Hastings contends that the Meta's church focus on "principle[s]" rather than over-specified "model[s] or pattern[s]" makes the model less rigid than cell-based churches (Hastings 2000, 236). Hastings also argues that the Meta Church model benefits from a better understanding of leadership development than the cell-church model, as its insights are "informed by adult education theory" (Hastings 2000, 236). Moreover, and perhaps most crucially, George's implementation of the systems perspective is total, whereas Neighbour relies on a much more piecemeal approach (Hastings 2000, 236–237).

Hastings concedes, however, that the model does have certain flaws. While the Meta Church approach appears "great on paper" it can prove difficult to implement. Hastings argues that the model also is hurt by its over-adherence to a pro-growth bias (Hastings 2000, 237). Hastings's point is clearly right here, as George's tendency to sell the Meta Church as the next new wave in church growth thinking is evident on virtually every page of *Prepare Your Church for the Future* and is ubiquitous in his last work, *The Coming Church Revolution* (1994). Moreover, the Meta Church model is designed to operate as a transitional approach to the "celebration-cell paradigm." As such, it is not designed for immediate, but rather gradual implementation over a period of many years. There is therefore a real potential for leadership burnout in the initial years of the program (Hastings 2000, 237). Moreover, two other potentially major issues exist with the model. First, the Meta Church model takes real intelligence to implement properly. If implemented by an ineffective pastor, the model likely creates more problems than it solves. Also, as a model steeped in Toyotist assumptions, Meta Church thinking can be faulted for a classic problem of lean production methods, which has been given the moniker "management by stress." Because the Meta Church model seeks for constant numerical growth and emphasizes qualitative improvement, it can create conditions that other Toyotist model institutions have led to, namely constant stress caused by unreasonable demands on the part of management for qualitative improvement (Sidorick 2009, loc. 628–712).

The debates over the need for economies of scale and efficient organizational practice that movements like the Meta Church model inspired did have a profound effect on the church. Some Christians have argued that the house church was the more biblical model of doing church (Jennifer G. Turner 2000, 50–51). Turner notes, however, that there were reasons for incorporating varying economies of scale in the church (Jennifer G. Turner 2000, 52–53), a sensible point for any institution that wants to successfully appeal to a customer base. The need to have efficient economies of scale also effect the size of small groups themselves and in part explain the increasing fascination with group dynamics in evangelical small group literature. Hastings notes that the initial popular understanding of small group dynamics within the movement held that groups should be no fewer than three people, and no more than around fifteen. Eight to ten people was seen as the optimal size for a small group. Later research in small group dynamics indicated that groups could be larger than this, depending on their composition and functional purpose. However, the movement did continue to promote the idea that small groups multiply after they reached the size of about ten people. Again, the issue here was as much about providing effective pastoral care as stimulating growth (Hastings 2000, 17).

Meta Church thinking tends to prize functionality over perceived outward formats of church. Ultimately the ministry is less concerned with the "programs, ministries, curriculums, and 'labels' of a church'" than it is with making sure the church's form of "organizational development" is sustainable. For certain churches, achieving effectiveness (i.e., quality control) involves utilizing "decentralized ministry through cells," while in other cases, the focus is on equipping larger organizational structures, such as congregations and celebration-sized events, for organizational effectiveness (George and Bird 1994, 280). Regardless of the "production model" employed, successful small group ministry depended on ministries continuously recruiting, training, and "equipping" leaders for church ministry. This in turn required a "layered" structure of leadership, especially in larger institutions, organizations, or simply networks. Thus, the need for effective leadership development is implicit in the adoption of any cell church or any large-scale adoption of the small group model. This requires the development of some form of "administrative support structure" and leadership delegation (Hastings 2000, 9). Thus, perhaps the most significant aspect of the Meta church model is that it created a systemized, highly rationalized approach to small group life within evangelicalism. Subsequent small group models have largely derived their view of group dynamics and ministry effectiveness from the Meta Church model and similar hyper-rationalized small group models developed during the heyday of the CGM.

Conclusion

Although not every aspect of previous church organizational models was adopted by the church growth movement, the CGM helped to systemize and operationalize many of the most efficient aspects of past organizational practices. Moreover, the CGM bears direct responsibility for the creation of the current marketized model that dominates evangelical churches. Understanding the CGM, therefore, is of vital importance if we are to understand how neoliberal ideals have come to dominate American Christianity.

2

The Church Growth Movement and the Birth of Modern Metricspirituality

The originator of the church growth movement was Donald McGavran. A Disciples of Christ missionary, McGavran's decision to apply social sciences methodology to the mission field came from hard experience (Cook 1998, 7–9). Although not a fundamentalist, McGavran believed that the promises of theological modernism were unequal to the task of evangelizing the world (Cook 1998, 23). While on the mission field, McGavran had had the opportunity to study the missions' practices of J. Watson Pickett, a British missionary. Pickett had conducted massive surveys of "mass movements" within Indian Christianity. McGavran became deeply involved in one of the studies that would follow from Pickett's work (Van Engen 1981, 326). Because of this study, a book called *Christian Missions in Mid-India* (1936), later re-titled *Church Growth and Group Conversion* (1962), was published (McIntosh 2004b, 11, 24). Crucially, Pickett introduced to McGavran the concept of mass movements, what McGavran later termed people movements (Rainer 1993, 30). In India, for many years, evangelists had success on the mission fields by converting people *en masse*, rather than viewing them in individual isolation (Cook 1998, 13). This kind of conversion aimed to create a snowball effect, in which one individual after another became Christianized after the initial elements of the people movement gained a foothold (Rainer 1993, 30; Cook 1998, 13).

People movements, however, could only start among willing populaces. Pickett and McGavran, along with their Indian colleague G.H. Singh, found that promoting church growth in India also relied on receptivity. The three men argued that for missions' efforts to work, specific receptive people groups had to be targeted for conversion (Cook 1998, 20; Rainer 1993, 30). McGavran and Pickett both contended that on a missions field with almost unlimited potential converts and limited resources, evangelists had to set priorities concerning financial and resource allocation (Rainer 1993, 30). Otherwise, the mission field ran the risk of becoming logistically and financially unmanageable.

From 1936 to 1954, McGavran's ideas about church growth crystallized into a consistent ideological framework (Cook 1998, 25). During the early 1950s, McGavran began working on a book called "How Peoples Become Christian." After much painstaking revision, it was published as *The Bridges of God* (1955) (McIntosh 2004b, 13). McGavran contended that the best way to win converts on the missions' field was not through the traditional "extraction" approach, but by utilizing preexisting bonds between families and other social groupings to win souls for Christ (Cook 1998, 30).

As Thomas Rainer points out, one of the most contentious aspects of McGavran's missiology was his emphasis on the corporate nature of evangelizing. Western missions' efforts were traditionally individualistic, modeling themselves on how first world evangelicals viewed faith commitments. But McGavran contended that the cultural situation of the developing world varied greatly from that which most first world citizens experienced (Rainer 1993, 35). A crucial means of gaining converts was to minimize the sense of cultural alienation caused by the conversion experience. The question was, how did one achieve this goal?

McGavran had an answer. In both *Bridges of God* and his later work *Understanding Church Growth* (1970), he advanced the idea of "the homogenous unit principle." McGavran contended that people "like to become Christians without crossing racial linguistic or class barriers" (McGavran 1990, loc. 64) and were attracted to churches where the membership physically, culturally, and/or linguistically resembled them (Rainer 1993, 255; Wagner 2010, 108–109). This simple principle had revolutionary implications. On the missions' field, it meant trying to connect similar cultural groups together in order to make the conversion experience easier and less painful to go through; by making these connections, it was hoped that the sense of alienation converts experienced would be mitigated (Jonathan C. Terry 1997, 90). McGavran aimed to further minimize such alienation by a distinction he made between discipling and perfecting. McGavran argued that the church's most important function was winning converts, who would then be brought into "active fellowship" with the church. The process of perfecting these people to be Christ-like was a distinct secondary stage (Rainer 1988, 41–42). He saw evangelization more as a process than an event, allowing for evangelicals to make successful conversions of individuals or people groups even when their behavior was, by evangelical standards, sub-optimal (Jonathan C. Terry 1997, 100).

McGavran accepted initially sub-optimal Christian behavior because his emphasis was on results, not efforts. He argued that traditional missions focused too much on what he called the "search principle," rather than the "harvest principle." The search principle's primary emphasis was on the effort put into missions, whereas those evangelizing from a "harvest principle" perspective were more concerned with the results of missions' efforts, whether in souls saved, church members gained, or other mission objectives accomplished (Jonathan C. Terry 1997, 75–77). Much of the church growth movement's tendency to embrace political conservatism also resulted from its commitment to the harvest principle. Pastoral and missions actions that did not lead to saved souls were seen as ancillary to the true function of the church. Thus, any appeal to the social gospel was seen as contrary to the church's mission (Jonathan C. Terry 1997, 83).

McGavran's affiliation with Pickett, as well as other influences, led him to promote the social sciences as a key to church growth. Initially, McGavran tested his church growth hypotheses on missions' trips overseas. Starting in the mid–1950s, he systematized his approach, devoting himself to rigorous reading, the use of questionnaire-based studies, and the promotion of lectures on church growth. The seminars, in particular, helped McGavran formulate an overriding ideological identity for the emerging church growth movement (Cook 1998, 32–34). Over the decades, the church growth movement's use of social science principles became much more confident and sophisticated, eventually embracing much of the cyborg sciences.

The church-growth movement promoted itself as a scientific and academic discipline (Wagner 1976, 40–41; Holvast 2009. 19). It viewed itself as an application of missiological principles. Critics, such as Samuel Escobar, contended that the CGM represented a "managerial missiology" (Holvast 2009, 19). In any case, the movement oriented itself towards theological and sociological pragmatism, and sought to combine the social sciences with evangelical ideology. It justified such pragmatism through its use of quantitative measurements of church growth and decline (Holvast 2009, 19). Later critics argued, not entirely with justification, that the movement ignored qualitative barometers of success.[1] It is true, however, that, at least in the beginning, the CGM had a pronounced desire to use demographic and quantitative analysis to advance Christian missions (Holvast 2009, 19). The sociological assumptions that the movement brought to the promotion of church growth had profound ramifications on how the movement and its descendants viewed governance. Because evangelical believers now saw themselves as seeking to convert people-groups, rather than individuals, evangelicalism became increasingly ecclesiocentric over the second half of the 20th century (Holvast 2009, 22–23).

Yet no academic discipline can develop without an institutional base to back it up. McGavran soon acquired such a base of operations, when the

Northwest Christian College of Eugene Oregon helped him found the Institute of Church Growth in 1961. In the Institute's formative years, it sought to lay out the ideological and missiological concepts that would motivate the movement. Through the well-respected William B. Eerdmans publishing company, McGavran began publishing the Church Growth Series. McGavran's publishing and outreach efforts soon gained him a wide hearing in the wider Protestant community. When the Iberville Consultation of 1963 was held, church growth theory received a groundswell of support, including the Consultation publicly supporting many of the major ideas behind early CG thinking. In 1965, McGavran transferred the Institute of Church Growth to Fuller Theological Seminary in Pasadena, California, where he was appointed dean of Fuller's School of World Missions. This gave McGavran a new, major power base from which to spread church growth thinking. Alan Tippet, a major early Christian anthropologist, joined McGavran at Fuller (Rainer 1993, 37–38). Fuller's School of World Mission eventually morphed into one of the most influential centers for missiology in the world. McGavran was soon joined by a talented group of Christian social scientists and missiologists, including J. Edwin Orr (1912–1987), Charles H. Kraft (1932–), Ralph Winter (1924–2009), C. Peter Wagner (1930–), and Arthur Glasser (1914–2009) (McIntosh 2004b, 15, 18; Rainer 1993, 51). Organizationally, the church growth movement benefited from a huge number of institutions that were built in the Pasadena area, including the William Carey library, which specialized in producing church growth literature; the Church Growth Book Club, whose cheap prices allowed for the wide dissemination of church growth literature; the Institute for American Church Growth, whose founder Win Arn (1923–2006) proved crucial to the spread of CGM ideas; the Missions Advanced Research and Communications Center (MARC), which played a crucial role in systemizing evangelical missions' efforts in the last quarter of the 20th century (Rainer 1988, 45–46; Holvast 2009, 25–26); and the U.S. Center for World Mission, whose founder Ralph Winter promoted some of the most adept evangelical missions' efforts in the last part of the 20th century (Rainer 1993, 38). By the time McGavran had published his magnum opus, *Understanding Church Growth* (1970), the movement's institutionalization within evangelical thought was assured (Rainer 1993, 38).

The institutionalization of the church growth movement led to the founding of many international, national, and local research facilities, whose goal was to develop "the most efficient and effective ways to do missionary work" (Holvast 2009, 25). Both MARC and the U.S. Center for World Mission (USWM) were prominent examples of this trend, as was *The Journal of Frontier Missions*, which USWM published (Holvast 2009, 25–26). McGavran emphasized repeatedly the importance of reliable research to achieving effective church growth. McGavran decried "inaccurate record keeping" and "administrators who do not think church growth matters." For McGavran accurate statistical analysis of church trends was not ancillary to the gospel mission, but central to it. As a consequence, he argued that the church must be held accountable for the results it obtained on the mission field (McIntosh 2005, 37–38).

Originally, the CGM's proponents, particularly McGavran, envisioned the movement primarily as a tool for the foreign missions' field (Wagner 2010, 89; McIntosh 2005, 44–45). However, CGM guru C. Peter Wagner and Win Arn saw America as a prime new target for church growth thinking (Wagner 2010, 89–90, 100–101). Initially, Wagner primarily spread church growth thinking through his classes, as well as his books and articles, whereas Arn promoted himself as a "field consultant," utilizing Church Growth seminars to spread the message of the movement to a national audience (Cook 1998, 63). After offering his first classes on church growth, Wagner realized the enormous potential church growth thinking had for the American market. Wagner used his class to promote church growth thinking and methodology to a wider and wider swathe of pastors and church leaders (Cook 1998, 68). A few years after the success of his course, Wagner penned *Your Church Can Grow* (1976), a major work in the church growth canon that played an important part in promoting its expansion in North America. Wagner then asked John Wimber, a former rock musician (Cook 1998, 90) turned influential preacher, to run the Charles E. Fuller Institute for Evangelism and Church Growth. The Institute became a central locus for church growth consultation. Wimber brought to the Institute a keen understand of business and evangelism, and was an innovator in the development of research tools for church growth and outreach. When Wimber left, Carl George, the man who would go on to create the influential metachurch model of small groups, took over in Wimber's place, staying head of the Institute till its closure in 1995 (McIntosh 2004b, 16–17; McIntosh 2005, 82).

Even after Wimber left the Institute, however, he still represented a significant influence on the CGM, though this fact is sometimes downplayed in otherwise reasonably objective histories of the CGM written by evangelicals who do not subscribe to Wimber's Third Wave Charismatic beliefs. When Wimber joined the Fuller Institute, he was not Charismatic. However, he struck up friendships with numerous Fuller faculty members sympathetic to the Pentecostal movement, such as McGavran and Charles Kraft. This caused him to rethink his beliefs (Cook 1998, 91–92). After breaking with the Calvary Chapel movement, the Vineyard churches that Wimber helped lead began promoting a form of healing evangelism called "power evangelism." Power evangelism emphasized the importance of spiritual "signs and wonders" in achieving church growth. From an evangelistic perspective, it was less head-driven and more focused on experiential concepts. Wagner soon gravitated to power evangelism as well, and by the 1980s, this would significantly shape how the CGM approached church growth (Cook 1998, 93–95).

Power evangelism, however, was not the only church growth pot that Wagner had his hands in. Starting in 1975, Fuller's School of Theology started offering a doctorate in ministry (D. Min) program. Wagner played a crucial role in the expansion of church growth into the D. Min program (McIntosh 2004b, 17). The new course offerings shifted the focus of Fuller from theological and more theoretical concerns to issues of praxis. Fuller's move in a pragmatic direction fit in well with the agenda of the CGM and thus provided the space needed for Wagner and McGavran to promote the growth of church growth thinking in American seminaries. Influential spokesmen for the CGM who received D. Min degrees from Fuller included Elmer Towns (1932–), Kent Hunter (1947–), John Vaughan, John Maxwell (1947–), Rick Warren (1954–), and Robert (Bob) E. Logan (1953–) (McIntosh 2004b, 17–18). The D. Min program graduated more than 1,150 American clergy by 1985 (McIntosh 2004b, 18).

Perhaps the most influential offshoot of Wagner's Church Growth classes at Fuller was the Institute for American Church Growth, which Win Arn established in 1974. Known as a skilled and effective leader with a knack for technological experimentation, Arn was intrigued by McGavran's missiological ideas, seeing them as ideal methods for expanding Protestant influence in the United States in a time of church decline. Arn decided to put his technological know-how to good use by establishing the Institute, even though he "had no visible means of support." When he told McGavran his plans for the Institute, McGavran allegedly remarked: "You'll lose your shirt. There's no money in church growth." Yet despite his misgivings, McGavran struck up a close friendship with Arn. The two men wrote a book entitled *How to Grow a Church: Conversations about Church Growth* (1973). Arn later decided to do a film of the same name and despite the misgivings of numerous film companies, went ahead and funded the movie himself. In spite of predictions of its cataclysmic failure, the film proved an important milestone in the expansion of the CG market; numerous clergymen saw it in the coming decades (McIntosh 2005, 46–50).

The initial success of the Institute for American Church Growth (IACG) resulted from both good strategy and a careful selection of strategically important Christian leaders, including World Vision's Vice President (later president) Ted Engstrom (1916–2006), C. Peter Wagner, and McGavran. The IACG's approach to the promulgation of the CGM was well thought out, reflecting long-standing CGM commitments to pragmatism and efficient organizing. The organization took a four-pronged approach to spreading CG practices. First, they ran a number of "seminars, workshops and training sessions to teach Church Growth" (Cook 1998, 105). The organization also tried to further refine the research and social science methods employed by contemporary church growth practitioners. Thirdly, Arn utilized his skills with communications technologies to further promote the message of church growth. Finally, the IACG set itself up as a church growth consultation service, paving the way for numerous such consultants that followed in the wake of the organization's initial success (Cook 1998, 106).

Of these methods, Arn was most successful with the church growth seminar. While McGavran had given such seminars before Arn entered the CGM, he lacked the necessary charisma to make church growth ideas engaging to a popular audience. Win Arn, by contrast was more innovative in his use of educational and communications technology and less didactic in his approach to teaching CG principles. He also benefited from the assistance of his son Chip Arn, whose technological skills were put to use on behalf of the IACG. Unlike much previous church growth literature, the material produced by the IACG did not rely heavily on the use of CGM jargon, allowing Arn to target far more viewers than previous church growth advocates had been able to reach (Cook 1998, 106–109).

In addition to its training seminars and mass media events, the IACG also frequently engaged in "diagnostic, research, and consultation services to churches" (Cook 1998, 127). Church growth diagnostics played a crucial part in IACG's ministry from the time the organization developed the Basic Growth Seminar. One diagnostic tool developed by the Arn's organization was the Advanced Growth Organizer. By making use of the devices, churches were told they could develop a precise knowledge of their "growth potential" (Cook 1998, 128). Reflecting the metricspiritual assumptions of CGM, computer monitoring and video training, then state-of-the-art technologies, were also incorporated into the program (Cook 1998, 129).

Thanks to programs like Arn's, the CGM's influence soon spread far beyond Pasadena. Also influential was Kent. R. Hunter, who established The Church Growth Center in 1977 and Elmer Towns, who was particularly interested in the application of CGM principles to Sunday School growth (Rainer 1993, 41). The movement's power base was also bolstered because of the influence of the International Congress on World Evangelization, which was held in 1974 in Lausanne. The Lausanne meeting served as a springboard by which CG ideas disseminated widely throughout the evangelical community. Increasingly, as well, the movement made common cause with the embryonic megachurches that began appearing in the 1970s. Many of these megachurches became symbolic exemplars for future church growth (Rainer 1993, 42). The CGM movement also intersected with many streams of lay evangelism during the period, such as Evangelism Explosion III and Campus Crusade for Christ. These combined influences, when united with the movement's impact on Neo-Pentecostalism, made its power felt throughout the length and breadth of evangelical Christianity (Rainer 1993, 42–43).

The CGM movement secured its position as the primary evangelical church outreach practice when, in late 1984, C. Peter Wagner was given the position of "Donald A. McGavran Chair of Church Growth at Fuller Seminary's School of World Mission." By 1985, the American Society for Church Growth had been founded, an organization designed to link academics, clergy, consultants, and denominational leaders. The organization soon had its own journal running and served as a bully pulpit for several major church growth advocates, notably George Hunter III, Charles Van Engen and Charles Arn (McIntosh 2004b, 18–19). Meanwhile, the Charles E. Fuller Institute of Evangelism and Church Growth (CEFI), no longer formally affiliated with Fuller Theological Seminary, began to develop a systematic consultation, training, and diagnostic philosophy under the leadership of Carl George. George started the first formal training regimen for church growth consultants—Diagnosis with Impact (McIntosh 2005, 83–85).

Halfway through the 1980s, the CGM had divided into multiple camps. One prominent division was between the North American and missions front. Those who followed the missions' approach to CG drew their ideas mainly from the School of World Mission at Fuller Seminary, and its offshoot missiological movements. In this regard, Jim Montgomery's Discipling a Whole Nation, which applied church growth missions' principles at a national level on the international missions field, and the U.S. Center for World Mission, were particularly influential. The other major force in church growth at the time were those church growth advocates committed to North American church outreach, of which Win Arn, Wagner, Wimber, George, and the organizations that they represented were the best examples (McIntosh 2004b, 18–19).

Wagner had been the heir-apparent for the CG movement (Rainer 1993, 51, 55) for more than a decade by the mid–1980s, but changes in his spiritual beliefs caused many to question his fitness to continue leading the movement. This change was most graphically demonstrated by a 1982 Fuller course Wagner nominally led called "MC 510: Signs, Wonders, and Church Growth." In actual fact, Wimber led the course. The use of healing ministry in post-class periods soon brought national attention to "MC 510." Critics charged that Fuller Seminary was moving into the Charismatic orbit. Wagner at the time claimed not to be Charismatically inclined (Cook 1998, 96). As the 1980s wore on, however, Wagner gravitated more and more into the Charismatic orbit. During the 1990s, this trend accelerated, so that by 1999 Wagner had adopted the doctrines of the Latter Rain Revival (Cook 1998, 97, Holvast 2009, 164). Wagner's 1980s excursion into signs and wonders theology not only preoccupied him, but brought many other CGM advocates into the same theological orbit, effectively creating a new strain of church growth

2. The Church Growth Movement and Modern Metricspirituality 103

thinking separate from more "mainstream" thought (Cook 1998, 97). Moreover, as my book *The New Apostolic Reformation: History of a Modern Charismatic Movement* (2016) makes clear, this Wagnerian strain of CG thinking became an increasingly dominant form of spiritual expression within evangelicalism in the ensuing decades (Weaver 2016, passim).

Due in large part to Wagner's exodus into Charismatic territory, the CGM became "fragmented and less centralized" during the 1990s (Holvast 2009, 27–28). As René Holvast relates, "this fragmentation was due in the first place to Church Growth's own success, spread throughout many denominations and geographical areas" (Holvast 2009, 27–28). Undertheorized hermeneutical methods and its over-commitment to relevance also hurt the CGM (Holvast 2009, 28). In North America, particularly among disaffected young people, church growth methods became a byword for inauthenticity in the 1990s and 2000s. Numerous attempts to reinvent church growth in a manner acceptable to younger members of Generation X, as well as millennials, failed to provide a reliable model of church growth for modern evangelicals to follow.

Various Christian leaders have taken up the role of spokesperson for church growth since Wagner stepped down from the McGavran Chair of Church Growth in 1999, but these individuals lacked the magnetism of Wagner and the influence and respect McGavran enjoyed. This led to a watering down of the concept of church growth. Modern models of church growth often are as likely to resemble the useful, but less systematically developed methods of "popular" church growth pioneered by pollsters like George Gallup and George Barna, or alternately McGavran's ideologically sophisticated contemporary Lyle Schaller, than the formal school of church growth that developed via the Pasadena Gang (McIntosh 2004b, 20). Moreover, as Win Arn's Church Growth Inc. (the updated version of the Institute for American Church Growth) declined in influence and The Fuller Institute for Evangelism and Church Growth ceased operating, outlets for formal, Pasadena-inspired church growth training became harder to promulgate. While some groups still publish church growth material modeled on McGavran's thinking, there is no longer a unified vision to the model, as there was in the 1970s and 1980s (McIntosh 2004b, 21). The success of the church growth model has also promoted what Gary McIntosh characterizes as an over-willingness on the part of "publishers to promote as Church Growth just about any book or product that speaks vaguely of growing a church" (McIntosh 2004b, 21). Much of this material lacks any strong theoretical grounding in church growth thought (McIntosh 2004b, 21), which weakens a movement that already is susceptible to charges of lax social science research and methodology.

Like many professional fields, upon entering its "maturity" in the 1990s, church growth had already started to diversify into a number of specialty areas. Church growth advocates, and simple profiteers began expanding into fields ranging from church planting and cell groups to conflict management and fund raising (McIntosh 2004b, 21). The label of church growth ministry became so terminologically vague as to be meaningless (McIntosh 2004b, 21). Two particular threads of church growth thinking (one claiming, on questionable grounds, to be distinct from church growth thought), developed into particularly widespread practices: the church health movement, whose most famous spokesperson is Christian Schwarz, and the increasing professionalization of church consultation practices. But before moving into these areas, we must look at the social science assumptions made by the CGM, for in those assumptions lie the foundations of the modern evangelical church's embrace of the cyborg sciences.

Church Growth Movement: Social Science and Governance Assumptions

The church growth movement historically mainly concerned itself with finding efficient mechanisms for marketing, outreach, and evangelism. This must be kept in mind when viewing the movement's approach to the social and cyborg sciences. Functionality, rather than theological conservatism, are the movement's overriding concern. This means that the movement's embrace of social science and cyborg science methodologies has come about largely out of rationalistic concerns, not unlike those that motivated public choice theory.

McGavran himself did not have extensive formal training in sociology or anthropology, though he tried to read widely in the various behavioral sciences (James Clappdale Smith 1976, 131). This led to criticisms of his social science methodology, particularly by professional anthropologists and sociologists, who resented his lack of terminological precision and carelessness towards proper citation methods (James Clappdale Smith 1976, 133). McGavran saw the social sciences as inherently neutral. In and of themselves, they were neither good or evil. Rather, it was how people applied social science methodology that made its use good or evil. He valued the social sciences because they provided a realistic model of how cultures change and develop (James Clappdale Smith 1976, 137). McGavran valued the potential of anthropology to break down what he saw as the "missionary's ethnocentricity," the tendency of missionaries to view the evangelized subject solely through the vantage point of the missionizing culture (James Clappdale Smith 1976, 142).

The church growth movement's ideology and methodology was criticized within and outside the United States. The "hegemony" of American thinkers inside the CGM was of major concern to those living outside the

U.S. Critics of America's hegemonic control of missions argued that the CGM promoted a leadership style "not unlike those of multinationals," in which top-down decision-making processes were emphasized. This encouraged an unrealistic approach to developing local evangelistic policy within the developing world. Instead of relying on local agencies and churches to achieve church growth, the CGM centralized all power within the American, or at least Anglo-American, church power structure. In the 1990s, this process replicated itself with the spiritual mapping movement (Holvast 2009, 26). The CGM's lack of terminological exactness also bothered critics, as did its reliance on fuzzy math and questionable statistics. Many critics contended that the research and development aspects of church growth, rather than bringing clarity, further mystified the process by which churches matured and developed. Again, this criticism repeated itself with spiritual mapping. Many critics, particularly prominent Latin American evangelicals, criticized the CGM's refusal to take seriously "the mandate of social work" in the mission of the church (Holvast 2009, 26–27).

The CGM's emphasis on social sciences had a large influence on missions' policy, where it was criticized for adopting a "managerial approach" to the missions' field (Holvast 2009, 28). Evangelicals involved in CGM envisioned conversion in geographic and territorial terms, rather than as a process between individuals (Holvast 2009, 28). This focus led to the development of the CGM's "'ecclesiocentric' missions" approach, one later copied in the AD 2000, spiritual mapping, and NAR adaptations of modern missions' work (Holvast 2009, 28). This increasing cartographic and ecclesiological tendency in evangelical missions' work was furthered by missions movements like Lausanne and research and academic organizations like Fuller Theological Seminary (Holvast 2009, 28).

There is no one-size fits all approach to governance within church growth theory. Early church management theories often borrowed from concepts derived from management by objectives (MBO) (Roddam 1997, 136). The MBO approach was most clearly articulated by business guru Peter Drucker (1909–2005), an important influence on Christian Right management theory, who emphasized that managers should be motivated by a task-emphasis rather than direction from an external authority. MBO advocates tried to walk a line between giving employees some autonomy and ensuring that the managerial class had the ultimate say in decision making (Wren and Bedain 2009, 424; Waring 1991, 88). Yet, as Stephen Waring points out, this task was perpetually a Sisyphean labor for MBO-supporting managers, because "when corporate interests conflicted with employee interests, those of the employee had to be sacrificed" (Waring 1991, 84).

The use of MBO techniques, along with strategic planning, formed the bedrock out of which modern evangelicalism embraced the cyborg sciences. In CGM, as well as its sister fields of church management and church health, this is most commonly seen through numerous variations on "faith goals" or church goal setting (Roddam 1997, 136). As an ideology, MBO supports setting goals that are "measurable, time-bound, and are established through a participatory approach" (Aswathappa, K. and Kardminer Ghuman 2010, 508). Church supporters have almost unanimously supported using this approach. For instance, in R. Daniel Reeves and Ronald Jenson's *Always Advancing: Modern Strategies for Church Growth* (1984), the two authors emphasize that "satisfactory goals must be measurable, manageable, and relevant," an approach to governance that clearly reflects MBO influence (Reeves and Jenson 1984, 41). Similarly, church growth guru C. Peter Wagner emphasizes that ideally church goals should be "relevant ... measurable ... significant ... manageable ... [and] personal" (Wagner 1987, 170–171). The number of church growth writers who embrace this goal setting approach is impossible to calculate, but represents a wide cross-section of important organizational thinkers in evangelicalism. Among other church growth writers, for instance, the reader could consult Rainer's *Book of Church Growth*, which simply reiterates Wagner's approach to church growth (Rainer 1993, 267). Rick Warren, similarly, believes that church purpose statements should be written in such a manner that they can be "biblical ... specific ... transferable ... measurable" (Warren 1995, 100–101). Within the field of church management literature, the same viewpoint is espoused. Kenneth O. Gangel (1935–2009) embraces a "ministry by objectives" approach that is essentially identical to secular MBO (see Gangel 1997, 279–285). These ministry goals are usually operationalized within the church's strategic plan.

Evangelical leadership quickly realized the benefits of applying systems approaches to strategic planning. This is due in large part to the influence of Ed Dayton. In the late 1960s, Dayton, who had been employed in the aerospace industry, suggested to World Vision leaders that there would be benefits to applying concepts from systems engineering to the missions field ("ASA Newsletter March 1968"; Dayton "Interview" n.d.). Dayton eventually wrote an influential manual on using the program evaluation and review technique (PERT) in the missions field (Manetsch 1967; "ASA Newsletter, March 1968"; see also Dayton and Fraser 1990, 296–297). PERT was an advanced method of modeling and assessing complex projects that was initially developed for the U.S. Polaris submarine project (Karrupan, et al. 2016, 84). PERT, along with Project Planning and Scheduling (PPS), became popular in the 1960s and 1970s in the national defense departments of various countries, as well as the U.S., and PPS was also particularly influential at NASA (Camilleri 2016, 6–7).[2] Dayton contended that one of the advantages of the PERT approach was that it not only allowed missions groups to determine the optimal time period to achieving their goals, but how those goals related to each other (Dayton and Fraser 1990, 297).

Moreover, the ten-step planning model that Dayton set up deliberately embraced feedback principles to optimize efficiency of missions' methods. The model did this by first setting operational priorities, then describing those priorities, figuring out the "means" and "methods" of the planning approach, carefully defining goals and "anticipat[ing] outcomes" and eventually acting on those outcomes (Dayton and Fraser 1990, 32–35). Crucially, this was followed by an evaluation of the whole approach, which would then feed back into future plans. As Dayton demonstrates, this last step is important to this "management for mission" approach, as it allowed the system to engage in "repetitive application" (Dayton and Fraser 1990, 37).

The principle of utilizing feedback, even if simply market feedback, to determine future courses of action is now a standard methodology of the CGM. This is seen in both outreach and evaluation efforts. For instance, Rick Warren writes, "Growing churches should always be asking, 'How can we do it better?' They are ruthless in evaluating their services and ministries. Evaluation is the key to excellence. You must continually examine each part of your service and assess its effectiveness" (Warren 1995, 275). Carl George and Robert Logan, similarly, set up a simplified three step process of "goal setting ... implementing ... [and] evaluating" which creates a feedback loop that hopefully will lead to continuous service improvement (see George and Logan 1987, 72).[3]

Thus, it must be understood that the CGM equipped itself with the toolbox that characterizes both modern management practice and the cyborg sciences. While critics of the CGM point out its similarities to secular management practices, they often fail to grasp how sophisticated the movement's use of these practices has been. Moreover, these critiques, particularly when coming from within the evangelical movement, fail to note how fundamentally the capitalist principles underlying the church growth movement have altered the evangelical movement's approach to both governance and the market.

One of the major problems with the CGM model of management was that its reliance on a business model of church leadership, rather than one founded in more traditional pastoral theology, encouraged the movement to adopt highly authoritarian leadership structures, which the movement believed hastened church growth (Crosby 1989, 344). In those elements of CGM thought attracted to "Signs and Wonders" or Third Wave Pentecostal theology, this preference for strong leadership led many churches to adopt the apostolic model of church governance. Frequently such churches ended up within the orbit of the NAR (Weaver 2016, 5–7). This has contributed greatly to the process of dedemocratization outlined in the introduction.

Moreover, the market model of the church that church growth offers has altered the nature of what constitutes democracy in evangelical churches. The consumer-orientation of the church growth movement creates a system in which church governance is based on *what the market wants, rather than what it needs*. This turns the church into a product or service, rather than a culture and way of life which brings with it mutual obligation to other human beings. A similar process, as documentarian Adam Curtis has noted, has occurred within secular governance, leading to the triumph of an "all-consuming self" which politicians seek to continuously placate at the expense of the common good (Curtis, 2007; Curtis, 2011; Curtis, 2002).

The CGM's marketized approach to Christian belief also created formulaic approaches to pastoral care that failed to meet the needs of congregants, a problem we see repeated from Chapter 1's description of the efficiency church movement. Because the CGM had a task-emphasis, rather than a pastoral emphasis, it sees issues of "soul care" as secondary. CGM advocates argued that a business-oriented church is a people-oriented church, but this assumption neglected the relational aspect of pastoral care and church discipline. Because of this preference for business, rather than relational, solutions to church problems, evangelical churches in the 1990s and 2000s proved increasingly willing to jettison principles and even common human decency when such values flew in the face of church management objectives. David Allen Crosby blamed this problem on the tendency of church growth proponents to evaluate church management decisions increasingly within terms of numerical categories, which he argued was a departure from historical Christian norms (Crosby 1989, 346–348). The growth in movements like biblical counseling and Christian integrationist psychology are partially a response to the increasing adoption of business methodology within the church, as well as in the corporate culture of the mental health industry; they have proven woefully inadequate, however, in dealing with the expanding influence of management practices into pastoral care (Weaver 2014, 19, 145–146). Indeed, in many ways, these movements have helped cause such an expansion.

CGM proponents never wedded themselves to one form of organizational management, freely adopting from the most sophisticated models they could utilize (Roddam 1997, 136). For Wagner, the ability to be flexible in adopting management ideas was of paramount importance. He condemned works, therefore, that claimed to have found "the biblically determined leadership style" (Wagner 1984, 97–98). As a result, the CGM freely borrowed from a wide range of management ideas. This allowed for the diffusion of such ideas into a wide variety of movements that were modeled after the CGM, such as AD 2000 and Beyond, the spiritual mapping movement, and the NAR.

One managerial model that got a good deal of attention was "total quality management," the model that most epitomized Oriental Systems Theory practices (Haberer 2001, 106). Leaders in industry and management circles had long known that quality control was important for product marketing (Wren and Bedian 2009, 476). However, in the immediate postwar period, quality control issues often proved secondary in the minds of manufacturers, who at the time felt more concerned about such issues as "human relations, the financial management of corporate portfolios, and unrelated product diversification" (Wren and Bedian 2009, 476). Western Electric quality control specialist Walter A. Shewhart (1891–1967) formulated many of the original principles of statistically based quality control, which were then further molded by William Edwards Deming (1900–1993), a long-time consultant on management practices who was particularly well known in Japan. Deming and fellow quality control experts argued that proper quality control sought to mitigate "variation, through continuous improvement," by figuring out what issues a product had, fixing those problems, and then continually evaluating the product for any signs of flaws in the production process (Wren and Bedian 2009, 476–482; Watts 1996, 17).

The kind of statistical methods and measurement instruments that TQM provided found widespread application within the church growth movement (Watts 1996, 23), and it is likely, though not certain, that even early borrowings in this area were conscious (later borrowings so closely reflect TQM literature that the influence can be assumed). Qualitative measuring instruments for church growth allowed the CGM to help "control variability" factors that came about from the process of church evangelism, expansion, and development (Watts 1996, 23). McGavran emphasized the importance of compiling accurate demographic figures on church growth, as well as the aforementioned geographical studies of potential areas for outreach, as crucial to effective church growth. The importance of effective diagnosis, both quantitative and qualitative, was a major influence on the movement as well. George Barna, for instance, suggested that churches hold review sessions to evaluate all aspects of their church services. This not only allowed churches to more effectively measure quality issues involved in church growth, but allowed churches the ability to decide what their "focus" or "vision" was for church development (Watts 1996, 23–24). Similarly, Diane Barber and the esteemed CGM advocate Kent R. Hunter, while acknowledging that statistical measures were not a one-size-fits-all solution to church growth, supported using statistical methods of monitoring congregational quality and numerical strength, and then comparing these monitored performance figures with perceived goals and objectives (Watts 1996, 25–26). Such diagnostic efforts, besides clarifying the objectives of church leadership teams, helped these teams to enforce "quality improvement and accountability" through periodic assessments of ministry effectiveness (Watts 1996, 24). Such thinking mirrored that of Walter A. Shewhart, who argued that, while error was inevitable in the production process, there should be "limits to ... random variation" on the factory floor, and that such limits could be controlled and improved upon via corrective action—what the church would call diagnosis or feedback (Wren and Bedian 2009, 477; Watts 1996, 23–24).

Because evangelicals generally agreed that qualitative instruments were harder to formulate for church growth than quantitative ones, much effort was expended in trying to create the former. One frequently used tool was "people flows." People flows tracked the "means by which unchurched families move toward responsible membership" (Watts 1996, 24). This kind of qualitative CG modeling led to the development of a wide range of measurement instruments, including a 3-phase conversion scale pioneered by Alan Tippett, a 3-tiered evangelism scale developed by C. Peter Wagner, McGavran's "receptivity axis," and others (Watts 1996, 24–25).

The model of church growth analysis offered up by church growth consultants and other church growth advocates was consumer oriented. In the TQM literature, quality represents what "the user or customer says it is" (Watts 1996, 26). Similar principles motivated the church growth movement and were even more present in the church health and marketing literature. As we saw in the Introduction, the closing decades of the 20th century saw the widespread application of managerialism to various aspects of Western life, such as NPM. The church growth movement was influenced by these same calls for "institutional effectiveness." In both secular and religious environments, the promotion of institutional effectiveness involved a continuous "process of evaluating data-based outcomes. Each outcome is related to a goal and each goal supports the institution's purpose. The analysis of the data determines actions and adjustments that will be made to improve outcomes" (Crites 2009, 58). The church health movement was particularly ardent in its embrace of the principles of institutional effectiveness. Sometimes movement proponents modeled their techniques based directly on the secular institutional effectiveness literature. As Crites notes, the model was viewed as a technique of "receiving God's vision, compiling appropriate strategies, implementing the strategies and evaluating the results" (Crites 2009, 58). This allowed for a continuous process of "circular" improvement based on the input and output of feedback (Crites 2009, 58).[4]

An important corollary idea followed from this embrace of institutional effectiveness, which is that if churches wanted to understand what represented quality to target religious consumers, they had to conduct outreach to those consumers. Churches had to understand the felt needs of religious consumers and seek to meet those needs. As a result, advocates of both church health and TQM-oriented approaches to church growth supported moving churches "from a message based approach to an audience-based approach" (Watts 1996, 26).

The consumer-oriented nature of churches that subscribe to church growth thought means that such churches frequently draw on marketing techniques including advanced ideas borrowed from marketing research. Here megachurches must be mentioned. Although church marketing campaigns long predated modern evangelicalism, the paradigmatic example of marketing strategies within contemporary evangelicalism is Willow Creek Community Church. Willow Creek subscribed to a number of revolutionary innovations in church praxis that defined its approach to evangelism. For instance, the church conducted a separate service for those it labeled "seekers." These services showcased "contemporary music, lots of creative entertainment, and relevant messages," in order to make the church as appealing as possible to non–Christians. A focus on high commitment from established members was also an important element of Willow Creek's program (Sargeant 1996, 87–89). Heavily influenced by the pro-therapeutic beliefs of Robert Schuller, a prominent church growth advocate, Willow Creek's message took on therapeutic overtones in order to attract seekers. Like Schuller, Willow Creek updated much modern psychological language, cloaking it in theological garb (Sargeant 1996, 92).

However, what proved most revolutionary about Willow Creek was its use of marketing surveys to discover why people did not attend church. Willow Creek then developed techniques based on these surveys to avoid the pitfalls respondents said prevented attendance (Sargeant 1996, 12). Subsequently, many other churches relied on similar marketing approaches to achieve church growth objectives. For instance, seeker churches frequently "depended on promotional letters, market research, special events and even name changes to increase their outreach potential" (Sargeant 1996, 12–13). Church growth proponents refined these techniques over the coming decades, holding competitions, engaging in statistical modeling, and developing church growth instructional material in order to gain the maximum religious market share possible (Wilford 2012, loc. 1107). Inevitably, this led not only to the further refinement of demographic research in the church, but to the application of psychographic techniques to church growth.

Demographic marketing practices have traditionally relied on segmenting people groups by population statistics ("Demographics"; Thorson and Duffy 2002, 42). Such population statistics can divide people by age group, gender, income, education, etc. (Thorson and Duffy 2002, 42). By contrast, psychographics segments people based on their "activities, interests, and opinions." The Values and Lifestyle (VALS), developed by SRI in the 1970s (Sivulka 2012, 299), is a particularly influential model in this regard. Where secular market research was going, evangelical marketing research did not lag far behind.

Psychographics fit in well with growing calls for more focused evangelism efforts. CGM proponents argued that one of the church marketing movement's prime uses would be as a tool for targeted outreach (David W. Fleming 2000, 76). This was a natural working out of McGavran's receptivity principle, which focused on reaching those populations most willing to be reached (David W. Fleming 2000, 6–7, 73). Church growth proponents contended that this should be done via a process of internal analysis, a process that proved particularly popular after the success of Rick Warren's *Purpose Driven Church*. Once a church had a specific population subset in mind, it developed theological products, services, and programs that could respond to the desires of that consumer base (David W. Fleming 2000, 76). Such careful market analysis was symptomatic of both Drucker's MBO approach (Waring 1991, 89), as well as the production processes associated with total quality management.

Drucker's MBO approach had oriented businesses to have management establish clear "operational objectives"—goals, in other words—which would determine not only management philosophy, but "Marketing, product innovation, output, resource allocation, personnel performance, corporate social responsibility, and performance measurement" (Waring 1991, 89). Lyle Schaller, Kirk Hadaway and C. Peter Wagner, all three of whom were important promoters of church growth thinking, similarly argued—in language infused with new paradigm assumptions—for the primacy of "vision-casting and goal setting" in the church's long-term strategic planning (David W. Fleming 2000, 6–7). This required accurate market research and self-assessment to evaluate the viability of the church's "vision" (David W. Fleming 2000, 67–70). CGM researchers claimed from their analysis of church growth that setting goals and objectives and furthering church growth were intrinsically tied together (David W. Fleming 2000, 69–70). Thus, some wedding of market research, modern management practices and CGM seemed imperative to movement leaders. Many CGM supporters felt that without church marketing practices, efficient strategic planning would be impossible. Thus, churches that supported the CGM model endeavored to apply ideas derived from market research to further church growth (David W. Fleming 2000, 11).

However, despite this, the necessity of developing strategic plans for church growth was considered so urgent that, if anything, the practice of strategic marketing took on a much more global outlook as the decades wore on. Initiatives such as AD 2000 and Beyond, the spiritual mapping movement that derived from AD 2000 and Beyond, as well as The Business as Mission movement all seem to have derived many of their ideas from the application of the practices of strategic marketing. According to Fleming, strategic marketing in churches is characterized by three shared values, common to almost all models. Most plans first try to delineate what flaws may exist within the organization, as well as organizational strong points. An analysis of the targeted locale is considered the second key point. Finally, strategic church marketers are encouraged to tailor specific marketing plans to specific market niches (David W. Fleming 2000, 83–85).

Virtually all church growth plans called for the use of demographics, and psychographics was also a fairly ubiquitous marketing tool (David W. Fleming 2000, 95, 102). Various reasons were given for the need for these new services. Ministries wanted to know how to tailor their worship style, resource allocation, and ministry services to the need of local religious consumers. Others simply wanted to have a better understanding of who their best likely target audience was. In addition to demographic and psychographic segmentation, geographic segmentation of targeted consumers was also employed (David W. Fleming 2000, 95–102). While psychographic profiling seems to have been quite popular, it seems to have particularly appealed to megachurches like Saddleback and Willow Creek (David W. Fleming 2000, 113–114), where new marketing innovations were constantly needed to both retain and increase membership.

The consumer model under which church marketing operated raised the ire of many critics outside the CGM (see for instance, Kenneson and Street, 2003 passim) and even some of those within the CGM questioned the increasing emphasis on marketing practice within church growth circles. For these concerned church growth advocates, the "association with selling and promotion" that surrounded church marketing made it an inappropriate tool for promoting church growth (David W. Fleming 2000, 109–110). As Fleming points out, however, whether church growth proponents admit to using church marketing principles is irrelevant. Advocates of church growth can call their practices whatever they want, but practically speaking, the CGM has relied extensively on "basic marketing principles and practices to improve the church's overall effectiveness in ministry" (David W. Fleming 2000, 110). Nor are such marketing practices entirely absent even from those Christian leaders and organizations most critical of Christian consumerism, a point that could be made today—with a great degree of truth—about the self-righteousness of some anti-capitalist advocates of the Emergent Church.

By the beginning of the 21st century, church growth thinkers and missiologists were beginning to consider new organizational paradigms for dealing with church outreach and evangelism. Churches were increasingly interested in retention. The focus on church health that crystallized in this period is reflective of these trends. A new emphasis was put on seeing organizations as "complex, living systems which often respond in counter-intuitive ways to growth interventions" (McMahan 1998, ii). But to implement that organizational strategy, church consultants—indeed Protestantism writ large—needed to adopt new terminology and strategies for dealing with and managing change. The remaining portion of this book examines how evangelicalism attempted to rise to this challenge and the strange church that resulted from it.

3

Cybernetics, Computers and Christ

How Systems Theory Helped Found the Modern Religious Right

This chapter explores the rise of various strains of systems theory, especially living systems theory, as dominant paradigms by which churches began to organize themselves in the latter part of the 20th century. The use of systems theory, along with the development of network models of doing church, reflected a new form of church in which the cyborg sciences played an increasing role in social control. This chapter explores the rise of general systems theory and computer science within Protestantism, thus lying the ground for Chapter 4's discussion of the growth of network models of Protestantism. This chapter argues, and subsequent chapters will demonstrate, that the insights of systems theory and the other cyborg sciences, particularly their insights on how to properly structure organizational networks, were eagerly and efficiently adopted by the Christian Right. Moreover, they play an important role in emergent, and "missional" congregations as well.

General Systems Theory: Overview

There are some disagreements about how to define systems, but a good definition of a system would be "a set of relationships between discrete things which together form some kind of coherent pattern and/or whole that is capable of maintaining itself through time" (Hammond 1997, 36). In General Systems Theory, this denotes a desire to understand the interconnections between systems and their environments (Hammond 1997, 19–20). Those unfamiliar with the intricacies of systems theory will often be amazed by the tremendous interdisciplinary scope of systems theory. Systems thinkers came from professional backgrounds as diverse as philosophy, sociology, biology, and physics, among numerous other fields (Skyttner 2001, 103). Despite the complex, interdisciplinary origins of systems theory, certain ideas are common throughout systems theorizing. All systems theory approaches arose as problem solving solutions to the issues faced by modern, industrial society (Hammond 1997, 19). This is true of religious approaches to systems theory as well, which have often sought to engage in the same sort of planned social change that characterized other forms of systems theory. The interdisciplinary nature of systems theory was necessitated by the increasingly complex interrelationships that characterized problem-solving in advanced industrial economies. As Hammond points out, the interdisciplinary nature of systems theory led the field to eclectically apply ideas from a number of different professional backgrounds to the solution of social and technological problems. Concepts from engineering, for instance, might be applied to sociology, while biological concepts often were fed back into engineering itself (Hammond 1997, 19).

Arguably the oldest world text that exhibits elements of a systems approach is the *I Ching*. Certain Pre-Socratic Western thinkers, notably Heraclitus, have in recent times been associated with contemporary systems approaches. Debra Hammond argues that there is some truth to this association. Whereas, the Pre-Socratics tended to emphasize "systemic conceptions with focus on interrelationships and dynamic processes," much of the Western tradition following the Pre-Socratics placed an emphasis on "systematic conceptions which are more concerned with order." The debate between those who focused on dynamism in systems and those who preferred order provides a crucial ideological dividing line in debates over systems theory (Hammond 1997, 12).

The more technocratic elements of systems theory, including its tendency towards supporting the idea of social planning and the "planned state," may have their origins in Plato's *Republic*, as well as Aristole's *Politics*. As Hammond notes, Michael Ghiselin has argued that both works created a "organismic conception of society" which has influenced how many intellectual disciplines, notably sociology, have approached both social analysis and systems theory (Hammond 1997, 12–13). More recent philosophical contributors to systems theory range from positivism and pragmatism to the works of Hegelian thinkers and philosopher Alfred North Whitehead (Hammond 1997, 13).

Two thinkers, Ludwig Von Bertalanffy and Norbert Wiener, played the biggest role in the modern acceptance of systems theory. Born in the Austrian-Hungarian Empire to a Hungarian noble family, Ludwig Von Bertalanffy was a student at the University of Innsbruck and later the University of Vienna. At the latter institution Von Bertalanffy ran across the thinking of the Vienna Circle. Von Bertalanffy was disturbed by the Vienna Circle's unwillingness to consider questions of value when conducting scientific analysis (Hammond 1997, 120). By the mid–1920s, von Bertalanffy had laid out his argument that organisms could best be viewed through a systems perspective. Most of von Bertalanffy's subsequent work elaborated on the huge intellectual consequences of this approach (Hammond 1997, 121).

Bertalanffy's grounded his systems theorizing in his belief that life was best understood through such common biological phenomena as "wholeness, organization and regulation" (Hammond 1997, 125). Bertalanffy was fascinated with organic life's dynamism and its tendency to organize around hierarchical patterns (Hammond 1997, 125). Bertalanffy's focus on the hierarchical nature of systems became a fundamental conviction of systems theory, which saw hierarchy as a universal organizing principle that extended from "inorganic nature" to organic and social life (Skyttner 2001, 60). Because complex systems tend to organize hierarchically, they also have an equally strong tendency to develop "control hierarchies." These control hierarchies become "structurally simpler the higher up the hierarchy one goes. Higher levels of the organization are responsible for regulating the 'behaviour of subsystems.'" Thus, in most complex systems, or hierarchies of systems, "less complex systems control more complex ones" (Skyttner 2001, 60). Bertalanffy's significant influence on attempts to develop efficient control mechanisms for system organization played an important role in the adoption of systems approaches by the Protestant establishment. Put quite simply, mainline Protestants and the Christian Right both desired to promote the most efficient forms of social organization possible within their movements. Religious ideologies which could not organize themselves effectively were likely to die out, and the advances that Bertalanffy and subsequent systems thinkers offered in organizational thinking provided a major impetus for the adoption of their model.

Knowing what control mechanisms work within a systems process is key if one wishes to predict how a rational system will behave. Western science's research into such automatic control systems predates the birth of Christ, but did not reach its height until the 1948 publication of Norbert Wiener's *Cybernetics: or Control and Communication in the Animal and the Machine* (Skyttner 2001, 69). Wiener, an American scientist working for MIT, developed the field of cybernetics. Wiener's approach elaborated principles governing engineering and organic life that could be applied to all systems (Skyttner 2001, 70). Cybernetics's concept of organismic biological thinking differed from Bertalanffy's in its willingness to elaborate on, rather than replace, "reductionist and mechanistic" scientific thinking. Cybernetics sought to apply ideas of "feedback, communication and control" across multiple types of systems (Hammond 1997, 67).

Cybernetics popularization of the concept of feedback is its most important contribution to the discourse surrounding systems theory. This is because feedback is a characteristic of many "natural and engineered systems" (Karl Johan Astrom 2008, 2),[1] allowing for such systems to "compensate for unexpected disturbances" (Skyttner 2001, 75). Cybernetics concerned itself with ideas of "control and communication." The goal of a cybernetic system was to maintain equilibrium, or "the maintenance of order." The equivalent of this idea in living systems was "homeostasis." Cybernetics central overriding concern, therefore, was maintaining stability within various types of systems. The advantage of well-run cybernetic control systems was that while expending only a small amount of energy, they were highly efficient. Cybernetic systems existed primarily to process information, rather than transform energy, allowing for this level of efficiency (Skyttner 2001, 71).

What made cybernetics controversial, however, was its theory of information. The intricacies of cybernetics' approach to information theory are beyond the purview of this text. However, what is crucial to understand is that cybernetics, as a field, was centrally concerned with the "science of messages." For Wiener and his colleagues, messages represented the central organizational pattern in both "animals and complex machinery." What made this concept troubling to many of Wiener's contemporaries was that as far as cybernetics was concerned, there was no difference between organic life and machines in the study of communication. The same principles that governed the organization of information in inorganic systems governed animal life as well (Hammond 1997, 73).

Although general systems theory (GST) and cybernetics are typically seen as identical, Bertalanffy contended there were important variances between the two approaches. The cybernetics approach, Bertalanffy charged, was narrower than that of GST, as it focused exclusively on feedback as the prime regulation mechanism for systems. Bertalanffy saw such an approach as self-limiting, as it ignored the potential of systems to be self-correcting, without need of input from external factors. Bertalanffy also was troubled by what he saw as the mechanistic tendencies of cybernetics. Cybernetics tended to emphasize the importance of keeping systems in equilibrium states, whereas GST put more emphasis on "nonequilibrium states" of systems organization. The cybernetic model, according to Bertalanffy, led to organisms responding reactively to their environment; GST, by contrast, saw the organism "as fundamentally active" (Hammond 1997, 143).

As a form of social control, cybernetics lends itself more easily to abuse than GST or the so-called "servomechanism" strand of feedback thought that has its roots in control engineering. The latter school has its closest affinities with industry and economics and its implications are most fully worked out in the research of Jay Forrester, whose investigations into industrial and urban dynamics led him to play a major role in the controversial Club of

Rome publication, *The Limits to Growth* (1972), a work of some relevance to the rise of systems theory in mainline Protestantism. However, as we shall see, even the servomechanistic approach's primary use is to judge between possible policy interventions into certain targeted systems (Hammond 1997, 74–80).

Living systems theory and systems thinking in ecology have had a particularly strong influence on the rise of systems theory among Protestants and thus also deserve some mention. A systems approach to ecology emerged during the beginning of the 20th century. As a field, ecology has had strong "normative" tendencies. Traditionally, ecological approaches to the environment have led either to positions that endorse the "presumed inherent balance of nature" or, alternately, have called for "a more managerial, interventionist view" (Hammond 1997, 83). The field of systems ecology, pioneered by Eugene and Howard Odum, produced some of the earliest approaches to systems theorizing in religious environments. Systems ecology developed ideas from Arthur Tansley's (1871–1955) ecosystem model and aligned them with emerging concepts in cybernetics. The systems ecology approach would gain a strong reputation for mechanistic and interventionist management practices in the coming decades; its economic conception of ecological principles led to accusations that systems ecology was little more than a tool of market capitalism (Hammond 1997, 86–87).

Living Systems Theory, as its connections with the organic and missional movements shows, also has potentially conservative applications. LST was founded by James Grier Miller (1916–2002). Unlike Bertalanffy, Miller did not think the distinction between GST and cybernetics was meaningful (Hammond 1997, 232–233). Miller integrated research from numerous fields into a comprehensive systems model that could encompass various aspects of human behavior as well as that of every living system. The principles Miller derived from this analysis would eventually evolve into the 20 subsystems of LST (Hammond 1997, 219). The LST model, simplified, contends that all living systems will have certain characteristics, whatever the system's "size, origin, and complexity." These common markers of all systems result from the fact that nature needs to "enhance and conserve order over time in a universe governed by uniform laws" (Skyttner 2001, 110).

Sociologically, the most contentious issue that Miller's variation on systems theory brings up is the question of the "decider," the control and coordinating node of the system which "form[s] the intentions of the system and send[s] out signals that control and coordinate the whole system" (Miller and Miller 1992, 229; Hammond 1997, 235). Obviously, when dealing with more advanced forms of organization, such as a society or a supranational system, who represents the "decider" is a question of major political, and not just scientific importance. Miller was criticized for his explanations of volition, since certain organizational systems that Miller described—the ecosystem, for instance—did not have a decider. Miller counterargued, in turn, that decision making was "diffuse" in such systems (Miller 1965a, 229; Hamond 1997, 236).

Miller also developed a model for theorizing power within systems models. For Miller, the control function of power was exhibited through the ability of a "'master' system" to "'influence in a specific direction the decision of a 'slave' system at the same or another level.'" (Miller 1965a, 229; Hammond 1997, 236). The systems able to acquire the most information will be those most likely to develop control over other systems within their environment. While at some points Miller contends that all types of systems have some degree of autonomy, he occasionally has contradicted this point (Hammond 1997, 238). Such questions about the use and extent of power within a systems model reoccur time and time again during the rise of systems theory in the Christian Right. Moreover, Miller's conflicted thinking on the degree of centralization necessary for the effective maintenance of effective systems became a frequent matter of debate in church growth and evangelical leadership circles during the latter part of the 20th century.[2] Such debates play a central policy role in evangelicalism today, as evangelical and mainline variations of systems theory all try to map out a new way of "doing" church in what they see as a "post–Christian" culture.

The Rise of the Systems-Based Church: Systems Theory Enters the Mainline

By the mid–1950s, systems theory and cybernetics played a prominent role in Western intellectual life. Intellectually, systems thinking coalesced in 1954 around the formation of the Society of General Systems Theory (later known as the Society for General Systems Research and today known as the International Society for the System Sciences, with Bertalanffy, Kenneth Boulding [1910–1993], Anatol Rapaport [1911–2007] and Ralph W. Gerard [1900–1974] as the initial main members [Christopher Scott Queen 1986, 43; "Society for General Systems" 2017]). The Massachusetts Institute of Technology proved to be a particularly important early adopter of systems theory. It developed a number of advanced computers to deal with pressing problems in areas like urban planning and global economics. Led by Jay Forrester, who would later go on to do the "'systems dynamics' modeling" for the Club of Rome project, M.I.T.'s efforts led to important developments in both "pure and applied research" (Queen 1986, 43–44).

Systems theory's adoption by mainline Protestantism occurred quickly and was centered initially in Cambridge, Massachusetts. The advancements in cybernetics and systems dynamics at M.I.T promoted a great deal of cross-disciplinary dialogue; this dialogue soon extended not only into religious studies generally, but into religion itself. The activism of Ralph Wendell Burhoe (1911–1997), who led the American Academy of Arts and Science (also in Cambridge) further contributed to the spread of the new cybernetics-based approach to church. Talcott Parsons' (1902–1979) influence on systems thinking in sociology meanwhile led to innovative, cybernetics-based approaches to religion from Harvard students Clifford Geertz (1926–2006) and Robert Bellah (1927–2013) (Queen 1986, 49).

Burhoe's founding of the Institute on Religion in an Age of Science (IRAS) proved especially foundational to the rise of system thinking in mainline Protestant churches. At the 1954 Star Island meeting, held off the shore of New Hampshire, a number of influential church leaders, theologians, and scientists gathered to discuss the role of religion in an increasingly secular era. Throughout the late fifties and early sixties, IRAS promoted itself through various venues, such as its annual Star Island conferences, symposiums, and its promotion of dialogue between scientists and religion scholars at the Boston University School of Theology. Most significant to the rise of systems theory, however, was the Institute's forming of *Zygon: Journal of Religion and Science*, in 1966. *Zygon* was characterized by a strong systems emphasis under Burhoe's leadership. Burhoe's own attempt to form a "scientific theology" was itself one of the most systematic early attempts to approach religious studies via systems theory (Queen 1986, 51–52).

By the late 1960s, Robert Bellah had advanced the use of cybernetic language as a tool for scientifically studying religion. Clifford Geertz, an anthropologist, had meanwhile used a theory of symbolic systems as a tool for interpreting religion. Expanding on this point, in Bellah's "Religious Evolution" and "The Sociology of Religion," Bellah interpreted religion as a "control system" which fused "'meaning and motivation'" (Bellah 1970, 6, 9–10; Queen 1986, 14). Bellah's essay "The Sociology of Religion" represented the first direct proposal to use systems theory as an academic tool to research the field of religion. Bellah framed his cybernetic view of religion as being constructed around "'action systems" composed of both "genetic and cultural information." Religion's role was to construct a bridge between meaning and motivation (Bellah 10, Queen 1986, 14). Bellah's cybernetic theory of religion had been influenced by sociologist Talcott Parsons, whose own thinking on systems was reflective of the strong interdisciplinary tendencies present in mid–20th century academia (Queen 1986, 14–15).

Simultaneous with the development of anthropological and theological approaches to appropriating systems theory for the field of religious studies, systems theorists themselves began examining possible means and models for exploring religious phenomena. For instance, Ervin Laszlo (1932–), a systems theorist who played a crucial role in advancing systems theory concepts in the religious community, was proposing systems-based interpretations of religious phenomena as early as 1969 (Queen 1986, 56). Even more interesting and telling was the work of ecologist Howard T. Odum, in his book *Environment, Power and Society*, published in 1971 (Queen 1986, 56, Chernayoka 2013, 14), which combined the study of energetics with that of belief systems (Chernayoka 2013, 14).

All these early thinkers were important innovators, whose work set the stage for the application of systems theory to the Protestant church. However, perhaps even more important to the growth of systems theory in Protestantism were the cultural debates surrounding the 1972 Club of Rome Study, *Limits to Growth*. The Club of Rome study not only provided religious leaders with new models for operating churches, but also gave these leaders new questions to ask themselves about how religious organizations could best be organized, and more importantly, sustained. Through the seemingly unrelated discussion about ecology and population growth conducted in the wake of *Limits to Growth*, religious leaders would get some of their first insights into a new, systems-oriented ecological conceptualization of church growth and development. The implications for Protestantism would be profound.

Limits to Growth: The Backstory to the Club of Rome Debate

It should surprise no one that the United States was the center of the church growth movement. From its beginnings, the United States has tended to promote pro-growth ideas in many areas of society. This pro-growth tendency in American culture is a result of the United States' unique history. The nation started off as an agrarian colony of a great industrial power and transformed itself into an urbanized, industrialized society that encompassed greater and greater land and power. Significantly, pro-growth ideology in the United States peaked during the mid–20th century, coinciding with both the foundation of the CGM as a formal movement and the rise of "unprecedented material prosperity" in the United States (see Nielsen 1997, Abstract).

One of the consequences of the United States' pro-growth outlook is that it has tended to take a dim view of Malthusian concepts. Thomas Malthus's *Essay on The Principle of Population* (1798) critiqued the rationalist utopianism of the Enlightenment, contending that in the wake of unchecked population growth, a "geometric" rise in population would result, one that could not be compensated for by the arithmetic rise of food production. Although Malthusian ideology argued that long-term increases in living standards were impossible and unsustainable, this idea appealed neither to the Founding Fathers nor to most early Americans, who found such Malthusian concepts absurd in a resource-blessed United States (Nielsen 1997, 16). Americans came to see Malthusian concepts as expressions of European decadence; the institutionalization of democratic values into the American governmental system, according to this belief, insulated the United States from the consequences of Malthusian ideas (Nielsen 1997, 17). Moreover, many early American social reformers presumed that pro-growth thinking was the cure to social ills (Nielsen 1997, 20).

Americans' concept of progress assumed a certain instrumental logic when viewing nature. America's embrace of progress prioritized "human control over nature" (Nielsen 1997, 26–27). The increasing abundance brought forth by technological progress encouraged Americans to believe that there were no limits to growth. No matter how much Americans had, they could always get more. Prior to World War II, even when there were calls for better resource use and conservation, these calls occurred under the shared American cultural belief in the permeance of material abundance (Nielsen 1997, 26–27).

These beliefs about the nature of growth profoundly shaped how Americans, and particularly American churches, reacted to the "limits to growth" debate the Club of Rome helped initiate in the early 1970s. In the 1950s, as the foundations for the "limits to growth" debate were being laid by economists, systems thinkers, and ecologists, most Americans paid little heed to the reality of economic limits. Even though some prominent American thinkers, such as the conservationist Samuel Ordway, had pointed out the likelihood that there were limits to growth (Nielsen 1997, 131–132), few Americans subscribed to this "long view" approach to resource conservation. Most Americans deferred the prospect of environmental conservation and strategic management of resources to a later time, since few Americans took anti-growth thinking seriously (Nielsen 1997, 145). As Frederick Nielsen points out, an even more fundamental problem by the end of the 1950s was that pro-growth thinking had become crucial to America's self-understanding. As a metaphor, the "'principle of Growth'" reinforced Americans' beliefs in their own national and cultural strength (Nielsen 1997, 148).

One of the major catalyzing agents for the spread of "limits to growth" ideology in the United States was the publication of Rachel Carson's (1907–1964) *Silent Spring* (1962). Carson warned that the combined threat of nuclear war and environmental degradation posed deadly perils to the United States (Nielsen 1997, 162). By drawing parallels between nuclear fallout and the use of chemical pesticides, Carson increased awareness of the interconnectedness between human beings and their environment. Her book also gave many Americans a new economics of scale in understanding the environment, helping Americans to understand the global nature of the environmental problems they faced (Eardley-Pryor 2014, 114–115).

The activism of environmentalists, ecologists, and pro-ecology advocates such as Carson dovetailed with a rise in concerns about overpopulation. Obviously, overpopulation plays a central role in Malthusian economics. Malthus's belief in the concept of "limits to growth," had been anticipated by the leading voice of classical economics, Adam Smith (1723–1790) and was shared by numerous 19th century classical economists, notably David Ricardo (1772–1823) and John Stuart Mill (1806–1873). Classical economists felt that population growth contributed to the exploitation of less fertile agricultural resources and led to "diminishing returns." Moreover, population growth contributed to the depreciation of wages due to the surplus supply of potential workers it gave employers (Hoff 2006, 3–4).

In the 20th century, the limits-to-growth perspective espoused by "Neo-Malthusians" faced internal challenges, brought about by the fact that its model of population growth was overly crude. The ecological movement, however, provided powerful new arguments in favor of Neo-Malthusianism, because it offered a more "holistic critique of the ecological footprint left by humans," particularly human patterns of consumption (Hoff 2006, 13). Faced with new neo-Malthusian arguments for population regulation and control, the American government, along with governments worldwide, faced the choice of how to instrumentalize this policy on a global scale. Historically, in the United States, there has been considerable ambivalence about the state's capacity to manipulate demographic trends. Although the United States does not have the explicit "population polic[ies]" that characterize parts of Europe, it has shown itself willing to use public policy to manipulate "demographic variables" of population growth and decline (Hoff 2006, 9). This same ambivalence, in the wake of the Club of Rome's push towards "limits to growth," would be reflected in both the church growth movement and its cousin church health movement's approach to the managerial instrumentalization of demographic methods by religious denominations, churches, pastors, church growth consultants, and other religious professionals. As we will see in our discussion of the church health movement, especially Christian Schwarz's Natural Church Development (NCD) model, this debate typically is reflected in debates surrounding whether qualitative or quantitative variables reflect the best tools of demographic manipulation (Hoff 2006, 9).

In the initial wake of the New Deal, the desire for an ideal population policy was modeled on two main concepts, "'reform eugenics' and a new 'social demography.'" The first concept involved distancing eugenics from its draconian and "hereditarian" values, which were wedded to often prejudiced assumptions about "qualitative" differences in population groups.

The new practice of social demography, ostensibly eschewing the eugenics practices of the past, marketed itself as a new potential vehicle for social reform (Hoff 2006, 42). Population policy, as interpreted through the lens of the welfare state, reflected a desire on the part of many Western nations to directly influence population trends (Hoff 2006, 42). With the simultaneous rise of the CGM and "limits to growth" discourse, social demography, if not reform eugenics, would increasingly take on this role within the evangelical church, dictating what kinds of population the church marketed to, and what populations were qualitatively preferred over others. Indeed, even the missional and emergent churches, with their emphasis on converting cultural leaders, reflect this trend; their evangelization strategy reflects a kind of "spiritual eugenics" in which the church's desire for qualitatively superior populations encourages churches to sacrifice some growth for quality.

By the 1950s, the main context for the debate over population policy was the population explosion in the developed world, which gave new life to Neo-Malthusianism (Hoff 2006, 112). However, this debate, much like the debate between the church health and church growth movements, came down to qualitative considerations. Just as important to the triumph of "limits to growth" thinking as its alarmist Neo-Malthusianism was the fear the movement expressed that population growth resulted in qualitative reductions to the standard of American living. The problem Americans faced, from this standpoint, was not simply that unlimited growth created scarcity, but that it led to overpopulation, reduced "wilderness conservation" and made Americans more conformist (Hoff 2006, 170). Though Americans wished to spread their standard of living to other countries, initial advocates of the "limits to growth" position, such as Fairfield Osborn and William Vogt, contended the spread of such standards was impossible, barring limitations on population growth (Nielsen 1997, 167–168).[3] By the mid-1960s, with the rise of the environmentalist movement, demographers, scientists, and economists were no longer simply concerned with the qualitative problems caused by population growth but had become worried that population growth reflected a major threat to the global ecosystem itself (Hoff 2006, 265). In response, a more "fundamentalist" version of "limits to growth" discourse appeared in the late 1960s, under the rubric of "zero population growth" (ZPG). An inherently malleable term, depending on the context, ZPG might imply the "immediate cessation of population growth," or alternately simply moving population growth to a replacement birth rate (Hoff 2006, 290). In any case, the message was stark. Without ZPG, the Earth's environmental outlook appeared bleak.

Two of the most ardent advocates of population control were Garrett Hardin (1915–2003) and Paul R. Ehrlich (1932–), whose writings influenced both the interpretation and reception of the Club of Rome's "Limits to Growth" model. Hardin's 1968 essay "The Tragedy of the Commons" set the tone for much of the policy debate surrounding growth during this period. Hardin believed that only a "new morality" would effectively solve the world's population problem. Hardin's "Tragedy of the Commons" idea held that when land or any other resources are held in common, each individual has an incentive to work the land as hard as he possibly can, since there is no benefit in conserving territory or resources that are held in common. Moreover, everyone else is operating under this assumption (Hoff 2006, 297). As a result, with everyone motivated to exploit the system, the whole system collapses. Extrapolating from this point, Hardin argued that non-coercive population controls were insufficient to limit growth. People must therefore be limited in their "'freedom to breed'" and thus Hardin argued for coercive population restrictions to family size. Moreover, Hardin forthrightly supported a "'lifeboat ethic'" in which the rich nations no longer gave aid to poorer nations, particularly unless they had accepted limits to population growth (Hardin 1974, 561–568; Hoff 2006, 297). As Hoff notes, according to Hardin, "some people need to be thrown off the lifeboat for the majority to survive" (Hoff 2006, 297).

Hardin's stark form of "limits to growth" thinking was mirrored in the writings of biologist Paul Ehrlich, whose book *The Population Bomb* (1968) helped turn the American population against growth in the years immediately preceding the publication of the Club of Rome's *Limits to Growth* study. *The Population Bomb* sold three million copies within 10 years of its publication, its sales eventually eclipsing all other environmental and conservation books (Nielsen 1997, 170). Although in many ways a derivative work, *The Population Bomb* proved significant. Ehrlich, unlike previous American opponents of growth, warned that environmental crisis was imminent, and not some vague projection of a future event. Moreover, Ehrlich focused as much on the problem of overpopulation in the first world as in the developing world and warned readers of the dangers of over-consumption (Nielsen 1997, 171–173). Perhaps even more important to understanding the influence of "limits to growth" thinking on both the Club of Rome and church governance was Ehrlich's suggestion that the federal government develop a federal Department of Population and Environment (DPE), whose mandate was to use whatever power necessary to ensure a reasonable population size (Nielsen 1997, 173). Suggestions such as Ehrlich's led to calls for new forms of governance to deal with environmental issues. It was within the context of the desire to create crisis management techniques for dealing with the environmental impact of "limits to growth" that the Club of Rome promoted its own Systems Analysis based approach to the global environmental crisis (see Jason Churchill 2006, 115–120).

The Club of Rome: Systems Analysis, Ecology and Protestantism Converge

The Club of Rome's approach to solving the ecological crisis was instrumentalist and managerial. As Rosalind Warner notes, this managerial approach to the environment has a long history in Western culture. During the 19th century, an embryonic globalized approach to interpreting the relationship between humans and nature was birthed. This approach's ideological inheritance was fundamentally European (Rosalind Warner 2005, 99). Some of this managerial Western impulse towards nature was a legacy of colonialism. While science's effect on colonial development and ecology was not uniformly negative, critical analysts have contended that at points, this scientific knowledge's main purpose was simply to aid in the exploitation of colonial resources for the home country (Rosalind Warner 2005, 99). Warner contends that this system of governance, which has similarity with what Richard Grove describes as "green imperialism," served as a form of "problem framing" under the aegis of imperial social control. Under this system of social control, environmental problems underwent a process of "rationalization, segmentation and institutionalization" (Rosalind Warner 2005, 98–99).[4]

Within the history of environmental management, the Club of Rome's *Limits to Growth* report represents a major turning point. *The Limits to Growth* report was the first attempt to create a global computer model of the Earth that took into account "human activity as an integral element of the planet system itself." Based on Jay Forrester's work in System Dynamics, *The Limits to Growth* report helped fuel a desire to manage the environment on a planetary scale (Irving Fernando Elichirigoity 1994, iii). This expansive desire to mold global environmental policy along lines derived from general systems theory and systems analysis would be promoted directly in the World Council of Churches (WCC), while the "limits to growth" discourse it promoted received considerable attention among evangelicals. This popularization of systems-based approaches to congregational problem solving among evangelicals and mainline Protestants, though not solely a result of the Club of Rome (COR) "limits to growth" report, played an important influence in raising the profile of GST and its various sub-branches among Protestant Christians.

Historian Jason Churchill contends that the COR's success at mobilizing support for its cause is largely attributable to Rachel Carson's influential writings, as well as the birth of the modern pro-ecology movement (Churchill 2006, 34). Crucial to Carson's importance in helping COR achieve its objectives was her promotion of environmental "interconnectedness." Carson's writing emphasized the "reciprocal relationship between humanity and the physical environment" (Churchill 2006, 34), a message that COR subsequently promoted in their own activism. Churchill notes that by 1972, when the first COR report emerged, the ecological movement had accepted the concept of interconnectedness (Churchill 2006, 34–38). Subsequently, the concept would be adopted by numerous other fields and ideological movements, including both mainline Protestantism and evangelicalism.

The guiding voice of COR was its co-founder Aurelio Peccei (1908–1984). Initially working for Fiat, Peccei's impressive contacts and anti-fascist leanings allowed him to become a major leader in the rebuilding of Italy's post–War economy (Churchill 2006, 12–13; Moll 1991, 50–51). Peccei expressed concern with the growing wealth inequities between North and South. He believed that such inequities could not be controlled unless growth limits were imposed. However, though Peccei's philosophy tended toward Malthusianism, scholar Peter Moll warns against reading his thinking as being entirely derived from Malthus (Moll 1991, 54).[5] By the mid-1960s, Peccei believed that advances in computerization and the information sciences threatened to fundamentally disrupt the world to a degree unseen even during the first industrial revolution (Churchill 2006, 14). Peccei termed the numerous sociocultural problems facing humanity at the dawn of the second industrial revolution as the "World Problematique" (Churchill 2006, 16). Early discussions among COR leaders divided over whether comprehensive and holistic strategies to solving the Problematique were truly viable. Along with his ally Alexander King (1909–2007), Peccei pushed strongly for holistic approaches to global problem solving, contending that only such a comprehensive approach could be used when dealing with such wide-ranging social problems (Churchill 2006, 54–57). According to Churchill, it was this need for a holistic approach to problem solving that led to the use of systems analysis within the "limits to growth" movement (Churchill 2006, iii). In the wake of its success with Limits to Growth, COR emerged as a major supporter of utilizing systems analysis in policy development (Churchill 2006, 107).

Some of the earliest attempts to effectively utilize systems theory's insights occurred at the United States Department of Defense and the RAND corporation in the 1950s and 1960s. The influence of systems analysis spread into business and industry by the early 1960s. In the search for a theory that could unite multiple disciplines, general systems theory (GST) was developed. For early GST promoters, such as Society for General Systems Research (SGSR) members, GST provided a flexible approach to relating parts to systems. It also did a good job highlighting the interconnectedness between systems and the environments that surrounded them (Eardly-Pryor 2014, 69, Skyttner 2001, 36). GST approached the scientific problems it dealt with from a different standpoint than traditional science. Traditional science thrived on reductionism, in which elements of the natural world were atomized into their "smallest components." This tendency towards atomization not only characterized how the objects of study were studied, both how the fields of study were divided. Because of the atomistic tendencies of traditional science, science had become highly compartmentalized and overly specialized by the mid–20th century. Promoters of GST, by contrast, wished to develop "generalized yet applicable frameworks" for studying widely differing fields of thought (Eardly-Pryor 2014, 69–70). The SGSR's ability to cut across various disciplines allowed it to engage in valuable dialogue between scholars from widely ranging fields, and likely was responsible for a great deal of the appeal of GST (Eardly-Pryor 2014, 70–71).

The success of systems scientists' approach to problem-solving led to widespread interest in utilizing "systems-based techniques" in the management of "social and technological systems" (Eardly-Pryor 2014, 72–73). The widespread adoption of digital computers quickened the spread of systems-based thinking. With the increasing prevalence of systems-based solutions to the problems of military defense, what Roger Eardly Pryor has termed a "systems discourse" came to shape Cold War culture. This discourse envisioned everything from battlefields, the world, and human societies as existing within "multilayered, closed systems" which could be manipulated and regulated by the proper application of various techniques derived from systems approaches (Eardly-Pryor 2014, 73–74).

From the beginning of the cybernetics movement, cyberneticists and their fellow travelers in other systems-based approaches had realized the revolutionary possibilities for social control that cybernetics presented. Wiener and his fellow cyberneticists contended that the same physical laws that governed the laws of physics and natural systems, were universally applicable, including in "human and mechanized environments." Improved and efficient organizations could be developed along cybernetic lines, as cyberneticists taught management new and improved techniques for dealing with "control and communication" in the business environment (Churchill 2006, 110). Norbert Wiener, founder of the cybernetics approach, noted that whether looking at biology or engineering, the "organizational and regulative processes" implemented by these approaches were largely governed by feedback concepts (Churchill 2006, 110–111). The efficient regulation of positive and negative feedback in global modeling became a key aspect of COR's approach to systems analysis (Churchill 2006, 110–111). However, systems analysis's goals were more expansive than cybernetics, as the field hoped to unify fields ranging from biology and economics, to ecology and policy research (Churchill 2006, 111).

Initial applications of GST, as forwarded by von Bertalanffy and Kenneth E. Boulding, limited themselves to inquiring into "specific aspects within scientific fields." Nonetheless, the Golden Fleece which all systems techniques wanted to acquire was a general "system of systems theory." Boulding, for one, was skeptical of both the possibility and desirability of applying such "system of systems" approaches to the human world. Boulding believed that human personality and organization involved systems phenomena whose complexity went well beyond the ability of science to successfully explore (Churchill 2006, 113–114). As a deeply religious Quaker (Hammond 1997, 23), Boulding also likely had moral objections to overly mechanistic applications of GST. Von Bertalanffy and Boulding's systems perspective towards science was motivated by both a scientific and moral concern at the mechanistic worldview adopted by the sciences from the Industrial Revolution to the beginning of World War II, and which received perhaps its fullest embodiment in Taylorism. Von Bertalanffy hoped that when perfected, GST would help lead the sciences into a more transdisciplinary, holistic, and "organismic" worldview, rather than the mechanistic worldview that he blamed for many of society's ills (Churchill 2006, 112–113).

Forrester's systems analysis perspective sought to advance "a theory of everything that went beyond the physical world" by developing a model of the basic principles regulating all systems. His approach differentiated itself from other systems perspectives by how it distinguished between open and closed systems (Churchill 2006, 116–117). Since Forrester's approach to feedback systems is directly reflected in Schwarz's approach to NCD, it is vital to see its importance in shaping COR policy. Forrester's definition of a feedback system was "one in which an action is influenced by the consequences of previous action." A closed system was a system in which "inputs and outputs interacted with each other." Two phenomena were particularly important in closed systems: negative and positive feedback loops. Within a closed system, these feedback loops outputs could subsequently change into inputs, thus highlighting the fact that prior actions could shape future ones. Open systems, which encompass many forms of physical systems, had outputs who enacted no influence on the initial inputs into the system. Open systems represent "non-historical systems" since the future results of outputs do not rely "upon past actions to affect the future outcomes" (Churchill 2006, 116–117).

Forrester noted that positive feedback loops grew exponentially until their resource base could no longer support them. Because of this, Forrester warned that positive feedback loops had the capacity to encourage "unstable and unsustainable exponential growth," beyond which a system could not sustain itself. By contrast, negative feedback loops reflected a system attempting to achieve equilibrium against forces aimed at it from outside the system. As a system strived for equilibrium, its efforts led to a more self-sustaining and stable process (Churchill 2006, 117–118). The perspective of systems analysis towards studying global processes had a natural affinity with the COR's approach to the Problematique. King and Peccei believed that the numerous problems facing the world at the height of COR's influence (the late 1960s to mid–1970s) could only be dealt with through a holistic viewpoint. Moreover, Peccei, like many of the founders of GST, decried a mechanistic outlook towards nature. He contended that such mechanistic approaches, not understanding the interrelatedness of human problems, exacerbated global dilemmas. Forrester therefore offered the right systems perspective at the right time for COR (Churchill 2006, 119–120). By 1970, enough support had crystallized in COR for Forrester to apply systems analysis to the Problematique (Moll 1991, 93; Churchill 2006, 122–123).

Eventually a COR-funded MIT study was published as *Limits to Growth* (1972). This study sought to explore the interconnected "global effects of industrialization, rapid population growth, widespread malnutrition, depletion of nonrenewable resources, and a deteriorating environment" (Nielsen 1997, 232). Because of the influence of Forrester and COR, as well as their own systems analysis perspective, the heads of the project, Dennis and Donella Meadows, approached these problems holistically, using some of the most advanced computer modeling of the time (Nielsen 1997, 232). The results of the study suggested that disaster threatened the industrial world. Given current trends in demographics, industrial output and consumption, pollution, agricultural production, and resource expenditure, the unsustainable rate of growth COR foresaw would cataclysmically end within a period sometime within 100 years of the publication of *Limits to Growth* (Nielsen 1997, 232–233). The MIT team proposed that the global economy immediately transition from a growth-based model towards a steady state, equilibrium model (Nielsen 1997, 232–233; Curtis 2011).

The political implications of the report, one of the most widely discussed books of the 1970s (see, on this score McCray 2013, 26–39), were immense. Forrester himself, as a pro-global equilibrium advocate, contended that the developing world might be better off with its current level of poverty. According to Forrester's reading, when environmental disaster hit, the developing world might be in a better position to cope with it. Forrester felt that for the sake of the global ecosystem, the developing world must tamper its desire for growth (Eardly-Pryor 2014, 255). The discourse of "limits to growth," along with the Global North's increasing attention towards environmental challenges and America's abandonment of the Bretton-Woods Agreement (which had provided the basis for the "post-war international economic order") led many countries in the developing world to fear that the West's new fascination with global environmental governance was just another means of imposing "no growth" policies on them (Eardly Pryor 2014, 259–261; Steger and Roy 2010, loc. 448).

In November 1971, in the leadup to the publication of *Limits to Growth*, a highly charged debate occurred at the United Nations. Miguel Ozório de Almeida, a Brazilian ambassador, condemned the increasingly strident "limits to growth" approach then apparent in the West. Not surprisingly, Almeida found the alarmist rhetoric of Ehrlich and Barry Commoner deeply troubling. Almeida contended that the no-growth ideology of American environmentalists as increasingly "anti-developmental." Almeida feared that the U.S. sought to impose international constraints on growth. In a later speech, Almeida pushed the nations of the developing world to adopt a sustainable development approach. For Almeida, the Problematique that COR focused on was a product of the industrial world's own making and should be dealt with by the West accordingly (Eardly-Pryor 2014, 236, 269–271). In the wake of heated criticisms of the "limits to growth" movement by leaders and activists in the developing world, a new gospel of sustainable development became the economic order of the day (Eardly-Pryor 2014, 251).

COR activism on behalf of "limits to growth" in the churches was extensive. Indeed, among Protestants, concerns about "limits to growth" preceded the WCC's engagement with COR. In the WCC, concern about humanity's effect on the environment started coming to center stage with the 1968 Conference on Church and Society, which took place in Geneva (Joseph Bush Jr. 1993, 16). Subsequently, a five-year study was commissioned, "The Future of Man and Society in a World of Science-Based Technology." The latter study involved a number of scientists, and discussion surrounding the study related directly to "limits to growth" (Joseph Bush Jr. 1993, 16). Even at the initial conference in Geneva, conference attendees, such as Charles Birch (1918–2009), showed a keen awareness of the key players in the population debate, such as Paul Ehrlich (Joseph Bush Jr. 1993, 155–156).

Birch is one of several crucial figures who paved the way for COR to influence WCC deliberations. Although a member of Ehrlich's ZPG movement, he disagreed with much of its policy, particularly its "life boat" draconian approach to solving population problems in the developing world (Steffes 2008, 354). While Ehrlich supported top-down approaches to limiting population growth, Birch thought a "bottom-up" grassroot approach would work better. Thinking this approach might work better among religious believers, Birch accepted an appointment to the WCC in 1970, where he immediately formed an alliance with Programme Director Paul Albrecht and anthropologist Margaret Mead (1901–1978). Birch credited Mead, an important influence on cybernetics, as herself a major influence on his own thinking, and Birch's own formidable scientific skills also inclined him to accept systems approaches to ecological problem solving (Hammond 1997, 66; Steffes 2008, 356). A major part of the initial agenda for the WCC was to facilitate discussions on the interrelationship between scientific and societal issues, with the goal being to model correct theology and praxis for local churches (Steffes 2008, 356).

Limits to Growth was a crucial point of discussion in the WCC's 1974 conference on Science, Technology for Human Development, held in Bucha-

3. Cybernetics, Computers and Christ 133

rest. Albrecht convinced Jørgen Randers (1945–), a member of the team that had conducted the study (Steffes 2008, 357), to help Birch explain the COR study's conclusions about the environmental problem to conference delegates (Steffes 2008, 356–358). Many of the key organizers within the Programme had been aware of the findings of *Limits to Growth* well before its publication, as Randers had spoken before them in 1970 (Steffes 2008, 357). Moreover, at the WCC's Nemi meeting, Randers had also spoken to delegates. One of the main points Randers made at this conference was that as humanity began to exceed the limits of their ecosystem, endemic social unrest would result. Randers warned the delegates that they faced a series of serious ethical dilemmas as a result of the ecological crisis, a warning later echoed by Jay W. Forrester in a speech before the National Council of Churches's Division of Overseas Ministries (Joseph Bush Jr. 1993, 182; Forrester 1972, 145).

Randers initial presentation at Nemi received mixed responses from the WCC, with some accepting the "limits to growth" argument and others rejecting it. Highlighting a problem that would be faced in the Bucharest conference, C.T. Kurien noted the questionable approach to the developing world of pro-limits advocates (Joseph Bush Jr. 1993, 174). Randers's presentation ended up being the most controversial aspect of the Nemi conference (Joseph Bush Jr. 1993, 182). At the Bucharest conference, when similar resistance was faced, Randers and Birch hit upon the idea of relabeling "limits to growth" into a new catchphrase: "ecological sustainable society." This new catchphrase soon caught on, spreading both the gospel of sustainability and the implicit systems perspectives that gave birth to that gospel, to a global audience (Steffes 2008, 5). Through much of the remainder of the debates at the WCC, the philosophy of "limits to growth" would be on the agenda (Joseph Bush Jr. 1993, passim).

Given the influence of the systems perspectives that motivated the Club of Rome, it is unsurprising that systems theory ended up becoming a major influence on mainline Protestants. Among those mainline Protestants and systems theorists who participated in the "limits to growth" debate, a number became significant influences on mainline Protestant thought. As an editor of *Zygon: The Journal of Religion and Science*, which fellow pro-cybernetics thinker Ralph Burhoe founded, Charles Birch became an influential voice in "science and religion studies" (Steffes 2008, 14–15). Meanwhile, Kenneth Boulding, a prominent Quaker thinker who had been in on the founding of GST, argued for a reformulation of the way traditional economic models were constructed; his system was predicated on the "limits to growth" perspective (Nielsen 1997, 210–211).The bizarre but influential systems theorist Ervin Laszlo, meanwhile, promoted the "limits to growth" movement among a host of religious ideologies, including mainline Protestantism, in his book *Goals for Mankind* (1978), another report to the Club of Rome (Laszlo 1978,

179–186). When the WCC's "Conference on Faith, Science and Future" was held at M.I.T., more than 400 influential thinkers, half of them scientists and many others theologians, participated. The "limits" debate again dominated the debate (Joseph Bush Jr. 1993, 577–578). Ecology, a science heavily informed by systems theory, was the major approach utilized at the conference (Joseph Bush Jr. 1993, 578). Historian Joseph Earl Bush, Jr., notes that the preparatory volume for the MIT Conference underlined the importance of both the Club of Rome and the limits to growth approach in developing the WCC's approach to sustainability (Joseph Bush Jr. 1993, 580–582). Meanwhile, COR supporter Frederic Vester's thinking in bio-cybernetics ended up influencing the development of Christian Schwarz's NCD model, the most influential paradigm within the church health movement (Schwarz 1999, 106, 233–236). Moreover, by playing such an influential role in spreading public consciousness about systems-based perspectives, the COR report and the "limits to growth" debate likely influenced the widespread adoption of various systems-based perspectives among mainline Protestants in the 1970s, such as those promoted by the Alban Institute.

Cybernetics Among the Evangelicals: The Limits to Growth Debate Enters the Embryonic Religious Right

Despite the Christian Right's anti-intellectual reputation, the movement did not lag much behind its mainline counterparts in seeing the potential of various systems perspectives. A 1966 JASA report on an Oxford Conference on "Science and Christian Faith," written by David Moberg (1922–), noted with some alarm the rise of cybernetic thinking (Moberg 1966, 21–23). Moberg, reporting on the thinking of Siegfried Bucholz of Germany, noted what he saw as several problematic aspects of the cybernetic outlook. One of the major problems, as Moberg and Bucholz saw it, was that the cybernetic approach tended to treat human consciousness as simply and solely an emergent quality of the brain. This led, in turn, to treating conscience as merely "the same as a psycho-hygienic control mechanism" (Moberg 1966, 21–23). Cybernetics' focus on "control processes" thus led to a deeply flawed theological anthropology. Some of the participants at the Oxford Conference felt that the feedback concept was more instructive as a metaphor for communication than as a metaphor for human experience writ large, objecting to what they saw as a mechanistic conceptualization of human nature (Moberg 1966, 21–23). Bucholz's theological reflections on the dehumanizing nature of cybernetics (with which Moberg appears to have agreed) reflected legitimate concerns that a number of prominent secular intellectuals raised against applying cybernetic theory too expansively. Such criticisms were rife in the writings of classic mid-century novelist Kurt Vonnegut, as well as in Bernard Wolfe's *Limbo* (1952), a classic American dystopian novel. Whatever the truth of their religious convictions, Bucholz, Moberg and many of the other conference participants clearly noted some of the more problematic aspects of cybernetics, while acknowledging that the theory might have some practical benefits (Moberg 1966, 21–23).

By 1967, writers for JASA were beginning to note the possible implications of cybernetics and system cybernation, particularly in verifying or debunking scientific hypotheses (Manetsch 1967, 77–86). Thomas J. Manetsch, who was familiar with Forrester's work, noted that the increased processing power of computers in the late 1960s was opening up new areas of scientific research, particularly in the social sciences, that had previously been unavailable. Manetsch expressed excitement about the possibilities of computer modeling and simulation. Manetsch believed that one of the most exciting possibilities the new simulation techniques offered up were in applying "control or cybernation" to systems; he explicitly noted that such control processes could be applied to human social life, as well as the physical universe. Manetsch felt simulation modeling of systems offered real possibilities but acknowledged that there were significant limitations. For instance, given the state of computer technology in the late 1960s, Mantesch realized that simulations could at best approximate the real world, nothing more. Moreover, due to the huge number of random factors that influence social systems, he believed that even the most perfect simulation could not exactly emulate the real-world system it simulated (Manetsch 1967, 77–86). Manetsch's essay then offered up an example of how simulations and feedback mechanisms could be utilized to more effectively evangelize, including elaborate modeling of how religious conversion systems operate. Through the model, Manetsch illustrates how increasing the percentage of "communicative believers" in a community in turns leads to an increase in proclamations of religious faith, which in turn alters the conversion rate. In other words, as Manetsch explicitly notes, this is a feedback loop. Moreover, although not directly stated, the implication would seem to be that if conversion techniques are properly implemented, they can lead to a positive feedback loop that allows the church to maximize its growth potential. Manetsch notes that such a model could, with care, be utilized in the real world, and could also yield the church important information on how, for instance, proclamation rates and "maturation delay" affect the speed of religious conversion. Manetsch believed that cybernetic techniques held "promise for increased understanding of the interaction of the Christian faith with the remainder of society" and therefore encouraged Christian academics to begin utilizing these new techniques. The CGM soon took him up on the offer (Manetsch 1967, 77–86).

An early and extremely important influence on the evangelical approach to cybernetics was Donald MacKay (1922–1987) (see Van Leeuwen 1988, 194–203 on MacKay's influence on Christian scientists). Mackay's influence on the relationship between 20th century science and Christianity cannot be overstated (Haas 1992, 55–61). As a research professor at the University of Keele in the United Kingdom, MacKay became an important authority on how brain organization relates to information processing (Haas 1992, 55–61). Mackay's work allowed him to hobnob with some of the finest minds in his field, frequently discussing cybernetics in the process (Haas 1992, 55–61). Mackay pioneered a school of thought, perspectivalism, which argued against Kuyperian theologies which required that there be such things as "Christian physics" or "Christian astronomy." For Mackay and his mentor, Reijer Hooykaas, it was important that "science be 'free,'" and not constrained by self-limiting religious dogma (Haas 1992, 55–61). Mackay, along with other Christian scientists, notably Richard Bube, utilized systems perspectives to help establish perspectivalism, also known as the "levels of explanation" approach, as one of the more robust forms of religion-and-science dialogue (Marvin McDonald 1990, 23–33). Perspectivalism had an enormous impact on how evangelicals approached science, because it allowed many evangelical scientists to avoid what they saw as needless theologizing about the sciences. As Eric Johnson and Stanton Jones note, those Christians who supported perspectivalism felt that combining science—they specifically reference psychology—with theology simply handicaps the "objectivity and integrity of the scientific method" (Johnson and Jones 2000a, 38).

It is difficult to determine how much perspectivalism influenced evangelical church growth proponents' adoption of system theory. The CGM definitely eschews the so-called "nothing buttery" approach to science which creates strict dualisms between the scientific method and biblical "truth." On the other hand, the CGM often appears to equally eschew strictly adhering to the scientific paradigm. However, CGM proponents would surely have been aware of perspectivalism and therefore the proponents of the systems perspective that adhered to the perspectivalist tradition are likely another early influence on the CGM's adoption of the systems perspective.[6]

However, even without the extensive references to cybernetics and systems theory found in JASA, the marks of the "limits to growth" debate, and the systems modeling that spawned it, are particularly evident in the approach evangelicals have taken to ecology and economics and these links become even more clear when one studies the intersection of ecological and economics discourses within the pro-sustainability movement.

According to most accounts, evangelicals first became engaged with the ecological crisis due to the publication of Lynn White Jr.'s "The Historical Roots of the Ecological Crisis" in 1967 (Ball 1997, 2, 63–64). In his essay,

3. Cybernetics, Computers and Christ

White argued that the cause of contemporary environmental problems was the promotion of humanity's dominion over nature by the Christian church. In response, evangelicals began attempting to offer biblical alternatives to this message, usually through what was called "the doctrine of stewardship." Francis Schaeffer's classic *Pollution and the Death of Man* [1970] became the foremost example of this line of reasoning (Larsen 2001, xi). Yet, Schaffer's approach was not the only one evangelicals applied to solving the ecological crisis. James Ball offers a useful typology of the approaches evangelicals took to the ecological debate. A number of evangelicals were concerned with what they saw as the pantheistic or "New Age" roots of the environmentalist movement, a refrain still commonly heard in evangelical circles. Much literature written in this vein was apologetic in nature, which extended into even less alarmist forms of evangelical ecological literature. Because the ecological crisis was a scientific crisis, evangelical scientists also were some of the main commentators on the environmental problems of the day. A third type of discourse centered on the close interaction between ecology and economic policy, leading to an economic debate between "markets-and growth" perspectives and "limits to growth" perspectives. Finally, the "stewardship" principles of Schaeffer and others also vied for dominance (Ball 1997, 61).

Evangelical writing on ecology shared a number of core themes, many of which directly reflected the movement's growing awareness of systems theory. Many evangelicals distanced themselves from the more overtly New Age appropriations of James Lovelock's Gaia theory, a controversial systems theory that advocates that Earth is a "living superorganism" (Ball 1997, 74–76; Skyttner 2001, 132). The key systems theory concept of interdependence was comfortably accepted by evangelicals, as many evangelicals felt the paradigm of interdependence suggests a "relational holism" consistent with biblical teachings (Ball 1997, 86). Evangelical approaches to the ecosystem from the 1970s into well into the 1990s were colored by an underlying assumption that balance—that is homeostasis—is the preferred state of any ecological system. Because of this focus on interdependence and homeostasis, much evangelical ecological literature adhered to COR's assumption that there were natural limits to growth, limits that if exceeded could lead to cataclysmic problems. Ball notes that, overall, evangelical ecological literature is characterized by a preference for balance that obfuscates the fact that ecological systems exist within linear temporality and thus do change over time. Ball contends that this has led evangelicals to create a dualistic division between "'nature' and 'history'"; for evangelicals, the only alterations to note in ecological systems are those deriving from humanity, without reference to the power of nature itself to evolve (Ball 1997, 86–90).

This ecologically conscious strain of evangelicalism directly influenced Schwarz's Natural Church Development and its influence can also be seen in the missional, organic, and emergent churches. While some of this influence merely relates to church window dressing, it also is reflected in the ecclesiological assumptions these movements accept and reject. Many members of the missional, emergent, and organic church movements feel personally burned by their experiences with the CGM; one of the attractions of these new forms of doing church is that they are seen as more community-driven than the supposedly more consumer-oriented approach of the CGM. However, Missionals, Emergents, and Organic churchers, despite their endorsement of the rhetoric of complexity theory, do share with the CH movement the assumption that negative feedback mechanisms are often preferable to the application of excess "positive feedback" mechanisms within church systems. This latter method, the modus operandi of the CGM movement, is now seen by many evangelical thinkers as leading to a dangerous amount of mission creep; church institutions built on "positive feedback" cycles are seen as being neither economically nor demographically sustainable when compared to the decentralized, smaller, and/or multi-site models that newer evangelical church plants now prefer (see, for instance, Hirsch 2006 on sustainability, 176).[7]

The economics discussions among evangelicals on the "limits to growth" model were particularly heated, as evangelicals split into "markets and growth" and "limits to growth" perspectives. "Markets to growth" supporters argued that pro-limits ideology would harm the planet, not help it. Technology, they contended, provided the needed solutions for pollution, while restricting growth might restrict developing nations financial and technological capacities to fight pollution effectively (Ball 1997, 92–93). Essentially, the movement was an extension of cornucopian ideology, which has had a fair share of support among futurists and libertarians. The limits approach took a similar position to that offered up by the COR Limits report. This approach argued that the world's resources were not infinite. Because of this, to be responsible for creation, humanity had to respect the ecosystem's "carrying capacity," particularly through the restriction of consumption and the promotion of ecologically sustainable government policies (Ball 1997, 93). Most of the evangelical literature written on ecology and growth subscribes to the "limits to growth" perspective. As Ball notes, however, much of this literature was written by ecologists or environmental activists (Ball 1997, 200), so it would probably be wise not to overestimate evangelical commitments to the "limits to growth" approach, which, given the generally pro-capitalist views of most evangelicals, almost certainly remains a minority position within the evangelical community. Those evangelicals who supported the "limits" approach were much more willing to sanction marketplace regulation for the sake of the environment than markets-and-growth supporters. They did not believe that the markets could solve the environmental crisis by themselves

(Ball 1997, 200). However, this position was not uniform. Some "limits" supporters preferred individualized solutions to the "limits" question rather than state regulation, a position that reflected a long-standing evangelical preference for individual solutions to social problems over structural ones (Ball 1997, 207; Emerson and Smith 2000, 104).

Evangelicals who supported the markets-to-growth perspective eschewed the ecological approach to growth, fearing that it inevitably led to a pro-limits perspective. The movement did not talk about sustainability and did not like the terms that derived from ecology's system-oriented approach to environmental problems (Ball 1997, 259). Many evangelical texts which discuss the "growth" debate, in particular those which did not concentrate on economics, blamed "economic growth" as the main engine of environmental decay. This dangerous economic growth, they charged, was fueled by rampant materialism (Ball 1997, 330). Markets-to-growth thinkers also expressed concern about materialism, but their personal concerns centered on the dangers to the individual's soul, not environmental decay (Ball 1997, 331).

The issue of materialism's effect on growth would, like most of the other debates that resulted from the "limits to growth" movement, be reflected in the debate between the CGM and the church health movement. CGM's approach, though not necessarily inherently a markets-to-growth approach, certainly has viewed materialism much more sympathetically than the church health movement. By contrast, church health advocates, along with missional, organic, and emergent church leaders, have tended to be skeptical of promoting materialism. The motivation for this is often cast in noble terms, and in many cases this self-critique may in fact be true. However, there are pragmatic strategic issues at work here as well. Significant leaders of the emergent, missional and organic movement, notably the aforementioned Alan Hirsch see the markets-to-growth approach to church growth as unsustainable.[8] Therefore, from the standpoint of the emergent/missional/organic alliance, the materialism that motivates the church growth movement is not only spiritually deleterious but, as a matter of praxis, inefficient.

Perhaps the most interesting sign of the *Limits* debate's influence on evangelical theories of governance and policy making were two conferences held towards the end of the 1970s: The "Consultation on Future Evangelical Concerns," which took place in Atlanta, Georgia, during December 1977 and the "Continuing Consultation on Future Evangelical Concerns," which was held in December 1978 (Hoke 1978a, iii). The conference was the brainchild of Billy Graham, Dr. Hudson Armerding (1918–2009), and Donald E. Hoke (1919–2006). All three men were influential figures in evangelicalism: Graham was then at the height of his power. Armerding was president of both Wheaton and the influential World Evangelical Fellowship; he had previously led the flagship organization of evangelicals, the National Association of

Evangelicals. Hoke, as a conference director, had led the International Congress for World Evangelization in Lausanne in 1974. Lausanne I, as it is now known, was one of the most important evangelical gatherings of the twentieth century (Hoke 1978a, ix–x, 167). The three men wanted an informed group of evangelicals to discuss the potential future courses of evangelical history over the remaining 23 years of the 20th century (Hoke 1978a, ix). The organizers also held the Consultation as a way of projecting possible future developments in both society and the church, where church leaders could "think futuristically and begin long-range planning for the church in the face of possible alternative futures" (Hoke 1978a, ix). But in contrast to secular stereotypes of evangelical futurism, the conference had virtually no concern for prophecy. Instead, conference organizers earnestly sought to establish realistic projections for the future course of the church, using the cyborg-science infused ideology of COR and other futurists.

A number of thinkers who were connected with secular future studies groups attended the conferences, among them E.V. Newland, an employee of the Royal Dutch Shell Corporation (Hoke 1978a, xiv). The Royal Dutch Shell Corporation was then famous for anticipating the 1973/1974 OPEC oil embargo by making use of scenario planning and had a formidable reputation in future studies (Begnston, Kubik and Bishop 2012). The 1978 conference included presentations from the eccentric but influential Willis Harman, employed by the Stanford Research Institute (see Hoke 1979, 27–37).[9] In addition, Peter Henriot, a member of the U.S. affiliate of the Club of Rome, was a speaker at the second conference (Henriot 1979, 47). At both conferences, but particularly the first, the "limits" debate was an important part of the agenda. For instance, at the first conference, Hoke gave an extensive presentation entitled "Views of the Future as Reflected in Reports to the Club of Rome" which gave the conference attendees a detailed account of COR's activities in the 1970s, almost uniformly in flattering terms (Hoke in Hoke 1978b, 3–9). Hoke's exposure to long-range planning had first occurred in the mid-1960s (Hoke 1978b, 3) and his report to the Conference shows a fairly thorough understanding of COR's objectives and methods, albeit with limitations imposed by Hoke's lack of mathematical training (Hoke 1978b 3–9). As a context for the remaining discussions at the conference, two films were then shown, one based directly on COR's "Limit to Growth" report (Hoke 1978b, 8).

Critics of the two Consultations have viewed them in somewhat conspiratorial terms, largely because of the influence of Willis Harman on the New Age movement.[10] Such responses are largely understandable, if perhaps misplaced, given the names of the major figures involved. Indeed, while evangelical critics of the Consultations have focused almost exclusively on the importance of Willis Harman and his connections to the New Age movement, they have failed to note that E.V. Newland is Ted Newland (Kleiner 2008, 131,

353). Newland is famous for working with Pierre Wack in pioneering scenario planning at Dutch Shell. Wack, like Willis Harman, was a profoundly spiritual person. He fused elements of Herman Kahn's futuristic vision with Eastern fused mysticism, what R. John Williams calls "Oriental Systems Theory" (R. John Williams 2016, 526). Wack had been heavily influenced by the spiritual teachings of G.I. Gurdjieff, from whom he developed a lifelong fascination with the concept of "seeing," as well as Indian spiritual teacher Svamiji Prajnanpad (Kleiner 2008, 134–135, R. John Williams 2016, 526–527). From a scholarly perspective, the most parsimonious explanation for the Consultations is twofold.[11] First, they served to promote the concept of voluntary simplicity among evangelicals, a concept that was heavily promoted at both SRI and Dutch Shell (Hoke 1978a, 11, 16, 18, 19, 21, 24). The reasons why SRI and Dutch Shell promoted voluntary simplicity in the late 1970s remain somewhat murky, although its usefulness as a tool for VALS market segmentation may have been one reason (see Kleiner 2008, 242–250). The second purpose, which is particularly clear at the first conference, is the appropriation of Dutch Shell scenario techniques by evangelical leaders (See Hoke 1978a, 1–25). In one particularly odd, brilliant and arguably totally immoral appropriation of Dutch Shell scenario techniques, Kenneth Kantzer utilized Pierre Wack's and Ted Newland's "muddling through scenario" for dealing with the OPEC crisis (Kantzer 1978, 137). In this scenario, Wack and Newland constructed a plausible future in which the West managed to "encourage energy saving ahead of time (reducing the demand for oil)," while also "find[ing] some leverage with which to get the OPEC countries to back down" (Kleiner 2008, 145). The evangelical church, Kantzer realized, had its own energy crisis. Previously the church had relied on believers as its energy source. But that source of material and spiritual energy could potentially be threatened—or alternately, benefited—by changes in the material cost of conversion. Successful missions and cultural renewal efforts required effective resource allocation, which meant that evangelical energy reserves—believers and potential believers—had to be allocated and/or extracted with a minimum of waste (Kantzer 1978, 136–137). While never explicitly stated, therefore, Kantzer is effectively redefining believers and potential converts as crude oil.[12]

There is no need to go into further detail here about the discussions held at both conferences. What is clear is that the two Consultations had an influence on evangelical leaders' willingness to adopt systems perspectives, as well as ideas from futurism (which has always been sympathetic to systems theory). Moreover, the conferences likely served as catalysts for the increasing number of evangelical programs, seminaries, authors and academics that incorporated long range and strategic planning into their deliberations. The various systems perspectives offered an ideal tool for implementing such long-range planning. When combined with the ubiquitous influence of the "limits" debate throughout the 1970s, the two consultations offered evangelicals yet another incentive to adopt systems theory as their modus operandi. And meanwhile, among mainline Protestants, a simultaneous movement towards adopting systems theory was occurring. At the center of it would be The Alban Institute.

The Alban Institute and the Adoption of Systems Theory in the Mainline

Of even more immediate importance to the spread of the systems perspective in the mainline than the *Limits* debate was the work undertaken by the Alban Institute. The Alban Institute represented one of several groups within mainline Protestantism which sought to promulgate advanced management techniques into mainline churches (see Mead 1981, 89–93). Practical management and human relations theory were among the most important influences on this school of Christian management thought, with the most influential figures being such individuals as Kurt Lewin and Peter Drucker. The National Training Laboratory (NTL), with its focus on small group relations, served as the center for much of this new vein of thinking (Mead 1981, 90). NTL's T-groups, which had been designed to improve individual communication and cooperation within organizations, had received much attention in the Episcopal Church because of the influence of Episcopalian leader Ted Wedell. Through an initiative called "The Church and Group Life Laboratory," the Episcopal Church began training the majority of its leaders in the adoption of human relations theory. Impressed by the training they received from NTL, two Episcopalian priests, George Peabody and Loren Mead, began applying concepts derived from organizational development into church life. This led to a grant-funded initiative called Project Test Pattern (PTP). Following the end of that initiative, Mead founded the Alban Institute (E. Bevan Stanley 2003, 13–14). Another early influence was the Grubbe Institute, which traces its lineage back to the Tavistock Institute of Human Relations, a prominent think tank. In 1975, Loren Mead persuaded Bruce Reed, the lead administrator for the Grubbe Institute, to begin an interchange between human relations specialists and church consultants. This led to an Alban-backed 1977 conference on religious systems (Warner Anderson Smith 2006, 50–51.).

The Alban Institute focused on promoting two major aspects of its church consultancy practice: the application of sociological theory to consultation, and the promotion of "organizational dynamics and systems theory." Even at the height of the "limits to growth" debate, the latter aspect of Alban marked it as unusual and forward-thinking, as systems-based perspectives had not yet spread significantly beyond the mainline (Warren Anderson Smith 2006,

53–55). By 2006, when Warner Anderson Smith composed his dissertation, Alban consultants and thinkers had written some 450 published works. Its consultancy spanned thousands of congregations throughout North America (Warren Anderson Smith 2006, 54), fueling the spread of the cyborg sciences within Protestantism.

Other organizations, both religious and secular, began offering their organizational development skills to churches during the late 1960s and early 1970s. One of the first was the Mid Atlantic Training Center, an organization started by John Dernham, specializing in human interaction and group dynamics training (E. Bevan Stanley 2003, 14). Meanwhile, the influential Lyle Schaller founded the Yokefellows Institute. NTL, like MATC, utilized its research skills to assist churches. Robert Gallagher's Church Development Institute, founded in the early 1980s, developed a successful training program based on the use of organizational development theory within church settings (E. Bevan Stanley 2003, 13–14).

The development of Alban's systems perspective to church consultation occurred against the backdrop of an increasing conviction among organizational researchers that organizations represented "complex systems with articulated goals or purposes" (E. Bevan Stanley 2003, 12). Five major psychological issues dominated these groups: communication, establishing normative standards for groups along with encouraging group growth, team solutions to problems, the issue of leadership and control, and cooperation and conflict between different groups. Among the initial efforts of mainline Protestants to deal with these group-centered issues were the Urban Training Centers, located in New York, Washington, D.C., Chicago, Cleveland, Atlanta, and Los Angeles. Along with this interest in group dynamics, came a growing awareness of the benefits of action research, an activity where consultants and those they advised both engaged themselves in organizational research. Speed Leas (1937–), who later became influential at Alban, was involved in one of these UTC efforts (E. Bevan Stanley 2003, 12).

The Episcopalian tradition, which helped birth PTP and thus Alban, was much more amenable to utilizing the social sciences and management theory—much of which was directly born from the cyborg sciences—than other Protestant faith traditions. The Episcopalian tradition helped pioneer the incorporation of the systems and organizational development perspectives into the practice of church consultation, with Alban deriving many of the benefits of Episcopalians' foresight in adopting the systems perspective (Warren Anderson Smith 2006, 55). This grounding in organizational development and systems theory became a "very significant portion of the toolkit used by Mead and later Alban consultants" (Warren Anderson Smith 2006, 108–109). For PTP, and for Alban, the dominating operating assumption would be the utilization of the social sciences to solve church organizational problems (Warren Anderson Smith 2006, 108–109). Throughout Alban material, concerns about spiritual life take a backseat to pragmatic concerns about organizational efficiency.

Part of Alban's unusually large influence can be attributed to both the age and the unusual background of its church consulting service. Unlike traditional church consultation teams, who grounded their practice in the beliefs of the CGM, Alban derived its practices from sociology and congregational studies. Thus, even at its beginning, Alban was more profoundly shaped by the social sciences than the CGM. Moreover, Alban's approach was ecumenical, allowing it to have broad appeal (Warren Anderson Smith 2006, 186–187). Thus, when the EMC (Emergent Missional Conversation) started, Alban material often provided valuable tools and inspiration for the application of systems approaches to church life.

Thanks in large part to the influence of Alban, systems theory soon found wide applications in a number of mainline congregations. Among the most influential texts among mainline Protestants were Peter Rudge's *Ministry and Management* (1968), E. Mansell Pattison's *Pastor and Parish—A Systems Approach* (1977), Alvin J. Lindgren's and Norman Shawchuck's *Management for Your Church* (1977), Thomas R. Hawkins's *Learning Congregation: A New Vision of Leadership* (1997), Peter L. Steinke's *Healthy Congregations: A Systems Approach* (1996), Ronald W. Richardson's *Creating a Healthier Church: Family Systems Theory, Leadership, and Congregational Life* (1996), *Understanding Your Congregation as a System* by R. George Parsons and Speed B. Leas (1993), *The Equipping Pastor* (1993), by R. Paul Stevens and Phil Collins, Norman Shawchuck's and Roger Heuser's *Managing the Congregation* (1996) and Peter L. Steinke's *How Your Church Family Works: Understanding Congregations as Emotional Systems* (1993) (See Ronald J. Allen 1999, 552–553). The clearest descriptions of the systems approach within mainline congregations is provided by scholar Ronald J. Allen, and since this model is influential not only in the mainline, but in evangelicalism, it is prudent to talk about it now.

Congregational systems, like all systems, have a number of common characteristics, including "input, output, transformation, environment, boundaries, and feedback" (Ronald J. Allen 1999, 555). Congregations can not only be systems but can also consist of systems within systems. In a congregational system, input can come from human beings, from technology, "organizational inputs" such as "innovations in organization or leadership style," and "social inputs" from the social environment surrounding the congregation (Ronald J. Allen 1999, 555–556). Moreover, the congregational system can produce outputs into its community, which are then reinputted to the congregation as inputs. There are numerous inputs into a congregation that can occur, such as money, materials, new or old doctrine, members, technology, and numerous other factors from outside the congregational system. Whatever the input, it always influences a congregation in more than one manner. Sermons, too, can be inputs into the congregational system, influencing doctrinal beliefs or interpersonal relationships (Ronald J. Allen 1999, 555–556). Inputs are eventually changed into outputs, that is the results of the inputs (Ronald J. Allen 1999, 557).

Outside of a congregational system exists its environment, the "larger world" with which a congregation must interact. As mentioned previously, this environment frequently produces inputs into a congregation of various kinds (Ronald J. Allen 1999, 563). For instance, a school shutting down may lead to increased participation in vacation bible school programs, or the construction of a new highway may increase the number of people visiting the church. Pastors informed by a systems perspective ideally try to help their congregations engage with such systemic issues, since an adequate understanding of faults within a congregational system will facilitate change (see Ronald J. Allen 1999, 563). Moreover, skilled pastors who work from a systems perspective can help their congregation or its leadership create informed response patterns to their environment, by helping them consider what they want to be outputting (see Ronald J. Allen 1999, 563–564).

Boundaries within a congregational system are slightly trickier issues. A congregation's confession of faith can serve as "a formal boundary marker" denoting it from other congregations. Worship styles, the types of pews used, the books that play the most important part in the service—all represent potential boundary markers. What is crucial about such boundary markers is that they delineate what constitutes legitimate input into a congregational system and what must be rejected (Ronald J. Allen 1999, 565).

Feedback within a congregational system lets a congregation know how effectively it is functioning. As we have seen, church growth theory borrows extensively from feedback concepts. Mainline Protestantism's use of feedback concepts is similar. If a congregation is skilled at interpreting the feedback it receives, it can "adjust its operation in order to account for the evaluation of persons and subgroups within the congregation, as well as from persons from outside the system" (Ronald J. Allen 1999, 566). Feedback can include the formal mechanisms detailed in church marketing and church growth literature but can also involve meetings between congregational leaders and key congregants, or the use of "pastor-parish relations committees" (Ronald J. Allen 1999, 566). In general, congregational systems that work effectively are characterized by certain factors, such as "high attendance, good morale, generous financial support, support of outreach ministries, and inflow of new members" (Ronald J. Allen 1999, 567).

In the final analysis, the goal of using systems theory with a congregation is to move it away from or towards homeostasis, depending on which state is considered more beneficial to the congregation. As Ronald J. Allen notes, most systems tend to move towards homeostasis, but such homeostasis can be detrimental in certain instances (Allen 1999, 568–569). And it is in this conflict between competingly relatively static and relatively dynamic visions of church organization that the most potential for abuse exists. A congregation that is democratically informed that its leadership is utilizing systems perspectives to improve congregational performance may benefit handsomely from the implementation of this perspective. However, the systems perspective, when misapplied, has real potential for abuse, through the use of feedback systems to ever-more regulate and monitor church members. Moreover, as detailed in the introduction, the misuse of feedback mechanisms by churches can lead to congregations whose values are no different than those of the neoliberal market. Such "responsive" congregations, as Kenneson and Street characterize them (Kenneson and Street 2003, 132), are unlikely to put up any prophetic resistance to the encroachment of neoliberal concepts on congregational life.

However, it has not been systems theory alone that has paved the way for the rise of a market-oriented "cyborg science"-infused gospel to triumph in contemporary Protestantism. Innovations in computer science, most of which have been profoundly aided by the development of systems theory, have also contributed to the rise of the market-oriented church. In the next section, we will explore the rise of computer science within evangelicalism and how innovations in this field helped create the modern evangelical church.

Computer Science and Evangelicalism

Religious leaders and scientists have expressed an interest in synchronizing the pursuits of digital technology and religion for far longer than is commonly understood. Following World War II, there was an expanded market for civilian use of computer technology, usually in accounting, education, and business. A number of projects emerged in 1951 to digitize holy texts. For instance, a Jesuit priest created a digital concordance of one canto of Dante's *Divine Comedy* on one of IBM's huge computers. At the same time, the Episcopal Rector John W. Ellison took advantage of IBM's computers to engage in cross-textual comparisons of biblical manuscripts. These projects, and those that followed, brought Christian theologians and engineers enough "social capital to assemble more ambitious teams of humans and computers toward more elaborate indexing projects" (Vincent Gonzalez 2014, 96). Such indexing projects later provided the foundation for much of the religious networking that I have outlined in my book *The New Apostolic Reformation: His-*

tory of a Modern Charismatic Movement. Vincent Gonzalez notes that even initial "digital religion" efforts ranged widely over a "diverse" range of endeavors (Gonzalez 2014, 96–97). He contends that most of the initial digital religion projects were not primarily evangelical in origin, since those theological groups who had enough "social capital" to utilize the major mainframes were unlikely to be evangelical (Gonzalez 2014, 98).

However, the utilization of computer systems by Protestant leaders, particularly conservative Protestants, has a longer history than even Gonzalez realizes. One of the first innovators in this venture was David B. Barrett (1927–2011), a former aeronautic engineer and hotshot test pilot turned missionary. Between 1946 and 1960, Barrett was responsible for the production of *Missionary Notes*, which used methods derived from science, particularly aeronautics, and applied them to missions. The publication made use of Colossus, the United Kingdom's first working computer, in its efforts. Years after being called to the mission field, Barrett found himself slogging through mountains of data for the initial edition of the World Christian Encyclopedia. Ed Dayton met with Barrett and suggested that Barrett acquire a microcomputer. Barrett's World Evangelization Research Center had already adopted advanced database technology by the time the World Christian Encyclopedia saw the light of day in 1982. Patrick Johnstone (1938–), another former scientist turned missionary, was also aided by Dayton's knowledge of computers; Dayton aided Johnstone's acquisition of a multi-use computer for the production of the 1986 edition of Operation World. Both of these research projects proved enormously influential in the missions' community (Jaffarian 2009, 33).

Barrett and Johnstone became major innovators in "quantitative missiology," which applies statistical metrics, as well as data analysis and modeling to the mission field. Not all computer-based research methodology is quantitative in nature (Samuel Wilson 803), but the early application of such methods to the missions' field was a major boon for the use of computer science in evangelical church outreach efforts. In particular, the field of missiometrics has expanded enormously due to the wealth of information now available via computer science. Missiologists realized that advances in computer technology could play an important role in sifting through the massive amounts of new data that were being generated by the Internet; the influence here of Barrett and Johnstone may thus have had a large impact on the relatively early and painless adaptation of systems theory through a wide variety of church outreach efforts (Barrett 2000, 636; Jaffarian 2009, 33).

Other key early adopters are also worthy of note. In 1960, Joseph E. Grimes undertook translation work in Mexico using a computer to perform language analysis. Missiologists in other fields utilized computer data to conduct analyses of everything from church growth efforts to the study of religious movements. In 1968, Edward Dayton compiled survey data from mission agencies into a computer for the North America Protestant Ministries Overseas Directory (Siewert 489). The influential Christian Right organizations World Vision and Campus Crusade for Christ also were trendsetters in the use of computer technology, which they exploited for accounting and other finance-related jobs. This allowed these organizations to derive major financial and time savings, creating a streamlining process that increasingly came to characterize the entire organizational apparatus of the Christian Right (see Jaffarian 2009, 33).[13]

Besides his important influence on both Barrett and Johnstone's adoption of computerized research methodology, Ed Dayton served as a crucial figure in the missions' community's entry into the computer age. Dayton was an important figure at World Vision, a major Christian relief and development organization. Dayton early on figured out that computers could be adapted for use by missions agencies. This led to the creation of the Missions Advanced Research Center (MARC) as a part of World Vision. MARC employed its computers to amass massive amounts of data for ten printings of *The Mission Handbook*, which would go on to become the most important North American missions guide. Dayton was a crucial figure at the 1974 Lausanne Congress on World Evangelization, which played a major role in crafting evangelical missions' strategy over the last quarter of the 20th century. Ralph Winter's U.S. Center for World Mission (USCWM), formed as a result of Lausanne, was likewise committed to the idea of "reaching the world's unreached people groups." MARC, partly as a result of Lausanne, formed a database of "unreached peoples" and subsequently issued a number of *Unreached Peoples* annuals, designed to identify and analyze groups targeted for evangelization (Jaffarian 2009, 33).

Two other missions organizations were also important. The first was the Summer Institute of Linguistics (SIL), which employed computers long before the PC revolution began. SIL compiled massive amounts of linguistic information, a portion of which it then printed in the Ethnologue series. The use of computers by SIL allowed it to efficiently sift through a "mountain of names, alternative names, facts, statistics and more that cried out for the organizing power of computer technology" (Jaffarian 2009, 33–34). In addition, to SIL, the efforts of missionary Jim Montgomery's "Discipling a Whole Nation" movement, better known as DAWN, also made use of computer technology. DAWN aimed to create a "living church that would be geographically and culturally accessible to every people group and community of the nation" (Jaffarian 2009, 34). Such an expansive dream required computer expertise. Montgomery therefore moved to his employer's (Overseas Crusades) headquarters, located in Silicon Valley, to become its lead research and development guru. Along with Bob Waymire, another influential figure

3. Cybernetics, Computers and Christ 149

in the evangelical adoption of computer technology, Montgomery acquired a computer for DAWN's research needs (Jaffarian 2009, 34).

It is important to understand that already by the beginning of the early 1980s, the Christian Right had begun to develop a sophisticated approach to information collection; moreover, evangelical leaders had innovative ideas in how to use such information to increase the efficiency of church outreach, evangelization, and missions work. Much of the early thinking on computer science by evangelical leaders was led by church growth advocates or movements influenced by the CGM. The Lausanne Movement had adopted church growth language and many of its methods during its 1974 meeting (Weaver 2016, 57). Ralph Winter's USCWM, with its common Fuller connections, was strongly committed to church growth principles; by C. Peter Wagner's account, Winter was a crucial figure in promoting the adoption of church growth at Lausanne (Wagner 2010, 110). Similarly, Ed Dayton of MARC collaborated with Wagner on the book *Unreached Peoples '79: The Challenge of the Church's Unfinished Business* (Jaffarian 2009, 37). Jim Montgomery, who was a major influence on Bob Waymire, was a former student of McGavran's and a strong proponent of church growth principles (Jaffarian 2009, 34).

The ease with which the Christian Right made use of computer technology during the 1980s and 1990s was in part a reflection of the personal computing revolution. During the late 1970s and early 1980s, pastors increasingly began using computerized research systems and concordances. Office keeping tasks in many churches were also digitized. In their quest for efficiency, churches made use of such technologies as PARSEC (Parish Secretary) and MMS (Ministry Management System) (Gonzalez 2014, 99). Gonzalez notes that in the 1980s, as in the 1950s, digital religious products were not simply derivative creations but were at the head of technological diffusion curves. For instance, the emergence of shareware, a major influence on PC gaming, was due to an experiment in digital religion by Jim Knopf, whose program PC-File was designed to maximize mailing efficiency for his local church (Knopf n.d., Gonzalez 2014, 104). Steve Hewitt, a prominent evangelical computer tech guru and the longtime editor of *Christian Computing Magazine*, traces the birth of the evangelical computing revolution to the Jesus Movement (Hewitt 2010, 25). The revolution in church worship that the JPM engendered, along with parallel worship innovations in the "coffee house" movement, led trend-setting churches to adopt new musical instruments, instruments that required more elaborate sound systems and lighting. Seeker-oriented churches like Willow Creek and Saddleback only hastened this urge to technological innovation. Churches began to realize that as "multi-media tools," computers were, as Hewitt puts it, "ground zero," allowing unparalleled efficiency (Hewitt 2010, 25).

Among the leading Christian software developers during this period were Bible Research Systems and NavPress Software. Initially Christian software development was mainly concerned with Bible translation, as we have seen, but by the early 1990s, the market had expanded "to include software hymnals, games and lesson planners" (Hawkins 1993, C1). Bible Research Systems became the first company to make the entire Bible accessible for home computers. Its creators, two former employees of Intel Corp by the name of Brown and Kent Ochel, had developed a digitized KJV in 1982 that was "revolutionary" and subsequently swiftly duplicated. Bible Research Systems eventually became among the first companies to transfer the Bible onto CD-Rom (Hawkins 1993, C1).

NavPress Software originally started as a mythical garage-based operation in 1987. Its founder Jim Sneeringer spun it off into a very successful enterprise, whose sales totaled $1 million a year by the end of 1993. Sneeringer's major accomplishment was to make a searchable Bible, which he then proceeded to "hawk" to interested purchasers. The Navigators' publishing division, NavPress, subsequently acquired Sneeringer's program and developed their own software division, NavPress Software. Sneeringer eventually bought it out and moved the business to Austin (Hawkins 1993, C1).

Meanwhile, on the American domestic front, church growth advocates had begun pioneering the use of computer technology in the late 1970s. Here, a crucial figure is Melvin F. Schell, Jr. Schell is a somewhat shadowy figure in the history of the Christian Right, but fortunately there is at least extensive biographical information about him. Schell was a church growth expert (and now serves as a church consultant) (Wagner 1988, 260–262; "Meet Mel Schell" n.d.). Born in the late 1930s, Schell entered the ministry in 1973. In the 1950s and 1960s, he had worked for IBM, where he was employed in the "use and marketing of the IBM small computer line." Schell has a BA in Bible and Psychology from Tennessee Temple and earned an MBA at Georgia State University. He also studied at Baptist Bible Seminary, Columbia Theological Seminary, and Emory University. Later he took advanced training in the Doctor of Ministry program at Fuller's School of World Mission (Wagner 1988, 260–262; "Meet Mel Schell" n.d.).

Schell's introduction to the church growth movement came when he began his evangelistic career at the First Alliance Church of Atlanta, Georgia. He soon found himself working for Evangelism Explosion's Atlanta headquarters. Schell studied under C. Peter Wagner and John Wimber. Eventually Evangelism Explosion International became Growth Ministries Inc. This organization served as a church consultancy and was closely linked with both Win Arn's American Institute of Church Growth and The Charles E. Fuller Institute of Evangelism and Church Growth. The latter fact is particularly significant, as Carl George, like Schell, would adapt systems theory to the church context (Wagner 1988, 260–261; "Meet Mel Schell" n.d.).

Schell, working through the Charles E. Fuller Institute of Evangelism and Church Growth (led by Carl George), developed a system called Total Church Growth which was implemented in several denominations, leading to impressive growth in a number of churches. Schell's advanced computer training influenced him in the creation of the Total Church Growth Model, which was designed to be a systems model of church growth (Wagner 1988, 171). The working assumption of the Total Church Growth Model was that "the local church is a cybernetic system" (Zenefski 1985, 6, 76). Ronald Zenefski, writing on the pilot version of the Total Church Model (Zenefski 1985, 99)[14] contended that while systems theory was vast, the makeup of the church could be explained in terms of systems theory. Cybernetic systems need program elements which control what acts a system can perform and how the components of the system operate to achieve desired objectives. According to Zenefski, the equivalent function to this in most congregations is the governing board. The program's function can be subdivided into two components. One is a command program, which is a "series of instructions directing the other system elements through a sequence of steps required to complete the desired operation." Most churches' expression of this component is their mission statement, sometimes also known as a church's vision statement. Process programs, in turn, provide instruction to the system on the way each operation will be performed. In most churches, the process program is the church's working ministry model (Zenefski 1985, 80–81).

Action elements in a cybernetic system correspond to those system elements which "align material and apply energy." In congregational life, these elements function through a church's "commission, work areas, and task forces." Sensing elements, on the other hand, find specific properties of a "processed item," and then "present that measurement in a form upon which the system can act." The measurements (feedback) that the system gains from sensors establishes if a process is fulfilling its objectives and can be used to provide corrective interventions. Typically, in a church this element operates via "congregational response" (Zenefski 1985, 81).

In cybernetic systems, decision elements represent those aspects of the system which utilize data obtained via sensors to gauge the effectiveness of system operations. In churches, this function is typically provided via a congregation's program board. Cybernetic systems also have control elements which determine how findings are implemented. In congregations, decision making procedures correspond to this element of cybernetic systems. These decisions, when implemented, lead to responses from the congregations (Zenefski 1985, 81–82).

Working with this understanding of church life, Schell developed a list of seven cybernetic principles which provided the basis for the operating parameters of the "Total Church Growth" model. First, churches had to collect accurate information on all elements of their church if they wanted to experience growth. Secondly, information must be communicated effectively throughout the church system. Moreover, those messages that were not sent were equally important with those that were. The "Total Church Growth" system assumed that changes to any part of the system had ripple effects across every other element of the system. A fourth principle of "Total Church Growth" contended that "futures changes within the system" could accurately be predicted via the use of cybernetic principles (Zenefski 1985, 87).

Schell and his fellow consultants understood that for this system to work, they had to have impressive data storage and information processing systems to improve system functionality. This assumption is foundational in much of the subsequent evangelical applications of systems theory to church outreach, growth, evangelization, and missions' efforts. Church systems that had these abilities survived, while those that did not died out. In Schell's and his colleagues' defense, this assumption seems to have largely proved accurate. Many of the evangelical movements that streamlined in this manner, particularly the NAR, proved to be remarkably efficient when compared to relatively ailing competitors (Zenefski 1985, 87).

Creating church growth required both understanding the subsystems of a church as well as, ideally, how the whole system functioned. Schell knew that churches could create effective sub-systems within congregational life if they delineated operational objectives, then monitored the created church subsystems using a feedback process.[15] This became his sixth operating principle. Finally, Schell's seventh assumption was that once a whole system was understood, the "sum of the parts is greater than the whole" (Zenefski 1985, 86). Schell emphasized that once cybernetic principles were applied to the life of the church, holistic strategies and programs could be developed that provided sustainable solutions for maintaining the "integrity" of the church's activities (Zenefski 1985, 86–87). Later evangelical systems theories, such as NCD and the organic church movement, put a similar emphasis on providing holistic, rather than piecemeal, solutions to the demands placed on the modern church (on Schell's holism, see Zenefski 1985, 86–87).

Schell's understanding of the rapidly changing nature of information communication technologies and the cyborg sciences that had helped nurture them to fruition helped lead to rapid evolutions in the Total Church Growth model. Zenefski published his dissertation in 1985. By the time *Church Growth State of the Art* (1986) was published, Schell had laid out even more detailed parameters for Total Church Growth. Many of these assumptions can also be seen in later evangelical systems theorizing, Schell argued that the church needed to standardize its data collection processes, echoing arguments long made by others in the CGM (Schell 1988, 177). Because the Christian Right, like other religious movements, had entered the modern information age, it needed to have efficient and standardized data collection methods if it wanted to win the religious "information wars" of the 21st century. Similarly, Schell wanted churches to standardize the means and measurements they used to determine "cause and effect relationships" dealing with church health and growth (Schell 1988, 178).

Most importantly, however, by 1986 Schell already perceived the need for more efficient development of church networks. This involved utilizing collected data from local churches and then communicating that data across local churches networks. Moreover, such networking required classifying the various kinds of churches within a network (Schell 1988, 178). The obvious implication was that the kind of efficient systems models that had been applied to individual churches could be successfully applied to networks of churches as well. Moreover, like other CGM proponents, Schell emphasized the importance of church leaders receiving accurate information and feedback about best practice church growth methods and goal setting. He also followed these CGM leaders in pushing for "continual research and publication" of collected information in order to accurately map and graph church trends (Schell 1988, 178).

Shortly after beginning his Church Growth Ministries organization, Schell became discouraged with the lack of systematic organizing principles for managing church analysis data. He felt without such a system it would be difficult to develop an effective means of implementing the findings of his data collection efforts. Schell believed that such a system needed to utilize at least a minimum amount of guidance if it was to be effective (Schell 1988, 177). He soon created the initial version of the "Total Church Growth" model, which organized information collected into four specific areas. Afterwards, Schell helped compile a seven-volume set that described how to create total church growth. These methods were subsequently "field-tested," to encouraging results. However, at the time the church growth movement was still collecting data via manual methods, making data collection and tracking ineffective. Schell felt the only way to overcome this barrier was via directly utilizing computers in churches. He then founded Omega Information Systems, Inc. in order to implement this strategy (Schell 1988, 179).

According to Zenefski, the purpose of the "Total Church Growth Model" was to implement "an apparatus" within churches that allowed leaders "to constantly assess, regulate and coordinate the separate programs and support systems [of the church] so that all work together to achieve the stated objectives" (Zenefski 1985, 93). The model utilized "'adaptive control'" mechanisms that allowed for effective communication between congregational leadership and their flocks. By doing so, this allowed leadership to model and implement procedures to create cross-group/program cooperation. Moreover, the "Total Church Growth Model" implemented an "'adaptive control' apparatus" which was "attitudinal and social" rather than mechanical. According to Zenefski, this mechanism was a "pre-determined mentality or way of seeing the church and a method of operation for the whole organization." The "attitudinal apparatus" of the church would then "be developed as members are aware of principles for efficient church management," in turn allowing for increased congregational "productivity." The insights gained through such attitudinal and organizational restructuring allowed the congregation to understand its own "organizational structures," so that it could more efficiently evaluate all church functions through the lens of the Total Church Growth model's cybernetic principles. Zenefski admiringly writes that the model's "detailed 'programming' of the attitudinal and social control apparatus" would allow for maintaining the church's "equilibrium" while moving towards "strategic changes" that would allow the church to achieve its objectives speedily and effectively (Zenefski 1985, 93–94).

Not surprisingly, given its origins in cybernetic theory, The Total Church Growth Model developed a streamlined program for congregational growth and change. This program involved "self-discovery, analysis, goal-setting, equipping and implementation," which was to be conducted over a three-year timespan. The model emphasized three forms of growth: internal growth, external growth, and operational growth (Zenefski 1985, 107). Implementing the model required a church growth consultant who, in consultation with the principal church members, formed a Church Growth Steering Committee to conduct workshops and seminars. In these seminars, congregations learned "important church growth strategies and principles" (Zenefski 1985, 95). The Steering Committee in turn formed three Task Forces for each of the three forms of church growth (internal, external, and operational). The Committee gave each of these task forces the job of data-collection and analysis for their respective growth areas; afterwards, the task forces advised the church administration on which "policies, strategies, and programs" would most likely result in church growth (Zenefski 1985, 95).

Schell's model also took deliberate steps to manage conflict. Committee members received extensive training in how to explain the Total Church Growth model to congregants. Strategically planned seminars were conducted to explain church growth ideology to parishioners. Moreover, after the completion of data analysis, an important seminar would be conducted, usually on a special retreat. This seminar determined the ministry's "statement of mission/philosophy of ministry," which in turn allowed the ministry to goal-set. This mission philosophy also determined the means of implementing congregational goals. The Task Forces, their jobs accomplished, then presented their findings to church leadership for approval (Zenefski 1985, 96–97). Before the Board gave its formal approval to the recommendation, the church would hold "equipping seminars" to address specific congregational policy questions that needed to be addressed because of the recommendations (Zenefski 1985, 97). This obviously both allowed for further indoctrination into CG principles while also giving congregants improved skill sets to address congregational deficiencies.

I have spent so much time delineating Schell's model for several reasons. First, as we shall see, the advantages of Schell's application of cybernetics did not take long to catch on. Reactions to Schell's pilot program were mainly positive, though members of one church complained that the church consultants seemed "'too smooth' and 'IBMish'" (Zenefski 1985, 117, 133–134). Secondly, Schell himself was clearly a major mover in the church growth world. Schell gained international recognition as an authority on church growth (Schell 1988, 172). Between 1974 and 1983, Schell conducted training programs that reached a total of 10,000 American church leaders. The Total Church Growth model was tested in many denominations and produced growth in the majority of those in which it was used ("Meet Mel Schell" n.d.). Schell later became CEO of Growth Ministries International, a church consultancy outfit ("Board of Directors" n.d.).

No longer a major player in evangelical power politics, Schell's time has passed. But his cutting-edge innovations in cybernetics would be only the first of a long line of evangelical applications of systems theory to church growth. However, while Schell was developing his vision of American church growth systems theory, missions theorists were not standing still. It is to those theorists we now return.

Missions Computing Redux

As Schell was working on increasing the computing power of American church growth, church growth specialists working on the missions' field followed a similar program. Engineering and computer expert Bill Dickson had expressed interest in missions, but felt discouraged by missions' agencies disengagement with his fields. At that point, Bob Coleman, an aide to Ralph Winter, encountered Dickson. Dickson realized that computerizing the missions field was a priority and soon was working with Waymire in utilizing the best technology Overseas Crusades could offer. Nor was Waymire inactive at this point (Jaffarian 2009, 34). In addition to his effort on the missions field, Waymire helped C. Peter Wagner develop a Church Growth Survey handbook. Although the book did not require computer technology to implement, its data collection methodology certainly showed that Waymire and Wagner anticipated the oncoming computer revolution (Waymire and Wagner 2006, passim).

Meanwhile Peter Holzmann, a Christian with a genius-level understanding of programming languages was finding employment in the high-tech industry as an independent consultant. At a meeting with Bill Dickson of Oversea Crusades, Holzmann encountered Bob Waymire. Waymire communicated to him the new technological potential that computer-generated mapping possessed for missions. Waymire wanted Holzmann to adapt this technology for the missions field. After a series of trials and errors, Holzmann created a map of Guatemala, which was used in evangelization efforts. As Jaffarian notes, instead of a "new technology shaping the Christian world mission," this new mapping technology was itself shaped by the demands of Christian missiologists (Jaffarian 2009, 34). Jim Montgomery in turn utilized these maps in evangelizing Guatemala, as well as numerous countries throughout the world (Jaffarian 2009, 34).

The data Montgomery had used on the Guatemalan mission field—a mission field that would be soaked with blood (see Weaver 2016, 194–199)—had come courtesy of the Global Research Database. This database, developed by Bob Waymire, served as a "comprehensive database of global missions-related information," which would be united with the mapping technology. Waymire hoped to produce an extensive database that could classify data on both nations and people groups via numerous different data groupings, such as religious status, the vitality of the Christian population, evangelization status, and the like (Jaffarian 2009, 34). Meanwhile, Bill Dickson had realized that mission agencies were in the market for computer experts, and many computer experts desired to work for missions' agencies. To unite these two objectives, Dickson founded DataServe in 1982 (Jaffarian 2009, 34).

In 1983, Bob Waymire formed the Global Mapping Project (GMP), which subsequently became Global Mapping International (GMI). GMP/GMI would initially be headquartered at the U.S. Center for World Mission,[16] where Ralph Winter's enthusiasm for both church growth and computer science made him an early major proponent of using computer science in missions. In Pasadena, Waymire collaborated not only with former associate Bill Dickson, but with a number of Christian computer tech experts that had been lured to the Global Mapping Project via Caltech Christian Fellowship. Meanwhile Holzmann, in between serving as a lead researcher at GMP and working in the commercial computer industry, found the spare time to develop the "first PC-based geographic information system" (Jaffarian 2009, 34). The technology that created ArcView, an important GIS software system, derived directly from Holzmann's research (Jaffarian 2009, 34).

The Global Mapping Project represented a major research and development effort on the part of the Christian Right's missions arm, with the specific design of evangelizing "unreached" people groups. Waymire's association with the Overseas Crusades organization and the U.S. Center for

World Mission had led him to adopt the missions' assumptions of the CGM. Among these assumptions, shared by almost all other early evangelical computer experts, was that more systematic data collection efforts were needed. The Global Mapping Project was birthed out of this vision. Waymire visited numerous locations to gain the data and expertise he needed to construct the database (Waymire 1984, 1). The GMP projected had three main goals. First, Waymire wished to create a comprehensive database on potential "harvest fields" and "harvest forces." Then he wanted to construct a "computerized mapping scheme that interacts with the database." Finally and crucially, Waymire realized that data was useless without proper networking and information distribution systems that could exploit the data. Therefore, Waymire proposed doing for international missions what Schell had essentially done for American church growth: Create a network, here international, to indigenize his research methods—which were those of the CGM—at a worldwide level. Waymire fully realized that computers had fundamentally altered "data management and communication" practices. Realizing that the ability to collect and manipulate data was now evolving at an almost exponential rate, Waymire believed that with enough money, such techniques could be powerfully implemented on the missions' field. Working with Dickson's Dataserve, also located at the U.S. Center for World Mission, Waymire's team developed numerous applications for the technology. "How To" guides were written for distribution, and Waymire's organization networked with other data collection agencies to obtain even more current data (Waymire 1984, 2).

Showing prescient foresight, Waymire realized that the essential advantage of such data collection was not the formation of centralized databases, despite their importance, but rather those functions which created decentralization and networking. From the first, the Global Mapping Project's design parameters called for its technological applications to be easily exportable. Waymire's concerns here made perfect sense. The globalized missions' agendas that evangelical missions agencies began to develop in the late 1980s almost all required the construction of not only technological networks, but also informational and political networks. With networked organizations increasingly becoming the dominant form of evangelical organization, inefficient information distribution systems were proving non-viable. National churches required accurate diagnostics of their church health and potential for growth if they were to successfully implement their church growth goals and objectives. Waymire therefore wanted to make sure that indigenous research functions were not primarily undertaken by outsiders. This did not simply represent an effort to promote indigenization of data collection practices, but also reflected an increasing trend in Information Age evangelical missions strategy to divest Western churches of the financial and training burden for developing world missions (Waymire 1984, 2). Thus, though the

Global Mapping Project was eager and open to working with national church leaders, it followed a general organizational principle of providing technology, training and information on the condition that the national churches provide the personnel, buildings, and hardware. To make this indigenization of research practices feasible, the GMP provided tools and books that helped standardize research practices. The organization also offered technical aid and inexpensive software to facilitate the project (Waymire 1984, 2–5).

North American missions' practices have from the 1970s on been criticized for their "managerial" approach to evangelization and church outreach (see Escobar 2000, 109). Despite Waymire's promotion of the indigenization of data collection and research practices, the continued centralization of Christian missions in the West threatened the developing world (Waymire 1984, 4). As Sarah Diamond describes in *Spiritual Warfare: The Politics of the Christian Right* (1989), by the late 1980s, southern California was honeycombed with dozens of high-tech missions' agencies. In these agencies sat hundreds of missions specialists, compiling statistics on everything from linguistic structures to local superstitions. Many of the people compiling this data had never met, let alone grown to understand, the populations they sought to convert. The information they collected was put in "main-frame computers the size of refrigerators where it is formatted, tabulated and crunched into final reports that pretend to describe human societies" (Diamond 1989, 205). Diamond's anger at these practices, which her ample documentation of missionary colonialism more than justifies, is easy to understand. Evangelical missionaries in the 1980s were involved in a large number of subversive activities against nations and people groups in the developing world (see Diamond 1989, 205–229, *passim*). Moreover, some of the organizations at the forefront of the evangelical computer science and systems theory revolutions were also heavily involved in colonialist exploitation of the developing world. SIL, for instance, which in 1988 had been provided $2 million dollars-worth of computer equipment to create a networked information-sharing system for its regional headquarters, had a well-deserved reputation for being CIA "'assets'" (Diamond 1989, 218). MARC, meanwhile, is connected to World Vision. World Vision has, like SIL, been repeatedly criticized for its problematic links with U.S. government intelligence and military assets (Diamond 1989, 211, 221–222). Although Diamond and other scholars conducted first class academic research that exposed the problematic colonialism characterizing evangelical missions' practices, their efforts failed to gain traction in the conservative climate of the Reagan-Bush era. As a result, when the religious right started forming its spiritual mapping and prayer networks in the 1990s, developing world populations often lacked credible information on evangelical missions' efforts and were left vulnerable to exploitation.

3. Cybernetics, Computers and Christ 159

Diamond's concern about the union of computer science and missions efforts was even more justified than she likely realized. This is powerfully demonstrated by a specific missions initiative to Silicon Valley undertaken by the DAWN campaign during the 1980s called RISE (Research in Strategic Evangelization). Traditionally, DAWN efforts aimed at reaching the top levels of church leadership first and then working their way down to implement the strategy at a grassroots level. RISE's plan involved working from the bottom up to try to change the culture of Silicon Valley. It thus was a considerable departure from traditional DAWN campaigns, which involved ministering to developing world populations (Daniel J. Griffeths 1992, iii–iv). Jim Montgomery, the leader of DAWN, had grown up in Santa Clara County, in the center of Silicon Valley, and thus felt a strong pull to evangelize the area (Griffeths 1992, 172). C. Peter Wagner told Daniel J. Griffeths that he gave the project less than a 30 percent chance of working. The problem that RISE faced, as far Wagner was concerned, was that DAWN lacked the proper missions' apparatus to reach first world populations, who in any case were not likely to be receptive to DAWN's evangelization efforts. Although Griffeths and Montgomery were irritated by Wagner, Griffeths later admitted that Wagner's comments were prescient (Griffeths 1992, 173–174). Nevertheless, Montgomery wanted to convert the Valley, as it obviously served as a growing cultural influence (Griffeths 1992, 175). Therefore, in 1986, RISE undertook what was then one of the most exhaustive research projects ever conducted by an American religious organization (Griffeths 1992, 203). The campaign leaders deciphered a number of reasons for the failure of evangelical churches in Silicon Valley, such as a lack of connection to Silicon Valley culture and an inability to reach Baby Boomers (Griffeths 1992, 208–211). Fortunately, in their subsequent campaign to evangelize Silicon Valley, the RISE campaign made mistakes of its own. For one thing, the campaign, assumed that local leadership would aid the campaign more than it did. Church planting was also underemphasized, according to Griffeths (Griffeths 1992, 252–253). As a result, it is clear, reading between the lines of Griffeth's dissertation, that the RISE campaign failed in its objective to take over Silicon Valley.

A campaign to promulgate Christianity in Silicon Valley that occurred at roughly the same time of the DAWN campaign was the "Mission: Silicon Valley" effort, a 3-year plan to evangelize the valley, which was initially headlined by Luis Palau and received the backing of local reverend Pat Robertson (no relation to the well-known Christian figure of the same name). Robertson aimed to get 13,000 people attending the Valley's local churches by the close of 1988 as part of what was described in news reports as a "long-range evangelistic strategy" (Joan Connell 1987, 11C). Such efforts at evangelizing Silicon Valley took on renewed urgency in the mid– to late 1990s and beyond, as we shall see in Chapter 5.

During the late 1980s, the GMP/GMI team worked with Norwegian evangelical leader Frank Kaleb Jansen and YWAM on the publication of *Target Earth*. The book was finished in 1989 and was showcased at Lausanne II. In the early 1990s, missionaries began utilizing the spiritual weapons of the PC revolution on the global missions' battlefield. Numerous databooks on different people groups were compiled. Noting the global mobilization of evangelization by various denominational and parachurch groups, Thomas Wang, head of the Lausanne Committee for World Evangelization, set in motion what would become the AD 2000 and Beyond Movement, headed by Luis Bush (1946–) (more details of which will be provided in Chapter 5). The plan's goal was "'a church for every people and the Gospel for every person by the year 2000.'" In order to implement this goal. Luis Bush asked Peter Holzmann to give him a visual iconographic representation of what key areas needed to be evangelized. Holzmann developed a number of maps which highlighted different target areas in need of evangelization. Bush concentrated on a geographical area stretching between the 10 and 40th parallels north of the equator, and thus the 10/40 window, one of the central conceits of the modern missions movement was born. And it had been computer science that had nearly single-handedly brought it to fruition (Jaffarian 2009, 35; Holvast 2009, 80–81).

Wanting good evangelization metrics for AD 2000 and Beyond, the AD 2000 Campaign set up an ad hoc group named Peoples Information Network (PIN), which later became a task force for the campaign. The group published works that "merged every major list of unreached peoples, or peoples that needed a church planting movement if the goal of a church for every people was to be met" (Jaffarian 2009, 35). Although an early draft publication of this listing was plagued by faulty research, subsequent research honed the AD 2000 Campaign's methodology. The Campaign set up a huge database designed to "assess all peoples of all countries and all sizes" (Jaffarian 2009, 35–36).

Waymire's GMI also helped optimize the evangelical movement's metric and mapping effectiveness. It sold its mapping software to The Navigators and Compassion International. Other clients included Wycliffe Bible Translators (WBI), the foreign missions arms of the SBC, the AOG, and World Vision. GMI also produced a number of then innovative products, including its global mapping software (Rabey 1991, 8). By the mid–1990s, the efforts of GMI and AD 2000 would lay the groundwork for the modern network-based evangelical movement that has come to dominate 21st century expressions of evangelical faith. Neither evangelicalism nor the world it inhabited would ever be the same. And meanwhile, a new wave of systems theorizing—this time imported from Germany—was about to wash over evangelicalism.

Church Health and Natural Church Development: Systems Theory Meets the Germans

In recent years, one of the biggest promoters of systems theory in the church has been Christian Schwarz, whose program Natural Church Development Survey has been utilized in 70,000 churches, as of 2016 ("About Natural Church Development" n.d.). Schwarz represents a stream of thought that has run parallel to the church growth literature, dubbed "church health," or occasionally the church health movement. While the literature promoting church health arguably predates the modern fascination with systems theory, much of the modern literature on the subject, particularly Schwarz's NCD program, utilizes systems theory quite openly.

References to church health occur in evangelical church growth materials beginning in the early 1970s (Day Jr. 2002, 2). Donald McGavran, C. Peter Wagner and Win Arn were all early writers in this genre. The early literature was largely forgotten, however, until writers such as Dann Spader, Gary Mayes, and Leith Anderson (1944–) began reemphasizing this aspect of church life. Ed Stetzer credits the rapid burgeoning of church health literature in the 1990s with the growing influence of pastors versus seminary professors among those influenced by the CGM (Stetzer "The Evolution of Church Growth" n.d., 12). Publications in church health by Rick Warren, Christian Schwarz, Mark Dever (1960–), and Steve Macchia (1956–) solidified the field's importance in the evangelical community (Day Jr. 2002, 2).

The acceptance of the church health movement in the late 1990s corresponded to an increasing emphasis on "institutional effectiveness" within evangelicalism, which had close ties to the rise of the cyborg sciences within the church. L. Thomas Crites calls this new era of church growth thinking a "strategic church period," characterized by a commitment to an "ongoing process of evaluating data-based outcomes" (Crites 2009, 58). The development of systems theory in the church health literature was meant to address the need for good outcome-based research within the Christian Right, a problem we saw bedeviled the CGM (Crites 2009, 58). Church health advocates often supported many of the same methods as experts in institutional effectiveness. Church health experts typically endorsed a strategy that included "receiving God's vision, compiling appropriate strategies, implementing the strategies, and evaluating the results" (Crites 2009, 58). Like the CGM, the church health movement is interested in affecting an aspect of "system output," but output is not necessarily viewed solely in numerical terms; rather, a more "holistic" approach is taken (Crites 2009, 58).

Early church health literature typically looked at differences between healthy and unhealthy churches. This was the approach, for instance, that characterized church consultant Lyle Schaller's work (Crites 2009, 59–60). Schaller's writing focused on the importance of correct health diagnostics in order to treat the church's "ailment"; subsequently, Schaller's methods would be copied by many other writers in the church health genre. However, much of the church growth and church health literature offered wildly varying ideas on both the church's ills and how to implement proper church health (Crites 2009, 60).

C. Peter Wagner, for instance, focused on the dangers of "ethnikitis" and "old age." The former problem was caused by changes in ethnic demographics that made once vibrant churches non-viable in whatever new context they happened to be in. The second problem was a result of a church simply atrophying from lack of membership and was a common affliction, Wagner claimed, in more rural locales (Day Jr. 2002, 6). Another early system, created by Stephen Macchia, relied on an "intuitive" list of 10 key aspects of church health; like many church health and church growth models, however, Macchia's list suffered from a lack of information about the scientific plausibility of its diagnostic measurements (Day Jr. 2002, 9–10). A popular contemporary model of church health is the 9 Marks model developed by Mark Dever, which has had a disproportionate influence on the Southern Baptist Convention in recent years (Crites 2009, 65–66).

William H. Day, Jr., notes three problems that proved a major stumbling block to the church health model. First, the model lacked scientific objectivity. Secondly, a lack of comparative analysis between criteria of church health prevented the church health model from coming to concrete answers about which church health criteria actually worked. Finally, Day Jr. pointed out that the lack of scriptural justification for the model was sparse (Day Jr. 2002, 10). Surprisingly, this last point may actually be unusually germane in discussing church health literature. Despite the Church Health Movement's (CHM) criticism of the church growth movement, its own pragmatism often is startling, even by the standards of church growth literature (see Warner Anderson Smith 2006, 115, 121 on this score).

Initially, the church health movement's chief promoters were members of the CGM, such as McGavran, Wagner, and Arn. However, church growth proponents endured heavy criticism because of their perceived focus on quantitative, rather than qualitative, methods of church outreach and growth. Moreover, many critics of traditional CGM methods argued that church growth literature was too committed to establishing universal models of church growth and church health (Pickering 2011, 30). Critics felt this was an unsustainable model for modern Protestantism, as it did not take sufficiently into account the particular local conditions churches faced (Pickering 2011, 30). Throughout the literature on church health, much as in church growth, there are perennial arguments against the imposing of "models" of church outreach; many evangelicals feel that such models tend to try to tame a spiritual process and submit it to the ordering of rational processes. For some Christians, the rationalism of church health, like the rationalism of church growth, appears antithetical to authentic Christian spirituality.

Because the church health movement was sensitive to criticisms of both its own pragmatism and that of church growth, church health movement proponents made a distinction between "principles" and "techniques" of church health; proper practice of church health ideas involved utilizing the former, rather than the latter. According to the ideology of church health, principles were seen as "universal"; because of the organic metaphors with which church health literature abounds, there is a strongly experiential character to these principles. However, the church health movement (CHM), much like the CGM, is focused on church outreach and growth. The distinction between the CHM and traditional church growth methods is that church health literature focuses more on the "maintenance" of existing churches, rather than the creation of new ones, to further its outreach (Pickering 2011, 26). Church health proponents (particularly Christian Schwarz) claim to offer a more biblically based, "natural" alternative to the CGM (Dadisman 2008, 51).

Crucial to the church health's movement's marketing campaigns and its rhetorical strategy is its condemnation of "technocratic" means of church control, which many CHM supporters argued was the root reason for the failure of church growth (Dadisman 2008, 51). There was also an implicit doctrinal critique, employed primarily for rhetorical effect, in the CHM's use of naturalistic and biological language. Such language stood in stark contrast to the church growth movement's often crass use of utilitarian logic in defense of any practice church growth proponents thought would increase growth. But in practice there has actually been little difference in this regard between church health and church growth supporters, lending some credence to the charge made by Gary McIntosh that the church health movement is just a more evolved form of church growth rhetoric (McIntosh 2004b, 22).

Despite the anti-technocratic bias of the church health movement, the sheer breadth of church health literature encouraged movement advocates to begin developing evaluative methods for interpreting church health. Many practitioners contended an empirically based approach was the way to proceed; these practitioners then began constructing "diagnostic instruments" which could be used to provide metrics for church health (Crites 2009, 67). The Rainer Group, founded by CGM supporter Thom Rainer, was an early proponent of this kind of methodology. According to L. Thomas Crites, Rainer and his subordinates typically focused on a particular church type they felt "worthy of study" and then determined what would be the "best practice" method of church growth for that type of church. As there was a "ready market" for this kind of research, Rainer gained a great deal of influence, leading him to eventually assume control of Life Way Christian Resources, the SBC's publication branch. Similarly, George Barna's Barna Research Group engaged in a number of such studies as well. Barna's practices were sometimes criticized for being too "market driven," as they focused on "describing user-friendly churches." Nonetheless, Barna continued to conduct his studies in the coming decades and emerged as a powerhouse figure in evangelical Christianity (Crites 2009, 68).

As we have seen, evangelicals had implemented systems theory in a number of fields as far back as the 1980s. This included the church growth movement, which played an important influence on church health. In addition to the CGM, mainline Protestant church health practitioners had already begun proposing systems-based approaches by the mid-1990s. For instance, Parsons and Leas applied systems theory to church health in their 1994 work on the "congregational life" of churches, *Understanding Your Congregation as a System*. Parsons and Leas work focused heavily on issues of authority; as with Leas's important influence on evangelical conflict management literature, evangelicals appropriated some of Leas's concerns in ways that would likely be deeply disturbing to Leas's supporters among mainline Protestants (Crites 2009, 68–69). Leas's work argued that for congregations to "think systemically" they needed to view individual congregations as systems, a point emphasized in much of the systems-based literature of the last twenty years. The ready adoption of systems theory by mainline supporters of Leas's and Parsons's works stands as testimony to the often-smooth transition systems theory has made between liberal and evangelical Protestants. Some of the more advanced forms of church-based systems theory, particularly the organic church, leave this standard division of Protestantism in shambles. What remains is a vestigial ecclesiastical organization that survives more by the use of effective psychological control mechanisms than anything else (Crites 2009, 68–69).

There have been numerous applications of systems theory in church health and church growth literature from the mid-1990s on. The initial place to start with the CHM, however, is Christian Schwarz's Natural Church Development model. NCD is often seen as the exemplar of the church health movement, so much so that most evangelicals who have heard of the CHM likely have done so through exposure to NCD-type churches or Schwarz's writings. In the process, we will see that Schwarz's work has led to some troubling questions about both the viability and the theological orthodoxy of church-based systems theory.

Natural Church Development: The Church Health Movement Goes Systems with a Smile

The Natural Church Development (NCD) church health model was the brainchild of Christian Schwarz. Schwarz first published on the ideas of church growth in a book he coauthored with his father, "Theologie des Gemeindeaufbaus" (*Theology of Church Development*) (Schwarz 1999, 11; Nel 2009, 235). In Germany, critics saw "Theologie des Gemeindeaufbaus" as a broadside against the church. The publication of "Theologie des Gemeindeaufbaus" led to a number of rejoinders against the work, a number of which were collected into a single volume. Schwarz's next work would be *Paradigm Shift in the Church* (1993; English translation 1999), a work that sought to simultaneously elaborate his ideas on church health and distance him from the CGM. Schwarz's work promised nothing less than a new reformation in the way church was conducted; such grandiose language, once one cuts through the formidable neo-orthodox theologizing of his work, tends to characterize virtually Schwarz's entire opus (not to mention many of his disciples) (Nel 2009, 235–236; Schwarz 1999, 11–12).

Warner Smith has noted that there is "little personal data" available on Schwarz (Warner Anderson Smith "A Neo-Orthodox Theology Applied: An Analysis of the Hermeneutics of Christian A. Schwarz's Natural Church Development" n.d.). Criticisms of Schwarz's secretiveness are fairly ubiquitous throughout the secondary literature critical of the NCD approach (see, for instance, Yeakley 1988, 83–92; Erwich 2004, 184). It is fairly hard to fault such critics; an early and persistent criticism of Schwarz was the lack of available material he made available on the research methodology he used to determine the "eight quality characteristics" for church health, crucial information considering the central role those quality characteristics played in NCD theory (Erwich 2004, 184). Like many church growth and church health advocates, Schwarz seems to have preferred operating behind the scenes; his lack of transparency is fairly typical within the field.

The secretiveness that characterizes Schwarz concerns many Protestants because of the wild popularity of his model. According to an NCD International website, his work was available in 84 nations as of 2016 ("About NCD International" n.d.). NCD's influence over North American Christianity was also widespread. It had been adopted by numerous SBC state conventions, Union Theological Seminary, and a number of other important church institutions (Smith "A Neo-Orthodox Theology Applied: An Analysis of the Hermeneutics of Christian A. Schwarz's Natural Church Development" n.d.). Fuller Theological Seminary incorporated elements of NCD into its curriculum; the influence of Schwarz's thought is apparent not only on a number of Fuller doctoral scholars, but on some of the more prominent church growth advocates as well, such as church consultant and church planting advocate Robert (Bob) Logan (Erwich 2004, 184, Warner Anderson Smith 2006, 17). In turn Logan, who figures prominently in evangelical adoptions of systems theory and modern church planting methods, retooled his Church Planters Toolkit to make it consistent with Schwarz's model and has served as NCD's licensed American distributor (Warner Anderson Smith 2006, 199). This toolkit has proven to be a major influence on the church planting movement (CPM), particularly within the SBC (Payne 2001, 2; see also Warner Anderson Smith 2006, 17), giving Schwarz a huge potential marketing venue. In addition, Logan, formerly presided over the American Society for Church Growth, the most important formal organization of Church Growth leaders, which has likely given Schwarz innumerable networking opportunities (Warner Anderson Smith 2006, 199). NCD workshops are attractive enough to bring in a lot of cash as well. Even in 2006, one Basic Training session cost $750.00, plus a $100.00 "processing fee for each code and [NCD] workbook" (Warner Anderson Smith 2006, 199).

Much of the success of NCD in conservative Protestantism, as well as much of mainline Protestantism, is attributable to the extent of Schwarz's research, which covered some 1000 churches in 32 different nations (Erwich 2004, 184). However, in the process, serious questions have been raised about both the theology and survey methodology that Schwarz employed. Both of these points must be covered in depth to understand why critics of the NCD method find it of such concern. But first, a description of the core principles of the NCD model, as well as some of the model's philosophical antecedents, is in order.

Schwarz argued that the church needed to promote what he called a "law of polarity." According to Schwarz, all forces were tied to counter-forces. In the process, two poles were formed, bringing to life what Schwarz dubbed "biotic potential." According to Schwarz, biotic potential represented "the inherent possibility of an organism to reproduce itself." Schwarz's goal was to apply this idea to the growth and health of the church. Schwarz argued that in order to do this, churches needed to "remove or reduce those factors which block or slow down the growth of the church." Schwarz therefore contrasted dynamic aspects of the church with static ones. Churches that swung too far in a dynamic direction were characterized by what Schwarz deemed a "spiritualistic" bias. Such spiritualism tended to lean towards "subjectivism" and "mysticism" and was inclined to the more experiential side of Christianity. Swinging too far towards the static pole led churches to embrace such features as dogmatism, fundamentalism, legalism, traditionalism, and universalism. Here churches took on what Schwarz calls a "monistic paradigm" (Schwarz 1999, 98–99; Erwich 2004, 181).

Schwarz argued that the one-sided static pole led to the danger of "technocratic" thinking. Here, "the external shapes and institutions" become the mechanisms of salvation or social improvement. By contrast, spiritualistic thinking tends to divorce spirituality from materiality, leading to an unsustainable "dualistic" vision of the church. The NCD model, by contrast, seeks to unite these divided aspects of the church into a more holistic paradigm. Schwarz takes issue with both liberal and conservative theological systems. Each ideological belief system is prone to both spiritualistic and technocratic thinking, it merely exhibits different forms of this thinking (Erwich 2004, 181; Schwarz 1996, 86).

Ecclesiologically, this tension is played out in a contrast between organism and organization. The dynamic pole of Schwarz's thinking expresses itself through "biological, organic terms" and takes as its starting point such New Testament expressions as the "body of Christ." By contrast, the static pole is the organizational aspect of the church; here the biblical motifs are scriptural references to "architectural and technical metaphors." Schwarz posits that in the New Testament these approaches "are in no way in competition with each other," existing in a balance. Indeed, so close is this union that the church existing in a paradoxical union of the organic and the inorganic, with scriptural references to "'living stones,'" or "'growing into a temple'" abounding (Schwarz 1999, 16).

The NCD model is extremely complicated and intricate. Crucial to understanding the model are its eight quality characteristics, six biotic principles, and its minimum factor. The eight quality characteristics were "empowered leadership, gift-oriented ministry, passionate spirituality, functional structures, inspiring worship service (s), holistic small groups, need-oriented evangelism, [and] loving relationships" (Schwarz 1996, 4). Not all these elements are particularly relevant to the more managerial aspect of NCD. Not surprisingly, given the church health movement's association with classical CGM, Schwarz strongly emphasizes the importance of small groups. Schwarz's views on need-oriented evangelism and inspiring worship services resemble that of traditional church growth, but with some moderate differences in emphasis. When it comes to worship services, for instance, Schwarz stresses that it is not the form of the worship service that promotes church growth—for instance, whether the service appeals to the more modern, seeker-sensitive congregants or those who prefer liturgical worship forms—but rather the effect the form has on worship participants that matters (Schwarz 1996, 30). Schwarz makes a similar point about need-oriented evangelism; he observes that there is an unfortunate tendency among Christians to blur "the distinction between methods of evangelism that may have been used successfully by one or many churches, and true principles of evangelism, which apply without exception to every church" (Schwarz 1996, 34).

Theologically, Schwarz expresses more interest in developing universal principles rather than models that can only be adapted to one particular church setting or set of church settings (see Schwarz 1996, 14). Underlying this focus on principles is Schwarz's promotion of "functional structures" as a key quality characteristic of successful churches. Successful structures, in Schwarz's model, embody those structures that enable the church to improve its self-organization and improve its ministry outreach (Erwich 2004, 182; Schwarz 1996, 28). Schwarz has claimed that this element of his research has tended to be the most controversial (Schwarz 1996, 28). He attributes this to the fact that many critics of functionally based arguments for church growth see this position as "untheological pragmatism" and, at its worst, "plain utilitarianism" (Schwarz 1999, 65). By contrast, Schwarz supports what he calls "functional dogmatics." Schwarz's method of biblical interpretation argues that doctrines should be judged primarily on whether they promote church development and outreach (Schwarz 1999, 109). Schwarz therefore rejects the idea that church doctrines are "static"; doctrine must adapt to the passage of time and different cultural contexts, even if the doctrine under discussion is the trinity or one of the historic church creedal formulas (Schwarz 1999, 109).

It is difficult to fault critics of Schwarz's "functional dogmatics." Warner Smith, a particularly perceptive critic of the problems inherent in Schwarz's model, points out that the church loses any ability to offer a prophetic critique of culture when all doctrinal elements are judged through the lens of functionality. Whether Schwarz admits it or not, his doctrinal beliefs essentially enshrine pragmatism as the core creedal formula by which the church should operate (Warner Anderson Smith 2006, 122). The NCD system therefore encourages the church to adopt any doctrinal position it wishes, without regard to the probability of its truth claim, its doctrinal orthodoxy, or its ethicality. Smith is primarily concerned with the tendency of this position to lead to doctrinal innovations on the part of parishioners, a point that this work does not dispute (Warner Anderson Smith 2006, 121). But furthermore, because of Schwarz's enshrinement of "functional dogmatics" as the core hermeneutical tool for NCD, his model runs the risk of sacrificing not only doctrinal truth, but moral behavior, in its search for the doctrines that work.

In any case, to implement the eight quality characteristics successfully, Schwarz posits that Christians must follow what he calls a "minimum strategy." That is, they should concentrate on one single area for growth, "the minimum factor." This idea, appropriated from the scientific work of biologist and chemist Justus von Liebig (1803–1873), argues that the weakest quality characteristic is the one that blocks growth the most. However, all the quality characteristics are important and cannot be ignored. Therefore, Schwarz argues that one should use the strongest elements of the church to improve on the weakest elements of the church, and thus leverage growth (Schwarz 1996, 49–60; Erwich 2004, 182–183).

The last foundational element of the NCD system is the 6 biotic principles: interdependence, multiplication, energy transformation, multi-usage, symbiosis, and functionality (Schwarz 1996, 66–77). The principle of interdependence argues that "the way the individual parts are integrated into a whole system is more important than the parts themselves." Whenever one acts on one part of the system, one acts on all eight parts; Schwarz contends that to deny this is to succumb to "linear thinking." A byproduct of seeing the church as an interdependent organism is that such interdependence at the organism-level should lead to structural interdependence as well. Such interdependence manifests itself by the creation of functional sub-systems within the larger structure which allow for "ongoing multiplication" of the church (Schwarz 1996, 66). When it comes to multiplication, Schwarz believes that "unlimited growth" is "profoundly unbiotic." Human beings do not see such growth in nature. Instead, when a tree grows large enough, it reproduces new trees, and those in turn multiply into still more trees. This emphasis on multiplication, versus size, therefore separates NCD from a more megachurch-oriented approach. Instead, growth via NCD comes through "continual multiplication" (Schwarz 1996, 68–69). Part of Robert Logan's fascination with the NCD model may derive from this point, as Schwarz's focus on multiplication fits in well with Logan's concern for rapid church planting.

Energy transformation, the third biotic principle, envisions the church "using destructive energy in productive ways" (Erwich 2004, 183). Rather than seeing conflict or catastrophe as a problem, this biotic principle assumes that these problems can be turned into solutions, by working with the nature of one's church rather than against it (Schwarz 1996, 70–71; Erwich 2004, 183). The multi-usage principle advances the point "that the results of work are transformed into energy, which in turn sustains the ongoing work" (Schwarz 1996, 72). Schwarz illustrates this principle via the example of church leadership. Rather than churches promoting leaders who are only focused on being better leaders, or alternately, promoting training programs to the exclusion of good leadership, churches should instead make use of leaders who create new leaders. The energy utilized therefore not only has more than one purpose, but allows for the production of more energy via multiplication of effective leadership (Schwarz 1996, 72–73; Erwich 2004, 183).

The fifth principle, symbiosis, is highly significant in terms of its relationship to Christian Right governance practices. Schwarz utilizes the term symbiosis in its traditional sense and contrasts it with two maladaptive models of organismic relationship: competition and monoculture. In competition, organisms fight against each other for dominance, while in monoculture, ecological diversity has been lost, and only one form of organism dominates. Schwarz contends that monoculture is a byproduct of technocratic means of thinking and exhibits itself in the church when Christians cling too tightly to the idea that "all churches belong to a single large denomination, employ the same liturgy, and hold to the same practices" (Schwarz 1996, 74). Schwarz argues that such monocultural ideas, and the competitive church practices that often accompany them, should be replaced by a more cooperative approach to church growth. Within congregations, this principle can exhibit itself via a commitment to balance the desires of individual congregants with those of the church as a whole. Schwarz says that this creates what secular managers dub a "win-win relationship," where nobody loses and the whole system benefits (Schwarz 1996, 74–75).

Finally, the sixth principle is functionality. Schwarz claimed that all parts of "God's creation" were fitted to particular functions. The church, like nature, should "bear fruit" and thus the best way to discern whether an outreach effort fitted in with the biotic principles was to "periodically examine" the effort (Schwarz 1996, 77). Functional church evaluation incorporated the same pragmatic ideology that encouraged Schwarz to develop functional church structures and hermeneutics, thus exhibiting the consistent drive towards pragmatism within Schwarz's writing.

All these theological principles and interpretative mechanisms only get at the surface level of NCD. The real, underlying foundation of the NCD model lies in a process called "'planned change,'" which has its roots in organizational development and organizational psychology. The latter field seeks to examine, then "develop," the behaviors of individuals and groups within organizations. Organizational psychology concerns itself with studying the interaction between organizations and individuals. Once an organization is adequately studied, the organizational psychologist can diagnose its ills and conduct an "intervention" in the organization, creating the process of planned change (Erwich 2004, 184). The idea of planned change was developed from Kurt Lewin's work in the 1950s (Erwich 2004, 190).[17] For organizational development to take place, an organizational diagnostic must be set in place (see Schalk 1999, 6). Schalk explains that the NCD church profiling is based on phenomenological methodology. Church profiles are created via "the perceptions of church members." These perceptions are then used as explanatory mechanisms of these individuals' behaviors and are viewed as the "normative" experience of the church (Schalk 1999, 11).

There are major problems in this model, problems it is difficult to believe Schwarz did not deliberately induce. As Erwich notes, such a model is inherently risky. The NCD model seeks to qualitatively examine church life, but it is difficult to establish reliable baseline measurements for church quality if analyses of church life are measured solely via "insider" perspectives. The NCD model's scientific effectiveness is hampered by the fact that only 30 congregants and the pastor are given a questionnaire. There are also questions about the selection process for questionnaires. A more random sampling would obviously be preferable, but arguably nominal members may not have sufficient knowledge of the church's nature to provide good feedback. On the flip side, if only key members are given the questionnaire (which seems all too likely to happen), then planned change becomes essentially whatever the leadership team wants it to be. Instead of moving ecclesiastical institutions away from authoritarianism, the original goal of much of Lewin's organizational research, the NCD model of planned change simply makes the authoritarianism of the church less transparent. Rather than create a liberatory church structure which encourages congregants and churches to exist in a symbiotic tensions—the ostensible goal of the NCD model—leadership-directed planned change is all too likely to merely make individuals conform to existing church bureaucratic structures (Schwarz 1996, 74–75; Erwich 2004, 184; Waring 1991, 110, 128). Schalk—and by extension Schwarz—are clearly aware that the very act of diagnosis itself can in turn affect the organization being diagnosed, as well as the individuals within it (Schalk 1999, 6–7).

Schalk and Schwarz's methodology suffers from a central flaw that characterized Kurt Lewin's work: Psychologism. A term invented by C. Wright Mills (1916–1962), psychologism refers to the "naïve attempt to explain society through interactions among individuals without taking into account the importance of institutions" (Waring 1991, 110). Sociological analyses of evangelicalism, even by evangelical social scientists, have long commented on evangelicalism's similar tendency to focus on individual rather than structural solutions to social problems (see, for instance, Emerson and Smith 2000, 104). Such approaches ignore the fact that large social institutions, whether corporations, churches, or governments are not simply "groups shaped by personal transactions," but also exist in bureaucratic structures that are "defined by a hierarchical division of power." Thus, promoting cooperation within institutions characterized by hierarchical stratification will likely normalize such stratification, not eliminate it. Lewin and his disciples promoted the idea that it was managerial style, not social structures, that created tensions between workers and management. Similarly, Schwarz and Schalk's methods rest on the implicit assumption that it is not the church itself that is the problem, but how effectively the church is managed. Indeed, Schwarz's belief in functional dogmatics is predicated on this assumption. Since Schwarz interprets both church structures and theology through the lens of functionality, those elements of the church that do not fit into this functional criteria must be "changed or eliminated." Thus, any element of church life that promotes church health can be rationalized as moral and normative. The question of whether there is something wrong with the institution of the church itself is thus conveniently sidestepped as irrelevant; the perfect church need not ask itself such a question, any more than a perfect corporation need question the institution of capitalism (Schwarz 1996, 28, 76–77; Waring 1991, 110).

Schwarz's connection to systems theory occurs courtesy of Frederic Vester, whose research into bio-cybernetics is the "frame of reference" for NCD (Schwarz 1999, 233). Vester's research contended that there were eight key biocybernetic rules. The first principle contends that "negative feedback cycles must dominate over positive feedback." Vester's second biocybernetic principle rested on the idea that a system's function must not rely on quantitative growth. Indeed, a system that relies on permanent linear expansion is doomed for disaster, because such unlimited expansion will collapse the system in the end (Bogner 2014, 171). This idea is reflected in Schwarz's continual disparaging of linear thinking and his preference for more systemic fixes to structural problems, as well as his preference for qualitative rather than quantitative fixes to churches' structural problems. Schwarz's principle of multiplication, for instance, follows Vester, in contending that unlimited growth of any organism is unsustainable, a "technocrat's dream" (Schwarz 1996, 68). A similar concept characterizes Cal George's Meta system; if one adds too many members to a small group, the group ceases to be manageable for the leader, potentially negatively affecting the group system and the organizational objectives it is meant to achieve (see George 1992, 125). Vester's third biocybernetic principle emphasizes that systems must be "function-oriented" rather than "product-oriented" (Bogner 2014, 171). Thinking must therefore be consistently function-oriented rather than product oriented. Obviously, this idea is paralleled in Schwarz's focus on functionality, particularly functional structures, where church form follows function, rather than function following form. Vester's fourth principle, the exploiting of existing forces, is nicknamed the jujitsu principle. Like jujitsu, this principle relies on opposing forces as controlling energy for the system. Energy put into the system should be used, rather than rejected. Schwarz's third biotic principle, "energy transformation," borrows this concept wholesale, even calling it the "jiu-jitsu principle" (Schwarz 1996, 70). The fifth principle of biocybernetics emphasizes that ideally, "products, functions, and organizational structures" must have "multiple uses." Products, functions and organizational structures that have multiple uses obviously have more long-term sustained viability than those "designed, produced, [or] sold" on their own, due to the fact that there would be far more energy expended for the same result. By reducing energy output, efficiency is increased (Bogner 2014, 171). The multiple-usage principle, like most of Vester's principles, is directly borrowed in Schwarz's work; his argument for the effectiveness of leaders training leaders, for instance, relies on the idea that this kind of in-service training creates higher leadership production yields for "smaller investment[s] of energy" (Schwarz 1996, 73). The sixth biocybernetic principle is recycling. If a system is to survive, it must recycle efficiently. Resources that are wasted lead to an imbalance in the system. Schwarz collapses this idea into the multi-usage principle, but does speak of the necessity of organismic recycling efficiency. Ideally, for instance, not only should a donor contribute to a project, but the project itself should contribute to its own financing: the energy expended on working on the project is the same energy that produces its funding. This, in turn, creates an economically sustainable model of church outreach and development (Bogner 2014, 171; Schwarz 1996, 73). The seventh principle of biocybernetics is symbiosis. The advantage of symbiosis to any cybernetic system is that it allows the pooling of "resources and functions" for the task of conducting work in a more efficient manner. Schwarz borrows this concept largely wholesale, which is not surprising given its central place in cybernetic and biocybernetic management practices (Bogner 2014, 171; Schwarz 1996, 74–75).

The eighth biocybernetic principle is particularly deserving of attention. This principle is "biological design." This argues that "products, processes, and forms of organization" should be designed through "feedback planning" (Vester 2007, 165). In principle what this means is that if a process occurring in the world is to be viable for any length of time, it must mimic natural processes, namely biological and ecological processes (Vester 2007, 165). Schwarz's distinction between the technocratic and the biotic is based on this distinction, and it is by no means inappropriate to see NCD as essentially a form of ecclesiastical biomimicry. For Schwarz, this means that the church should think in a "systemic" and "holistic" manner, paying attention to the natural "ecology" of the church. He uses a Malthusian analogy borrowed directly from Vester, in which a group of elephants is saved from extinction and placed in a nature preserve. The herd population stabilizes and then increases. However, because the elephants were being protected from their natural predators and diseases, the herd population increases too quickly. The maximum herd population is exceeded and the whole herd dies. Schwarz argues that this process—a variant on the Tragedy of the Commons—is fundamental in a wide variety of systems, including the church. Reliance on technocratic solutions to church development and outreach led to quick fixes that did not address systemic issues that plagued the "functional structures" of the church. Mechanistic methods of determining structural faults in the church relied on reductionist ideas. Here, the focus was on exact information. The biotic approach, again borrowing from Vester, is less reliant on "precise information" and more reliant on how systems operate. Simple models were to be preferred over complex ones; therefore, for church consultants wishing to implement planned church growth knowing details was less important than having effectively worked out principles. This affects the diagnostic procedures of those who practice the NCD model. Schwarz's team asks many questions of its clients, but its motive for doing so is quite different from that of traditional church growth consultants. Schwarz's consultancy does not rely on establishing "detailed, pre-programmed instructions for each area of the church," but instead relies on finding two or three leverage points that need to be addressed if church outreach is to be effective. For the church to survive, its functionality must conform to how functional processes work in the natural world. Thus the "structural principles" of the church must conform to these natural processes. Structural effectiveness, rather than a detail orientation, distinguishes the NCD model from more primitive methods of CG (Schwarz 1999, 224–226).

In embracing a biocybernetic approach to church outreach and development, Schwarz sought to apply the NCD approach as a corrective to traditional CG thinking. Focusing on numerical expansion was fine, but such expansion could not continue indefinitely. The amount of resources (potential believers) which the church could call upon was finite. Moreover, seeking to keep the herd (the church) ecologically cocooned in some sort of ecclesiastical nature preserve was unlikely to work. Resource depletion would set in. Thus, if the church was to be an evolutionarily viable social structure, it had to be concerned not simply with numerical growth, but with fixing structural inefficiencies that made it an ineffective cybernetic system. By utilizing NCD principles, Schwarz attempted to apply a model of sustainable development to church outreach, evangelism, and organization. More advanced than earlier evangelical cybernetic models, the NCD approach would be refined to a science in the coming two decades.

Systems Theory Among Evangelicals: Other Applications

Evangelicals have been quick to realize the potential of systems theory. As we have seen, Edward R. Dayton's application of systems analysis methods to missions and strategic planning was an early application of the principles of systems theory in the evangelical church. Much evangelical management literature and church growth literature borrows either directly or indirectly from such insights. For instance, R. Daniel Reeves and Ronald Jenson's *Modern Strategies for Church Growth* applies insights from systems theory to develop strategies for dealing with barriers to church growth (Reeves and Jenson 1984, 45–51). Charles L. Chaney's and Ron S. Lewis's *Design for Church Growth* shows a clear awareness of the "limits to growth" debate and its potential effect on church growth patterns (see Chaney and Lewis 1978, 23–43 passim). The strategic planning model utilized by Robert E. Logan is indebted to feedback concepts borrowed from systems theory (see Logan 1990, 182).[18] In recent years, both Nelson Searcy and Andy Stanley have helped popularize highly simplified, cookie-cutter versions of systems concepts to a wide evangelical audience (Searcy n.d., loc. 55–105; Andy Stanley 2011). A leading evangelical church management manual, *Management Essentials for Christian Ministries*, utilizes systems and feedback concepts constantly (Anthony and Estep Jr. 2005, passim, but especially 3–4, 28–29, 115, 121, 209–210) Most significantly, *Leading Congregational Change: A Practical Guide for the Transformational Journey* (2000), by Jim Herrington, Mike Bonem, and James H. Furr, one of the most influential works in recent church organizational literature, extensively utilized concepts derived from systems theory borrowed from a number of thinkers, including Gregory Bateson and Peter Senge, thus diffusing systems concepts throughout evangelical and mainline churches (Herrington, Bonem, and Furr 2000. 143–157).

At a deeper level, however, the entire design of church marketing, church growth, and church health all depended on principles derived from systems theory, particularly in their use of feedback systems. To understand just why this is the case, however, we need to return to the issue of institutional effectiveness. Much of the institutional effectiveness literature was derived from the field of liberation management, whose most famous proponent was Tom Peters.[19] Proponents of liberation management contended that public managers had the skill set necessary to deal with institutional problems but were handicapped by inefficient systems of control, regulations, and other "red tape" (Larry D. Terry 1998, 195). As we have seen, in the wake of the rise of managerialism, a whole range of effectiveness literature arose in the evangelical movement, much of it tied to the church health movement (Crites 2009, 58). This literature had focused on using data to improve future performance through the use of feedback and feedback response, creating an "internal, circular, and ongoing process which involves identifying and updating the church's vision" (Crites 2009, 58). As Kennesson and Street note, church marketing practices, from which CHM and CGM literature frequently borrowed, focus on creating predictable systems. For church marketing to be effective, churches must be ready to assess their ministry programs success at some future date. To do this, however, churches must be able to have metrics that are definable and measurable, since without such metrics, they cannot set long-term goals (Kenneson and Street 2003, 110–112). Thus, the use of the principle of feedback and responsiveness, both of which are based on at least a basic understanding of systems theory, are utterly necessary if churches are to have any effective strategy for confronting the future. This, as Kenneson and Street note, is predicated on a practice of risk management in the face of market uncertainty (Kenneson and Street 2003, 116). By defining systems of measurement, assessment, and feedback, church marketers—and again, by extension, church growth and church health advocates—are able to set up systems of control, but those systems depend on the ability of churches to operationalize measurements of institutional effectiveness (Kenneson and Street 2003, 121). This assumption in church growth and church health literature is problematic, however, because it reduces virtually all aspects of spiritual life to quantifiable phenomena (Kenneson and Street 2003, 121). Crites, in his study of church health literature, found that the underpinning logic of the movement "aligned with the findings of systems theorists" (Crites 2009, 82). Thus, whether consciously or not—and much CGM and CHM literature was quite conscious in this regard—both movements borrowed implicitly from systems perspectives to create ideally optimizable forms of governance.

But the most important advocate of systems theory within the evangelical movement would be the Leadership Network. And through that Network, the systems perspective helped create one of the most divisive debates within modern evangelicalism; for from the insights of systems theory, a group of young evangelicals and mainliners were about to embark on a new "conversation." This conversation helped create the emergent church and the missional "conversation" that now so shape evangelical culture.

The Rise of the EMC Conversation

Of all the Protestant movements that sought to adopt systems theory, none adopted it more completely than the emergent church and its sister missional movement. The EMC's fascination with the systems perspective originated both from its theological presuppositions and the movement's managerial philosophy, which had been shaped by Bob Buford's Leadership Network. Without understanding these two forces, it is impossible to understand why the emergent and missional movements represent a transformative moment in Protestantism's relationship to management philosophy.

The Missional Movement's theological suppositions were largely shaped by the thought of Anglican bishop Lesslie Newbigin (1909-1998). In his book *The Other Side of 1984*, Newbigin challenged the church to think of the West as a mission field (Doornenbal 2012, 4). Newbigin argued that once Christian leaders accepted this assumption, the church would have to restructure its approach to its mission environment (Doornenbal 2012, 4). The missional movement thus came to see itself as living in a "post–Christendom" environment. In "post–Christendom," Christian ideological and theological assumptions were no longer dominant within the West. Christian terminology no longer represented the West's "lingua franca." Rather than focusing on regaining the church's historical moment, however, the missional movement instead tries to "contextualize" itself to a new post–Christendom context, by adopting "paradigms of church, mission, and leadership" that are more culturally appropriate for a post–Christendom world (Doornenbal 2012, 105, 117). This requires the church to become more outward-focused and missionary in its outlook, with pastoral care taking a secondary, if still important role.

One of the questions the EMC sought to address was what effect the switch to a missional mindset would have on church organization and leadership (Doornenbal 2012, 104–105).

Missiologically, adopting a missional mindset fundamentally alters the church's ecclesiological assumptions. The church, in the Christendom model, was an attractional entity, calling people to come to it. In the missional movement, by contrast, the church's orientation is to come to others first. EMC adherents therefore believe that static institutional structures are no longer sufficient for the church. As a result, they support a missionary outlook that focuses on utilizing "organic structures" as an organizing paradigm. A natural outgrowth of this organicism is that the movement has chosen to adopt living systems theory (LST) as an organizational philosophy (Doornenbal 2012, 106).

Newbigin believed that Western culture was becoming paganized. This led him to maintain a robust publishing schedule. He also took part in the foundation of the "Gospel and Our Culture Network" (GOCN), a network of Christians that emerged in the 1980s in response to his publications (Stewart 2013, 14; Doornenbal 2012, 4). Beginning in the early 1990s, GOCN began bringing its message to Christian cultural elites. The movement sponsored the publication of a number of books, which were united by the belief that the church needed to move away from the CGM-inspired marketing ideology of the time to a missional attitude (Doornenbal 2012, 4–5).

The missional movement brought about seismic changes to Christian consciousness. Into this wake stepped the Emerging Church Movement. Doornenbal argues that the move towards the Emerging paradigm was the result of "three contextual shifts." First, the ecumenical movement influenced early adopters of the Emerging Church model to rethink how they viewed "ecclesiology, mission, and worship." Secondly, the church faced a new theological climate after the post–Vatican II liberalization of the Catholic Church. This liberalization had a profound effect on the emerging church movement's willingness to adopt "high church" practices. Finally, due to decolonization, Western church leaders began to realize how much their own theological heritage was a product of inbuilt cultural assumptions (Doornenbal 2012, 33). In response to these cultural changes as well as the academic discussions going on in missional circles, evangelical groups in New Zealand and the UK began implementing new worship forms in the late 1980s and early 1990s. These new movements were termed "alternative worship" and "fresh expressions of church," but also were sometimes labeled "emerging church" due to American influence (Doornenbal 2012, 34–35). These new forms of church experimented with quite original liturgies, many of them purloined from British club culture and sought to be both multimedia in format and respectfully worshipful at the same time (Stockdale 2013, 89–90). These new worship styles began influencing Christian leaders in the English-speaking world (Stockdale 2013, 89–90).

As the Baby Boomer generation began giving way to Generation X, many pastors saw what they considered a disturbing trend. Unlike Baby Boomers, who typically left church early on in life only to re-enter it at some later point, the members of Generation X were less likely to return to church once they had left (Tony Jones 2011, 44). At this point, the Dallas-based organization, the Leadership Network began calling for a new approach to doing church. The organization hired up-and-coming evangelical leader Doug Pagitt in 1997 to form a "Young Leadership Network," which was tasked with forming a response to an increasingly postmodern culture (Tony Jones 2011, 45). Pagitt began recruiting leaders he felt could create the kind of innovative thinking the Leadership Network was promoting. However, according to Jones, tensions arose between the Leadership Network and Young Leadership Network (YLN) about the direction of the former organization. Many leaders within YLN, for instance, were willing to consider more theologically liberal concepts than Leadership Network leaders felt comfortable with (Tony Jones 2011, 45–46). Although Leadership Network and YLN leaders attempted to heal this rift, none of these efforts succeeded. In response, the organization Emergent Village formed to serve as the hub of Emerging Church organizing (Stockdale 2013, 96).

Yet, despite its break from the Leadership Network, many of the organizational and ecclesiological assumptions that shape Emerging Church thinking originated from its original interactions with the Leadership Network. Without an understanding of these assumptions, as well as the history of the EMC conversation's relationship with them, it is difficult to comprehend just how pervasively management ideology has shaped the movement. Founded by Bob Buford, the Leadership Network has been shaped by the thought of influential management guru Peter Drucker; Buford himself was a prominent Drucker disciple and eventually founded the Peter F. Drucker Foundation for Non-Profit Management. The Leadership Network sought to apply Drucker's approach to "leadership, management and innovation" to a church setting (Frye 2011, 109). Leadership Network's publishing efforts played a significant role in the spread of systems theory and complexity science within evangelical and mainline circles, publishing numerous titles invoking these themes. What was not evident to many of the readers of these texts was where these new innovations in church structure and leadership practices were coming from.

A number of important leaders in secular management circles helped shape the Leadership Network's management philosophy in the 1990s. Their influence was often direct, with the LN frequently inviting such individuals to speak at their conferences. Most of the thinkers who spoke at these conferences feature prominently in the writings of EMC writers and practically always in flattering terms. One of the most important thinkers to influence the movement was Everett Rogers (1931–2004). Rogers was an expert in researching the diffusion of innovations: that is, the means by which innovations are adopted. Rogers' model of diffusion is influential, with fields as diverse as communications, history, economics, education, political science, and healthcare policy all utilizing Rogers' model (Sahin 2006, 14; Godin 2014, 33). Rogers five stage model of innovation adoption became particularly influential among EMC leaders. The five adopter categories that Rogers proposed were innovators, early adopters, early majority, late majority and laggards. Innovators are the creative individuals who introduce new ideas into society. Because of their creativity and forward-thinking nature, innovators are not always respected by the rest of society, even though they produce the technological innovations and cultural trends that the rest of society eventually accepts. The second group, early adopters, tend to conform more to societal norms, often holding leadership positions within the wider society. Early adopters therefore represent a crucial adopter category. Early adopters help ease the acceptance of an innovation by more resistant cultural elements, often through their influence in social networks (Sahin 2006, 18–19). The early majority is composed of those individuals who are just ahead of the curve in adopting innovations. Such individuals often have important societal roles but are not necessarily in key positions of leadership. Nevertheless, their ability to network, like that of the early adopters, is still important. The Late majority represents a fairly large bloc of individuals who are somewhat behind the curve of innovation. Eventually, however, these individuals adopt an innovation, either because of social or economic pressures. The final group in Rogers' model are the laggards. Laggards are culturally resistant to change, usually lacking both the resources and the leadership roles necessary to effectively adopt a new innovation (Sahin 2006, 19–20; Godin 2014, 32; Rogers 1983, 247–251).

The Leadership Network early on realized the advantage of networking with Rogers. In May 1999, LN sponsored a two-day workshop where Rogers presented ideas on how to introduce innovations within a church context ("The Diffusion of Innovation Workshop" 8). A crucial insight that LN took from Rogers model, not incorrectly, was that it was crucial to mobilize Christian innovators and early adopters first, if productive change was going to be introduced into Christianity. LN's assumption was that once this was done, other Christians would fall behind the efforts of these innovators and early adopters (Travis 1999a, 12). Dave Travis, an influential member of the Leadership Network, noted several other lessons that Rogers' presentation gave the Leadership Network. One of the most crucial of these insights was that innovations often proved most successful when they were implemented alongside other innovations. Moreover, Travis pointed out two other important points to Leadership Network's supporters: First, innovations would not succeed if they did not give adopters an adaptive advantage. Although the Emergent church in many ways did not learn this lesson, those who adopted the missional and "organic" church models clearly did. In both those movements, but particularly the organic church, much more careful attention was paid to messaging the EMC dialogue in a way that would not alienate Christian moderates and conservatives. Travis also noted that simpler innovations were more likely to be adopted, which may account for the relatively simplified versions of complexity theory and systems theory that most EMC authors promoted among their supporters (Travis 1999b 49). Because LN found Rogers book on diffusion too technical, they later promoted Malcolm Gladwell's *Tipping Point* as an adjunct to Rogers's writing, while still acknowledging the movement's indebtedness to Rogers's thinking (Travis 2000, 202).

Rogers's model predicated itself on the assumption that good social networks are a must for innovations to be effectively introduced. He believed that innovations were judged less by their base scientific or economic value than by how they were received by those within a potential adoptee's social circle (Rogers 1998, 15). Rogers therefore told Leadership Network leaders and thinkers that understanding the communication networks they had established was crucial to implementing any change. He contrasted two models of networks. The first, radial networks, were networks in which people with different characteristics are connected. The second form of networks, interlocking networks, formed around people with similar characteristics. Radial networks, he contended, tended to be better at information gathering and were useful for those individuals who wanted to implement change, while interlocking networks helped provide individual members with "social support and consensus" and were thus not a useful source of innovation. Rogers's focus on social networks came at a precipitous moment in American technological history, as the Internet began to harness its potential. After the leaders of the YLN split from LN, many of them continued to utilize Rogers' diffusion model, and the model served as an organizing paradigm for much of the missional movement as well.[20] Rogers's thought was particularly influential on the widely used Missional Change model for converting churches to a missional model (Roxburgh and Romanuk 2006, 80).

In addition to diffusion theory, systems theory and a number of complexity theories figured heavily in the rhetoric of the EMC. Complexity theory—which is more appropriately spoken about as a group of theories, representing a body of theoretical concepts, research models and theories that originate in fields ranging from meteorology to mathematics—is particularly important to understanding the EMC conversation. More and more, academics and organizational professionals are seeing complexity theory as an ideal platform from which to launch organizational change (Burnes 2005, 73). This new interest in complexity theory arose because of a shared conviction among academics and management professionals that late 20th and 21st century organizations face an unprecedented amount of change. Yet such change has historically been difficult to implement, and many of the older models, such as those offered up by Kurt Lewin and promoters of organizational development, have garnered a good deal of criticism in recent years. This has led many organizations to adopt change models that focus on "continuous transformation"; at the heart of these models lie efforts to implement complexity theory towards the task of organizational change (Burnes 2005, 73–75). In the natural sciences, adherents of complexity theories contend that "disequilibrium (chaos) is a necessary condition for the growth of dynamic systems, but that such systems are prevented from tearing themselves apart by the presence of simple order-generating rules" (Burnes 2005, 74). In organizational theory, supporters of complexity theories advance the argument that organizations function exactly like natural complex systems. This means that these systems are dynamic and non-linear. Thus, the results of a system are not predictable, but are bound by the same order-generating rules that characterize natural systems. Thus, organizations that wish to survive must learn to live on what has been termed "'the edge of chaos." Overly stable organizations lack sufficient flexibility to adapt proactively to change. Overly chaotic organizations, however, risk falling apart due to the pace of change they are enduring. Thus, the key is to derive a new form of order-generating rules (Burnes 2005, 74).

Although there are numerous models of organizational change, most of these models can be divided into two categories: planned change and the emergent approach to organizational change.[21] During the initial post–World War II period, the planned approach dominated. Building on the work of Kurt Lewin and his intellectual descendants in the organizational development movement, the planned approach emphasized "participative, group- and team-based programmes of change" (Burnes 2005, 74–75). However, due to the energy crisis of the 1970s and the increasing economic challenge presented by Japan, organizations in the 1970s and 1980s began advocating for more radical approaches to organizational development. The approach of planned change came to be seen as too incremental for a rapidly developed mass media culture (Burnes 2005, 74–75). By contrast, those who supported an emergent model argued that the requirements of the modern marketplace required organizations to "change continuously in a fundamental manner" (Burnes 2005, 76).

Leadership theorist A. Keene has advanced the proposition that traditional organizations have found themselves overly bound to the mechanistic management practices they have inherited from scientific management

(Aaron Smith 2004, 90), a belief that is shared by key voices in the EMC, such as Kester Brewin and Brian McLaren (Doornenbal 2012, 75–76).[22] Because of this mechanistic worldview, traditional management theory tries to segment systems into their component parts. This assumption, in turn has led management theorists to adopt complexity theories, as a new non-reductionistic alternative to problem solving (Aaron Smith 2004, 90).

Before looking at specific complexity theories, and their corresponding applications in the EMC, it is important to understand that the application of complexity theory to "the science and practice of management" is by no means uncontested. Aaron Smith contends that management theory's application of complexity theory has suffered from "confusing academic rhetoric, slick 'consultant-speak' and misleading gossip" (Aaron Smith 2004, 90). Multiple scholars have suggested that complexity theory has offered up few practical benefits as an organizational theory (Aaron Smith 2004, 90). Indeed, the application of complexity theories to organizational life present numerous problems. For instance, as Smith notes, the concept of "surfing on the edge of chaos" can be faulted for the degree of nebulousness it presents managers and organizational thinkers. The model offers few clues as to how to successfully differentiate between surfing the chaos and falling into "the 'black hole'" that the chaos represents. Thus, keeping an organization from verging too far in the direction of either chaos or equilibrium is difficult, particularly since the whole "'edge of chaos'" paradigm is predicated on the assumption that non-linear systems are ultimately unpredictable. Thus, even if an organization develops a successful method for dancing on the "edge of chaos," the method is unlikely to be replicable, which calls into question the organizational utility of the whole "edge of chaos" concept (Aaron Smith 2004, 94).

A further criticism of complexity theory's organizational usefulness applies to its frequent use of computer modeling. In general, computer modeling seeks to construct straightforward behavioral principles which can be used to describe "macro behavior[s]" (Burnes 2005, 81). The problem is that real world scenarios rarely conform to such straightforward modeling (Burnes 2005, 81). Doornenbal has raised a similar point when applying complexity theory to the EMC. He points out that at its root, complexity theories are "highly mathematical" and may not be appropriate to apply to ecclesiological or organizational questions, due to the number of variables they cannot account for (Doornenbal 2012, 158).

From Doornenbal's standpoint, the division some complexity theorists and most EMC adherents make between biological and mechanistic paradigms is dubious. Biology, as Doornenbal notes, can itself be reductionistic. Moreover, the sociological application of biological metaphors, even more common in the EMC than among predecessor movements like the CHM and NCD, has had a dubious historical record, making it questionable how appropriate it is to apply such metaphors in the absence of any strong support for their validity (Doornenbal 2012, 158).

In terms of understanding the EMC's appropriation of complexity theory, a few key concepts are important: complex adaptive systems, self-organization and non-linearity, emergence, chaos theory, and dissipative structures (Doornenbal 2012, 148–153; Burnes 2005, 80). In complex adaptive systems (CASs), numerous agents operate under sets of rules which govern how they interact with other agents. This in turn requires "each agent to adjust its behavior to that of other agents" (Burnes 2005, 78–79). Complexity theorists point out that all organisms are CASs (79). By their very nature, CASs are "self-organizing." The behavioral nature of the system arises from the interactions of the component agents within it. Because of this capacity to self-organize, CASs have the ability to proactively react to their environment, though the original or initiating environment of CASs plays a formidable role in their subsequent development (79). EMC adherents who subscribe to complexity theory frequently characterize the church as a CAS (Doornenbal 2012, 149).

The concept of self-organization is even more key to EMC adaptations of complexity theory. Self-organization is the ability of systems to produce order through the utilization of a few simple "order-generating rules." These rules allow for a finite amount of chaos, while still promoting a relative amount of stability for the system (Burnes 2005, 80). This ability to produce self-organization is what allows complex, non-linear, self-organizing systems to skirt the edge of chaos, despite variations in the environment a system is located within (Burnes 2005, 80). For the EMC, the concepts of self-organization and non-linearity suggest that when knowledge and innovative ideas are pooled by the movement, the sum of the parts will often be different than expectations predict (Doornenbal 2012, 150).[23]

In the context of complexity theory, emergence can mean many things. However, for the purpose of understanding the theory's application to the EMC context, Doornenbal provides the most succinct definition: "In general, the term 'emergence' is used by scientists to describe the spontaneous appearance of unprecedented orderliness in nature" (Doornenbal 2012, 152). Within organizations, this can lead to major and sometimes unexpected increases in organizational effectiveness. From the standpoint of organizational theorists, as well as many supporters of the EMC, this leads to a major reshaping of organizational leadership theory. Leaders no longer seek to provide stability to churches, but to destabilize them. The leadership is far less concerned with innovating or creating change than encouraging and interpreting these processes. Finally, leadership's role ceases to be controlling people and instead becomes "managing words" (Doornenbal 2012, 152–153).

Chaos theory refers to systems whose processes look random, but whose actual operation takes place as the result of "'precise scientific laws'" (Lorenz 1979 qtd. in Burnes 2005, 78; Burnes 2005, 78). The processes chaos theory references are inevitably dynamic, persistently and irreversibly altering themselves in an evolutionary fashion (Burnes 2005, 78). Chaos theory accepts non-linear causality, while standing against "Newtonian, mechanical laws." Within a chaotic system, small alterations in an environment can create major alterations to the behavior of a system. Yet at some point, systems begin to self-organize and produce a new "high-order structure," often called a "dissipative structure." This term refers to structures whose stability will inevitably dissipate barring the external input of energy to uphold them. As with chaos itself, dissipative structures operate according to non-linear logic. In some cases, such structures have the ability to withstand a great deal of force from external factors, while in other cases, minute alterations can break up the entire system. Dissipative structures, like chaos theory, concentrates on "whole systems and populations" and thus the study of such structures differs from the approach taken by students of CASs, which look at individual behavioral factors within systems or demographic groups (Burnes 2005, 78).

Frequently referenced in popular culture, it is not surprising that many of chaos theory's concepts have been appropriated by the EMC. EMC organizational and leadership literature frequently references such popularizations (Doornenbal 2012, 135). For instance, Neil Cole appeals to chaos theory in his book *Organic Church* (Cole 2005, 123–124), while Phyllis Tickle also sought to use chaos theory to promote theological discussion within the church (Jones 2014, 26). Particularly influential in this regard is the work of Australian missiologist Alan Hirsch, whose book *Forgotten Ways* has an entire appendix on chaos theory (Doornenbal 2012, 135–136).

Robert Doornenbal has severely criticized the EMC for its appropriation of chaos theory. Doornenbal contends that EMC leaders tend to "uncritically embrace the newest scientific, or scientific sounding, ideas, especially those that criticize reductionism and modernity" (Doornenbal 2012, 136). In the process, these leaders produce a problematic binary between, on the one hand, reductionism and modernity, and on the other hand, postmodernism and organic thinking. Instead of using chaos theory as an "illustrative analogy or suggestive metaphor" when applied to church life, EMC authors grant it the argumentative force of an ironclad scientific principle. This grants chaos theory a far greater influence over church policy than the chaos metaphor can productively support. EMC authors' preference for holism over reductionism can be faulted on similar grounds (Doornebal 2012, 136). Doornenbal is particularly worried about references to holism in EMC thinking, as he has noted that the utilization of holistic metaphors as ideological metaphors has had a long and dubious history—including the appropriation of such metaphors by Nazi Germany (Doornenbal 2012, 138). Doornenbal's point echoes similar concerns I have about the problematic embrace of holistic ideals in the NCD model.

Despite the problems associated with the holistic metaphor and other misapplications of complexity theory, the application of complexity theory to both secular organizations and the EMC is widespread. Many organizational thinkers describe organizations as CASs, which have self-organizing potentiality. Because of the rejection of mechanistic modalities of management and the embrace of holism, management theorists currently promote decentralized power structures and reject "top down, command-and-control styles of management." Numerous writers also advance the proposition that effective organizations must begin operating along democratic lines, which means, among other things, they must have the ability to voluntarily self-organize (Burnes 2005, 81–83). Peter Senge's (1947–) concept of learning communities, a popular idea within the EMC, is important here. Moreover, those who apply complexity theory to organizational life usually argue for a destabilization of hierarchal systems, the use of relational networking, the promotion of diversity and uncertainty, and the application of "organic and ecological metaphors" to organizational life (Doornenbal 2012, 148).

The rejection of hierarchical thinking and the embrace of decentralization within the EMC is notable here and serves quite specific ideological functions. Alan Hirsch's writing is instructive in this regard. For Hirsch, the move towards decentralization plays a crucial role in the EMC's message. He contends that previous reform efforts within Christianity have failed because they have addressed "software" problems in the church, without addressing the fundamental "hardware" questions—that is structural dilemmas—that the church faces (Hirsch 2006, 52). Traditional modes of church organization, which Hirsch associates with denominationalism, favors the "command and control" model of organizational life that complexity theorizing explicitly rejects.[24] Hirsch, by contrast, prefers an apostolic mode of governance, that allows for a more dynamic approach to organizational development (Hirsch 2006, 52–58).

This apostolic mode of control is attractive to EMC leaders for many reasons. Most notably, the ideological justification for the EMC movement's critique of the institutional church rests on its rejection of the culture of Christendom. Christendom, for Hirsch, remains steeped in institutionalism. Although the birth of Christendom allowed Christianity to become culturally dominant, it was, by the standards of the EMC, a disastrous event for the "Jesus movement,"[25] because it turned a dynamic and innovative religious movement into a formalized and codified rule making system (Hirsch 2006, 59–60). Thus, a theologically consistent critique of Christendom would on its own likely cause the EMC movement to reject institutionalism and embrace a more apostolic mode of leadership.

Some have accused EMC leaders, particularly Alan Hirsch, of presenting a thinly disguised version of NAR-model apostolic governance, where apostles have dictatorial control over their followers (Metzger). It must be said in Hirsch's defense, however that the dominant model of leadership in the EMC focuses more on facilitating change rather than directing that change from on high (Doornenbal 2012, 177–180). In that sense, New Apostolic leadership paradigms do not fit in to the leadership philosophy that the EMC purports to uphold (see, on this score, Doornenbal 2012, 171 for his comments on EMC leadership styles). EMC thinkers argued against leadership predicated on institutional authority or scholastic achievement. The movement shies away from ordination and rejects the control of the church masses by an ecclesiastical intelligentsia (Doornenbal 2012, 177). Power is meant to be shared through relational networking. What is key for the EMC, whose ideas of leadership were shaped by the organic leadership movement common in secular organizational literature is that the focus of leadership is on the principle of leadership itself, rather than on a specific leader. Thus, within EMC and organic leadership models, leadership is diffused throughout an entire system, and decisions are typically arrived at through consensus (Doornenbal 2012, 187–191). Nevertheless, even Doornenbal acknowledges that there is a potential for abuse within this model (Doornenbal 2012, 179). Regardless of its motivations, by organizing authority around apostolic figures, the EMC runs the risk of creating an authoritarian leadership, but one untied to any form of organizational structure. As I have argued in *The New Apostolic Reformation: History of a Modern Charismatic Movement*, this is not an ideal state of affairs. One of the major advantages of denominational bureaucracies, seldom acknowledged in either EMC or NAR writings, is that they provide institutional breaks against power-hungry individuals. Without these democratic checks and balances, it is easy to see how EMC churches could fall prey to dictatorial control.

The agenda of decentralization within the EMC also fits two other long-term goals of the evangelical movement: cost-cutting and the creation of networked church cultures. Alan Hirsch is again particularly instructive in this regard. Hirsch and his colleague Michael Frost (1961–) have noted, in line with the thinking of Christian Schwarz, that Christian leaders should focus less on size, and more on sustainable growth practices (Cronshaw 2009, 56). The reason for this focus on sustainability is that church systems, like any systems, face "limits to growth." Brian McLaren (1956–), the dominant voice within the Emerging Church movement, notes that while churches have an unlimited growth potential, their leadership typically cannot get them to grow beyond a certain size without either trading one form of growth for another, or engaging in "multiplication." The most effective church organizations, in McLaren's reading, are those capable of utilizing multiple forms of reproduction, rather than just one (McLaren 2000, 46–47).

For evangelicalism to be sustainable long-term, however, it must be cost-effective. Given the declining amount of religious adherence in the United States, it behooves the evangelical movement to develop techniques for promoting cost-effectiveness. Therefore, structures and institutions that do not provide sufficient cost effectiveness are being called into question. EMC leader Neil Cole, for instance, has attacked the megachurch on these grounds. From Cole's vantage point, the megachurch leads to an overemphasis on expensive buildings, leaders, and services, as well as the corresponding increase in cost for advertising, land use, and other expenses. The church can no longer extract enough resources from its local environment to make such a growth model sustainable or cost-effective (Cole 2010, 50–51). Cole therefore focuses on creating new churches that are "self-perpetuating and 'self-propagating.'" Such churches are not dependent on other ecclesiastical organizations/organisms for their support; moreover, they can start new organizations that will in turn produce additional organizations of their own. In such a growth model, maintaining low overhead allows for the evangelical movement to continue its global growth even in a period of relative ecclesiastical economic decline (Cole 2010, 83).

The EMC shares with the NAR the conviction that only a new organizational model can allow the church to structurally compete with other modern institutions. And, as with the NAR, the model organizational system that EMC churches seek to base themselves on is the network. Hirsch concedes that this organizational schema may seem an unnatural fit with New Testament models, but argues that it actually is closer to the way New Testament Christians envisioned church than the models offered up by post–New Testament (a.k.a. Christendom) culture (Hirsch 2006, 200). EMC organizations, like most networked groups, focus on direct action, make extensive use of digital communications, and try to structure themselves in an organic manner (Doornenbal 2012, 195).

The EMC models much of its operating agenda on computer technology, with websites like Wikipedia serving as models for church organization. This new form of church emphasizes relationships, interconnectedness, and flexibility. References to the church being an open source are frequent. EMC leader Karen Ward has argued that the model of church that emergent and missional churches support has many affinities with Linux, but less so with Windows. In Linux, all people can become coders, whereas in Windows the coding of structure—here church structure—is largely pre-set by a select group of individuals (Gibbs and Bolger 2006, 162).[26] Thus, the church is changeable and adaptable to the extent that it literalizes these computational metaphors.

When it comes to the idea of networks themselves, however, EMC churches borrow from some of the most sophisticated network theories currently available. Two thinkers, John Arquilla (1954–) and David Ronfeldt, have particularly influenced how EMC leaders approach networks. Arquilla and Ronfeldt were researchers at the RAND Corporation, when they penned their influential work *Networks and Netwars*, which is seen as a pioneering text on the netwar concept. While the U.S. military-industrial complex was already focused on specific applications of network theory to the global battlefield, the netwar concept explored how information networks might affect non-military forms of conflict, as well as militarized ones (Weber 2004, 11) Netwars are thus not limited to just traditional military conflicts but can embrace all forms of "network-based conflict and crime." Netwar theory can thus be applied to conflicts with "nonstate 'actors,'" thus giving the theory an added saliency in a post–9/11 world dominated by asymmetrical warfare (Weber 2004, 11). Ronfeldt and Arquilla construct a typology of three major network types. Chain or line networks consist of components that are tied together in a "linear, sequential manner." In such networks, communication between actors is "More or less fixed" from "end to end." The second type of network is alternately referred to as "the hub, star, or wheel network." In these networks, all the components connect through a central hub by which "communication must pass." Nevertheless, this central hub does not exert hierarchal control. Finally, all-channel and full-matrix networks are constructed out of components that are interconnected without having a centralized hub (Weber 2004, 12). Depending on the context, differing forms of networks can be combined in response to environmental stimuli. The commonality between all these network forms is that organizationally, they are centered around horizontal rather than vertical principles. Netwar theory predicts, therefore, that the "all channel" style of networking will be particularly unique, due to its highly dispersed and non-hierarchical nature (Weber 2004, 12). One of the major advantages of converting to "all channel" networking is that it eliminates the ability of enemies to knock out an organization by taking out a centralized command and control system. All channel networks are organized in such a manner that cutting off the head of an organization, still leaves the remaining components intact and functional, making such networks much more difficult to control. A further implication of netwar theory, as outlined by Arquilla and Ronfeldt, is that organizational leadership structures based on verticality are giving way somewhat to horizontally organized institutions based on netwar principles (Weber 2004, 13).

As Marieke Goede notes, the discourse surrounding networks is not without its problems. Network theory can be faulted for exposing threats that it itself actually creates and then controls (see Goede 2012, 215–216). Discussions of network interconnectivity therefore do not simply conduct objective threat assessments, but themselves "constitute and actualize dangers, select risks, and prioritize threats" (Goede 2012, 216). Thus, insofar as the EMC utilizes network theory as an organizational ideology, it serves a policing role within the movement, allowing it to analyze potential dangers to Christian security and cultural consensus. The tremendous potential for this organizational ideology to be turned towards conservative ends is not acknowledged in EMC literature.

This literature, moreover, promotes the netwar theory quite openly. Neil Cole, after citing Arquilla and Ronfeldt, notes that Christians would do well to organize their churches around "all channel networks." However, according to netwar theory, for these all-channel networks to be truly effective, they need to share a motivating ideological, doctrine, or organizational identity that can unite them in a fundamental manner (Cole 2010, 95). Therefore, in NAR churches, which share many of the characteristics of "all channel networks," organizational identity is shaped by a shared vision usually brought about by the lead apostle or prophet. Although the apostle or prophet often exerts profound influences within these movements, his power is based on charisma rather than centralized command and control abilities. Cole seeks to operationalize a similar form of unitary ideological identity for so-called organic churches, the iteration of the EMC that he backs (Cole 2010, 97–98). Hirsch similarly notes the specific advantages of not utilizing a centralized command and control structure and promotes horizontal rather than vertical organizational structures (Hirsch 2006, 201). Hirsch also draws analogies between the (purported) network structures of the early church and the highly decentralized structures of "international terrorist networks like Al Qaeda" (Hirsch 2006, 206). For Hirsch the important lesson that Christian churches can take from Al Qaeda is to focus on decentralization and emphasize localized, easily "multipliable" cell groups that can replicate the same ideological convictions in vastly differing environmental contexts (Hirsch 2006, 206).

One key component in the EMC's approach to creating such all channel networks is its utilization of living systems theory. Undergirding virtually the entire organic church conversation and much of that surrounding the EMC writ large is the metaphorical comparison of the church to a living system (Doornenbal 2012, 145). Within the broader systems framework, living systems theory (LST) posits that there are certain uniform principles true of all life, "regardless of their size origin and complexity"; moreover, these principles are not necessarily replicable in artificial systems. Living systems are characterized as "purposive" because they are "complex, adaptive, [and] open." Like other open systems they have the ability to bring in and export energy from their surrounding environment. Such systems must therefore be capable of self-regulation and self-repair. A relatively controversial aspect of LST is that Miller applies his theory not simply to organisms but to social groupings, such as communities, nations, and alliances. However, current social theory has been unable to determine whether such entities actually have "a real existence 'in nature' or not." Because of this, a number of scientists contend that such social entities are better seen as organizational metaphors or "theoretical constructs" rather than as entities with actual natural existence (Skyttner 2001, 113). Moreover, scientists also debate whether "systems at levels above the organism can be considered alive" (Skyttner 2001, 114), since they lack physical connections between different parts.

Nevertheless, for the EMC, one of the major advantages of complexity theory as an organizational tool is that it helps legitimize the use of organic and holistic metaphors to EMC adherents (Doornenbal 2012, 153–154). Various major writers in the EMC, including Leonard Sweet, Joseph Myers, Neil Cole, and Erwin McManus invoke such organismic language to push forward the movement's ideological and organizational beliefs (Doornenbal 2012, 154–155). LST largely entered the EMC conversation through the influence of the Leadership Network, which has promoted several prominent secular supporters of its application to organizations. Particularly influential in this regard, as Doornenbal notes, is prominent management guru Margaret Wheatley, one of the key organizational gurus promoting new paradigm management.[27] Don Zimmer, writing for a Leadership Network publication in 2001, noted that Wheatley influenced him to move away from "organizational practices" that emphasized "control, predictability, division and reductionism" (Zimmer 2001, 433). Wheatley spoke before a Leadership Network conference entitled "Exploring the Map" and her books have been heavily promoted in LN material (Wheatley 2000, 43–44; Sweet 2000, 50–53; Explorer 2000, 50–53). In keeping with much of the organizational thought surrounding complexity theory, Wheatley promotes a "radical" application of chaos theory to organizational life, primarily through fostering "interdependence, networked relationships and grassroots dreaming and planning" within organizations (Cronshaw 2009, 57).

Wheatley contends that organizations "are not just living systems, but they are literally alive" (Doornenbal 2012, 162). Many EMC authors follow her line of reasoning. Yet, as Doornenbal points out, this appropriation of LST by the emergent and missional movements often obfuscates the many negative aspects of human life that characterize such systems. In the process, as Douglas Griffin has warned, this kind of "idealistic holistic philosophy" risks becoming reified into its own form of highly ideological thinking, while at the same time claiming that it is the end of ideology. Since the application of organismic metaphors to the church has a New Testament lineage, it can be all too easily used to emphasize power relationships that emphasize, rather than subvert, authority structures (Doornenbal 2012, 162–163).

A number of other authors share Doornenbal's concern about the increasing appropriation of organismic metaphors by church health and EMC advocates. Jeremy Posadas, for instance, has expressed concern that church health discourse—he particularly notes the NCD model—appeals to biomedical discourse in its description of church life, but in practice obtains data about demographic target groups through application of the human and social sciences. In the church health model, particularly as advanced by NCD, church leaders are explicitly attempting to gain "scientific knowledge about Christian congregations." Posadas suggests that one of the implicit goals of such research is to instrumentalize a form of social control on congregations' social life, using biomedical categories as both justifications for this instrumental control and metrics for measuring it. Posadas contends, not unreasonably, that there is little practical difference between this kind of population management and the forms of "regulatory biopower" that governments use to shape their own biomedical policies. In both cases, the main concern is to "normalize," as well as "optimize," demographic groups via the application of scientific research. Therefore, while acting as an engine of organizational innovation and creativity, the purpose of CH, NCD, and EMC discourse can be seen in one sense as deeply reactionary (Posadas 2012, 160–163). All three discursive methodologies seek to operationalize a biomedical rationality that limits, rather than enhances, "consumer" choice, and that still seeks to manage population groups via more subtler means than were available to the CGM.

Lyndon Shakespeare, in his book *Being the Body of Christ in the Age of Management* (2016), expresses similar concerns about the use of biomedical discourse in the church. Shakespeare warns that this discourse runs the risk of appealing to physicalist principles that have their roots in scientific naturalism. For Shakespeare, this represents a rejection of the liberating aspects of Christianity in favor of a form of ecclesiastical control that, despite claims to the contrary, has its roots in "managerial practices of efficiency, calculability, predictability and control" (Shakespeare 2016, loc. 154). Managerialism thus promotes "operations and practices" which seeks to qualify and quantify human life into increasingly segmented categories. When applied to the life of the church, the inevitable result is the adoption of a corporate-oriented managerial philosophy (Shakespeare 2016, loc. 204–227). Shakespeare expresses the concern that by adopting the managerial techniques and philosophies of secular managerialism, EMC advocates and their allies in other veins of Christian managerial philosophy, run the risk of changing the church from a service provided to a community, to a product sold to one. In the process, the church's lineage as a heritage for Christians to adhere to is reduced to a commodified object (Shakespeare 2016, loc. 1597–1622).

The concerns expressed by Doornenbal, Posadas, Shakespeare, and others should not be lightly ignored. Perhaps the most obvious example of how

EMC leadership practices can be transformed into simple managerialism is in the movement's approach to conflict and organizational change. The EMC movement has developed a specific change model to deal with congregational change: The Missional Change Model (MCM). The MCM is based on Rogers's diffusion of innovation model. The leaders who constructed the MCM realized that implementing congregational change in a church context was not an easy process; resistance to new ideas and change was part and parcel of any large-scale cultural transition. To ease this process, the movement adopted insights they had gleaned from Rogers.

The movement based its five stages of successful transition on a similar stage model presented by Rogers. The first stage is to raise awareness of an issue that the leadership thinks needs to be changed. The second stage employs conversation to make people understand that change is needed. In the third stage, the church evaluates its congregational expectations in order to see what church practices fit the model of "missional innovation" that the church wants to employ. Crucial to the success of this stage is reassuring the congregation that while experimentation will occur (especially in the fourth stage of the model), much of the fundamental character of the church will remain the same. The fourth stage of the MCM employs experimentation to set the stage for "missional innovation." Roxburgh argues that the changes made in the congregation must be more than programmatic or organizational but must affect the congregation at the cultural level. Finally, in the last stage of the MCM model the church accepts its new model of doing church (Roxburgh and Romanuk 2006, 79–103).

Given the assumptions of Rogers diffusion model, which focuses on first gaining the support of innovators, the MCM model also centers on gaining a crucial base group of support who are receptive to the innovation the church wants to introduce. Once this beachhead in the church is established, the dialogue stage of the MCM is used to bring others into the fold. By three years into the introduction of the missional innovation, the leadership has built up a base support of 25 percent, at which stage any resistance can no longer effectively stop the innovation. Over "a third 18 month period," most of the remaining congregation will commit to the change, while a small core of resisters and laggards refuses to change. Some of these individuals will end up leaving the church, but the church in the end will have successfully converted to the new MCM model it wishes to use (Roxburgh and Romanuk 2006, 103–105).

The MCM represents but one of several congregational change models that are now offered up by church consultants. There are other examples, for instance Herrington, Bonem, and Furr's Congregational Change model (see Herrington, Bonem and Furr 2000, passim). What makes the MCM such a potentially effective tool for overcoming resistance to congregational change is that it applies sociological and anthropological insights from secular change models to a church context, often without congregations being consciously aware of this happening. Because of this, the MCM model, and other congregational change models, invite abuse by leadership teams who want to use them to introduce changes that benefit leadership first and sincere Christian adherents last. In the process, churches run the risk of utilitarianism, with the theological ends justifying the means.

Conclusion

The ecclesiological changes that managerial logic has wrought on American Protestantism over the last century and a quarter have been profound. Starting from the triumph of Taylorist principles over more traditional soul care, American Protestantism has more and more taken on the image and even the methodology of secular businesses. As I have argued in Chapter 1, this does not necessarily reflect any unprincipled behavior on the part of church leaders, particularly those at the turn of the 20th century. Protestantism's transition to a congregational culture based on secular business models was likely inevitable. What should give Protestants pause, however, is how uncritically the insights of secular business models have been adopted, oftentimes with only the thinnest veneer of theological gloss surrounding them.

In the next chapter, we will examine the range and influence of the network idea within American evangelicalism. For it is network organizational principles that have proven foundational to the success of the modern evangelical movement. The rise of the new, network model of doing church has forever transformed evangelicalism. Yet whether that change really benefits believers is a highly disputable question, one which Chapters 4 and 5 endeavor to answer.

4

Networked Churches and the Rise of Church Toyota

As the 20th century ended, two closely connected forms of church organization came increasingly to the fore. Each form of organization built itself on top of the other and could not exist without the organizing ideology that sustained its fellow movement. The first of these new forms of church organization, the church network, has its origins in Pentecostal apostolic networks. In the United States, these Charismatic apostolic networks originally sprouted from the shepherding networks of the 1970s, while British apostolic networks mainly evolved out of their house church movement (Hocken 2009, 30–31). The second element of church organization that arose during this time period, which was used as a support system for the many new forms of church organization being implemented during the last few decades of the 20th century, was the rise of what I have termed the "Toyotist" church.

This latter term requires some explanation. Despite my frequent disagreement with William Kay, I am indebted to his use of Manuel Castells in this regard. Castells analysis of modern corporations in *The Rise of the Network Society* notes a number of important trends that characterize modern corporations. These corporations have a "process" orientation rather than a task-based one. Organizationally, modern corporations prefer "flat" hierarchies and "team management." The metric for success in such corporations typically is its "customer satisfaction." Moreover, training occurs throughout every level of the corporation. As Kay notes, apostolic networks embrace many modern corporate elements, including flat organizational structures, process-oriented approaches to production (i.e., ministry), team ministry, and continuous training (Kay 2007, 289). However, a few other elements of Castells analysis that Kay fails to mention are also important. Modern corporations, which derive much of the inspiration for their production process from Toyota, seek to implement "'total quality control'" when they produce goods, usually with the hope of arriving "at near-zero defects and best use

4. Networked Churches and the Rise of Church Toyota 195

of resources" (Castells 2010a, 169). Toyotism encourages "decentralized initiative" and "greater autonomy of decision on the shopfloor" (Castells 2010a, 169). While this speaks to Kay's point about the use of flat organizational structures in both modern corporations and apostolic networks, the move towards decentralization and localization of all procedures also speaks to a move away from centralized planning. This move towards decentralization is characteristic of most forms of neo-liberalism. Moreover, the emphasis on quality control is also seen in numerous churches. More than one church thinker has argued that Protestants should borrow Toyotist ideas, particularly Total Quality Management (TQM), outright. Even those who have not suggested such open appropriation of secular business practices have pushed for an increasing emphasis on quality in ministry.

Most of the churches that I classify as Toyotist here would fall somewhere within the new paradigm church (NPC) moniker coined by Donald E. Miller. Miller's *Reinventing American Protestantism: Christianity in the New Millennium* (1997) argued that a new form of church—the new paradigm church—was emerging during the second half of the 20th century (Donald E. Miller 1997, 11). Miller dates the beginning of this change to the emergence of the JPM (Donald E. Miller 1997, 11). New Paradigm Churches are characterized by a number of significant traits. Small groups are heavily emphasized in new paradigm churches (Donald E. Miller 1997, 14). Church planting is strongly emphasized. The typical NPC empowers lay members to create new ministries on their own, with "enormous latitude" given to lay members in how they fulfill this goal (Donald E. Miller 1997, 15–16). NPC churches deemphasize seminary training, while contemporary worship is put at the forefront (Donald E. Miller 1997, 19–20). Miller also notes the tendency of NPC congregations to embrace a modified form of the therapeutic gospel, which takes some of the values of the sixties' encounter groups but mixes them with more biblistic, direct, and even "confrontational" Christian pastoral care (Donald E. Miller 1997, 21).

From an organizational perspective, the most important element of the NPC church, as Miller defines it, is its "anti-establishment" nature. Bureaucratic regulations and institutionalism face significant resistance from NPCS. Not surprisingly, NPC churches, tend to focus on "lean" staffing methods, a characteristic that they share with Toyotist corporations (Donald E. Miller 1997, 22). Moreover, like church networks (of which they are often a part), NPC churches and groups organize around a "highly decentralized" model. In most NPC churches, infused with New Paradigm and neospiritual assumptions, the pastor is responsible for casting a vision for the organization, but delegates responsibility for most church programs to his staff and lay members (Donald E. Miller 1997, 138). NPC churches can more rapidly adapt to cultural changes than more bureaucratically centered mainline and evangelical churches because of the low-cost method they utilize to initiate new programs and ministries. Existing in what is essentially a deregulated religious economy, such ministries suffer relatively few restrictions in NPCs versus traditional churches (Donald E. Miller 1997, 139). Although Miller accentuates the benefits of such an arrangement, the deregulation of church ministries does have its downsides. One of the more significant problems such ministries encounter is a tendency to hive off into little authoritarian subcultures within the wider church body. Moreover, the deregulated nature of NPC churches' religious economies means that there is insufficient accountability for abuses that occur within their walls.

New Paradigm Churches tend to have most of the characteristics of a business start-up. Miller contends that because of their "decentralized leadership," organizational innovation and creativity is encouraged in a manner not possible for traditional church structures. Those structures aim for what Miller calls "'sure' success," but risk losing out on "product innovation" in the process. To ensure that bureaucracy is not institutionalized, NPC churches implement a leadership system characterized by relational links between leaders, rather than bureaucratic rules (Donald E. Miller 1997, 142–143).

However, while Miller's NPC terminology is useful, it has severe limitations. The foremost problem with the terminology is how Miller approaches the issue of democratization and new paradigm churches. For Miller, new paradigm churches represent the triumph of certain democratic impulses within Protestantism (Donald E. Miller 1997, 15, 145–147). Miller contends that the organizational change that NPC churches have implemented has helped to connect lay people "to the sacred," making NPC churches formidable barriers to the increasing hierarchicalization of church organizational structure (Donald E. Miller 1997, 146–147). Miller's argument here conflates the reduction of bureaucracy with democratization. However, the argument that deregulation of any market, including the "religious market," automatically leads to increased democratization is of dubious validity. Governments have been more than willing to implement authoritarian measures in the name of de-bureaucratization, and bureaucracy is not necessarily antithetical to democracy. Indeed, in some cases bureaucratic regulation is absolutely necessary to the maintenance of democratic structures.

The promotion of flat organizational structures as politically empowering is one of many points of agreement between William Kay and Miller, though Kay is considerably more sophisticated in how he employs this idea. Kay takes great pains to acknowledge that bureaucracy is not always synonymous with "religious decline" (Kay 2007, 287). However, Kay suggests that religious bureaucracies have several elements in their organizational structure that make them unideal starting points for molding 21st century churches. Bureaucracies are, in Kay's eyes, "hierarchical, rational, ordered, procedurally

4. Networked Churches and the Rise of Church Toyota 197

orientated ... painstaking, slow, and often unimaginative and committee-led" (Kay 2007, 287–288). Contemporary management theory, with the assistance of complexity theory, often contends that we are now in an era of discontinuous change, where change is both incredibly fast and intrinsically unpredictable.[1] Because of that, many leaders in Toyotist churches argue that bureaucracy-heavy churches are not suited to deal with the contemporary religious environment the church finds itself in (see Wagner 2010, 206–207 and Gibbs 2000, 234). To compete with the other unregulated institutions that are the product of NPM and neo-liberalism, churches, according to this line of reasoning, must take on the organizational structures that characterize other neo-liberal institutions.

In describing British apostolic networks, Kay puts forward the argument that while such networks reject hierarchalism, this does not mean that they embrace voting. Indeed, he notes that apostolic networks are characterized by a rejection of "all forms of balloting." Instead of the committee-based approach to decision making favored by denominational structures, apostolic networks rely on the use of spiritual gifts and charismatic authority by the apostle in the envisioning and implementation of leadership decisions (Kay 2007, 266–267). C. Peter Wagner, one of the leading lights of the New Apostolic Reformation (NAR) in the United States, indicates that authority operates in a similar manner among American NAR apostles (Wagner 1999b, 75). Wagner, like many evangelical leaders, portrays this move to increased authoritarianism as spiritually liberating, contending that "authority is invested in individuals as contrasted to bureaucracies ... and similar groups formed to make decisions" (Wagner 1999b, 75). Strategically, Wagner argues that such investment of authority in apostolic leadership is necessary to ensure the unity of organizational objectives (Wagner 1999b, 75–77). For Wagner, the democratization of churches has made them organizationally weak (Wagner 1999b, 89–90). Rick Warren concurs in this assessment, arguing that words like committees and elections are not found in the New Testament, and have led churches to force "an American form of government on the church and, as a result, most churches are as bogged down in bureaucracy as our government is. It takes forever to get anything done" (Warren 1995, 377). This organizational red tape, according to Warren, is harmful, because it makes pastors so detailed-focused that they cannot engage in the leadership responsibilities which are the driving purpose of their ministry (Warren 1995, 378).

Yet despite the relatively forthright claims of de-democratization made by leaders like Wagner and Warren, it is not uncommon to find evangelical leaders extolling networked churches as new embodiments of democratic values. For instance, Eddie Gibbs, in *Leadership Next: Changing Leaders in a Changing Culture* (2005), states that networks, unlike "hierarchal organizations," are "flexible, responsive, and empowering precisely because they have no control center and are able to grow exponentially" (Gibbs 2005, 62). Gibbs further claims that in networks, pastors and leadership teams "cultivate" rather than "control" their followers (Gibbs 2005, 62–63). Alan Hirsch and Dave Ferguson make similar claims for networked churches, claiming that they will create "new forms of ecclesia" which will allow the "Imagineering" of new types of churches which will be "highly creative, multicultural, multidimensional, diverse, [and] highly innovative," values most readers associate with democratized institutions (Hirsch and Ferguson 2011, loc. 890–895). Dwight Friesen, similarly casts networked individuals as perfect intermixtures of "premodern, modern and postmodern" values, whose situated perspective within a network allows them to both support "human agency" while acting in favor of social justice and "prophetic" witness as members of a wider community (Friesen 2009, 64–65).

Frequently such claims of the liberating possibilities of networked churches rest on the idea that decentralized organization allows for more freedom, spontaneity, self-expression, and other values associated with democracy. Examples of this appeal to the democratic value of decentralization are ubiquitous in church management and church growth literature. For instance, in *The Minister's MBA* (2006), a work recommended by NAR apostle Os Hillman (*Minister's MBA* 2006, blurbs), writers George S. Babbes and Michael Ziagarelli argue that a "decentralized approach" to ministry can "be very useful," particularly because it allows churches to engage in more niche marketing and better quality-control practices, while simultaneously allowing church workers to feel a sense of "empowerment" and "ownership over what they produce" (Babbes and Ziagarelli 2006. 25). Kenneth O. Gangel's *Team Leadership in Christian Ministry* (1997) suggests a similar approach to team ministry, with team leaders decentralizing and delegating authority to followers (Gangel 1997, 243–244). Gangel's carefully written and systematic work, while not totally opposed to bureaucracy,[2] condemns over-centralization, particularly when the church is engaged in planning (Gangel 1997, 303). Robert Logan similarly supports the decentralization of churches, arguing that bureaucratically centralized churches are "dependent on narrow organizational functions for survival" (Logan 1990, 119). Decentralization is also emphasized in Wagner's *Churchquake*, where he supports a move from "control"-based organization to "coordination"-based organizing. Wagner argues that NAR networks are similar to the kind of flat "organizational patterns" he claims are characteristic of Northern Italian local governments, while the typical denominational structure has more in common with the hierarchical structure of authority present in Southern Italy (Wagner 1999b, 71).

Augusto Rodriguez, a New Apostolic pastor who has documented the rise of NAR networks (Rodriguez 2003, vi, 4), has written extensively on how the NAR views decentralization. Rodriguez notes that decentralization, be-

4. Networked Churches and the Rise of Church Toyota 199

sides being an explicit rejection of centralized organizational schemas—is a reaction against institutionalism. In his reading of the NAR, the NAR and other movements committed to deinstitutionalization are motivated by a move away from "institutional help" for problems to "selfhelp" [sic]. Rodriguez contends that this does not make these movements anti-institutional, but simply reflects a tendency to question how effectively current contemporary institutional models are working (Rodriguez 2003, 104–105). Decentralization allows movements to more effectively engage in local organizing and thus avoid a "'top down'" approach (something typically associated with centralization in NAR, church growth, and general business literature) (Rodriguez 2003, 106–107).

Rodriguez claims that centralization poorly fits both democratized and socialistic cultures. Centralized planning, in his reading, leads to harmfully high costs to state social services, ultimately handicapping the state's ability to provide adequate care for its population. For Rodriguez this handicap of centralized planning leads democratic institutions to adopt representative forms of government rather than participatory ones. Participatory democracy, he contends, has numerous advantages over representative democracy. Because participatory democracy is more responsive to employee, voter and customer feedback, it is easier for participatory institutions to achieve common goals. Moreover, since the leadership has a better idea of what followers want in a participatory democracy, they should theoretically become better and more efficient leaders (Rodriguez 2003, 107). These assumptions, of course, track very well with those held in neospiritual and secular New Paradigm management circles.

For the NAR and many of the Christian movements that adopted its network organization, network structures were typically organized around small groups or cells. This form of organization provided two main organizational advantages. First, cell organizations allowed for more efficient resource allocation and resource distribution. This effectiveness was achieved through outsourcing much of the clerical labor to volunteers and lay leadership. With the lay leadership taking care of this lower-level labor, the church staff can move their attention to other areas. The second benefit of cell structure is again, decentralization. Ministries, according to NAR organizational theory, become less dependent on individuals when utilizing a cell structure, allowing for pastors to build an overarching vision for the church, while allowing "substantial autonomy to individual staff members in overseeing specific programs" (Rodriguez 2003, 297; Donald E. Miller 1997, 138).

The focus on the effectiveness and democratically participatory nature of networked and decentralized Christians organizations has been repeatedly justified through references to one particular concept in the cyborg sciences, that of computer networking, particularly Internet-mediated networks.

One-time EMC writer Kester Brewin, for instance, justifies EMC organizational strategies by noting their congruence with the popularly accepted narrative of the Internet's development. Brewin points out that the Internet was developed as a "dispersed network of computers" whose purpose was to help America's defense forces to survive nuclear war. Dispersed networks would be less vulnerable to nuclear annihilation because "even if a number of individual computers were taken out by the blast, the military network could still function normally because the 'knowledge'—or data—was distributed across hundreds of different 'cells' in different parts of the country'" (Brewin 2004, 85). Centralized systems, Brewin argued, have centralized power structures, and thus he echoes Rodriguez's issues with centralized planning. Brewin, however, given his EMC background, is more concerned with the centralization of knowledge distribution that he claims occurs in organizations that fail to adopt the decentralized organizational model of distributed systems. Thus, the Emergent Church will model itself on the Internet by not centrally storing organizational knowledge or power in one particular node, but instead adopting the structure of a distributed network to prevent abuses of authority (Brewin 2004, 86). Eddie Gibbs, a more mainstream evangelical figure who is nevertheless sympathetic to the EMC, contends that distributed network structures are increasingly necessary for all organizations as they enter the information age. Gibbs draws a biblistic analogy, arguing that the churches of the New Testament "operated as clusters and networks rather than as a centralized hierarchy" (Gibbs 2005, 96-98). This organizational form was necessary because the spread of information was too slow in the Mediterranean world (Gibbs 2005, 98). To gain any advantage in an information war, one side has to have more efficient processing power than another. Moreover, as Brewin correctly points out, adopting a distributed network structure makes an organization more invulnerable from attack. Gibbs draws on similar ideas by noting that the "networked-cluster structure" of the early church, lacking any centralized hierarchy, could not be easily destroyed (Gibbs 2005, 98). He warns, however, echoing Wagner's ideas in *Churchquake*, that network structures lack "control" loci. This means that networks must establish strong relational alliances through community building if they are not to fragment (Gibbs 2005, 98).

David Cannistraci, a prominent NAR thinker, has also appeared to the Internet as a liberating force for apostolic organization. Cannistraci argues that the current use of "networking principles in our world is nothing short of revolutionary" and points to computer networking and the Internet as two of his prime examples (Cannistraci 1996b, 186). He then goes on to lay out a case for network structures based on "minimal legal and financial" central control, again mimicking the rhetoric of distributed networks (Cannistraci 1996b, 190). Peter Hocken similarly notes that "the self image of the new [net-

4. Networked Churches and the Rise of Church Toyota

worked] churches is of flexible networks without top-down authority patterns" (Hocken 2009, 39)—in other words a model of church networks based on the principles associated with distributed networks. Yet, if distributed networks are characterized by participatory democracy and a lack of centralized control, why have New Apostolic churches and other network-based churches been so often accused of promoting authoritarian and control-based ecclesiology? To understand this apparent dilemma, we must first look at contemporary rhetoric surrounding the Internet.

As Kester Brewin correctly notes, the Internet had its origins in Arpanet. The technology that made the dream of the World Wide Web a reality was packet switching. Packet switching allows for "the simultaneous use of a single communication line for a number of different data communication sessions" (Panzaris 2008, 76–77). RAND researcher Paul Baran developed the concept of packet switching as a way of implementing distributed networks with built-in redundancy. The aim was to make such networks virile enough to survive the loss of multiple nodes or links while maintaining functionality. Baran noted that in order for this to happen, messages would have to be broken up into small pieces called packets, "routed across the nodes of the network," and then "reassembled at the destination" (Panzaris 2008, 89). Packets are units of information containing data payload and information on how to deliver this payload to the destination. The major mode of forming a telecommunications network then available was circuit-switching. Circuit-switching relied on communication links based on "dedicated connection[s] between users" (Russell 2014, 167). The multi-nodal and decentralized nature of networks that utilized packet-switching made their resistance to attack much more robust than those networks that utilized circuit switching (Russell 2014, 167). Nevertheless, Arpanet, like many information networks, was itself a "closed system" which could be subjected to "centralized control" (Russell 2014, i). Starting in the 1970s, American and European engineers started developing new network design strategies. This led them to develop a very influential approach to the concept of "openness." The emerging promoters of the digital world emphasized several ideological imperatives, with "entrepreneurship, technological innovation, and participatory democracy" being key (Russell 2014, i). The problem with this rhetoric is that it obfuscates the fact that the Internet, like previous "'open' systems'" is quite reliant on "hierarchical forms of control" (Russell 2014, i).

Although the discourse of "openness" has a long history, the discourse of "open systems" got its most profound and systemized push from fields like cybernetics and systems theory. These concepts were also strongly evident in organization studies (Russell 2014, 11). Theoretically, the thinkers who systematized open systems discourse into a viable intellectual model—intellectuals like Karl Popper (1902–1994), Norbert Wiener and Ludwig von Bertalanffy—

shared a number of ideological assumptions that shaped their work. Russell argues that though these men seldom commented on the political culture of their era, their "ideological commitments to individualism, democracy and market economies were as strong as they were implicit" (Russell 2014, 11). Open systems discourse contended that cultures could not be profitably sequestered from each other (Russell 2014, 11). Totalitarianism was strongly antithetical to their worldview, as it slowed scientific progress. Open systems discourse valued peaceful interaction between peoples based on such values as "political freedom, scientific progress, and personal autonomy" (Russell 2014, 11).

It is therefore problematic to argue that the Internet and open systems discourse are predicated on ideological neutrality. From its start, "open systems" ideology was predisposed to promote decentralization over "centralized control" (Russell 2014, 11). The decentralized organizational structure that open systems ideology modeled was congruent with similar organizational structures promoted within both neo-liberal and conservative circles that arose at the height of "open source" discourse in the 80s and 90s. For instance, as we have seen, NPM became a major form of neo-liberal social governance in the public sector during the 80s and 90s. Moreover, at the same time, as Sara Diamond notes, the Christian Right was moving to a "decentralized" and localized organizational model, as a result of the failure of more centralized organizations, such as the Moral Majority, to achieve the movement's objectives (Diamond 2000, 32). The open systems ideology that shaped the Internet was molded by a support for globalization and multiculturalism, an ardent opposition to centralized control systems, and a belief that the dreams of the systems movement [s] could be obtained through "cooperation and standardization" (Russell 2014, 14). Thus, the application of open systems discourse, including the creation of the Internet, are based on an implicit "faith in market capitalism" (Russell 2014, 24). This organizational philosophy embraced three somewhat contradictory core beliefs that shaped most Americans' perception of technology. First, the power of corporations must be held back. Secondly, entrepreneurialism must be promoted (Russell 2014, 157). Finally, the new "broad-based ideological consensus" towards technology contended that "efficiency and innovation" should be promoted via "market competition" instead of "government planning" (Russell 2014, 157).

Parallels to how church management practices have developed should be fairly obvious to most discerning readers. Just as hackers, academics, and scientists tried to limit corporate control over the development of the Internet,[3] the move away from denominationalism and the decline of mainline Protestantism in the 70s and 80s reflected a similar distrust of organizations that had codified their organizational philosophies around the corporate ideology of "scientific management." Entrepreneurialism obviously was the motivating impulse behind the entire CGM, and was evident throughout the church's adoption of Toyotist principles. It has become particularly noticeable in recent years with the growing influence of church planting movements, whose organizational philosophy is eerily similar to Silicon Valley start-ups. The emphasis on innovation is also evident in much of church growth, EMC, and organic church literature, and accounts for much of the adoption of secular models by leaders within these movements.

As Russell points out, the actual history of the Internet does not support the popular thesis that the formation of the Internet relied on "distributed control and participatory democracy that emerged organically from the interactions of Internet engineers" (Russell 2014, 231). Indeed, it was the Internet's main initial competitor, Open Systems Interconnection which relied on democratic organizational principles, principles that unfortunately in the OSI's case made the organization relatively "slow" and "unwieldy" (Russell 2014, 231). In contrast, the Internet's formation was predicated on "autocratic and centralized control over system architecture and standardization" (Russell 2014, 231). Indeed, the leaders of the emerging "Internet community" that helped form its current form and structure stood firmly opposed to "basic formalities of democracy such as membership and voting rights" in the creation of the Internet (Russell 2014, 232). As opposed to OSI, the Internet community, in the words of pioneer David Clark, rejected "'kings, presidents, and voting" while embracing "'rough consensus and running code.'" (Russell 2014, 253) While Internet pioneers supported majority-rule, they did not embrace crucial elements of democratic decision making in their standardization practices, including formal votes or governance by presidents. To Internet pioneers such features of democratic governance appeared antiquated. Their preferred model, "rough consensus," left proposals open to criticism, but allowed these proposals to be acted on quickly if they enjoyed "vast majority" support within the Internet Engineering Task Force (IETF). In contrast to OSI, the Internet created the architecture of its networks via a "well-funded and homogenous environment" which was relatively immune from "commercial and political pressures" (Russell 2014, 258). The protocol standards that the Internet developed were thus the product of the synergetic fusion of market forces and U.S. government support (Russell 2014, 24, 258).

What this meant practically for the claim of networked democracy, both within the Internet and the church, can now be elaborated. Fred Brooks, a software engineer for IBM, in a 1975 essay, pointed out the problems that democratization posed for emerging Internet pioneers. Brooks view of system design held that system designs were best left to a "singular" individual or a "small design team," as this allowed for "conceptual clarity" in the design process. Obviously, the more potential voices are admitted into the design of any technical system, the greater chance there is of a design flaw being introduced into that system. However, paradoxically, once a system design is introduced, "important adaptations, innovations, and fresh concepts" are very like to come "from implementers and users"—the masses of system design. Brooks held that conceptual clarity had the more overriding importance in system design, a point that many supporters of the Internet came to share by the late 1990s (Russell 2014, 259).

The designers of apostolic networks and their successors based their structures on similar organizational principles. Even though churches within the AD 2000 movement and the NAR supported, even encouraged "user-developed" innovations on the part of lay members and the rank and file, the system architecture of NAR networks and churches—their mission statements, their organizational structure, and modes of governance—were not created through the formal structures of democratic organizations. Moreover, it is unclear how much churches within these movements have supported other principles of democratic governance, such as guaranteed liberties and rights for organization members. And just as in the creation of the Internet, NPC, NAR, and AD 2000 churches and networks were created under organizational principles that promoted pastors and apostles, or ministry teams, as the primary originators of system design, with lay followers having, at best, limited control over church design and usually little to no control over church network design. In part to demonstrate this point, as well as the power of network ideas within evangelical culture, we will now look briefly at the history of Protestant church networks.

Network Architecture in the AD 2000 Movement and NAR

Although apostolic networks predate the beginning of the NAR by several decades, the movement's modern form and influence is largely the product of the AD 2000 movement. The system design and architecture of the AD 2000 movement and the movements that it influenced and gave birth to are a product of a number of influences. One of the most important of these influences however was the Global Consultation on World Evangelization (GCOWE I), a preliminary meeting held before the huge Lausanne II conference. The meeting, which took place in January 1989, aimed to complete the Great Commission—that is the church's mission to evangelize the world—by the close of the 20th century. The idea of the AD 2000 and Beyond movement began to be formalized at this meeting (Holvast 2009, 80). Enthusiasts for the new vision of GCOWE I realized that it required a global reach to implement, and they aimed to use network structures to facilitate cooperation in the achievement of this vision (Holvast 2009, 80) Organizationally, some movement leaders within Lausanne II felt that GCOWE I was trying to compel the wider Lausanne movement to implement its agenda, an agenda not universally agreed to by the whole movement. In order to facilitate cooperation between Lausanne II and GCOWE I enthusiasts, the GCOWE I movement was given a specific subset "of workshops ('track[s]') within the framework of the Lausanne II conference" (Holvast 2009, 81). These workshops were well publicized and led to the creation of the AD 2000 & Beyond movement under the leadership of Luis Bush (Holvast 2009, 81). The movement's formal goal was to implement the objectives outlined by GCOWE I, by reaching "the world before 2000 through the empowerment of Christians for world evangelization" (Holvast 2009, 82).

Luis Bush, the founder of the AD 2000 movement, believed strongly in the importance of "catalytic" individuals who would spur on innovation for their movement. Interestingly, the ideal model Luis Bush took for such a catalytic leader was John R. Mott (Bush 2002, 65–78). Mott had been chairman of the Interchurch World Movement, a group that aimed to achieve many of the same organizational goals that both GCOWE I and the AD 2000 movement did, albeit less successfully (Jonathan J. Edwards 2015, 57–58). Mott, like Bush, realized the importance of utilizing conferences to mobilize movement support (Luis Bush 2002, 76). Bush also notes with approval Mott's organizational ability, as well as his ability to juggle the leadership of multiple organizations without losing effectiveness (Luis Bush 2002, 77). But it was Mott's catalytic ability as a mobilizer that was key (Bush 2002, 65–78 passim). Bush's own organizational philosophy focused most strongly, however on the "catalytic" aspect of movements and movement leadership. According to C. Peter Wagner's description of Bush's role in the AD 2000 Movement, Bush "unquestionably had the final decision-making authority in AD 2000" but was skilled at delegating authority, responsibility, and freedom to the AD 2000 track coordinators. Wagner characterizes these individuals as the "middle level of management" within the movement; by granting these individuals autonomy, Wagner argues, Bush allowed them to utilize their creativity in achieving organizational objectives (Wagner, 2010, 169). In other words, Bush conceptualized his leadership role implicitly, if not explicitly, through the lens of diffusion theory. Bush was the catalyst, one of the innovators, along with men like C. Peter Wagner and George Otis. These elite innovators' job was to introduce new organizational models to early adopters, who then spread this organizational model throughout a wide breadth of the evangelical movement. Similarly, the AD 2000 movement's role itself was as a catalyst movement. For the leadership of the spiritual mapping movement that partially supplanted AD 2000 and Beyond, and for the NAR, which inherited many followers and organizational ideas from both these movements, organizations ceased to be important once they had fulfilled their stated objectives. Movement leadership thus had little problem in organizationally supplanting AD 2000 once the organizational needs it had fulfilled were met by those movements it had catalyzed (Holvast 2009, 86–87; Luis Bush 2002, 135).

The network architecture that developed under the AD 2000 movement emphasized a number of key points. Like the historically contemporary development of the Internet, the AD 2000 movement adopted an "anti-institutional" outlook, an outlook that in any case had a long history among many of the Pentecostal and Charismatic members of the movement, some of whom had held such beliefs since the Latter Rain Revival (Holvast 2009, 86–87; Weaver 2016, 28–29). The movements that sprang out of the AD 2000 movement, such as spiritual mapping, focused on the promotion of individual initiative in the achievement of organizational objectives (Wagner 2010, 169; Holvast 2009, 101). Bush believed that the creation of a global missions movement like AD 2000 required "synergistic effort" (Luis Bush 2002, 144). This was because the AD 2000 vision required a great deal of coordination, cooperation, and effective movement mobilization and resource allocation, all while at the same time allowing for individual initiatives to maintain their "particular distinctives and autonomy" (Luis Bush 2002, 144). It is fairly easy to see why Bush saw such synergy as a necessity; the AD 2000 movement, although disproportionately influenced by neo-Pentecostals, cooperated with numerous denominations as well (see Luis Bush 2002, 137, 143–144, 175). Moreover, it was a global movement which sought to reach a diverse group of individuals. Given these realities, movement unity was of primary consideration (Luis Bush 2002, 144).

Although not the first Protestant or evangelical movement to utilize "flat network" structures, the AD 2000 movement did represent the first and likely the most systematic attempt to implement such organizational structures on a global scale (see Luis Bush 2002, 146). Leadership in the AD 2000 movement was ostensibly based on relational rather than "hierarchical structure" (Luis Bush 2002, 146). Bush noted that one of the organizational objectives in utilizing relational leadership structures was to persuade Two-Thirds world cultures—that is, the cultures of the developing world—to align themselves with the movement. Bush, himself from Argentina (Luis Bush 2002, 312), believed that relational leadership structures "corresponded with the typical way of relating within these [developing world] cultures" (Bush 2002, 88). There is certainly some truth to Bush's claim. As Doornenbal notes, writers on leadership, both secular and religious, are increasingly interested in the leadership practices of "non-Western" and "pre-modern" cultures (Doornenbal 2012, 188), likely as a result of the influence of globalization and the consequently greater need for sensitivity to cultural diversity. However, relational leadership practices also fit into the emerging practice of "organic leadership," a moniker developed by Gayle Avery to describe a widely influential contemporary leadership style (Doornenbal 2012, 185–186). In organizations that utilize organic leadership practices, leadership is distributed rather than centralized in "specific positions and roles." Leaders who utilize an organic leadership style frequently take on the metaphorical role of "teacher … mentor … steward or servant" (Doornenbal 2012, 187). Within organic leadership models, "authority and power reside in the collectivity of the organization" (Doornenbal 2012, 187); rather than centralizing power at the top, power is distributed through the organization. Because of this, "a diversity of opinions" are given weight. Organizational objectives within organically led organizations are the product of "intensive and continuing interactions between [organizational] participants." This leads organically led organizations to frequently adopt network structures, ones utilizing "simple and flexible structures" that can respond quickly to discontinuous change. The lack of support for "hierarchy and bureaucracy" among supporters of organic styles of leadership also is related to "specific cultural factors" within contemporary society. In contemporary culture, relationships between leaders and followers tend to be more informal than in the past, and organic leadership structures tend to capitalize on this practice. Such leadership structures are much more open to rapid organizational and cultural change and tend to follow more "feminine" styles of leadership which accentuate "cooperation and good working relationships" (Doornenbal 2012, 188).

As Doornenbal notes, organic leadership styles are not "mutually exclusive" with other forms of leadership (Doornebal 2012, 189). Within the evangelical movement, the organic style is most strongly present in the EMC conversation, as Doornenbal documents (see Doornenbal 2012, 192–193). However, the leadership practices of the AD 2000 movement and the NAR also share many similarities with organic leadership, along with the slightly earlier "visionary paradigm of leadership." The influence of the visionary paradigm, however is most forceful within the NAR, which borrows from the visionary model's emphasis on "inspiring and charismatic leader[s]" who are cast in heroic terms by organizational leadership and followers alike; this role is obviously that held by the apostle in the NAR (Weaver 2016, 88, 90; Doornenbal 2012, 186–187). Visionary leaders' emphasis on "emotions, intuitions, values and moral issues" is also strongly characteristic of NAR leadership practices, as it is of most Pentecostal leadership practices (Doornenbal 2012, 186–187).

For the AD 2000 movement, but even more so for the spiritual mapping and NAR movements that it generated, the adoption of a fused combination of visionary and organic leadership practices had major organizational implications. Within the network church structures that developed in the 1990s, religious "consumers" bore little "responsibility" for the success or failure of an organization. The responsibility for developing an organizational vision usually lay in the hands of the leader, although the leader might coordinate his approach to ministry with other members of the organization, such as its board or "apostolic team." Once organizational objectives were laid out through such "vision-casting," or "visioneering," the network's mission was then brought to the public. The starkest rhetorical difference between the NAR and the movements that evolved after it usually occurs at this point. The EMC and the organic church, influenced by the Leadership Network's approach to organizational development and change, tend to promote a vision-casting process that *appears* entirely democratic. Such leadership practices fit more into organic leadership styles than the visionary model. By contrast, within the spiritual mapping movement and the NAR, "There was no democratic decision-making process, and no accountability structure for strategies and policies used" (Holvast 2009, 87). This meant that while there might be some board supervision of the network, and peer-to-peer network relationships and accountability, the locus of authority remained with the apostle, or in some cases, the apostolic team (Holvast 2009, 87). The wider "public" in the AD 2000 movement (and later the NAR) was paternalistically conceptualized as "clients" by movement leadership (Holvast 2009, 87). Characteristic of both movements, however, was the appropriation of the "soft skills" that Nigel Thrift has emphasized were central to the triumph of New Age and New Paradigm business methods.

The NAR movement further refined this concept of peer-to-peer network relationships by distinguishing between two groups of leaders: vertical and horizontal apostles. Vertical apostles directly lead ministries and have other ministries, congregations and/or individual people under their "spiritual 'covering'" (Wagner 2012, 77–78). Horizontal apostles, by contrast, typically did not exercise authority in this manner, but instead helped other "peer-level leaders" establish interconnectivity between each other (Wagner 2012, 79). This system of management reinforced mutual accountability among members while also insulating the movement from outside critiques that might cast a poor light on its leadership structure. Because of the covering system, the faults of apostles are typically cast as the problems of individuals, rather than more systemic faults in the way NAR churches are organized.

The development of church network structures in the AD 2000 movement, NAR, Leadership Network, and other more modern forms of networked churches, served a number of important functions. Holvast, writing about the AD 2000 movement, lists a number of the advantages the network structure brings. First, network structures allowed for more effective information sharing and communication. The adoption of networked organizational structures also allowed for increased emphasis on collaborative projects. While these projects were not always successful, the network structure allowed for

4. Networked Churches and the Rise of Church Toyota

improved advertising practices and often "impressive worldwide mobilization" of individuals within networked movements like AD 2000. Networking also allowed for improved public relations practices. Public relations was also strengthened by the AD 2000 movement's mobilization of individuals around specific well-known leaders, who frequently referenced other allied leaders. This practice, frequently utilized by the NAR as well, led to an increased sense of unity among members and contributed to the solidarity of movement leadership as well, since leaders shared each other's rhetorical "platforms" (Holvast 2009, 87–88). Mutual accountability was another impetus for the creation of network structures. Because AD 2000 leaders, and even more so NAR apostles, did not believe in democratic governance, there was no ability to hold leadership accountable without a system of mutual accountability. In the NAR, the function of horizontal apostles theoretically provided this accountability (Holvast 2009, 87–88).

According to movement proponents, one of the main advantages to the network structure is that it prevents the "routinization" of religious practices (Christerson and Flory 2017, loc. 921–935). As we have seen, Charismatic churches have typically tried to prevent charismatic spirituality from being routinized (Poloma 2003, 15–16). From a theological perspective, such routinization is seen as a challenge to the Holy Spirit. In pragmatic terms, it also represents a poor business practice, since routinization may stifle innovations in doctrine, dogma, worship, and other forms of spiritual expression. Without such innovations, routinizers may find themselves increasingly unable to compete against more freeform or decentralized forms of Christian spirituality. Furthermore, network structures, because of their (ostensible) lack of bureaucratic organization, may be less dependent on particular leaders or families to perpetuate an organization. Instead, the network itself provides new leadership through a constant process of leadership development (Christerson and Flory 2017, loc. 921–935).

When AD 2000 developed its form of networked organization, it concentrated on developing each of its "tracks" into "semi-autonomous unit[s]." While this development obviously improved the resilience of the network against malfunctioning networks or netwar attacks (such as proselytization or infiltration by rival religious groups), it also gave the movement other adaptive advantages that should not be overlooked. In order to keep solidarity between movement leaders, "annual meetings with track and task force leaders" were organized. Track leaders were encouraged to work out potential disagreements and conflicts of interest themselves and to embrace efforts at reducing "redundancy," while increasing any synergistic forces (Luis Bush 2002, 149). From Wagner's description of the AD 2000 networks, movement leaders tended to view themselves primarily as facilitators. Thus, while they rejected democratic governance, they also had little problem letting followers, particularly the "middle level of management," bypass regulatory bodies that slowed them down (Wagner, 2010, 169). These organizational innovations allowed the movement organizational adaptivity when fulfilling organizational objectives.

Whether these innovations, however, actually helped reduce bureaucracy in the church, as some proponents of apostolic governance have maintained, is more open to question. Hocken maintains that as apostolic networks have expanded, they have taken on some of the accouterments of denominational structures. Large headquarters, for instance, are not uncommon. Many networks also establish their own educational institutions. The real difference between networks and denominations, in Hocken's view, is the prominence of the "charismatic leader for life" (Hocken 2009, 38). Hocken is dubious of the contention that networks are flexible. Rather, he contends, their organizational advantage comes from the fact that apostolic governance allows "emerging structures" to be continuously "subordinated to mission" (Hocken 2009, 38). In other words, what apostolic networks really do for movement leadership is allow them a means for clearly and quickly clarifying and implementing organizational objectives. This ability to cut through red tape, while potentially very detrimental to movement members, allows for faster information "processing power" on the part of those individuals who are designing the implementation protocols—worship services, sermons, conferences, books, meetings, etc.—for the network, while buffering movement leadership from any potential criticism they might receive for these implementation protocols. Put simply, the framework design for networked churches is far more efficient than that utilized by denominational churches, giving them a major advantage.

It is not surprising, therefore, that with all these organizational advantages, plus the institutional backing afforded network churches by Lausanne II, that this new organizational schema quickly spread throughout conservative Protestantism. AD 2000 had effectively started in January 1989, but received its "formal establishment" in 1991. A headquarters for the movement was built in Colorado Springs. The movement rapidly took on global proportions, with "large segments of the Evangelical and Pentecostal world" adopting its mission (Holvast 2009, 98). To establish organizational unity, the movement prioritized reaching the so-called "10/40 Window"—the part of the world "between ten degrees and forty degrees north latitude"—with the gospel. This area spanned a vast portion of the globe, reaching deep into Northern Africa as well as to locations like Japan and the Philippines (Luis Bush 2002, 138). Massive international prayer campaigns were organized, designed to mobilize millions of individuals to pray for the 10/40 Window (Holvast 2009, 100). The AD 2000 movement also widely promoted the practice of spiritual mapping, a form of territorial "spiritual warfare" against perceived demonic entities (Holvast 2009, 16). As I have argued in *The New Apostolic Reformation: History of a Modern Charismatic Movement*, spiritual mapping gave the AD 2000 movement a number of organizational advantages, foremost of which may have been what amounted to "free intelligence" from those engaged in mapping practices (Weaver 2016, 78).

Conferences and consultations were held to promote the theology of AD 2000 (Luis Bush 2002, 86–87). One of the most important was the Global Consultation on World Evangelization II (GCOWE 95), held in Seoul in 1995. The Conference involved some 4,000 individuals from 186 countries, most of them from outside the West (Holvast 2009, 104). However, shortly after the conference, the attention of crucial movement leader C. Peter Wagner, shifted away from AD 2000 and towards the NAR, which perfected the innovations the AD 2000 movement had brought to networked churches. Wagner's devotion to this new form of Christian organization crystalized at the May 1996 National Symposium of the Postdenominational Church, which he helped organize. The conference focused on looking at "what it called 'new paradigms' of church structures, relations between local churches, financial organization, communication, evangelism, leadership training, prayer and dealing with supernatural powers'" (Holvast 2009, 106). The conference had over 40 major speakers and eleven panels and attracted 500 delegates (Augusto Rodriguez 2003, 139). Conference participants were handed a copy of conference speaker David Cannistraci's *The Gift of the Apostle* (1996) (Rodriguez 2003, 139).

Cannistraci's work is considered a fairly important theoretical text within NAR circles. The blurbs for the book featured such major future NAR leaders as Bill Hamon, Lawrence Khong, and John P. Kelly (who would eventually take over the leadership of Wagner's ICAL, the most influential apostolic network) (Cannistraci 1996b, blurbs). From an outsider's perspective, it is sometimes difficult to understand Cannistraci's influence, as he is not nearly as sophisticated or even plain spoken as C. Peter Wagner. However, what Cannistraci's work did do was legitimize the structure of church networks in language that most Charismatic evangelicals could find acceptable. In addition, Cannistraci's work offered up a well-written and in many ways prescient understanding of the role apostles should play in NAR churches. Cannistraci's work outlined most of the elements and terminology of the AD 2000 movement and Leadership Network, particularly the need for catalytic leadership and minimal regulatory oversight (Cannistraci 1996b, 100–103, 185–191).

It is important to note that apostolic networks predated Wagner's embrace of apostolic language. Too much popular writing on the NAR, and even some academic writing, assumes that Wagner "founded" the movement. But as I have pointed out in *The New Apostolic Reformation*, the term

New Apostolic Reformation is a "description of an organizational philosophy and a theological and political ideology.... It is not, however, an organization, much less a denominational structure" (Weaver 2016, 89). Networks can adopt different "brands" while still adhering to the movement's core philosophical and organizational presuppositions. Because of this, the NAR presents an adaptive organizational model, which can be tailored to prevailing local conditions. This has allowed even opposing Christian movements to adopt some of the organizational insights of the NAR and AD 2000 without adopting the theological commitments that come with it (Weaver 2016, 88–89).

By 2016, the NAR played a major role in global Christianity. The movement's success was reinforced by its attempts to appeal to a broad base of constituents, including women and minorities. The movement, while ostensibly claiming to be socially transformative, promoted an economically conservative ideology. NAR apostles, notably C. Peter Wagner, called for a "Great Wealth Transfer" in which the wealth of "the world" would be transferred to believing Christians. Some of the major facilitators of this transfer of wealth would be workplace apostles, leaders within the workplace who had apostolic authority over their employees (Weaver 2016, 145-151). The advantages of such an economic ideology to supporters of neo-liberal economics should be obvious and it is not at all surprising that the movement found both Democratic and Republican supporters willing to embrace its message (Tabachnick 2013a). The success of the NAR, moreover, had by this point spurred a number of other organizations to promote network organizational frameworks.

The most prominent of these organizations was the Leadership Network (LN). Founded in 1984, the Leadership Network draws much of its organizational philosophy from management guru Peter Drucker. LN's founder Bob Buford was a disciple of Drucker, and would go on to found the Peter F. Drucker Foundation for Non-Profit Management (Frye 2011, 108). Buford believed that the leadership practices of modern churches were substandard and thus sought to improve churches' managerial expertise and "organizational innovation." Buford is a hugely influential figure in evangelicalism. When D. Michael Lindsay interviewed a huge swathe of evangelical leadership for his book *Faith in the Halls of Power*, he found that 20 percent of his interviewees mentioned Buford as a major figure in their lives (Lindsay 2007, 197). LN sought to promote strategic partnerships, sometimes of an interdenominational nature, in the hopes of creating better ministry strategies for evangelical churches (Frye 2011, 109).

One of the Leadership Network's first major initiatives was a huge research effort aimed at compiling a comprehensive list of important pastors with the aim of inviting them to LN events. This effort was undertaken by

Norman Shawchuck (1935–2012), a prominent early supporter of applying systems theory to church life (Richard Lee Olson 1988, 1). The list, compiled between August of 1987 and May of 1988, eventually included some 1548 congregations (Olson 1988, 2). A special "Lotus file was written to an ASCII file" and then uploaded to a mainframe computer to be broken down and investigated (Olson 1988, 47). Many denominations proved reluctant to cooperate with the initiative, which forced the Leadership Network's researchers to rely on a telephone-based study methodology (Olson 1988, 153). Nevertheless, the study showcased the Leadership Network's considerable organizational ability and influence.

One of Buford's important early efforts was his "Forum for Pastors." These forums focused on mobilizing pastors of major congregations—those with 800 people or more. The Forums offered no particular agenda, instead focusing on peer-to-peer networking and ministry. Beginning in April 1984 at Glen Eyrie, these forums grew to encompass some 12 forums a year by the late 1980s. Because of LN's particular ideological commitments, the forums did not focus on theological or doctrinal issues, but instead were aimed at providing the kind of pragmatic training and organizational networking that emerging evangelical leaders needed to promote their churches and ministries (Olson 1988, 170).

The Leadership Network also established the Summit Conference, a biannual to triannual event that gave would-be evangelical leaders access to the crème-le-crème of Christian Right leadership. As with the Forums, these conferences strongly encouraged peer-to-peer networking. The Summit Conference networked with high-profile leadership figures in both management and religious circles, including Lyle Schaller, Martin Marty (1928–), John Stott (1921–2011), and Peter Drucker (Olson 1988, 170). In addition, even in the late 1980s, the Leadership Network had already developed several other major initiatives, including a Leadership Challenge devoted to mobilizing 25–40 year olds for the purpose of teaching "social ... responsibility," as well as a specially tailored Leadership Course (Olson 1988, 171).

During the 1990s, LN served as the catalyst for a number of movements. As we have seen, it played a crucial role in the birth of the EMC conversation. LN also promoted New Apostolic ideas from the very inception of the movement. George Hunter III, for instance, writing for LN's publication *Next*, proclaimed that the church was entering a "new apostolic age" (Hunter 1996, Vol. 2.2, 29). Hunter III, a prominent supporter of the church growth movement, placed a premium on many of the same features of church life that Wagner promoted, including a focus on contextualized worship and a prioritization of lay ministry. Like Wagner, Hunter III also noted the importance of developing effective social networking within churches, which, with the support of other CG advocates, helped pave the way for LN's mobilization of churches on behalf of the networking concept (Hunter 1996, 2). Towards the end of the 1990s, the Leadership Network directly excerpted passages from C. Peter Wagner's *Churchquake*, further promoting the spread of NAR theology (Wagner 1999b, 1–2).

Although difficult, it is possible to gain a fairly accurate picture of the Leadership Network's approach to network theory. As Christerson and Flory note in *The Rise of Network Christianity: How Independent Leaders are Changing the Religious Landscape*, it is sometimes difficult to pinpoint who precisely LN has influenced, because LN prefers to work without a huge infrastructure or "denominational name branding" (Christerson and Flory 2017, loc. 1190–1195). This indicates that LN has adopted much of the organizational philosophy that motivated lean production practices. With that comes a particular approach to conceptualizing networked culture that can best be characterized as digital or cyber libertarianism.

Much of the fusion of digital libertarianism with Christian right ideology can be traced to *Wired* magazine. *Wired* Magazine's first issue came out in March of 1993 and proclaimed the beginning of a new ""Digital Revolution"" (Frederick C. Turner Jr. 2002, 255). *Wired*'s founder Louis Rossetto (1949–) helped the magazine see the computer and the digital innovations it produced as representing far more than merely new technologies. Rather, *Wired* promoted the idea that these new technologies were creating a totally different, if not entirely new, form of social organization than had existed for most of the 20th century. The ability to communicate on the Internet via "peer-to-peer" connections mirrored "the possibilities of peer-to-peer markets" (Fred Turner 2002, 257).

Politically, *Wired* argued that these new technologies threatened the political establishment because they allowed the citizenry to bypass the government's totalizing control of political discourse. The digital utopians of *Wired* and other digital libertarian groups argued that modeling society around computer networks and the codes that helped run them was a perfect basis for a new form of social governance. In this new utopia, the "government made its rules and got out of the way," with both "computational and governmental" systems working to create fulfilled, self-actualized persons. Because of this particular political interpretation of the Net, *Wired* not only served as a platform for the ideas of new technological innovators, but also promoted libertarian and Republican leaders who embraced its ideology, including Newt Gingrich (1943–) and George Gilder (1939–) (Fred Turner 2002, 256–257).

Wired promoted a theme that would have been quite familiar to LN's pro-church growth advocates: the need for decentralization. The writers of *Wired* therefore saw libertarians not as advocates of corporate oppression, as some on the left might have classified them, but rather as social engineers

4. Networked Churches and the Rise of Church Toyota 215

who earnestly aimed for the same vision of "non-hierarchical" social structures that *Wired* itself envisioned (Turner Jr. 258–259). A crucial connecting point between the Christian Right and *Wired* was Kevin Kelly (1952–). Kelly was a born-again Christian (Fred Turner 2002, 196–197) who was perhaps the foremost digital libertarian network theorist. Kelly saw organisms, ecologies, corporations, and computers as being governed by systems rules that were essentially the same. Kelly promoted the idea that the modern era was "epochal," a great transition point before a new and better form of "social evolution" appeared (Fred Turner 2002, 13–15). Kelly argued that the humanity's main organizational unit was "not the individual, but the information system" (Fred Turner 2002, 16). In the 1990s, spurred on in large part by Kelly (an acolyte of Stewart Brand, the founder of the well-known *Whole Earth Catalog*), *Wired* simultaneously promoted counterculture approaches to digital technology while serving as a platform for a host of New Right leaders who subscribed to *Wired*'s pro-digital deregulation, anti-big government beliefs. These leaders, in turn, promoted a vision of how digital libertarianism and the countercultural viewpoints that had inspired *Wired* magazine could be successfully fused into a coherent whole (Fred Turner 2002, 313). Among these supporters was George Gilder. Gilder was featured prominently in *Wired* Magazine on several occasions, largely flatteringly (Fred Turner 2002, 301–305). A prominent right wing economic theorist, Gilder was a pro-supply side celebrity, a believing Christian, and most perplexingly considering the ideology of Silicon Valley, the founder of the Discovery Institute, the leading think tank for the intelligent design movement (Fred Turner 2002, 301–303). Gilder and Kelly bonded over their shared belief in bionomics, an economic theory designed by Michael Rothschild in 1990. Rothschild believed that the market could be used to model biological systems and that this process could also be inverted. Rothschild's viewpoints were widely influential in Silicon Valley, where his economic theories provided a "natural meeting point for representatives of the New Right, such as Gilder, and of the Whole Earth's New Age tradition" (Fred Turner 2002, 302).

Proof that the Leadership Network has been heavily influenced by digital libertarianism is not hard to find. For instance, George Gilder was a major influence on Reggie McNeal, an important writer aligned with LN (McNeal 2003, acknowledgments). LN's founder Bob Buford quotes approvingly and frequently from Gilder and Kelly in his book *Stuck in Halftime* (Buford 2001, loc. 63, 445, 741–747, 876–890). Given LN's influence over EMC theology it is important to note that Kevin Kelly is quoted approvingly in numerous works of EMC writers, such as Bob Roberts, Jr. (Roberts Jr. 2007, 27), Joseph R. Myers (Myers 2003, 76–77) and Leonard Sweet (Sweet 1999, 83, 153). During the 1990s, LN specifically recommended *Wired* magazine to its readers in its flagship publication NEXT, claiming that *Wired* had a "well-deserved reputation as the hottest magazine start up in U.S. history." Moreover, *Next*'s PR staff argued that *Wired* was a vital resource for those seeking "to understand the 21st-century world and culture being shaped by electronic communications" ("Leadership Network Recommends" 1996: 21). LN also publicized the Global Business Network, led by immensely influential Internet pioneer and *Wired* ally, Stewart Brand ("Web. Watch" 1996, 11). The reader should understand that this support would have been welcomed by *Wired* and other digital libertarians in the 1990s, and not just because of LN's ability to tap into grassroots support for digital libertarianism. What may have really mattered more to those who publicized themselves within LN's journals was Buford's close connections with Peter Drucker. Given Buford's friendship with Drucker (see Buford 2014, passim) and Drucker's preeminent position in American management circles, many management theorists and Silicon Valley entrepreneurs likely saw Buford as an important ally. Those who aspired to grander political visions, such as Kevin Kelly, may have also been impressed by LN's already impressive ability to serve as the catalyst for major Christian Right movements. Unlike other Christian Right organizational efforts, LN's management philosophy and various initiatives would likely have struck many non–Christian management theorists as representative of "best practices" in the field.[4]

Perhaps most germane to understanding digital libertarianism's effect on LN was an extensive excerpt taken from Kevin Kelley's writings on the 12 rules of the network economy (NEXT chose to focus on seven of these rules). In the excerpt, Kelly argued that society had now entered a network-based economy. Kelly realized, largely correctly, that communications innovations and improvements were now even more important than improvements to hardware. However, Kelly drew a number of somewhat expansive conclusions from this realization. The first was that "innovation, not optimization" was where wealth would be generated in the modern economic order. Kelly contended that marginal improvements to products simply were no longer enough to maintain market share (Kelly 1997, 6–9). LN's constant attempts to "surf the edge of chaos" and to catalyze innovative movements reflected this bias for innovation over optimization.

Perhaps most crucially for understanding the emergence of networked Christianity, Kelly's article emphasized the importance of distributed networks, connected by the "dumb power" of the "distributed bottom" through exploiting "decentralized forces" that promoted connectivity. Kelly's oeuvre clearly indicates that he had a politically expansive vision of the influence of dumb power (Kelly 1997, 7). A corollary to Kelly's faith in "dumb power" and distributive networks was his support for increasing network power through, whenever feasible, adding network nodes. Kelly noted that when "the number of nodes in a network increases arithmetically, the value of the network increases exponentially. Adding a few more members can dramatically increase the value for all members" (Kelly 1997, 7). Thus copies—whether it be of software, of a methodology, or any other innovation—could "shrink ... marginal costs" and thus reduce scarcity, while increasing the value of the network and its services (Kelly 1997, 7). The Leadership Network has perfected this technique, allowing it to promote organizational models that are easily transferable from one church, ministry, or leadership team to another. This, in turn, fits into LN's goal to serve as a catalyst for organizational efficiency in evangelical circles.

Kelly also had very strong views on diffusion theory. Borrowing insights from epidemiology, Kelly compared the spread of innovations to the spread of infection. Kelly contended that "in biology, the tipping points of fatal diseases are fairly high, but in technology, they seem to trigger at much lower percentages of victims or members." Due to the "fixed low costs, insignificant marginal costs, and rapid distribution" of technologies within networked economies, Kelly advanced the proposition that society was increasingly facing lower and lower tipping points for the diffusion of innovation. It was thus increasingly imperative to discern what innovations would be adopted before they happened, rather than after (Kelly 1997, 7).

As we partly saw in Chapter 3, LN took this advice to heart. Everett Rogers had suggested to LN interviewers (and readers) that one practical way of increasing the likelihood of innovation adoption was to center the marketing of the innovation at a particularly receptive group of individuals and thereby gain a "critical mass" of supporters. According to Rogers diffusion theory, once this "critical mass point" was achieved, the innovation's adoption was almost inevitable (Rogers 1998, 15). LN was by no means slow to realize the implications of Rogers' insights for network organization. In the magazine *NetFax*, LN promoted a somewhat bastardized form of Kuhnian thinking to introduce its audience to how diffusion theory could be applied to networks. *NetFax* noted that the church was going through a series of rapid "paradigm shifts" due to the pressure to innovate and adapt to increasingly complex organizational and cultural dilemmas. *NetFax* noted that the battle for the group between 10 percent and 20 percent adoption was critical if an idea was to be successfully diffused through a social network. The magazine therefore perceptively suggested to LN supporters that churches should "identify the innovators and early adopters in their congregation or organization and know their personal networks" ("Diffusion of Innovation" 1996: 91). Like LN-inspired EMC authors would later do, Kelly promoted the importance of discontinuous change. Most interesting, however, is the fact that Kelly directly promoted bionomic concepts of ecologically modeled economies within LN's publications. While bionomic economic ideas may not have entered the EMC conversation, it is perfectly obvious that biologically derived justifications for organizational change are part and parcel of that conversation.

Thanks to the influence of Kelly and others, in the 1990s, LN began to formalize its approach to networking. LN, much like the NAR, adopted the idea of a "network of networks" to maximize its utility to the Christian Right. Three primary networks were established to implement this vision. A church leader network served as the "primary customer base of [the] Leadership Network." This network consisted of those individuals, primarily pastors and other Christian leaders, who were at the head of the diffusion curve and thus best able to implement change at the congregational level. Moreover, LN contended in its publicity material—likely truthfully—that local congregations could help LN develop insights into "'best practice churches.'" Moreover, the church leader network provided the peer-to-peer networking and organizational conferences that allowed LN to disseminate its ideology to a wide consumer base ("We're a 'Network of Networks'" 1997: 3). The Church Leaders Network, according to then-director Brad Smith (writing in 1997), sought to first find the best church leaders it could and then organize networks around those leaders. Smith contended that to not do this essentially turned the Church Leader's Network into little more than a think tank; as LN's mandate was not simply to advise, but to mobilize, such a devolution in Church Leaders Network's mission would indeed have fit in poorly with the Leadership Network's goals (Brad Smith 1997, 4). This allowed LN to keep itself financially solvent while also maximizing its potential range of influence within the evangelical movement.

LN also established an "interventionist network. This network existed to promote 'best practices'" among church consultants, denominational leaders, church suppliers and the like. Interventionist networks sought to improve the quality of church intervention practices, in the hope that church interventionists, in turn, would prove increasingly productive in supporting local congregations ("We're a Network of Networks" 1997: 3). LN also sought to connect church suppliers and consultants with potentially receptive "markets," thus giving the organization powerful leverage with church consultants (Travis 1997, 5). Besides the obvious financial advantages this gave LN, LN's efforts to establish a dominating presence in church consulting circles—which clearly have had widespread success, given the massive influence of the various movements LN has helped birth or nurture—effectively gave the movement a dominating interest in what organizational literature was produced within Christian Right circles. The far greater sophistication of LN material vis-à-vis the church growth literature that proceeded it—which itself was by no means unsophisticated—testifies to how fundamentally LN altered the depth and quality, if not the honesty, of church growth and church management literature.

The Leadership Network's information network, meanwhile, sought to promote both the ministry and the organizational insights that LN was getting from management and information tech gurus through a range of publications, as well as public relations efforts ("We're a Network of Networks" 1997: 3). The Information Network sought to distribute "ideas and innovations" through as many channels as possible, most likely in order to achieve a broad enough diffusion of these innovations to ensure their adoption once a critical mass had been achieved (Childress 1997, 6). Like most of LN's efforts in the 90s, this was self-evidently a success. The organization's newsletter, for instance, now reaches 60,000 Christian leaders worldwide, if LN's figures are to be believed (Christerson and Flory 2017, loc. 1186–1187).

The Leadership Network promoted some of the networking ideology of Eddie Gibbs as well. In 1998, LN excerpted a short part of a Gibbs' speech, in which he advocated for modern networking to be done relationally, rather than via "power-seeking controllers" who sought to be coercive leaders. Gibbs specifically invoked the NAR as a good organizational model to follow, and commended the power of decentralization and the lack of command and control centers as ideal methods for evolving the church into a new form of leadership and governance (Gibbs 1998, 17). While Gibbs' early insights into network theory seem at times to be somewhat contradictory, his later works show a clear and quite perceptive understanding of the implications of network theory.

Early LN publications such as *NetFax* expressed a marked preference for the promotion of strong network ties over weak ties. Weak ties are the connections formed between an individual and acquaintances. Strong ties are those formed between an individual and intimate friends and family. In social network theory, these ties are primarily defined via "the frequency of interaction" (Kadushin 2012, 30). LN contended, plausibly if banally enough, that the increasing prominence placed on weak ties in the Information Age (think here, for instance, of social media) was leading people to feel "disconnected" from each other. Socially, LN saw a number of benefits to strong ties, including the fact that such ties allowed for greater intimacy between individuals and greater stability. *NetFax* contended that strong ties brought a greater "sense of connectedness and belonging, whereas weak ties engender a sense of loneliness and [a] lack of emotional support." The only real concern *NetFax* had with strong ties at the time was their tendency to be "exclusionary," as this made admittance into strongly tied networks difficult for new individuals, an obvious problem for a movement seeking to mobilize church growth ("Strong Ties, Weak Ties" 1999: 34).

NetFax's understanding of social network theory is here fairly dubious, though it does serve clear organizational objectives. Weak ties, contrary to *NetFax*'s contentions, serve a variety of important purposes. Individuals who lack sufficient weak ties are often "deprived of information from distant parts of the social system," which lessens the likelihood of them being exposed to opinions and information from individuals outside their social circle. Scientific social network theory also maintains that weak ties often aid a culture's ability "to integrate social systems." Those social systems that do not have a sufficient number of weak ties are typically "fragmented and incoherent," a point that directly contradicts LN's understanding of social network theory (Kadushin 2012, 31). Nevertheless, later LN publications strongly emphasized the disconnected nature of contemporary culture ("The End" 1999: 48).

This focus on disconnectedness strongly shaped the EMC conversation that LN largely gave birth to. Within the EMC, church leaders forsook the role "of a public performer" and instead concentrated on adopting the role of "networker" (Doornenbaal 2012, 32). The EMC's focus on the promotion of personal authenticity (Doornenbal 2012, 3) and more meaningful interconnectivity between individuals was a byproduct of the LN's analysis of the faults of weak ties. EMC literature is rife with jeremiads about people's need to find meaningful and satisfying relationships in a postmodern world.[5] While there certainly is some truth to both the LN's and EMC's analysis of the problems associated with weak ties, it should also be noted that the LN and EMC organizations are major beneficiaries of weak ties through their practice of organizational networking. Moreover, the movements' promotion of Christianity as the place to find meaningful relationships (strong ties) often is used to obfuscate the fact that both the LN and the EMC maintain much of their power through the extensive use of peer-to-peer networking based on weak ties.

In any case, LN represents a formidable influence in contemporary evangelicalism. Buford's promotion of "'leadership communities' and 'innovation labs'" has allowed him to synergize his ministry with a number of major megachurch pastors. His network has garnered the support and/or active participation of leaders ranging across the evangelical spectrum, including "Rick Warren, Bill Hybels, Tim Keller, Mark Driscoll and Erwin McManus" (Christerson and Flory 2017, loc. 1182–1190). According to LN, more than a million of its books have been purchased and as of 2012, sales by LN-affiliated churches had topped $1 billion (Christerson and Flory 2017, loc. 1182–1190). Given its influence over the EMC, the organic church movement and, to a lesser extent, New Calvinism, the LN represents perhaps the most underrated and understudied organization on the Christian Right. LN is the purveyor *par excellence* of change management within evangelicalism. Both evangelicals and non-evangelicals ignore the organization at their peril.

Church Planting Networks and the Rise of Reformed Networking

Church planting has arguably existed for centuries.[6] The movement's contemporary popularization can be partially accredited to such churches as Calvary Chapel and Vineyard Christian Fellowship. The Calvary Chapel and Vineyard movements were able to spread rapidly due to their use of church planting practices (Boy 2015, 14). In terms of its organizational approach, much of the modern CPM movement traces its roots to Steve Ogne, and in particular, Robert Logan, who helped systemize the modern approach to church planting (Stetzer 2005, 3). Logan's influence, in particular, deserves comment. By the early 1990s, Logan was considered one of the foremost evangelical authorities on church planting; his approach to church planting received rave reviews from such well-known figures as C. Peter Wagner and Kevin Mannoia (Stetzer 2003, 14). Logan initiated what was called the Church Planting System (CPS) approach to church planting, which he agreed to implement in the SBC with the aid of the Home Mission Board (HMB) (Stetzer 2003, 15). While it is difficult to find a complete description of the framework of this system-based approach to church planting, Kevin Mannoia described how the system worked in 1994. As Stetzer notes, Mannoia's description is of great use in understanding how CPM movements function today, whatever tweaks the movement may have undergone in the meantime (Stetzer 2005, 4–5).

Mannoia contended that a parent church network (PCN) was often helpful in establishing a church planting vision. PCN's generally organized in "cluster" groupings consisting of up to five congregations (Stetzer 2003, 23). The second element that Mannoia describes as essential to a church planting system was a "profile assessment system" which engaged in psychological profiling of potential candidates in order to ensure church planters were put in productive positions (Stetzer 2003, 23; Stetzer 2005, 5–6). Such psychological profiling was not necessarily meant to be an invasive procedure, but rather was conducted because of growing concerns about the need for better leadership recruitment and retention practices (J. Allen Thompson 1995, 3). American church planting thus relied on techniques derived from social science methodology, particularly "diagnostic assessment." Denominations founded or made use of assessment centers to help with this process, a technique recommended by Robert Logan (J. Allen Thompson 1995, 6; Logan 1990, 54–55).

Another component of church planting systems is a New Church Incubator (NCI). The NCI allows for mentoring and oversight by a coach figure (Stetzer 2005, 6). Stetzer indicates that NCI's are meant for "fellowship" and thus they involve a good deal of peer-to-peer networking, as well as vertical networking (see Stetzer 2005, 6; Logan 2006, 158). In a typical NCI, multiple planters, along with mentors and coaches, gather together for peer-to-peer bonding (Logan 2006, 158–159).

A third component of a church planting system (CPS) is the "pastor factory." Designed to create and foster new leaders, the pastor factory idea is influenced by both the assessment technique ideas that Logan and others promoted, as well as cell church methodology. In order to facilitate this form of leadership development and also promote small groups, initial CPS systems also strongly emphasized the importance of meta-church concepts (Stetzer 2003, 24).

There were four other crucial components to the organization of CPS. Church Planter's Summits, held annually, served as both "basic training" and welcome meetings for new planters (Stetzer 2003, 24). Again, the purpose here was probably to increase the likelihood, as well as the value, of peer-to-peer networking. Yet another part of the church planting system that Mannoia describes is the Maturing Church Cluster. This organization was designed to help churches who had moved beyond their first-year transition beyond the initial church planting stage. This was a crucial step, organizationally, because the needs of established churches changed significantly from what those churches had desired as initial church plants (Stetzer 2003, 24). Strategic Planning Networks were also established to make sure such transitions occurred smoothly. Finally, there was the idea of Harvest 1000, which centered on CPM-focused fundraising (Stetzer 2003, 24).

Obviously, not every CPM system exactly fits this model. Stetzer contends, however, that "this system, in its nascent form, was what most denominations began to adapt for their own contexts" after its introduction in the 1990s (Stetzer 2005, 7–8). Church planting thus morphed into a systems-based approach, with a primary emphasis on leadership development, recruitment, assessment and mentoring (Stetzer 2005, 8). Perhaps the biggest influence the CPM movement had, however, was in transitioning evangelical churches away from a reliance on denominational structures to a newly formed mode of organizational governance: the network.

The Calvary Chapel and Vineyard movements played a crucial role in this transition. Over the course of the 1990s and 2000s, numerous new networks formed, such as the Acts 29 Network, CtC, Stadia, Association of Related Churches, Sojourn Network, Glocal.net and NewThing. Networks could center on national or global outreach, but most tried to operate in both these arenas. For most networks, their primary concern was founding new churches; loyalty to particular denominational creeds, was of much less importance, leading to increasing conflict between denominations and networks from the 1990s onwards (Boy 2015, 15). CPM networks are not without their drawbacks. They tend to be monocultural in outlook and often have little ability to support the social mission of the church that more traditional denominations

4. Networked Churches and the Rise of Church Toyota 223

engage in (Stetzer 2005, 9–10). Moreover, the very success of church planting networks has led many of them to take on some of the organizational features of denominational structures, such as the need for increased specialization on the part of network members (Stetzer 2005, 10).

Philosophically and organizationally, CPM networks today are united by a number of central features. First, they are based primarily on relational allegiances, usually promoted through mentoring, coaching, as well as "boot camp" type meetings (Stetzer and Bird n.d., 29). CPM networks also are heavily missiologically focused (Stetzer and Bird n.d., 29). This is likely the result of the increasing missional focus of evangelical churches, one that has crossed the barrier from the EMC conversation into the evangelical mainstream. Most CPM networks aspire to be contextually relevant to their local community; Stetzer and Bird indicate, however, that many CPMS tend to reflect the character of their network, instead of their surrounding culture (Stetzer and Bird n.d., 29). The most successful leaders of CPM networks, much as in the NAR, tend to be charismatic figures (Stetzer and Bird n.d., 30). CPM networks have been particularly effective at "reproducing" churches due to their focus on utilizing church planting teams, rather than relying on solo leadership (Stetzer and Bird n.d., 31–32). Networks today function as "learning platforms," helping to "stimulate new ideas" (Stetzer and Bird n.d., 32). Many advocates of CPM networks promote what is seen as a new math for doing churches, one that focuses on church multiplication, rather than addition. Stetzer and Bird, for instance, support, this idea in their book *Viral Churches: Helping Church Planters Become Movement Makers* (2010) (Stetzer and Bird 2013, 36). This involves a move away from focusing on church growth per se to focusing on the multiplication of churches (Stetzer and Bird 2013, 40; Stetzer 2014). The church, in this model, is intended to spread virally, with the help of a new and more efficient form of congregational support system: the network (Stetzer and Bird 2013, passim).

Church planting networks have been particularly vital in the emergence of two major modern evangelical movements. The first is the EMC conversation. The second is the movement commonly referred to as New Calvinism (Boy 2015, 16–17). Whereas the EMC focuses on experimentation, New Calvinism prides itself on its theological conservatism. Some of the movements chief supports include John Piper, Tim Keller (founder of Redemmer Presbyterian Church), and the Gospel Coalition. For much of the movement's early existence, Mark Driscoll was also a crucial figure. Redeemer City to City (Ctc) and the Acts 29 Network are two CPM networks that formed under the aegis of New Calvinist leadership; both continue to reflect New Calvinist values, even with the exit of Mark Driscoll from New Calvinist circles (see Boy 2015, 17). These two networks have attracted a number of younger supporters into Reformed ranks and played a crucial role in helping perpetuate the Reformed movement, a movement which has historically had trouble generating as much grassroots support as that expressed for Charismatics (Boy 2015, 17).

Understanding both the influence of New Calvinism in contemporary evangelicalism as well as the controversy it engenders is crucial to grasping the movement's singular importance as an example of church networking practices. New Calvinism is the central pillar of modern complementarianism, a pro-patriarchal evangelical theology which models its views of gender roles based on "female submission and male headship" (Joyce 2010, ix–x). Though not all complementarians are New Calvinists, New Calvinism as a whole is primarily a complementarian ideology. There is sometimes debate about whether New Calvinism is itself perhaps primarily a "fad," a product of hype more than substance (Oppenheimer). Collin Hansen, a New Calvinist whose book *Young, Restless, Reformed: A Journalist's Journey with the New Calvinists* (2008) is the most well-known popular Christian text on the movement, has noted a number of traits he believes characterizes the movement.

One of the major traits that separates New Calvinism from "Old" Calvinism is that it is much more open to charismatic tendencies than its more theologically conservative sister movement. Traditional Calvinism is cessationist, and does not emphasize the "gifts of the Sprit," such as speaking in tongues or prophecy. New Calvinism, by contrast, is more markedly experiential. This has a number of real-world implications. First, New Calvinism's movement away from traditional Calvinist rationalism means that the movement is much more oriented in the direction of evangelism and missions than previous variants of Calvinist theology, which explains the movement's tendency to support CPMS. This has led some old Calvinists to see New Calvinism as too markedly revivalistic; New Calvinism has led to many modern Calvinists embracing "Calvinist sotereiology but not necessarily the broader Reformed tradition of Covenant theology, including infant baptism" (Hansen 2009, 103, 109–110). Strategically speaking, however, this move towards experientialism made a lot of sense for New Calvinists as it allowed the movement to incorporate elements of popular culture—notably newer music forms—that had previously been frowned upon within New Calvinist circles. Much like the church growth movement of the seventies and eighties, New Calvinists believed that their movement needed to engage with younger believers/seekers, their commitment to doctrinal purity non-withstanding.

Hansen also notes similarities that characterize major New Calvinist leaders, such as Mark Dever and C.J. Mahaney. Among these similarities are a fondness for the Puritans, a commitment to the welfare of the local church, and a corresponding elevation in the importance of the issues of church membership and church discipline (Hansen 2009, 106). The church discipline aspect of New Calvinism has received widespread promotion among New Calvinist leaders in the wake of the child abuse scandals that have occurred in these churches over the last ten years. Such disciplinary practices, however, are much more often directed at alleged victims than at alleged perpetrators.

The few scholarly articles examining New Calvinism have mainly come from evangelical journals, and point to other commonalities shared by New Calvinist churches. Drew Curley, writing in *The Journal of Dispensational Theology*, has noted that New Calvinism has strongly emphasized a city-based theology, in which evangelicals "missionally" entering into cities as a center point of cultural transformation (Curley 2014, 234). Much of this city-emphasis can be attributed to the incredible sway Tim Keller holds over New Calvinism, particularly the increasingly influential Gospel Coalition, a powerful network of evangelicals with a strong New Calvinist presence. Keller, pastor of Redeemer Church in New York City, is seen as a major success story for the New Calvinist brand. Theologically, Keller's emphasis on "city theology" derives from his belief that major culture-shaping professions—the arts, law, business, education—tend to be disproportionately located in cities (Hart 2013, 221). This means that New Calvinists are increasingly concerned with targeting cultural elites for conversion, rather than the masses, since only through converting the elites can the masses be brought back into the fold; contrary to the contentions of movement critics, such beliefs reflect simple pragmatic realizations about the nature of cultural influence rather than elitism. This has had major implications for how New Calvinists implement church planting.

One aspect of New Calvinism that many scholars, critics, and supporters have noted is its networked nature: both church networks and computer networks. Myron Penner, writing in the Mennonite Brethren journal *Direction*, emphasizes that part of New Calvinism's strength lies in its trans-denominational nature, which has led to the rise of trans-denominational networks and the creation of distinctly non-denominational New Calvinist congregations. This expansion has been fueled by the particular emphasis New Calvinists have placed on church planting. Three of the most influential church planting networks for much of New Calvinism's history have been Sovereign Grace Ministries (formerly led by C.J. Mahaney); the Acts 29 network (co-founded by the now disgraced Mark Driscoll); and Redeemer City to City, which arose in the late 1990s from Tim Keller's Redeemer Presbyterian Church. Sovereign Grace Ministries and Acts 29 require explicit New Calvinist theological leanings from their church planters; Redeemer's qualifications are slightly broader, but are certainly Reformed in outlook. As of 2013, Acts 29 claimed to be a network of nearly 500 churches; Sovereign Grace Ministries, meanwhile had a network of 82 churches at its height, though now its numbers are apparently somewhere in the seventies ("About Us" *Sovereign*

Grace Ministries n.d.; Penner 2013), while Redeemer City to City has some 170 churches in 35 cities around the world (Penner 2013).

More influential than any of these church planting networks is the Gospel Coalition, which plays an important part in "resourcing both established and new churches" (Penner 2013) The Coalition was founded by Tim Keller and Don Carson in 2006. Churches enter the Coalition's "network" once they endorse its confessional statement and vision for ministry (Penner 2013). As Penner points out, The Gospel Coalition has distinctly New Calvinist beliefs, pointing specifically to its emphasis on a Calvinist understanding of the gospel and its support for "complementarian male-headship theology" (Penner 2013). For New Calvinist networks, the Gospel Coalition serves as a valuable tool for gaining increased resource allocation and funding and also assuredly provides the same peer-to-peer networking opportunities that the more explicitly church-planting focused New Calvinist networks (such as Acts 29) offer (Penner 2013). A variety of Reformed heavyweights are or have been council members of the Coalition, including famous Reformed pastor Alistair Begg; Thabiti Anyabwile, a leading African American supporter of New Calvinism; Mark Dever, head of the influential 9 Marks movement; Kevin DeYoung; Ligon Duncan, Chancellor of Reformed Theological Seminary; Al Mohler, one of the foremost Reformed leaders within the Southern Baptist Convention; Russel Moore, another significant Southern Baptist leader with Calvinist leanings; John Piper; and David Powlison, a leading proponent of biblical counseling, among numerous other Reformed elites (Penner 2013; "About the Council" 2018).

One of the major factors in the success of New Calvinist networks has been the utilization of new technological innovations. James K.A. Smith, an influential and relatively independent Calvinist theologian, has pointed out that "[t]he New Calvinism is very much a wired Calvinism—it is more of a network than a movement, finding its coherence in websites more than buildings" (James K.A. Smith 2011, 12). John Boy, perhaps the most objective chronicler of New Calvinism to explore the movement in depth, has noted the movement's fondness for electronic technologies such as church websites (Boy 2015, 18). Blogging is also heavily promoted by New Calvinists, particularly by such groups as The Biblical Counseling Coalition and The Gospel Coalition; such promotion is not always without risk, however, given the vociferous criticism New Calvinists have received from survivor groups. As James K.A Smith notes, the real unifying focus of the Gospel Coalition is as much its complementarian, pro-patriarchal identity as it is any other aspect of the Reformed tradition (James K.A. Smith 2011, 12).

Practically all the great sexual abuse scandals of the 2000s and 2010s, as well as those involving domestic abuse and rape occurred in churches that

4. Networked Churches and the Rise of Church Toyota   227

subscribed to Christian patriarchal theology writ large, and often complementarian theology specifically. The scandals at Sovereign Grace Ministries and within the Acts 29 Network both came directly out of New Calvinism and involved other players in the New Calvinist movement that were not necessarily affiliated directly with the networks: The Christian Counseling and Educational Foundation (CCEF) in the case of SGM and biblical counseling in general in the case of both networks. Furthermore, New Calvinist and complementarian teachings on female subordination, through the influence of the biblical counseling movement, played an influence on the sex abuse scandals at Bob Jones University (see GRACE 2014, 62, 85, 95–97 on the influence of CCEF and Ed Welch over counseling at Bob Jones) and may also have influenced Patrick Henry College's approach towards sexual abuse. The evangelical sex abuse scandals therefore cannot be understood without reference to the influence of New Calvinism.

Although both the Acts 29 network and Sovereign Grace Ministries (SGM) have received extensive—and primarily negative—media coverage, there has been relatively little attention paid to their approach to networking, including in academia. I will therefore focus my attention on Reformed networking practices through looking at Tim Keller's CtC network. Tim Keller started Redemmer Presbyterian Church in 1989. Located in Manhattan, the church may have as many as 5,000 members and visitors attending any given service, an astonishing number for a church located in the heart of secular New York ("Bio: Timothy Keller" 2014). Keller's CtC had, as of 2016, started 250 congregations in almost fifty cities. Sales of his various works have exceeded a million copies, including translations into fifteen different tongues. An urbane intellectual, Keller received his training at "Bucknell University, Gordon-Conwell Theological Seminary, and Westminster Theological Seminary" ("Bio: Timothy Keller" 2014).

As conceptualized by Keller and refined by others, CtC sees its mission as providing "'leadership development'" services for other congregations (Boy 2015, 20: "Bio: Timothy Keller" 2014). CtC also has made a place for itself in the Faith at Work movement and seeks eagerly to recruit and develop effective urban leaders (Boy 2015, 20–21). CtC serves as both a "central node" for its network, but with its individual involvement in church plants ranging anywhere from serving as a catalyst to simply being a nominal ally of a ministry. Those congregations within CtC may fit themselves tightly into the network or be only loosely aligned with it; in most cases, congregations gain support from entities outside the network as well as inside, including denominations, churches with similar organizational agendas, or networks outside the CtC (Boy 2015, 22–23). In any case, CtC's role in the Reformed community in many ways mirrors that of the Leadership Network (on a smaller scale), in that it serves as a "skunk works" for various Reformed CP initiatives.

CtC views its main purpose as the promotion of leadership training through "the provision of workshops, and opportunities for … professional development" (Boy 2015, 70). When Boy visited CtC's midtown Manhattan offices, staffing included approximately 12 individuals, among them aides to the organization's regional directors, various PR and communications specialists, and fundraisers (Boy 2015, 70). In order to facilitate both public relations and peer-to-peer networking, CtC provides "network leaders" (25 individuals at the time Boy conducted his interviews with the organization), who specialize in peer-to-peer networking with other network members on behalf of CtC. Not only are these individuals well trained in mobilizing attendees to large conferences, but they also engage in efforts at more small-scale mobilization, such as local meetings conducted with the aid of their regional partners, often with other networks (Boy 2015, 71). CtC tries to maintain a great deal of flexibility against what it perceives to be the "greater rigidity" of "institutional structures" such as denominations. This obviously represents a politically wise move for CtC, as it allows the organization to avoid the infighting of denominations while also bypassing denominational rules and regulations set up to limit the effectiveness of the network's objectives (see Boy 2015, 71).

From a missiological perspective, CtC is united by a common "DNA." Boy interprets the CPM's vision of the DNA ideas as referring to "the manner in which doctrinal principles are articulated in contextualized ways in individual church plants without ultimately compromising them" (Boy 2015, 81). Boy emphasizes that it is the ability of churches to successfully negotiate issues of contextualization that defines how networked churches will relate to each other. Moreover this ability to negotiate the need for contextualization in radically different contexts also allows networked churches to "stay coordinated without resorting to centralized authority," giving them—in CPM theory generally and CtC's organizational vision specifically—a perceived major advantage over traditional church authority structures (Boy 2015, 81). Boy productively references Alex Galloway's ideas on protocol to point out how decentralization in church planting networks does not necessarily "indicate an absence of power relations" (Boy 2015, 81). From Boy's perspective, the protocol system that exists in church networks is the concept of church DNA or as Keller alternately refers to it, "middleware." Such network DNA is not developed casually, but rather through a process of discussion between pastors and their chief advisors or leadership teams. These leaders, in turn, frequently borrow ideas from books or "case studies" that have occurred in similar church environments.[7] The members of the church planting team, most of which will take important positions in the plant, provide the framework for the church's DNA, thus ensuring a high degree of "genetic" replication of the parent network's vision. Thus, these meetings, which practically

4. Networked Churches and the Rise of Church Toyota   229

always reinforce conservative ides about the church through peer-to-peer dialogue, allow for the organizational protocol to be spread throughout the entire network (Boy 2015, 81–82). These network protocols are reinforced by a number of other supporting mechanisms present in CtC—as well as most other church planting networks. For instance, CtC and other church planting networks offer leadership development and training to leaders in their networks. In addition to helping future network and church leaders develop useful skill sets, such training regimens allow these leaders to relate their own leadership practices to other leaders within the movement. Since the movement serves as the "frame of reference" for how most movement leaders want to interpret the Christian life, these training regimens serve as a means of norming individuals into accepting the network's "protocol." Moreover, the conferences that CtC holds—another practice that it shares with other church planting networks—ensure that its membership sees itself as participating cooperatively in a much grander mission for the church. Thus, as Boy notes, it is a mistake to believe that networks operate without governing protocols, regardless of the rhetoric such networks propagate (Boy 2015, 81–82).

Keller's vision for church planting was specifically an urban one. He was influenced by missiologist Harvie Conn, who contended that Christians should not concede urban areas to the forces of secularism (Boy 2015, 89–90). Keller believes that the "technological revolution" brought about by information technology had led to an increasing prioritization of urban life over rural areas. Moreover, the spread of digital technologies had greatly extended the influence of urban culture, creating an environment in which the whole planet was becoming one big cityscape (Keller 2012, 154). Major cities and the metropolitan areas surrounding them were leading cities to take on more cultural influence than the governments they paid obeisance to. Keller notes that governments were increasingly losing out in influence to networked organizations and multinational corporations because they were no longer able to effectively command "the flow of capital and information" (Keller 2012, 155). The most important element in Keller's promotion of urban ministry, however, is his belief that in order to reach "cultural elites," evangelical churches must be willing to aim their ministries at where these elites live: the city (Keller 161). For Keller, as Boy notes, gaining cultural capital is of vital importance (Boy 2015, 185).

In order to ensure that the church gains a firm foothold in urban areas, Keller relies heavily on the influence of social science methodology. Keller's early church planting manuals focused on using demographic and ethnographic techniques to develop people group profiles, which could then be used to strategically plan how to best approach a particular urban evangelism opportunity. The focus on ethnography also led Keller to advocate a move away from a "one size fits all approach for church planting," in favor of relying heavily on contextualization. Like other church planting network (CPN) advocates, Keller realized that the number of potential factors influencing the success or failure of a church plant were almost infinite. Therefore, one key to helping church plants thrive was to make sure planters realized that no model was perfect for every cultural scenario the church faced (Boy 2015, 95). Although not perfectly clear from Keller's work, his ministry also clearly relies on elements of diffusion research to promote its agenda. The desire to capture "cultural capital" through gaining access to cultural elites shows Keller's preference for developing "in-house" cultural innovators and early adopters. Moreover, throughout Keller's work, as well as many other advocates of church planting, there is repeated reference to Malcolm Gladwell's works, especially the *Tipping Point*, a book that popularized the ideas behind diffusion research (Keller 2012, 376–377; Keller 2011, 117; Gladwell 2002, 12).[8] Keller argues that in urban areas, the church must so effectively spread the gospel that the local environment reaches an "ecosystem tipping point" in which urban church planting becomes "self-sustaining" and thus leads to a revived evangelical urbanism. The ultimate endgame is to make urban churches so effective that there influence as a citywide culture-shaper is acknowledged (Keller 2012, 376–377).[9]

New Calvinist networking has enjoyed some staggering successes, but the poor level of peer-to-peer accountability practiced in New Calvinism may well prove its downfall. This lack of accountability among leaders has alienated many rank-and-file New Calvinists and produced tremendous backlash within fundamentalist and Reformed circles. This backlash has become all the more problematic in the light of the abuse scandals that have rocked New Calvinist churches. Part of the problem for New Calvinist leaders may have been that they failed to realize the difficulty of contextualizing the network ideal for a Reformed audience. The Reformed movement, as a rule, has been more resistant to networking than many other adherents of evangelicals. Moreover, a huge problem that Reformed networks have faced is that their complementarian theology appears to have left their adherents far more vulnerable to sexual and physical abuse than the far more female-friendly theology that motivates the NAR. Whether New Calvinism can overcome these organizational vulnerabilities remains an open question. While the movement has a formidable rank of intellectuals in its ranks, it also has to face increasing amount of criticism from evangelical survivor groups and discernment ministries, many of whom have shown much greater expertise at using networking ideas than New Calvinists have themselves (Harris 2014). Unless New Calvinists find a method of appeasing or silencing their critics, their likely future influence in evangelicalism may be minimal, given how much their "brand" has been tarnished in recent years.

Willow Creek and Networking

A prominent and early example of "network governance" among evangelicals was the Willow Creek Association (WCA), centered around Bill Hybels's Willow Creek Community Church. Hybels was one of the formative voices in the seeker-sensitive movement and helped pioneer many of its techniques. Hybels organized the WCA in 1991 to promote his seeker-sensitive ideas to a wider audience. The main organizational advantages of joining the WCA include the ability to engage in peer-to-peer networking with other leaders, as well as taking advantage of the numerous conference and workshop offerings the WCA promotes. The WCA does not promote a formal "franchis[ing]" process, but instead serves as an ecclesiological port-of-call for those who want to utilize the seeker sensitive techniques it helped perfect, for which the WCA offers extensive resources and products. As of 2010, the network numbered some 9,000 congregations (Christerson and Flory 2017, loc. 1161–1177).

When the WCA was founded in 1991, it specifically targeted major urban areas, including, when possible, major cities outside the U.S. The WCA was specifically interested in getting pastors to copy its particular model for reaching "unchurched individuals," one which would become widely emulated in evangelical circles (Branaugh 2008; Pritchard 1994, 3–6; "Willow Creek Repents" 2007). In addition to the standard conferences that Willow Creek utilized, the network also made sure to provide similar training for small groups and its "Network" ministry. The WCA marketed its organizational model as being highly modular, and therefore both encouraged other churches to adopt it and served as a mentoring church in this adoption process (Pritchard 1994, 5).

In order for Willow Creek to spread its model, it developed a form of organizational governance that borrowed heavily from corporate structures, with the church splitting its different roles into "pastoral, administrative, and programming responsibilities" divided initially among three departments (Sargeant 1996, 170). A corporate board of directors oversaw the senior pastor. Willow Creek also divested senior pastors of much of their teaching responsibility, so that they could concentrate on management-oriented tasks. By the time Kimon Sargeant investigated Willow Creek in 1996, the organization's methods were highly refined. Staff-people's lives were governed by the same prioritization of performance targets that governed corporations. The church's organizational outlook also relied on including the laity in its mission. This was the purpose of the ministry's "Network" program which sought to find out laity members' skill sets and then match them to organizational needs (Sargeant 1996, 170).

The WCA continues to be an important, though now embattled, network. Moreover, many of the organizational innovations that Willow Creek adopted have since become a standard part of most church network organizations. For instance, Willow Creek was famous for promoting specialization of leadership functions. Senior pastoral leaders were referred to as directors and typically their skill set lay in their area of specialization, not the ministry (Sargent 1996, 172). Hybels, like C. Peter Wagner, deemphasized the importance of seminary training in leadership development (Sargent 1996, 172–173).[10] As a network, WCA provided for many of the same needs that other churches had traditionally looked to denominations for. It proved adept at giving advice to other churches on such topics as "church leadership, management and vision" and was seen by these churches as an important distributor of leadership resources and training. Willow Creek's emphasis on "hands-on" training gave it a distinct advantage against denominational churches that had not adopted to the new networked economy (Sargent 1996, 281–282). These organizational advantages, combined with Willow Creek's pioneering approach to marketing, thus were of crucial importance in spreading network models of governance throughout the evangelical movement, and particularly to Willow-Creek's fellow seeker-sensitive churches.

In addition to the numerous Toyotist production and governance practices that I have discussed in this section and those preceding it, networked churches have also borrowed from several other Toyotist ideas. Space prevents me from detailing all of these innovations, which would take a small volume. But one particular innovation, the multisite church, must be discussed. Otherwise, the significance of the evangelical church's embrace of ICTs cannot be readily understood.

Multisites

A prominent example of innovation in church organizational networking is the multisite church. Multisite churches, often known as "'satellite" or "franchise"-based churches (Smietana 2005, 61), at their most basic represent the idea of having one church which gathers at multiple different locations for its service (Frye 2011, 15). In short, in its most basic form, multisite churches literally represent franchisable churches. While the multisite model has arguably had a long history, it was only recognized as a movement in the wake of a major LN-sponsored conference on multisites held on 9/11 (Frye 2011, 1, 5). Embryonic forms of the multi-site idea had appeared in the 1980s in a number of locations. The movement was prominent enough by the early 1990s to catch the attention of CGM enthusiast Elmer Towns (Frye 2011, 7). By the early 2010s, multisites were becoming an established institution within evangelical Christianity. A cottage industry developed around multisites, in-

4. Networked Churches and the Rise of Church Toyota

volving conferences, lectures, and a burgeoning list of book titles (Frye 2011, 9). Much of the organizational impetus for multisite churches has come from the Leadership Network (Frye 2011, 108–109). In 2002, The Leadership Network helped established an influential "Multi-site Leadership Community" among important promoters of the multisite model, which served as an organizational skunk works for refining multisite theory and organizational techniques. The Leadership Network also helped facilitate organizational connections between important innovators and early adopters of the modern multi-site model. Since many of these individuals became the most influential supporters of the multi-site idea within evangelicalism, LN's role within the multisite movement was foundational (Frye 2011, 110–115).

For the evangelical movement as a whole, multisite churches represent a perfection of Toyotism's application of "kan-ban" or "just in time" production. In the business world, just-in-time production reduces inventory size by making sure that suppliers meet the needs of the production line "at the exact required time and with the characteristics specified" by line workers (Castells 2010a, 169). Multisites and the house churches that have originated out of the EMC both represent differing approaches to dealing with the problem of "large inventories" that megachurches present. Because of their greater size, megachurches require a disproportionate investment of financial resources into their buildings (Smietana 2005, 62), staffing, and other aspects of their ministries (Frye 2011, 267–268). Because multisites are typically smaller than megachurches, they help ministries avoid costly zoning battles (Smietana 2005, 62–63). With growing concerns among evangelicals about the ability of the evangelical movement to financially sustain the megachurch model, multisite churches offer an alternative to both the "go small" approach of EMC house churches and the "go big" model of classical megachurches. Moreover, multisite advocates, such as Life Church's Craig Groeschel, argue that multisite churches create the communal experience that small churches provide, with many of the advantages that larger megachurches provide (Smietana 2005, 61).

Multisites rely heavily on digital and ICT (information communication) technologies to make their "just in time" production process a reality (Frye 2011, 85–86). Even at the level of organizational innovation, the multi-site movement was dependent on the increasing ability of church leaders, "innovators," and "implementers" to create the catalytic forces needed to transform the multisite paradigm from an idea to a movement (Frye 2011, 86). The multisite model succeeded because American evangelicals fully embraced the technological possibilities of television, the Internet, and other forms of electronic media. The full extent of this embrace will be detailed in the next two chapters, but it is important to note certain aspects of that embrace here. Due to the invention of the television and advanced recording technologies, evangelicals were increasingly able to take advantage of pre-taped sermons, worship services, and other forms of Christian ministry. Moreover, these recordings could be replayed, and the ability and durability of such recordings has increased almost exponentially in recent years (Frye 2011, 91). With the advent of the Internet and advanced multimedia presentation technologies, church services soon benefited from "increased speed and proficiency of communication ... throughout the church body (gathered and distributed), and out into the community" (Frye 2011, 91). The use of PowerPoint, for instance, notably improved congregational worship and aided church outreach efforts, both to members and to non-believers. The advent of social media meant that "spatial limitations and boundaries" mattered far less than they had in previous eras. Evangelical churches also readily adopted technologies like Skype, Google Talk, and Google Docs, which allowed them to maintain both regional and international presences with undreamed-of efficiency. Churches eventually came to realize that with the development of all these new technologies, the multisite model was becoming an increasingly feasible means of doing business, one with many advantages (Frye 2011, 91–92).

ICT technologies were important in making just-in time production practices feasible for multisites. For instance, at Groeschel's Life Church, the worship program is synchronized to the last second, with a "countdown clock" constantly serving as a reminder of the need for organizational sychronization. To further this organizational standardization, multisites rely heavily on video technologies, such as satellite links, DVDS, and now streaming, as a key aspect of their teaching ministry. In some churches, video teaching is the preferred method, while other churches utilize campus-specific pastors, an instructor who is a member of a rotation of leaders, or one pastor who travels between each individual satellite location (Smietana 2005, 62).[11] Each campus of Groeschel's multisite has a full-time pastor who helps to create "social networks" for the area he has been delegated (Smietana 2005, 61). Multisites hope that the providing of staff pastors at satellite locations will help alleviate any feelings of alienation from church leadership (Smietana 2005, 62).

The prevalence of ICT technology in multisite churches has not just altered how evangelical parishioners relate to their pastors, it also has fundamentally changed the church's geographical understanding of itself. For the multisite church, "geography is no longer the defining factor" in how it approaches ministry (Surratt, Ligon, and Bird 2006, 27). Frye notes that historically evangelical churches—indeed all Christian congregations—faced "geographical limits" in their outreach; even older attempts at multi-site ministries that predated the modern ICT revolution were unable to fully address such deficiencies. However, because of the advances in ICT technology (and to a lesser extent transport), the geographical limitations churches face are now minimal, if not non-existent (Frye 2011, 139).

The franchisability of multisites that this overcoming of geographical and technological limitations affords is a key aspect of the model's appeal. Bob Smietana posits that multisites are successful for the same reasons that chain stores are. An ideal multisite will "take a system that works, and duplicate it over and over.... When a new location starts up, leaders don't have to reinvent children's ministries or small-group programs" (Smietana 2005, 63) Such franchisability allows congregations to take on aspects of both churches and church networks simultaneously. They create a powerful incentive for further standardization of church ministries, staffing practices, and even doctrinal commitments. Such standardization can have far more massive implications if a multisite is involved in a church network, a "network of networks," or if the church has become a major "teaching church" for other churches and church leaders.[12] As Frye notes, multisite churches borrow heavily from modern business franchising practices, and bear an "astounding" resemblance to such franchises in "areas of shared branding, accounting, quality controls, management, training, product, and services" (Frye 2011, 79). Just as church planting networks like CtC utilize the idea of "DNA" as their network protocol, multisites are similarly invested in ensuring that all satellite campuses within their system are on track with the central information processor of the multisite network: the home church. Thus, as Heath Kahlbau notes, "the same core values … must be present at each campus" of a multisite network (Heath Kahlbau 2014, 112). The increasing uniformity that evangelicals have noted since the beginning of the rise of network-based churches is at least partly attributable to the kind of standardization that the multisite movement has afforded evangelicalism.

Such uniformity obviously has its benefits. Better resource allocation and decreased production costs are major advantages of multisite networks over more traditional forms of church planting (or for that matter, megachurches).[13] Greg Ligon, one of LN's major promoters of multisites, notes that church plants represent more of an organizational gamble (church venture capitalism, if you will). This, in turn, affords church plants less peer-to-peer and congregation-to-congregation networking than is provided in multisite networks. Moreover, because multisites are so closely connected to all their satellite campuses, every campus "has a stake in making sure they all thrive" (Smietana 2005, 63), thus decreasing the likelihood of infighting and providing an incentive for the creation of positive "working"—i.e., believing—environments.

Moreover, multisites also provide better customer service for congregants than that afforded by many other types of churches. Lean production techniques, which Toyotist practices helped perfect, are predicated on effective customer service (see Castells 2010a, 176). Thus, a consumerist model of doing church is likely to attract more customers than a producer-oriented approach. Multi-sites are far more modular in their approach to doing church than the models offered up by the house church movement or megachurch movement. For every need, the multi-site movement tries to offer an option (Frye 2011, 73–74). During the organizational revolution of the 60s and 70s, many organizations had realized that they needed to reach out to their customers rather than wait for their customers to come meet them (Frye 2011, 75). The Multisite movement, much like EMC churches (some of whom are also multisite), has realized that it must be incarnational, rather than attractional, if it wants to bring new sheep into the fold.

The advent of multisites has had important implications for the organization of church polity as well. One of the reasons why multisite churches have been controversial among many evangelicals is because of contemporary evangelicalism's preoccupation with church governance structures (Frye 2011, 196). The type of polity—congregational, Presbyterian, or episcopal—that a normal church adopts has major implications for both how much freedom individuals have within the church and how much regulatory oversight exists over church leaders.

Some evangelicals contend that the multi-site model naturally lends itself to Episcopalian governance, in which the lead pastor serves as "a bishop over the multisite church or a group of churches" (Frye 2011, 196). This understanding of multisite governance practices has led concerned critics to contend that the pastors of multisites function as little more than glorified CEOS (Frye 2011, 196–197). Frye notes that the combination of Episcopalian governance and the multisite approach does have some problems, when such fears come true. Churches in which governance is centralized in one leader or a small leadership team run the risk of taking away many important "decision making roles" that typically are the provenance of congregations (Frye 2011, 198).

Frye contends that Presbyterian governance structures fit well with the multisite approach (Frye 2011, 204–205). He notes that the governance system of multisites resembles the relationship between "ruling" and "teaching" elders in Presbyterian polities. Frye explains that:

> Within the presbyterian system, the teaching elder, who is considered, the lead pastor of a session, is principally responsible for the Word and the sacraments, and ruling elders generally handle pastoral responsibilities. In a similar way, in many multi-site arrangements, campus pastors handle pastoral roles at their respective campuses as ruling elders, and the lead pastor of a multi-site church (or in some cases, lead pastors) whether in person or by video assume(s) primary teaching responsibility [Frye 2011, 207–208].

Frye's point here is a significant one. The desirability of Presbyterian governance structures in multisite churches for many church leaders is reflective of an increasingly widely shared view in evangelical Protestantism that distrusts congregational government. Multisite churches present a particular challenge to democratic governance because, as Frye correctly notes, they split "a single church body into multiple locations," making the possibility of congregants' effective participation in a church's governmental life dubious at best (Frye 2011, 209). What Frye does not note is how congenial such a development would be to the multisite model's chief promoter, the Leadership Network, whose already-noted allegiance to network governance concepts makes it a natural enemy of democratic leadership practices. Moreover, as an early supporter of the NAR, LN helped further the dedemocratization of evangelicalism in the 1990s. Multisite churches may simply be another refinement of that strategy.

Moreover, even if the goal of the multisite movement is not dedemocratization, there are other organizational challenges that it presents evangelical churches. Multisite organizational structures resemble "matrix model[s]" rather than the "traditional hierarchal system." Those hierarchies that exist often involve ministry team members reporting to multiple superiors (James Howell Edwards II 2016, 41–42). In most matrix-oriented leadership systems, "flexibility and adaptability" are key to organizational effectiveness (James Howell Edwards II 2016, 41–42); as we have seen, the promotion of flexibility is a central narrative of network governance within evangelicalism and therefore the adoption of matrix organizational structures in multisite churches will likely predispose future multisites to adopt most other aspects of network governance. Therefore, if it is LN's goal to dedemocratize Protestant Christianity, the adoption of matrix organizational structures will likely accelerate the process of dedemocratization started in the 1990s. At this point, where that process ends is anyone's guess. But given the increasing concerns about disaffection among evangelical believers, particularly youth, it is likely that the combination of multisite and matrix organizational patterns will lead to the increasing narrowing of possibilities for organizational dissent within evangelical churches. With dissenting believers geographically fragmented, their choices will increasingly be either absolute compliance or total disaffiliation. Many Christians who cherish their faith will not be willing to pay the latter cost, but the consequences for not doing so may be almost as damaging to the church as any forced exodus would be.

Conclusion

The development of church networks based on Toyotist principles remains one of the major organizational achievements of evangelical Christianity in the late 20th century. But the achievements of these networks would not have been possible without crucial innovations in organizational theory and, in particular, computer technology. The next two chapters will delve into this latter topic, showing how the evangelical movement has developed a profoundly underestimated technological infrastructure that leaves it well prepared to tackle the challenges of the 21st century. Unless the full extent of this technological infrastructure is understood by the movement's critics and opponents, reforming or challenging the movement will continue to prove impossible.

5

The Christian Right's Technological Infrastructure

In the 1990s, a seemingly new ideology, centered in Silicon Valley, came to dominate discussions surrounding the Internet. This ideology had many names—"cyber-libertarianism," and the "Californian ideology" are two of the most well-known. This philosophy had a number of underlying assumptions about what the Net did. According to this line of thinking, the Internet tends to flatten hierarchies, creating a decentralized society, and therefore leads the world to adapt the ideals of neoclassical economics. The decade witnessed a drive towards computerization, with every group in American society attempting to out-digitize its opponents. At the same time, this new form of "digital libertarianism" or cyber-libertarianism played an important role in legitimizing right-wing policies aimed at reducing government size and regulatory powers. Comingled with these changes were important assumptions about how corporate hierarchies should be run, as well as what new "production and distribution patterns in business" would now dominate the global economy (Fred Turner 2002, 4). A particularly influential proponent of this new form of cyber-libertarianism was *Wired* magazine. For *Wired*, everyone from Newt Gingrich, the formulator of the Contract with America to Bill Gates were engaged in a massive project of social engineering involving cyberspace. But this project of social engineering was cast in the tones of human liberation and self-actualization. The new society that these ideologues of cyber-libertarianism promoted would be an open one and based on rapid social decentralization. Coupled to these concepts was an understanding of human nature in which human and machine nature began to blur (Fred Turner 2002, 5).

For some digital libertarians, such as John Perry Barlow, this means that human nature must be reconceptualized: People, in Barlow's reading, "have become information" (Fred Turner 2002, 8). This has also fundamentally altered the nature of politics. For the rhetoricians of cyberspace, the struggle over resources is meaningless, because the main resource they are concerned with—information—is unlimited. Conflict is no longer primarily conceptualized in terms of "states and armies ... since there are no bodies to conscript" (Fred Turner 2002, 8). Thus, for cyber-libertarians, the Internet is more than simply a "network of networks"—instead, it presents a fundamental model, which has correspondences in nature, of how to organize social systems in the physical world (Fred Turner 2002, 8–9; Adam Curtis 2011).

Barlow's understanding of the Net has broad appeal in Silicon Valley. For instance, Esther Dyson (1951–), daughter of famed physicist Freeman Dyson (the man who gave us the vision of the Dysonsphere) was attracted to aspects of the cyber libertarian vision. For the younger Dyson, what proved revolutionary about the Net was that its value came from its "citizens," not its "institutions" (Dyson, 1997, 279; Fred Turner 2002, 307). For Dyson, online markets promised to revolutionize the world by giving people the capability to engage in "peer-to-peer interactions between entities that are not in fact peers in the material world" (Fred Turner 2002, 9). Dyson believes that this creates revolutionary potential for online markets because it gives all individuals access to potentially unlimited amounts of data, allowing individuals the ability to compete with large corporations on equal terms, at least in the online environment. Moreover, the radically more egalitarian information distribution the Net creates incentivizes both consumers and producers to mutually "co-create" products that each benefit from (Fred Turner 2002, 10). Governance is not imposed on the system, but is created by the system as "an emergent property" (Fred Turner 2002, 10). The electronic marketplace thus becomes the arbiter of the new global order, an order characterized by "conversation, cooperation, [and] coevolution" that replaces the old coercive relationships "between buyers and sellers" (Fred Turner 2002, 11). The market becomes simply an information processor that enacts the will of its members (Curtis, *Trap* DVD).[1]

Many of the spokesman of the Californian Ideology clustered around networks originating from Stewart Brand, a countercultural figure in the 1960s and 1970s who ran the Global Business Network (GBN), a consulting firm with an explicitly futurist outlook (Fred Turner 2002, 34). Brand was most famous for editing the *Whole Earth Catalog*. From its formation in 1968, the *Whole Earth Catalog* served as a meeting place for two worldviews that in the late sixties *seemed* wildly divergent. The first was the new cybernetic ideology of industry, while the second was the Eastern religious orientation, mystical New Age beliefs, and communal organizing of the counterculture (Fred Turner 2002, 110). In the *Catalog*'s early formative years—a period ranging from roughly 1968 to 1971—contributors from four distinctive groups were of particularly importance: Thinkers in academia, government, and corporate-based science and technology; the avant garde

5. The Christian Right's Technological Infrastructure 241

art scenes of New York and San Francisco; The Bay Area counterculture, specifically its "psychedelic community"; and the various communes that had begun in the United States in the late 1960s (Fred Turner 2002, 111). While these communities had always interacted with each other, Stewart Brand was one of the few individuals who had participated significantly in all four. Prior to his work on the Catalog, Brand had collaborated with computer scientists at SRI and studied under leading Stanford University–based biologists, notably doom-and-gloom ZPG advocate Paul Ehrlich (Fred Turner 2002, 111; Rowe 2011, 429). Brand's countercultural "cred" was equally significant, including a stint with Ken Kesey's Merry Pranksters. Due his extensive traversing of the American Southwest, Brand was able to "spot points of commonality and possibility for collaboration" between various communes that other, more limited organizers might have missed (Fred Turner 2002, 111–112).

Organizationally, both the Catalog and the network that surrounded it drew inspiration from two divergent influences: the systems theories then being promulgated in cybernetics and ecology, as well as commune-supported "notions of distributed government and disembodied community" (Fred Turner 2002, 112). By the early 1970s, *Whole Earth Catalog* writers, along with their writers at spinoff periodical *CoEvolution Quarterly* began to see the formation of neoliberal ideology, but rather than reject its tenets, they began to jump onboard. *Whole Earth Catalog* writers believed that emerging new technologies, particularly information technologies, could not just serve as a form of self-actualization, but could help individuals escape the tyranny of irresponsive bureaucratic structures (Matt Garite 2013, 49). Even at this relatively early date, the *Whole Earth Catalog* adamantly supported gurus of the emerging neo-liberal order, writing glowing reviews of works like Milton Friedman's *Capitalism and Freedom* (1962) and Ayn Rand's *Atlas Shrugged* (1957) (Garite 2013, 112). Though the areas of interest in which *Whole Earth Catalog* writers engaged in were wide reaching, Brand managed to promote a good deal of overtly pro-computer rhetoric into the magazine, influencing many people who were interested in what the computer industry was doing (Josh Rowe 2011, 428). The *Whole Earth Catalog*, as Steve Jobs ones noted, served an analogous role to Google for many early computer innovators. The "mission, function, and culture" of the *Catalog* helped shape how many tech companies envisioned their mission, while the values the *Catalog* promoted, such as the importance of "free information, personal exploration, and community formation" served as a kind of technological benchmark which other high-tech innovators hoped to both give voice to and improve upon (Rowe 2011, 434).

What made the *Catalog* revolutionary was that it divorced itself from previous linear communication models. Traditional models of authorship, as

Turner describes them, involve a three-step process of "production, text, and reception," where a:

> raw material (a "news event" in journalism; "imagination" in fiction) meets a processor (a reporter, a novelist), who transforms the raw material into a "product" (a news story, a novel) within a geographically isolated production facility ... and then distributes it through appropriate institutional channels ... to an audience which in turn "consumes" it [Fred Turner 2002, 150].

The problem with this model, as Brand realized, was that it conceptualized the audience as a passive receptor of products, rather than as potential producers. The *Whole Earth Catalog*, by contrast, served as a networking site which went beyond simply selling goods; it thus called for a fundamental reconceptualization of the relationship between producer and consumer (Fred Turner 2002, 150, 152, 157). The managerial practice of Brand and his associates, both at the *Catalog* and its quarterly *Supplement* embraced New Age approaches to social organization that sought to level hierarchies and bypass conflicts embedded in traditional structures of social organizing. Within the *Catalog* in particular, Brand sought to avoid hierarchal power relationships by empowering reviewers, letter writers, and even the products the *Catalog* sold. Yet Brand ultimately had the final say in what was produced by the *Catalog*. He just preferred to exercise his power by constructing the initial "protocol" of the catalog, rather than using a more directive approach (Fred Turner 2002, 167–169).

Like many of the thinkers explored in *Technology, Management and the Evangelical Church*, Brand's vision of technology was profoundly informed by the Cold War. Brand's studies under Ehrlich had led him to conclude that in a situation in which two species competed for the same ecological niche, one would inevitably force the other out. Brand found this a depressing and deeply hierarchical worldview. In Brand's mind this hierarchical vision was emblematic of both the Soviet Union and politics as a whole. Looking for an alternative worldview, Brand believed that both the *I Ching* and the insights of environmental biology offered an alternate vision of the world that allowed for mutual co-existence of individuals. Brand contended that "invisible forces—mystical, in the case of the *I Ching*, and natural in the case of environmental biology" would in this alternate vision allow people to "pursue their own identities while functioning as unique members of ever more varied systems" (Fred Turner 2002, 115).

Brand found this vision liberating. It allowed him to envision a world not trapped in the "Cold war dualisms" that had shaped so much of his generation's thinking. Rather than forcing order on nature from above, as the Kremlin seemed to do to human beings through the application of "force from above," the biological order of the natural world suggested to Brand that

5. The Christian Right's Technological Infrastructure 243

such order could be replicated in human society, but originating not from above, but below. Thus, applying analytical insights from ecology and evolutionary biology, Brand, argued that the threat posed by the Soviet system and the threat directed at individuals by rigidly tiered social orders were the same: "Both were monocultures, systems devoted to reducing the individual variations that helped ecosystems evolve" (Fred Turner 2002, 116). Like many other digerati, Brand's ideology was rooted in systems philosophies, including the social cybernetic movement that had taken its inspiration from Norbert Wiener. Among this movement's most avid supporters were Gregory Bateson (1904–1980) and Heinz von Foerster (1911–2002). What distinguished their form of second-order cybernetics was that it took into account the observations of the observer as "an essential feedback node" within a system (Rowe 2011, 437). Thus second-order cybernetics invited grandiose visions of "holistic inclusion of entire environmental, social and psychological systems" into over-arching wholes. Bateson and von Foerster thus fundamentally shaped Brand's worldview (Rowe 2011, 437).

The mixture of counterculture ideology and hi-tech cybernetic thought that Brand embraced may be perplexing to some. As Rowe points out, it is not immediately apparent how a magazine like *The Whole Earth Catalog*, "devoted to radical individual freedom" could easily reconcile itself to the belief that humans are just "programmed systems" (Rowe 2011, 445–446). But this apparent irreconcilability is an illusion. What Brand was able to derive from cybernetic thought was a profound philosophy of "self-programming" (Rowe 2011, 445). Within this philosophy, human beings were "self-direct[ing] systems" (Rowe 2011, 446). Rather than obviate free will, this ideology in Brand's reading called into question the effectiveness of "large scale human enterprises like Government and War," as such programs were based on the thinking of "imperfect and vulnerable machines," namely human beings (Rowe 2011, 446).

Over a period stretching 30 years, Stewart Brand built a relational network of individuals and publications that connected the San Francisco counterculture with Silicon Valley. *The Whole Earth Catalog* served as the hub of that network, and the shared ideology of "cybernetic utopia" became the ideology by which the counterculture embraced Silicon Valley (Rowe 2011, 455–456). Although the influence of the counterculture over computing may have been exaggerated in some works, even critical scholars like Josh Rowe acknowledge that this fusion of counterculture and Silicon Valley ideology did exist and concede that the counterculture likely "played a very important part in bringing personal computing to public recognition" (Rowe 2011, 455–456). In the process of turning into a networking organization "par excellence," the *Whole Earth Catalog* and the other networks Brand formed largely betrayed their counterculture origins. Rather than fight for the downtrodden,

Brand and his colleagues allowed their vision to be subsumed behind those of global capitalist interests (Fred Turner 2002, 184–185).

Yet, this move could have easily been predicted. As early as 1970, fellow *Whole Earth Catalog* staffer Jay Bonner had publicly criticized Brand for his depoliticized worldview. In Brand's somewhat desultory response, he legitimized his form of activism by contending that the "top down politics" of the past was no longer viable. The individual, not the group, was central to political change. Brand's vision of reform was therefore profoundly localist (Fred Turner 2002, 185). This is important to understand if we are to come to an adequate understanding of the surprising amount of networking that Brand and his associates engaged in with evangelicals and even with the Christian Right writ large (Fred Turner 2002, 184–185).

The links between the Christian Right and the *Whole Earth Catalog* can be traced back to the foundation of the Whole Earth "Lectronic" Link (the WELL), which began in 1985. Started by Stewart Brand and doctor and tech enthusiast Larry Brilliant (1944–), WELL was one of the first "'virtual' communities," and played an enormously important role in developing public perceptions of the Internet. Turner convincingly contends that WELL's whole organizing methodology borrows from specific "countercultural and cybernetic ideals," particularly in its approach to organizational philosophy and relational networking (Fred Turner 2002, 189–190, 212).

But the founders of WELL faced a radically different world than that that had confronted the counterculture in the 1960s. The network society discussed in Chapter 4 had arisen. The experimentation that had characterized the counterculture had a marginal place in this new world. Any attempt to promote a "back-to-the-land" philosophy was now seen as embarrassingly anachronistic. Brand and his colleagues networked with a new emerging group of thinkers, including hackers, science fiction novelists, and reporters. The WELL was their meeting ground, and at that meeting ground Whole Earth ideology engaged in yet another fusionist project, this time with the promoters of the new digital economy (Fred Turner 2002, 191–192). Prior to the creation of the WELL, one of the most important contacts Brand had made was with Kevin Kelly, a born-again Christian. Kelly's abiding love for cybernetics came through his interactions with his father, who had been employed in systems analysis (Fred Turner 2002, 196–197). Kelly would play a pivotal role in fusing New Right, Christian Right, and cyber-libertarian ideology into a comprehensive ideological package in the mid-1990s.

Halfway through 1984, Brand and his associates at the *Whole Earth Catalog* made overtures to the hacker community. Through this outreach effort, the first Hackers' Conference was organized (Fred Turner 2002, 199). Brand's view of hackers had been heavily influenced by Steven Levy (Fred Turner 2002, 203–204), who contended that hackers were united by several overarching values, including easy access to computing, the need for information to be free, the promotion of decentralization, a mistrust of authority, a belief in meritocratic valuations of hacking ability (irresponsive of race, gender, age, etc.), and a fundamental core belief that computers could allow individuals to self-actualize (Fred Turner 2002, 202; Levy 1984, 27–33). The hacking ethic and the philosophy of the *Whole Earth Catalog* fitted together seamlessly. Both espoused a belief in the power of tools to fundamentally improve the world. Moreover, both philosophies arose from a "systems"-based worldview. Fundamentally, both hackers and *Catalog* writers valued the importance of decentralized organizing (Fred Turner 2002, 203). The Christian Right's embrace of systemic decentralized organizing in the 1990s made the movement a natural potential ally for the WELL's organizers and its allies, who by that time included *Wired* magazine (on *Wired*'s connection to Brand, see Fred Turner 2002, Chapter 5). Moreover, much of the Christian Right, particularly Christian Reconstructionists, had promoted a belief in localized, decentralized organizing for as long as the counterculture had; the fusion of these ideologies is hardly odd, but instead an almost inevitable outworking of both movement's core socioeconomic and ideological principles.

The conference served a number of functions for Kelly and Brand. First, as an act of "cultural scouting," the Hackers conference was peerless. Brand and Kelly engaged in peer-to-peer networking with an emergent group of intellectuals that they foresaw would shape the coming generation of hi-tech thinking (Fred Turner 2002, 285). Furthermore, the conference clarified some of the overarching issues that the computer industry was dealing with at the time. Perhaps the foremost of these was the new approaches to business that the computer industry was forcing onto the global economy. Brand realized that the industry faced a dilemma as to how to structure itself. On one hand, business insiders wanted information dissemination to be expensive, so that they could get the most value out of their products. On the other hand, the cost of information distribution was sinking dramatically, which offered the industry tempting new markets if it could overcome the profits loss associated with making information less expensive to acquire (Fred Turner 2002, 206). The conference did not come to any consensus on the right approach to hacking, but as publicity, it served to soften the image of hackers in the public imagination. From the perspective of those committed to the *Whole Earth* vision, the conference gave them valuable insights and social links with the computing world that they were able to exploit. Moreover, through careful public promotion, Brand recast the ideals of the hacker community as a furthering of the countercultural vision that the *Whole Earth Catalog* had embodied (Fred Turner 2002, 208–210). In the ensuing coverage of the conference, Brand became symbolic of the hacking community, and by extension, of an emerging hi-tech industry (Fred Turner 2002, 211).

After the formation of the WELL, the platform served as an organizational nexus around which disparate communities organized and communicated through cyberspace. The WELL, like the *Whole Earth Catalog*, was at the same time an act of commercial exercise and community-formation, all ruled over through cybernetically oriented governance (Fred Turner 2002, 213). Organizationally, WELL ran on some of the same principles of "rough consensus and running code" that dominated early Internet enterprises. The organization embraced a Whole Earth ethos associated with "tools, not rules" that encouraged the working out of relational difficulties via the application of the WELL's PicoSpan Unix–based software (Fred Turner 2002, 216). Moreover, the WELL's embrace of Whole Earth thinking meant that it also inherited the principles of second-generation cybernetics that the Whole Earth "network" had embraced in the mid–1970s. Within second generation cybernetics, the observer must always realize that he or she is a component of whatever system is under observation. This has huge implications for managerial philosophy. A manager appropriating the principles of second order cybernetics sets the initial "boundary conditions for the 'system'" and then simply observes what happens once the experiment is conducted. Given the *Whole Earth* understanding of ecology and its relationship to cybernetics, this meant trying to create a balanced social order by first setting the initial conditions of a relational ecosystem and then ensuring that, within the limits of that ecosystem, there was free room for intellectual interaction (Fred Turner 2002, 218–219). In short, as Alexander Galloway has pointed out, it is protocol that controls this form of organizational ideology—it is diffused through distributed networks rather than centralized and thus is a power that is very hard to combat (see Galloway 2001, iv, 1, on the use of protocol as an organizational principle for distributed networks).

By the beginning of the 1990s, the WELL was a central organizational platform through which Whole Earth ideology then infiltrated the public's consciousness and became the default language by which people addressed the nature of networked computing (Fred Turner 2002, 233). Those who participated in the WELL experience became major voices in redefining the new network era. John Perry Barlow, for instance, would pioneer the idea of viewing networking of computer systems on a large scale as an "electronic frontier" (Fred Turner 2002, 234). In the process, the reality of the Internet and its representation ceased to have much correspondence. This allowed for a good deal of "creative destruction" of old organizations, organizational principles, and groups, many of which had been aligned with the left.[2]

Along with WELL, another crucial organization that Brand founded in the 1980s was the Global Business Network (GBN). GBN, despite some conspiratorial renderings of the organization, is most parsimoniously explained as simply "an elite corporate strategy firm" that engaged in strategic planning/scenario planning to aid larger organizations in managing future changes better. GBN's clientele has included Apple, DuPont, Shell, BP, GM, Citicorp, GE and numerous other firms. However, this is not what really makes GBN noteworthy. Rather, it is the impressive number of future-oriented experts and thinkers that are associated with GBN that truly denoted the Network's potential. Among them are Esther Dyson, cyberpunk writers Bruce Sterling (1954–) and William Gibson (1948–), John Perry Barlow, Howard Rheingold (1947–), Kevin Kelly, and Francis Fukuyama (1952–), a secular conservative author who would prominently ally with the Christian Right on biotechnology issues (Garite 2013, 69 "Green Futures").[3] Through these contacts, GBN helped promote green approaches to capitalism that had long been prominent in the pages of the *Whole Earth Catalog* (Garite 2013, 60).

But however influential GBN has been, its influence pales when compared against another offshoot of Whole Earth thinking: *Wired* magazine (Garite 2013, 62). *Wired* Magazine's cultural influence is easily discernable, as are the reasons for it. As Matt Garite points out, *Wired* articulated a variant on Fukuyama's "end of history" paradigm, in which Western capitalism had transcended its past and was creating a new "globalized, postindustrial economy" (Garite 2013, 72).

Wired Magazine played a particularly important role in legitimizing a new view of the United States' economic structure. In previous eras, technology had been used to legitimate interventionist agendas, including the application of centralized planning to numerous aspects of society, such as corporations and the economy. It had also furthered a vision of corporations that were based on hierarchies, but in which workers could reasonably expect permanent employment. This discourse, however, had long since served its purpose. Instead, the discourse surrounding technology that *Wired* magazine promoted and which succeeded in no small part thanks to the efforts of many evangelicals (Kevin Kelly, George Gilder, Leadership Network, and the Discovery Institute in particular) sought to legitimize a completely different form of organizing social relations. In this new order, the state had no place and must withdraw from market regulation. The economy was to be globalized, and businesses were to go through a rapid process of "dehierarchization and decentralization," characterized by production and labor flexibility (Fisher 2007, 2–3). Eran Fisher persuasively contends that the "digital discourse" that characterizes cyber-libertarianism serves a legitimizing function in the contemporary socioeconomic sphere. The heroes of the digital culture are our heroes, the terminology of the digerati our terminology. Some of this language has become such common parlance in popular culture that it has readily penetrated many other ideologies and discourses, some of which are only tangentially related to digital discourse (Fisher 2007, 36). *Wired* magazine, however, is notable for "crystallizing" this view in particularly explicit terms (Fisher 2007. 42).

Wired's legitimation of the new social order reinvented the corporate business world, members of the New Right, libertarians, and futurists as the next generation of cultural revolutionaries. Particularly under the leadership of founder and editor Louis Rosseto, the magazine promoted a "digital discourse" that characterized computers as hierarchy-destroyers, with the power to create new organizational forms based on computer networking. At the same time, Wired promoted the myth that "the peer-to peer communications of Internet users" was representative of the possibilities of markets, which were also based on "peer-to-peer" relationships. Furthermore, networks would facilitate the role of collective organizing and thus serve to delegitimize the power of governments to organize people's lives. This, ideally, would cut off the "monopoly on political power" that governments held. In place of outmoded forms of government organizing, the computer network would serve as the organizational model for a new form of governance in which the protocols for running the system would be set by governments, which would then get out of the way of the markets (Fred Turner 2002, 257). Markets, as Philip Mirowski states in Adam Curtis's documentary *The Trap*, were seen in this ideology as the best "information processors" and thus an ideal mechanism to replace traditional governmental governance, with all its attendant problems (Curtis 2007).

Wired magazine promoted its vision as the return of a reinvigorated counterculture ideology, one which idealized the "digital discourse" that Fisher describes (Fisher 2007, 2–3, Fred Turner 2002, 258). Just as the '60s counterculture had built communes, so too did the writers and readers of *Wired* build digital communes, virtual communities operating on the same organizational principles on which the communes had been modeled. In this vision, computer companies were the builders of a better tomorrow, as were libertarians and pro-tech politicians (Fred Turner 2002, 258). According to the logic of *Wired*, pro-tech conservative leaders, such as evangelical neoconservative George Gilder or Newt Gingrich were aiming for the same goal as the counterculture rebels of Silicon Valley, if occasionally using different aims to achieve it (Fred Turner 2002, 258–259).

While Louis Rossetto and Jane Metcalfe were the founding editors of *Wired*, the magazine was deeply shaped by Stewart Brand and the network(s) he spawned. Crucially, both for *Wired*'s own history and for the history of evangelicalism's relationship to network technology, one of their first hires was Kevin Kelly. Kelly, a central player in the GBN, WELL, and the crucially important Electronic Frontier Foundation (Fred Turner 2002, 260), would, with a number of other important individuals shape the public consciousness surrounding the net. While these individuals had vastly variant biographies, they were all shaped to varying degrees by a "complex set of allegiances to systems theory and the counterculture" (Fred Turner 2002, 261). *Wired* presented groups like The Media Lab, the Electronic Frontier Foundation, the WELL and GBN as representing a new type of world order and then legitimized that social order through cybernetic rhetoric borrowed from the Whole Earth movement. This reading of cyberspace was largely accepted by the public and contributed strongly to debates about computer networks and the "'new economy'" (Fred Turner 2002, 261). *Wired*, as the chief champion of "digital discourse" would frequently be seen as the main embodiment of the "'new' economy" and Kevin Kelly is typically seen as the main spokesperson for that economy (Fred Turner 2002, 4–5, 261; Best and Kellner 2000, 375–376).

Wired promoted a glossy vision of the future, one that was both overseen and sponsored by deans of the hi-tech industry. The magazine utilized the language and discourse of futurism, and promoted well known voices in the futurism "industry" such as John Naisbitt (1929–), Esther Dyson, Alvin and Hedi Toffler, and George Gilder, all of whom were quite friendly to industry. For the most part, the messaging on digital technology has stayed consistent, claiming that the changes the industry brings are both necessary and inevitable (Garite 2013, 68). Gone was the Whole Earth movement's concern with ecology. In its place was a cornucopianism on steroids. Reflecting a trend that runs through most veins of pro-capitalist systems theory, the magazine deeply opposed the idea of "limits and constraints," an anti–Malthusian ideology that Wired and its allies could take to absurd lengths (Garite 2013, 69). Faced with the limits the ecosystem places on all human beings, *Wired* just reimagined these limits as evolutionary pressure points that would force the human species to develop new tools or new ways of being human in order to advance; progress was the overriding gospel of the magazine. Interviewees and writers in *Wired* fantasized endlessly on every form of gimmicky near future or far future technological device, ranging from superhuman robots to cold fusion (Garite 2013, 70).

To understand the connections that have developed between cyber-libertarianism and the Christian Right, it is particularly important to study the works of Kevin Kelly. It is not totally clear whether Kelly's claims to be a born-again Christian should be taken at face value. What is clear is that regardless of whether Kelly actually is born again, he is perceived as such by evangelicals who know of his work; moreover, Kelly has served as a nexus point for cyber-libertarians and the religious right, irrespective of whether his faith claims are accepted at face value.[4]

Kelly's approach to economic and social organization are shaped fundamentally by his beliefs about complexity theory. Embracing the *Wired* ethos that he has done so much to shape, Kelly contends that we are moving to a "neo-biological civilization," in which power comes from below and is exercised diffusely. Control in this complexity outlook is exerted through distributed networks that are "highly pluralistic, open, and decentralized" (Best and Kellner 2000, 375). The theoretical backing for this ideology was first set out in Kelly's *Out of Control: The Rise of Neo-Biological Civilization* (1994), which served as a paean to the benefits of emerging technologies and the "new economy" that has birthed them. Kelly's work, much like that of the LN, reflected a shift in understanding organizational ideology that characterized many academic fields in the 1990s, in which virtually every aspect of human existence was characterized as "'complex" or "self-organising" (Best and Kellner 2000, 376). Whatever the value of these theoretical insights, they also served as powerful means of social control, precisely because they served as tools to "mystify" these systems of control (Best and Kellner 2000, 376).

Kelly predicated *Out of Control* on core ideological assumptions of the Whole Earth movement. Foremost of these was an assumption—one he shared with Stewart Brand[5]—that the modern world was characterized by an increasing convergence between the biological and the mechanical. As Kelly put it, this trend was reflected concretely in two ways: "Human-made things are behaving more lifelike, and.... Life is becoming more engineered" (Kelly 1994, 7–8). What this made evident to Kelly, much as it had to previous generations of cybernetic enthusiasts, was that the line between the organic and the mechanical was an illusory one (Kelly 1994, 7–8). Kelly therefore characterized both types of existence as "vivisystems" (Kelly 1994, 8). For Kelly, vivisystems were characterized by a "universal law," namely that "higher-level complexities cannot be inferred by lower-level existences" (Kelly 1994, 15). This meant that no ideology, mind, system of math, or computer could discern emergent patterns without first letting them run their course (Kelly 1994, 15).

In response to this law of vivisystems, Kelly advocates the need for "creative and flexible paradigms" that could respond to the needs of a world increasingly characterized by "complex, co-evolving systems" (Best and Kellner 2000, 377). As an advocate of Whole Earth ideology, Kelly steeped himself in "holistic systems theory and cybernetics" (Best and Kellner 2000, 377). However, he felt alienated from cybernetics' control tradition, which as we have seen in Chapter 3, sought movement towards equilibrium. Instead—in a move very consistent with both his Christian and cornucopian beliefs—Kelly contended for a "counter-cybernetics" that distanced itself from "systems steering and control" (Best and Kellner 2000, 377). He believed that systems that were left to steer their own course would create their own form of self-organization, independent of control (Best and Kellner 2000, 377–378).

Using then hot scientific research into memory, Kelly describes memories in oversimplified terms as operating like "emergent vents summed out of many discrete, unmemory-like fragments stored in the brain" which, like computers, are dependent on the properties of "distributed computing" to work effectively (Kelly 1994, 15–19).

Although such bio-technical speculations may not seem to have political implications, in reality they are highly politicized conceptualizations of the universe. Kelly uses technical discourse to legitimate a certain form of "network economics" that is reified as natural and therefore inevitable by its apparent grounding in complexity science (Best and Kellner 2000, 379). Vivisystems, in Kelly's reading, can organize in one of two ways. One way of doing so is by creating systems based on "sequential operations," a model that Kelly associates with the assembly lines of factories—a classic Taylorist image. This is a clock-like approach to organization which is characteristic of most mechanical systems (Kelly 1994, 21). In contrast, the "swarm model" of organization has radically different motivating principles. A swarm-like system operates in "a patchwork of parallel operations," which closely resembles the operations of neural networks or certain insect colonies. In this system, there is no chain of command, nor is there any neat system of "cause and effect." In a swarm system, it is not individual actions that matter but the "collective pattern" generated out of a multitudinous amount of such actions (Kelly 1994, 21). This leads to a system of causality that is highly non-linear and characterized by "high connectivity between the subunits" within the swarm (Kelly 1994, 21). Kelly contends that this form of swarm activity creates a high level of adaptivity, evolvability, system resilience (based on the fact that the parallel processing within the network creates built in redundancies), and innovation (what Kelly terms "novelty"). Moreover, in a swarm system, unlike in a linear system, continuous positive feedback loops do not lead automatically to the collapse of order, because the swarm builds new order on top of the positive feedback. As Kelly puts it, "spontaneous order helps create more order. Life begets more life, wealth creates more wealth, information breeds more information, all bursting the original cradle. And no bounds in sight" (Kelly 1994, 21–22).

All these characteristics of swarm systems obviously fit in ideally with the "new economy" concept that *Wired* promotes; moreover, its values are almost "line-for line" consistent with both the values of neo-liberalism and the "biblical economics" worldview that characterizes much of the Christian Right (see Fisher 2007, 66 and 89).[6] Kelly's vision of the new economy is interpreted, through the legitimizing lens of digital discourse, as a vision of a network economy. For Kelly, intelligence within a network can only reside in the network itself, not its constituent members. It is the "swarm" abilities created by the new network economy, and nothing else, that allows for society to now take "collective rational action" (Fisher 2007, 67). Paradoxically, this network rationality is created through the interconnections of various "simple, irrational nodes" in which the "dumb power" of these nodes allows for massive qualitative improvements once they are effectively digitally networked to other nodes (Fisher 2007, 67). Kelly centrally contends that human consciousness is itself the product of cooperation between "dumb neurons." Fundamentally, this means within a neural network, that no neuron is smart, but the network itself can be. Intelligence, therefore, can only reside in networks, not in constituent parts, because no individual part can understand the "complexity of the network's rationality" (Fisher 2007, 68). Kelly's motto in understanding this approach to network rationality (borrowed from the Doblin Group's Larry Keely) is "No one is as smart as everyone" (Kelly 1998, 14). Ideologically, this contention serves a very important purpose in legitimating free markets and is built on the same assumptions that drove Von Hayek, RCT, and the wider neo-liberal approach to markets. Since no individual, no node, can possibly understand the workings of the entire market system, any attempt by any agency or individual to understand or control markets is doomed to failure (Fisher 2007, 68).

This approach to networks and markets, legitimated in digital discourse as scientifically neutral, serves as a form of ideological bridge-building between cyber-libertarians and neoliberal discourse. In particular, cyber-libertarians and neoliberals are united by a shared concern over the proper interpretation of concepts of "spontaneous order and chaos" (Fisher 2007, 90). Spontaneous order is perhaps the most fundamental theoretical precept of neoliberalism. In the minds of neoliberal theorists, the order we see in society does not come from planning, but springs up spontaneously. The free market is perhaps the most representative institution that helps create such spontaneous order. The market has no "directing hand," but order is nevertheless created spontaneously through the interaction of the various dumb neurons in the market network (Fisher 2007, 90–91). Individual units within that market operate out of a "selfish and narrow rationale," each adhering to their own interests (Fisher 2007, 90–91). Yet the combined production of all this selfish action is the creation of an overarching order which is "socially rational and benevolent" (Fisher 2007, 91). Spontaneous order, in the vision of neoliberalism, can create far more efficient order than any planned system is capable of producing, because unlike humans, it is "universally rational and beneficial, a-political, and most significantly, it is a self-regulating mechanism" (Fisher 2007, 91). The corollary of this principle is a convenient ideological justification for corporate greed everywhere: By interfering in the market, regulators and planners are interfering in a natural, self-regulating benevolent order. Neoliberalism therefore suggests that if the benevolent order they envision is to be brought about, it must be done through protecting markets from planning and centralization (Fisher 2007, 91). Moreover, the implications of managerialism and new public management suggest that neoliberalism, as an ideological project, seeks to marketize all aspects of human existence, so that interactions between individuals in schools, hospitals, *and churches* is predicated on the assumption that all human beings are ultimately selfish agents only out for themselves.

As Eran Fisher notes, the parallels here between neoliberalism and the digital discourse associated with *Wired* and cyber-libertarianism are "uncanny" (Fisher 2007, 98). Moreover, *Wired*'s support of the market's rationality in some ways mirrors the philosophy of Hayek. Hayek's philosophical predilections were largely anti-rationalist. However, Hayek contended that "both social traditions and marketplace interactions" gave people the ability to act on a greater depth of information than they could ever possibly acquire on their own. Thus, the market and tradition allowed for rationality in a way that would not otherwise be possible for finite and epistemologically limited human beings (Fisher 2007, 92; on Hayek's view of market rationality, see Burgin 2012, 112). For *Wired*'s network concepts, and Hayek's market paradigm, rationality derives from the irrationality of constituent parts/nodes of a network or market. This rationality cannot be foreseen, planned, or directed. It can be recognized, after the fact, however, by "evaluating the pragmatic results of spontaneous formations" (Fisher 2007, 92). In the neoliberal vision that Hayek, and later *Wired*, supported, this led to a "spontaneous order" in which self-interested agents each sought for their optimal gain. Though the actions of individual agents might be irrational, the sum total of the free market would be rationality (Fisher 2007, 91). This concept of rationality, however, is no longer seen as a concept with historical boundaries and antecedents (largely derived from the Cold War and game theory), but is instead viewed by almost everyone as part of the economy's natural order (Curtis 2007). In the modern world, built as it is on the triumphs of science, to claim that a view is scientific or in some sense rational is to nearly automatically imbue such a concept with the weight of moral authority. Thus, uniting the digital discourse of spontaneous order with the neoliberal discourse of such order serves the ideological projects of both cyber-libertarians and the neoliberal movement (see Fisher 2007, 92).

As with spontaneous order, there are important similarities between neoliberal and cyber-libertarian visions of the chaos paradigm. Hayek's neoliberal vision of equilibrium differed markedly from the classical liberal vision of equilibrium. In classical liberalism, the invisible hand of the market created "harmony and homeostasis" (Fisher 2007, 98). By contrast, for Hayek markets were not inclined to create economic equilibrium, but "disharmony" (Fisher 2007, 98). The market's job, therefore, was not to create equilibrium

(Fisher 2007, 98). As we have seen, Kelly's approach to cybernetics was also fundamentally predicated on preferring disequilibrium states.[7]

As Fisher notes, the "digital discourse" that *Wired* and its cyber-libertarians promote is closely allied to Joseph Schumpeter's concept of creative destruction (Fisher 2007, 98). That Kelly supports the concept is unsurprising. The regimes of Ronald Reagan, Margaret Thatcher, and Bill Clinton were all predicated on "neo-Schumpeterian" discourses which sought to obliterate the concessions Keynesianism made to planned economies and replace the Keynesian model with a ruthless promotion of the market. And as Steve Best and Douglas Kellner note, Kevin Kelly and fellow evangelical George Gilder were two of the most prominent spokesmen for this ideology (see Best and Kellner 2000, 390). As we have seen in the Introduction and Chapter 4, the concept of creative destruction was predicated on the belief that capitalism is structured around states of disequilibrium, not equilibrium. Moreover, such disequilibrium is to be celebrated, not condemned, as it creates "new wants and products" while always helping destroy "older wants, commodities, and jobs" (Fisher 2007, 98). According to this line of reasoning, without creative destruction, the economy loses an important component of economic growth. Economic turbulence, therefore, is a sign that the markets are working, not the reverse. Thus, whether society is prosperous or not, the fundamental governmental response to markets should be the same: Benevolent non-interference, even if the social disruptions caused by market imbalance are severe (Fisher 2007, 99–100).

However, this view of the market has deep problems associated with it. First, it is questionable how much modern economies could successfully develop without some intervention from the state. The state is necessary, for instance, to support the military. Moreover, if the state did not provide social safety nets for those whose lives have been undermined by creative destruction, would this form of disequilibrium economics work so effectively? Furthermore, Kelly's worldview promotes the power of humanity's digital creations to such an extent that it ignores the destruction element of the creative destruction equation, thus running the risk of creating a truly "out of control" situation that disequilibrium systems have no more solution to than economies molded around the principle of maintaining equilibrium[8] (Best and Kellner 2000, 384). But the worldview of cyber-libertarians has no place for these concerns about creative destruction. Like other neo-liberals, they simply propose that the market must be protected from the "democratic political process," since the market will only run efficiently when it is free of the pesky regulatory procedures inherent in that democratic process (see Fisher 2007, 99–100). The human and social costs of skirting "the edge of chaos" are simply ignored in Kelly's rhetoric nor are the possibilities inherent in planning models seriously considered (Best and Kellner 2000, 391). Kelly's blind support of disequilibrium in "economic systems" allows him to underrate the value of social stability as a mechanism for promoting the maintenance of order (Best and Kellner 2000, 391).

Regardless, what Kelly offers up is a biological rationale for post–Cold War capitalism supported by appeals to natural law. The spontaneous order of nature provides the ideological justification for the superiority of capitalism over centralized Soviet planning. Capitalism is based on the logic of nature, while Soviet-style centralized planning is dependent on machine-style behaviors. To survive disequilibrium, therefore, both cultures and individuals must function with the same operating rationale as nature itself. As Garite notes, once this "universal logic is decrypted, it breaks down into a single, business-friendly message, abrupt enough to fit on a bumper sticker: DEREGULATE EVERYTHING [capitalization in the original]" (Garite 2013, 83). Garite contends the appeals to nature that Kelly makes are quite similar to those found in cyberpunk. William Gibson, for instance, draws heavily on the neo-Darwinian ideas embodied in the work of Richard Dawkins (1941–) and Edward O. Wilson (1929–), who extended neo-Darwinian evolutionary concepts to every form of "information system," including culture, that is predicated on "competitive or 'selective' methods of replication" (Garite 2013, 84). The now popularized concept of the meme—a favorite buzzword of *Wired* in the 1990s—was a direct outgrowth of this information-centered approach to evolutionary theory (Garite 2013, 84).

Under this extreme form of what I would term as biological informationalism that Kelly and his allies inherited from Richard Dawkins, life forms are simply gene carriers. In the process, life is given a "stingy reductive definition … as mere 'programmed matter'" (Garite 2013, 85). From a neoliberal perspective, this allows for much profitable obfuscation of the connections between culture and biology. Most notably, whether Dawkins or Wilson concede it or not, their philosophies are reflective of previous Social Darwinist thinkers, such as Herbert Spencer (1820–1903), whose work was utilized as ideological justification for "'selfish' forms of behavior'" (Garite 2013, 85). When this ethos is embodied in popular fiction, such as cyberpunk, it often serves as a cleverly constructed justification for the "New Economy" ideals that Wired and Kelly promoted. Since markets are part of nature, and the flesh is now digitized, the borders between capital and nature are collapsed. In this reading of the world, both capital and nature are "reducible to information" (Garite 2013, 86). Capitalism is thus rendered unassailable. By naturalizing the capitalist order, Kelly and his allies seek to depoliticize potential resistance to that order. Implicit in this form of informationalism is a deeply secular worldview that would seem to be utterly inconsistent with evangelical Christianity. But to understand why this is the case, we must turn to the strange life of George R. Price.

George R. Price: The Strange Story of How an Evangelical Helped Create Richard Dawkins

The theoretical rationale for this new extreme form of Social Darwinism was laid in large part by George R. Price (1922–1975), whose reaction to this neo-Darwinian paradigm highlights the problematic nature of evangelicalism's embrace of cyber-libertarianism in the starkest detail. For neo-Darwinians, the selfishness of the market embraced by game theorists, neoliberals, rational choice theorists and the Christian Right is not hard to explain. Natural selection serves to get rid of the weak, while benefiting the strong. Selfish behavior is therefore adaptive. Theoretically, altruism has always been something of a perplexity in the Darwinian paradigm. Darwin's solution to this dilemma was group selection, in which natural selection operated on groups, in addition to individuals. Darwin's descendants, however, are skeptical about the potential of group selection (Schwartz 2000, 1). As renowned evolutionary biologist Jerry Coyne notes, group selection has not found much support in contemporary evolutionary research for a number of reasons. Fundamentally, its explanation for trait selection is not efficient enough. Moreover, as Coyne notes, "group selection" is a relatively implausible force for explaining the existence of altruism or "pro sociality" (Coyne 2011). It is more likely, rather, that there was "direct selection" of those organisms who engaged in "reciprocal support" (Coyne 2011).

The most cogent explanation for the existence of altruism was offered up by William D. Hamilton (1936–2000) and is called "nepotistic altruism." According to Hamilton's theory, "all apparently altruistic behavior is directed exclusively toward genetic relatives. True selflessness ... almost never happened" (Schwartz 2000, 1). Two human beings stood out to Hamilton as interesting challenges to this assumption. One was Mother Theresa. The other was his colleague and friend, George R. Price (Schwartz 2000, 1). Price made three revolutionary contributions to evolutionary theory. First, he developed the Price Equation, which allowed biologists to engage in a "hierarchical analysis of natural selection" (Steven A. Frank 1995, 373). Hamilton later used this equation to develop his approach to kin selection and group selection; the equation has also been utilized to cast light on a whole host of other dilemmas that have beset evolutionary biology, ranging from "quantitative genetics to the abstract properties of natural selection" (Steven A. Frank 1995, 373). Price also revolutionized evolutionary theory by being the first individual to demonstrate that game theory could be productively applied to animal behavior. This would, in turn, influence Maynard Smith's classic work, *Evolution and the Theory of Games* (1982). Price also laid important groundwork to settling the correct significance and interpretation of R.A. Fisher's fundamental

5. The Christian Right's Technological Infrastructure 257

theorem of natural selection (Steven A. Frank 1995, 373; see also Harmon loc. 4130–4141, 6013).

Yet Price's contributions to evolutionary biology, though acknowledged, are often met with silence. To understand why this is the case, we must look to Price's incredibly strange life history, which intersects with evangelicalism's history in the most revealing of ways. By training a journalist and chemist, Price had worked on the Manhattan Project and also served as a medical researcher. Price's first marriage ended in divorce, at least in part because of contentions over religion with his devoutly religious wife Julia. In the mid-1950s, he published his first journalistic article, a highly critical look at the notion of ESP. In the late 1950s, Price exchanged a number of letters with influential Senator, later presidential candidate Herbert Humphry, in which Price advocated the use of game theory to solve diplomatic problems with the Soviets. Humphry was reputedly enthralled. Eventually Price went back to work for IBM, where he participated in the development of mainframe computers and helped mathematically model free markets (Schwartz 2000, 1).

Towards the end of 1967, Price ran across an article by W.D. Hamilton, "The Genetical Evolution of Social Behavior," now considered a classic text in evolutionary biology. The traditional Darwinian model of fitness did a good job of explaining evolutionary traits that clearly benefited an individual organism; what it had problems doing was offering up an explanation for behaviors that were prosocial but did not aid an individual organism's own chance for survival. Group selection was therefore seen as the most realistic model for dealing with this problem. Evolution acted on two levels by helping "better adapted individuals (who left more progeny), on the one hand, and better adapted groups, on the other" (Schwartz 2000, 1). Although selfish individuals as a rule might leave more offspring, groups composed largely of altruists would tend to have higher growth rates than those that did not. Hamilton felt this approach was wrong-headed. Natural selection, he contended, could explain altruism. Hamilton felt the previous definitions of fitness had been too narrow and therefore advocated an approach called "inclusive fitness" (Schwartz 2000, 2). In this approach, fitness involved not only an organism's own offspring, but also the "progeny of his relatives, fractionally weighed according to how closely they were related" (Schwartz 2000, 2). This viewpoint explicitly depended on a "gene's eye" model of organisms. In this line of evolutionary reasoning, what mattered for adaptation was not the survival of the organism, but the survival of specific genes. The gene carrier—the organism—was not as important as the individual genes. This view was later popularized by Richard Dawkins in *The Selfish Gene* (1976). Price wrote Hamilton for a copy of his article and over a number of months totally redrew the mathematics of natural selection that Hamilton had envisioned. The equation was so elegant and parsimonious that it could be applied to all forms of selection, whether it was selecting a television station or genetic selection (Schwartz 2000, 2).

At the crux of the evolutionary questions that Hamilton and Price asked was a deep philosophical quandary. If it could be demonstrated that altruism had an adaptive function, then it must serve a "utilitarian purpose." This could theoretically reduce altruism and the emotions associated with it to simple "natural metrics" which arose at the deepest level out of genetic self-interest. And if this was so, could altruism, or love, or compassion, be said to really exist? (Oren Harman 2010, loc. 130–134). Love, the last thriving religion, would be dethroned; and without that religion and the myths it perpetuated, social order might be destabilized. What the Price equation did that was so revolutionary was spell out in great detail the specific conditions which would allow group interests to trump individual interests (Schwartz 2000, 2). This effectively delineated both the lines and limits of the emotion we call love.

But then a strange thing happened. Even though Price had, as Adam Curtis notes in his documentary *All Watched Over by Machines of Loving Grace*, effectively mathematically demonstrated the manifest unlikeliness of a totally altruistic God, he converted to an evangelical form of Anglicanism (Schwartz 2000, 3). Price had begun to notice what he thought were amazing coincidences that had led him to develop The Price Theorem (Oren Harman 2010, loc. 3735). Price soon found himself engaged in spiritual conversations with John Stott, one of the most prominent and widely respected evangelicals in the world (Oren Harman 2010, loc. 3800–3807). At the same time, Price began a search for hidden codes in the Bible; he was convinced that human beings must determine specifically what God required of them, free of ecclesiastical "misinterpretation." Not surprisingly, Stott and Price soon butted heads (Oren Harman 2010, loc. 3809–3812).

The extremely paradoxical nature of Price's research became stronger and stronger over the remaining years of his life. In September 1970, Price wrote Billy Graham, pleading with Graham to find a way of helping end the Vietnam conflict by intervening with Richard Nixon (Oren Harman 2010, loc. 4216–4220). By the end of 1972, Price and John Maynard Smith together published "The Logic of Animal Conflict." While Smith actually wrote the paper, many of the fundamental insights behind the paper originated with Price, which is why Smith offered to credit Price as co-writer. In the late sixties, Price had realized that game theory could be profitably used to explain animal conflict. Price then experienced a conceptual breakthrough of staggering proportions; he noted that the most "genetically optimal behavior for an animal could depend on the behavior of other animals. In a population made up of animals genetically programmed to make war, for example, an animal programmed to retreat from a threat might actually be an advantage." The paper played a key role in legitimizing evolutionary game theory (Schwartz 2000, 4). Borrowing a page straight from John von Neumann (1903–1957), the founder of game theory, Maynard Smith and Price, argued that whether talking about "poker, nuclear proliferation, or for that matter—Vietnam—animal conflict could be modeled as a game; the trick was to see that the strategy of each 'player' depended on the other" (Oren Harman 2010, loc. 4361–4371). What Price had done, along with other game theorists, was provide devastating support for one of Darwin's fundamental insights: Morality was a byproduct of nature (Oren Harman 2010, loc. 4510–4511). Game theory could therefore not only be used to explain conflicts like Vietnam; theoretically, it could even be applied to modeling why Billy Graham picked the particular pro-Nixon conflict strategy he had used during the Vietnam War.

Yet, at the very time "The Logic of Animal Conflict" was being published, Price was moving further and further into evangelical Christianity (Schwartz 2000, 4). Price had become strongly attracted to the works of C.S. Lewis (Oren Harman 2010, loc. 3840–3857). While working on clarifying the mathematics of "Fisher's Fundamental Theorem" and thus making his third major contribution to evolutionary theory, Price simultaneously exchanged correspondences with Henry Morris (1918–2006), the founder of the Creation Research Center (CRC), the dean of the creation science movement (Oren Harman loc. 2010, 4089; Numbers passim). Price initially praised Morris's work, but their relationship degenerated *after Price critiqued Morris for being insufficiently rigorous in his Christian belief* (Oren Harman 2010, loc. 4080–4112). At the same time that Price was "penetrating the thought of the twentieth century's greatest evolutionary sage," he was also engaged in intense philosophical debates with Morris over the exact extent of the flood. Was it global or merely local? Nor did Price necessarily see these two research agendas as being in conflict. He believed the skill set he brought to bear on cracking Fisher could be productively applied to biblical hermeneutics, thus solving age old theological questions (Oren Harman 2010, loc. 4113–4119).

Price's life shifted radically towards the end of 1972. He experienced a deep religious crisis where he felt he had not truly understood the message of Christ. Rather than promote biblical study, he felt that he needed to engage in the "care and love of people." He started to invest his energies into helping the destitute. He worked at old age homes and started giving away all his wealth to homeless alcoholics, even encouraging them to stay with him in his flat. He apologized to his daughter Annamarie for his fatherly failings. Midway through 1973, Price abandoned his flat and began drifting around as an itinerant. He gave away the last of his possessions to the poor (Schwartz 2000, 5). Yet, as time went on, Price became increasingly despairing about his work with this itinerant population. Price was increasingly unsure whether true altruism was possible (Oren Harman 2010, loc. 5059–5064).

In 1975, Price committed suicide. Shortly before his death, he wrote his daughter and told her that he was being pursued by the "Hound of Heaven" referring to a popular poem by English poet Francis Thompson (Oren Harman 2010, loc. 5608–5622). As Adam Curtis notes, "The Hound of Heaven" is a profound assertion of man's powerlessness—his lack of free choice—against the forces of a totally loving God. Yet, ultimately, do we know what was in Price's mind before he died? Was the hound still God, or was it the informationalist, totally rationalized vision of nature that he had done so much to help promote?[9] Yet, as implausible as Price's life story is, its implications for the history of the evangelical movement are even wilder than Price's colorful biography. Price, disturbed by the implications of his evolutionary mathematics, had embraced evangelical Christianity as an escape from informationalism. But thirty years later, the evangelical movement would embrace the "new economy" and informationalism and would directly use both philosophies to build the vanguard institution of the intelligent design movement: The Discovery Institute. Moreover, Price had in all likelihood embraced evangelical faith to avoid the Social Darwinist implications of the Price Theorem and the evolutionary applications of game theory to animal behavior; by contrast, both the Discovery Institute and Kevin Kelly embraced a thinly veiled form of Social Darwinism to support their pro-capitalist vision of evangelical belief. But to understand how these seemingly impossible beliefs coalesced into a coherent intellectual whole, we must again look at the life of Kevin Kelly, and in particular explore Kelly's relationship with George Gilder, co-founder of the Discovery Institute.

The God of the Wired: Kevin Kelly, George Gilder, Cyber-Libertarians and the Discovery Institute

News coverage of *Wired* depicts Louis Rosetto and Jane Metcalfe as the magazine's dominant voices. This is not incorrect, but throughout their time at the magazine, both Rosetto and Metcalfe relied heavily on a number of individuals and institutions that Stewart Brand had networked, Kelly being perhaps the most notable example (Fred Turner 2002, 260). Nicholas Negroponte (1943–), for instance, had given much of the seed money for *Wired*. Many of the writers for stories, as well as the individuals quoted within them, were part of Brand's huge social network. These included Mitch Kapor, John Perry Barlow, Peter Schwartz, and Brand himself (Fred Turner 2002, 260–261). While there were variations of thought among these individuals, they were still heavily socially networked and united, as mentioned previously through a "complex set of allegiances to systems theory and the counterculture" (Fred Turner 2002, 261). Whole Earth models of organization therefore

5. The Christian Right's Technological Infrastructure 261

were heavily promoted in the pages of *Wired* (Fred Turner 2002, 299). This served several purposes that brought the movement into alignment with the New Right. For one, the call to "deregulate everything" led to the promotion of calls for telecommunications deregulation and limited government. Thus, *Wired* did not simply serve as a prototype for the Whole Earth movement, but it also promoted a vision of governance that was in line with much of the New Right's motivating agenda. Thus, it is hardly surprising that the magazine played host to a number of New Right ideologues and politicians (Fred Turner 2002, 298–299).

The web of links between Esther Dyson, George Gilder, and then-House Speaker Newt Gingrich demonstrates the alliance between the New Right and cyber-libertarians most clearly. Each one of these figures provided a legitimating discourse for the activities of the others. Gilder and Dyson alternately served as sources for *Wired*, the topics of coverage, and even, in the case of Dyson, an interviewer. At the same time this "mutual legitimation" took place, these three figures were engaged in a number of other mutual endeavors. One of the most significant of these occurred in August 1994, when Gilder and Dyson met at a conference held under the auspices of the Progress and Freedom Foundation; this foundation had strong ties to Newt Gingrich. At the conference, Gilder and Dyson came together with famous futurist Alvin Toffler (1928–2016) and George Keyworth, who had served as a science advisor to Ronald Reagan. Together they came together to support one of the most influential deregulatory documents of the 1990s, "Cyberspace and the American Dream: A Magna Carta for the Knowledge Age" (Fred Turner 2002, 299–300).

Following a longstanding editorial practice of the Whole Earth movement, *Wired* would simultaneously help lay the groundwork for such meetings and then engage in celebrations of them. Therefore, as Silicon Valley's movers and shakers, the Whole Earth network, and the New Right started to network with each other, individuals from all these groups appeared in *Wired* magazine. As Turner points out, this served as a form of legitimization for each of these movements and their members. Moreover, the cultural capital that leaders in one movement held could be used or leant to allies in another part of this alliance, when it proved necessary (Fred Turner 2002, 302).

By the early 1990s, Gilder's and Kelly's lives had started to intersect. Both men had been keynote speakers at the yearly Bionomics conference in San Francisco. These conferences were the brainchild of Michael Rothschild, author of the book *Bionomics: The Inevitability of Capitalism* (1990). According to the theory of bionomics, the biological world could be modeled onto market systems and the same process could also be undertaken in reverse (Fred Turner 2002, 302). For Kelly, bionomics was a natural fit, as the cybernetics-infused thinking of the Whole Earth movement fully agreed with Rothschild's contention that "natural and social systems could model one another" (Fred Turner 2002, 302). But Gilder, too, was intrigued by the vision of bionomics. In an interview with Kevin Kelly, Gilder notes that the Internet represented a working out of the "metaphor for spontaneous order" (Gilder 1993). Turner notes that Gilder borrows specifically from bionomic views of ecology to construct a vision of how the libertarian concept of the free market operates (Fred Turner 2002, 303).

Gilder claimed to believe that the bionomics model offered a revolutionary new approach to capitalism, one that "revitalized the economics of freedom and prosperity" (Gilder 1990, F1). In the spirit of Ronald Reagan, Rothschild had teared "down the wall separating economics from the rapidly advancing biological sciences" (Gilder 1990, F1). What attracted Gilder to Rothschild was his (correct) belief that if bionomics was correct, capitalism was "not merely desirable, or efficient, or productive; it is as essential to life as sex" (Gilder 1990, F1). Gilder condemns equilibrium economic models. To Gilder, bionomics demonstrates that "all economic and biological growth and change are the non-linear impulses of disequilibrium" (Gilder 1990, F1), a rather broad claim to make, depending on the definition of equilibrium to which he subscribes. Taking on a Social Darwinian tone, Gilder suggests that for "both biology and bionomics" the cruel reality is that "competition weeds out the weak and ill and reduces parasitism" (Gilder 1990. F1).[10] The sum total of Gilder's fawning review of Rothschild's work amounts to little more than a thinly veiled glorification of Schumpeterian creative destruction through praise of disequilibrium states (Gilder 1990, F1)[11]; following Rothschild's reading, Gilder sees governments as parasites that follow a "tapeworm dynamic of bureaucratic growth" that allows them to spread "in the bowels of capitalism ... until, as in the Soviet Union, it threatens to kill its host" (Gilder 1990, F1). The only conclusion to be drawn from Gilder's crass writing is that he views government as a form of chronic organizational constipation, that must be excreted from the body of capitalism if the economy is to remain healthy.

Building on this stimulating idea, both Rothschild and Gilder were suspicious of Newtonian worldviews because they saw such views as preventing innovation and encouraging the support of planned economies and what Rothschild characterized as "managerial intervention" (Bryant 2006, 259; Gilder 1990, F1). Gilder therefore preferred "non-linear chaos theory" because its model of the world was more consistent with "the spontaneous order of markets and ecologies" (Gilder 1990, F1). Rothschild (who helped shape Gilder's view on the importance of chaos theory. See Gilder 1990, F1), similarly, criticized economics for historically distancing itself from biology (Rothschild 1990, 44). As Paulina Borsook notes, however, this point was not actually true. Evolutionary thinking had been vitally important to the research of Robert Solow, and the entire field of evolutionary economics had been around "for a very long time" (Borsook 2000, 31).

In any case, once one cuts through the excess verbiage and capitalist backslapping of Rothschild's work, bionomics represents little more than an excuse to glorify unrestricted global capitalism (Bryant 2006, 262). Rothschild emphasizes that capitalism, like evolution, "*was not planned*" (Rothschild 1990, xi, my emphasis). It is created spontaneously because it is a force of nature, and thus is best understood as "a living ecosystem" (Rothschild 1990, xi). According to this ecological logic, government's only role in the economy is to protect the capitalist system from "interference" (Bryant 2006, 259–260). Government therefore simply grows the economy, cultivating it like a gardener (Bryant 2006, 260). Borsook notes that the essential ecological message of Bionomics is to not mess with the capitalist rain forest; a similar message also characterizes Kelly's work. Borsook lambasts this point: "Never mind that people have been messing with ecology (acting like big bad government) since forever: controlled burning to increase forest health or, oh, even doing things like farming" (Borsook 2000, 32–33). In short, even many basic human activities involved interference in our ecology in a manner that could be directly characterized as planning.

But at least Rothschild's support of an unplanned capitalism is internally consistent. Gilder's support for this position leads to almost comically absurd contradictory positions. Gilder was the co-founder of The Discovery Institute, the leading think tank for Intelligent Design (Flank 2007, 150). Founded in 1990, the Institute supported numerous conservative political projects, including "Free-market economics … opposition to the animal-rights movement, and opposition to human stem cell research and human cloning" (Flank 2007, 150). To really understand the ideological influences that shaped the Discovery Institute, we must look to the organization that parented it: The Hudson Institute.

Discovery was a spinoff of the Hudson Institute, which likely played more than a slight role in the organization's unusually futurist orientation (Herb Robinson 1991, A10). The Hudson Institute had been founded by Cold War futurist Herman Kahn, a former employee of the RAND Corporation (Sardar 2013, 32). Kahn is rightly considered one of the most controversial of the futurists, which is something of an accomplishment in a field characterized by larger than life personalities. Kahn had risen to prominence with his *On Thermonuclear War* (1960), a brutally pragmatic book about how a nuclear war could be won. According to Kaya Tolon, an early scholarly chronicler of the futurist movement, Kahn's "discussion of how megadeaths might affect military strategy and how they might impact humanity were unapologetic" (Tolon 2011, 63). It was Kahn who provided one of the major inspirations for the character of Dr. Strangelove in the Kubrick film of the same name (Menand 2005). Kahn was bullish about the future, and his projections typically were strongly optimistic, with an implicit belief that, given the means, technology could find solutions to most human problems. A corresponding belief of the Hudson Institute, which again is characteristic of both Gilder specifically and The Discovery Institute generally, is robust economic growth (Sardar 2013, 32).

Kahn's work took an increasingly conservative turn as time went on (Menand 2005). During the 1970s, Kahn, according to New Yorker writer Louis Menand, "became a dealer in the futurology business" (Menand 2005). The Hudson Institute, at Kahn's instigation, attacked advocates of the limits-to-growth approach to future projections. He projected that humanity probably would build colonies in outer space and began waxing eloquent about Ronald Reagan in the 1980s (Menand 2005). The cornucopian, pro-growth, pro-free market, and futurist orientations that characterized the Hudson Institute would in turn also characterize The Discovery Institute.

Discovery's split with Hudson was an amicable one; the members of Hudson's Seattle branch, as well as their economic backers, simply wanted more control over "programs and staffing" (Herb Robinson 1991, A10). The entire local Hudson staff, as well some new associates, agreed to sign up with the Institute. Bruce Chapman, the co-founder of Discovery (Flank 2007 150), had also had important roles in the conservative intellectual sphere. He had previously directed the U.S. Census Bureau and worked as a White House aide (Robinson 1991, A10). Other Hudson Institute holdovers included Mark Helprin, who had worked as a contributing editor at the Wall Street Journal and Glenn Pascall, a would-be financial guru. Discovery originally hoped to use a variety of venues—conferences, seminars, books, and articles—to promulgate their vision for public policy and innovation (Robinson 1991, A10).

Although the Discovery Institute was initially described as a who's-who of liberal Republicans (see Robinson 1991, A10), the organization's ideology was fundamentally right-wing in the 1990s. George Gilder, for instance, contended that the image of capitalist entrepreneurs as "fat cats" was simply wrong. Entrepreneurs were actually responsible spenders committed to virtues of "discipline and self control, hard work and austerity that exceed that of any Washington think tank, school of social work or congregation of bishops" (Gilder 1992, A17). Gilder contended that greed was not a capitalist vice, but a socialist one, as it was predicated on gaining "unearned pay" from the exercise of "government action"; this was what made "wealth creation" anathema to those who advocated government planning (Gilder 1992, A17). Thus, Gilder presented the deregulatory, anti-taxation policies of the New

5. The Christian Right's Technological Infrastructure 265

Right as being a solution for the problems of the poor, not an obstacle to the economically disadvantaged (Gilder 1992, A17).

In the mid–1990s, Discovery Institute began to take on the issue for which it is now most known: intelligent design (ID). Along with ID advocate Stephen C. Meyer, Bruce Chapman met with liaisons of Howard and Roberta Ahmanson in the summer of 1995, a prominent Christian Right couple who have funded many Christian Right organizations (Wilgoren 2005). This led to the Institute receiving $750,000 in funding from the Ahmansons to start a Center for Science and Culture. With this start-up investment, the path was set for the Institute to make its mark on American education and science debates. The organization's organizational strategy, highlighted in the famous Wedge Document, drew an elaborate plan for infiltrating the public consciousness with ID. The first phase consisted of establishing a body of research and publications supportive of the movement (Flank 2007, 158). In the second stage, the Institute sought to mold public opinion. Finally, in the third stage, the movement engaged in "cultural confrontation and renewal," utilizing both the courts and the public-school system to achieve this objective. As the Institute itself admitted, its elaborate social networks created powerful opportunities for the ID movement to shape public opinion (Flank 2007, 159).

But the Institute's activities in the 1990s were hardly confined to ID, despite frequent public misperceptions on this score. Discovery also sought to network with economic trendsetters in Seattle. This involved a bullish promotion of the need for Seattle to engage in strategic networking with trend-setting institutions and communities around the world. In the May 1993 conference "International Seattle," sponsored by the Discovery Institute, a number of public policy and business figures laid out the steps by which Seattle could take on this position. Washington's governor Mike Lowry, for instance, promoted closer trade ties with Russia, as did Pat O'Malley, the Port Commissioner of Tacoma. O'Malley further contended that these ties should be supplemented with "sister-port relationships" linking Seattle with Tianjin and Shanghai. Such new strategic networking involved fundamentally reshaping the state's relationship to urban areas. Neil Peirce, a columnist who spoke at the conference, contended that cities would increasingly take on roles "normally assigned to national governments" (Boyle 1993). At the same time, corporate leaders, such as Douglas Beighle of Boeing, condemned the regulatory powers of state governments, including Washington's, leading Lowry to promise he would institute a "regulatory efficiency reform group' to cut the red tape'" (Boyle 1993).

Gilder, while helping Discovery Institute gain its organizational footing, was also being promoted by *Wired* and its libertarian purveyors. Gilder was featured on *Wired*'s cover in 1996 (Bronson 1996). The magazine profile while not entirely laudatory, did promote a vision of Gilder as a tech guru par-excellence (Bronson 1996; Fred Turner 2002, 305–306). As Turner notes, given the editorial practices of the Whole Earth movement, there is a clear process of "legitimation" at work here, in which Gilder's vision of technology is normalized within the wider "'computational metaphor'" utilized by the Whole Systems movement (Fred Turner 2002, 306). *Wired* was also promoting Esther Dyson through an article by Paulina Borsook, who had not yet distanced herself from *Wired* and its cyber-libertarian politics. As with *Wired*'s coverage of Gilder, computational metaphors took on tremendous importance and helped legitimize Dyson as an important figure in Silicon Valley (Fred Turner 2002, 307; Borsook 1993).

Dyson eventually became closely aligned with the Whole Earth movement. Her association with GBN was long-lasting; she had become a member in 1988. Dyson also ended up serving as an important piece in the Electronic Frontier Foundation (EFF), while serving on its board of directors. The EFF had formed in 1990 under the aegis of John Perry Barlow and Mitchell Kapor (both of whom had originally networked through Stewart Brand's WELL bulletin board. See Fred Turner 2002, 34). Because of the EFF, Dyson had maintained a network of contacts that included Brand, Barlow, Kevin Kelly, and others. In 1995, Dyson took over the role of board chairperson for the EFF, while also associating herself with Brand's futurist-oriented Long Now Foundation (see below). Meanwhile, both Dyson and Gilder were worming their way into the heart of the Republican establishment (Fred Turner 2002, 34, 309). These connections were particularly fostered by the 1994 Atlanta Conference *Cyberspace and the American Dream*, which occurred under the aegis of the Progress and Freedom Foundation (PFF). Dyson's trip to the conference, which had been arranged by George Gilder, allowed her to meet with Alvin and Heid Toffler, as well as Newt Gingrich. Dyson found that she had underestimated Gingrich, whose intimate understanding of the Net was quite impressive. Moreover, she thought that Gingrich understood that the Net was not simply a means "to make current government structures more efficient, but … an agent of political change in its own right" (Fred Turner 2002, 309–310).

The Manifesto that Dyson, Gilder, and the Tofflers produced was shaped by these organizational affinities. Organizationally, much of the sponsorship of PFF during the time of Dyson's visit to the Atlanta conference was underwritten by a number of "telecommunications and cable firms, including AT &T, Bell South, Turner Broadcasting System, and Cox Cable Communications" (Fred Turner 2002, 309–310). PFF's ideological agenda has largely been shaped by "Toffleresque ideology" (Mosco and Foster 2001, 222). Alvin Toffler's theories concerning the "third wave" position the changes brought about by the "information revolution" as lead-

5. The Christian Right's Technological Infrastructure 267

ing to a need for a technologically reshaped politics. PFF espouses a belief that the liberating force of technology, when given to the people through ICTs, can help them liberate themselves from the power of heartless organizational bureaucracies, especially those created by politics (Mosco and Foster 2001, 222). In addition to standard cyber-libertarian efforts to combat government regulation, the organization sought to make crucial distinctions between old bureaucratic means of governance—characteristic of "'second wave" economies—and the new means of governance that digital discourse was envisioning. Thus, PFF, in Toffleresque fashion, sought to unite "information technology and capitalism" (Mosco and Foster 2001, 222). Mosco and Foster plausibly reason that PFF's vision of ICTs offers up the promise of a capitalism that claims it can "end all injustice and create a world where all are equally free to pursue life as entrepreneurs" (Mosco and Foster 2001, 222). A corollary of this belief is the assumption that government will no longer be necessary in this new form of Internet-based governance, and thus will eventually dissolve because of its own inadequacies (Mosco and Foster 2001, 222). Ideologically, therefore PFF's agenda seems little different from that of other proponents of the "new economy." PFF had underwritten a good deal of Gingrich's academic and talk show activity. What Dyson and her co-authors would do would be to create a libertarian-cum-cybernetic-cum-countercultural fusion of metaphors that would help legitimate libertarian and deregulatory policies, particularly for the telecommunications industry (Fred Turner 2002, 310).

To achieve the union of disparate ideological traditions ranging from cybernetics, the Whole Earth movement, to libertarianism, futurism, and the New Right, "Cyberspace and the American Dream a Magna Carta for the Knowledge Age" (henceforth "Cyberspace and the American Dream") drew on the language that had helped legitimate each tradition (Fred Turner 2002, 310–311). For instance, cyberspace was conceptualized by Dyson, Gilder and the Tofflers as an "ecosystem" or "bioelectronic environment," one which was "inhabited" by the organism known as "knowledge" (Dyson et al. 1994). Such concepts obviously have more than a tenuous connection to those promoted via the Bionomics Institute. The document also drew on the rhetoric of participatory involvement/democracy that has become a hallmark of digital discourse. In the American Constitutional framework, Dyson et al. assert, "power resides with the people" (Dyson et al. 1994). This rhetoric, as Turner notes, legitimizes governance of cyberspace by the people by simultaneously confusing the notions of cyberspace and marketplace (Dyson et al. 1994) (see Fred Turner 2002, 316–318). This conflation, as the documentarian Adam Curtis and much of the writing of Thomas Frank has suggested, has allowed the markets to be socially re-imagined and legitimated as a force of liberation, rather than control, with the Internet and the idea of the self-organizing system as the central metaphors for this new form of informationalist capitalism.[12] *Wired* specifically covered Gingrich in 1995, through a "convened" interview between Dyson and Gingrich (Fred Turner 2002, 314). As Turner points out (Fred Turner 2002, 314), Dyson does express considerable reservations about Gingrich (Dyson 1995). However, it is debatable how seriously such reservations should be taken. In any case, as Turner points out, by the time Gingrich and Dyson met, many of the areas of agreement between *Wired* editorial policy and New Right politics had been spelled out in *Wired* for a long time. The most central of these points—that businesses were now mechanisms for "social change, of the digital world as the new metaphor and tool" for the business world, and the importance of decentralization—had been promoted so effectively by *Wired*'s editors that they were not only the common parlance of *Wired* (see Fred Turner 2002, 315), but of much organizational literature of the period, including church growth movement literature.

Gilder and his allies at Discovery Institute continued to network with Silicon Valley throughout the 1990s. For instance, in 1995, Discovery Institute brought together John Perry Barlow and George Gilder to discuss the pros and cons of Internet deregulation (Paul Andrews 1995, B2). Both Barlow and Gilder indicated that regulatory answers to the Internet were counterproductive (Paul Andrews 1995, B2). Bruce Chapman, at the same time, advocated the Reaganite position towards the Net that had been espoused in "Cyberspace and the American Dream," in which the Net was people-directed (This position was epitomized in Reagan's phrase "let the people rule." See Curtis 2002), while noting—quite accurately—that there were some areas of the Net that would need at least modest regulation for the promotion of the public good (Chapman 1995, A13). Indeed, coping with regulatory efforts seems to have been one of Discovery Institute's chief contributions to the promoters of digital discourse. In 1996, an international task force, called the Internet Law Policy Forum was formed; its goal was to help solve central dilemmas that Internet providers were facing concerning "content and online commerce." A number of prominent companies were part of the group, most notably Microsoft, Netscape, AOL, AT &T, and MCI. Discovery Institute helped instigate the effort; the original idea, for it, however, came from lawyer Peter Harter, a Netscape employee who was spooked by government attempts at Net regulation (Flash 1996, A1). In January 1997, a Discovery Institute conference entitled "Toward 2000: The Next Four Years in Government Politics" attracted Bill Gates, Jr., father of Microsoft-founder Bill Gates and president of the Technology Alliance, Ed Meese, President Reagan's infamous attorney general, and Netscape Communication's Corp's general counsel, Roberta Katz. Discovery Institute speakers, meanwhile, spoke on issues of "technological policy and 'Social Security reform'" (P-I Staff 1997, B8).

5. The Christian Right's Technological Infrastructure 269

At the height of Gilder's and the Discovery Institute's influence over Silicon Valley, his influence over the high-tech world would have surprising consequences. In September 1998, Bill Joy (1954–), chief scientist and cofounder of Sun Microsystems attended one of Gilder's Telecosm Conferences held in northern California (Garreau 2005, 137, 142; Joy 2000). Joy was one of the two chief presenters at the conference; the other was Ray Kurzweil, one of the most futuristic techno-utopians that commands widespread respect in Silicon Valley (see Joy). At the conference, Joy listened to one of Kurzweil's most radical predictions: given the rate of computer development, computers would soon "supersede humans in the next step of evolution" (Garreau 2005, 142). Joy discussed the predictions with John Searle, a prominent philosopher attending the conference who is a well-known skeptic about the feasibility of A.I. Kurzweil walked in on the discussion, and a debate between Searle and Kurzweil ensued. Joy was rather skeptical of the benefits of Kurzweil's envisioned techno-utopia. As he memorably relates, at one point he found himself nodding in agreement with one of the critics of techno-utopianism that Kurzweil discussed, only to find out that this critic was Theodore Kacyzynski, the infamous Unabomber (Joy 2000; Garreau 2005, 142–144). Joy pointed out that the modern world was increasingly characterized by systems that were "complex, involving interaction and feedback between many parts" (Joy 2000). The potential for systems to act in fundamentally unpredictable ways was thus obviously greatly increased. Furthermore, Joy saw clear parallels between Kurzweil's ideas of the technological ascendancy of A.I. and those promoted by Hans Moravec, another technoutopian who commands respect in certain Silicon Valley circles (Joy 2000).[13] Joy feared that this storm of potentially negative technological forces could easily lead to a situation in which humanity faced not simply the contemporary threats of WMDS, but also what Joy characterized as "knowledge enabled mass destruction (KMD)"; the problem with KMD and the systems that employed it was that its power would be massively amplified due to its "power of self-replication" (Joy 2000). Joy envisioned a world in which nanotechnology could be used to selectively target certain "genetically distinct" racial groups (Joy 2000). He therefore proposes giving up certain particularly dangerous forms of GNR technology (Joy 2000). Given that Joy's essay is written for *Wired*, a magazine not exactly known for its commitment to the finer points of professional journalistic ethics,[14] it is difficult to know how seriously to take Joy's point here. But Joy's fears and the fact that he developed them at one of Gilder's conferences is important to the history of cyber-libertarianism's relationship to the Christian Right for three reasons. First, it simply highlights the breadth and depth of Gilder's influence; Joy's essay on the conference and its effects on him, "Why the Future Doesn't Need Us," have become legendary in the high-tech industry and are well known outside of Silicon Valley. Secondly,

Joy's fears pointed to an emerging form of techno-apocalypticism, often fatalistic in its orientation, that would increasingly characterize certain elements of the Christian Right. Finally, the fears that Joy expressed in his 2000 *Wired* article triggered a great deal of concern at the Discovery Institute, which led to the publication of a rather strange volume entitled *Are We Spiritual Machines? Ray Kurzweil vs. the Critics of Strong A.I.* (2002).

Are We Spiritual Machines? is, at one level, an attempt to legitimize Christian spirituality in the face of the possible development of Strong A.I. Such efforts are understandable, given the often-expressed cultural belief that the development of Strong A.I. would effectively delegitimize the theological beliefs of the Christian Right. As Gilder and Jay Richards note in their introduction to the volume, on one level, Kurzweil's utopian view of A.I. can be seen as a "substitute vision for those who have lost faith in the traditional objects of religious belief" (Gilder and Richards 2002, 11). This obviously would be of great concern to evangelicals, even if evangelicals were not inclined to dispute the potential development of Strong A.I. on theological grounds.

But the actual reasons for Discovery's engagement with Kurzweil are subtler than this. Despite what are apparent criticisms, Gilder and Richards are in many ways quite laudatory of Kurzweil, seeing his worldview, with its inherent hopefulness and cornucopian outlook, as closer to the Christian belief in the "transcendent" than "the handwringing of Bill Joy or the reductionist Darwinian materialism of the previous century" (Gilder and Richards 2002, et al. 11). Kurzweil presents two almost irresistible attractions for the Discovery Institute, both of which are related to the Institute's cornucopian outlook. Much of Gilder's techno-utopian rhetoric revolved around his cornucopian interpretations of Moore's Law. The fundamental assumption of Moore's law rested on the observation that "the power of information technology will double every 18 months, for as far as the eye can see" (Garreau 2005, 49). While this belief, in Gilder's vision, has a quasi-spiritual dimension, hard evidence does tend to back it up (Garreau 2005, 51). Gilder utilized the apparent certitude of chip development built into Moore's law to cast opponents of his positions as technological "luddites" who were hurting innovation. This was tied into his more general opposition to regulation, which might handicap the fulfillment of Moore's predictions about chip development (see Gilder "Life After Television" n.d. and Gilder "Angst and Awe" n.d. in particular). Gilder went further, however, promoting what he would eventually characterize as Gilder's Law. Gilder contended that the planet's "total supply of bandwidth will double roughly every four months—or more than four times faster than the rate of advance in computer horsepower" (Rivlin 2002). When this assumption proved to be erroneous, Gilder arrived at a slightly longer figure of six months (Rivlin 2002). While Gilder, according to *Wired*, likely got the time frame wrong, his point that "infinite bandwith" was going to

5. The Christian Right's Technological Infrastructure 271

have implications almost as revolutionary as those of the "microprocessor" were seen as foundational truths of the computer industry, truths that Gilder was given considerable credit for advancing (Rivlin 2002).

From the standpoint of the Discovery Institute and the intelligent design movement, Moore's Law had certain attractions. First, Moore's Law, in Gilder's estimation, demonstrated that intelligently designed systems worked "way faster than evolution" (Metcalfe 2007). The temptation to apply this kind of faster equals better approach to the development of life is clear in much I.D. literature, because it makes God a more efficient designer than evolution. As reporter Michael S. Malone points out, Gilder conceptualized the chip not simply as a "landmark invention but a transcendent vehicle for reordering human nature" (Michael S. Malone 2002, 171). Gilder, like much of the hi-tech industry, had "found redemption in Moore's law," a point Malone characterizes—correctly—as heretical, given Gilder's evangelical views (Michael S. Malone 2002, 171). Gilder served as the intellectual guru of a subset of Silicon Valley leaders who believed that Moore's Law was now the market's "Invisible Hand," one which helps global society reach a "Valhalla of cultural equilibrium, perpetual innovation, and general enlightenment and prosperity" (Michael S. Malone 2002, 171).[15] Thus, the microchip, for Gilder, helps legitimize the neoliberal political orientation of the Discovery Institute. Moreover, by promoting the economic cornucopianism that motivates Silicon Valley entrepreneurs, with its fundamental denial of the second law of thermodynamics Gilder neatly fuses the agenda of the hi-tech world with the promotion of a common argument of the creationist movement. Creationists contend that evolution asserts that "small, less complex organisms" inevitably lead to "larger more complex ones" (Flank 2007, 112). From their standpoint, this is a "violation of the Second Law of Thermodynamics, which, they claim specifies that no system can move from a state of simplicity to more complexity. Therefore, evolutionary progression of life, they conclude, could not have happened without some sort of 'intelligent intervention'" (Flank 2007, 112). Thus, the creation of ever greater amounts of complexity, from a creationist standpoint, serves as a direct refutation of physical law, in which systems cannot move from simplicity to complexity (Flank 2007, 112). The cornucopianism expressed by both Moore's law and Silicon Valley therefore finds a natural bedfellow with George Gilder and the Discovery Institute, since that cornucopianism also predicates itself, often explicitly and always implicitly, on a similar denial of the implications of the Second Law of Thermodynamics As Flank correctly points out, the creationist reading of the Second Law of Thermodynamics is based on a grossly simplistic misreading of the Second Law of Thermodynamics; the law only applies in "thermodynamically 'closed system[s],'" which is not the condition that life operates with on Earth (Flank 2007, 112–113). As Flank notes, the ID movement dropped the creationist fascination with thermodynamics, but oftentimes simply used new terminology to come to the same conclusions that the creationist movement had arrived at (Flank 2007, 112–113). Thus, whatever official position Discovery Institute takes at any given time to the issue of the second law of thermodynamics's relationship to evolution, the Institute is fundamentally motivated by an economic rejection of the second law that is fully consistent with everyone from Old Earth Creationists to Silicon Valley enthusiasts. The opponents of Discovery Institute—Flank, in large part excluded—have made the mistake of seeing the Institute's opposition to evolutionary theory as rooted primarily in biology and religious belief; however, a close inspection of the Institute's motivating impulses indicates that it is opposition to the potential economic implications of the Second Law of Thermodynamics, rooted in neoliberal rejections of the concept of "limits to growth," which most fundamentally shape the Institute's mission. Gilder, for instance, has vocally rejected the "view of a thermodynamic world economy, dominated by 'natural resources' being turned to entropy and waste by human extraction and use" (Discovery Institute Staff 2013). Thus, if the left is going to combat the scientific beliefs of the Christian Right, one important implication of this understanding of the Institute is to realize that it is the implications of the Second Law of Thermodynamics, as much as evolutionary theory, that currently shape policy debates between the scientific community and the Christian Right; moreover, these debates, whatever the language employed, are rooted as much in the economic beliefs of the Right as they are in its commitment to cultural conservatism.

This brings us back to the ironies of Gilder's career. Gilder, as we have seen saw governments as parasitic organisms that infected "the bowels of capitalism" till it risked the death of the "host" organism (Gilder 1990, F1). They were the central planners, the "managerial intervention" that Rothschild had warned against (see Bryant 2006, 259). Yet Gilder made his reputation promoting the existence of intelligent design, a system fundamentally predicated on the notion that there is some sort of central planner who set the Earth's ecosystem in motion; if one takes a conservative Christian position (as Gilder does), Gilder's view of planning becomes even more inconsistent, even sacrilegious. For, if central planners are to be opposed in the physical world, why not in the spiritual world? Does this make God into the ultimate expression of the "tapeworm dynamics of bureaucratic growth" (Gilder 1990, F1)? Will God have to be excreted from the "bowels of capitalism" because he threatens his current host body, capitalism? I do not pose these questions to offend, but rather to point out how easily Gilder's ideology could be shaped to fuel an anti-Christian, rather than pro-Christian, agenda. Neoliberalism has only one God, and that is not Christ incarnate.

It is the market.

Conclusion: God Is the Machine

Ever the technological proselytizer, Kevin Kelly would at the beginning of the 2000s promote the most radical fusion of digital and theological discourse. In his essay "God is the Machine," Kelly contended that the new "digital physics" suggested that the universe is "nothing but 1s and 0s. The physical world itself is digital" (Kelly 2002). This "new science of digitalism" in turn, saw the "the universe itself" as "the ultimate computer" (Kelly 2002). Kelly contended that this vision turned computation into a nearly "theological process," one in which all choice is reduced to "yes or no, the fundamental state of 1 or 0" (Kelly 2002). Kelly then offered up a vision of theology, fused with the ethos of transhumanist-sympathizing hubris, that proclaimed:

> After stripping away all externalities, all material embellishments, what remains is the purest state of existence: here/not here. Am/not am. In the Old Testament, when Moses asks the Creator, "Who are you?" the being says, in effect, "Am." One bit. One almighty bit. Yes. One. Exist. It is the simplest statement possible [Kelly 2002].

In this fusion of cyber-libertarian and evangelical ideology, metricspirituality received perhaps its most extreme expression. God no longer simply planned code. Fundamentally, God *was* code. The original vision of metricspirituality, as proclaimed by church growth advocates, was to put numbers at the service of God. Kelly's formulation reduced this to putting the numbers at the service of one ultimate number: Jehovah himself. In the process, while metricspirituality in the hands of Gilder and Kelly had elevated humanity to a position near God, it had reduced God to a machine.

6

The Evangelical Web

The Emergence of the Evangelical Web

Evangelical use of Internet communication can be traced to the use of BBS systems, which were one of the earlier forms of Internet communication, predating the web. Evangelicals made use of early computer communication systems, notably BBS (Gonzalez 2014, 109). This was a part of a wider Christian engagement with the Internet that originated in the 1980s. The UMC formed the Church Computer Users Network (CCUN) in the 1980s, an ecumenical outreach effort, which led to several spinoff BBS discussion groups (Heidi Campbell 2005, 62). The UMC was also responsible for the pioneering efforts in email newsletters (Heidi Campbell 2005, 62). Midway through the 1980s, a number of online computer networking groups existed, including Computer Applications for Ministry Network (CamNet), Religious Associates, which was a software discussion group, as well as PresbyNet (Heidi Campbell 2005, 61). Another major effort was Ecunet, which launched in 1986 as the first online ecumenical network (Heidi Campbell 2005, 62).

Two technologies proved particularly instrumental in the 1990s information revolution: the World Wide Web and CD-ROM. The former was especially significant in its ability to create connectivity among a diverse range of religious participants. CD-ROMS, meanwhile, enormously enhanced the data storage and distribution of archived material. This, in turn, allowed for the creation of vast religious databases with heretofore unheard-of amounts of easily accessible data (Gonzalez 2014, 109–110). These technologies created "spaces of contact" as well as potential information markets, for distributors and disseminators of evangelical informational material (see Gonzalez 2014, 109–110).

Religious groups quickly exploited the opportunities afforded them by the World Wide Web, with a number of communities forming in 1994, a year after the public launch of the Web. Most of these groups had engaged in previous forms of digitized networking through antecedents of the Web's communication systems (many of which involved TCP/IP network protocols) (Gonzalez 2014, 112). By 1996, religion had already gone "viral" on the Web (Gonzalez 2014, 114). An Internet Evangelism Coalition (IEC) crystallized in 1997, which networked 70 major ministries (Gonzalez 2014, 114–115). The Coalition sought to create collaborative efforts between various ministry partners, as well as facilitating "strategic thinking and resource development for internet evangelism" (Heidi Campbell 2010, 139–140). The IEC developed training workshops and "resource sharing sessions" to help facilitate this process (Heidi Campbell 2010, 140). Campus Crusade for Christ developed similar "e-vangelism" outreach efforts (Heidi Campbell 2010, 140). At the same time, due to concerns expressed about the social effects of Web technology, a market emerged for "content filtering services and software." Sites like "Integrity Online" and "Safeplace.net" were formed to cater to this consumer concern (Gonzalez 2014, 115), which also played a major role in debates surrounding Internet regulation (see Strub 2010, 273). By the late 1990s, Christian groups had created a number of outreach-oriented websites, such as crosswalk.com and gospel.com (Heidi Campbell 2010, 23).

In the 1990s, much of the growth in "hi tech" evangelicalism was spurred by the need to optimize efficiency on the mission field. Utilizing the "Internet, email and emerging technologies," evangelicals began to create a "global electronic blanket" that interconnected all their ministries (Richard Scheinn 1997, 1E). This new web of relationships allowed Christian leaders to interact via email, engage in relational networking, and collectively brainstorm new ideas. Radio broadcasters made use of the technology to optimize their distribution practices and avoid redundant broadcasts. Peter Holzmann has plausibly contended that the coordination of the AD 2000 and Beyond Movement would have been impossible without the Internet (Scheinn 1997, 1E). Perhaps the most grandiose and coordinated expression of this effort was the World Prayer Center (WPC), formed in 1998. According to Deborah Caldwell the WPC included a "situation room full of data and computers" and was designed to be "the nerve center of an emerging worldwide evangelical prayer movement" that utilized "phone, fax, and Internet" to engage in targeted prayer for people in 120 nations. The effort attempted to connect some 50 million Christians in these countries together (Caldwell 1998, 3E). Like much other activity led by the AD 2000 movement, the WPC was motivated by a desire to reach the 10/40 Window. Organizers of the WPC, specifically noted to Caldwell its geographical proximity to Cheyenne Mountain, where the North American Aerospace Defense Command (NORAD) is located. According to Caldwell, she was told by organizers that the WPC was to serve as a "spiritual NORAD" (Caldwell 1998 3E). Within this spiritual defense complex was a "'war room with restricted access'" for movement prayer warriors (Caldwell 1998, 3E). In the room, prayer warriors "read e-mail and faxes from missionaries requesting urgent prayer in countries that are hostile to Christianity" while simultaneously engaging in worldwide data distribution to other Christians (Caldwell 1998, 3E).

For the AD 2000 movement, the WPC Observatory, founded in 1998, was intended to play the role of "repository for research and intercession" (Holvast 2009, 151). The Observatory's purpose was to function as a global "'switchboard" for the spiritual mapping movement, complete with "conferences and seminars, an interactive website, a collection of Spiritual Mapping reports and a library" (Holvast 2009, 151). Originally run as a joint project by Ted Haggard and C. Peter Wagner's Global Harvest Ministries (GHM), Ted Haggard's New Life Church took over the WPC "by the end of 2002," and the Observatory was closed (Holvast 2009, 154). After Haggard took charge, the WPC shifted emphasis, and became a "more general prayer centre" (Holvast 2009, 154–155). An attempt to launch a new interactive website failed to win traction (Holvast 2009, 154–155).

Meanwhile, the demand for religious information online was robust; in the year 2000, alone, for instance, 35 million Americans conducted searches for religiously oriented information. Browser-accessible Bibles were ubiquitous by this point. Congregations were quick to realize the influence of the Internet in people's daily lives. Some 20,000 congregational websites had already formed by the dawn of the millennium, coupled with emerging new forms of "church management software" that promised to revolutionize the way churches did business (Gonzalez 2014, 118).

Sometime during the late 1990s, an increased demand for miniaturization of digital religious products occurred, a "presaging" of contemporary demands for smartphones. Vincent Gonzalez dates the birth of pocket computing among digital religion enthusiasts to the creation of the Olive Tree Bible for Palm organizers and the PocketBible, both birthed in 1998. *Mobile Ministry Magazine* was formed in 2004 to improve ministry and outreach efforts that made use of mobile digital technology (Gonzalez 2014, 122–123; "Mobile Ministry" n.d.).

Evangelical groups expressed concern about falling behind in the technological arms race. At a 2005 conference, Walter Wilson, a prominent evangelical tech guru, contended that evangelicals needed to master their approach to web searches in order to facilitate "search engine optimization" (Buseck 2015, 18). Wilson emphasized that the church must realize that technology in many fields was enjoying a rapid "convergence" and that they must be ahead of that curve. Wilson therefore advocated a technologically savvy approach to ministry and emphasized that the church must engage in increasingly byte-sized ministry to interested seekers (Buseck 2015, 18). George Barna noted that same year that the desire for ICT excellence was leading to a monetary increase in expenditures for ICT technologies (Buseck 2015, 22).

The need for ICT professionals led to the creation of specialized courses and degrees for church tech specialists (Buseck 2015, 22).

The evangelical ICT revolution penetrated almost every aspect of church life, particularly in megachurches. Churches now have technology that allows them to create massive management systems, optimizing their ability to engage in monitoring finances and minimizing their staffing needs (Cone 2005, 47). Willow Creek Communiy Church, for instance, had a tech budget exceeding a million dollars as of 2005. Its IT staff included 15 people to help manage 50 servers and 600 personal computers, as well as two full timers dedicated solely to its web-based ministry, and a massive number of volunteers to supplement this paid workforce (Cone 2005, 47). Another church seeking to optimize its ability to provide quality care to its congregants, Fellowship Church of Grapevine Texas, created its own management software. The church then created its own company, Fellowship Technologies, to meet other churches demands, accumulating $3 million in revenues per year (Cone 2005, 47).

Naturally, Church ICT professionals have expressed great interest in leveraging new ICT technologies, particularly social networking, for evangelism. RelevantMagazine.com managing editor Jess Carey, in an interview with Buseck, states "For people that are really comfortable sharing their faith in normal situations, you can literally see it by going into their Facebook or their MySpace. A lot of times people can post files about themselves, or have their quotes, or they can have worship songs playing. They can be very direct" (Buseck 2015, 116). Carey further notes that social networking can allow for greater effectiveness in organizing and message-promulgation, areas of digital technology that many social movements have wanted to explore (Buseck 2015, 116).

Congregations of all American religious movements embraced social media aggressively, though not always without issue. The emergence of social media technology, particularly Facebook, led to something of a drop-off in the creation of congregational websites. As early as 2010, 40 percent of churches were making use of Facebook, which as Thumma correctly notes, is a "staggering" rate of adoption. One problem that many congregations suffered was a lack of relevant information distribution on their Facebook pages. As Thumma notes, "Facebook is great for congregational insiders, but may well be less functional as a yellow-pages ad for those shopping for a new faith community home" (Thumma 2010, 3).

By 2010, religious congregations—especially evangelical congregations—were employing a bizarre myriad of technologies. Sermons could be spread via CD, DVD, or cassette tape. Streaming sermons were available. Churches utilized Google calendars, maps and docs, Analytics, YouTube, and texting to optimize their outreach efforts. E-newsletters were particularly common, and a number of churches had begun working with online giving (Thumma

2010, 3). And, as we shall see, the very infrastructure of churches was being changed by the need to incorporate new technologies, and more importantly, new technological workers, into church staffs and ministry teams.

Information Infrastructures of Evangelical Churches

Information management is a crucial mechanism of any church or ministry. Indeed, arguably, effective IT is even more relevant in Protestant houses of worship than in the for-profit world, since Christian organizations are ostensibly supposed to operate out of a "values bases" rather than profit-based, model. Churches, as we have seen, have very particular recruitment and training needs, a byproduct of the fact that they subsist as volunteer-supported organizations. This, while affording congregations unique outreach opportunities, also requires a unique skill set on the part of management (Heist 2011, 1–3).[1] As James Heist notes, this is particularly true of Christian organizations. IT helps to promote financial accountability, as well as "service excellence and cost efficiency," without which any Christian ministry's mission is likely to be badly crippled (Heist 2011, 1–3).

To create an effective IT infrastructure for a church or ministry, one of the first goals most congregations seek to reach is the formation of a strategy for technological use. Ideally, this strategy expresses the ministry's IT strategy while defining what knowledge workers the church can call on to achieve this objective in the desired time frame. There are quite important reasons for ministries to methodically strategize in this regard. Churches that avail themselves of IT services can find significant price discounts if they are able to network with non-profit-centered sellers. Obviously, the creation of an effective church website and tech team can help improve ministry support services. As Heist notes, one of the prime barriers non-profits face in the implementation of effective IT strategy is their reliance on non-skilled, semi-skilled, and sub-skilled volunteer staff. This places major burdens on staff and professionally skilled volunteers. Thus, acquiring professional-quality volunteer staffs remains an issue of critical importance for many churches, especially if they are to remain operationally competitive with rival congregations or forms of entertainment. Moreover, in addition to all these uses, IT is also useful in strategic planning, which despite criticisms to the contrary by the likes of Henry Mintzberg, is still utilized in many business organizations (Heist 2011, 49, 52).

Church multimedia and IT professionals and volunteers—as Michael D. Lee terms them, "creatives" (Michael D. Lee 2016, 5)—are obviously crucial elements to any ministry's long-term viability. IT professionals and other "creatives" typically network through online communities, as well as conferences dedicated to "church tech" concerns (Michael D. Lee 2016, 2). The move to network church tech professionals can be traced to the conferences of groups like the National Association of Broadcasters (NAB), as well as media magazines, many of which now cater to evangelical clientele. But prior to the Internet, networking of creatives involved mainly audio engineers, who could network through secular trade organizations like NAB (Michael D. Lee 2016, 56). Evangelicals have been quick to exploit the power of digital media to network church tech professionals and other creatives (Michael D. Lee 2016, 55–56). Social media allows creatives to relationally network and helps the church tech industry set normative benchmarks for industry excellence (Michael D. Lee 2016, 78). Furthermore, such networking creates a sense of community among church tech professionals which helps mitigate any sense of alienation they may feel from the wider church community (Michael D. Lee 2016, 83).

Church tech professionals face certain unique industry concerns. Creatives emphasize the importance of staying current with contemporary technology and tend to be "early adopters" (Michael D. Lee 2016, 77). In general, for instance, sound engineers often report to the worship team or the worship leader. Avoiding tension between these two groups is a key component to achieving a successful media ministry (Michael D. Lee 2016, 94–95). Hewitt, although he does not explicitly address this point in *Windows PCs in the Ministry* (2010), also seems to believe that a great deal of conflict in contemporary churches is caused by "control" issues surrounding the implementation of ICT technologies, which threaten to divide more tech-savvy younger believers from their elders (Hewitt 2010, 8). Many church tech professionals grumble about the non-creative community's lack of appreciation and understanding for their particular ministry concerns (Michael D. Lee 2016, 96).

Success, for church tech purveyors, has both spiritual and pragmatic dimensions. On the spiritual side, such purveyors view themselves as "ministers of sound," a role most take quite seriously. More pragmatically, however, church creatives, much like church management professionals, are concerned with numbers. These metrics involve both purely technical and consumer-oriented concerns (which are not necessarily divorced). For instance, a frequent measure of success for church creatives is attendance (Michael D. Lee 2016, 11–12). Because contemporary churches follow a business-model, satisfactory customer service and production excellence is a must. The desire to provide comfort and relevance, therefore, is still a motivating factor for church creatives (Michael D. Lee 2016, 12), even if such rhetoric may be officially downplayed by certain elements of the evangelical movement. This means that church creatives often do not merely reflect market trends, but set them, particularly in their skilled use of audio technologies (Michael D. Lee 2016, 16–17).

At the congregational level, much of the Christian Right's ICT infrastructure is provided through publications such as *Technologies for Worship Magazine* (TFWM). The magazine, which originated in the early publication *Religion*, formed in 1995. It aims directly at servicing congregations, particularly in the technological arena. *TFWM*, though starting as a small, family-oriented enterprise, serves as a valuable networking tool from which church tech writers can pool their skills. Much of the material in the magazine is educationally driven and is promoted in alliance with the manufacturers of worship technology (Laurie Baker 2015, 14). As an "advertising driven" media platform, *TWFM* aims to make advertisers aware of the opportunities it offers them in the emerging worship market. From 1993 onward, this has led the magazine to run two conferences, Inspiration East and West. *TFWM* was an innovator in this regard, and their attempt to connect marketers with consumers coincided with growing interest in the Christian Right about utilizing ICT technology to facilitate church growth (Baker 2015, 15). Christian Right activists viewed emerging ICT technologies as a means of "amplifying their message," thus allowing them to potentially target a far wider group of "potential congregants" (Baker 2015, 15). Due to constant technological innovations, such conferences are held more and more frequently and have led to the creation of a "niche" market for those interested in purchasing media ministry equipment (Baker 2015, 15). In addition, *TFWM* and its conferences have promoted enhanced training among media ministry specialists (Baker 2015, 15).

The technological infrastructure of most churches are dependent on volunteer workforces, which explains why the push for equipping or freeing the laity is so radically emphasized. This emphasis on volunteer work, coupled with grueling production demands, has led most churches to favor creating "established relationships," usually with brand name manufacturers or other groups that set industry benchmarks (Baker 2015, 114–115).

Not surprisingly, the evangelical movement has also extensively employed the Internet as a tool for so-called "digital evangelism." This evangelism involves utilizing the Internet to promulgate Christianity, typically via whatever means the evangelist finds most effective. The tools involved include podcasts and YouTube, Facebook, Google Plus, Twitter feeds, discussion boards, chat rooms, Instagram and Pinterest pages, as well as personal blogs (Stamper 2013, 4). Many digital evangelism ministries got their start in the period between 1997 and 2000, as church leaders and concerned Christians became aware of the evangelistic potential of the Internet. Mark Kellner's *God on the Internet* (1996) and Tony Whittaker's *Web Evangelism Guide* (1997) became influential texts in the digital evangelism explosion. Perhaps even more influential is the frequently quoted *E-vangelism: Sharing the Gospel in Cyberspace*, by Andrew Careaga (1999). Careaga, along with

6. The Evangelical Web 281

fellow Christian Net theorist Vernon Blackmore began to speculate on how they could contextualize the Christian message for the Web medium. In April 1999, the Billy Graham Institute sponsored the first Internet Evangelism Conference, noting evangelicalism's increasing prioritization of the Internet as a new evangelism tool (Stamper 2013, 51). Meanwhile, Campus Crusade for Christ developed an effective bridge strategy, since widely copied (Stamper 2014, 118), which involved creating websites whose design mirrored that of popular secular platforms like Salon, but whose "content and interactive options" served as proselytization tools (Stamper 2013, 51). Bridge sites were developed for a host of issues, including sports, the sciences, and apologetics (Stamper 2013, 51).

Digital evangelism or the e-vangelism movement shares a number of common features.[2] Obviously, the movement's willingness to utilize the Internet indicates a "wholehearted" support for the Net as a ministry tool; the movement further offers prescriptive and descriptive "techniques" that can help movement leaders achieve these ministry ends (Campbell 2010, 137, 139). The e-vangelism movement also has a missions-orientation (Campbell 2010, 139), which aligns it with the movement to incarnational evangelism within the EMC. The movement's understanding of missions is also fundamentally relational. In the words of church web consultant Richard Helsby (who has worked for such prominent web-based ministries as CBN.com) the church needs to learn to "leverage the network effect" of the Internet (Buseck 2015, 109). Church tech guru Tony Whittaker echoed this point as well, noting that well-run evangelical sites produce "welcoming interactivity" that creates a genuine "sense of community" among those who participate in them (Buseck 2015, 110). Moreover, digital evangelists, like the Leadership Network and those participating in the EMC, understand that we now live in a digitized world. Digital technology's social effects must be comprehended, therefore, if digital evangelism is to be effective (Campbell 2010, 139).

Stamper notes that website architecture, as well as the desire to get "hits," directly contributes to the success or failure of a digital evangelism outreach. For instance, sites have very deliberate "'strategies of channeling and directing navigation'" which may be utilized to direct and limit not only the searches undertaken, but also the possible interpretative meanings which can result from them (Stamper 2013, 76). For instance, websites which are heavily textual but offer little indication as to how the content may be viewed promote a careful reading of material, whereas text-light or image-centric websites promote a much faster movement through material. Moreover, websites that offer "many menu options, links to external websites, video content, chat features, or discussion boards encourage slower movement by prioritizing exploration" (Stamper 2013, 77). In an interview with Buseck, leading church ICT thinker Tony Whittaker calls this approach a "pull strategy," in which websites aim to meet the "'felt needs'" of the seeker, "pulling them toward the answers they are searching for" (Buseck 2015, 104). Therefore, even at the level of website architecture churches aim to optimize their sites for incarnational, rather than attractional, ministry.

Moreover, Stamper contends that the technological and theological presuppositions from which Christian web designers approach constructing their websites has enormous implications for the potential effectiveness of web-based evangelism ministries specifically (and, one might add, online Christian websites generally). She notes that

> many evangelistic websites promote exclusively one-on-one contact between the user and a mentor who is able to be contacted via chat or email. This type of interactivity allows for an extreme amount of control in terms of what information might be shared and what type of feedback the user receives. It also establishes a clear hierarchy in which the mentor becomes the prime source of information and teacher, and the user is positioned as a student. By contrast, evangelistic websites that have open discussion boards potentially are more inclusive of a variety of opinions, perspectives, and viewpoints. In addition, discussion boards may allow users to answer each other's questions or engage in discussion without the mediating hand of a designer. The extent to which dialogue is controlled and which perspectives are allowed to appear has implications for the ability of users to exist and behave in certain ways within the space [Stamper 2013, 89–90].

Stamper's point here is extremely salient when considering the current and potential future uses of web technology by the Christian Right. Currently, one of the major problems evangelicals face is the difficulty they will face in successfully appropriating open source technology and organizing ideologies to their purposes. Because most evangelicals believe in a closed biblical canon, they tend to be more favorably inclined to information control than many of their ideological opponents. Steve Hewitt, one of evangelicalism's leading computer gurus, has also noted that issues of technological control may reflect a generational divide between older ministry members and the younger generation, one that handicaps intergenerational connection (Hewitt 2010, 8). While there may not be anything inherently wrong with such uses of information control—there are cases in which information control is obviously necessary for the greater good—the web's tendency to promote dehierarchalizing rhetoric means that such attempts at information control will prove ineffective. Moreover, when referencing website design specifically, the increased focus on information control may make evangelical websites less usable than their secular counterparts.[3]

Reading church tech literature, one gets the impression that creatives are frustrated by the lack of good website design on the part of the evangelical movement.[4] Perhaps the most comprehensive available text on website architecture written from an evangelical perspective is Steve Hewitt's Win-

6. The Evangelical Web 283

dow's *PCs in the Ministry* (2010). Though the book is now several years out of date, it clearly indicates that website functionality is Hewitt's overriding concern. Hewitt warns against using animated gifts on websites, distracting backgrounds, and the overuse of "bold and capital letters" (Hewitt 2010, 121–122). This last characteristic is particularly telling, since anyone who has been on a large number of evangelical websites realizes that such lettering often denotes that a church or individual espouses a radically fundamentalist or, alternately, conspiracist, worldview; for many image-conscious church creatives, these are fellow religious travelers that the evangelical movement is better off without. Most of Hewitt's other recommendations involve maximizing functionality and browser satisfaction. Techniques that he suggests to do this involves keeping the home page short, putting basic information up front, and providing a welcome platform for members (Hewitt 2010, 123, 125).

Church communication theorists emphasize that at the congregational level, churches must develop a multichannel communication approach. One level involves what such specialists call the "PR Communication level," while the second level involves "the ministry communication production level." Because of this multichannel approach, it is crucial that congregations reach consumers of their information at both a print and digital level (Prehn 2016, 5). The PR communications level would involve such aspects of the church as its logo, primary bulletin, newsletter, and church website. These activities are usually overseen by someone on staff, though in some ministries, a volunteer might suffice (Prehn 2016, 6). In addition to communication production, the PR Communications specialist is also responsible for educational instruction for staff and volunteers, so that the outflow of materials from the church is not disrupted (Prehn 2016, 6). At the core level of PR communication, "communication standards" are somewhat strict, mainly because the "reputation of the church or a ministry within the church" may be at stake (Prehn 2016, 6). Prehn suggests, however, that ministry communication standards beyond the first tier of communications be "flexibile," in order to promote employee morale as well as avoiding employees going (figuratively) rogue and simply doing "their own communication pieces" without reference to the needs of the church office (Prehn 2016, 6).

At the ministry communication production level, a somewhat different form of information protocols operates. The ministry communications production level is responsible for all communications activities not covered under the public relations communication level's purview. This could include anything from "simple notices, lessons, flyers and announcements to more complex communication projects" (Prehn 2016, 6). Much of the emphasis at this level seems to be on niche-oriented ministries within the church (see Prehn 2016, 6). Prehn emphasizes that while there should be one key communication producer—either a staff member or an important volunteer—that individual alone cannot handle communications. It is therefore imperative that a ministry also develop individual communications ministry members for each department or ministry. Typically, these individuals are volunteers overseen by one of the staff members of the church ministry's communication staff, who serves as a coach and mentor (Prehn 2016, 6). Flexibility is even more strongly encouraged at the church ministry communication level (Prehn 2016, 6). Prehn does not spell out the reason for this, but it is likely that churches, like most non-profit organizations are grateful for whatever volunteers they can get, and are not overly concerned with how a job gets done, so long as it is done quickly and (hopefully) responsibly.

Evidence indicates that such divisions of church communication also affect website architecture. Steve Hewitt contends that church websites should have a multi-layered approach to website design:

> First there should be content for your members. Second, there should be a place for new residents who are Christians and have recently moved into your area and are seeking a new church home. And third, it needs to be designed for those who are seekers—people that have turned to the Internet to find solutions to a present crisis in their lives [Hewitt 2010, 125].

This multi-level functionality reflects the consumer-orientation of church creatives. Such functionality promotes a maximum amount of consumer satisfaction and also, ideally, maximizes the advantages churches derive from the appropriation of ICT technologies. Such multi-level functionality has not been without its problems, however. The more information churches and ministries make accessible online, the greater potential there is for leaks. The disastrous implosion of a number of complementarian ministries in the 2010s can be largely attributed to the loss of information control that the Internet facilitated (Harris 2014). In recent years, this has led to a pronounced minimalist approach to website design, with an increasing amount of information being unavailable to interested people or even congregants.

The need to set up effective information protocols and other industry best practices has led to calls for the development of industry standards among church creatives. The industry literature available from Christian ICT professionals indicates that management practices in the profession mirror those of other church management gurus, albeit with a greater emphasis on the importance of data systems. ICT professionals recommend that churches utilize technology to spread work allocation in a more efficient manner. Getting relevant customer feedback from potential congregants is also a must. Measurement and evaluation processes are therefore recommended (Steve Caton 2015, 25), which hints at likely organizational affinities with MBO and perhaps even TQM performance evaluation systems. Walter Wilson, a prominent evangelical Internet guru, contends that "ministries need to establish rules of productivity and measurements of deliverables [for the online side of their ministry] because the rules and measurements are important to track what is happening and how people are responding to the Gospel" (Buseck 2015, 7).

There has been a push among industry professionals to set industrial benchmarks for excellence in church tech. Buseck's book version of his dissertation, *Netcasters* (2010) is but one prominent example of this trend. Research by church technology expert Drew Goodmanson indicates that there are certain optimal ICT standards that churches should follow. Goodmanson's firm, Monk Development, found that visitors were the primary audience for church's web-based ministry. Research has indicated that people who visit the websites of Christian houses of worship spend only around 90 seconds on them. In order to maximize the potential of the church's evangelistic outreach, Monk Development's research team and the church cooperative it associated with suggested several industrial benchmarks, including a welcome video for the church and a banner section that displays the house of worship's vision statement (Goodmanson 2009, 25). The cooperative found that people strongly desired connectivity from church online media, particularly the abilities to let other online users know of their prayer requests, as well as the abilities to find ministry opportunities, access the church directly, participate in some sort of fellowship group, and/or pool resources (Goodmanson 2009, 25).

To facilitate these felt needs and perhaps to optimize their ability at information control, churches have begun developing web applications that facilitated private communication between individuals, while still maintaining a social media outreach. Monk's research found that those who implemented these private spiritual communication systems often faced a lack of participation in this aspect of the church, though polls indicated many congregation members did indeed see the benefits of private communication within the church. This problem appears to have been caused in part by the extensive time investment people were already making in other forms of social media (Goodmanson 2009, 26). This lack of participatory involvement with the church obviously poses long-term issues of viability within evangelical congregations.

The embrace of ICTs by the modern church does create certain management problems for pastors as well. As mentioned previously, computer systems are used in evangelical churches to correlate financial data, as well payroll and other "'corporate' work" (Grinter, Wyche, Hayes, Harvel 2011, 7). However, the need for this technology creates unique problems for pastors, particularly revolving around "issues of control" (Grinter et al. 2011, 7). Because of the expense of ICTs, churches frequently had to receive financial backing for these technologies from the laity. Moreover, many ministries also depended on the laity for their ICT infrastructure as well (Grinter et al. 2011, 8). This has led to an important change in the balance of power within churches, and indeed has created a sort of new leadership caste. Ministries have become very reliant on IT workers for support services for many facets of church life. However, because IT is becoming so central to every aspect of church operations, unskilled volunteers are increasingly left without any job function, potentially demotivating the laity (Grinter et al. 2011, 8). This need for a technologically literate workforce is likely responsible for the increased adoption of Toyotist management practices in church, particularly team ministries. The need to have enough knowledge workers to run the evangelical church's religious economy means that evangelical ministries, particularly parachurch groups like LN, willingly commit significant resources into workforce development.

Ministers also report that the adoption of ICTs can cause significant dissension in churches, with some congregants complaining that they turn church into simply spectacle. Many pastors have adopted the solution of dividing church services into traditional and contemporary formats (Grinter et al. 2011, 10). These conflicts mirror similar divisions that occurred in the 1990s over the embrace of worship music. Many pastors may not wish to embrace such technology out of fears of a repeat of the "worship wars" that divided evangelicals during that period.

Nevertheless, many ministers do embrace ICTs. Ministers are very impressed with ICTs ability to engage in better demographic targeting. Ministers can, for instance, "tailor their content towards what they thought their audience would prefer, such as removing old language and updating to new" (Grinter et al. 2011, 10). Perhaps even more importantly, most ministers realize they need ICTs if they are to successfully engage in youth recruitment (Grinter et al. 2011, 11). Tellingly, in their study of southeastern Protestant churches, Grinter et al. found that pastors were nearly "uniformly interested in leveraging ICTs" for the purpose of "managing the relationship that a minister seeks to have with each member of the laity" (Grinter et al. 2011, 12). This was seen as guaranteeing "the type of connection that builds community and commitment to the faith" (Grinter et al. 2011, 12). As we have seen previously, churches are concerned about retention, and ICTs provide powerful support to this process (Grinter. Et al. 2011, 20). Ministers at large churches frequently employ ICTs to create "social structures" that allow them to manage their relationship with the laity (Grinter et al. 2011, 12). ICTs have also increasingly optimized the quality of pastoral care, by allowing pastors greater connectivity and coordination of pastoral care efforts (see. Grinter et al. 2011, 13).

Regardless of whether pastors want ICTs in their churches or not, the new information technology is here to stay. The real issue is now how well Protestants leverage such technology for the benefit of their community. Because ICTS are disruptive innovations that shake up the balance of power within Protestant communities, they threaten to fundamentally reshape the meaning and even the message of Protestant Christianity. The Protestantism that is birthed from these trends may be fundamentally alien from anything we have seen before, with important consequences for American religious life and democratic institutions.

The Church and Big Data

The infiltration of managerialist assumptions into the Christian Right's use of ICT technology, meanwhile, is well advanced. In particular, evangelicals are fully aware of the potential revolution that Big Data is helping underwrite. Russ McGuire, a writer for *Christian Computing*, has called this new emerging era "The Intelligence Revolution" and argues that it will help individuals develop a better understanding of the world, while also allowing "companies to better serve us based on the correlation and analysis of data from the interrelation of people, things, and content" (McGuire 2015, 22). Nevertheless, McGuire admits to some concerns about Big Data. McGuire fears that an overreliance on Big Data may end up exposing the evangelical church, and the theology it represents, to criticism, if churches rely too greatly on the storage and manipulation of congregant data. McGuire, along with one of his interviewees, also worries that "the types of information being collected and the inferences being made from it" are potentially worrisome to the evangelical church's reputation (McGuire 2015, 23). McGuire's point should not be seen as insincere. Rather, what McGuire points to is the dilemmas all nonprofits face when confronted with the temptation of Big Data. The information can be utilized for tremendous good in improving services, but non-profits also run the risk of using Big Data as nothing more than a marketing ploy or recruitment tool, something McGuire is clearly averse to doing.

In any case, whatever qualms the Christian Right has in using big data are becoming increasingly minor, as the advantages it presents for movement mobilization expand exponentially. This was dramatically demonstrated in the leadup to the 2016 election. In the months leading up to the 2014 midterm election, the common cultural consensus within the Beltway was that both the Christian Right and the evangelical movement were finished. But as the Left was preparing for yet another of its premature burials of the religious right, conservative Christian leaders were busy plotting strategy. A number of evangelical groups got together and plotted out an "aggressive voter mobilization campaign" which took full advantage of the new technologies churches had at their disposal. There were briefings for pastors, and simulcast rallies held at mega-churches. Collectively, the goal of such meetings was to mobilize right wing rage at what was perceived as assaults by the ungodly on religious liberty. These "battles" between Christians and the secular world were cast in apocalyptic terms (Blake 2014).

The main group backing this 2014 voter mobilization effort was United in Purpose, a group that was backed by a number of rich Silicon Valley evangelicals (Blake 2014). UIP utilized finely honed data-mining techniques to develop a database of unregistered voters who were evangelical, born-again, or conservatively Catholic. Then the organization worked with Christian Right organizers and pro-life groups to recruit voters to their cause. The profiles drawn from UIP's databases allowed the movement to engage in extremely specific market targeting, with email and video outreach efforts that were tailored to the specific interests of each likely potential voter (Gold and Hamburger 2011). Among the leading backers of UIP was Ken Eldred, a leading Christian advocate of Business as Missions (see Weaver 2016, 232) who had also played a crucial role in financing the infamous *Transformations* movie, *Uganda: An Unconventional War* (Weaver 2016, 230).

In March of 2014, United in Purpose held a Mobilization Strategy Summit to network this effort and create a voter mobilization strategy. According to Blake, United in Purpose was a "behind-the-scenes technology and communications group with deep dominonist ties" (Blake 2014). Moreover, the group was very effective at utilizing ICT technologies such as videos and voter mobilization apps, to mobilize the Christian Right's base. After the summit meeting, the FRC and Vision America, a Texas organization, engaged in regular clergy policy briefings, as well as slickly produced major events designed to heighten voter mobilization (Blake 2014).

In the fall of 2014, a number of Christian Right organizations gathered together to sponsor a Value Voters Summit and by mid-October had networked with United in Purpose to deliver a simulcast entitled iPledge Sunday. Again, there were warnings about attacks on religious liberty. These were coupled with pristinely filmed videos of David and Jason Benham, two former HGTV hosts who had become a Christian cause célèbre after their show had been axed due to disputes with HGTV over their family's opposition to homosexuality.[5] Within the iPledge Sunday broadcast, the battle between Christianity and its opponents was increasingly cast in Manichean terms of light and darkness. Tony Perkins encouraged Christians who watched the video to "visit 123Vote.org, where they can pledge to 'vote biblical values' and can use the technical tools developed by United in Purpose to find unregistered Christians and get them to sign up" (Blake 2014).

Fast forward two years. In May 2016, Bill Dallas, the head of United in Purpose met with Donald Trump (Burke 2016), along with Ben Carson, Tony Perkins, and a number of other Christian leaders (Burke 2016). Dallas spoke with Trump before a crucial speech he gave to evangelicals in June 2016 as well (Milligan 2017). Trump successfully courted the evangelical voters that Dallas represented and won the evangelical vote by the largest margin in its 12-year recorded history (Milligan 2017). United in Purpose was by no means shy in taking credit for part of this victory (see, for instance "Election Poll" 2017). The Christian Right realized that big data had won them the election ("Election Poll" 2017). With both the political will and the increasing ability to optimize such technologies, the Christian Right has a major head start over left wing efforts at movement mobilization; this superiority is likely to remain uncontested so long as the left continues to believe that the Christian Right is technologically unsophisticated. Moreover, in the first half of 2016, there were credible and convincing, but unconfirmable reports that United in Purpose was behind a massive data breach that put 191 million American registered voters at risk (Schulz 2016; Fox-Brewster 2016; Kovacs 2016). Regardless of whether or not United in Purpose was ultimately culpable for the data breach—which will likely remain unconfirmable—the possibility of unscrupulous groups on the CR [Christian Right] combining both the movement's powerful technology and its mobilization abilities remains undeniable. What the results of such a synergy of big data and bad ethics might mean is anyone's guess, but such a synergy is unlikely to promote what lingering trust remains for the American electoral system. And this is a development no one in our country, whether evangelical or not, should welcome.

God in Silicon Valley

The successful utilization of Big Data by evangelicals represents just one action in a long-term Christian Right attempt to leverage the power of Silicon Valley to advance evangelical interests. Given the cultural importance of Silicon Valley since the 1980s, it is not surprising that the campaigns that DAWN and Mission: Silicon Valley first undertook in the 1980s led to further evangelical outreach campaigns in the 1990s and 2000s. The most prominent evangelist to target the Valley was none other than Billy Graham. In October 1996, Graham visited the wider Bay Area, including San Jose and Oakland, in order to motivate the local church community. Christians in Silicon Valley saw Graham's mission as a spiritual gauntlet thrown down against the perceived technocratic ideals of the Valley. Graham networked with Peter Wilkes, who led South Hills Community Church and Pat Robertson (again, not the famous Robertson) of CityTeam Ministries to bring Graham to San Jose (Scheinn 1E, 1997; Quinn 1997, B4). Eventually, a letter writing campaign was organized to persuade Graham that there was indeed enough backing in the Valley to make this crusade a reality (Scheinn 1E, 1997).

Graham wanted to capture the feeling of Silicon Valley in attracting the local jet setters, so he hired CKS Partners, a prominent local marketing group famed for its work in promoting microchips and the Internet, to help him with his Silicon Valley marketing. CKS Partners then created a parody ad of Microsoft's well-known tag line–"'Where do you want to go today?'"—but asked the question "'Where do you want to go tomorrow?'" Campaign organizers tried to promote a version of a hip Graham whose message was a "step ahead." Microsoft itself was less than impressed with the Graham Crusade's activities and wanted to get a photo of one of the Crusade's signs, so they could ask them formally to "'cease and desist'" (Michelle Quinn 1997, B4).

In recent years, such investments in converting the "Technorati" have begun to pay fruit. Data available from the Association of Religion Data Archives indicated that by 2015, several Protestant denominations had actually begun to grow in San Francisco County (Gaus 2015). As Annie Gaus correctly notes, such success does not come without careful planning. The SBC, for instance, utilized Linda Bergquist as their "lead Bay Area catalyst" for their efforts in the region (Gaus 2015). In addition to being a skilled church planter with a long history of ministry in California ("Linda Bergquist" 2018), Bergquist is among the most adept church planting strategists on the Christian Right. Her book, *Church Turned Inside Out* (2009), is a theoretically sophisticated work, published under the aegis of the Leadership Network (Bergquist 2010, passim). Given the increasingly corporate model of church planting—followed both inside and outside of Silicon Valley—Silicon Valley church planting efforts are quite intentional in their application of business principles, and behave in much the same way as "any other start-up in the nation's technology hub" (Gaus 2015). There are a number of outreach efforts in the Bay Area that have proven successful in recent years. For instance, Reality SF markets itself to millennials through a tech-oriented ministry, and hosts groups like "Praxis, a 'kingdom-centered' business accelerator" (Gaus 2015). Reality SF gives a lot of advice on the ins and outs of the Christian single life but tries to avoid alienating Bay Area residents on issues such as LGBT life or premarital sex. Instead, the ministry seeks to optimize its ability to connect with young people by providing relational networking. Gaus notes that "it's clear that Reality understands its congregation: it accepts tithing in the form of stock and reported a budget of $2.3m[illion] in 2014" (Gaus 2015).

A perhaps more problematic church plant than Reality SF is C3 SV (C3 Silicon Valley). C3 is pastored over by Adam Smallcombe, an Australian participant in the C3 Global movement (once known as Christian City Church International). The movement started in 1980 and has since spread worldwide, birthing a number of megachurches (Tiku 2016). The ministry, like Reality SF, focuses on group activities, offers a mobile app and bus service. Tithing is heavily emphasized in the church. Smallcombe's eventual goal is for the church to serve as a "start-up" model for numerous other C3 church plants and ministries around the world (Gaus 2015). The constitutional apparatus of Christian City Church International, according to reporter Nitasha Tiku, explicitly "encourages a sort of modular adaptability" for ministry outreach efforts, in which "each individual church can be dressed up to blend into its environment" (Tiku 2016). Functionally, C3 churches are not defined by particular styles, but by a desire to be contextually relevant to whatever market group they are seeking to reach (Tiku 2016). Thus, Smallcombe and his wife sell "religion like a software product" (Tiku 2016). The church's website looks like any other startup's website, while "its donations page starts with the words 'INVEST IN ETERNITY' and could just as easily work as crowdfunding for a cryogenics company" (Tiku 2016).

What is problematic about the C3 movement's outreach efforts in Silicon Valley is C3 Global's connections to theology that lies outside the borders of mainstream classical Pentecostalism. Some of these problematic ties involve dalliances between movement leader Phil Pringle and David Yonggi Cho, a fellow traveler with, if not participant in, the New Apostolic Reformation. Pringle was also the mentor of Kong Hee, a well known Singapore pastor who fell from grace in 2015 after being found guilty by a Singapore court of misusing church funds (Weaver 2016, 249–251; Sam Hey 2010, 111–112; Heng 2013; Pringle 2008, blurbs; Pringle 2014, blurbs; Woods 2015; Klett 2015). Moreover, because the C3 movement is strongly influenced by Word of Faith teachings, there have been more than a few leaders allied with the movement who have engaged in financial irregularities.[6]

Another ally of Cho's is Ken Eldred, who even serves as an elder in Yoido Full Gospel Church (Bruce Wilson 2015). He is one of Silicon Valley's most "strategic funders" of Christian Right interests and his organization the Living Stones Foundation Charitable Trust has been particularly active in this regard. The Foundation has helped fund the American Family Association, an anti-gay group; the Sentinel Group, which produced the infamous *Transformations* films that advanced NAR interests in Africa; Ed Silvoso's Harvest Evangelism, another major NAR ministry; Campus Crusade for Christ; and the Alliance Defending Freedom/Alliance Defense Fund, a well-known Christian legal group (Bruce Wilson 2015).[7] Besides his funding efforts, Eldred also wrote *God Is at Work* (2009), one of the most important texts within the Business as Missions movement (BAM), whose extensive influence on Christians missions' policies I have previously documented (Weaver 2016, 230–232).

Another prominent voice in hi-tech evangelicalism is Walter Wilson. Wilson was an important executive for three decades in various Fortune 100 companies, notably Apple Computer (Bob Mims 2000, C2). Wilson is the creator of Global Media Outreach (GMO), one of the most well-known digital evangelism platforms. Although GMO is organizationally small—with only 22 members—it has had a major effect online, registering some 10 million conversions (or re-conversions) to Christianity in 2009 alone (Jennifer O'Connell 2010, no pagination). Wilson's book, *The Internet Church* (2004), meanwhile, has made him a well-known advocate for the powers of digital technologies.

An important Silicon Valley executive aligned with the evangelical movement is Michael Yang, a South Korean immigrant who entered the U.S. in 1976 and subsequently graduated from the University of California Berkley. Yang worked for a number of high-tech firms over the years, including Xerox and Samsung, before eventually founding MySimon.com, a comparative shopping website that he later sold for $700 million (Carnes 2001, 35; "Michael Yang" 2013). Yang has been a speaker at Silicon Valley Prayer Breakfasts, prominent evangelical networking events in the Valley ("Speaker Info" n.d.).

Passionate advocates of the more anti-democratic forms of evangelicalism, such as the NAR, can also be found in Silicon Valley. Chen Wen-Chi, head of Via Technologies, is a major evangelical hi-tech voice. Wen-Chi joined Via Technologies in 1987 and by 1993 he had become the company's CEO (Carnes 2001, 36–37). Chen Wen Chi is married to Cher Wang, the founder of VIA technologies, also an evangelical Christian ("Keep the Faith" 2016; "HTC Investors" n.d.). Cher Wang is the richest woman in Taiwan. She leads HTC, a major Taiwanese smartphone manufacturer, as its chairperson and CEO ("Keep the Faith" 2016; Linder 2018). As of 2011, HTC made one in every six smartphones sold in the American market (Ungerleider 2011). Wang's father was Wang Yung-Ching, considered a "god of management" for his skill in running the Formosa Plastics Group, Taiwan's top petrochemicals conglomerate; Yung-Ching also played a crucial role in attempting to facilitate harmony between Taiwan and the People's Republic of China (Ungerleider 2011: "Keep the Faith" 2016). Wang's sister, Charlene Wang, helped found First International Computer in 1980 (Lev-Ram 2014). Cher Wang frequently talks about how important the scriptures are to her, even in business interviews ("Keep the Faith" 2016). She routinely runs prayer sessions with other executives before making crucial decisions and makes sure to have copies of Bibles on hand whenever possible in case she meets someone who is interested in the Good Book ("Keep the Faith" 2016).

Wang has engaged in some concerning activities. Her opponents have charged that she is responsible for pouring billions of Taiwanese dollars into Bread of Life Church, a megachurch in Taiwan that embarked on a high-profile campaign to stop same-sex marriage from coming to the country (Linder 2018). J. Michael Cole, the editor of the Taiwan Sentinel and a former intelligence official with the Canadian Security Intelligence Service

6. The Evangelical Web 293

(CSIS) (J. Michael Cole 2017b) has written extensively on the troubling connections between American Christian Right activists and anti-gay activism in Taiwan. During the conflict over a proposed amendment which would legalize gay marriage, the Taiwanese Christian right recited a predictable litany of reasons for opposing gay marriage, including that it would "spread AIDS, confuse children, encourage orgies, condone bestiality, [and facilitate incest]." This effort in Taiwan was spurred on by the International House of Prayer (IHOP), a radical NAR group and had strong links to the Wagner Leadership Institute (WLI), another organization which advocates New Apostolic theology (Cole 2013). A foundation that Cher Wang directs sponsored one of IHOP's leaders to come to Taiwan; there are also indications that she was responsible for facilitating training sessions for Christian Taiwanese at one of IHOP's U.S. locations (Cole 2013). Wang also helped bring IHOP leader David Sliker, a prominent participant in IHOP's ministry activities, to Taiwan (Cole 2016).

However, there are potentially even more troubling connections. Cole has contended that Wang's support for a closer relationship with China may be partly motivated by her sponsorship of The Forerunner College in the Guizhou region of China. Wang donated some $28.1 million dollars to start the college; Wen Chi-Chen also helped found the college (J. Michael Cole 2017a, 73–74). Furthermore, GFC is sponsored by a number of other high-tech companies, including Hewlett Packard and Microsoft, as well as the Marriott Hotel Group ("Guizhou Forerunner College" n.d.). As I have documented in my work on the NAR, the NAR, and Mike Bickle's IHOP ministry in particular, have gravitated to the idea of forerunner ministry leaders.[8] That Wang is using the term Forerunner in naming the Guizhou area college therefore is deeply troubling, given the historical associations forerunner terminology has with the most theologically conservative and aberrant elements of the wider NAR.

There are also more direct signs of NAR involvement in Silicon Valley. One evangelical group that has been particularly adamant at directly transforming high tech culture to a Christian worldview has been the organization Transforming the Bay with Christ (TBC), the brainchild of VMware CEO Pat Gelsinger. Gelsinger hopes his movement can serve as the catalyst for the birth of a 1,000 church plants in the Bay Area by 2024 (Vaccarello 2015, loc. 219). Gelsinger gathered together an elite team of venture capitalists and Christian leaders, including Kevin Compton, one-time employee of Kleiner Perkins; Promod Harque, employed by Northwest Ventures; John Ortberg of Menlo Park Presbyterian Church (MPCC), Chip Ingram, another noted evangelical preacher; and Reformed pastor Francis Chan (Vaccarello 2015, Loc. 672–676). The group hoped to serve a societally transformative role in Silicon Valley (672–676). What is not so clear from their material is the apparent links to NAR apostle and transformationalist leader Ed Silvoso, who served on the advisory board of the group ("TBC Advisory Board").

Allied with TBC is Menlo Park Presbyterian Church. MPCC's outreach efforts in Silicon Valley represent one of the most long-term Christian projects of cultural transformation within the area. MPPC started in 1873 with some 13 members as a mission church. The ministry ebbed dangerously low in membership at some points in its early history, yet also attracted the attention of prominent citizens of the Bay Area, such as Jane Lanthrop Stanford (Hackett 2009, 35–36). What ultimately saved the ministry, however, was not the attention paid to it by Stanford—which was relatively brief—but the postwar "boom period" that the surrounding area experienced after World War II (Hackett 2009, 36). Walter Gerber would take over the church in 1974 and would play a prominent role in shaping its future ministry. Gerber instituted many farsighted reforms at MPPC that increased its competitive viability vis-à-vis other congregations. Under Gerber's leadership, Menlo began adopting modern worship styles that he had himself learned in southern California. Gerber also relied heavily on small groups to broaden the church's appeal, adopting a "therapeutic" style of ministry that catered to the wealthy. Gerber's ministry was innovative enough for the church to reach a membership of some 5,000 by the time of his retirement (Hackett 2009, 40–41, 45) Among MPPC's many claims to fame is that it helped facilitate the conversion of Paul Ely, a major executive at Hewlitt-Packard (Vaccarello 2015, 291–322, 375, 395–406). Ely would subsequently channel his efforts into helping Walt Wilson's Global Media Outreach (GMO) ministry (Vaccarello 2015, loc. 415).

Menlo Park Presbyterian Church was at the forefront of networking Silicon Valley. It held a Faith Online Conference in 1996 which attracted the likes of Jack Sculley, the son of powerful Apple Executive John Sculley (Sandy Kleffman 1996, 1B). An even more important conference occurred in 2006, when the church hosted Techevangelism '06. Walt Wilson spoke at the conference and encouraged participants to view computer networks as the new battleground for "the minds and souls of people across the world" (Mike Langberg 2006, 1C). Peter Holzmann, who by now had become the director of the International Christian Technologists Association, also spoke at the conference and pressed for Silicon Valley Christians employed in high-tech to leverage their positions for their faith. Holzmann, tellingly, also thought Christian engineers should think about "God's purpose" when implementing the "product development process" (Langberg 2006, 1C). Holzmann had started to form "spirit-led technology groups" to think about "the intersection of work and faith" (Langberg 2006, 1C). MPCC is also known among evangelicals for its promotion and utilization of the ICT-mediated multisite model (see Frye 2011, 9).

Evangelicalism, therefore, has a robust presence in Silicon Valley. Indeed, this chapter has only dug at the surface of some of the most obvious connections. Whether the evangelical movement can effectively capitalize on these connections, of course, is anyone's guess. Given the movement's genius for organizational innovation, however, the long-term outlook for evangelical outreach into Silicon Valley remains promising. The movement has been careful and strategic in how it targets the area, and in this game of souls, even winning a few influential adherents may reap the movement many long-term advantages. In a time of increased uncertainty about the long-term viability of evangelicalism, gaining the support of such key individuals may prove critical to the movement's long-term success.

Conclusion

While Protestant Christianity certainly faces challenges in utilizing ICTs effectively in the coming years, it would be foolish to underestimate the commitment of evangelical Christians to successfully transitioning into the information age. As we have seen, evangelicals have invested massive amounts of funding and resources into making this dream a reality. For progressives, viewing evangelicals as technologically deprived is dangerously short-sighted. In reality, the movement has proven reasonably adept at adopting the technologies of the information age. If the non-evangelical world does not come to realize the power of the cyborg sciences within evangelical thought, it may come to regret its underestimation of the Christian Right, with consequences that are detrimental both to the United States and the entire world.

Conclusion
Managing the Future

> "In the past, politicians promised to create a better world. They had different ways of achieving this, but their power and authority came from the optimistic visions they offered their people. Those dreams failed, and today people have lost faith in ideologies."
> —Adam Curtis, *The Power of Nightmares*

Ultimately, evangelicalism's endeavors in management are as much about managing the future as they are about managing the present. Or, put a different way, managing the future can be a technique for managing the present (Andersson 2018, 8). Within the evangelical church there have been significant debates as to how the future is to be managed and what techniques of managing that future are and are not acceptable. At their center, these debates reflect concerns over the changing nature of workplace culture since the 1970s.

The Consultation on Future Evangelical Concerns and the Continuing Consultation on Future Evangelical Concerns were perhaps the first notable attempts by evangelical leaders, along with secular thinkers, to transition evangelical culture into the new workplace culture that came to characterize the New Economy. At the latter conference, Willis Harman described the transition between what he termed the "outmoded 'warfare between science and religion'" viewpoint (Willis Harman 1979, 34). Harman noted what he perceived as a growing "suspicion" that both "traditional religion and conventional science alike are both partial and flawed and due to be superseded by a more unified view of reality" (Willis Harman 1979, 34–35). Harman gave examples of what he perceived as "once taboo" fields that now were gaining wider cultural currency, including: "hypnosis ... unconscious processes ... psychosomatic illness ... sleep and dreams ... creativity ... biofeedback training ... psychic phenomena ... states of consciousness" (Willis Harman 1979,

35). Harman also noted even more exotic fields, such as "'remote viewing,' precognition, and psychokinesis" that were being explored with "renewed interest" and speculated on the increased interested in prayer and meditation as well (Willis Harman 1979, 35). Harman's interests in these various questionable fields of scientific research, many of which scholars would classify as "'fringe science,'" eventually evolved into a unique New Age discourse surrounding the "New Science."[1]

As the introduction highlighted, this discourse associates itself with legitimate fields of scientific inquiry, such as quantum physics and complexity theory, while often putting a New Age or Eastern gloss on these particular subjects. The New Science includes many of the fields discussed earlier in this work, including "the study of chaos, complexity, emergence, fractals, non-linear systems, the implications of quantum physics, and self-organization" (Doornenbal 2012, 147). Both the promoters of the New Science and New Age Science support the move towards "holism" in the natural sciences and object to scientific reductionism and or the "Newton[ian]" paradigm (Doornenbal 2012, 147; Dyer-Witherford 2017, 26, 37–38, 44–45). The New Age movement has tended to appropriate scientific discourses to justify its own discursive agendas. It is particularly interested in quantum theory, the scientific use of self-organization, the "holographic paradigm" of the universe developed by David Bohm and Karl Pribam, and (especially) James Lovelock's Gaia theory (Dyer-Witherford 2017, 44–45). Therefore, discussion in evangelical churches surrounding the agenda of the church growth movement reflected wider issues than simply how church was organized. Instead, they reflected deep concerns about the possibility of theological innovations being introduced into the evangelical church via the innovations of the church growth movement, the Leadership Network, and the EMC. At the root of these concerns were two issues. The first, the debate over pragmatism, has been more or less discussed throughout this book. The second issue was the fear that, in borrowing mainstream management's use of the "new science," evangelicals would inadvertently borrow from New Age Science as well. These fears powerfully shaped much of the debate surrounding the management of the future that is present in evangelical culture. To explore this discourse, this concluding chapter looks at evangelical appropriations of futurist techniques and Oriental Systems discourses in evangelicalism.

The Futures of Yesterday's Religion: Evangelical Futurism

The reader should note that the term futurism in this chapter refers to evangelical appropriations (sometimes simply glosses) of secular futurist techniques, not the more commonly known prophetic techniques of the evangelical community (some of which do have a passing similarity to secular futurism). Evangelical futurism is an evolving field. The field in large parts owes its existence to Lyle Schaller, whose functionalist theology allowed his ideas a wide currency in evangelicalism, despite the fact that he straddled a liminal area between mainline Protestantism and evangelicalism. Schaller's first futurist work was *The Impact of the Future* (1969). Schaller noted the research of Herman Kahn and Anthony J. Wiener, but while respectful of their work, remained unconvinced of the essentially static nature of the future projected by Kahn and Wiener (Schaller 1969, 18). Schaller also engaged in a fairly serious attempt to articulate an effective and ethical response to the needs of the disaffected youth culture of the Vietnam Era. At the same time, Schaller appeared open to more gradualist approaches to implementing social change, particularly those articulated by Peter Drucker (Schaller 1969, 169–175). On the whole, therefore, Schaller showed a fairly sophisticated understanding of how potential future trends in society were likely to impact churches, particularly mainline churches. While Schaller's work was geared more to mainline audiences, it is widely conceded that he was influential throughout Protestant Christianity (Warren Anderson Smith 2006, 57–58).

Schaller's second book, *Understanding Tomorrow* (1976) continued the evolution of Schaller's futuring career. *Understanding Tomorrow*, like many evangelical and mainline appropriations of secular futurist techniques, can be seen as glorified trends analysis. Indeed, secular futurism itself can be productively read through that lens (with some qualifications). Significantly, by 1976 Schaller was beginning to see signs of the shift from a textually based society to an image-based society, a theme that would come to dominate much of the evangelical and mainline futurist literature that followed (Schaller 1976, 53–54, 56, 57). *Understanding Tomorrow* was relatively unsophisticated compared to the more serious strategizing between secular futurist leaders and evangelical elites that was highlighted in Chapter 3; after all, those meetings were likely meant to set, as well as sell, policy, unlike Schaller's work, which does only the latter. Schaller did, however, foresee a particular need on the part of the church to more comprehensively develop an understanding of voluntarism, a point that became significant in the thought of Peter Drucker and the Leadership Network in the 1990s (Schaller 1976, 94–95, 97, 103, 108–109; Trueheart 1996, 5; "Converting Geography into Community" 2001, 126–128). In the 1990s, established as one of the most influential church consultants in the United States (see Warner Anderson Smith 2006, 28), Schaller again appropriated futurist techniques in his *The New Reformation: Tomorrow Arrived Yesterday* (1995) and *Discontinuity and Hope: Radical Change and the Path to the Future* (1999). Again, both works are largely glorified trends analysis and seek to legitimize changes in church organizational life brought about by the transition to a post–Fordist economy. Schaller thus serves largely the same role for the church market as promoters of the New Economy did in the 1990s: promoting a bull market in church futures.

Two other voices, Hiley H. Ward and Howard Snyder, also emerged as supporters of church futurism in the 1970s. Ward's *Religion 2101 A.D: Who or What Will Be God?* (1975) did not endorse any particular Christian or even religious viewpoint and it is unclear whether Ward even considered himself a Christian. Nevertheless, Ward's work is a treasure-trove of information about innovative forms of church expression that were occurring in the 1970s. In the process, however, Ward engages in some of the wildest speculation associated with church futurism. For instance, Ward interviews Harvey Cox; Cox speculated on the possibility of transmitting sermons via thoughts. Ward expresses excitement at this prospect and makes the obligatory references to mind-reading experiments conducted at SRI, which have since become fodder for conspiracy theorists.[2] Ward also indulges in the fantasy of "mind over matter in healing" (Ward 1975, 24), with speculations on "'channeling energies,'" "mind suggestion," and Unitarian church "'energy'" sessions (Ward 1975, 25). Much of this form of spirituality would be par for the course by the early 21st century, but was cutting edge at the time Ward was promoting it.

Howard A. Snyder played a much greater role in church futurism, particularly the evangelical variety. Snyder's *The Problem of Wineskins: Church Structure in a Technological Age* (1975), published by the evangelical publisher Intervarsity Press, was a radical rethinking of church structure, one geared to making the evangelical church more institutionally sustainable (Snyder 1975, 61, 67, 69–73). Snyder's works extensively reference the work of ecological economists, along with other figures associated with a pro-limits view of the world's resources, including Jeremy Rifkin and E.F. Schumacher (Snyder 1975, 115–121; Snyder 1983, 21, 27–30, 33–34, 264). Snyder was promoting a vision of the church closely aligned with those associated with organizational ecology (see Morgan 1986, 66–71). The church was to be remodeled on ecological, or at least biomimetic, terms. The models that came to be associated with Snyder's approach to church organization either borrowed directly from organizational ecology or alternately from a fairly wide number of theories associated with the "organismic metaphor" of organizations that Gareth Morgan describes in his book *Images of Organization* (See Morgan 1986, 39–71, passim). Such viewpoints, though not always borrowing from Snyder, dominated church organizational thinking by the late 1990s because of the rise of "open systems" ideology in the United States (Russell 2014, 11–17). Snyder's association with the so-called "Au Sable" theology (see Larsen 2001, 203–204) of the evangelical environmentalist movement undoubtedly influenced the Emergent Church and Missional Movements. The EMC, after all, has shown a marked preference for distributed networking, environmentalism and smaller churches and institutional forms (this is particularly true in those EMC churches that subscribe to the organic church or simple church models). Snyder's articulation of the need for, and possibilities of, a more institutionally and ecologically sustainable church thus remain relevant today. The groundbreaking nature of Snyder's work was recognized even in the 1970s, when Gene Getz proclaimed it "one of the most perceptive [books] to date" on "church renewal," a movement out of which much of the innovative uses of smaller, more sustainable churches came from (Getz 1979, 67–68). Snyder also contributed to the evangelical version of church futurism with his book *Foresight: 10 Major Trends That Will Dramatically Affect the Future of Christians and the Church* (1986), co-authored with Daniel V. Runyon. *Foresight* remains historically significant as one of the pioneering works of evangelical church futurism, but in many ways is actually less path breaking than Snyder's ostensibly non futurist works, such as *Liberating the Church: The Ecology of Church & Kingdom* (1983). Much like Lyle Schaller's work, *Foresight* engages in glorified trends analysis. John Naisbitt, a populist futurist, is the futurist most engaged with in the work, though Snyder and Runyon also briefly touch on the futurism of Herman Kahn, who Snyder views negatively (Snyder and Runyon 1986, 12–13, 25, 62–63, 66 150–151). Snyder found a "number of philosophical or quasi-theological assumptions" within Kahn's work that made its modeling techniques suspect in his eyes (Snyder 1983, 262–263). This viewpoint on Kahn's cornucopianism continues to be widely held in environmental history, and certainly represents the majority viewpoint among many environmentalists. Kahn gave a platform to the economic thought of Cornucopian thinker Julian Simon, a favorite figure within anti-environmentalist circles. (On Simon and Kahn, see Paul Sabin's *The Bet: Paul Ehrlich, Julian Simon, and Our Gamble Over Earth's Future* [2013].)

David McKenna joined Howard Snyder in promoting church futurism in the 1980s, publishing *Mega Truth: The Church in The Age of Information* (1986). The book's title was an obvious takeoff on John Naisbitt's *Megatrends* (1982) and McKenna, much like Snyder, largely apes Naisbitt's work. *Mega-Truth* lacks the originality of Snyder's more radical projective analyses of the problems confronting the evangelical church at the close of the 20th century and instead apes both *Foresight* and *Megatrends* in being a typical exercise in trends analysis.

One other futurist began actively promoting his work in the 1970s: Tom Sine. Sine is perhaps the most significant evangelical church futurist. Sine's work in the field dates at least to the late 1970s, where he served at the Consultation on Future Evangelical Concerns as a facilitator of "working-group discussions" (Hoke 1978a, xi). In Sine's *Mustard Seed Conspiracy*, he advanced an economic agenda grounded largely in the assumptions of ecological economics. This agenda held much in common with similar Protestant and evangelical works at the time. For evangelicals committed to environmental justice, the most significant figures in this line of reasoning would be Ron Sider, Jeremy Rifkin (who was not an evangelical, but co-wrote several books with Ted Howard, who, according to John Hyde Evans [Evans 1998, 336], is a Pentecostal), Richard Foster, and Bob Goudzwaard. Outside of evangelicalism, significant figures included Herman Daly and Nicholas Georgescu-Rogan (Caradonna 2014, 8, 117, 128). Like other evangelical left authors in this school, Sine named the "energy-extravagant lifestyles" and the excessive consumerism of the West as major problems that the United States would have to deal with. His worry—which proved to be correct—was that the Reagan administration was moving in the opposite direction, promoting an unsustainable "high growth national lifestyle" associated with the mid-century boom years (Sine 1981, 48). Throughout *Mustard Seed Conspiracy*, Sine's training in foresight techniques[3] and intelligence are clearly evident. His projections about the future development of the American economy were accurate more often than not and were certainly more sound than those provided by more ideologically driven members of the evangelical left, such as Jim Wallis and Ron Sider. Moreover, Sine's later futurist works, such as *Mustard Seed vs. McWorld* (1999) and *The New Conspirators: Creating the Future One Mustard Seed at a Time* (2008), reflected a far more consistent ideological commitment to the original vision of the evangelical left than that seen in either Wallis's or (especially) Sider's works.

In practical terms, Carl George was the most significant church futurist of the 1990s, particularly in his *Prepare Your Church for the Future* (1992). The first chapter of George's work was entitled "Prepare for Future Shock" clearly playing off the name of Alvin and Heidi Toffler's similarly titled *Future Shock* (1970). George showed a familiarity with a number of futurists, most of them "popular" futurists. Among the futurists he cites are John Naisbitt, Joel Barker, David McKenna, Lyle Schaller, and Howard Snyder (George, 1992 15–18). George warned Christians to prepare for "an extended future" rather than simply a rapture. Part of this preparation involved restructuring how church was organized which was where, of course, the meta-church model came in (Carl George 1992, 19–25). As George has been covered extensively earlier in this work, there's no need to linger on him here. It should be noted, however, that George's work, much like Snyder's, was actually far more innovative in its futurism than works that more explicitly fell within the futurist camp. George, like Snyder, not only saw the organizational problems the evangelical church faced, but also provided workable techniques for circumventing those problems.

Although not the only other church futurist in the 1990s, Leonard Sweet represents the most significant for the purpose of this chapter. Sweet, in his books *Quantum Spirituality* (1991), *FaithQuakes* (1994), and *SoulTsunami*

(1999), outlined a highly influential version of church futurist thinking. Sweet is a borderline evangelical church futurist. He is a professor at Drew University and was formerly dean there ("Leonard Sweet Biography" n.d.). Dissertations from Drew run the gamut from fairly orthodox evangelical theology towards EMC theology all the way to quite liberal forms of Protestant thought.[4] However, a number of Sweet's books, including *SoulTsunami*, have been published with evangelical publishers. Moreover, Sweet has been a target for criticism because of his involvement with the Leadership Network and the EMC. Sweet represents an interesting figure in the history of modern evangelicalism because of his promotion of quantum mysticism and other Eastern systems concepts, within his works. By the 2010s, quantum mysticism and Eastern Systems theory would play a significant role in a number of new spiritual outreach efforts, including the NAR's appropriation of quantum mysticism (now well advanced), contemplative prayer, and the use of enneagrams in churches (particularly via contemplative prayer).

Quantum Theology and the Rise of Evangelical Zen

Leonard Sweet outlined the major concepts that came to define evangelical quantum mysticism in the first of his major works, the aforementioned *Quantum Spirituality: A Postmodern Apologetic* (1991). In *Quantum Spirituality*, Sweet distinguishes between a "New Light" form of spirituality, a basic shorthand for everything positive developing in spirituality, and more traditional church. The influences on Sweet's work include a number of figures that are either significant players in the New Age movement or significant influences on it, including Matthew Fox, Ken Wilber, David Bohm, and Willis Harman (Sweet 1991, xviii–ix). Sweet's work is almost totally derivative of "New Paradigm" and "Oriental Systems Discourse." Sweet embraces the emerging trend of non-linearity (Sweet 1991, 3). He shows a marked preference for New Age physics—the foundation point of quantum mysticism—by his favorable mentions of David Bohm, Fritjof Capra, and Gary Zukav (Sweet 1991, 3). According to Sweet, the "New Light apologetic's essence" was grounded in a "holistic" view of the world that embraced "planetary spirituality" (Sweet 1991, 10). Like many popularizers of quantum mysticism, Sweet engaged in gross simplifications of quantum theory, particularly the "observer" effect (Sweet 1991, 26). The work, in other words, clearly represented a form of Christian mysticism.

This point is important to understand in contextualizing Sweet's condemnation of online discernment ministries (ODMs). Sweet argues that ODMs misunderstand him and argues that ODMS have engaged in "'guilt by association" by misunderstanding his use of quotations within Quantum

Spirituality (Sweet 2007). Within the work, Sweet argues, his quotation of New Age Leaders did not necessarily imply agreement (Sweet 2007). Furthermore, Sweet notes that his faith has changed and matured since that time (Sweet 2007).

There are significant reasons, however, to question Sweet's narrative of these events. First, as already demonstrated, Sweet did indeed borrow significantly from New Age physics—indeed, this work has had to condense significantly the similarities between New Age quantum mysticism and Sweet's quantum mysticism due to space limitations. Secondly, the Acknowledgments section of *Quantum Spirituality* calls the New Light Leaders he acknowledges "personal role models" (Sweet 1991, viii). It is therefore completely understandable why ODMs would be concerned with an evangelical ministry claiming Willis Harman and Ken Wilber, clear participants in the New Age movement, as role models (see Sweet 1991, viii–ix). Moreover, despite Sweet's claims of a change of heart in his faith, his later work *SoulTsunami* was still promoting elements of Eastern systems theory and New Paradigm thinking a decade later. Here, he was using the metaphors of chaos and complexity theory, plus "chaordic leadership" (a term popularized by Dee Hock), but, as the Introduction showed, chaos and complexity theory were in part disseminated via New Age networks and Leadership Network served a similar function among evangelicals, including promoting Peter Senge, whose allegiance to Eastern Systems concepts is well known.[5] In any case, the workplace culture that Sweet was trying to justify in both *SoulTsunami* and in his work with Leadership Network could not have been understood as anything other than New Paradigm Management. This is particularly noticeable in Sweet's explicit promotion of bionomics (Sweet 1999, 81, 242–243). The church, for Sweet, must become biomimetic and so naturally Sweet approvingly quotes from Christian Schwarz, who was trying to do exactly that (Sweet 1999, 253). Sweet's explanation of Schwarz's model is highly deceptive as well, talking about how it will help "release the growth hormones through which God builds the church" without mentioning that Schwarz's thinking is rooted in the application of organizational development and biocybernetic concepts that most congregants cannot plausibly be expected to understand, bringing up questions of informed consent to congregational organizational practices (Sweet 1999, 253).

In any case, however genuine Sweet's purported change of heart was, quantum mysticism and other theological elements of Eastern systems theory play an increasingly important role within the evangelical movement. The most clear signs of quantum mysticism have occurred within the NAR, particularly the Revival Alliance, and the EMC. *The Physics of Heaven* (2012), an NAR anthology edited by Judy Franklin and Ellyn Davis, is particularly explicit in its appropriation of quantum mysticism. The book praises the healing power of dolphins, a common New Age refrain (Franklin and Davis 2012, loc. 341–347). The most important chapter in the book is chapter 12, entitled (appropriately enough) "Quantum Mysticism." Written by Ellyn Davis, the chapter outlines what Davis sees as a Christian response to quantum mysticism. Davis notes that many of the ideas promoted by New Age proponents of quantum mysticism are consistent with scripture, but notes dissent on four points: "Where God, Jesus and the Holy Spirit fit into the picture … what constitutes sin … where the Bible fits into the picture: and … what happens after we die" (Franklin and Davis 2012, loc. 1771–1778). To misquote Bateson, this is the difference that does not make a difference. Franklin practically admits as much, saying that "there is much that we [Christians] can agree on" with quantum mystics and noting the repeated arguments within *The Physics of Heaven* that "there are many precious 'God-truths' hidden in Quantum Mysticism for us [Christians] to claim as our own" (Franklin and Davis 2012, loc. 1778). The endorsements of quantum mysticism in the text represent a critical inroad of New Age thought into the NAR. Among the significant NAR leaders who are excerpted in the *Physics of Heaven* are Bill Johnson, head of Bethel Church and one of the most influential figures in the NAR today; Beni Johnson, Bill Johnson's wife; Cal Pierce, a prominent NAR advocate for healing ministry; and David Van Koevering, another leading proponent of quantum mysticism within the Charismatic movement.

There are a number of other promoters of quantum mysticism within the NAR. The most notable advocates are Patricia King, Aiko Hormann (who teaches on "quantum field miracles"), and in particular Phil Mason. Hormann is a significant advocate because of her association with Bethel's sozo healing technique (Weaver 2014, 50, 55). Hormann espouses the idea that "[the] quantum field" is "the bridge between the spirit realm and the physical and material realm" (Hormann 2015a). Jesus, according to Hormann, is a "bilocate[ed]" being, since He operated "in the spirit realm with the Father, but physically he was on this earth [when he was incarnated]" (Hormann 2015b). Such rhetoric obviously is consistent with the mystification of physics that characterizes New Age and management practices, as delineated in the Introduction. Patricia King, meanwhile, has promoted the quantum mysticism of David Van Kovering ("Quantum Healing—David Van Kovering" 2015). Phil Mason, the most prominent NAR supporter of quantum mysticism claims to be writing a "biblical response" to New Age quantum mysticism, but his book is transparently an effort to appropriate New Age quantum spirituality for the Revival Alliance (Mason 2010, 25–26). Mason's book received accolades from a number of prominent NAR figures (mostly participants in Revival Alliance), including Che Ahn, Beni Johnson, Wesley Campbell, Bill Johnson, and Rolland Baker (Rolland Baker 2010, Foreword; Bill Johnson 2010, Foreword; Mason 2010, blurbs).

The evangelical discernment site Herescope has characterized a number of modern prophetic voices as falling into what it calls a "postmodern prophetic paradigm"[6] and has expressed concern at the fusion of extreme elements of this paradigm—notably teachings connecting Nephilim to UFOS— with quantum mysticism (Discernment Research Group 2012a). While Herescope probably paints with too large a brush here, there is significant overlap between the teachings of some prophets associated with this trend of modern prophecy belief and quantum mysticism (both in its evangelical and New Age variety). For instance, author Josh Peck exhibits a fairly common quantum mystic fixation on the similarities between quantum physics and alchemy (Peck 2017, loc. 4155). Influential prophecy teacher Chuck Missler, in his book *Beyond Perception*, endorses the New Age concept that the universe may be a hologram and is much taken with David Bohm's idea of the implicate order, a favorite concept of the New Age movement (Missler 2016, loc. 865–899). Missler contends in the classic mystifying style of Christian physics popularizers, that "[t]he Bible is like a hologram. If it's illuminated by the same light that created it, we see an image of Jesus Christ" (Missler 2016, loc. 914). Despite Missler's affirmation of the holographic model, the model is probably best understood as a variant of *Naturphilosophie* and thus not primarily concerned (if not unconcerned) with upholding scientific truth claims (Hanegraff 1996, 64–68). What is ultimately concerning about Missler and other physics popularizers in the postmodern prophecy paradigm is less their questionable physics—which is not always a problem anyway, particularly with Missler (who has a fair degree of scientific training in his past)—as is their conflation of potentially racially explosive concepts with prophetic and millennialist themes. As Paul Thomas notes, popularizers of "apocalyptic alternative history" promote a view of the biblical Nephilim myth in which the Nephilim are read as a hybrid species and the creation of sinister scientific experiments (Thomas 2012, 317–319). This is an essentially alchemical reading of the Nephilim which views them as Satanic Frankenstein monsters. The writers at Herescope, though sometimes themselves prone to what might be deemed fringe beliefs by the cultural mainstream, have noted with great concern the development of this connection, which they believe may lead readily to the embrace of the "serpent seed" doctrine favored by the NAR (Discernment Research Group 2013; Discernment Research Group 2012b). As detailed in my book on the New Apostolic Reformation, the serpent seed doctrine has powerfully influenced the NAR; the concept has been used in the NAR to justify the existence of a racial elite, but with race interpreted as a spiritual rather than biological or cultural concept (Weaver 2016, 25–26, 36– 38). Because Pentecostal history intersects with the racist Christian Identity movement in some significant ways, elements of serpent seed doctrine have found their way into racist and anti–Semitic formulations concerning Reptoid extraterrestrials (Barkun 2013, 125). While such esoterica may seem far removed from the realities of everyday politics, the increasing prominence of serpent seed doctrines in racist right, Pentecostal, and UFO enthusiast circles lends a significant amount of credibility to the concerns expressed by scholars such as Thomas and internal movement critics such as the Herescope discernment group.

Critics have also raised concerns about the Eastern influences on the practice of contemplative prayer and centering prayer. This discourse is often associated with the quantum mystical tradition. The modern practice of contemplative prayer derives in large part from the teachings of Thomas Keating (Conti 1994, 1). Keating teaches what is called centering prayer, a form of prayer that can be conceptualized as a "contemporary *via negativa*" (Conti 1994, 2). Keating, according to Conti, fuses Western esoteric teachings about the "Primordial tradition" with an eclectic mixture of other ideas from inside and outside the Catholic church, including "The Carmelite mystical tradition ... transpersonal psychology, and themes in liberation theology" (Conti 6). Keating also sought to dialogue with Eastern mystics (Conti 1994, 43–44). This is in part due to Keating's desire for interfaith dialogue (Conti 1994, 125), but Keating did draw on certain Eastern spiritual ideas, notably the kundalini concept that is so central to Taoism, Buddhism, and Hinduism (Conti 1994, 43–45, 81).

Contemplative and centering prayer have gained increasing prominence in evangelical circles in recent years. These practices have been promoted in a number of books published by evangelical presses, including Adele Ahlberg Calhoun's *Spiritual Disciplines Handbook* (Calhoun 2005, passim, but especially 208), Phileena Heuertz's *Mindful Silence: The Heart of Christian Contemplation* (Phileena Heuertz 2018, Mindful passim) and Heuertz's *Pilgrimage of a Soul: Contemplative Spirituality for an Active Life* (2010) (Phileena Heuertz 2010, passim). In addition, a number of authors writing for evangelical publishers have promoted the enneagram idea, famous in the West largely as a result of esoteric teacher G.I. Gurdjieff, as a form of personality profiling. The use of the enneagram for such personality profiling has a long history in the Catholic tradition, originally deriving from Jesuit appropriations of the device (Wellbeloved 2003, 65). Representative titles in this expanding genre include Alice Fryling's *Mirror for the Soul: A Christian Guide to the Enneagram* (2017), Christopher Heuertz's *The Sacred Enneagram: Finding Your Unique Path to Spiritual Growth* (2017), Ian Morgan Cron's and Suzanne Stabile's *The Road Back to You: An Enneagram Journey to Self-Discovery* (2016) and Stabile's other title, *The Path Between Us: An Enneagram Journey to Healthy Relationships* (2017). As we saw in Chapter 3, Gurdjieff's teachings can be seen as what R. John Williams labels as a form of "Oriental Systems theory," though the relationship between Eastern systems and temporal systems concepts is complex and often—as is typical with Gurdjieff—ambiguous (R. John Williams 2016, 488–493). That a Gurdjieffian technique is now finding a ready home in evangelicalism might seem bizarre, but such syncretic fusions of Christian and esoteric tradition are increasingly common in evangelical circles. Indeed, such syncretism may ultimately be unavoidable, given the gigantic if unacknowledged influence of Western esotericism on the spiritual and cultural life of the West.[7]

A certain amount of syncretism is inevitable in any religious tradition, despite the claims to doctrinal purity that are common throughout the Western monotheistic faiths. It should be noted, too, that the Christian tradition has had its own contemplative and mystical side, particularly in the Eastern Orthodox tradition. The increasing rapprochement between Western Christianity and Eastern Orthodoxy represents an often-unacknowledged influence (particularly in discernment ministry discourse) on the respect accorded esotericism and mysticism in the Western church. While it is certainly true that much of the evangelical contemplative tradition has been strongly influenced by Eastern systems concepts, as well as Eastern approaches to temporality, discernment ministries and other evangelical critics of the contemplative tradition have often handicapped their own (often excellent) arguments against these practices by engaging in highly reductionist anti–New Age or anti–Catholic assessments of the contemplative tradition.

One other aspect of quantum mysticism in evangelicalism should be noted: There are a number of Christian science fiction authors who have endorsed or promoted variants of quantum mysticism. Quantum mysticism has a significant prehistory in Christian science fiction. Charles Williams, a prominent member of the Inklings writing group, advocated the idea of co-inherence, an idea that bears significant similarities to ideas about interconnectedness popularized by systems theorists, the New Age movement, and New Paradigm management advocates (see Lindop 2015, 311; Morrison 2007, 27–28). Thematically, Stephen Lawhead's later work, particularly the *Bright Empires* series, and almost all of Ted Dekker's science fiction, most readily showcase the pronounced influence of quantum mysticism over evangelical science fiction. Lawhead's *Bright Empires* series is a thinly veiled Teilhardian take on the concept of the multiverse, while Dekker's *Circle* series and *Paradise* trilogy embrace "mind over matter" readings of reality that are strikingly similar to New Age and contemporary Gnostic formulations of reality. In particular, Thomas Hunter, the lead character in the Circle series, is a Christian pastiche of *The Matrix*'s Neo. As Lawhead and Dekker are two of the most significant writers in evangelical science fiction today, this represents a significant trend. In addition, Ted Dekker's daughter Rachelle Dekker shows signs of verging into this territory, while Dekker's sometimes cowriter Tosca Lee shows similar preoccupations with esotericism. Like Ted Dekker and Lawhead, Rachelle Dekker and Lee are significant and skilled writers of contemporary Christian speculative fiction and thus may be pointing the way to a sea-change in the way that evangelical speculative fiction engage with quantum mysticism and Oriental Systems theory. Such mysticism, however, does face opposition within the evangelical science fiction community. Kathy Tyers and Christopher Walley have produced significant works challenging the "esotericiziation" of evangelical faith that move significantly beyond relatively simplistic depictions of esotericism in early evangelical science fiction (on Tyers, in particular, see Burnett 2014). Tyers, Walley, and a fair number of other voices in evangelical science fiction (most notably Steve Rzasa) have embraced a critical, yet often highly nuanced critique of esoteric trends in contemporary Christian culture. Whether this trend (which resembles Tolkien's negative view of esotericism more than Williams's[8]) or the quantum mystical trend pioneered by Lawhead and Dekker, will gain ascendance, is difficult to tell. But both trends speak to the continuing infusion of New Paradigm and neo-spiritual views into the wider evangelical subculture.

Far-Future Evangelical Futurism: Foresight into the Posthuman Era

After 2000, the majority of church futurists were associated with the Leadership Network, The Discovery Institute, or the EMC. As a number of these futurists have been covered in depth in previous chapters, there is no need to deal with them here. However, mainstream evangelical discourse surrounding posthumanism and transhumanism deserves some brief mention, as it is the public face that evangelicalism has emphasized in its approach to managing the future.

A number of books published by evangelicals—as well as the wider Christian Right—have addressed the problems that so-called GRIN technologies (Genetics, Robotics, Information, and Nanotechnology) (Garreau 2005, 115) present to the Christian faith. These works create an alarmist impression of GRIN technologies and their ability to disrupt future human development. Representative titles include the anthology *Cutting Edge Bioethics: A Christian Exploration of Technologies and Trends* (2002), Wesley Smith's *Consumer's Guide to a Brave New World* (2004), the anthology *Human Dignity in the Biotech Century: A Christian Vision for Public Policy* (2004), Joni Eareckson Tada's and Nigel M. De Se. Cameron's *How to be Christian in a Brave New World* (2006), and C. Ben Mitchell, et. al.'s *Biotechnology and The Human Good* (2007). The most alarmist of these works, *How to Be a Christian in a Brave New World*, gives an alchemical reading of transhumanism that resembles that of the postmodern prophetic paradigm. Joni Eareckson Tada insinuates that transhuman beings may in fact be Nephilim (Tada and Cameron

2006, 173–174). Smith's *Consumer's Guide to a Brave New World* also brings up the specter of controversial philosopher Joseph Fletcher, who advocated the creation of a chimeric slave species, thus replicating the alchemical reading present in Tada and Cameron's works (Wesley J. Smith 2004, 20). The most responsible of these works is *Cutting Edge Bioethics*, as well as the aforementioned *Are We Spiritual Machines?*. In *Cutting Edge Bioethics*, a number of contributors try to realistically appraise high-tech advances from a Christian perspective. However, much of this assessment is hurt by highly simplistic renderings of recent developments in hi-tech industries, with the description of cybernetics provided by C. Christopher Hook being of particularly poor quality (Hook 2002, 52–70). Such simplistic analysis has led secular commentator Antony Alumkal to argue that Christian Right bioethical discourse is significantly underdeveloped (Alumkal 2017, loc. 2319–2337). Alumkal is an excellent scholar, but he does not appear to be cognizant of the possibility that such underdevelopment may be intentional, rather than accidental. As noted in Chapters 5 and Chapter 6, the reaction of evangelicals to "high tech" industries is not simply reactionary; in many cases, the Christian Right works in concert with these industries or even attempts to make significant inroads into their activities. Having rank-and-file evangelicals informed on biotech issues may thus not serve the long-term policy objectives of movement leadership.

Christian speculative fiction has also obviously influenced discourse on posthumanism within the Christian community. Here, the Inklings are the obvious major influence, particularly C.S. Lewis's bioethical classic *The Abolition of Man* (1943), which represents a work of general, not merely evangelical, historical significance. Most of the best subsequent evangelical science fiction that has engaged in debates surrounding posthumanism or bioethics is either directly or indirectly indebted to the Inklings. Such trends, for instance, are particularly strong in Steve Rzasa's *Face of the Deep* series and Chris Walley's *Lamb Among the Stars* trilogy. Both works strongly resemble Lewis's *Abolition of Man* in their concerns over the increasingly instrumentalist and transactional nature of human interactions. These Christian speculative fiction authors tend to engage far more seriously with secular posthuman and transhuman ideology than contemporary bioethicists. From the standpoint of Rzasa's and Walley's work, what is truly troubling about the increasing tendency towards instrumentalization in modern culture is not how it perverts physical nature, but how it perverts human nature itself.

In a real sense, this book ends as it began. It was Chris Walley, author of the *Lamb Among the Stars* trilogy, who convinced me years ago to reevaluate the techno-utopianism of transhumanism. Like many techno-utopian academics of my generation, I became—and remain—disillusioned about the dream palaces of future bliss that transhumanism seeks to tempt the world with. Academic Joel Dinerstein has wisely observed that "the posthuman is an escape from the panhuman," the latter being the "creolized" multiracial and multicultural identity that Dinerstein hopes humanity, as a species, can eventually aspire to (Dinerstein 2006, 592). Walley's work represents one of the most sincere attempts by an evangelical science fiction writer to come to terms with such panhuman aspirations. What neither Walley nor I anticipated, however, was how thoroughly the instrumentalized assumptions that characterize the posthuman ethos have seeped into evangelicalism. The evangelical embrace of both Silicon Valley and contemporary management culture have in large part paved the way for this conjunction of influences. In the modern world, sometimes church is stranger than science fiction. And the dreams churches offer may turn out to be little more than fantasy, so long as evangelicalism fails to acknowledge both the social benefits and the social costs extracted from the Christian Right's continued embrace of managerial culture. That embrace can be either a catalyst for humane social transformation or a tool of social control. Which direction evangelical churches will take their managerial culture, however, remains veiled behind mists of their own making.

Glossary

Californian Ideology—The Californian ideology arose in the Bay Area as a fusion of countercultural ideas and pro-computer empowerment rhetoric and was popularized by key segments of the counterculture, especially supporters of Whole Earth discourse (Barbrook and Cameron 1996, 1, 3; Turner 2002, 25, 34–35). The ideology combined its countercultural ideals with technological utopian beliefs derived from "the convergence of media, computing and telecommunications" (Barbrook and Cameron 1996, 3). Proponents of the Californian ideology within the evangelical community included George Gilder and Kevin Kelly. The Californian ideology also influenced the ideas of the Leadership Network. This book also refers to this discourse as cyber-libertarianism.

Chaos Theory—Chaos theory refers to systems whose processes look random, but whose actual operation takes place as the result of "'precise scientific laws'" (Lorenz 1979 qtd. in Burnes 2005, 78; Burnes 2005, 78). The processes chaos theory references are inevitably dynamic, persistently and irreversibly altering themselves in an evolutionary fashion (Burnes 2005, 78). Chaos theory is frequently invoked by participants in the EMC.

Charismatics—In typical evangelical parlance, Charismatics are usually seen as Pentecostals-lite, that is, the less radical element of the wider Charismatic/Pentecostal movement. In reality, however, if one is defining Charismatics by the more technical sense of those who indulged in the Charismatic Renewal, the exact opposite impression emerges. In general, Charismatic is used in the popular sense of the term (or alternately to refer to the entire Charismatic/Pentecostal movement), since it's so ubiquitous, but readers should remember that denominational Pentecostalism is in many ways less radical than its Charismatic descendants. Regardless, if one is talking about the Charismatic movement, Charismatic Renewal, or Pentecostalism all three groups are characterized by a strong belief in the gifts of the spirit, such as speaking in tongues, prophecy, and the casting out of demons.

Church Futurism—Church Futurism is a form of futurist discourse, found in both mainline and evangelical churches, that like much—if not all—of secular futurism, seeks to render the future controllable (see Andersson 3 on this aspect of secular futurism). Secular futurism has tended to put its faith in quantitative survey research as well as "computer led simulation and modeling" (Andersson 2018, 3). Church futurist research has tended to mainly utilize quantitative survey data without resort to extensive computer modeling. Much of this discourse is characterized by the application of techniques similar to those deployed in trends analysis.

Church Growth Movement—The church growth movement was a movement pioneered by evangelical thinker Donald McGavran, which sought to maximize the growth of evangelical churches. McGavran concluded that the key to doing this was by mobilizing large "people movements" by which people made collective decisions to commit their community to Christianity (Holvast 17, 18). Equally important to McGavran was the homogenous unit principle, defined by NAR and church growth guru C. Peter Wagner as the "ability for non–Christians to convert without having to cross 'racial, linguistic or class barriers'" (Wagner 2010, 109; Weaver 2016, 262). The church growth movement played a crucial role in the spread of managerial ideology within evangelicalism and even, to a lesser extent, within mainline Protestantism.

Church Health Movement—The church health movement is a movement within primarily evangelical churches that focuses, contra the church growth movement, on qualitative improvements to church life, as opposed to quantitative increases to church membership. It should be noted that some critics of the church health movement, such as Gary McIntosh, have charged that the church health movement largely just rebranded church growth rhetoric (McIntosh 2004b, 22), a point that this book largely concurs with.

Closed System—A system that is resistant to incorporating external input into its internal processes as means of adapting. Such systems are usually self-regulated through negative feedback loops.

Closed Systems Church Strategy—An organizational strategy where the management places strategical constraints on the church's growth.

Complexity Theory—Complexity science is a field, really a set of scientific fields, devoted to studying how "systems adapt, evolve, and self-organize not in spite of crisis but through the very means of crisis" (Cooper 2011, 373; Burnes 73). Complexity theory and various related scientific discourses, such as chaos theory, form the bedrock of the so-called "'new science'" or "'new sciences'" (Doornenbal 2012, 147). These new sciences are characterized by a rejection of so-called Newtonian science in favor of a more holistic approach to understanding the world (Doornenbal 2012, 147). Complexity theory, like the New Sciences generally, plays a major role in discussions of church governance within both the Leadership Network and the EMC.

Cyber-Libertarianism—See Californian Ideology.

Cybernetics—Cybernetics is a science of "control and communication in the animal and the machine" (Wiener 1948, Title Page). Cybernetics's concept of organismic biological thinking differed from Bertalanffy's General Systems Theory (GST) in its willingness to elaborate on, rather than replace, "reductionist and mechanistic" scientific thinking. Cybernetics sought to apply ideas of "feedback, communication and control" across multiple types of systems (Hammond 1997, 67). Like general systems theory, cybernetics has found application in evangelical and mainline churches, though applications of GST to church life tend to have been more dominant.

Cyborg Sciences—The cyborg sciences is a term utilized by Philip Mirowski to refer to a number of disciplines, including (but not limited to), "information theory, molecular biology ... computer science, artificial intelligence, operations research, systems theory ... sociobiology, artificial life, and ... game theory" that "shared an incubation period" with cybernetics (Mirowski 2002, 12). This book uses the term in roughly the same sense, showing how the cyborg sciences were popularized in evangelical churches. In addition, this book extends this analysis to fields such as complexity theory and futurism, which shared similar scientific preoccupations (and were also utilized by evangelicals and mainline Protestants).

Emergent Missional Conversation (EMC)—There is no universally accepted definition of the EMC. In general, churches that adhere to the model emphasize flexibility, the importance of community, decentralized power structures, a fondness for technology, and postmodern hermeneutics (Doornenbal 2012, 3, 10, 12–13). EMC churches have been at the forefront of promoting digital technology, systems theory, and complexity theory within both evangelical and mainline congregations.

Feedback—The modification, adjustment, or control of a process or system (as a social situation or a biological mechanism) by a result or effect of the process, especially by a difference between a desired and an actual result (O.E.D.).

Feedback Loops—Feedback loops are the part of a system that "can enhance or buffer changes that occur in a system" ("Feedback Loops"). Positive feedback loops "enhance or amplify changes; this tends to move a system away from its equilibrium state and make it more unstable." Negative feedback loops "tend to dampen or buffer changes; this tends to hold a system to some equilibrium state making it more stable" ("Feedback Loops"). In general, church growth ideology, with its emphasis on quantitative growth, privileged positive feedback. The church health movement's position has been more complex. Its espousal of open systems ideology would normally align the movement with ideologies that emphasize governance via positive feedback mechanisms. However, the church health movement's emphasis on qualitative over quantitative improvements to church life position the movement as one that has more use for the application of negative feedback loops than the church growth movement. The church health movement and EMC see permanent unrestrained growth of churches as unsustainable. This position is often informed by the same considerations concerning unrestrained population growth that characterized the Club of Rome's *Limits to Growth* (1972) report. Some proponents of these models, such as Christian Schwarz and Howard Snyder, have developed their application of these ideas directly from ecological economics and other environmental discourses that admit the reality of ecological limits to growth. However, the degree to which such models are applied to actual economic life, as opposed to the life of the church, varies. Snyder, for instance, is more consistent on this score than other church health and EMC authors, notably Leonard Sweet, whose support for a bionomic model of the economy (i.e., unlimited economic growth and the positive feedback implicit in such a system) is a transparent justification for unrestrained free market capitalism

Fordism and post-Fordism—Post-Fordist scholarship posits a transition from a Fordist production "regime of accumulation" which emphasized the "industrial, assembly-line factory pioneered by.... Henry Ford ... with its associated institutions of mass consumption and the national welfare state" to a post–Fordist ideology which centers on the application of "cybernetic technologies, new management techniques, transnational supply chains and neoliberal governance" (Dyer-Witherford 2017, 24). Post-Fordist or Toyotist practices within the church are exemplified by organizations such as the Leadership Network.

Fundamentalism—Fundamentalism was a conservative Protestant movement that, during its period of national prominence during the 1920s, opposed theological modernism and evolutionary theory (Marsden 2006, 3–4). Detwiler lists "insistence on the Virgin Birth, the miracles of the Bible, the bodily resurrection of Jesus, and the power of Jesus' sacrificial death to remove the stain of sin from us," along with personal conversion, as the main markers of fundamentalism (Detwiler 1999, 151). Fundamentalists are chiefly distinguishable by their wholehearted support for biblical inerrancy (in the original Biblical texts), creationism, and traditional as opposed to higher critical hermeneutical strategies.

General Systems Theory—GST is a science that seeks to understand the interconnections between systems and their environments (Hammond 1997, 19–20). In short, it is an attempt to create a science of systems that seeks to discover the principles governing all systems (Jackson 2000, 52). It has had a profound influence on both evangelical and mainline appropriations of management theory, influencing church organizational gurus such as Christian Schwarz, Carl George, and Norman Shawchuck.

Homogenous Unit Principle (HUP)—This central principle of the church growth movement, advocated by the movement's leading guru Donald McGavran, contends that people "like to become Christians without crossing racial linguistic or class barriers" (McGavran 1990, loc. 64) and were attracted to churches where the membership physically, culturally, and/or linguistically resembled them (Rainer 1993, 255; Wagner 2010, 108–109).

Mainline Protestant—For the purpose of this book, mainline Protestants are defined as members of the seven core mainline denominations, who generally but not universally subscribe to politically liberal and theologically modernist beliefs. Mainline Protestants, like evangelicals, have adapted significant parts of secular management theory, systems theory, and complexity theory.

Management by Objectives/Ministry by Objectives (MBO)—MBO is a theory of management that charges that managers should motivate their employees by a task-emphasis rather than direction from external authority. MBO advocates have historically walked a line between giving employees some autonomy and ensuring that the managerial class had the ultimate say in decision making (Wren and Bedain 2009, 424; Waring 1991, 88). Early church management theories often borrowed from concepts derived from management by objectives (MBO) (Roddam 1997, 136), and the influence of MBO—both as a management ideology and a social theory—can still be felt in much modern church organizational literature, particularly that developed by the Leadership Network.

Managerialism—There is no universally held to definition of managerialism. However, for the purpose of this work, I build off of the research of Jean Isabel Matthews, who contends that managerialism "generates the notion that organizational order ceases to be pre-ordained and is the arena for management intervention and control" (Matthews 2000, 7). This notion is centered in the belief "that systems are controllable and should be controlled," leading to a "machine like perspective of the organization and a partiality for cybernetic and ideological philosophies of management" (Matthews 2000, 7). This book argues that managerialism, along with its "partiality for cybernetic and ideological philosophies of management," characterizes large aspects of Christian management ideology as well.

Multisite churches—A multisite church is a single individual church that gathers at multiple different locations for its service. At its most basic, a multisite church is essentially a franchisable church. Multisite churches have played an increasingly important role within Protestantism, particularly among evangelicals. The Leadership Network has played a particularly significant role in promoting the multisite concept (Smietana 2005, 61; Frye 2011, 110–115).

Neo-evangelicalism—Neo-evangelicals are characterized by a "conversion experience" similar to other evangelicals, but would not (necessarily) have the hardline position on inerrancy and creationism that fundamentalists would have, nor the emphasis on spiritual gifts that is a part of Charismatic and sometimes Holiness practice (Detwiler 153). The term is a nebulous one in many ways and the rule of thumb that an evangelical "was [once defined as] anyone who identified with Billy Graham" (Marsden 2006, 234) still holds some validity even today.

Neoliberalism—Neoliberalism is an economic ideology characterized by support for "strong private property rights, free markets, and free trade" in the ideological interest of creating "individual entrepreneurial freedom" (David Harvey 2005, 2). In neoliberal ideology, the state serves as a bulwark for the nation's currency and as a support for national defense. The state also plays a significant role in shaping judicial policy. However, intervention into the market is generally frowned upon (David Harvey 2005, 2; Slobodian 6).

Network (computing)—A system of computers and peripherals that are able to communicate with each other ("Network" Webster).

Network (people)—A group of people who exchange information and contacts for professional or social purposes ("Network" Oxford)

New Apostolic Reformation (NAR)—The New Apostolic Reformation is a movement of evangelicals, primarily from the Charismatic tradition, who seek to restore the role of the apostles to contemporary church life. In practice, what this means is a different vision of church ecclesiology, focusing on relational networks over close denominational affiliations and controlled through the natural charisma and authority invested in the apostle (on the point of relational networking, see Holvast 159). Holvast relates that in the NAR, one is not "led by a group but by an individual apostle. It was this divinely appointed apostle as opposed to a board or presbytery, a democratic vote or institution who was seen bearing responsibility for making decisions and guiding adherents" (Holvast 2009, 159).

New Calvinism—New Calvinism is a contemporaneous form of Reformed Theology that places a strong emphasis on gender complementarianism and a greater Reformed emphasis on the gifts of the Spirit. New Calvinists also tend to be more attuned to digital technology than other members of the Reformed movement and have strongly embraced the idea of church networking.

New Paradigm Management—A form of management that emphasizes the importance of "soft-skills" and employs the rhetoric of both the "New Science" and New Age scientific concepts (Thrift 2005, 41, 63). New Paradigm Management began to have a significant influence on the evangelical movement in the 1990s due to the promotion of New Paradigm managerial ideas within the Leadership Network.

New Public Management—New Public Management (NPM) is a form of management that emphasizes "administrative efficiency, effectiveness, and accountability" (Steger and Roy, 2010, 13). NPM practices are mirrored within contemporary church governance practices as well.

Open System—A system that incorporates external input to help regulate its internal processes. Such systems typically self-regulate through positive feedback loops and are more likely to experience growth than closed systems.

Open Systems Church Strategy—An organizational strategy where the management places no practical constraints on the church's growth.

Oriental Systems Theory—Oriental Systems Theory is a form of systems theory that R. John Williams contrasts with the "computationalist, rationalist" cybernetics tradition. Oriental Systems Theory, contra the cybernetics tradition, emphasizes "narratological, avant-garde," quasi-mystical thinking that is generally indebted to Eastern thought in some way (R. John Williams 2016, 477–478). Some aspects of contemporary church life, such as contemplative prayer, the influence of enneagram personality testing, and quantum mysticism, show the clear influence of Oriental Systems thinking. I use the term Oriental Systems Theory in this text as a synonym for neospiritual and New Paradigm management practices. New Paradigm churches represent a slightly different phenomena, but many practices of New Paradigm churches do overlap with New Paradigm management and neo-spiritual organizational practice.

Parachurch—This book follows Rachel Tabachnick's parsimonious and accurate definition of parachurch groups as "religious organizations not associated with a particular denomination" (Tabachnick 2008). Parachurch organizations have been particularly influential in the evangelical movement and account for the movement's early adoption of networked organizational forms.

Pentecostalism—A major subset of modern Christianity characterized by a strong belief in the gifts of the spirit, such as speaking in tongues, prophecy, the casting out of demons, etc. Pentecostalism can most productively be contrasted with Charismatic belief by pointing out Pentecostalism's stronger allegiances to traditional denominational structures, something that's becoming less and less a characteristic of Charismatic practice. Charismatic spirituality and ecclesiology also tend to be more ecumenical than traditional Pentecostalism, so long as the groups the Charismatic church allies with reflect conservative moral values.

Quantum Mysticism—Quantum Mysticism represents a discourse, initially popular primarily in New Age circles, which emphasized the mixing of ideas from quantum physics with mystical, primarily Eastern, spiritual concepts. As a discourse, quantum mysticism tends to privilege "holistic and vitalistic" interpretations of the natural universe over "mechanism, determinism and/or reductionism" (Asprem 2013, 260–261; Burwell 2013, 354–355). Over the last twenty years, quantum mysticism has proven increasingly popular in evangelical communities as well, particularly in the NAR and EMC.

Rational Choice Theory (RCT)—RCT is a form of decision science that advances a theory of human agency in which "rational agents" display a "consistent set of preferences and act to obtain that which they most prefer" (Amadae 2003, 5). RCT emphasizes the importance of individuals motivated by "self-interest" though it takes into account individuals' "altruistic preferences" as well (Amadae 2003, 5–6) RCT can be used to describe, understand, and foresee the activities of purported rational agents (Amadae 2003, 5–6). While there are relatively few references to RCT and game theory in church growth or church management literature, the fundamental assumptions of these fields regarding human nature are reflected through much of the church growth movement's (CGM), church health movement's (CHM), EMC movement's, and Leadership Network's approach to church governance. In particular, most of these movements, particularly the church growth movement and the Leadership Network, share the ideological preference of neoliberalism and RCT for modeling human agency based on noncooperative assumptions.

Reformed Christianity—Reformed Christianity is a theological system that is much too complex to simply and neatly define. However, in popular evangelical usage today, it typically refers to those evangelicals who draw their theological inspiration from the "teachings of John Calvin" (Detwiler 1999, 154), or, much more rarely, one of the other early Reformed leaders, such as Guillaume Farel. Opponents of Reformed Christianity often simplify its core doctrines to simply a belief in predestination or the famous, and frequently misused, TULIP designation (Total depravity, Unconditional election, Limited atonement, Irresistible grace, and Perseverance of the saints). However, Reformed beliefs go beyond such simplifications. As Molly Worthen notes, the Reformed tradition focused on "the depravity of humankind, the awesome sovereignty of God, and the Christian mandate to transform earthly society according to God's command" (Worthen 2013, loc. 276). Central to most modern Reformed thought (outside of now mainline Reformed denominations), is a strong belief in the value of pastoral care, a firm belief in the value of church discipline, and a preoccupation with correct ecclesiology.

Self-Organization—The ability of systems to produce order through the utilization of a few simple "order-generating rules." These rules allow for a finite amount of chaos, while still promoting a relative amount of stability for system (Burnes 2005, 80). The idea of self-organization plays a prominent role in the EMC (Doornenbal 2012, 150), as well as among many promoters of team ministry.

Shepherding movement—The shepherding movement, sometimes called the discipleship movement, put a particular emphasis on "accountability and submission to church leaders." Churches were centralized under a "pyramid-like authority structure," with progressively higher levels of shepherds, submitting to progressively even higher levels of leadership above them. There were widespread complaints of abuse and cultic manipulation against the shepherding movement, which continues to this day. Two of the major shepherding leaders were also major leaders within the deliverance "movement," namely, Derek Prince and Don Basham (Balmer 2002, 523–524). Shepherding practice significantly influenced the NAR and the memory of shepherding has significantly shaped how evangelical leaders deal with church governance issues.

Small Group Movement—Within evangelicalism, the small group movement refers to a movement within evangelical churches that focused on the providing of church social services, recreational activities, therapy, and numerous other aspects of social life in relatively tiny groups of people (typically no more than 10 or 15 people). The small group movement played a crucial role in the development of church growth and church health ideology.

Spiritual Mapping—A movement, primarily among evangelicals and "neo-Pentecostals," "that specialized in the use of religious techniques to wage a territorial spiritual war against unseen non-human beings" (Holvast 2009, 1).

System—There are many ways of defining systems. This book utilizes a definition of systems used by Debora Hammond, which notes that a system is "a set of relationships between discrete things which together form some kind of coherent pattern and/or whole that is capable of maintaining itself through time" (Hammond 1997, 36).

Taylorism—Taylorism is the name for a set of managerial practices, as well as a management ideology, that emphasizes on creating harmony between management and labor via setting a "common productive goal." Taylorism claims to be non-ideological, but in fact emphasizes the "naturalness of capitalism." Within Taylorist ideology, the good of company and society are emphasized primarily via an emphasis on "productive growth and efficiency" which can be measured apolitically and dispassionately using "scientific calculations" that appealed to economic rationalism (Waring 1991, 11–12; Sheldrake 2002, 16–17). Taylorism, though still often the dominant management ideology, today is often masked under the rhetoric of the ostensibly more progressive human relations school (which goes under various other names today, such as Theory Y management or Humanistic Management). Taylorism played a prominent role in the development of bureaucratic structures in both evangelical and (especially) mainline Protestant churches.

Toyotism—Toyotism is a management ideology and practice characterized by "just in time" supply systems which help reduce inventory sizes, better quality control practices that ideally lead to "near zero defects"; better resource allocation; greater worker involvement in the production process; particularly through the incorporation of ideas of teamwork; and "flat" governance structures (Castells 2010a, 169). Churches often follow Toyotist organizational principles in surprising ways, particularly after the triumph of the new paradigm church organizational structure in the 1990s.

Whole Systems Discourse—The Whole Systems Discourse is a body of thought, most famously articulated via Stewart Brand and the *Whole Earth Catalog*, that sought to promote a view of nature and technology as harmonious, rather than in conflict. Stewart Brand, the primary articulator of the discourse, sought to legitimate forms of technology which he believed could productively interact with their natural environment. Ironically, this discourse became a central ideological underpinning of neoliberal ideology in the 1990s. Evangelicals, particularly George Gilder and Kevin Kelly, played a significant role in advancing this re-articulation of Brand's originally counterculutral vision.

Chapter Notes

Preface

1. See, for instance, James Delingpole's hyperbolic comparison of Adam Curtis to David Icke, which is available at: https://www.spectator.co.uk/2016/10/gloriously-compulsive-and-maddening-adam-curtiss-hypernormalisation-reviewed/.
2. See for instance, S.M. Amadae's account of game theory's influence on modern neoliberalism in *Prisoners of Reason*, which almost entirely concurs with the analysis of Curtis in *The Trap*.
3. These disagreements center mainly on his adoption of what Peter Watkins characterizes as the "monoform." On the monoform, see Watkins "The Media Crisis."

Introduction

1. For instructive insights into mainline Protestant debates about the nature of liberal theology, see Gary Dorrien's *Social Ethics in the Making: Interpreting an American Tradition* (2011), particularly his extended treatment of Christian Realism in Chapter 4.
2. See, for instance, Murphy, on this score, who highlights that such powerful denominations as the Episcopal Church, the Presbyterian Church USA, Unitarians, and the United Church of Christ have among the highest levels of education of most religious or non-groups, including atheists.
3. See, for instance McIntosh 2009, 105–106.
4. For an overview of the concept of institutional isomorphism, see Paul J. Dimaggio and Walter W. Powell, "The Iron Cage Revisited: Instiutional Isomorphism and Collective Rationality in Organizational Fields," 147–160.
5. On the public's preference for mystified physics, see Leane 2007, 24–25

Chapter 1

1. Later laboratories were modeled on the Group and Life Laboratory. See Braun 1960, 223.
2. For concision, S. David Moore is hereafter referred to as Moore, unless otherwise noted.
3. An important influence on the YFC, though not a founding member. See Hunsicker 1998. 342.
4. See Wagner 1999, 155–180, on the need for contextualized worship.
5. Note that Yeakley is talking specifically about discipling in the Churches of Christ, but his comments are consistent with other forms of shepherding practice as well.
6. Note Walker 1998, 94 in which he contends that British Restorationism in its entirety held to the SM model.
7. Note that Kay makes this point specifically about the house church movement, which he sees as heavily influenced by American shepherding but not necessarily synonymous with discipling practice writ large. My own view, however, is closer to that of Andrew Walker, who sees shepherding as characteristic of both the American shepherding movement and the British house church movement. Kay's contention that the FLF did not directly preside over the British apostles seems plausible enough, however, and thus I would contend that Walker's decision to view the two movements as separate parts of a wider movement

is the most plausible means of reconciling these viewpoints. In any case, Kay believes that shepherding and discipling was central to at least the R1 half of the British house church networks. See Walker 1998, 94 and Kay 2007, 32, 195–197.

8. For examples of the cell multiplication idea, see Patterson and Scoggins 2002, 210 and Comiskey 1999, 48–50.

9. On George's views of "limits to growth" concepts as applied to church growth, see George and Bird 1993, 129–181.

10. It should be remembered that George was a prominent advocate of the church growth movement and therefore quite sympathetic to the idea of "seeker-sensitive" churches.

Chapter 2

1. See, in particular, Christian Schwarz's *Natural Church Development: A Guide to Eight Essential Qualities of Healthy Churches* (1996). Schwarz's work will be covered in greater detail in Chapter 3.

2. PPS would later evolve into the Critical Path Method [CPM], which would have an important influence on the construction industry. CPM would be utilized to complete large construction and engineering projects in numerous settings during the 1960's and 1970's, where the ability of the method to handle large-scale endeavors was very much valued. See Camilleri 2016, 6–7.

3. There are numerous examples of this view of feedback and evaluation in church growth and church management literature. Reeves and Jenson advocate the use of Dayton's approach (Reeves and Jenson 1984, 35–36). Wagner, who usually knows a good thing when he sees it, also embraces this model (Wagner 1987, 95). R. Henry Migliore, whose work straddles the church growth and church management literature, supports the continuous use of evaluation and feedback as well (Migliore 1988, 18–19).

4. For paradigmatic examples of church effectiveness literature, see George Barna's *The Habits of Highly Effective Churches* [1999], Christian A. Schwarz's *Natural Church Development: A Guide to Eight Essential Qualities of Healthy Churches* [2000], and Lyle Schaller's *Concepts and Skills for Leaders Getting Things Done* [1986]. Rick Warren's *The Purpose Driven Church* (1995) has clear affinities with the institutional effectiveness literature, as does Walt Kallestad's *Total Quality Ministry*, which is based on TQM models. Most church health literature, with the exception of some extremely spiritualized models, appears to draw from the concepts of "institutional effectiveness" to one degree or another.

Chapter 3

1. I am quoting from the digital review copy of Astrom's work, as its explanation of feedback is somewhat simpler than the final version. Please see the print copy for a more detailed description of the concept.

2. See Hammond 1997, 236–237 on Miller's conflicted thinking on centralization.

3. Nielsen notes that though the population crisis was framed in "global terms," Osborn and Vogt were not averse to addressing America's own issues with population growth. See Nielsen 1997, 167–168.

4. Warner rejects what she considers a "simplistic identification between the projects of political and environmental imperialism," a position that I can understand, but nevertheless partially reject in the following sections. I would be the first to admit, however, that the imperialism implicit in some Club of Rome and evangelical approaches to environmental management is not necessarily the norm for either political actors or environmental activists. See Warner 2005, 99.

5. For one thing, Peccei was too much of a technological optimist to fit entirely into a Malthusian worldview. See Moll 1991, 54.

6. The reader should note, however, that while Leeuwen in her article "North American Evangelicalism and the Social Sciences: A Historical and Critical Appraisal" points out that it is in the academic social sciences, rather than applied social sciences, that one tends to find the most Christian perspectivalists. See Mary Van Leeuwen 1988, 194–203.

7. James Bragan makes a somewhat similar point in his thesis "The Educational Role of the Church for a Just and Sustainable Society," when referring to the tendency of the CGM to blindly favor pro-growth policies solely for the sake of growth. Bragan understandably saw this tendency in the early CGM as reflective of the church's surrender to a consumeristic mindset. See Bragan 48.

8. For examples of such critiques, as well as a variety of reasons for them, see J.B. Watson Jr., and Walter H. Schalen, Jr., "'Dining with the Devil': The Unique Secularization of American Churches," which concentrates on the representative par excellence of the markets-to-growth model of evangelical churches, the megachurch.

9. Harman was responsible for directing the rather bizarre Institute of Noetic Sciences from 1977 until 1996. The Institute is famous for its influence on author Dan Brown. It should be noted that connections between such respected institutions as SRI and fringe organizations like the Institute of Noetic Sciences were not necessarily uncommon in the 1960's and 1970's. Esalen's connection to various dubious aspects of the counterculture is perhaps the most well-known example of such mainstream-fringe connections. See Erdmann 2009, 34 and Kleiner 2008, 155–185, 226–268 passim.

10. Examples of discernment sites that have warned about the Consultations include Herescope and Crossroad. See Discernment Research Group 2005, and Kjos, n.d., "Mysticism and Global Mind Change."

11. Note that I do not reject every discernment ministry criticism of the New Age influences that the conference helped promote among evangelicals. I simply lack the space and time to confirm or debunk them. The (rather extensive) evidence I have collected leads me to conclude that at least some of the concerns of discernment ministries are, from their perspective, valid on this score, if exaggerated. Such criticisms tend to be more accurate when dealing with the aftereffects of the Consultations than when dealing with the Consultations themselves.

12. It should be noted that the focus on images at both the Consultations on the Future and the Continuing Consultation on the Future may in part explain the presence of Harman as well. In his address to the first Consultation, Leighton Ford makes reference to Fred Polak's research. Polak is the author of *The Image of the Future* (1961; English abridged edition 1973) (Ford 1978 31). Polak's work played a significant role in shaping the *Changing Images of Man*, which Ted Newland alludes to at the first Consultation (Fosbrook 2017, 131). Polak's view of futurism emphasized the importance of creating powerful eidetic imagery to mold people's opinions (Polak 1973, 11–15). Polak's work can be read as simply a sophisticated form of propaganda theory, a point that can also be made about *The Changing Images of Man*. This does not mean, of course, that either work was intended to serve such purposes, merely that their focus on eidetic imagery lend these works fairly easily to such uses. Interestingly, Polak's work, much like *The Changing Images of Man*, is full of references to Western Esoteric traditions (Polak 1973, 6–7, 48–49, 82).

13. On the organizational apparatus streamlining, please refer to Chapter 4.

14. Note that the program details were almost exactly identical in Zenefski's description and in that provided by Schell in Wagner, so the Total Church Model in both was still obviously a cybernetic model, even though Schell does not mention this in Wagner.

15. Note that while feedback in church subsystems often refers to verbal feedback, Schell is almost certainly using the technical definition of feedback that cybernetics employs, which incorporates not only verbal feedback, but other forms of information feedback. Most church marketing and church growth literature is aware of and utilizes both aspects of the feedback concept.

16. It is now closed. See http://www.gmi.org/

17. Note that while the modern planned change model was developed by Lewin, it only became fully articulated after his death. Erwich fails to note that Lewin died in 1947. On Lewin and planned change, see Cummings and Worley 23–24.

18. Note that Logan does not acknowledge the systems influence here, but his strategic planning model is clearly based on feedback principles as anyone who is conversant with management theory would instantly recognize.

19. Peters has been a significant influence on evangelical thinkers. See for instance Logan 1990, 118.

20. Representative examples of the use of the diffusion model in EMC writings include Hirsch and Ferguson 2011, loc. 1391–1396, Dreier 2007, 208–209, and Alan Roxburgh and Romanuk 2006, 80.

21. This is not to be confused with the Emerging Church movement, which does nevertheless share a similar fascination with the concept of emergence and emergent systems.

22. Also see Hirsch 2006, 286 on the

costs and benefits of mechanistic views of leadership.

23. The implication in most EMC material I have read is that the sum of this self-organizational ability will be greater than its constituent parts, a common assumption within holistic thinking.

24. Note that Hirsch specifically refers to this problem as one of "command and control."

25. Hirsch refers here to the biblical Jesus Movement, not the modern Jesus Movement, which confusingly use the same terminology.

26. See also Doornenbal 2012, 175 for a short discussion on Ward's place in the EMC.

27. See Doornenbal 2012, 147, 162 on Wheatley's influence in the EMC.

Chapter 4

1. See McKelvey 1999, 1–9 and Hindle 2008, 31 on the popularity of discontinuity concepts

2. On Gangel's relatively complex views of bureaucracy, see Gangel 1997, 86–90

3. On this score, see Russell 2014, Chapters 5–8 passim.

4. Interestingly, the Drucker Foundation, which Buford led [see Frye 2011, 108], also hosted influential cyber libertarian supporter Esther Dyson at one of their conventions. Leadership Network recommended the convention. See "Leadership Network Recommends" Vol 4.5, 7.

5. On the centrality of the "relational" paradigm in the EMC, see Doornenbal 2012, 11.

6. On the resemblance of church planting to biblical models of starting new churches, see Ebbie C. Smith 2000, 202–203.

7. Keller even refers to the specific theo-environmental systems that churches are a part of as "gospel ecosystems." See Keller 2012, 374.

8. For other New Calvinists endorsement of Gladwell, see Hansen 2013, as well as Wax 2007. Gladwell has also been a speaker at the important evangelical Q conferences (see Gladwell "Legitimacy" n.d.)

9. Other examples of CP and CPN advocates of diffusion principles are numerous. For instance, David Garrison, a pioneer in international church planting, was clearly aware of the importance of developing tipping points for cultural diffusion (Garrison 2004, 22). Neil Cole, Alan Hirsch, and Dave Ferguson, important voices in the EMC as well as universally respected church planting advocates, are all strong supporters of this idea as well (Cole and Helfer 2012, 147–148).

10. For Wagner's view of seminaries, see Wagner 1999a, 222–239.

11. On multisites and debates about streaming, see Daley. As I will demonstrate in the next chapter, many of the most significant debates about evangelicalism's relationship to technology are occurring not among creationists, ID advocates, and their opponents, but among ministry tech enthusiasts.

12. See Sargeant 1996, 281–282 on the phenomenon of teaching churches.

13. Note that church planting and the multi-site idea are not mutually exclusive models. See Frye 2011, 274–279.

Chapter 5

1. On this score, see economist Philip Mirowski's comments to Adam Curtis in the documentary *The Trap*.

2. For a description of how the ideology of the electronic frontier helped further conservative business interests, see Frank 2000, 78–87, which details how cyberspace became the utopia of "market populism," that is the belief that markets "in addition to being mediums of exchange" were also "mediums of consent" which "expressed the popular will more articulately and more meaningfully than did mere elections" (Frank 2000, xiv). As Frank notes, there was nothing inevitable about this reactionary reading of the net (see Frank 2000, 78).

3. For Fukuyama's influence on the Christian's right's views of biotechnology see Fukuyama's *Our Posthuman Future*. To see Fukuyama's intersection with the Christian Right, I refer the reader to Cromatarie 2002; Hertz 2002; Hertz 2001; and Wesley J. Smith. Fukuyama was also on the President's Council for Bioethics from 2001–2004 (See "Francis Fukuyama" N.D). The Council was widely seen as a tool of both Christian conservatives and the neoconservative movement with which it had allied. See, for instance, Meltzer 2008, as well as Bibbee and Viens 2007.

4. Kelly has claimed to be a Christian in a recent article published by the *Atlantic*

Monthly. According to the *Atlantic Monthly* he was raised Catholic. Turner, as we have seen describes Kelly as "born again." See Merritt 2017. Kelly identifies as an evangelical. See Krattenmaker 2013, 169.

5. On Brand's similar ideas about mechanical and biological convergence, see Fred Turner 2002, 269.

6. On Biblical economics, also known as biblical capitalism, see Tabachnick, "Biblical Capitalism." For another overview of this understudied topic, I would refer readers to Montgomery's "Biblical Economics."

7. On this point, see Fisher 2007, 85, 98–99.

8. I am specifically referring to equilibrium in a narrow sense here, in regard to the process of innovation and its effects on the economy. I am not referring to market equilibrium as understood by Adam Smith's invisible hand.

9. On this, point see Adam Curtis's interpretation of Price's life in *All Watched Over by Machines of Loving Grace.*

10. Note that Gilder is likely misreading Rothschild on this score. See Rothschild 1990, 343–350 and Bryant 2006, 267–268.

11. Gilder does note approvingly Rothschild's points of disagreement with Schumpeter. But even the most cursory reading of Rothschild shows that he simply embraces Schumpeterian theory as he claims to criticize it. See Rothschild 1990, 74–75. Nothing Gilder describes in his review of Rothschild and little that Rothschild describes in *Bionomics* is inconsistent with Schumpeterian theory.

12. My understanding of "market populist" liberationist rhetoric has been shaped by two of Curtis's documentaries, *All Watched Over by Machines of Loving Grace* and *The Trap,* as well as Thomas Frank's *One Market Under God.* Among market populists, Gilder's work and Walter Wristan's *The Twilight of Sovereignty* [1992] are perhaps the most explicit in outlining this vision.

13. But not necessarily in mainstream research. On this score, see Robert Geraci's interesting description of the puzzled reaction of Moravec's colleagues to some of his published works, 39–41, Kindle Edition.

14. On *Wired*'s rather unusual approach to journalism, see Fred Turner 2002, Chapter 5 passim.

15. I would note that Malone is specifically referring to cultural equilibrium here, not economic equilibrium, where Gilder supports disequilibrium models. As a noted critic of feminism and supporter of Intelligent design, Gilder clearly is a supporter of equilibrium cultural models, as opposed to disequilibrium ones. See Malone 2002, 171.

Chapter 6

1. I have used Heist, despite the fact that he publishes through Walden University (a school not known for stellar academics) because of the obvious excellence of his work. Heist's work is comparable with, and even sometimes superior to, some of the elite scholars of Christianity and new media, such as Heidi Campbell and Vincent J. Gonzalez.

2. Note that the digital evangelism idea extends beyond the evangelical community, though digital evangelism is perhaps most prominent among evangelicals. See Campbell 2010, 137, 139.

3. Focusing on a narrower subset of evangelical Christians—prophecy believers—Robert Glenn Howard's *Digital Jesus* (2013) has reached similar conclusions about information control on evangelical websites. Howard notes how prophecy websites sought to utilize a form of "ritual deliberation" which deliberately "excludes those not able to deliberate about the End Times." As far back as the early 1990's, prophecy believers have taken advantage of "network technologies" to isolate dissenting viewpoints. See Howard 2013, 55–56.

4. See, for instance, Hewitt 2010, 120–121. See also Clifford 2012 and Jerod Clark 2015.

5. On this opposition, see Tashman 2014.

6. See, for instance: "Asheville Pastor" 2012; see also Wetzstein 2015 on Pringle's ally Kong Hee. Pringle serves as an "advisory pastor" for Kong Hee. Among Hee's other prominent supporters is Pentecostal leader Mary Hudson, the mother of American pop star Katy Perry (Wetzstein 2015).

7. On the Transformations films links to the NAR, see Weaver 2016, 96–97, 131–132, 227–230.

8. See Weaver 2016, Chapter 1 passim for repeated iterations of this concept, as well as Weaver 2016, 134–138

Conclusion

1. See Hanegraaff 1996, 62 on New Age Science.

2. I should make clear that the mind-reading experiments that Ward refers to are different from the ones that have gained most of the attention of conspiracy theorists and paranormal enthusiasts.

3. For the clearest evidence of Sine's training in futurism, particularly for those familiar with the history of scenario planning, I refer the reader to Sine's *Mustard Seed vs. McWorld* (1999).

4. To provide some context, Asbury Theological Seminary, another major seminary in the Wesleyan tradition, tends to be far more consistently associated with the evangelical branch of Methodism.

5. On this point, see Thomas Frank 2000, 196. Frank wryly notes that Senge makes his major points via "an endless pitter-pat of quotations from the *Bhagavad Gita*, Sufi tales, explications of Chinese symbols, and fawning remarks about the wisdom of the East and of simple unaffected indigenous peoples" (Frank 2000, 196). It should be noted that Frank's point in no way represents disrespect for any of these cultures, but rather the weariness that many readers of management theory feel at the gross simplifications and reductionist explanations of these cultures offered by popular management gurus.

6. For various discussions of this paradigm, see herescope.blogspot.com. That this paradigm represents a body of thought is largely conceded in academic literature as well. It is referred to by Paul Thomas via a similar moniker: "apocalyptic alternative history." See Thomas 2012, 311.

7. On the influence of Western esotericism on the West, see Bogdan 2008, 7. Bogdan contends that "Western esotericism can ... be viewed as a third pillar of Western culture, a form of thought that took a middle position between doctrinal faith and rationality" (Bogdan 2008, 7).

8. On Tolkien's dislike of esoteric and occult traditions, particularly as exemplified in the works of Charles Williams, see Zaleski and Zaleski 2015, 231.

Works Cited

"About Che Ahn." n.d. *Wagner Leadership Institute.* Web. 6 May 2013. http://wagnerleadership.com\Che.htm.
"About Natural Church Development (NCD)." n.d. *NCD.international.org.* http://www.ncd-international.org/public/natural_church_development.html.
"About NCD International." n.d. *NCD.international.org.* http://www.ncd-international.org/public/international.html.
"About the Council" 2018. *Gospel Coalition.* Web. 8 Aug 2018. https://www.thegospelcoalition.org/about/council/.
"About Us" n.d. *Sovereign Grace Ministries.* Web. May 2014. http://www.sovereigngraceministries.org/about-us/default.aspx (no longer available).
"About Us" n.d. *TMS Global.* Web. 8 Jul 2017. https://www.tms-global.org/about/vision-and-beliefs.
"Adam Curtis: Awards" 2017. *Imdb.com.* 7 Sep 2017. https://www.imdb.com/name/nm0193231/awards.
Alden, Jenna Feltey. 2012. "Bottom-Up Management: Participative Philosophy and Humanistic Psychology in American Organizational Culture, 1930–1970." Dissertation: Columbia University.
Allen, Jere, ed. 1981. *Consultations.* Atlanta: Home Missions Board.
Allen, Ronald J. 1999. "Preaching in the Congregational System." *Encounter* 60.4: 551–583.
Alumkal, Antony. 2017. *Paranoid Science: The Christian Right's War on Reality.* New York: New York University Press.
Amadae, S.M. 2003. *Rationalizing Capitalist Democracy.* Chicago: The University of Chicago Press.
Amadae, S.M. 2015. *Prisoners of Reason: Game Theory and Neoliberal Political Economy.* New York: Cambridge University Press.
American Scientific Affiliation. 1968. "News." *American Science Affiliation.* Vol 10.1 (March). http://www.asa3.org/ASA/topics/NewsLetter5960s/MAR68.html (listed as ASA newsletter March 1968 in in text-citations).
Andersson, Jenny. 2018. *The Future of the World: Futurology, Futurists, and the Struggle for the Post Cold War Imagination.* Oxford: Oxford University Press.
Andrews, Paul. 1995. "Cyber Thinkers Debate Cyber Law, Internet." *Seattle Times.* 1 Nov. B2. Academic Newsbank.
Anthony, Michael. 2005. "Ministry by Objectives" In *Management Essentials for Christian Ministries.* Edited by Michael J. Anthony and James Estep, Jr. Nashville: B & H.
Anthony, Michael J., and James Estep Jr., eds. 2005. *Management Essentials for Christian Ministries.* Nashville: B & H.
"Asheville Pastor Pleads Guilty in Bank Fraud Case." 2012. *WITN.Com.* 11 Jan. Web. 8 Jan 2018.
Asprem, Egil. 2013. "The Problem of Disenchantment: Scientific Naturalism and Esoteric Discourse, 1900–1939." Dissertation: University of Amsterdam.
Astrom, Karl Johan. 2008. *Feedback Systems: An Introduction for Scientists and Engineers.* Version 2.7. (later published by Princeton: Princeton University Press).

Aswathappa, K., and Kardminer Ghuman. 2010. *Management: Concepts, Practices, and Cases*. New Delhi: Mcgraw Hill India.
Baker, Laurie M. 2015. "Spiritual Economies of Evangelical Worship: Technology, Stewardship and Experience." Dissertation: York University (Canada).
Baker, Rolland. 2010. Foreword. In *Quantum Glory: The Science of Heaven Invading Earth*. By Phil Mason. Maricopa, AZ: XP Publishing. 19–20.
Ball, James Gregory. 1997. "Evangelical Protestants, the Ecological Crisis, and Public Theology." Dissertation: Drew University.
Balmer, Randy. 2002. *Encyclopedia of Evangelicalism*. Louisville: Westminster John Knox Press.
Barbrook, Richard, and Andy Cameron. 1996. "The Californian Ideology." *Science as Culture* 9 (1), 5–40. This book utilizes the version of the essay available at: http://www.comune.torino.it/gioart/big/bigguest/riflessioni/californian_engl.pdf.
Barkun, Michael. 2013. *A Culture of Conspiracy: Apocalyptic Visions in Contemporary America*. Berkley: University of California Press.
Barna, George. 1988. *Marketing the Church*. Colorado Springs: NavPress.
Barna, George. 1992. *Church Marketing: Breaking Ground for the Harvest*. Ventura, CA: Regal.
Barna, George. 2002. *A Fish Out of Water: Strategies to Maximize Your God-given Leadership*. Brentwood, TN: Integrity.
Barna, George. 2013. *The Power of Team Leadership*. Colorado Springs: Waterbrook Press.
Barrett, David B. 2000. "Missiometrics." *Evangelical Dictionary of World Missions*. Ed. A. Scott Moreau. Grand Rapids, MI: Baker Books.
Bebbington, D.W. 1989. *Evangelicalism in Modern Britain: A History from The 1730s to The 1980s*. London: Unwin Hyman.
Bell, Matthew. 2017. "The Biggest Megachurch on Earth and South Korea's 'Crisis of Evangelism.'" *PRI's the World*. May. Web. 8 Sep 2017. https://www.pri.org/stories/2017-05-01/biggest-megachurch-earth-facing-crisis-evangelism.
Bellah, Robert N. 1970. *Beyond Belief: Essays on Religion in a Post Traditional World*. New York: Harper Row.
Bengston, David N., George H. Kubik and Peter C. Bishop. 2012. "Strengthening Environmental Foresight: Potential Contributions of Futures Research." Ecology and Society 17(2):no pagination.
Bergler, Thomas E. 2000. "Winning America: Christian Youth Groups and the Middle-Class Culture of Crisis, 1930–1965." Dissertation: University of Notre Dame.
Bergquist, Linda, and Allan Kerr. 2010. *The Church Turned Inside Out: A Guide for Designers, Refiners, and Re-Aligners*. San Fransisco: Josey-Bass.
Best, Steve, and Douglas Kellner. 2000. "Kevin Kelly's Complexity Theory: The Politics and Ideology of Self-Organizing Systems." *Democracy and Nature* 6.3: 375–399.
Bibbee, Jeffrey R., and A.M. Viens. 2007. "The Inseparability of Religion and Politics in the Neoconservative Critique of Biotechnology." *American Journal of Bioethics* 7.10 (October): 18–20.
"Bio: Timothy Keller." 2014. Timothykeller.com. April 8. Web. 2016. http://www.timothykeller.com/author/.
Bird, Warren. 2016. "4 Important Salary Benchmarks You Might Not Know About." 6 April. Web. 8 Aug 2018. http://leadnet.org/10-important-salary-benchmarks-you-might-not-know-about/.
Blake, Mariah. 2014. "How the Christian Right Is Using Hobby Lobby and 'Duck Dynasty' to Take Back America: Evangelicals Are Mobilizing for Mid-Terms." *Mother Jones*. 31 October. Web. 8 Aug 2017. https://www.motherjones.com/politics/2014/10/evangelical-hobby-lobby-duck-dynasty-election/.
Blumenthal, Max. 2004. "Avenging Angel of the Religious Right: Quirky Millionare Howard Ahmanson, Jr., Is on a Mission from God to Stop Gay Marriage, Fight Evolution, Defeat 'liberal' Churches—and Reelect George W. Bush." *Salon*. 6 Jan. Web. 19 May 2018. https://www.salon.com/2004/01/06/ahmanson/.
"Board of Directors" n.d. *Growth Ministries International*. http://gogmi.org/about-us/board-of-directors/.
Bogdan, Henrik. 2008. *Western Esotericism and Rituals of Initiation*. Albany, NY: SUNY Press.

Bogner, Michael, et al. 2014. "Cybernetic Aspects in the Agile Process Model Scrum." *ICSEA 2014: The Ninth International Conference on Software Engineering Advances*.167–172.
"Books That Have Shaped Leadership Network" 2013. 24 Sep. Web. 8 Mar 2017. http://leadnet.org/books_that_have_shaped_leadership_network_part_21/.
Borsook, Paulina. 1993. "Release: Some Have Called Esther Dyson the Most Powerful Woman in Computing, but Is Her Fascination with Eastern Europe Leading to Eclipse on Her Home Turf." *Wired Magazine*. 1 May. https://www.wired.com/1993/05/dyson-3/.
Borsook, Paulina. 2000. *Cyberselfish: A Critical Romp Through the Terribly Libertarian Culture of Hi-Tech*. New York: Public Affairs.
Boy, John D. 2015. "Blessed Disruption: Culture and Urban Space in a European Church Planting." Dissertation: City University of New York.
Boyle, Alan. 1993. "A Seattle Blueprint for Trade." Seattle Post-Intelligencer. 7 May. Newsbank.
Bragan, James Harris. 1979. "The Educational Role of the Church for a Just and Sustainable Society." Dissertation: School of Theology at Claremont.
Branaugh, Matt. 2008. "Willow Creek's 'Huge Shift': Influential Megachurch Moves Away from Seeker-sensitive Services." *Christianity Today*. May 15. Web. 9 April 2018. https://www.christianitytoday.com/ct/2008/june/5.13.html.
Branson, Mark Lau. 2004. *Memories, Hopes and Conversations: Appreciative Inquiry and Congregational Change*. Herndon, VA: The Alban Institute.
Braun, Dorothy. 1960. "A Historical Study of the Origin and Development of the Seabury Series of the Protestant Episcopal Church." Dissertation: New York University.
Brewin, Kester. 2004. *The Complex Christ: Signs of Emergence in the Urban Church*. SPCK: London.
Brittain, Christopher Craig, and Andrew McKinnon. 2011. "Homosexuality and the Construction of 'Anglican Orthodoxy.': The Symbolic Politics of the Anglican Communion." *Sociology of Religion* 72.3: 351–373.
Bronson, Po. 1996. "George Gilder: Does He Really Think Scarcity Is a Minor Obstacle on the Road to Techno-utopia?" *Wired*. 1 March. https://www.wired.com/1996/03/gilder-5/.
Brouwer, Steven, Paul Gifford and Susan D. Rose. 1996. *Exporting the American Gospel: Global Christian Fundamentalism*. New York: Routledge.
Brown, Candy Gunther. 2012. *Testing Prayer*. Cambridge University Press.
Bryant, William Harold. 2006. "Whole System, Whole Earth: The Convergence of Technology and Ecology in Twentieth-Century American Culture." Dissertation: University of Iowa. Proquest.
Buford, Bob. 2001. *Stuck in Halftime: Reinvesting Your One and Only Life*. Grand Rapids, MI: Zondervan.
Buford, Bob. 2014. *Drucker and Me: What a Texas Entrepreneur Learned from the Father of Modern Management*. Brentwood, TN: Worthy Publishing.
Bullers, Finn. 1999. "A Theological Debate: Digital Doom?" *The Kansas City Star* (31 Jan). A19. Newsbank.
Burgess, Stanley M., and Eduard M. Van Der Maas. 2002. *The New International Dictionary of Pentecostal Charismatic Movements*. Grand Rapids, MI: Zondervan.
Burgin, Angus. 2012. *The Great Persuasion: Reinventing Free Markets Since the Depression*. Cambridge, MA: Harvard University Press.
Burke, Caitlin. 2016. "Trump Meeting with More Evangelical Leaders as Part of 'United in Purpose' Efforts." *CBN News*. 25 May. Web. 8 Aug 2018. http://www1.cbn.com/cbnnews/us/2016/may/trump-meeting-with-more-evangelical-leaders-as-part-of-united-in-purpose-efforts.
Burnes, Bernard. 2005. "Complexity Theory and Organisational Change." *International Journal of Management Reviews* 7.2: 73–90.
Burnett, E. Stephen. 2014. "Kathy Tyers: Defeating Gnostic Forces in Fantasy Fiction." *Speculative Faith*. 4 Sep. Web. 10 Jun 2019. http://speculativefaith.lorehaven.com/kathy-tyers-defeating-gnostic-forces-in-fantasy-fiction/.
Burwell, Jennifer. 2013. "Figuring Matter: Quantum Physics as a New Age Rhetoric." *Science as Culture* 22.3: 344–366.
Bush, Joseph Earl, Jr. 1993. "Social Justice and the Natural Environment in the Study Program of the World Council of Churches, 1966–1990." Dissertation: Drew University.

Works Cited

Bush, Luis. 2002. "Catalysts of World Evangelization." Dissertation: Fuller Theological Seminary.

Bustraan, Richard. 2014. *The Jesus People Movement: A Story of Spiritual Revolution Among the Hippies*. Eugene, OR: Pickwick Publications.

Caldwell, Deborah Kovac. 1998. "Spiritual Defense Center, New World Prayer Center in Colorado Springs, Colorado, Arms Itself with Technology in Its Evangelical Quest." *The Wichita Eagle*. 26 Sep. Newsbank. 3E.

Calhoun, Adele Ahlberg. 2005. *Spiritual Disciplines Handbook: Practices That Transform Us*. Downers Grove, IL: Intervarsity Press.

Camilleri, Emanuel. 2016. *Project Success: Critical Factors and Behaviors*. New York: Routledge.

Campbell, Heidi. 2005. *Exploring Religious Community Online: We Are One in the Network*. New York: Peter Lang.

Campbell, Heidi. 2010. *When Religion Meets New Media*. London: Routledge.

Campbell, Iain D., and William M. Schweitzer. 2013. *Engaging with Keller: Thinking Through the Theology of an Influential Evangelical*. Grand Rapids, MI: EP Books.

Cannistraci, David. 1996a. *Apostles and the Emerging Apostolic Movement*. Ventura, CA: Renew Books.

Cannistraci, David. 1996b. *The Gift of Apostle*. Ventura, CA: Regal.

Cannon, Douglas F. 2015. "What Do You Say That I Am? a History of How Religious Communicators Have Often Avoided 'Public Relations.'" *Journal of Public Relations Research* 27: 280–296. Ebscohost. Accessed 8 Jul 2016.

Caradonna, Jeremy L. 2014. *Sustainability: A History*. Oxford: Oxford University Press.

Carnes, Tony. 2001. "The Silicon Valley Saints: High-Tech Christian Executives Are Bringing Biblical Values into a Mecca of Mammon." *Christianity Today* (6 August): 34–40.

Castells, Manuel. 2010a. *The Rise of the Network Society*. Malden, MA: Wiley-Blackwell.

Castells, Manuel. 2010b. *The Power of Identity*. 2nd edition. Malden, MA: Wiley.

Caton, Steve. 2015. "Four Steps to a Visitor-Centric Connections Ministry." *MinistryTech* (October): 24–25.

Chandler, Matt. 2014. "Reliance." Sermon. 2 Mar. Web. 8 Aug 2018. https://www.tvcresources.net/resource-library/sermons/reliance.

Chaney, Charles R., and Ron S. Lewis. 1978. *Design for Church Growth*. Nashville: Broadmen Press.

Chapman, Bruce. 1995. "Individuals, Not Governments, Should Shape Internet's Future." Seattle Post Intelligencer. 20 Oct. A13. Editorial. Academic Newsbank.

Chaves, Mark. 1998. "Denominations as Dual Structures: An Organizational Analysis." In *Sacred Companies*. Editor N.J. Demerath. New York: Oxford University Press. 175–194.

Chernyakova, Irina. 2013. "Systems of Valuation." Thesis: M.I.T.

Childress, Carol. 1997. "Information Network" Interview by Next Magazine. *NEXT Magazine* 3.3. (December): 6.

Cho, Paul Yonggi. 1981. *Successful Home Cell Groups*. South Plainsfield, NJ: Bridge Publishing.

Christerson, Brad, and Richard Flory. 2017. *The Rise of Network Christianity: How Independent Leaders Are Changing the Religious Landscape*. Oxford: Oxford University Press.

Churchill, Jason Lemoine. 2006. "The Limits to Influence: The Club of Rome and Canada, 1968 to 1988." Dissertation: University of Waterloo.

Clark, Jerod. 2015. "Modern Church Website Design." *Churchjuice*. 9 Jul. Web. 8 Aug 2018. https://churchjuice.reframemedia.com/blog/modern-church-website-design.

Clarkson, Frederick. 2006. "The Battle for the Mainline Churches." *Public Eye* (Spring): 10–14.

Clarkson, Frederick, and Rachel Tabachnick. 2005. Personal Communication. 19 August.

Clifford, Paul Alan. 2012. "Seven Sins of Bad Church Website Design" ChurchMag. 4 Sep. Web. 8 Aug 2018. https://churchm.ag/7-sins-of-bad-church-website-design/.

Coalter, Milton, et al., eds. 1992. *The Organizational Revolution: Presbyterians and American Denominationalism*. Louisville, KY: Westminster John Knox Press.

Cole, J. Michael. 2013. "The Perpetrator as Victim." *Far Eastern Sweet Potato* (blog). 18 December. Web. 8 Jun 2018. http://fareasternpotato.blogspot.com/2013/12/the-perpetrator-as-victim.html.

Cole, J. Michael. 2016. "Thousands Protest as Taiwan Inches Closer to Legalizing Same-Sex

Marriage." *Hong Kong Free Press*. 18 November. Web. 8 Jun 2018. https://www.hongkongfp.com/2016/11/18/thousands-protest-taiwan-inches-closer-legalising-sex-marriage/.
Cole, J. Michael. 2017a. *Convergence or Conflict in the Taiwan Strait: The Illusion of Peace*. New York: Routledge.
Cole, J. Michael. 2017b. "U.S. Hate Group MassResistance Behind Anti-LGBT Activities in Taiwan." Taiwan Sentinel. 2 Jan. Web. 8 Jun 2018. https://sentinel.tw/us-hate-group-anti-lgbt/.
Cole, Neil. 2005. *Organic Church: Growing Faith Where Life Happens*. San Francisco: Josey Bass.
Cole, Neil. 2010. *Church 3.0: Upgrades for the Future of the Church*. San Francisco: Josey Bass.
Cole, Neil, and Phil Helfer. 2012. *Church Transfusion: Changing Your Church Organically from the Inside Out*. San Francisco: Josey Bass.
Collins, James M. 2009. *Exorcism and Deliverance Ministry in the Twentieth Century: An Analysis of the Practice and Theology of Exorcism in Modern Western Christianity*. Eugene: Wipf and Stock.
Comiskey, Joel. 1999. *Reap the Harvest: How a Small-Group System Can Grow Your Church*. Houston: Touch Publications.
Comiskey, Joel. 2014. *2000 Years of Small Groups: A History of Cell Ministry in the Church*. Moreno Valley, CA: CCS Publishing.
Cone, Edward. 2005. "MegaChurch, Megatech: Nowadays, Spreading the Word Involves a Lot of Sophisticated Information Technology. Here's How IT Works in a Very High-Growth Enterprise." *CIO Insight*. 05 Nov. Web. 8 Aug 2018. Ebscohost.
Connell, Joan. 1987. "Evangelist Targets Silicon Valley Three Year Program Aims at 13,000 Unchurched Residents." *San Jose Mercury News*. 24 Jan. 11C
Conti, Joseph Gerard. 1994. "The 'Inner Worldly Mysticism' of Thomas Keating: A Paradigm of Renewal of Catholic Contemplativism." Dissertation: University of Southern California.
"Converting Geography into Community" 2001. *Explorer: Field Notes for the Emerging Church*. No. 28 (15 Jan).
Cook, David Lowell. 1998. "The Americanization of the Church Growth Movement." MA Thesis. Auburn Univeristy. Print. Proquest.
Cooper, Melinda. 2011. "Complexity Theory After the Financial Crisis." *Journal of Cultural Economy* 4.4: 371–385, DOI: 10.1080/17530350.2011.609692.
Cowan, Douglas E. 2003. *The Remnant Spirit: Conservative Reform in Mainline Protestantism*. Westport, CT: Praeger.
Coyne, Jerry. 2011. "Can Darwinism Improve Binghamton?" New York Times: Sunday Book Review. 9 Sep. Web. 2 Jun 2018. https://www.nytimes.com/2011/09/11/books/review/the-neighborhood-project-by-david-sloan-wilson-book-review.html.
Crabb, Larry. 1977. *Effective Biblical Counseling*. Grand Rapids, MI: Zondervan.
Crisman, Karl-Dieter. 2015. "Open Source Software and Christian Thought." *Perspectives on Science and Christian Faith* 67.1 (March): 3–13. https://www.asa3.org/ASA/PSCF/2015/PSCF3-15Crisman.pdf.
Crites, L. Thomas (Tom). 2009. "Four Core Principles for Enhancing Ministry Effectiveness: A Factor Analysis Evaluating the Relationship Between Select Variables and Church Health Observed in Churches of the Georgia Baptist Convention." Dissertation: Southeastern Baptist Theological Seminary.
Cromaterie, Michael. 2002. "Our Posthuman Future: A Conversation with Francis Fukuyama." *Christianity Today: Books and Culture*. July\August. https://www.booksandculture.com/articles/2002/julaug/4.9.html.
Cron, Ian Morgan, and Suzanne Stabile. 2016. *The Road Back to You: An Enneagram Journey of Self-Discovery*. Downers Grove, IL: IVP Books.
Cronshaw, Darren John. 2009. "The Shaping of Things Now: Mission and Innovation in Four Emerging Churches in Melbourne." Dissertation: Melbourne College of Divinity.
Crosby, David Allen. 1989. "Church Government in the Church Growth Movement: Critique from a Historic Baptist Perspective." Dissertation: Baylor.
Cummings, Thomas G., and Christopher G. Worley. 2008. *Organization Development and Change*. 9th ed. Mason, OH: Cenage.

Cuneo, Michael. 2001. *American Exorcism: Expelling Demons in the Land of Plenty*. New York: Doubleday.
Curley, Drew. 2014. "New Calvinism 1, Part I: An Historical Understanding and Theological Critique." *Journal of Dispensational Theology* (Winter): 225–269.
Dadisman, Jeffrey Mark. 2008. "Results of the Implementation of Turnaround Strategies for the Maquoketa United Methodist Church Based on Natural Church Development." Dissertation: Asbury Theological Seminary.
Daley, Dan. 2012. "How This Multisite Church Created an Immersive A/V/L Experience: Forrest Hill Church Uses Physical Media to Leverage Its Weekend Services with a Life-size Projection of the Pastor to Satellite Locations." *Worship Tech Director*. 23 Jul. Web. 8 Aug 2018. http://www.worshiptechdirector.com/article/how_this_multisite_church_created_an_immersive_experience.
Daly, Lew. 2000. *A Moment to Decide: The Crisis in Mainstream Presbyterianism*. New York: Institute for Democracy Studies.
Daly, Lewis C. 2001. "A Church at Risk: The Episcopal 'Renewal' Movement." *IDS Insights* 2.2 (December): 1–9, 12. Institute for Democracy Studies.
Darrand, Tom Craig, and Anson Shupe. 1983. *Metaphors of Social Control in a Pentecostal Sect*. New York: Edwin Mellen.
Day, William H., Jr. 2002. "The Development of a Comprehensive Definition of Church Health." The Ola Farmer Lenaz Lecture. Submitted to New Orleans Baptist Theological Seminary. 19 Dec.
Daystrom, Edward. 1976. *The Art of Management for Christian Leaders*. Waco, TX: Word Books.
Dayton, Edward. n.d. "A Conversation with Dr. Edward Dayton." Translation from an interview by Miss Jean Liu. Kairos Communication Services. *Interflow*. Vol 92-11.
Dayton, Edward R., and David R. Fraser. 1990. *Planning Strategies for World Evangelization*. Revised Edition. Grand Rapids, MI: Eerdmans and Missions Advanced Research and Communication Center.
Delingpole, James. 2016. "Gloriously Compulsive and Maddening: Adam Curtis's *Hypernormalisation* Reviewed." *The Spectator*. 29 Oct. Web. Accessed 8 Sep 2017.
Demereth, N.J., et al., eds. 1998. *Sacred Companies*. New York: Oxford University Press.
"Demographics." 2014. *Oxford English Dictionary*.3rd Edition. March.
Detwiler, Fritz. 1999. *Standing on the Premises of God: The Christian Right's Fight to Redefine America's Public Schools*. New York: New York University Press.
Diamond, Sara. 1989. *Spiritual Warfare: The Politics of the Christian Right*. Boston: South End Press.
Diamond, Sara. 1995. *Roads to Dominion: Right Wing Movements and Political Power in the United States*. New York: Guilford Press.
Diamond, Sara. 2000. *Not by Politics Alone: The Enduring Influence of the Christian Right*. New York: Guilford Press.
"Diffusion of Innovation." 1996. *NetFax* 53.2 (September): 91.
"The Diffusion of Innovation Workshop with Everett Rogers." 1999. *NEXT Magazine*. Advertisement. Vol 5 (1). January–March. 8.
DiMaggio, Paul J., and Walter W. Powell. 1983. "The Iron Cage Revisited: Institutional Isomorphism and Collective Rationality in Organizational Fields." *American Sociological Review*, Vol 48, No. 2 (Apr.), pp. 147–160. JSTOR. http://www.jstor.org/stable/2095101.
Dinerstein, Joel. 2006. "Technology and Its Discontents: On the Verge of the Posthuman." *American Quarterly* 58.3. (September): 569–595.
Discernment Research Group. 2005. "Willis Harman Consults with Evangelical Leaders Circa 1979." *Herescope*. 20 Sep. Web. 8 Aug 2018. http://herescope.blogspot.com/2005/09/willis-harman-consults-with.html.
Discernment Research Group. 2012a. "Cosms, Codes, and Cryptologies, Part 7." *Herescope*. 30 May. Web. 8 Aug 2019. Http://herescope.blogspot.com/2012/05/quantum-prophecy.html.
Discernment Research Group. 2012b. "The Serpent Seed and the Nephilim: Nephilim Eschatology, Part 2: A Crash Course in the Emerging Endtime Prophecy Heresy" *Herescope*. 21 July. Web. 8 Aug 2018.

Discernment Research Group. 2013. "A New Cosmology for the Church, Part 6: Alien Encounters, a Book Review." *Herescope*. 23 Aug. Web. 8 Aug 2018.
Discovery Institute Staff. 2013. "Discovery Institute Announces 2013 Intelligent Design Summer Science Seminars." Discovery Institute. 15 April. Web. 8 Aug 2018. https://www.discovery.org/a/20531/.
Dochuk, Darren. 2011. *From Bible-Belt to Sun-Belt: Plain Folk Religion, Grassroot Politics, and the Rise of Evangelical Conservatism*. New York: Norton.
"Donald E. Miller: Leonard K. Firestone Professor of Religion." 2017. USC Dornsnife. https://dornsife.usc.edu/cf/faculty-and-staff/faculty.cfm?pid = 1003537. Accessed 8 Sep.
Doornenbal, Robert. 2012. *Crossroads: An Exploration of the Emerging-Missional Conversation with a Special Focus on 'Missional Leadership' and Its Challenges for Theological Education*. Delft, Netherlands: Eburon Academic Publisher.
Dorrien, Gary. 2003. *The Making of American Liberal Theology: Idealism, Realism & Modernity: 1900–1950*. Louisville: Westminster John Knox Press.
Dorrien, Gary. 2011. *Social Ethics in the Making: Interpreting an American Tradition*. Malden, MA: Wiley-Blackwell.
Dreier, Mary Sue Dehmlow. 2007. "An Old New Church in the Marketplace: The Evangelical Lutheran Church in America (ELCA) into the Twenty-First Century." In *The Missional Church in Context: Helping Congregations Develop Contextual Ministry*. Ed. Craig Von Gelder. Grand Rapids, MI: Eerdmans. 189–218.
Dyer-Witherford, Anne. 2017. "Neospirituality, Social Change, and the Culture of the Post-Fordist Workplace." Dissertation: University of Waterloo.
Dykstra, Craig, and James Hudnut-Beumler. 1992. "The National Organizational Structures of Protestant Denominations: An Invitation to a Conversation." In *The Organizational Revolution: Presbyterians and American Denominationalism*. Edited by Milton J. Coalter, et al. Louisville, KY: Westminster John Knox Press.
Dyson, Esther. 1995. "Friend and Foe." *Wired*. 01 August. https://www.wired.com/1995/08/newt/.
Dyson, Esther. 1997. *Release 2.0: A Design for Living in the Digital Age*. New York: Broadway Books.
Dyson, Esther, George Gilder, George Keyworth and Alvin Toffler. 1994. "Cyberspace and the American Dream: A Magna Carta for the Knowledge Age." *Future Insight* 1.2 (August). Web. 8 Aug 2018. http://www.pff.org/issuespubs/futureinsights/fi1.2magnacarta.html.
Eardly-Pryor, Roger. 2014. "The Global Environmental Moment: Sovereignty and American Science on Spaceship Earth, 1945–1974." Dissertation: University of California, Santa Barbara.
Edwards, James Howell II. 2016. "Leadership Structures and Dynamics in Multisite Churches: A Quantitative Study" Dissertation: Southern Baptist Theological Seminary.
Edwards, Jonathan J. 2015. "Superchurch: The Rhetoric and Politics of American Fundamentalism." East Lansing: Michigan State University Press.
"Election Poll Results of Christian Conservative Voters Pt.2" 2017. *Wallbuilders*. 20 Jan. http://wallbuilderslive.com/president-trumps-win/.
Elichirigoity, Irving Fernando. 1994. "Towards a Genealogy of Planet Management: Computer Simulation, Limits to Growth and the Emergence of Global Spaces." Dissertation: University of Illinois Urbana–Champaign.
Ellas, John, and Flavil Yeakley. 1999. "Natural Church Development" Review. *Journal of the American Society for Church Growth* (Spring): 83–92.
Emerson, Michael, and Christian Smith. 2000. *Divided by Faith: Evangelical Religion and the Problem of Race in America*. New York: Oxford University Press.
"The End" 1999. *Netfax* 139 (Dec 20): 49.
Erdmann, Martin. 2009. "The Spiritualization of Science, Technology, and Education in a One-World Society." *European Journal of Nanomedicine* 2 (January): 31–38.
Ernst, Eldon Gilbert. 1968. "The Interchurch World Movement of North America, 1919–1920." Dissertation: Yale.
Erwich, Rene. 2004. "Missional Churches: Identical Global 'Plants' or Locally Grown 'Flowers.'" *Transformation* 21.3: 180–191.
Escobar, Samuel. 2000. "Evangelical Missiology: Peering into the Future at the Turn of the

Century." In *Global Missiology for the 21st Century*. Ed. William D. Taylor. Grand Rapids, MI: Baker Academic. 101–122.

Eskridge, Larry. 2005. "God's Forever Family: The Jesus People Movement in America, 1966–1977." Dissertation: University of Stirling.

Evans, John Hyde. 1998. "Playing God? Human Genetic Engineering and the Rationalization of Bioethics 1959-1995)." Dissertation: Princeton University.

Ewan, Stuart. 1996. *PR!: A Social History of Spin*. New York: Basic Books.

Explorer ... Field Notes for the Emerging Church. 2000. 12.5.

Farnsley, Arthur. 2016. "The Rise of Congregational Studies in the USA." Congregational Studies in the U.K: Christianity in a Post-Christian Context. Ed. Matthew Guest, Karen Tusting, and Linda Woodhead. New York: Routledge. 25–38.

"Feedback." 2019. *Oxford English Dictionary*.

"Feedback Loops." 2019. Carleton College. 22 Jan. Web. 27 Sep 2019. https://serc.carleton.edu/introgeo/models/loops.html.

Felts, Robert Walter. 1989. "A Critical Analysis of Dawson Trotman's Methodology of Discipleship for Contemporary Mission Strategy Among North American Evangelical Mission Agencies." Dissertation: Southwestern Baptist Theological Seminary.

Fenimore, James A., Jr. 2009. "High Tech Worship: Digital Display Technologies and Protestant Liturgical Practices in the U.S." Dissertation: Rensselear Polytechnic Institute. Proquest.

Fey, Harold E. 1945. "'What About Youth for Christ?'" *The Christian Century* 62 (20 June): 729–731.

Fineman, Stephen. 2006. "On Being Positive: Concerns and Counterpoints." The Academy of Management Review, Vol 31.2 (April): 270–291.

Fisher, Eran. 2007. "The Spirit of Networks: *Wired* Magazine and the Discourse on Technology in Post-Fordist Society." The New School. Dissertation. Proquest.

Flank, Lenny, Jr. 2007. *Deception by Design: The Intelligent Design Movement in America*. St. Petersburg, FL: Red and Black Publishers.

Flash, Cynthia. 1996. "Task Force Trying to Develop Internet Guidelines—High Powered Group Hopes Code Would Reduce Government Role." *The News Tribune* (Tacoma, Washington). 26 May. Newsbank. A1.

Fleming, David W. 2000. "The Use of Demographics and Psychographics in the Development of Intentional and Contextualized Strategies for Evangelistic Outreach Through the Local Church." Dissertation: New Orleans Baptist Theological Seminary.

Fleming, Travis Dean. 2006. "An Analysis of Bill Bright's Theology and Methodology of Evangelism and Discipleship." Dissertation: Southern Baptist Theological Seminary. Proquest.

Ford, Leighton. 1978. "Images of the Future: An Evangelical Perspective." In *Evangelicals Face the Future*. Ed. Donald E. Hoke. Wheaton, IL: William Carey Library. 29–41.

Forrester, Jay W. 1972. "Churches at the Transition Between Growth and World Equilibrium" *Zygon* 7.3 (September). Republished from *Toward Global Equilibrium: Collected Papers*. Ed. Dennis Meadows. Cambridge, MA: Wright-Allen Press, 1972. DOI: 10.1111/j.1467-9744.1972.tb00204.

Fosbrook, Bretton. 2017. "How Scenarios Became Corporate Strategies: Alternative Futures and Uncertainty in Strategic Management." Dissertation: York University.

Fowler, Frank Lincoln III. 1983. "Lyman Coleman and the Serendipity Movement in Christian Education: 1954–1980." Dissertation: New York University.

Fox-Brewster, Thomas. 2016. "Right Wing Company of Convicted Embezzler Turned Christian Linked to Huge Leaks of US Voter Records." *Forbes*. 4 Jan. https://www.forbes.com/sites/thomasbrewster/2016/01/04/191-million-leak-bill-dallas-christian-anti-abortion/#7425c23c78f7.

"Francis Fukuyama." n.d. Stanford University https://fukuyama.stanford.edu/.

Frank, Steven A. 1995. "George Price's Contribution to Evolutionary Genetics." *Journal of Theoretical Biology* 175: 373–388.

Frank, Thomas. 2000. *One Market Under God: Extreme Capitalism, Market Populism and the End of Economic Democracy*. New York: Doubleday.

Franklin, Judy, and Ellyn Davis, eds. 2012. *The Physics of Heaven*. Shippensburg, PA: Destiny Image.

Friesen, Dwight J. 2009. *Thy Kingdom Connected: What the Church Can Learn from Facebook, the Internet, and Other Networks*. Grand Rapids, MI: Baker Books.
Frye, Brian Nathaniel. 2011. "The Multi-Site Church Phenomenon in North America: 1950–2010." Dissertation: Southern Baptist Theological Seminary.
Fryling, Alice. 2017. *Mirror for the Soul: A Christian Guide to the Enneagram*. Downers Grove, IL: Intervarsity.
Fukuyama, Francis. 2002. *Our Posthuman Future: Consequences of the Biotechnology Revolution*. New York: Picador.
Galloway, Alexander. 2001. "Protocol, Or, How Control Exists After Decentralization." Dissertation: Duke University.
Gangel, Kenneth. 1997. *Team Leadership in Christian Ministry: Using Multiple Gifts to Build a Unified Vision*. Revised Edition. Chicago: Moody.
Garite, Matt. 2013. "Green Futures: A Cultural History of Ecotopia from the Cold War to the Present." Dissertation: SUNY Buffalo.
Garreau, Joel. 2005. *Radical Evolution: The Promise and Peril of Enhancing Our Minds, Our Bodies—and What It Means to Be Human*. New York: Doubleday.
Garrison, David. 2004. *Church Planting Movements: How God Is Redeeming a Lost World*. Midlothian, VA: WIGtake Resources.
Gaus, Annie. 2015. "Hipster Churches in Silicon Valley: Evangelicalism's Unlikely New Home: Netflix Fasts, Coffee Vouchers, Plaid-Wearing Worshipers Is What It Takes for 'Church Transplants' to Make Their Home in the Affluent Bay Area." *Guardian*. 29 Jan. Web. 8 Aug 2018. https://www.theguardian.com/us-news/2015/jan/29/hipster-churches-sillicon-valley-evangelical-new-home.
Gelder, Craig von. 2007. *The Missional Church in Context: Helping Congregations Develop Contextual Ministry*. Grand Rapids, MI: Eerdmans.
George, Carl. 1992. *Prepare Your Church for the Future*. Tarrytown, NY: Revell.
George, Carl, and Robert Logan. 1987. *Leading and Managing Your Church*. Old Tappan, NJ: Revell.
George, Carl, and Warren Bird. 1993. *How to Break Growth Barriers: Capturing Overlooked Opportunities for Church Growth*. Grand Rapids, MI: Baker.
George, Carl, and Warren Bird. 1994. *The Coming Church Revolution*. Grand Rapids, MI: Revell.
Geraci, Robert M. 2010. *Apocalyptic A.I.: Visions of Heaven in Robotics, Artificial Intelligence, and Virtual Reality*. New York: Oxford University Press.
Getz, Gene. 1979. "The Future of the Church: Its Nurture, Form, and Function." In *An Evangelical Agenda: And Beyond*. Pasadena, CA: William Carey Library.
Gibbs, Eddie.1998. "Effective Leaders and Models of the 21st Century Church." *Netfax* 112 (Dec 7): 17.
Gibbs, Eddie. 2000. *ChurchNext*. Downers Grove, IL: Intervarsity.
Gibbs, Eddie. 2005. *LeadershipNext: Changing Leaders in a Changing Culture*. Downers Grove, IL: Intervarsity.
Gibbs, Eddie, and Ryan K. Bolger. 2006. *Emerging Churches; Creating Christian Community in Postmodern Cultures*. Grand Rapids, MI: Baker Academic.
Gilder, George. n.d. "Angst and Awe on the Internet." *Forbes ASP*. Reprinted on Discovery Institute. http://www.discovery.org/a/25/.
Gilder, George. n.d. "Life After Television, Revisited." *Forbes ASAP*. Reprinted at Discovery Institute. http://www.discovery.org/a/39/.
Gilder, George. 1990. "Principles of Business Transformed into the Laws of Nature." Washington Times. 24 Dec. F1.
Gilder, George. 1992. "Rich and Famous—Bless the Entrepeneurs—Defenders of Capitalism Say It Wouldn't Survive Without a Few Fat Cats." *Seattle Times*. 8 Nov. Newsbank.
Gilder, George. 1993. "George Gilder: When Bandwidth Is Free." Interviewed by Kevin Kelly. *Wired Magazine*. 1 Apr. https://www.wired.com/1993/04/gilder-4/.
Gilder, George, and Jay Richards. 2002. "Introduction: Are We Spiritual Machines? the Beginning of a Debate." *Are We Spiritual Machines?*. Editor Jay Richards. Seattle: Discovery Institute. 1–11.
Gilliand, Dean. 2000. "Contextualization." In *Evangelical Dictionary of World Missions*. Ed. A. Scott Moreau, et al. Grand Rapids, MI: Baker Books.

Gjelten, Tom. 2016. "Anglican Communion Temporarily Suspends U.S. Episcopal Church." *All Things Considered*. NPR. 15 Jan. Web. 8 May 2017. https://www.npr.org/2016/01/15/463224168/anglican-communion-temporarily-suspends-u-s-episcopal-church.
Gladwell, Malcolm. n.d. "Legitimacy." *Q Ideas*. http://qideas.org/videos/legitimacy/.
Gladwell, Malcolm. 2002. *The Tipping Point: How Little Things Can Make a Big Difference*. Boston: Back Bay Books.
"GMI Is Now Closed" 2018. *Global Mapping International*. Web. 10 May 2018. https://www.gmi.org/.
Godin, Benoit. 2014. "The Vocabulary of Innovation: A Lexicon." Project on the Intellectual History of Innovation. Working Paper. Volume 20.
Goede, Marieke de. 2012. "Fighting the Network: A Critique of the Network as a Security Technology." *Distinktion: Scandinavian Journal of Social Theory* 13.3: 215–232.
Gold, Matea, and Tom Hamburger. 2011. "Silicon Valley Gives Conservative Christians a Boost: A Group of Venture Capitalists Is Backing United in Purpose, an Ambitious Project That Seeks to Affect the 2012 Election by Registering 5 Million New Conservative Christians to Vote." *Los Angeles Times*. 15 Sept. http://articles.latimes.com/2011/sep/15/nation/la-na-evangelical-outreach-20110916.
Gomez, Nile. 2012. "The Anglican Mission in the Americas: Background, Beginnings, and Barriers." Dissertation: Regent University.
Gonzalez, Vincent J. 2014. "Born Again Digital: Exploring Evangelical Video Game Worlds." Dissertation: University of North Carolina Chapel Hill.
Goodmanson, Drew. 2009. "Website Wisdom: New Research, Cooperative Reveal Best Practices for Church." *Your Church* (November\December): 24–27. Christianity Today International.
GRACE. 2014. "For the Investigatory Review of Sexual Abuse Discourses and Institutional Responses at Bob Jones University." December 11.
Graebner, William. 1986. "The Small Group and Democratic Social Engineering, 1900–1950." *Journal of Social Issues* 42.1: 137–154.
Graebner, William. 1987. *The Engineering of Consent: Democracy and Authority in Twentieth-Century America*. Madison: University of Wisconsin Press.
Griffeths, Daniel Jay. 1992, "The RISE of DAWN in the Silicon Valley" Dissertation: Fuller Theological Seminary.
Grinter, Rebecca E., Susan P. Wyche, Gillian R. Hayes and Lonnie D. Harvel. 2011. "Technology in Protestant Ministry." Reprinted in Computer Supported Cooperative Work 20.6. (December 2011): 449–472.
Growth Ministries International. "Overview of the Consulting Division." Web. http://gogmi.org/coaching-consulting/consulting/.
Guest, Matthew, Karen Tusting and Linda Woodhead, eds. 2016. *Congregational Studies in the U.K: Christianity in a Post-Christian Context*. New York: Routledge.
Guffin, Scott Lee. 1999. "An Examination of Key Foundational Influences on the Megachurch Movement in America, 1960–1978." Dissertation: Southern Baptist Theological Seminary.
"Guizhou Forerunner College" n.d. *Guizhou Forerunner College*. Web. 8 Jun 2018. http://www.forerunnercollege.com/en/Menus.aspx?id = 6.
Haas, J.W., Jr. 1992. "Donald MacCrimmon MacKay (1922–1987)." *Perspectives on Christian Faith*. PSCF 44 (March). 55–61. http://www.asa3.org/ASA/PSCF/1992/PSCF3-92Haas.html.
Haberer, Jack. 2001. *Godviews: The Convictions That Drive Us and Divide Us*. Louisville, KY: Geneva Press.
Hackett, Jennifer E. Campbell Goodloe. 2009. "Nurturing the Capacity to Think Theologically About Moral Issues: An Empirical Study of Christian Moral Formation in Four Presbyterian Congregations." Dissertation: Princeton Theological Seminary.
Hadaway, C. Kirk, Francis M. Dubose and Stuart A. Wright. 1987. *Home Cell Groups and House Churches*. Nashville, Broadman Press.
Hammond, Debora Ruth. 1997. "Toward a Science of Synthesis: The Heritage of General Systems Theory." Dissertation: Berkley.
Han, Ju Hui Judy. 2009. "Contemporary Korean/American Evangelical Missions: Politics of Space, Gender, and Difference." Dissertation: Berkley.

Hanegraff, Wouter J. 1996. *New Age Religion and Western Culture: Esotericism in the Mirror of Secular Thought*. Leiden: E.G. Brill.
Hankins, James Douglas, Jr. 2011. "Following Up: Dawson Trotman, the Navigators and the Origins of Discipleship Making in American Evangelicalism, 1926–1956." Dissertation: Trinity Evangelical Divinity School.
Hansen, Collin. 2009. *Young, Restless, and Reformed: A Journalist's Journey with the New Calvinists*. Wheaton: Good News Publishers.
Hansen, Collin. 2013. "Gladwell on Power and the Weapons of the Spirit." *GospelCoalition. org*. 10 Nov. Web. 8 May 2018. https://www.thegospelcoalition.org/article/gladwell-on-power-and-the-weapons-of-the-spirit/.
Hardin, Garret. 1974. "Living on a Lifeboat." *Bioscience* 24 (October): 561–568. Garrett Hardin Society. Reprint. Fall 2001. Web. Accessed 8 Aug 2018. https://www.garretthardinsociety.org/articles_pdf/living_on_a_lifeboat.pdf.
Harman, Willis. 1979. *An Evangelical Agenda: And Beyond: Addresses, Responses, and Scenarios from the 'Continuing Consultation on Future Evangelical Concerns' Held in Overland Park, Kansas, December 11–14, 1979*. Ed. Donald E. Hoke. Pasadena, CA: William Carey Library. 27–37.
Harmen, Oren. 2010. *The Price of Altruism: George Price and the Search for the Origins of Kindness*. New York: Norton.
Harris, Alissa. 2014. "'Survivor' Bloggers Join Forces to Reveal Christian Fundamentalist Abuses: They Collect Documents, Interview Sources and Get Thousands of Facebook Shares. Meet the Army of Ex-Fundamentalists Exposing the Misdeeds of the Organizations They Left." *The Daily Beast*. 23 Mar. Web. 9 Aug 2019. https://www.thedailybeast.com/survivor-bloggers-join-forces-to-reveal-christian-fundamentalist-abuses.
Hart, D.G. 2013. "Looking for Communion in All the Wrong Places: Tim Keller and Presbyterian Ecclesiology." Editors Campbell, Iain D. and William M. Schweitzer. *Engaging with Keller: Thinking Through the Theology of an Influential Evangelical*. Grand Rapids, MI: EP Books. 211–238.
Harvey, David. 2005. *A Brief History of Neoliberalism*. Oxford: Oxford University Press. Kindle Edition.
Harvey, Paul William. 1992. "Southern Baptists and Southern Culture." Dissertation: Berkley.
Hassett, Miranda Katherine. 2004. "Episcopal Dissidents, African Allies: The Anglican Communion and the Globalization of Dissent." Dissertation: University of North Carolina Chapel Hill.
Hastings, Walter G. 2000. "A Critical Analysis and Comparison of Models for Small Group Ministry." Dissertation: Fuller Theological Seminary.
Hawkins, Lori. 1993. "Scriptures on Screen—Software Developers Bring Bible Study into the Computer Age." Austin American-Statesman. December 10. C1. Newsbank.
Heist, James. 2011. "Information Technology Management, Business Processes, and Strategic Planning in the Church." Dissertation: Walden University.
Heng, Michelle. 2013. "Phil Pringle: God of the Turnaround—City Harvest Advisory Pastor Phil Pringle Reminded the Congregation of God's Power to Turn Things Around Even When a Situation Looks Headed for Disaster." *City News* (Singapore). 9 Apr. Web. 8 Aug 2018. https://www.citynews.sg/2013/04/phil-pringle-god-of-the-turnaround/.
Henriot, Peter J. 1979. "A Dystopian Perspective on the Future: Challenge for the Churches." In *An Evangelical Agenda: And Beyond: Addresses, Responses, and Scenarios from the 'Continuing Consultation on Future Evangelical Concerns' Held in Overland Park, Kansas, December 11–14, 1979*. Pasadena, CA: William Carey Library.
Herrington, Jim, Mike Bonem and James H. Furr. 2000. *Leading Congregational Change: A Practical Guide for the Transformational Journey*. San Francisco: Josey Bass.
Hertz, Todd. 2001. "'Only Cellular Life'?: Christians, Leaders, and Bioethics Watchdogs React to the Announcement That Human Embryos Have Been Cloned." *Christianity Today* (Web Only). 1 Nov. Web. 1 Jun 2018. https://www.christianitytoday.com/ct/2001/novemberweb-only/11-26-41.0.html.
Hertz, Todd. 2002. "Biotech Backlash: New Coalition Rallies Against Human Cloning." *Christianity Today*. 7 Jan. Web. 1 Jun 2018. https://www.christianitytoday.com/ct/2002/january7/9.17.html.

Heuertz, Christopher L. 2017. *The Sacred Enneagram: Finding Your Unique Path to Spiritual Growth*. Grand Rapids: Zondervan.
Heuertz, Phillena. 2010. *Pilgrimage of a Soul: Contemplative Spirituality for the Active Life*. Downers, Grove, IL: Intervarsity.
Heuertz, Phillena. 2018. *Mindful Silence: The Heart of Christian Contemplation*. Downers Grove, IL: Intervarsity.
Hewitt, Steve. 2010. *Windows PCs in the Ministry*. Nashville: Thomas Nelson.
Hey, Sam. 2010. "God in the Suburbs and Beyond: The Emergence of an Australian Megachurch and Denomination." Dissertation: Griffith University.
Hindle, Tim. 2008. *Guide to Management Ideas and Gurus*. London: Economist.
Hirsch, Alan. 2006. *The Forgotten Ways: Reactivating the Missional Church*. Grand Rapids, MI: Brazos Press.
Hirsch, Alan, and David Ferguson. 2011. *On the Verge: A Journey into the Apostolic Future of the Church*. Grand Rapids, MI: Zondervan. Kindle Edition.
Hocken, Peter. 2009. *The Challenges of the Pentecostal, Charismatic, and Messianic Jewish Movements*. New York: Routledge.
Hoff, Derek Seabury. 2006. "Are We Too Many? the Population Debate and Policymaking in the Twentieth-Century United States." Dissertation: University of Virginia.
Hoke, Donald, ed. 1978a. *Evangelicals Face the Future: Scenarios, Addresses, and Responses from the 'Consultation on Future Evangelical Concerns' Held in Atlanta, Georgia, December 14–17, 1977*. Wheaton, IL: William Carey Library.
Hoke, Donald, ed. 1979, *An Evangelical Agenda: And Beyond: Addresses, Responses, and Scenarios from the 'Continuing Consultation on Future Evangelical Concerns' Held in Overland Park, Kansas, December 11–14, 1979*. Ed. Donald E. Hoke. Pasadena, CA: William Carey Library.
Hoke, Donald E. 1978b. "View of the Future as Reflected in Reports to the Club of Rome." *Evangelicals Face the Future: Scenarios, Addresses, and Responses from the 'Consultation on Future Evangelical Concerns' Held in Atlanta, Georgia, December 14–17, 1977*. Wheaton, IL: William Carey Library.
Holifield, E. Brooks. 1983. *A History of Pastoral Care in America: From Salvation to Self-Realization*. Eugene, OR: Wipf & Stock.
Holvast, Rene. 2009. *Spiritual Mapping in the United States and Argentina, 1989–2005: A Geography of Fear*. Boston: Brill.
Hook, C. Christopher. 2002. "Cybernetics and Nanotechnology." In *Cutting-Edge Bioethics: A Christian Exploration of Technologies and Trends*. Grand Rapids, MI: William B. Eerdmans.
Hormann, Aiko. 2015a. "Quantum Field Miracles—Part 1" Did We Love. 27 Mar. Youtube. 8 Apr 2019. https://www.youtube.com/watch?v = qbnBQsWdsRQ
Hormann, Aiko. 2015b. "Quantum Field Miracles—Part 2" Did We Love. 28 Mar. Youtube. 8 Apr 2019.
Horn, Thomas. 2015. "Tom Horn on Transhumanism, Grin [sic] Tech, and the Future of Man and Beast." *Charisma*. 29 Sep. Web. 8 Aug 2018. https://www.charismanews.com/opinion/52307-tom-horn-on-transhumanism-grin-tech-and-the-future-of-man-and-beast?showall = &limitstart =
Howard, Robert Glenn. 2013. *Digital Jesus: The Making of a New Christian Fundamentalist Community on the Internet*. New York: New York University Press.
Howell, Leon. 2003. *United Methodism @ Risk: A Wake-Up Call*. Kingston, NY: Information Project for United Methodists.
"HTC Investors" n.d. *HTC*. Web. 8 Jun 2018. http://investors.htc.com/phoenix.zhtml?c = 148697&p = irol-govBio&ID = 224272.
Hunsicker, David B. 1998. "The Rise of the Parachurch Movement in American Protestant Christianity During the 1930s and 1940s: A Detailed Study of the Beginnings of the Navigators, Young Life and Youth for Christ International." Dissertation: Trinity Evangelical Divinity School.
Hunt, Stephen. 2009. *A History of the Charismatic Movement in Britain and the United States of America: The Pentecostal Transformation of Christianity*. 2 Volumes. Lewiston, NY: Edwin Mellen.

Hunter, George III. 1996. "Church for the Unchurched" (excerpt). *NEXT Magazine* 2.2. (August).
Hutcheson, Richard G., Jr. 1979. *Wheel Within the Wheel: Confronting the Management Crisis of the Pluralistic Church.* Atlanta: John Knox Press.
Ingersoll, Julie. 2015. *Building God's Kingdom: Inside the World of Christian Reconstruction.* New York: Oxford University Press.
Irish, C.M., and C.B. Fulton, Jr. 2002. "Acts 29 Ministries" *New International Dictionary of Pentecostal Charismatic Movements.* Revised and Expanded Edition. Ed. Stanley M. Burgess and Eduard M. Van Der Maas. Grand Rapids, MI: Zondervaan.
Jackson, Michael C. 2000. *Systems Approaches to Management.* Boston: Kluwer Academic Publishers.
Jaffarian, Michael. 2009. "The Computer Revolution and Its Impact on Evangelical Mission Research and Strategy." *International Bulletin of Missionary Research.* Vol 33.1 (January): 33–37.
Johnson, Bill. 2010. Foreword. Mason, Phil. *Quantum Glory: The Science of Heaven Invading Earth.* Maricopa, AZ: XP Publishing. 17–18.
Johnson, Eric, and Stanton L. Jones,ed. 2000. *Psychology and Christianity: Four Views.* Downers Groves, IL: Intervarsity.
Johnson, Eric, and Staon L. Jones. 2000a. "A History of Christians in Psychology" In *Psychology and Christianity: Four Views.* Downers Groves, IL: Intervarsity. 11–53.
Johnson, Tommy Dale, Jr. 2014. "The Professionalization of Pastoral Care Within the Southern Baptist Convention: Gaines Dobbins and the Psychology of Religion." Dissertation: Southwestern Baptist Theological Seminary, 2014.
Jones, Tony. 2011. *The Church Is Flat: The Relational Ecclesiology of the Emerging Church Movement.* Minneapolis: JoPa Group.
Jones, Tony. 2014. *Phyllis Tickle: Evangelist of the Future.* Brewster, MA: Paraclete Press.
Joy, Bill. 2000. "Why the Future Doesn't Need Us." *Wired Magazine.* 01 Apr. Web. 8 Aug 2018. https://www.wired.com/2000/04/joy-2/.
Joyce, Kathryn. 2010. *Quiverfull: Inside the Christian Patriarchy Movement.* Boston: Beacon Press.
Kadushin, Charles. 2012. *Understanding Social Networks: Theories, Concepts, and Findings.* Oxford: Oxford University Press.
Kahlbau, Heath. 2014. "Is Anything New Under the Sun? a Comparative Evaluation of the Ante-Nicene Patristic Episcopacy and Common Polity Models Within the Contemporary Multi-Site Church Movement." Dissertation: Southeastern Baptist Theological Seminary.
Kallestad, Walter P., and Steven L. Schey. 1994. *Total Quality Ministry.* Minneapolis: Augsburg.
Kantzer, Kenneth S. 1978. "The Future of the Church and Evangelicalism." In *Evangelicals Face the Future.* Ed. Donald E. Hoke. Pasadena, CA: William Carey Library.
Kaoma, Kapya. 2009. "Globalizing the Culture Wars: U.S. Conservatives, African Churches, and Homophobia." Somerville, MA: Political Research Associates.
Kaoma, Kapya. 2009."The U.S. Christian Right and the Attack on Gays in Africa." *Political Research Associates.* 1 Dec. Web. 1 Jun 2018. http://www.politicalresearch.org/2009/12/01/the-u-s-christian-right-and-the-attack-on-gays-in-africa/#sthash.jtZf2w08.73wQpsFY.dpbs.
Karrupan, Corrine, Nancy E. Dunlap and Michael Waldrum. 2016. *Operation Management in Healthcare: Strategy and Practice.* New York: Springer.
Kay, William K. 2007. *Apostolic Networks in Britain: New Ways of Being Church.* Eugene, OR: Wipf & Stock, 2007.
"Keep the Faith: Cher Wang Counts on Virtual Reality and the Bible to Revive HTC." 2016. *Week in China.* 4 Mar. Web. 8 Jun 2018. https://www.weekinchina.com/2016/03/keep-the-faith/.
Keller, Timothy. 2011. *Counterfeit Gods.* New York: Riverhead Books.
Keller, Timothy. 2012. *Center Church.* Grand Rapids, MI: Zondervan.
Kelly, Kevin. 1994. *Out of Control: The Rise of Neo Biological Civilizationl.* New York: Perseus.
Kelly, Kevin. 1997. "New Rules for a New Economy." Excerpt. *Next Magazine* 3.2. (November): 6–9.
Kelly, Kevin. 1998. *New Rules for the New Economy: Radical Strategies for a Connected World.* New York: Viking.

Kelly, Kevin. 2002. "God Is the Machine." *Wired Magazine*. 1 Dec. Web. 8 Aug 2018. https://www.wired.com/2002/12/holytech/.

Kelly, Kevin. 2016. "Spiritual Guidance for Artificial Intelligences." *Q Ideas*. Youtube. 23 Sep. Web. 8 Aug 2018. https://www.youtube.com/watch?v = iZFih-VJ2fQ.

Kenneson, Phillip D., and James L. Street. 2003. *Selling Out the Church: The Dangers of Church Marketing*. Eugene, OR: Cascade Books.

Kidder, Annemarie. 2010. *Making Confession, Hearing Confession: A History of the Cure of Souls*. Collegeville, MN: Liturgical Press.

Kilner, John F., C. Christopher Hook and Diann B. Uustal, eds. 2002. *Cutting-Edge Bioethics: A Christian Exploration of Technologies and Trends*. Grand Rapids, MI: Eerdmans.

Kim, Kyoung Pan. 2009. "An Analysis of Dissertations on Church Growth Published During the Past Five Years (2004–2008)." Dissertation: Liberty University.

Kjos, Berit. n.d. "Mysticism and Global Mind Change" *Crossroad*. http://www.crossroad.to/articles2/007/global-mind-1.htm.

Kleffman, Sandy. 1996. "Faith On-Line Nearly 475 Attend Conference Designed to Help Christians Harness the Power of Cyberspace in Spreading the Gospel Don't Be Left Out, Organizers Warn." *San Jose Mercury News* (24 March 1996): 1B.

Kleiner, Art. 2008. *The Age of Heretics: A History of the Radical Thinkers Who Reinvented Corporate Management*. 2nd edition. San Francisco: Josey-Bass.

Klett, Leah Marieann. 2015. "City Harvest Church Pastor Kong Hee, Wife Sun Ho Update: Advisory Pastor Says 'New Days Are Unstoppable Despite Guilty Verdict.'" *Gospel Herald*. 2 November. Web. 8 Jun 2018. http://www.gospelherald.com/articles/59358/20151102/city-harvest-church-pastor-kong-hee-wife-sun-ho-update.htm.

Klikauer, Thomas. 2015. "What Is Managerialism?" *Critical Sociology* 41.7–8: 1103–1119. http://journals.sagepub.com/doi/abs/10.1177/0896920513501351?journalCode = crsb.

Knopf, Jim. n.d. "The Origin of Shareware." *Association of Software Professionals*. http://www.asp-software.org/users/history-of-shareware.asp.

Kovacs, Eduard. 2016. "Second Database Exposing Voter Records Found Online." *Security Week*. 4 Jan. Web. 8 Aug 2018. https://www.securityweek.com/second-database-exposing-voter-records-found-online.

Krattenmaker, Tom. 2013. *The Evangelicals You Don't Know: Introducing the Next Generation of Christians*. Lanham, MD: Rowman and Littlefield.

"Lambeth Conference: Resolution Archives from 1998." n.d. Anglican Communion Office. 2005. Web. 8 Jul 2017. http://www.anglicancommunion.org/media/76650/1998.pdf.

Langberg, Michael. 2006. "Faith Is Only a Mouse Click Away—Christians Learning to Spread the Word Online." *San Jose Mercury News* (16 March): 1C. Newsbank.

Lantzer, Jason. 2012. *Mainline Christianity: The Past and Future of America's Majority Faith*. New York: New York University Press. Kindle.

Larsen, David Kenneth. 2001. "God's Gardeners: American Protestant Evangelicals Confront Environmentalism, 1967–2000." Dissertation: University of Chicago.

Laszlo, Ervin, et al. 1978. *Goals for Mankind*. Updated and Revised Edition. Bergenfield, NJ: New American Library.

"Leadership Network Recommends" 1996. *Next Magazine*. Vol 2.2. (April).

"Leadership Network Recommends" 1998. *Next Magazine* Vol 4.5. (September\October).

Leane, Elizabeth. 2007. *Reading Popular Physics: Disciplinary Skirmishes and Textual Strategies*. Hampshire, England: Ashgate.

Lee, Laura Kim. 2002. "Changing Selves, Changing Society: Human Relations Experts and the Invention of T Groups, Sensitivity Training and Encounter in the United States, 1938–1980." Dissertation: University of California, Los Angeles.

Lee, Michael D. 2016. "Making Church Sound; Contemporary Christian Discourse and Practice About Audio Production and Religious Experience" Dissertation: Indiana University.

"Leonard Sweet Biography." n.d. Web. 8 Jun 2019. https://leonardsweet.com/about/.

Lethem, John. 2016. "It All Connects: Adam Curtis and the Secret History of Everything." *New York Times Magazine*. 27 Oct. Web. Accessed 7 Jul 2017. https://www.nytimes.com/interactive/2016/10/30/magazine/adam-curtis-documentaries.html.

Lev-Ram, Michael. 2014. "Cher Wang: A Visionary Tech Founder Returns." *Fortune*. 7 Jul. Web. 8 Jun 2018. http://fortune.com/2014/07/07/cher-wang-htc/.

Levy, Steven. 1984. *Hackers: Heroes of the Computer Revolution.* Garden City, N.Y: Anchor Press/Doubleday.
"Linda Berquist: NAMB Church Planting Catalyst." 2018. California Southern Baptist Conference. http://www.csbc.com/team/linda-bergquist.
Linder, Alex. 2018. "HTC Boss Cher Wang Bilked of a Few Million Dollars by Church Mates and Long Time Friends." 5 May. Web. 8 Aug 2018. http://shanghaiist.com/2016/02/14/htc-cher-wang/.
Lindop, Grevel. 2015. *Charles Williams: The Third Inkling.* Oxford: Oxford University Press.
Lindsay, D. Michael. 2007. *Faith in the Halls of Power: How Evangelicals Joined the American Elite.* New York: Oxford University Press.
Logan, Robert. 2006. *Be Fruitful and Multiply.* St. Charles, IL: Churchsmart Resources.
Logan, Robert E. 1990. *Beyond Church Growth: Action Plans for Developing a Dynamic Church.* Old Tappan, NJ: Fleming H. Revell Company.
Lohr, Eileen. 2015. "Cold War Teenitiative: American Evangelical Youth and the Developing World in the Early Cold War." *The Journal of the History of Childhood and Youth* 8.2 (Spring): 295–317. Project Muse. Web. Accessed 2 Feb 2017.
Loohauis, Jackie. 1999. "Y2K—An All Purpose Fear—More Than a Computer Glitch, the Millennial Bug Has Become an Opportunity to Sell, Defraud, Scare, and Even Prepare." *Milwaukee Journal Sentinel* (12 September): 1. Academic Newsbank.
Lorenz. E. 1979. "Does a Butterfly's Wing in Brazil Set Off a Tornado in Texas?" Address at the American Association for the Advancement of Science, Washington.
Lowe, Kevin. 2013. "Baptized with the Soil." Dissertation. Pennsylvania State University. Proquest.
Magoola, Robert Joshua. 2015. "Preemptive Restorying as a Means of Mitigating Costly Conflict: The Case of the Anglican Mission in America and the Anglican Church of Rwanda." Dissertation: Asbury Theological Seminary.
Malone, Michael S. 2002. *The Valley of Heart's Delight: A Silicon Valley Notebook, 1963–2001.* New York: Wiley.
Manetsch, Thomas J. 1967. "A New Approach to Studying Some Social Processes." *Journal of American Science Affiliation (JASA)* 19 (September): 77–86. http://www.asa3.org/ASA/PSCF/1967/JASA9-67Manetsch.html.
Manetsch, Thomas J. 1978. "Goal Setting in a Christian Congregation." *Journal of American Science Affiliation* (JASA) 30 (September). http://www.asa3.org/ASA/PSCF/1978/JASA9-78Manetsch.html.
Mantyla, Kyle. 2016. "Ted Cruz Welcomes Endorsement of Mike Bickle, Who Believes Oprah Is a Forerunner to the Antichrist." *Right Wing Watch.* Jan 22. Web. 8 May 2018. http://www.rightwingwatch.org/post/ted-cruz-welcomes-endorsement-of-mike-bickle-who-believes-oprah-is-a-forerunner-to-the-antichrist/.
Marishane, Jeffrey. 1991. "Prayer, Profit, and Power: US Religious Right and Foreign Policy" *Review of African Political Economy* 52 (Nov): 73–86.
Marsden, George. 1984. "Introduction: The Evangelical Denomination." *Evangelicalism and Modern America.* Edited by George Marsden. Grand Rapids, MI: Eerdmans. vii-xix.
Marsden, George. 2006. *Fundamentalism and American Culture.* New York: Oxford University Press.
Marsden, George, ed. 1984. *Evangelicalism and Modern America.* Grand Rapids, MI: Eerdmans.
Martin, William. 2005. *With God on Our Side: The Rise of the Religious Right in America.* Revised ed. New York: Broadway.
Mason, Phil. 2010. *Quantum Glory: The Science of Heaven Invading Earth.* Maricopa, AZ: XP Publishing.
Matthews, Jean Isabel. 2009. "Power, Management and Complexity in the NHS: A Foucauldian Perspective." Dissertation. University of Glamorgan. http://dspace1.isd.glam.ac.uk/dspace/handle/10265/435.
McCray, W. Patrick. 2013. *The Visioneers.* Princeton: Princeton University Press.
McDonald, Gordon. 1978. "Social Relations and Alternative Future Paths." *Evangelicals Face the Future: Scenarios, Addresses, and Responses from the 'Consultation on Future Evangelical Concerns' Held in Atlanta, Georgia, December 14–17, 1977.* Wheaton, IL: William Carey Library. 84–90.

McDonald, Marvin. 1990. "Exploring 'Levels of Explanation' Concepts Part II: Levels in Science-Religion Dialogue." *Perspectives on Christian Faith*. PSCF 42 (March): 23–33. http://www.asa3.org/ASA/PSCF/1990/PSCF3-90McDonald.html.

McElligot, Ann Elizabeth Proctor. 1995. "The Business of Teaching Christians: National Education Leadership in the Episcopal Church, 1945–1976." Dissertation: New York University.

McGavran, Donald. 1990. *Understanding Church Growth*. Edited by Peter Wagner. 3rd Edition. Grand Rapids, MI: Eerdmans.

McGinn, Bernard J., John J. Collins and Stephen J. Stein. 2003. *The Continuum History of Apocalypticism*. New York: Continuum. pp. 467–492.

Mcguire, Russ. 2015. "The Intelligence Revolution for Churches (Part 2)" *Christian Computing* 27.1. (January): 22–25.

Mcintosh, Gary. 2004. *Evaluating the Church Growth Movement*. Grand Rapids, MI: Zondervan.

Mcintosh, Gary L. 2004b. "Why Church Growth Can't Be Ignored." In *Evaluating the Church Growth Movement*. Edited by Gary Mcintosh. Grand Rapids, MI: Zondervan.

Mcintosh, Gary L. 2005. "The Impact of Donald A. McGavran's Church Growth Missiology on Selected Denominations in the United States of America, 1970–2000." Dissertation: Fuller Theological Seminary.

Mcintosh, Gary L. 2009. *Taking Your Church to the Next Level*. Grand Rapids, MI: Baker Books.

McKelvey, Bill. 1999. "Complexity Theory in Organization Science: Seizing the Promise or Becoming a Fad?" Emergence 1.1: 5–32.

McKenna, David. 1986. *Mega Truth: The Church in the Age of Information*. San Bernardino, CA: Here's Life Publishing.

McKinley, Angus Richards. 1999. "The Cell Church Strategy of Ralph W. Neighbour in Evangelism and Discipleship." Dissertation: Southwestern Baptist Theological Seminary.

McKinney, Jennifer, and Roger Finke. 2002. "Reviving the Mainline: An Overview of Clergy Support for Evangelical Renewal Movements." *Journal for the Scientific Study of Religion* 41.4: 771–783.

McLaren, Brian. 2000. *Church on the Other Side*: Grand Rapids, MI: Zondervan.

McMahan, Martin Alan. 1998. "Training Turn-Around Leaders: Systemic Approaches to Reinstating Growth in Plateaued Churches." Dissertation: Fuller Theological Seminary.

McNeal, Reggie. 2003. *The Present Future: Six Tough Questions for the Church*. San Francisco: Josey Bass.

McNeill, John T. 1951. *History of the Cure of Souls*. Harper & Row.

McPhee, Arthur G. 2007–2008. "How Research Became a Signature Factor in Church Growth and Evangelism." *Journal of the Academy for Evangelism in Theological Education* 23: 43–57.

McVicar, Michael J. 2010. "Reconstructing America: Religion, American Conservatism, and the Political Theology of Rousas John Rushdoony." Dissertation: Ohio State University.

Mead, Frank S., and Samuel Hill. 1990. *Handbook of Denominations in the United States*. Nashville: Abingdon Press.

Mead, Loren. 1981. "Consultants—What They Are and What They Are Good For" In *Consultations*. Edited by Jere Allen. Atlanta: Home Missions Board. 89–98.

"Meet Mel Schell." n.d. Growth Ministries International. http://gogmi.org/about-us/board-of-directors/mel-schell/.

Meltzer, Leslie A. 2008. "Human Dignity and Bioethics: Essays Commissioned by the President's Council on Bioethics." *New England Journal of Medicine* 359.6 (August): 660–661. Book Review.

Menand, Louis. 2005. "Fat Man: Herman Kahn and the Nuclear Age." *New Yorker*. 27 Jun. Web. 2 Jun 2018.

Merritt, Jonathan. 2017. "Is AI a Threat to Christianity?: Are You There, God? It's I, a Robot." *Atlantic Monthly*. 3 Feb. Web. 2 Jun 2018. https://www.theatlantic.com/technology/archive/2017/02/artificial-intelligence-christianity/515463/.

Metcalfe, Robert M. 2007. "It's All in Your Head." *Forbes*. 20 Apr. Web. 8 Aug 2018. https://www.forbes.com/forbes/2007/0507/052.html#2f0fe94847d3.

Metzger, Gregory. 2012. "A New Apostolic Movement? the Need for Discernment." *Christianity Today: Books and Culture*. July\August. https://www.booksandculture.com/articles/2012/julaug/apostolicmovement.html.

"Michael Yang, Silicon Valley Entrepreneur Talks About His Faith." 2013. *Finding God in Silicon Valley*. 27 Feb. Web. 8 Aug 2018. https://findinggodinsiliconvalley.com/michael-yang-silicon-valley-entrepreneur/.
Migliore, R. Henry. 1988. *Strategic Planning for Ministry and Church Growth*. Tulsa, OK: Harrison House.
Miller, Donald E. 1997. *Reinventing American Protestantism*. Berkley: University of California Press.
Miller, James, Grier. 1965b. "Cross-Level Hypotheses." *Behavioral Science* 10 (1965).
Miller, James Grier. 1965a. "Living Systems Basic Concepts." *Behavioral Science* 10: 193–237.
Miller, James Grier, and Jessie L. Miller. 1992. "Cybernetics, General Systems Theory, and Living Systems Theory," in Ralph L Levine and Hiram E. Fitzgerald, eds. *Analysis of Dynamic Psychological Systems, Vol. 1: Basic Approaches to General Systems, Dynamic Systems and Cybernetics*. New York: Plenum Press.
Milligan, Susan. 2017. "Trump's Spiritual Journey: Once Skeptical, the Religious Right Is Now Singing the Praises of President Donald Trump." *U.S. News and World Report*. 5 May. Web. 8 Jun 2018. https://www.usnews.com/news/the-report/articles/2017-05-05/president-trumps-spiritual-journey-delivers-for-the-religious-right.
Milton, Joyce. 2002. *The Road to Malpsychia: Humanistic Psychology and Our Discontents*. San Francisco: Encounter Books.
Mims, Bob. 2000. "Is the Internet an Instrument of God?—Computer Exec Turned Evangelical Writer Says Cyberspace Guided by the Hand of the Almighty." *Salt Lake City Tribune*. 18 March: C2. Newsbank.
Mintzberg, Henry. 2013. *The Rise and Fall of Strategic Planning*. New York: Free Press.
Mirowski, Philip. 2002. *Machine Dreams: Economics Becomes a Cyborg Science*. New York: Cambridge University Press.
Missler, Chuck. 2016. *Beyond Perception*. Coeur d'Alene, ID: Koinonia House.
Moberg, David O. 1966. "A Brief Report on Cybernetics, Determinism, and Free Will." *Journal of the American Scientific Affiliation (JASA)* 18 (March): 21–23. http://www.asa3.org/ASA/PSCF/1966/JASA3-66Moberg.html.
"Mobile Ministry Magazine." n.d. *Mobile Ministry Magazine*. Accessed 8 Aug 2018. http://www.mobileministrymagazine.com/.
Moll, Peter. 1991. *From Scarcity to Sustainability: Future Studies and the Environment: The Role of the Club of Rome*. Peter Lang: Frankfurt am Main.
Montgomery, Peter. 2015. "Biblical Economics: The Divine Laissez-Faire Mandate." *Political Research Associates*. 21 Apr. Web. 8 Aug 2018. http://www.politicalresearch.org/2015/04/21/biblical-economics-the-divine-laissez-faire-mandate/#sthash.49Q1lFlM.ydr7NAb2.dpbs.
Moore, S. David. 2003. *The Shepherding Movement*. London: T &T Clark.
Moore, William Gene. 2003. "The Gospel Ministry from English Separatism of the Late Sixteenth Century to the Southern Baptist Convention of the Early Twentieth Century." Dissertation: Southern Baptist Theological Seminary. Proquest.
Moorhead, James H. 2003. "Apocalypticism in Mainstream Protestantism, 1800 to the Present" In *The Continuum History of Apocalypticism*. Ed. Bernard J. McGinn, John J. Collins, and Stephen J. Stein. New York: Continuum. 467–492.
Moreau, A. Scott, et al., eds. 2000. *Evangelical Dictionary of World Missions*. Grand Rapids, MI: Baker.
Morgan, Gareth. 1986. *Images of Organization*. Newbury Park: Sage.
Moriarty, Michael. 1992. *The New Charismatics: A Concerned Voice Responds to Dangerous New Trends*. Grand Rapids, MI: Zondervan.
Morrison, Mark S. 2007. *Modern Alchemy: Occultism and the Emergence of Atomic Theory*. Oxford: Oxford University Press.
Mosco, Vincent, and Derek Foster. 2001. "Cyberspace and the End of Politics." *Journal of Communication Inquiry* 25.3 (July): 218–236.
Murphy, Caryle. 2016. "The Most and Least Educated U.S. Religious Groups." *Pew Research Center*. 4 Nov. Web. Accessed 8 Jun 2017. http://www.pewresearch.org/fact-tank/2016/11/04/the-most-and-least-educated-u-s-religious-groups/.
Myers, Joseph. 2003. *The Search to Belong: Rethinking Intimacy, Community, and Small Groups*. Grand Rapids, MI: Zondervan.

Naughton, Jim. n.d. "Following the Money." A Special Report from the Washington Window. Private Collection.
Neighbour, Ralph W., Jr. 1990. *Where Do We Go from Here? a Guidebook for the Cell Group Church.* Houston: Touch Publications.
Nel, Malan. 2009. "Congregational Analysis Revisited: Empirical Approaches." *HTS Teologiese/ Theological Studies* 65 (1) (January): 230–242.
"Network." n.d. Lexico (Oxford). https://www.lexico.com/en/definition/network.
"Network." n.d. *Merriam-Webster.* https://www.merriam-webster.com/dictionary/network.
Nielsen, Frederick H. 1997. "Doubters in the Land of Plenty; the Limits to Growth Movement in the United States." Dissertation: University of Kansas.
O'Connell, Jennifer Oliver. 2010. "Global Evangelism Meets Twenty-First Century Technology." *Los Angeles Examiner.* 12 March. No pagination. Newsbank.
Olson, Richard Lee. 1988. "The Largest Congregations in the United States: An Empirical Study of Church Growth and Decline." Dissertation: Northwestern University.
Oppenheimer, Mark. 2014. "Evangelicals Find Themselves in the Midst of a Calvinist Revival." *New York Times.* 3 Jan. https://www.nytimes.com/2014/01/04/us/a-calvinist-revival-for-evangelicals.html?_r = 0.
"Our Best Reports and Downloads from 2016" 2016. Web. 2018. http://leadnet.org/our-best-reports-and-downloads-from-2016/.
P-I Staff. 1997. "Meese to Address Discovery Institute's Public Policy Conference." *Seattle Post Intelligencer.* 7 Jan. Newsbank. B8.
Panzaris, Georgios. 2008. "Machines and Romances: The Technical and Narrative Construction of Networked Computing as a General-Purpose Platform, 1960–1995." Dissertation: Stanford University.
Patterson, George, and Richard Scoggins. 2002. *Church Multiplication Guide: The Miracle of Church Reproduction.* Pasadena, CA: William Carey Library.
Pattison, E. Mansell. 1981. *Pastor and Parish—A System Approach.* Philadelphia: Fortress Press.
Payne, Jervis David. 2001. "An Evaluation of the Systems Approach to North American Church Multiplication Movements of Robert E. Logan in Light of the Missiology of Roland Allen." Dissertation: Southern Baptist Theological Seminary.
Peck, Josh. 2017. *Unraveling the Multiverse: The Christian's Guide to Quantum Physics, Entities from Higher Realities, Strange Technologies, and Ancient Prophecies Being Fulfilled Today.* Defender Publishing. Ebook.
Penner, Myron A. 2013. "The Rise of New Calvinism Among Canadian Mennonite Brethren." *Direction Journal* (Fall): 148–165. http://www.directionjournal.org/42/2/rise-of-new-calvinism-among-canadian.html.
"Pentecostal and Charismatic Research Initiative." n.d. *Center for Religion and Civic Culture.* Web. 6 Jun 2017. https://crcc.usc.edu/pcri/.
Pickering, Matthew, Daniel. 2011. "The Picture of Health: A Study of Church Health in the Central New York District of the Wesleyan Church" Dissertation: Asbury Theological Seminary.
Pietsch, Brendan. 2011. "Dispensational Modernism." Dissertation: Duke University.
Piper, John. 2004. "How God and Christians Treasure Christ." *Desiring God.* Web. 8 Aug 2018. https://www.desiringgod.org/articles/how-god-and-christians-treasure-christ-part-2.
Polak, Fred. 1973. *The Image of the Future.* Translated and abridged by Elise Boulding. Amsterdam, Netherlands: Elsevier.
Poloma, Margaret. 2003. *Main Street Mystics: The Toronto Blessing & Reviving Pentecostalism.* Walnut Creek, CA: Altamire Press.
Posadas, Jeremy D. 2012. "The Body of Christ Worships in the Era of Biopower: Towards a Liturgical Somatics." Dissertation: Emory University.
Prebble, Edward. 2012. "Invigorating the Church for Mission: Action Research with Local Parishes." Dissertation: The University of Waikato.
Prehn, Yvonne. 2016. "How to Effectively Use Volunteers to Create All the Communications Your Church Needs." *MinistryTech* (Jun): 4–7.
Primer, Ben. 1979. *Protestants and American Business Methods.* Ann Arbor, MI: UMI Research Press.
Pringle, Phil. 2008. *But God.* Lake Mary, FL: Christian Life.

Pringle, Phil. 2014. *Inspired to Pray*. Grand Rapids: Chosen.
Pritchard, Gregory. 1994. "The Strategy of Willow Creek Community Church: A Study in the Sociology of Religion." Dissertation: Northwestern.
"Programs." 2017. *Leadership Network*. 29 Jul. Web. 8 Aug 2018. http://leadnet.org/programs/. Retrieved at https://web.archive.org/web/20170729044913/http://leadnet.org/programs/.
Putnam, Robert. 2000. *Bowling Alone: The Collapse and Revival of American Community*. New York: Simon & Schuster.
"Quantum Healing—David Van Kovering."2015. 31 Jul. *Youtube*. 8 Apr 2018. https://www.youtube.com/watch?v = qRkY6VyrD40.
Queen, Christopher Scott. 1986. "Systems Theory in Religious Studies: A Methodological Critique." Dissertation: Boston University.
Quinn, Michelle. 1997. "Crusade Promotes the Microsoft Way." *Ledger-Enquirer* (Columbus, Georgia). 15 Nov. B4.
Rabey, Steve. 1991. "Religious Groups in Springs Lure Mapping Firm—GMI Takes Refuge from High Business Costs of California." Gazette Telegraph (Colorado Springs). 12 Jul. *Newsbank*. 8 (Business section).
Rainer, Thom. 1988. "An Assessment of C. Peter Wagner's Contributions to the Theology of Church Growth." Dissertation: Southern Baptist Theological Seminary.
Rainer, Thom. 1993. *The Book of Church Growth: History, Theology and Principles*. Nashville: Broadman.
Reeves, R. Daniel, and Ron Jenson. 1984. *Always Advancing: Modern Strategies for Church Growth*. San Bernardino, CA: Here's Life Publishers.
Reifsnyder, Richard W. 1984. "The Reorganizational Impulse in American Protestantism: The Presbyterian Church (U.S.A.) as a Case Study (1788–1983)." Dissertation: Princeton Theological Seminary.
Reynolds, Jeffrey Paul. 2014. "Dawson Trotman's Personal Spiritual Disciplines as the Foundation for His Great Commission Ministry." Dissertation: Southern Baptist Theological Seminary.
"Richard Flory: Associate Professor (Research) of Sociology" 2017. *USC Dornsife*. Web. Accessed 1 Sep 2017. https://dornsife.usc.edu/cf/faculty-and-staff/faculty.cfm?pid = 1018147.
Richards, Jay, ed. 2002. *Are We Spiritual Machines?*. Seattle: Discovery Institute.
Richey, Russel E. 2013. *Denominationalism Illustrated and Explained*. Eugene, OR: Cascade Books. Kindle Edition.
Rivlin, Gary. 2002. "The Madness of King George: George Gilder Listened to the Technology, and Became Guru of the Telecosm. the Markets Listened to His Newsletter, and Followed Him into the Global Crossing Abyss. Yet He's Never Stopped Believing." *Wired*. 01 Jul. Web. 8 Aug 2018. https://www.wired.com/2002/07/gilder-6/.
Roberts, Bob, Jr. 2007. *Glocalization: How Followers of Jesus Engage a Flat World*. Grabd Rapids, MI: Zondervan.
Robinson, Herb. 1991. "Ideas from the Region's Best and Brightest." *The Seattle Times*. 27 Sept. Editorial.
Roddam, John W.R. 1997. "Quality Ministry in the Local Church." Dissertation: Fuller Theological Seminary. Proquest.
Rodriguez, Augusto. 2003. "New Apostolic Churches in Greater Los Angeles: Renewal, Mission, and Growth." Dissertation: Fuller Theological Seminary.
Rogers, Everett M. 1983. *Diffusion of Innovations*. 3rd Edition. New York: Free Press.
Rogers. Everett M. 1998. "Leadership and Diffusing Innovation." Interviewed by *Netfax*. Netfax 110 (9). 15.
Rothschild, Michael. 1990. *Bionomics: The Inevitability of Capitalism*. New York: Henry Holt and Company.
Rowe, Josh. 2011. "The Public Life of Information." Dissertation: Princeton University.
Roxburgh, Alan, and Fred Romanuk. 2006. *The Missional Leader*. San Francisco: Josey Bass.
Rubenstein, Mary Jane. 2008. "Anglicans in the Postcolony: On Sex and the Limits of Communion." *Telos* 143 (Summer): 133–160.
Rubin, Julius H. 1994. *Religious Melancholy and Protestant Experience in America*. New York: Oxford University Press.

Works Cited

Russel, Andrew L. 2014. *Open Standards and the Digital Age: History, Ideology, and Networks*. New York: Cambridge University Press.

Sabin, Paul. 2013. *The Bet: Paul Ehrlich, Julian Simon, and Our Gamble Over Earth's Future*. New Haven: Yale University Press.

Sahin, Ismail. 2006. "Detailed Review of Rogers' Diffusion of Innovations Theory and Educational Technology-Related Studies Based on Rogers' Theory." *The Turkish Online Journal of Educational Technology* 5.2 (April): 14–23.

Sardar, Ziauddin. 2013. *Future: All That Matters*. London: Mcgraw Hill.

Sargeant, Kimon Howland. 1996. "Faith and Fulfillment: Willow Creek and the Future of Evangelicalism." Dissertation: University of Virginia.

Schalk, Christoph A. 1999. "Organisational Diagnosis of Churches: The Statistical Development of the 'Natural Church Development' Survey and Its Relation to Organizational Psychology." Institute for Natural Church Development, Germany.

Schaller, Lyle E. 1969. *The Impact of the Future: Trends Affecting the Church of Tomorrow*. Nashville: Abingdon Press.

Schaller, Lyle E. 1976. *Understanding Tomorrow*. Nashville: Abingdon.

Schaller, Lyle E. 1995. *The New Reformation: Tomorrow Arrived Yesterday*. Nashville: Abingdon Press.

Schaller, Lyle E. 1999. *Discontinuity and Hope: Radical Change and the Path to the Future*. Nashville, Abingdon Press.

Scheinn, Richard. 1997. "Digital Evangelism Fundamentalists Harness the Net to Spread the Word." *The Mercury News* (San Jose, California). 18 Oct. Newsbank. 1E.

Scheitle, Christopher. 2008. "Beyond the Congregation: Christian Nonprofits in the United States." Dissertation: Pennsylvania State University. Proquest.

Schell, Melvin F. 1988. "Using Computers to Support Total Church Growth" In *Church Growth State of the Art*. Editor C. Peter Wagner. Wheaton, IL: Tyndale.

Schell, Melvin F. 2015. "The Bible and Cybernetics." *Growth Ministries International*. 17 Jun. http://gogmi.org/the-bible-and-cybernetics/. Accessed Jun 8, 2018. For More bibliographic information on this entry, see http://gogmi.org/?s = %22bible+and+cybernetics%22.

Schell, Melvin F. 2017. "Understanding Total Church Systems." Manual. Growth Ministries International.gogomi.org/wp-content/,, ,.TCS-TotalChurchSystems-Instruction-Manual-151101.docx. Accessed 8 Apr 2017.

Schlect, Christopher. 2015. "Onward Christian Administrators." Dissertation: Washington State University.

Schulz, G.W. 2016. "Are Christian Conservatives Behind Breach of 18 Million Voter Records." *Reveal*. 2 Mar. Web. 8 Jun 2018.

Schwartz, James. 2000. "Death of an Altruist: Was the Man Who Found the Selfless Gene Too Good for This World?" *Lingua Franca* 10.5 (July/August): no pagination, so I have used pdf pagination for reader convenience.

Schwarz, Christian. 1996. *Natural Church Development: A Guide to Eight Essential Qualities of Healthy Churches*. Carol Stream, IL: ChurchSmart Resources.

Schwarz, Christian. 1999. *Paradigm Shift in the Church; How Natural Church Development Can Transform Theological Thinking*. Carol Stream, IL: Churchsmart Resources.

Schweiger, Beth Barton. 1994. "The Transformation of Southern Religion: Clergy and Congregations in Virginia, 1830–1895." Dissertation: University of Virginia. Proquest.

Scotland, Nigel. 2000. *Charismatics and the New Millennium: The Impact of Charismatic Christianity from 1960 into the New Millennium*. Guildford, UK: Eagle.

Searcy, Nelson. N.D *Healthy Systems, Healthy Church*. Ebook.

Senter, Mark Houston. 1989. "The Youth for Christ Movement as an Educational Agency and Its Impact Upon Protestant Churches: 1931–1979." Dissertation: Loyola University of Chicago.

Shakespeare, Lyndon. 2016. *Being the Body of Christ in the Age of Management*. Eugene Oregon: Cascade Books. Kindle Edition.

Sheetz-Willard, Julia. 2007. "Seeking More Light: Contemporary Debate About Homosexuality in the Presbyterian Church (U.S.A.)" Dissertation: Temple University/.

Sheldrake, John. 2002. *Management Theory*. Second Edition. London: Cenage Learning EMEA.

Shires, Preston. 2007. *Hippies of the Religious Right: From the Countercultures of Jerry Garcia to the Subculture of Jerry Falwell.* Waco, TX: Baylor University Press.
Sidorick, Daniel. 2009. *Condensed Capitalism: Campbell Soup and the Pursuit of Cheap Production in the Twentieth Century.* Ithaca, NY: Cornell University Press. Kindle Edition.
Siewert, John. 2000. "Information Technology." In *Evangelical Dictionary of World Missions.* Ed. A. Scott Moreau. Grand Rapids, MI: Baker Books.
Sine, Tom. 1981. *The Mustard Seed Conspiracy: You Can Make a Difference in Tomorrow's Troubled World.* Waco, TX: Word Books.
Sivulka, Julian. 2012. *Soap, Sex, and Cigarettes: A Cultural History of American Advertising.* Boston: Wadsworth (Cenage).
Sizer, Aaron W. 2012. "'A Beautiful Prophecy Awaiting Fulfillment': The Presbyterian New Era Movement and Religious Reconstruction, 1918–1925." Dissertation: Princeton.
Skyttner, Lars. 2001. *General Systems Theory: Ideas and Applications.* River Edge, NJ: World Scientific.
Slobodian, Quinn. 2018. *Globalists: The End of Empire and the Birth of Neoliberalism.* Cambridge, MA: Harvard University Press.
Slocum, Robert. 1990. *Maximize Your Ministry: How You as a Lay Person Can Impact Your World for Jesus Christ.* Colorado Springs, Colorado: NavPress.
Smietana, Bob. 2005. "High Tech Circuit-Riders." *Christianity Today* (September): 60–63. Ebscohost.
Smietana, Bob. 2012. "Anglican Mission in the Americas Confronts a New Power Struggle with Rwandan Patrons." *Huffington Post* (Religion News Services). 10 Feb. https://www.huffingtonpost.com/2012/02/10/anglican-mission-in-the-americas-rwanada_n_1266831.html.
Smith, Aaron C.T. 2004. "Complexity Theory as a Practical Management Tool." *Organization Management Journal.* 1.2: 91–106.
Smith, Brad. 1997. "Church Leaders Network." Interview by *Next Magazine. NEXT* magazine 3.3. (Dec): 4.
Smith, Ebbie C. 2000. "Church Planting." Evangelical Dictionary of World Missions. Ed. Scott Moreau. Grand Rapids, MI: Baker Books. 202–203.
Smith, James Clappdale. 1976. "Without Crossing Barriers: The Homogenous Unit Concept in the Writings of Donald Anderson Mcgavran." Dissertation: Fuller Theological Seminary. Proquest.
Smith, James K.A. 2011. "The 'New Calvinism' … How New Is It." *Christian Courier: A Reformed Biweekly.* 11 Apr. 12.
Smith, Kevin John. 2002. "The Origins, Nature, and Significance of the Jesus Movement as a Revitalization Movement." Dissertation: E. Stanley School of World Mission and Evangelism (Asbury Theological Seminary).
Smith, Nils. 2016. "Setting Up Your Social Media Profile." Podcast. 7 Sep. Web. 8 Aug 2018. http://leadnet.org/setting-up-your-social-media-profiles-podcast-189/.
Smith, Warner Anderson. n.d. "A Neo-Orthodox Theology Applied: An Analysis of the Hermeneutics of Christian A. Schwarz's Natural Church Development." Web. 8 Mar 2016. http://warnersmith.org/archives/153.
Smith, Warner Anderson. 2006. "An Analysis of Church Consultation in the North American Church, 1960–2003." Dissertation: Southern Baptist Theological Seminary.
Smith, Wesley J. 2004. *Consumer's Guide to a Brave New World.* San Francisco: Encounter Books.
Smith, Wesley J. 2016. "Bioethics in the Age of Trump." *Weekly Standard.* 26 Dec. Web. 8 Aug 2018. http://www.discovery.org/a/25321/.
Snyder, Howard A. 1975. *The Problem of Wineskins: Church Structure in a Technological Age.* Downers Grove, IL: Intervarsity.
Snyder, Howard A. 1983. *Liberating the Church; the Ecology of Church & Kingdom.* Basingstoke, UK: Intervarsity.
Snyder, Howard A., and Daniel V. Runyon. 1986. *Foresight: Major Trends That Will Dramatically Affect the Future of Christians and the Church.* Nashville: Thomas Nelson.
"Society for General Systems Research (SGSR\ISSS)." 2017. *BCSS. Bertalanffy Center for the Study of Systems Science.* Web. 8 Aug 2017. http://www.bcsss.org/the-center/legacy/system-movement/society-for-general-systems-research-sgsrisss/.

Works Cited

"Speaker Info." n.d. Silicon Valley Prayer Breakfast. http://www.svpb.net/speaker-info.html.
Stabile, Suzanne. 2018. *The Path Between Us: An Enneagram Journey to Healthy Relationships*. Downers Grove, IL: Intervarsity.
Stamper, Amber M. 2013. "Witnessing the Web: The Rhetoric of American E-Vangelism and Persuasion Online." Dissertation: University of Kentucky, Lexington.
Stamper, Amber M. 2014. "Building the Narrow Gate: Digital Decisions for Christ and the Draw of Rhetorical Space." *Journal of Religion, Media, and Digital Culture (JRMDC)* 3.2 (August): 116–151.
Stanley, Andy. 2011. *Catalyst: Andy Stanley Systems*. 11 Jun. Web. 8 Aug 2018. https://vimeo.com/24979087.
Stanley, Charles. 2001. *Charles Stanley's Handbook for Christian Living: Biblical Answers to Life's Tough Questions*. Revised Edition. Nashville: Thomas Nelson.
Stanley, E. Bevan. 2003. "Organizing the Congregation: The Use of Community Organizing Techniques in the Training of Congregational Leaders." Dissertation: Hartford Seminary.
Steffes, David Michael. 2008. "The 'Eco-Worldview' of Charles Birch: Biology, Environmentalism and Liberal Christianity in the 20th Century." Dissertation: University of Oklahoma Graduate College.
Steger, Manfred B., and Ravi K. Roy. 2010. *Neoliberalism: A Very Short Introduction*. Oxford: Oxford University Press. Kindle Edition.
Stetzer, Ed. n.d. "The Evolution of Church Growth, Church Health, and the Missional Church: An Overview of the Church Growth Movement From, and Back To, Its Missional Roots. Alpharetta, GA: North American Mission Board (NAMB). Https:\\www.christianitytoday.com\assets\10231.pdf.
Stetzer, Ed. 2003. "The Impact of the Church Planting Process and Other Selected Factors on the Attendance of Southern Baptist Church Plants." Dissertation: Southern Baptist Theological Seminary.
Stetzer, Ed. 2005. "Church Planting: Observations on the State of North American Mission Strategies." Originally published in *Journal of Evangelism and Missions*. http://churchplanting.net/FreeDownloads/General%20Church%20Planting/Church%20Planting%20Trends%20in%20North%20America.pdf.
Stetzer, Ed. 2013. "Understanding the Charismatic Movement: Over 300 Million People in the World Are Considered Charismatic Christians." *Christianity Today: The Exchange*. 18 Oct. Web. 8 May 2018. https://www.christianitytoday.com/edstetzer/2013/october/charismatic-renewal-movement.html.
Stetzer, Ed. 2014. "Moving Toward Church Multiplication Movements: 4 Steps for Developing Multiplication Leaders." *Christianity Today: The Exchange*. 7 Apr. https://www.christianitytoday.com/edstetzer/2014/april/4-steps-for-developing-multiplication-leaders.html.
Stetzer, Ed, and Warren Bird. n.d. "The State of Church Planting in the United States: Research Overview and Qualitative Study of Primary Church Planting Entities." https://www.christianitytoday.com/assets/10228.pdf.
Stetzer, Ed, and Warren Bird. 2013. *Viral Churches: Helping Church Planters Become Movement Makers*. San Francisco: Josey-Bass.
Stewart, Joe Randall. 2013. "The Influence of Newbign's Missiology on Selected Innovators and Early Adopters of the Emerging Church Paradigm." Dissertation: Southern Baptist Theological Seminary.
Stockdale, Todd J. 2013. "Ecclesiological Contributions of Emerging Churches for Their Parent Communities." Dissertation: University of Edinburgh.
"Strong Ties, Weak Ties, and Social Networks." 1999. *Netfax*. No. 129 (2 Aug).
Strub, Whitney. 2010. *Perversion for Profit: The Politics of Pornography and the Rise of the New Right*. New York: Columbia University Press.
Surratt, Geoff, Greg Ligon, and Warren Bird. 2006. *The Multi-Site Church Revolution: Being One Church in Many Locations*. Grand Rapids: Zondervan.
Swecker Stephen. 2005. *Hard Ball on Holy Ground: The Religious Right Vs. the Mainline for the Church's Soul*. North Berwick, ME: Boston Wesleyan Press.
Sweeney, Douglas. 2005. *The American Evangelical Story: A History of the Movement*. Grand Rapids, MI: Baker Academic.

Sweet, Leonard. 1991. *Quantum Spirituality: A Postmodern Apologetic*. Dayton, OH: Whaleprints,.
Sweet, Leonard. 1999. *Soultsunami*. Grand Rapids, MI: Zondervan.
Sweet, Leonard. 2000. "New Maps for an Ancient Future." *Explorer. .. Field Notes for the Emerging Church* 12.5. 51–54.
Sweet, Leonard. 2007. "A Response to Recent Misunderstandings (2007)." Web. 29 Nov 2016. https://leonardsweet.com/response-recent-misunderstandings-2007/.
Tabachnick, Rachel. 2008. "Spiritual Mapping and Spiritual Warfare—Muthee and the Transformations Franchise." Talk to Action. 30 Oct. Web. 23 Sep 2019. http://www.talk2action.org/story/2008/10/27/115813/98.
Tabachnick, Rachel. 2011. "Biblical Capitalism: The Religious Right's War on Progressive Economy Policy." *Talk to Action*. 1 Feb. Web. 1 Jun 2018. http://www.talk2action.org/story/2011/2/1/132159/0192/Front_Page/Biblical_Capitalism_The_Religious_Right_s_War_on_Progressive_Economic_Policy.
Tabachnick, Rachel. 2013a. "Anti-LGBTQ, Anti-Union 'Apostles' Fielding Another Democratic Candidate." *Political Research Associates*. 31 Oct. http://www.politicalresearch.org/2013/10/31/anti-lgbtq-anti-union-apostles-fielding-another-democratic-candidate/#sthash.5NMxu0aG.0yIhl6UO.dpbs.
Tabachnick, Rachel. 2013b "Spiritual Warriors with an Antigay Mission: The New Apostolic Reformation." *Political Research Associates*. 22 Mar. Web. 8 Aug 2014. https://www.politicalresearch.org/2013/03/22/spiritual-warriors-with-an-antigay-mission/.
Tabachnick, Rachel. 2014. "Profiles on the Right: Mike Bickle, Founder of the International House of Prayer." *Political Research Associates*. 24 Mar 2014. http://www.politicalresearch.org/2014/03/24/profiles-on-the-right-mike-bickle-founder-of-the-international-house-of-prayer/#sthash.i9yaCu8q.cn3ILwYp.dpbs.
"Table of Statistics of the Episcopal Church." 2017. Office of the General Convention. Web. 9 Jul 2017. https://www.episcopalchurch.org/files/table_of_statistics_english_2015.pdf.
Tada, Joni Eareckson. and Nigel M. De S. Cameron. 2006. *How to Be a Christian in a Brave New World*. Grand Rapids, Michigan: Zondervan.
Tashman, Brian. 2014. "HGTV Picks Anti-Gay, Anti-Choice Extremist for New Reality TV Show." *Right Wing Watch*. 6 May. Web. 8 Aug 2018. http://www.rightwingwatch.org/post/hgtv-picks-anti-gay-anti-choice-extremist-for-new-reality-tv-show/.
Taylor, William D., ed. 2000. *Global Missiology for the 21st Century*. Grand Rapids, MI: Baker Academic.
"TBC Advisory Board." 2017. *TBC*. 8 Jun. Web. 8 Aug 2018. http://www.tbc.city/about2/ (Note: The Original link has since been taken down).
Terry, Jonathan C. III. 1997. "A Liberationist Critique of the Church Growth Movement." Diss. Temple University. Print. Proquest.
Terry, Larry D. 1998. "Administrative Leadership, Neo-Managerialism, and the Public Management Movement." *Public Administration Review* 58.3 (May\June): 194–200.
"Terry Schlossberg." n.d. Linked In. https://www.linkedin.com/in/terry-schlossberg-b6a78018.
Thomas, Paul. 2012. "Meme Splicing Genesis 6:1–4 and the Apocalypse of 2012." *Journal of Religion and Popular Culture* 24.2 (Summer): 310–325.
Thompson, J. Allen. 1995. "Church Planter Competencies as Perceived by Church Planters and Assessment Center Leaders: A Protestant North American Study." Dissertation: Trinity International University.
Thorson, Esther, and Margaret Duffy. 2002. *Advertising Age: The Principles of Advertising and Marketing Communication at Work*. Mason, OH: South-Western. Kindle Edition.
Thrift, Nigel. 2005. *Knowing Capitalism*. London: Sage Publications.
Thumma, Scott. 2012. "Virtually Religious: Technology and Internet Use in American Congregations." *American Congregations 2010. Faith Communities Today*. Hartford Institute for Religion Research. Hartford, CT: Hartford Seminary.
Tiku, Nitasha. 2016. "Silicon Valley's Hippest Church Is Going Public: How Do You Market Religion to the Worker Who Has Everything? with Startup Buzzwords, a Slick Website, and Cathy Music." *Buzzfeed*. 31 Jul. Web. 8 Aug 2018. https://www.buzzfeed.com/nitashatiku/c3-silicon-valley-church?utm_term = .owmKxaa7N#.gnn1oJJb7.
Tipton, Steven. 2007. *Public Pulpits: Methodists and Mainline Churches in the Moral Argument of Public Life*. Chicago: University of Chicago Press.

Tolon, Kaya. 2011. "The American Future Studies Movement (1965–1975): Its Roots, Motivations, and Influences." Dissertation: Iowa State University.
Travis, Dave. 1997. "Interventionists Network" Interview by *NEXT Magazine*. *NEXT Magzine*. Vol 3.3. (Dec): 5.
Travis, Dave. 1999a. "Church Champions Update." *Church Champions Archive*. 12 Mar. 12.
Travis, Dave. 1999b. "Church Champions Update." *Church Champions Archive*. May 21 1999. 48.
Travis, Dave. 2000. "Church Champions Update" Church Champions Archive. 7 Apr. 202–205.
Trueheart, Charles. 1996. "Welcome to the Next Church." *NEXT Magazine*. Vol 2.4. (Dec).
Tucker, Arthur Roger. 2003. "An Investigation of the Development of the Cell Church Concept in the Western Cape." Dissertation: University of Pretoria.
Tucker, Michael G. 1998. "Total Quality Ministry Tools for Building a Great Commission Church." Dissertation: Fuller Theological Seminary.
Turner, Frederick (Fred). 2002. "From Counterculture to Cyberculture: How Stewart Brand and the Whole Earth Catalog Brought Us *Wired* Magazine." Dissertation: University of California, San Diego.
Turner, Jennifer G. 2000. "Small Groups in the Structure of the Local Church." Dissertation: Fuller Theological Seminary.
Turner, John G. 2005. "Selling Jesus to Modern America: Campus Crusade for Christ, Evangelical Culture, and Conservative Politics." Dissertation: Notre Dame.
Ungerleider, Neal. 2011. "The Most Influential Women in Technology 2011—Cher Wang." *Fast Company*. 10 Jan. Web. 8 Aug 2018. https://www.fastcompany.com/3017000/the-most-influential-women-in-technology-2011-cher-wang.
Utzinger, John Michael. 2000. "Yet Saints Their Watch Are Keeping: Fundamentalists, Modernists, and the Development of Ecclesiology in the Evangelical Protestant Establishment, 1887–1937." Dissertation: University of Virginia.
Vaccarello, Skip. 2015. *Finding God in Silicon Valley: Spiritual Journeys in a High-Tech World*. San Diego: Creative Team Publishing.
Valentine, Gil, Robert M. Vanderbeck, Joanna Sadgrove, Johan Andersson and Kevin Ward. 2012. "Transnational Religious Networks: Sexuality and the Changing Power Geometries of the Anglican Communion." *Transactions*. Web. 8 Jul 2018.
Van Engen, Charles Edward. 1981. "The Growth of the True Church." Dissertation. Vrije University, Amsterdam (The Netherlands).
Van Leeuwen, Mary Stewart. 1988. "North American Evangelicalism and the Social Sciences; a Historical & Critical Appraisal." *Perspectives on Science and Christian Faith*. PSCF 40 (December): 194–203. http://www.asa3.org/ASA/PSCF/1988/PSCF12-88VanLeeuwen.html.
Vester, Frederic. 2007. *The Art of Interconnected Thinking*. Munich, Germany: Malik Management.
Vieregge, Quentin. 2011. "Narratives of Architectural Revolution in Online Christian Rhetoric." Dissertation: University of South Florida.
Vizant, Don. 1988. "Historical Roots of the Discipling Movement Among Churches of Christ." In *The Discipling Dilemma*. Ed. Flavil Yeakley, Jr. Nashville: Gospel Advocate Co.
Von Buseck, Craig. 2015. "Netcasters: An Analysis of the State of Christian Digital Evangelism." Dissertation: Regent University.
Wagner, C. Peter. 1976. *Your Church Can Grow*. Ventura, CA: Regal.
Wagner, C. Peter. 1977. "Culturally Homogenous Churches and American Social Pluralism: Some Religious and Ethical Implications." Dissertation: University of Southern California.
Wagner, C. Peter. 1984. *Leading Your Church to Growth*. Ventura, CA: Regal.
Wagner, C. Peter. 1987. *Strategies for Church Growth*. Ventura, CA: Regal.
Wagner, C. Peter. 1999a. "Another New Wineskin. .. the New Apostolic Reformation." Excerpt from *Churchquake*. Next from Leadership Network. 5.1:2.
Wagner, C. Peter. 1999b. *Churchquake!*. Ventura, CA: Regal.
Wagner, C. Peter. 2002. "Third Wave." *The New International Dictionary of Pentecostal and Charismatic Movements*. Revised and Expanded Edition. Eds. Stanley M. Burgess and Eduard M. Van Der Maas. Grand Rapids, MI: Zondervan. Print. 1141.
Wagner, C. Peter. 2010. *Wrestling with Alligators*. Ventura, CA: Regal.

Wagner, C. Peter. 2012. *Apostles Today.* Bloomington, MN: Chosen Books.
Wagner, C. Peter, et al. 1988. *Church Growth: State of the Art.* Wheaton, IL: Tyndale House.
Walker, Andrew. 1998. *Restoring the Kingdom: The Radical Christianity of the House Church Movement.* Guildford, U.K: Eagle.
Ward, Hiley. 1975. *Religion 2101 A.D.: Who or What Will Be God?.* Garden City: Doubleday & Company.
Ware, S.L. 2002. "Restorationism in Classical Pentecostalism." In *The New International Dictionary of Pentecostal and Charismatic Movements.* Revised and Expanded Edition. Ed. Stanley M. Burgess and Eduard M. Van Der Maas. Grand Rapids: Zondervan. Print 1019–1021.
Waring, Stephen P. 1991. *Taylorism Transformed: Scientific Management Theory Since 1945.* Chapel Hill: University of North Carolina Press.
Warner, Lloyd, ed. 1967. *The Emergent American Society: Large-Scale Organizations.* New Haven, Conneticut: Yale University Press.
Warner, Rosalind. 2005. "Discourses of Global Environmental Governance from Colonialism to the 21st Century" Dissertation: York University.
Warren, Rick. 1995. *The Purpose Driven Church.* Grand Rapids, MI: Zondervan.
Watkins, Peter. 2014. "The Media Crisis." http://pwatkins.mnsi.net/Intro_MedCr.htm. Accessed 7 Sep 2017.
Watson, J.B., Jr., and Walter H. Schalen Jr. 2008. "'Dining with the Devil': The Unique Secularization of American Evangelical Churches." *International Social Science Review* 83.3–4, 171–180.
Watts, Laurie Story. 1996. "An Analysis of the Relationship Between the Utilization of Total Quality Management Concepts and Principles and Growing Churches in the Alabama Baptist State Convention." Dissertation: New Orleans Baptist Theological Seminary.
Wax, Trevin. 2007. "Book Review: Blink" 18 Apr. Web. 9 May 2018. https://www.thegospelcoalition.org/blogs/trevin-wax/book-review-blink/.
Waymire, Bob. 1984. "The Global Mapping Project. an Interview with Bob Waymire." Interview by Bruce Graham. July 30. http://www.ijfm.org/PDFs_IJFM/01_2_PDFs/1_2%20Graham%20and%20Waymire%20global%20mapping%20fixed2.pdf.
Waymire, Bob, and C. Peter Wagner. 2006. *The Church Growth Survey Handbook.* OC International.
"We're a Network of Networks" 1997. *NEXT Magazine* 3.3. (December): 3.
Weaver, Andrew, Nicole Siebert and Fred Kandeler. 2005. "When Good News Is Bad News or Working on a Coup D'etat." In *Hard Ball on Holy Ground.* North Berwick, ME: Boston Wesleyan Press. 58–68.
Weaver, John. 2013. *Evangelicals and the Arts in Fiction: Portrayals of Tension in Non-Evangelical Works Since 1895.* Jefferson, NC: McFarland.
Weaver, John. 2014. *The Failure of Evangelical Mental Health Care.* Jefferson, NC: McFarland.
Weaver, John. 2015. "Big Questions About Templeton." *Public Eye.* Summer. 14–21. http://www.politicalresearch.org/2015/08/12/big-questions-about-templeton-how-the-philanthropic-giant-legitimizes-faith-healing/#sthash.hSYFd2uC.mFISIAl1.dpbs.
Weaver, John. 2016. *The New Apostolic Reformation: History of a Modern Charismatic Movement.* Jefferson, NC: McFarland.
"Web.watch" 1996. *Next Magazine* 2.2. (August): 11.
Weber, Samuel. 2004. "Targets of Opportunity: Networks, Netwar, and Narratives." *Grey Room* 15 (Spring): 6–27.
Wellbeloved, Sophia. 2003. *Gurdjieff: The Key Concepts.* New York: Routledge.
Wells, Jason. 2009–2010. "The Church Needs Hackers." *Dynamic Link: Christian Perspectives on Software Development* 2: 2–5.
Wetzstein, Cheryl. 2015. "Singapore Megachurch Founder Kong Hee on Trial in Religious Freedom Test Case: A.R. Bernard Among Supporters of City Harvest Church Pastor Facing Corruption Charges." *Washington Times.* 8 Feb. Web. 8 Jun 2018. https://www.washingtontimes.com/news/2015/feb/8/kong-hee-singapore-megachurch-founder-on-trial-in-/.
Wheatley, Margaret. 2000. "The Real Work of Leadership… a Conversation with Margaret Wheatley." Interview by Explorer Magazine. *Explorer Magazine.* 10.8.

Wiener, Norbert. 1948. *Cybernetics: Or Control and Communication in the Animal and the Machine*. Cambridge, MA: M.I.T. Press.
Wikipedia. n.d. "Wikipedia: Neutral Point of View." *Wikipedia*. https://en.wikipedia.org/wiki/Wikipedia:Neutral_point_of_view.
Wikipedia. n.d. "Wikipedia; Verifiability." *Wikipedia*. https://en.wikipedia.org/wiki/Wikipedia:Verifiability.
Wilford, Justin G. 2012. *Sacred Subdivisions: The Post Suburban Transformations of American Evangelicalism*. New York: New York University Press, 2012.
Wilgoren, Jodi. 2005. "Intelligent Design Debate Flows from Conservative Think Tank." New York Times (appearing in Ocala Star Banner, Florida). 22 Aug. Newsbank.
Williams, R. John. 2016. "World Futures." *Critical Inquiry* 42 (Spring): 473–546.
"Willis Harman Consults with Evangelical Leaders Circa 1979." *Herescope*. http://herescope.blogspot.com/2005/09/willis-harman-consults-with.html.
"Willow Creek Repents? Why the Most Influential Church in America Now Says 'We Made a Mistake.'" 2007. *Christianity Today International*. October\November. http://www.christianitytoday.com/pastors/2007/october-online-only/willow-creek-repents.html.
Wilson, Bruce. 2015. "From U.S. to S. Korea to Africa, Christian Anti-Gay Activism Led by the NAR." *Truth Wins Out*. 28 Jun. Web. 8 Aug 2018. https://twocare.org/from-uganda-to-south-korea-the-global-vanguard-of-christian-anti-lgbt-activism-the-new-apostolic-reformation/.
Wilson, Samuel. 2000. "Quantitative Missiology" *Evangelical Dictionary of World Missions*. Ed. A. Scott Moreau. Grand Rapids, MI: Baker Books. 803–804.
Woods, Mark. 2015. "Kong Hee and City Harvest Church: How a Music 'ministry' Led to a Megachurch Pastor's Downfall." *Christian Today*. 21 Oct. Web. 8 Aug 2018. https://www.christiantoday.com/article/kong-hee-and-city-harvest-church-how-a-music-ministry-led-to-a-megachurch-pastors-downfall/68317.htm.
Worthen, Molly. 2013. *Apostles of Reason*. Oxford: Oxford University Press.
Wosh, Peter J. 1988. "Bibles, Benevolence, and Emerging Bureaucracy: The Persistence of the American Bible Society, 1816–1890." Dissertation: New York University. Proquest.
Wren, Daniel A., and Arthur G. Bedian. 2009. *The Evolution of Management Thought*. 6th edition. Hoboken, NJ: Wiley.
Wright, Lela Susan. 1968. "A Study of the Adult Laboratory School of the American Baptist Convention." Dissertation: Indiana University.
Wuthnow, Robert. 1994. *Sharing the Journey: Support Groups and America's New Quest for Community*. New York: The Free Press.
Yeakley, Flavil, ed. 1988. *The Discipling Dilemma*. Nashville: Gospel Advocate.
Young, Shawn David. 2011. "Jesus People USA, the Christian Woodstock, and Conflicting Worlds: Political, Theological, and Musical Evolution, 1972–2010." Dissertation: Michigan State University.
Zaleski, Philip, and Carol Zaleski. 2015. *The Fellowship: The Literary Lives of the Inklings, J.R.R. Tolkien, C.S. Lewis, Owen Barfield, Charles Williams*. New York: Farrar, Strauss, and Giroux. Kindle Edition.
Zenefski, Ronald Harry. 1985. "The Total Church Growth Model and the United Methodist Church: A Way Up from the Decline." Dissertation: School of Theology at Claremont.
Zigarelli, Michael, and George Babbes. 2006. *The Minister's MBA: Essential Business Tools for Maximum Ministry Success*. Nashville: B & H Publishing Group.
Zimmer, Don. 2001. "Leadership and the New Science: Margaret Wheatley." Church Champions Update. Ed. Dave Travis. Apr 23. 433–435.

Filmography

Curtis, Adam. 2002. *Century of the Self*. BBC Four.
Curtis, Adam. 2004. *The Power of Nightmares*. BBC.
Curits, Adam. 2007. *The Trap: What Happened to Our Dream of Freedom*. BBC.
Curtis, Adam. 2011. *All Watched Over by Machines of Loving Grace*. BBC.

Index

Acts 29 network 222-227
AD 2000 and Beyond Movement 44, 105, 108, 112, 160, 204-212, 275-276; *see also* New Apostolic Reformation (NAR)
Ahmanson, Howard 265
Al Qaeda 189
Alban Institute 19, 47, 134, 142-144
Albrecht, Paul 132-133
American Bible Society (ABS) 29-31, 39
American Society for Church Growth 166
apostolic networks 74, 89, 146-147, 158, 194-195, 197-199, 203-212, 315; *see also* New Apostolic Reformation (NAR)
Anderson, Leith 161
Arn, Win 100, 103, 161
Arpanet 201
Association of Reformed Churches 222
Austrian School Economics 1, 18-19, 252-254, 262, 323*ch5n*11

Barlow, John Perry 10, 21-22, 239-240, 246-247, 260, 266-268
Barna, George 103, 109, 164, 276
Barrett, David B. 147-148
Basham, Don 74, 317
Bateson, Gregory 175, 243, 304
Baxter, Ern 72, 74
Bellah, Robert 121
Bergquist, Linda 290
Bernays, Edward 34-35
Bertalanffy, Ludwig von 116-120, 129-130, 201-202, 312
biblical counseling movement 76, 108, 226-227
bionomics 10, 215, 217-218, 261-263, 267, 303, 313, 323*ch5n*11
Bionomics Institute 267
Birch, Charles 132-133
Bohm, David 297, 302, 305
Bonem, Mike 175, 192
Borsook, Paulina 266

Boudinot, Elias 30
Boulding, Kenneth 120, 129-130, 133
Brand, Stewart 10, 21, 215-216, 240-246, 248, 250, 260, 266, 318, 323*ch5n*5; *see also Whole Earth Catalog*; Whole Systems Discourse
Brewin, Kester 181-182, 200-201
Bright, Bill 56, 65-66, 70
Buford, Bob 176, 178, 212-213, 215-216, 220, 322*ch4n*4, ; *see also* Leadership Network
Burhoe, Ralph Wendell 121, 133
Bush, Luis 160, 205-206

Californian ideology 21-22, 239-255, 311
Calvary Chapel 68-69, 99, 221
Campus Crusade for Christ 9, 58, 60, 65-66, 101, 148, 275, 281, 291
Cannistraci, David 200, 211
Capra, Fritjof 302
Carson, Ben 286
Carson, Rachel 123-124, 127-128
Castellanos, Cesar 79
cell groups\cell church 9, 72, 77-93, 199, 222
Chaos theory 20, 183-184, 190, 262, 311-312
Chapman, Bruce 264-265, 268
Charles E. Fuller Institute of Evangelism and Church Growth 86, 99, 102, 150-151
Cho, David Yonggi 79-81, 291
Christian Reconstructionism 11-12, 245
Church Computers User Network (CCUN) 274
Church Growth Inc. 103
Church Growth International 79
Church Growth Ministries 152
church growth movement (CGM) 4, 9, 18-19, 22-23, 32, 38, 40, 44-46, 58-59, 60, 62, 70-71, 79, 87, 92, 94-114, 122, 124-125, 135-136, 138-139, 144-145, 147-157, 161-168, 173-177, 191, 198, 203, 214, 218, 224, 232, 268, 273, 297, 312-314, 317-318, 320*ch1n*14,

Index

320*ch*1*n*15, 320*ch*2*n*3, 320*ch*3*n*7, 321*ch*3*n*15
church health movement (CHM) 9, 18, 71, 82, 104, 106, 110-111, 124-125, 134, 139, 153, 157, 163-176, 190-191, 312-313, 317-318, 320*ch*2*n*4
church networks 9-10, 48, 53-54, 68, 74, 78, 89, 153, 157-158, 160, 176, 178-180, 188, 194-232, 235, 315
church planting movement (CPM) 9, 160, 166, 169, 195, 203, 221-225, 228-230, 235, 290, 322*ch*4*n*9, 322*ch*4*n*13; *see also* New Calvinism
Clarkson, Frederick 1-2, 12
Club of Rome (COR) 9, 118-127, 132-134, 140, 313, 320*ch*3*n*4
Cole, J. Michael 292-293
Cole, Neil 184, 187, 189, 322*ch*4*n*9
Coleman, Lyman 83-84
Commoner, Barry 132
Compassion International 160
Complex Systems Theory/Complexity Science 2, 18-19, 113, 117, 138, 178, 180-183, 185, 190, 197, 249-251, 297, 303, 312-314
Computer Applications for Ministry Network 274
contemplative prayer 306
creationism 52, 271-272, 314-315, 322*ch*4*n*11
Curtis, Adam 2, 22, 108, 258, 260, 267-268, 296, 319pr1*n*1, 319pr1*n*2, 323*ch*5*n*9, 323*ch*5*n*12
cyber-libertarian 10, 20-22, 214-218, 239-256, 260-262, 265-267, 269, 273, 311, 322*ch*4*n*4
cybernetics 2, 8, 9, 14-15, 18, 20, 21, 117-121, 129, 132, 134-136, 151-155, 172-174, 201-202, 240-241, 243-244, 246, 249-251, 254, 261-262, 267, 303, 309, 312-316, 321*ch*3*n*14, 321*ch*3*n*15

Dawkins, Richard 255-257
Dayton, Ed 106-107, 147-149, 174, 320*ch*2*n*3
Dekker, Rachelle 307
Dekker, Ted 307-308
Dever, Mark 161-162, 224, 226
Dewey, John 36
Diamond, Sara 9, 53, 158-159
Dickson, Bill 155-157
diffusion of innovation 19, 179-180, 192, 205, 217-219, 230, 320*ch*3*n*20, 322*ch*4*n*9
"digital" evangelism 280-282
digital libertarian *see* cyber-libertarian
Discipling a Whole Nation (DAWN) 102, 148-149, 159, 289
Discovery Institute 10, 215, 260, 263-266, 268-272, 308
Dobbins, Gaines 36-37

Dominionism 12
Driscoll, Mark 223-224
Drucker, Peter 48, 105, 112, 142, 178, 212-213, 216, 298; *see also* Buford, Bob; Leadership Network
Dyson, Esther 10, 240, 247, 249, 261, 265-268, 322*ch*4*n*4
Dyson, Freeman 240

Ehrlich, Paul R. 125-126, 132, 241-242
Eldred, Ken 288, 291
Electronic Frontier Foundation 248-249, 266
Ely, Paul 294
emerging church *see* Emergent Missional Conversation
Emergent Missional Conversation (EMC) 4, 9, 13-15, 18-19, 60, 82, 97, 119, 138-139, 144, 164, 176-193, 200, 203, 207-208, 213, 215-217, 220, 223, 225, 233, 236, 281, 297, 299-300, 302-303, 308, 311-313, 316-317, 320*ch*3*n*20, 321*ch*3*n*21, 321*ch*3*n*23, 322*ch*3*n*26, 322*ch*3*n*27, 322*ch*4*n*9
Emerson, Harrington 36
Emmanual Movement 36
encounter groups 9, 49, 83-84
Engstrom, Ted 100
enneagram 306-307
Esalen 48, 321*ch*3*n*9; *see also* Human Potential Movement
Escobar, Samuel 97, 158
Evangelical Alliance 39, 41
evangelical bioethical literature 308-310

Ford, Henry 40
Fordism 81, 85-87, 91, 313-314; *see also* post-Fordism; Toyotism
Forrester, Jay 118, 120, 127, 130-131, 133, 135; *see also* Club of Rome; *Limits to Growth* (book)
Fort Lauderdale Five (FLF) 72, 74-75
Fosdick, Harry Emerson 40
Friesen, Dwight 198
Frisbee, Lonnie 68
Fukuyama, Francis 247, 322*ch*5*n*3
Fuller School of World Missions 98, 102
Furr, James H. 175, 192
futurism 2, 138, 140-142, 240, 248-249, 261, 263-264, 266-267, 297-302, 308-313

Gaia theory 137, 297
Gallagher, Robert 143
game theory 2, 17-18, 22, 253, 256-260, 313, 317, 319*n*2
Gangel, Kenneth O. 106, 198, 322*ch*4*n*2
Geertz, Clifford 121
Gelsinger, Pat 293

Index

General Systems Theory (GST) 15, 115-120, 127, 129-130, 312, 314
George, Carl 86-92, 99, 102, 107, 150-151, 172, 301, 314
Georgescu-Rogan, Nicholas 301
Gibbs, Eddie 197-198, 200, 219
Gibson, William 247, 255
Gilder, George 10, 214-215, 247-249, 254, 260-272, 311, 318, 323*ch*5*n*10, 323*ch*5*n*11, 323*ch*5*n*12, 323*ch*5*n*15
Gingrich, Newt 214, 239, 248, 261, 266-268
Gladwell, Malcolm 180, 230, 322*ch*4*n*8
Glasser, Arthur 98
Global Business Network (GBN) 216, 240, 246-249, 266
Global Mapping Project (GMP) 156-158, 160
Global Media Outreach (GMO) 291-292, 294
Glocal.net 222
Gospel and Our Culture Network (GOCN) 177
Gospel Coalition 223, 225-226
Goudzwaard, Bob 301
Graham, Billy 56, 59-60, 65, 139, 258, 289-290, 315
Groeschel, Craig 233-234
Grubbe Institute 142
Gurdjieff, G.I. 141, 306

Hamilton, W.D. 256-258
Hardin, Garrett 125-126
Harman, Willis 140-141, 296-297, 302-303, 321*ch*3*n*9, 321*ch*3*n*12
Hayek, Friedrich von 18-19, 252-254; *see also* neoliberalism
Herrington, Jim 175, 192
Hewitt, Steve 149, 279, 282-284
Hillman, Os 198
Hirsch, Alan 139, 184-189, 198, 321*ch*3*n*20, 322*ch*3*n*24, 322*ch*3*n*25, 322*ch*4*n*9
Hoke, Donald E. 139-140
Holzmann, Peter 155-156, 160, 275, 294
Hudson Institute 263-264
Human Potential Movement 20, 48-49
Hunter, Kent R. 100-101, 109-110
Hunter, George III 102, 213-214
Hybels, Bill 220, 231-232; *see also* Willow Creek Association (WCA); Willow Creek Community Church

I Ching 116, 242
Institute for American Church Growth 100-101, 103, 150
Institute of Church Growth 98
Institute of Social and Religious Research (ISRR) 44

Institute on Religion in an Age of Science (IRAS) 121
Intelligent Design 215, 260, 263, 265, 271-272, 323*ch*5*n*14; *see also* creationism
Interchurch World Movement (IWM) 41-44, 205

Jesus People Movement (JPM) 9, 67-72, 74-78, 91, 149, 195
Johnson, Bill 304
Johnson, Torrey 60, 62
Johnstone, Patrick 147-148
Joy, Bill 269-270

Kahn, Herman 141, 263-264, 298, 300
Kaoma, Kaypa 2
Keller, Tim 223, 225-230, 322*ch*4*n*7
Kelly, John P. 211
Kelly, Kevin 10, 215-218, 244-245, 247-255, 260-263, 266, 273, 311, 318, 322*ch*5*n*4
Kraft, Charles H. 98-99
Kurzweil, Ray 269-270

Laszlo, Ervin 121-122, 133
Latter Rain Movement\Latter Rain Revival 12, 72, 102
Lawhead, Stephen 307-308
Laymen's Missionary Movement 41-42
Leadership Network 1, 4-5, 9-10, 18-19, 48, 176, 178-180, 190, 211-220, 232-233, 235, 237, 247, 250, 281, 286, 290, 297-298, 302-303, 308, 311-315, 317, 322*ch*4*n*4; on Young Leadership Network 178, 180
Leas, Speed 143-144, 164
Le Bon, Gustave 40
Lee, Tosca 307
Lewin, Kurt 9, 49-50, 142, 170-171, 181, 321*ch*3*n*17
Lewis, C.S. 61, 259, 309
libertarian 10, 18-22, 214-218, 239-241, 244, 247-256, 260-262, 265-267; *see also* neoliberalism
Liebig, Justus von 168
Limits to Growth (book) 119, 122, 126-128, 131-133, 313
Lippmann, Walter 40-41
Living Systems Theory (LST) 15, 115, 119-120, 177, 189-190
Logan, Robert (Bob) 100, 107, 165-166, 169, 174, 198, 221-222, 321*ch*3*n*18
Lovelock, James *see* Gaia Theory

Macchia, Steve 161-162
MacKay, Donald 136
Mahaney, C.J. 224-225
mainline Protestantism 14-15, 17-19, 38, 41, 46-53, 84-85, 117-121, 127-128, 133-134,

142-146, 164, 166, 175, 178, 202-203, 298, 311-314, 317-318
Management by Objectives/Ministry by Objectives (MBO) 48, 105-106, 112, 284, 314; *see also* Drucker, Peter
"managerial missiology" *see* Escobar, Samuel
Maslow, Abraham 49
Matthews, Shailer 33-34, 43
Maxwell, John 100
McClusky, Evelyn 62-63
McGarrah, Albert F. 34
McGavran, Donald 79, 95-101, 103-104, 109-110, 112, 161-162, 312, 314
McLaren, Brian 181-182, 186-187
McManus, Erwin 190, 220
Mead, Loren 142-143
Mead, Margaret 132
Meadows, Dennis 131
Meadows, Donella 131
Mears, Henrietta 65
Men and Religion Forward Movement 41-43
Menlo Park Presbyterian Church 293-294
Meta Church model 81, 85-94, 99, 222, 301
Metcalfe, Jane 248, 260
Mid Atlantic Training Center 143
Miller, Donald E. 3, 9-10, 19-20, 195-196
Miller, James Grier 119-120
Missional Change Model (MCM) 180, 192-193
Missionary Education Movement 41-42
Missions Advanced Research and Communications Center (MARC) 98, 148-150
Moberg, David O. 134-135
Montgomery, Jim 102, 148-149, 156, 159
Moody, D.L. 41-42, 57-58
Moravec, Hans 269
Morris, Henry 259
multisites 232-237, 294, 315, 322*ch*4*n*11
Mumford, Bob 74, 77

Naisbitt, John 249, 300-301
National Association of Evangelicals (NAE) 61-62
National Training Laboratory (NTL) 9, 49-52, 59, 142-143
Natural Church Development (NCD) 9, 124, 130, 134, 137, 152, 161, 164-174, 182, 185, 191; *see also* church health movement (CHM)
Navigators 9, 55-60, 62-63, 68, 83, 150, 160
NavPress Software 150
Nee, Watchman 70, 72
Neighbour, Ralph 80-81, 92
neoliberalism 1, 3, 9-10, 16-19, 21-22, 146,

239-241, 252-256, 271-272, 315, 317-318, 319*Pref*n2
Neo-Malthusian 124-126, 132
neospirituality 20, 195, 199, 316
netwar theory 188-189, 209
Network Christianity 9-10, 53-54, 68, 115, 153, 157-158, 160, 186-188, 193, 197-198
network democracy 203
network economy 216, 251-252; *see also* new economy
network theory 2, 70, 80, 88, 180, 188-189, 197-201, 214-220, 227-229
New Age Movement 20, 137, 140-141, 208, 215, 242, 296-297, 302-307, 321*ch*3*n*9, 321*ch*3*n*12
New Apostolic Reformation (NAR) 13, 15, 23, 70-71, 73-89, 105, 107-108, 146-147, 152, 186-187, 189, 194, 197-200, 203-212, 214, 237, 291-294, 303-306, 315, 317-318, 323*ch*6*n*7; *see also* AD 2000 and Beyond Movement; apostolic networks; Shepherding Movement
New Calvinism 9-10, 23, 220, 223-230, 315, 322*ch*4*n*8
new economy 10, 21, 249-252, 255, 260, 267, 296, 299
New Paradigm Churches (NPC) 3, 9-10, 85, 87, 112, 195-196, 204, 316, 318
New Paradigm Management 20, 190, 195-196, 199, 208, 302-303, 307-308, 316
New Public Management 17-18, 47, 110, 197, 202, 252-253, 316
New Thing 222Newbigin, Lesslie 176-177
Newland, Ted 140-141, 321*ch*3*n*12
Nixon, Richard 258-259

Odum, Howard T. 119, 122
Open Systems Discourse 201-202, 299, 302
organic church movement *see* Emergent-Missional Conversation (EMC)
organic leadership model 186, 206-208
Oriental Systems Theory 20, 109, 141, 297, 302-308, 316

Palau, Luis 159
parachurch movement 8-9, 30-31, 38, 41, 52-57, 59-66, 70, 72, 286, 316
Parsons, George R. 144, 164
Parsons, Talcott 121
Peccei, Aurelio 128, 130-131, 320*ch*3*n*5
Peters, Tom 175, 321*ch*3*n*19
Pew, J. Howard 53
Pickett, J. Waskom 44, 95-97
Piper, John 223, 226
Political Research Associates (PRA) 1-2
post–Fordism 20, 298-299, 313-314; *see also* Toyotism

Prajnanpad, Svamiji 141
Price, George R. 255-260, 323*ch5n*9
Prince, Derek 74, 77, 317
program evaluation and review technique (PERT) 106
Progress and Freedom Foundation (PFF) 261, 266-267
Project Planning and Scheduling (PPS) 106, 320*ch2n*2
Project Test Pattern (PTP) 142-144
Promise Keepers 42

Quantum mysticism 20, 297, 301-308, 316-317

Rainer, Thomas 106, 163-164
RAND Corporation 128, 188
Randers, Jorgen 133
Rational Choice Theory (RCT) 17-18, 252, 256, 317
Rayburn, Jim 63
Reagan, Ronald 158, 254, 264, 268, 301
Redeemer Ctc network (Ctc) 222, 223, 227-229, 235
Reeves, R. Daniel 106, 174, 320*ch2n*3
Research in Strategic Evangelization(RISE) 159
Rieff, Philip 48
Rockefeller Jr., John D. 41, 43
Rogers, Carl 49
Rogers, Everett 19, 179-180, 192, 217
Rossetto, Louis 214, 248
Rothschild, Michael L. 215, 261-263, 272, 323*ch5n*10, 323*ch5n*11
Royal Dutch Shell Corporation 140-141, 247
Rzasa, Steve 308-309

Saddleback Church 113, 149
Schaeffer, Francis 137
Schaller, Lyle 103, 112, 143, 161-162, 213, 298-301
Schell, Melvin (Mel) 150-155, 157, 321*ch3n*14,321*ch3n*15
Schuller, Robert 111
Schumpeter, Joseph 19, 254, 262, 323*ch5n*11
Schwarz, Christian 9, 71, 104, 124, 130, 134, 137-138, 161, 163-174, 186, 303, 313-314, 320*ch2n*1, 320*ch2n*4
Searcy, Nelson 174
Senge, Peter 15, 20, 175, 185, 303, 324*con*6
Serendipity small group model 81, 83-85, 91
Shawchuck, Norman 144, 212-213, 314
shepherding movement 9, 52, 57, 66-67, 69-78, 194, 317-318
shepherding networks 74, 78, 194
Sider, Ron 301
Simpson, Charles 74, 77

Sine, Tom 300-301
small group movement 9, 28, 47-50, 52, 59, 66-67, 78-94, 167, 195, 222, 231, 318
Smith, Adam 124, 322*ch5n*8
Smith, Chuck 68-69, 71
Smith, Maynard 256, 258-259
Smith, Wesley J. 308-309
Snyder, Howard A. 299-301, 313
Social Darwinism 255-256, 260, 262
Social Gospel 31, 33, 38, 42-43
Sojourn Network 222
Southern Baptist Convention (SBC) 10, 32-34, 36-37, 45, 162-166, 221, 226, 290
Sovereign Grace Ministries (SGM) 225-227
spiritual mapping movement 44, 105, 108, 112, 158, 205-208, 210-211, 276, 318
Stadia 222
Stanford, Jane Lanthrop 294
Stanford Research Institute (SRI) 111-112, 140-141, 299, 321*ch3n*9
Stanley, Andy 174
Stetzer, Ed 161, 223
Stott, John 213, 258
Student Volunteer Movement 41-42, 55
Summer Institute of Linguistics (SIL) 148, 158
Sweet, Leonard 215, 301-303, 313,
systematic finace 35
systems analysis 126-131
systems dynamics 8, 120, 127, 130-131
systems ecology 119
systems engineering 106
systems theory 2, 8-9, 15-16, 20-21, 48, 79-81, 84, 86-87, 90-92, 106, 115-122, 126-130, 134, 136-138, 141-147, 150-155, 158, 160-161, 164, 166, 172-177, 186-187, 212-213, 249, 302-308, 312-314, 316, 318
systems thinking 120-121

Tabachnick Rachel 1-2, 9, 316, 323*ch5n*6, 323*concn*2
Tansley, Arthur 119
Tavistock Institute of Human Relations 142
Taylor, Frederick W. 33
Taylor, Hudson 55
Taylorism 4, 8, 33-34, 36-37, 41, 44-45, 87, 130, 318
Templeton Foundation 3, 19-20
Tickle, Phyllis 184
Toffler, Alvin 249, 261, 266-267
Toffler, Heidi 249, 266-267
Total Church Growth Model 151-155
Total Quality Management (TQM) 109-112, 195, 284
Towns, Elmer 100-101, 232
Toyotism 9-10, 19-20, 54, 80-82, 85, 89,

356 Index

91-93, 194-197, 199-233, 235-237, 286, 313-314, 318
Transforming the Bay with Christ (TBC) 293-294
Trotman, Dawson 55-60, 65-66
Tyers, Kathy 308

United in Purpose 288-289
U.S. Center for World Mission 98, 102, 148-149, 156-157

Values and Lifestyles Marketing 111-112, 141
Vester, Frederic 9, 134, 172-173
Vineyard Churches\Vineyard Movement 69, 99, 221-222

Wack, Pierre 141
Wagner, C. Peter 71, 79, 86, 98-100, 102-103, 106, 108, 110, 112, 149-150, 155, 159, 161-162, 197-198, 200, 205, 209, 211-214, 221, 232, 276, 312, 320*ch2n*3, 322*ch4n*10
Wagner Leadership Institute 293
Walley, Chris 308-310
Wang, Cher 292-293
Ward, Hiley H. 299, 323*concn*2
Ward, Karen 187
Warren, Rick 100, 106-107, 112, 161, 197-198, 220
Waymire, Bob 148-149, 155-158, 160
Western Esotericism 20, 121-122, 133, 137, 140-141, 208, 215, 242, 296-297, 302-307, 321*ch3n*9, 321*ch3n*12
Wheatley, Margaret 20, 190, 322*ch3n*27
Whole Earth Catalog 20-21, 240-246, 265-266, 318

Whole Earth "Lectronic" Link (WELL) 244-246
Whole Systems Discourse 20-22, 246, 249-250, 260-262, 265-267, 311, 318
Wiener, Norbert 116-118, 129, 201-202, 243, 312
Williams, Charles 307-308
Willow Creek Association 9, 231-232
Willow Creek Community Church 9, 62, 111, 149, 231, 277
Wilson, Bruce 1
Wilson, Edward O. 255
Wilson, Walter 276, 284-285, 291-292, 294
Wilson, Woodrow 41
Wimber, John 69, 71, 73, 86, 99-101, 150
Winter, Ralph 98, 148-149, 155-156
Wired magazine 10, 214-216, 239, 245, 247-249, 251-255, 260-261, 265-271, 323*ch5n*14
Word of Faith (WOF) 12, 291
World Council of Churches (WCC) 127, 132-134
World Vision 100, 106, 148, 158, 160
Wriston, Walter 22
Wycliffe Bible Translators 160
Wyrtzen, Jack 60

Yoido Full Gospel Church 79, 291
Young Life 63
Youth for Christ (YFC) 60-64

Zero Population Growth (ZPG) 125-126, 132, 241
Zygon: Journal of Religion and Science 121, 133